MASTERPLOTS

AMERICAN FICTION
SERIES

MASTERPLOTS

Revised Category Edition

AMERICAN FICTION SERIES

1

A-Grea

Edited by

FRANK N. MAGILL

SALEM PRESS

Englewood Cliffs, N.J.

Library of Congress Cataloging in Publication Data
Masterplots: revised category edition, American
fiction series.
Includes index.
1. America—Literatures—Stories, plots, etc.
2. America—Literatures—History and criti-
cism—Addresses, essays, lectures. 3. Fiction—
Stories, plots, etc. 4. Fiction—History and crit-
icism—Addresses, essays, lectures. I. Magill,
Frank Northen, 1907–
PN843.M15   1985   809.3   85-1936
ISBN 0-89356-500-8
ISBN 0-89356-501-6 (volume 1)

The material in this three-volume set includes all digests and critical evaluations dealing with American fiction that appear in MASTERPLOTS, *Revised edition. The 343 titles included herein are reprinted exactly as they appear in the revised* MASTER-PLOTS *volumes, except for updated research, minor editorial alterations, and format changes. Digests of fiction by authors from Canada and Latin America are included in this set.*

THE PUBLISHER

LIST OF TITLES IN VOLUME 1

MASTERPLOTS

AMERICAN FICTION
SERIES

ABSALOM, ABSALOM!

Type of work: Novel
Author: William Faulkner (1897–1962)
Type of plot: Psychological realism
Time of plot: Nineteenth century
Locale: Mississippi
First published: 1936

> Principal characters:
>> THOMAS SUTPEN, owner of Sutpen's Hundred
>> ELLEN COLDFIELD SUTPEN, his wife
>> HENRY and
>> JUDITH, their children
>> ROSA COLDFIELD, Ellen's younger sister
>> GOODHUE COLDFIELD, Ellen's and Rosa's father
>> CHARLES BON, Thomas Sutpen's son by his first marriage
>> QUENTIN COMPSON, Rosa Coldfield's young friend
>> SHREVE MCCANNON, Quentin's roommate at Harvard

The Story:

In the summer of 1909, when Quentin Compson was preparing to go to Harvard, old Rosa Coldfield insisted upon telling him the whole infamous story of Thomas Sutpen, whom she called a demon. According to Miss Rosa, he had brought terror and tragedy to all who had dealings with him.

In 1833, Thomas Sutpen had come to Jefferson, Mississippi, with a fine horse and two pistols and no known past. He had lived mysteriously for a while among people at the hotel, and after a short time, he had disappeared from the area. He had purchased one hundred square miles of uncleared land from the Chickasaws and had had it recorded at the land office.

When he returned with a wagon load of wild-looking blacks, a French architect, and a few tools and wagons, he was as uncommunicative as ever. At once, he set about clearing land and building a mansion. For two years he labored, and during all that time he rarely saw or visited his acquaintances in Jefferson. People wondered about the source of his money. Some claimed that he had stolen it somewhere in his mysterious comings and goings. Then, for three years, his house remained unfinished, without windowpanes or furnishings, while Thomas Sutpen busied himself with his crops. Occasionally he invited Jefferson men to his plantation to hunt, entertaining them with liquor, cards, and savage combats between his giant slaves—combats in which he himself sometimes joined for the sport.

ABSALOM, ABSALOM! by William Faulkner. By permission of the author and the publishers, Random House, Inc. Copyright, 1936, by William Faulkner.

At last, he disappeared once more, and when he returned, he had furniture and furnishings elaborate and fine enough to make his great house a splendid showplace. Because of his mysterious actions, sentiment in the village turned against him. This hostility, however, subsided somewhat when Sutpen married Ellen Coldfield, daughter of the highly respected Goodhue Coldfield.

Miss Rosa and Quentin's father shared some of Sutpen's revelations. Because Quentin was away in college, many of the things he knew about Sutpen's Hundred had come to him in letters from home. Other details he had learned during talks with his father. He learned of Ellen Sutpen's life as mistress of the strange mansion in the wilderness. He learned how she discovered her husband fighting savagely with one of his slaves. Young Henry Sutpen fainted, but Judith, the daughter, watched from the haymow with interest and delight. Ellen thereafter refused to reveal her true feelings and ignored the village gossip about Sutpen's Hundred.

The children grew up. Young Henry, so unlike his father, attended the university at Oxford, Mississippi, and there he met Charles Bon, a rich planter's grandson. Unknown to Henry, Charles was his half brother, Sutpen's son by his first marriage. Unknown to all of Jefferson, Sutpen had got his money as the dowry of his earlier marriage to Charles Bon's West Indian mother, a wife he discarded when he learned she was part black.

Charles Bon became engaged to Judith Sutpen. The engagement was suddenly broken off for a probation period of four years. In the meantime, the Civil War began. Charles and Henry served together. Thomas Sutpen became a colonel.

Goodhue Coldfield took a disdainful stand against the war. He barricaded himself in his attic and his daughter, Rosa, was forced to put his food in a basket let down by a long rope. His store was looted by Confederate soldiers. One night, alone in his attic, he died.

Judith, in the meantime, had waited patiently for her lover. She carried his letter, written at the end of the four-year period, to Quentin's grandmother. Sometime later on Wash Jones, the handyman on the Sutpen plantation, came to Miss Rosa's door with the crude announcement that Charles Bon was dead, killed at the gate of the plantation by his half brother and former friend. Henry fled. Judith buried her lover in the Sutpen family plot on the plantation. Rosa, whose mother had died when she was born, went to Sutpen's Hundred to live with her niece. Ellen was already dead. It was Rosa's conviction that she could help Judith.

Colonel Thomas Sutpen returned. His slaves had been taken away, and he was burdened with new taxes on his overrun land and ruined buildings. He planned to marry Rosa Coldfield, more than ever desiring an heir now that Judith had vowed spinsterhood and Henry had become a fugitive. His son, Charles Bon, whom he might, in desperation, have permitted to marry his daughter, was dead.

Rosa, insulted when she understood the true nature of his proposal, returned to her father's ruined house in the village. She was to spend the rest of her miserable life pondering the fearful intensity of Thomas Sutpen, whose nature, in her outraged belief, seemed to partake of the devil himself.

Quentin, during his last vacation, had learned more of the Sutpen tragedy. He now revealed much of the story to Shreve McCannon, his roommate, who listened with all of a northerner's misunderstanding and indifference.

Quentin and his father had visited the Sutpen graveyard, where they saw a little path and a hole leading into Ellen Sutpen's grave. Generations of opossums lived there. Over her tomb and that of her husband stood a marble monument from Italy. Sutpen himself had died in 1869. In 1867, he had taken young Milly Jones, Wash Jones's granddaughter. After she bore a child, a girl, Wash Jones had killed Thomas Sutpen.

Judith and Charles Bon's son, his child by an octoroon woman who had brought her child to Sutpen's Hundred when he was eleven years old, died in 1884 of smallpox. Before he died, the boy had married a black woman, and they had had an idiot son, James Bond. Rosa Coldfield had placed headstones on their graves, and on Judith's gravestone she had caused to be inscribed a fearful message.

In the summer of 1910, Rosa Coldfield confided to Quentin that she felt there was still someone living at Sutpen's Hundred. Together the two had gone out there at night and had discovered Clytie, the aged daughter of Thomas Sutpen and a slave. More important, they discovered Henry Sutpen himself hiding in the ruined old house. He had returned, he told them, four years before; he had come back to die. The idiot, James Bond, watched Rosa and Quentin as they departed. Rosa returned to her home, and Quentin went back to college.

Quentin's father wrote to tell him the tragic ending of the Sutpen story. Months later, Rosa sent an ambulance out to the ruined plantation house, for she had finally determined to bring her nephew, Henry, into the village to live with her so that he could get decent care. Clytie, seeing the ambulance, was afraid that Henry was to be arrested for the murder of Charles Bon many years before. In desperation she set fire to the old house, burning herself and Henry Sutpen to death. Only the idiot, James Bond, the last surviving descendant of Thomas Sutpen, escaped. No one knew where he went, for he was never seen again. Miss Rosa took to her bed and died soon afterward, in the winter of 1910.

Quentin told the story to his roommate because it seemed to him, somehow, to be the story of the whole South, a tale of deep passions, tragedy, ruin, and decay.

Critical Evaluation:
Absalom, Absalom! is the most involved of William Faulkner's works, for

the narrative is revealed by recollections years after the events described have taken place. Experience is related at its fullest expression; its initial import is recollected, and its significance years thereafter is faithfully recorded. The conventional method of storytelling has been discarded. Through his special method, Faulkner is able to re-create human action and human emotion in its own setting. Sensory impressions gained at the moment, family traditions as powerful stimuli, the tragic impulses—these focus truly in the reader's mind so that a tremendous picture of the nineteenth century South, vivid down to the most minute detail, grows slowly in the reader's imagination.

This novel is Faulkner's most comprehensive attempt to come to terms with the full implications of the Southern experience. The structure of the novel, itself an attempt by its various narrators to make some sense of the seemingly chaotic past, is indicative of the multifaceted complexity of that experience, and the various narrators' relationship to the material suggests the difficulty that making order of the past entails. Each narrator has, to begin with, only part of the total picture—and some parts of that hearsay or conjecture—at his disposal, and each of their responses is conditioned by their individual experiences and backgrounds. Thus, Miss Rosa's idea of Sutpen depends equally upon her Calvinist background and her failure to guess why Henry Sutpen killed Charles Bon. Quentin's father responds with an ironic detachment, conditioned by his insistence upon viewing the fall of the South as the result of the workings of an inevitable Fate, as in Greek drama. Like Quentin and Shreve, the reader must attempt to coordinate these partial views of the Sutpen history into a meaningful whole—with the added irony that he must also deal with Quentin's romanticism. In effect, the reader becomes yet another investigator, but one whose concern is with the entire scope of the novel rather than only with the Sutpen family.

At the very heart of the novel is Thomas Sutpen and his grand design, and the reader's comprehension of the meaning of the work must depend upon the discovery of the implications of this design. Unlike the chaos of history the narrators perceive, Sutpen's design would, by its very nature, reduce human history and experience to a mechanical and passionless process which he could control. The irony of Sutpen's failure lies in the fact that he could not achieve the design precisely because he was unable to exclude such human elements as Charles Bon's need for his father's love and recognition. Faulkner, however, gains more than this irony from his metaphor of design. In effect, Sutpen's design is based upon a formula of the antebellum South which reduces it to essentials. It encompasses the plantation, the slaves, the wife and family— all the external trappings of the plantation aristocracy Sutpen, as a small boy from the mountains, saw in his first encounter with this foreign world. Sutpen, who never really becomes one of the aristocracy his world tries to mirror, manages, by excluding the human element from his design, to reflect only what is worst in the South. Unmitigated by human emotion and values, the

Southern society is starkly revealed to have at its heart the simple fact of possession: of the land, of the slaves, and, in Sutpen's case, even of wife and children. Thus, Faulkner demonstrates here, as he does in his great story "The Bear," that the urge to possess is the fundamental evil from which other evils spring. Sutpen, trying to insulate himself from the pain of rejection that he encountered as a child, is driven almost mad by the need to possess the semblance of the world that denies his humanity, but in his obsession, he loses that humanity.

Once the idea of the design and the principle of possession in *Absalom, Absalom!* is established, Sutpen's treatment both of Charles Bon and Bon's mother is more easily understood. In Sutpen's distorted mind, that which is possessed can also be thrown away if it does not fit the design. Like certain other Faulkner characters Benjy of *The Sound and the Fury* being the best example Sutpen is obsessed with the need to establish a perfect order in the world into which he will fit. His first vision of tidewater Virginia, after leaving the timeless anarchy of the mountains, was the sight of perfectly ordered and neatly divided plantations, and, like a chick imprinted by its first contact, Sutpen spends his life trying to create a world that imitates that order and a dynasty that will keep his spirit alive to preserve it. His rejection of Bon is essentially emotionless, mechanical, and even without rancor because Bon's black blood simply excludes him from the design. Similarly, the proposal that Rosa have his child to prove herself worthy of marriage, and the rejection of Milly when she bears a female child are also responses dictated by the design. Thus, Sutpen, and all whose lives touch his, ultimately become victims of the mad design he has created. Sutpen, however, is not its final victim: the curse of the design lives on into the present in Jim Bond, the last of Sutpen's bloodline.

Sutpen's rejection of Charles Bon and the consequences of that rejection are at the thematic center of *Absalom, Absalom!* In the fact that Charles is rejected for the taint of black blood, Faulkner very clearly points to the particularly Southern implication of his story. Bon must be seen, on one level, to represent the human element within Southern society that cannot be assimilated and will not be ignored. Faulkner implies that the system, which inhumanely denies the human rights and needs of some of its children, dehumanizes all it touches—master and victim alike. In asserting himself to demand the only recognition he can gain from his father—and that only at second hand through Henry—Charles Bon makes of himself an innocent sacrifice to the sin upon which the South was founded. His death also dramatizes the biblical admonition so relevant to *Absalom, Absalom!*: a house divided against itself cannot stand.

Sutpen's history is a metaphor of the South, and his rise and fall is Southern history written in one man's experience. The Sutpens, however, are not the only victims in the novel. Each in his own way, the narrators too are victims and survivors of the Southern experience, and each of them seeks in Sutpen's history some clue to the meaning of their own relationship to the fall of the South. Their narratives seek to discover the designs which will impose some order on the chaos of the past.

THE ADVENTURES OF AUGIE MARCH

Type of work: Novel
Author: Saul Bellow (1915–   )
Type of plot: Modern picaresque
Time of plot: 1920–1950
Locale: Primarily Chicago
First published: 1953

Principal characters:

AUGIE MARCH, the narrator and protagonist
SIMON MARCH, Augie's older brother
CHARLOTTE MAGNUS, Simon's wife
GEORGIE MARCH, Augie's feeble-minded younger brother
WILLIAM EINHORN, Augie's friend and employer
MRS. RENLING, a woman who wants to adopt Augie
THEA FENCHEL, Augie's sometime mistress
STELLA CHESNEY, Augie's wife

Saul Bellow's *The Adventures of Augie March*, which won for him his first National Book Award in Fiction, is a novel that quickly impresses the reader that he must be ready to read and understand the book at several levels, and each of these levels is completely meaningful in itself and yet unmistakably intertwined with the others.

At the simplest and most obvious level of reading, the novel is in the picaresque tradition, telling the adventures, often comic, of a rascal born out of wedlock to a charwoman, reared in the poverty of a down-at-heels Chicago neighborhood, and early addicted to taking life as it comes. Augie March the adult, thus seen, is a ne'er-do-well hanger-on to people of wealth and, at times, a thief, even a would-be smuggler. As a child of poverty, he learned from the adults about him and from his experience that a ready lie told with a glib tongue and an air of innocence is often profitable. Growing older, he learned that many women are of easy virtue and hold the same loose reins on their personal morality as Augie himself. Love of a kind and easy money seem, at this level, to be Augie's goals in life. While he may dream of becoming a teacher, even take a few courses at the University of Chicago and read widely in an informal way, Augie stays on the fringes of the postwar black market, where he finds the easy money he needs to live in what he regards as style.

When viewed at the literal level, *The Adventures of Augie March*, like Bellow's earlier fiction, is largely in the Naturalistic tradition. In his choice of setting, in his pessimistic choices of detail and character, in his use of a wealth of detail, and in the implicit determinism apparent in the careers of Augie March, his relatives, and his friends, one notes similarities to the fiction of Zola, Norris, Dreiser, and other giants of the Naturalistic tradition in literature. One notes also a kinship with the novels of Nelson Algren and James T. Farrell. At times, Augie March seems little more than a Jewish boy from Chicago's Northwest Side who is one part Farrell's Studs Lonigan and one part the same author's Danny O'Neill. from Chicago's South Side Irish neighborhood. With Farrell's characters, Augie March shares an immigrant background, a loss of meaning in life, degrading poverty, and a grossly hedonistic view of life.

Unlike many Naturalistic novelists, however, Saul Bellow seeks meaning in facts; he is not confined to the principle that the novelist is simply an objective, amoral reporter of life as he finds it, a recorder of life among the lowly, the immoral, the poverty-stricken. Nor does he permit his character Augie March to be merely a creature of environment, molded by forces outside himself, or within himself, over which he has no control. *The Adventures of Augie March* can be read at a deeper level than environmental determinism. Augie is capable of intellectual activity of a relatively high order, of knowing what he is struggling with and struggling for. Throughout his life, he learns that other people want to make him over. Grandma Lausch, an elderly Russian-Jewess of fallen fortunes who lives with the Marches, tries to form the boy, and he rebels. Later Mr. and Mrs. Renling, well-to-do shopkeepers in a fashionable Chicago suburb and Augie's employers, want to make him over, even adopt him, but he rebels. Augie's brother Simon, who achieves wealth and considerable respectability, tries to make a new man of Augie and finds Augie rebellious. Various women in Augie's life, including Thea Fenchel, Augie's erstwhile mistress (whom he follows to Mexico to hunt iguanas with an eagle), try to recast Augie's character. They, too, fail, because above all, Augie refuses to be molded into someone else's image of what he ought to be.

What does Augie want to be, that he refuses to be cast in any mold suggested by the people about him? He wants to become something, for he is always searching—but he never seriously accepts any goal. He wants always to be independent in act and spirit, and some sort of independence he does achieve, empty though it is. He wants to be someone, to achieve all of which he is capable, but he never finds a specific goal or pattern. By refusing to commit himself to anything, he ends up accomplishing virtually nothing. It is a sad fact of his existence that he comes to be a bit envious of his mentally deficient brother Georgie, who has mastered some of the elements of shoe repairing. Saul Bellow seems to be saying through Augie that it is possible to have a fate without a function, but as he presents the character the result is, ironically, to show that without a function no one, including Augie March, can have a fate. Whether or not the irony is intentional, the reader cannot be sure.

Another view of the novel that is both logical and fruitful is to regard it at the level of social comment. Most remarkable at this level is the section of American society in which Augie March moves. Augie is a Jew; that fact is literally beaten into him by neighborhood toughs, including those among the Gentiles he thought his friends, while he is a child. As he grows up, takes jobs, finds friends and confidants, seeks out women to love, Augie moves almost always in the company of Jews. The respectability toward which he is pushed is always the respectability of the Jewish middle classes, particularly that of the Jews who have lost their religion and turned to worshiping the quick success in moneymaking which is mirrored in their passion for fleshy women, flashy cars, and too much rich food. While in one sense Bellow's novel is a novel of an adolescent discovering the world, it is a restricted world in which Augie makes his discoveries. He seems never to understand the vast fabric of American culture which lies about him. If his is a sociological tragedy, and many readers will find it so, it is not an American tragedy in the broad sense. Rather, it is the tragedy of a Jewish child who sees only the materialism of Jews who have forsaken their rich tradition and who have found nothing to replace it.

While some readers will most readily grasp the tragic elements in *The Adventures of Augie March*, others will grasp more readily the comic aspects. Following as it does in some ways the picaresque tradition, the novel is bound to have a wide strain of the comic. Neither Augie nor his creator take some of the character's deviations from conventional standards of conduct very seriously. Augie bounds in and out of crime and sin with scarcely a backward glance. If his loves seem empty, his women unfaithful, Augie accepts the results with comic aplomb. If to be unheroic, to give in with little or no struggle, to be weak and ineffectual is comic (and thus it has long been viewed), Augie is a comic protagonist and the novel a comic work. The comic spirit, however, is also used traditionally for serious, often satiric, purpose. It is here that the reader well may be puzzled. While the comic elements are undeniably in the novel, adding to the richness of its texture, one wonders at their purpose. The novel seems at times to be offering satiric comment on the foibles of mankind, but such comment seems alien, if not contradictory, in the framework of Bellow's work, unless it is there to show that the creator of Augie March shares the character's belief in the irrational nature of man, society, and the universe.

Indeed, Augie seems at times to be a symbol of the irrational; this symbolic value is mirrored by the eaglet that Augie and Thea Fenchel trained to hunt. The young bald eagle, fierce in appearance, proved to be an apt pupil; he seemed marvelously equipped, with powerful wings, beak, and claws, to be an instrument of destruction, and he learned well how to attack a piece of meat tendered by his trainers. Yet, when a live creature, even a tiny lizard, put up resistance, he turned away from the attack; he refused to do what he was capable of doing, defying his very nature. Like the eagle, Augie March failed, too. Young, handsome, charming, and intelligent, Augie refuses to face life, always seeing it as something someone else wants him to do. When life hit back at him, Augie turned away from what he was prepared to do. He strikes the reader as being left without purpose, like the eagle, to exist, to look at, and to be fed. That the character sees this as "living" is perhaps the greatest irony of all. Augie has become an antihero; he is not so much comic as pathetic. As narrator, he realizes, however vaguely, that while he has denied the traditional goals which people have held up for him, he has failed to find a goal for himself that he can regard as worthwhile. In trying to live, he has found little but a meaningless existence.

THE ADVENTURES OF HUCKLEBERRY FINN

Type of work: Novel
Author: Mark Twain (Samuel L. Clemens, 1835–1910)
Type of plot: Humorous satire
Time of plot: Nineteenth century
Locale: Along the Mississippi River
First published: 1884

> *Principal characters:*
> HUCKLEBERRY FINN
> TOM SAWYER, his friend
> JIM, a black slave

The Story:

Tom Sawyer and Huckleberry Finn had found a box of gold in a robber's cave. After Judge Thatcher had taken the money and invested it for the boys, each had a huge allowance of a dollar a day. The Widow Douglas and her sister, Miss Watson, had taken Huck home with them to try to reform him. At first, Huck could not stand living in a tidy house where smoking and swearing were forbidden. Worse, he had to go to school and learn how to read. He did, however, manage to drag himself to school almost every day, except for the times when he sneaked off for a smoke in the woods or to go fishing in the Mississippi.

Life was beginning to become bearable to him when one day he noticed some tracks in the snow. Examining them closely, he realized that they belonged to the worthless father whom Huck had not seen for more than a year. Knowing that his father would be back hunting him when the old man learned about the six thousand dollars, Huck rushed over to Judge Thatcher and persuaded the judge to take the fortune for himself. The judge was puzzled, but he signed some papers, and Huck was satisfied that he no longer had any money for his father to take from him.

Huck's father finally showed up one night in Huck's room at Widow Douglas' home. Complaining that he had been cheated out of his money, the old drunkard took Huck away with him to a cabin in the woods, where he kept the boy a prisoner, beating him periodically and half starving him. Before long, Huck began to wonder why he had ever liked living with the widow. With his father, he could smoke and swear all he wanted, and his life would have been pleasant if it had not been for the beatings. One night, Huck sneaked away, leaving a bloody trail from a pig he had killed in the woods. Huck wanted everyone to believe he was dead. He climbed into a boat and

THE ADVENTURES OF HUCKLEBERRY FINN by Mark Twain. Published by Harper & Brothers.

went to Jackson's Island to hide until all the excitement had blown over.

After three days of freedom, Huck wandered to another part of the island, and there he discovered Jim, Miss Watson's black slave. Jim told Huck that he had run off because he had overheard Miss Watson planning to sell him down south for eight hundred dollars. Huck swore he would not report Jim. The two stayed on the island many days, Jim giving Huck an education in primitive superstition. One night, Huck rowed back to the mainland. Disguised as a girl, he called on a home near the shore. There he learned that his father had disappeared shortly after the people of the town had decided that Huck had been murdered. Since Jim's disappearance had occurred just after Huck's alleged death, there was now a three hundred dollar reward posted for Jim's capture, as most people believed that Jim had killed Huck.

Fearing that Jackson's Island would be searched, Huck hurried back to Jim, and the two headed down the Mississippi. They planned to leave the raft at Cairo and then go on a steamboat up the Ohio into free territory. Jim told Huck that he would work hard in the North and then buy his wife and children from their masters in the South. Helping a runaway slave bothered Huck's conscience, but he reasoned that it would bother him more if he betrayed such a good friend as Jim. One night, as they were drifting down the river on their raft, a large boat loomed before them, and Huck and Jim, knowing that the raft would be smashed under the hull of the ship, jumped into the water. Huck swam safely to shore, but Jim disappeared.

Huck found a home with a friendly family named Grangerford. The Grangerfords were feuding with the Shepherdsons, another family living nearby. The Grangerfords left Huck mostly to himself and gave him a young slave to wait on him. One day, the slave asked him to come to the woods to see some snakes. Following the boy, Huck came across Jim, who had been hiding in the woods waiting for an opportunity to send for Huck. Jim had repaired the broken raft. That night, one of the Grangerford daughters eloped with a young Shepherdson, and the feud broke out once more. Huck and Jim ran away during the shooting and set off down the river.

Shortly afterward, Jim and Huck met two men who pretended they were royalty and made all sorts of nonsensical demands on Huck and Jim. Huck was not taken in, but he reasoned that it would do no harm to humor the two men to prevent quarreling. The Duke and the King were clever schemers. In one of the small river towns, they staged a fake show which lasted long enough to net them a few hundred dollars. Then they ran off before the angered townspeople could catch them.

The Duke and the King overheard some people talking about the death of Peter Wilks, who had left considerable property and some cash to his three daughters. Wilks's two brothers, whom no one in the town had ever seen, were living in England. The King and the Duke went to the three daughters, Mary Jane, Susan, and Joanna, and presented themselves as the two uncles.

They took a few thousand dollars of the inheritance and then put up the property for auction and sold the slaves. This high-handed deed caused great grief to the girls, and Huck could not bear to see them so unhappy. He decided to expose the two frauds, but he wanted to insure Jim's safety first. Jim had been hiding in the woods waiting for his companions to return to him. Employing a series of lies, subterfuges, and maneuverings that were worthy of his ingenious mind, Huck exposed the Duke and King. Huck fled back to Jim, and the two escaped on their raft. Just as Jim and Huck thought they were on their way and well rid of their former companions, the Duke and King came rowing down the river toward them.

The whole party set out again with their royal plots to hoodwink the public. In one town where they landed, Jim was captured, and Huck learned that the Duke had turned him in for the reward. Huck had quite a tussle with his conscience. He knew that he ought to help return a slave to the rightful owner, but, on the other hand, he thought of all the fine times he and Jim had had together and how loyal a friend Jim had been. Finally, Huck decided that he would help Jim to escape.

Learning that Mr. Phelps was holding Jim, he headed for the Phelps farm. There, Mrs. Phelps ran up and hugged him, mistaking him for the nephew whom she had been expecting to come for a visit. Huck wondered how he could keep Mrs. Phelps from learning that he was not her nephew. Then to his relief, he learned they had mistaken him for Tom Sawyer. Huck rather liked being Tom for a while, and he was able to tell the Phelps all about Tom's Aunt Polly and Sid and Mary, Tom's brother and sister. Huck was feeling proud of himself for keeping up the deception. When Tom Sawyer really did arrive, he told his aunt that he was Sid.

At the first opportunity, Huck told Tom about Jim's capture. To his surprise, Tom offered to help him set Jim free. Huck could not believe that Tom would be a slave stealer, but he kept his feelings to himself. Huck had intended merely to wait until there was a dark night and then break the padlock on the door of the shack where Jim was kept; but Tom said the rescue had to be done according to the books, and he laid out a most complicated plan with all kinds of storybook ramifications. It took fully three weeks of plotting, stealing, and deceit to let Jim out of the shack. Then the scheme failed. A chase began after Jim escaped, and Tom was shot in the leg. After Jim had been recaptured, Tom was brought back to Aunt Sally's house to recover from his wound. Then Tom revealed the fact that Miss Watson had died, giving Jim his freedom in her will. Huck was greatly relieved to learn that Tom was not really a slave stealer after all.

To complicate matters still more, Tom's Aunt Polly arrived. She quickly set straight the identities of the two boys. Jim was given his freedom, and Tom gave him forty dollars. Tom told Huck that his money was still safely in the hands of Judge Thatcher, but Huck moaned that his father would likely be back to claim it again. Then Jim told Huck that his father was dead; Jim had seen him lying in an abandoned boat along the river.

Huck was ready to start out again because Aunt Sally said she thought she might adopt him and try to civilize him. Huck thought that he could not go through such a trial again after he had once tried to be civilized under the care of Widow Douglas.

Critical Evaluation:

Little could Mark Twain have visualized in 1876 when he began a sequel to capitalize on the success of *The Adventures of Tom Sawyer* that *The Adventures of Huckleberry Finn* would evolve into his masterpiece and one of the most significant works in the American novel tradition. Twain's greatest contribution to the tradition occurred when, with an unerring instinct for American regional dialects, he elected to tell the story in Huck's own words. The skill with which Twain elevates the dialect of an illiterate village boy to the highest levels of poetry established the spoken American idiom as a literary language and earned for Twain his reputation—proclaimed by Ernest Hemingway, William Faulkner, and others—as the father of the modern American novel. Twain also maintains an almost perfect fidelity to Huck's point of view in order to dramatize the conflict between Huck's own innate innocence and natural goodness and the dictates of a corrupt society.

As Huck's own story, the novel centers around several major themes, including death and rebirth, freedom and bondage, the search for a father, the individual versus society, and the all-pervasive theme of brotherhood. Huck's character reflects a point in Mark Twain's development when he still believed man to be innately good but saw social forces as corrupting influences which replaced, with the dictates of a socially determined "conscience," man's intuitive sense of right and wrong. This theme is explicitly dramatized through Huck's conflict with his conscience over whether or not to turn Jim in as a runaway slave. Huck, on the one hand, accepts without question what he has been taught by church and society about slavery. In his own mind, as surely as in that of his southern contemporaries, aiding an escaped slave was clearly wrong both legally and morally. Thus, Huck's battle with his conscience is a real trauma for him, and his decision to "go to Hell" rather than give Jim up is made with a certainty that such a fate awaits him for breaking one of society's laws. It is ironic that Huck's "sin" against the social establishment affirms the best that is possible to the individual.

Among the many forms of bondage, ranging from the widow's attempt to "civilize" Huck to the code of "honor," which causes Sherburn to murder Boggs and the law of the vendetta which absolutely governs the lives of the Grangerfords and Shepherdsons, that permeate the novel, slavery provides Twain his largest metaphor for both social bondage and institutionalized injustice and inhumanity. Written well after the termination of the Civil War,

Huckleberry Finn is not an antislavery novel in the limited sense that *Uncle Tom's Cabin* is. Rather than simply attacking an institution already legally dead, Twain uses the idea of slavery as a metaphor for all social bondage and injustice. Thus, Jim's search for freedom, like Huck's own need to escape both the Widow and Pap Finn, is as much a metaphorical search for an ideal state of freedom as mere flight from slavery into free-state sanctuary. Thus, it is largely irrelevant that Twain has Huck and Jim running deeper into the South rather than north toward free soil. Freedom exists neither in the North nor the South but in the ideal and idyllic world of the raft and river.

The special world of raft and river is at the very heart of the novel. In contrast to the restrictive and oppressive social world of the shore, the raft is a veritable Eden where the evils of civilization are escaped. It is here that Jim and Huck can allow their natural bond of love to develop without regard for the question of race. It is here on the raft that Jim can become a surrogate father to Huck, and Huck can develop the depth of feeling for Jim which eventually leads to his decision to "go to Hell." But, while the developing relationship between Huck and Jim determines the basic shape of the novel, the river works in other structural ways as well. The picaresque form of the novel and its structural rhythm are based upon a series of episodes on shore, after each of which Huck and Jim return to the peaceful sanctuary of the raft. It is on shore that Huck encounters the worst excesses of which "the damned human race" is capable, but with each return to the raft comes a renewal of spiritual hope and idealism.

The two major thrusts of Twain's attack on the "civilized" world in *The Adventures of Huckleberry Finn* are against institutionalized religion and the romanticism which he believed characterized the South. The former is easily illustrated by the irony of the Widow's attempt to teach Huck religious principles while she persists in holding slaves. As with her snuff taking—which was all right because she did it herself—there seems to be no relationship between a fundamental sense of humanity and justice and her religion. Huck's practical morality makes him more "Christian" than the Widow, though he takes no interest in her lifeless principles. Southern romanticism, which Twain blamed for the fall of the South, is particularly allegorized by the sinking of the Walter Scott, but it is also inherent in such episodes as the feud where Twain shows the real horror of the sort of vendetta traditionally glamorized by romantic authors. In both cases, Twain is attacking the mindless acceptance of values which he believed kept the South in its dark ages.

Many critics have argued that the ending hopelessly flaws *The Adventures of Huckleberry Finn* by reducing its final quarter to literary burlesque. Others have argued that the ending is in perfect accord with Twain's themes. Nevertheless all agree that, flawed or not, the substance of Twain's masterpiece transcends the limits of literary formalism to explore those eternal verities upon which great literature rests. Through the adventures of an escaped slave and a runaway boy, both representatives of the ignorant and lowly of the earth, Twain affirms that true humanity is of men rather than institutions and that everyone can be aristocrats in the kingdom of the heart.

THE ADVENTURES OF TOM SAWYER

Type of work: Novel
Author: Mark Twain (Samuel L. Clemens, 1835–1910)
Type of plot: Adventure romance
Time of plot: Nineteenth century
Locale: St. Petersburg on the Mississippi River
First published: 1876
Principal characters:
TOM SAWYER
AUNT POLLY, Tom's aunt
HUCKLEBERRY FINN and
JOE HARPER, Tom's friends
BECKY THATCHER, Tom's girl
INJUN JOE, a murderer
MUFF POTTER, a village ne'er-do-well

The Story:

Tom Sawyer lived securely with the knowledge that his Aunt Polly loved him dearly. When she scolded him or whipped him, he knew that inside her breast lurked a hidden remorse. Often he deserved the punishment he received, but there were times when he was the victim of his tale-bearing half brother, Sid. Tom's cousin, Mary, was kinder to him. Her worst duty toward him was to see to it that he washed and put on clean clothes, so that he would look respectable when Aunt Polly took Tom, Sid, and Mary to church on Sunday.

A new family had moved into the neighborhood. Investigating, Tom saw a pretty, blue-eyed girl with lacy pantalets. She was Becky Thatcher. Instantly the fervent love he had felt for Amy Lawrence fled from his faithless bosom to be replaced by devotion to the new girl he had just beheld.

She was in school the next day, sitting on the girls' side of the room with an empty seat beside her. Tom had come late to school that morning. When the schoolmaster asked Tom why he had been late, that empty seat beside Becky Thatcher caught Tom's eye. Recklessly he confessed he had stopped to talk with Huckleberry Finn, son of the town drunk. Huck wore castoff clothing, never attended school, smoked and fished as often as he pleased, and slept wherever he could. For associating with Huckleberry Finn, Tom was whipped by the schoolmaster and ordered to sit on the girls' side of the room. Amid the snickers of the entire class, he took the empty seat next to Becky Thatcher.

Tom first attracted Becky's attention by a series of drawings on his slate. At length, he wrote the words, "I love you," and Becky blushed. Tom urged

THE ADVENTURES OF TOM SAWYER by Mark Twain. Published by Harper & Brothers.

her to meet him after school. Sitting with her on a fence, he explained to her the possibilities of an engagement between them. Innocently, she accepted his proposal, which Tom insisted must be sealed by a kiss. In coy resistance she allowed Tom a brief chase before she yielded to his embrace. Tom's happiness was unbounded. When he mentioned his previous tie with Amy Lawrence, however, the brief romance ended. Becky left her affianced with a haughty shrug of her pretty shoulders.

That night, Tom heard Huck's whistle below his bedroom window. Sneaking out, Tom joined his friend, and the two went off to the cemetery, Huck dragging a dead cat behind him. They were about to try a new method for curing warts. The gloomy atmosphere of the burial ground filled the boys with apprehension, and their fears increased still more when they spied three figures stealing into the graveyard. They were Injun Joe, Muff Potter, and Doctor Robinson. Evidently they had come to rob a grave. When the two robbers had exhumed the body, they began to quarrel with the doctor about money, and in the quarrel, Potter was knocked out. Then Injun Joe took Potter's knife and killed the doctor. When Potter recovered from his blow, he thought he had killed Robinson, and Injun Joe allowed the poor old man to believe himself guilty.

Terrified, Tom and Huck slipped away from the scene they had just witnessed, afraid that if Injun Joe discovered them he would kill them too.

Tom brooded on what he and Huck had seen. Convinced that he was ill, Aunt Polly dosed him with Pain Killer and kept him in bed, but he did not seem to recover. Becky Thatcher had not come to school since she had broken Tom's heart. Rumor around town said that she was also ill. Coupled with this sad news was the fear of Injun Joe. When Becky finally returned to school, she cut Tom coldly. Feeling that there was nothing else for him to do, he decided to run away. He met Joe Harper and Huck Finn. Together they went to Jackson's Island and pretended to be pirates.

For a few days they stayed happily on the island and learned from Huck how to smoke and swear. One day they heard a boat on the river, firing cannon over the water. Then the boys realized that the townspeople were searching for their bodies. This discovery put a new aspect on their adventure; the people at home thought they were dead. Gleeful, Tom could not resist the temptation to see how Aunt Polly had reacted to his death. He slipped back to the mainland one night and into his aunt's house, where Mrs. Harper and Aunt Polly were mourning the deaths of their mischievous but good-hearted children. When Tom returned to the island, he found Joe and Huck tired of their game and ready to go home. Tom revealed to them an attractive plan which they immediately decided to carry out.

With a heavy gloom overhanging the town, funeral services were held for the deceased Thomas Sawyer, Joseph Harper, and Huckleberry Finn. The minister pronounced a lengthy eulogy about the respective good characters of the unfortunate boys. When the funeral procession was about to start, Tom, Joe, and Huck marched down the aisle of the church into the arms of the startled mourners.

For a while, Tom was the hero of all the boys in the town. They whispered about him and eyed him with awe in the schoolyard. Becky, however, ignored him until the day she accidentally tore the schoolmaster's book. When the irate teacher demanded to know who had torn his book, Tom confessed. Becky's gratitude and forgiveness were his reward.

After Muff Potter had been put in jail for the murder of the doctor in the graveyard, Tom and Huck had sworn to each other they would never utter a word about what they had seen. Afraid Injun Joe would murder them for revenge, they furtively sneaked behind the prison and brought Muff food and other cheer; but Tom could not let an innocent man be condemned. At the trial, he appeared to tell what he had seen on the night of the murder. While Tom spoke, Injun Joe, a witness at the trial, sprang through the window of the courtroom and escaped. For days Tom worried, convinced that Injun Joe would come back to murder him. As time went by and nothing happened, he gradually lost his fears. With Becky looking upon him as a hero, his world was filled with sunshine.

Huck and Tom decided to hunt for pirates' treasures. One night, ransacking an old abandoned house, they watched, unseen, while Injun Joe and a companion unearthed a chest of money buried under the floorboards of the house. The two frightened boys fled before they were discovered. The next day, they began a steady watch for Injun Joe and his accomplice, for Tom and Huck were bent on finding the lost treasure.

When Judge Thatcher gave a picnic for all the young people in town, Becky and Tom were supposed to spend the night with Mrs. Harper. One of the biggest excitements of the merrymaking came when the children went into a cave in the riverbank. The next day, Mrs. Thatcher and Aunt Polly learned that Tom and Becky were missing, for Mrs. Harper said they had not come to spend the night with her. Then everyone remembered that Tom and Becky had not been seen since the picnickers had left the cave. Meanwhile the two, having lost their bearings, were wandering in the cavern. To add to Tom's terror, he discovered that Injun Joe was also in the cave. Miraculously, after spending five days in the dismal cave, Tom found an exit that was five miles from the place where they had entered. Again he was a hero.

Injun Joe starved to death in the cave. After searchers had located his body, Tom and Huck went back into the cavern to look for the chest which they believed Injun Joe had hidden there. They found it and the twelve thousand dollars it contained.

Adopted shortly afterward by the Widow Douglas, Huck planned to retire with an income of a dollar a day for the rest of his life. He never would have stayed with the Widow or consented to learn her prim, tidy ways if Tom had not promised that he would form a pirates' gang and make Huck one of the bold buccaneers.

Critical Evaluation:

Beginning his writing career as a frontier humorist and ending it as a bitter satirist, Mark Twain drew from his circus of experiences, as a child in a small Missouri town (who had little formal schooling), as a printer's apprentice, a journalist, a roving correspondent, a world traveler, silver prospector, Mississippi steamboat pilot, and lecturer. He was influenced, in turn, by Artemus Ward, Bret Harte, Longstreet, and G. W. Harris. Beginning with the publication of his first short story, "The Celebrated Jumping Frog of Calaveras County," in 1865, and proceeding through his best novels—*Innocents Abroad* (1869); *Roughing It* (1872); *The Guilded Age* (1873), brilliant in concept but a failure in design and execution; *The Adventures of Tom Sawyer* (1876); *Life on the Mississippi* (1883); *The Adventures of Huckleberry Finn* (1885); *A Connecticut Yankee in King Arthur's Court* (1889); and *The American Claimant* (1892)—Twain developed a characteristic style which, though uneven in its productions, made him the most important and most representative nineteenth century American writer. His service as delightful entertainment to generations of American youngsters is equaled, literarily, by his influence on such twentieth century admirers as Gertrude Stein, William Faulkner, and Ernest Hemingway.

Twain's generally careful and conscientious style was both a development of the southwestern humor tradition of Longstreet and Harris and a departure from the conventions of nineteenth century literary gentility. It is characterized by the adroit use of exaggeration, stalwart irreverence, deadpan seriousness, droll cynicism, and pungent commentary on the human situation. All of this is masked in an uncomplicated, straightforward narrative distinguished for its wholehearted introduction of the colloquial and vernacular into American fiction that was to have a profound impact on the development of American writing and also shape the world's view of America. Twain, according to Frank Baldanza, had a talent for "paring away the inessential and presenting the bare core of experience with devastating authenticity." The combination of childish rascality and innocence in his earlier writing gave way, in his later and posthumous works, to an ever darkening vision of man that left Twain bitter and disillusioned. This darker vision is hardly present in the three Tom Sawyer books (1876, 1894, 1896) and in his masterpiece, *The Adventures of Huckleberry Finn.*

Twain's lifelong fascination with boyhood play led to the creation of *The Adventures of Tom Sawyer*, a book of nostalgic recollections of his own lost youth that has been dismissed too lightly by some sober-sided academics as "amusing but thin stuff" and taken too analytically and seriously by others who seek in it the complexities—of carefully controlled viewpoint, multiple irony, and social satire—found in *The Adventures of Huckleberry Finn*, begun in the year *The Adventures of Tom Sawyer* was published. Beyond noting that *The Adventures of Tom Sawyer* is a delicate balance of the romantic with the realistic, of humor and pathos, of innocence and evil, one must admit that the book defies analysis. In fact, Twain's opening statement in *The Adventures of Huckleberry Finn* is, ironically, more applicable to *The Adventures of Tom Sawyer*: "Persons attempting to find a motive in this narrative will be prosecuted; persons attempting to find a moral in it will be banished; persons attempting to find a plot in it will be shot." *The Adventures of Tom Sawyer* is purely, simply, and happily "the history of a boy," or as Twain also called it, "simply a hymn, put into prose form to give it a worldly air." It should be read first and last for pleasure, first by children, then by adults.

For *The Adventures of Tom Sawyer* is also, as even Twain admitted para doxically, a book for those who have long since passed from boyhood: "It is *not* a boy's book at all. It will be read only by adults. It is written only for adults." Kenneth S. Lynn explicates the author's preface when he says that *The Adventures of Tom Sawyer* "confirms the profoundest wishes of the heart"; as does Christopher Morley, who calls the book "a panorama of happy memory" and who made a special visit to Hannibal because he wanted to see the town and house where Tom lived. During that visit, Morley and friends actually whitewashed Aunt Polly's fence. Certainly there can be no greater testimony to the effectiveness of a literary work than its readers' desire to reenact the exploits of its hero.

Tom is the archetypal all-American boy, defining in himself the very concept of American boyhood, as he passes with equal seriousness from one obsession to another: whistling, glory, spying, sympathy, flirtation, exploration, piracy, shame, fear—always displaying to the utmost the child's ability to concentrate his entire energies on one thing at a time (as when he puts the treasure hunt out of his mind in favor of Becky's picnic). Tom is contrasted to both Sid, the sanctimonious "good boy" informant who loses the reader's sympathies as immediately as Tom gains them, and to Huck. As opposed to Huck's self-reliant, unschooled, parentless existence, his love of profanity, his passive preference for being a follower, his abhorrence of civilization, Tom is shrewd in the ways of civilization, adventurous and a leader. He comes from the respectable world of Aunt Polly, with a literary mind, with a conscious romantic desire for experience and for the hero's part, an insatiable egotism which assists him in his ingenious schematizations of life to achieve his heroic aspirations—and a general love of fame, money, attention, and "glory." The relationship between the two boys may be compared to that between the romantic Don Quixote and the realist Sancho Panza. It was Twain's genius to understand that the games Quixote played out of "madness" were, in fact, those played by children with deadly seriousness. Lionel Trilling summarizes Twain's achievement in this book when he says that *"The Adven-*

tures of Tom Sawyer has the truth of honesty—what it says about things and feelings is never false and always both adequate and beautiful." Twain's book is an American classic, but a classic that travels well as an ambassador of American nostalgic idealism.

THE AGE OF INNOCENCE

Type of work: Novel
Author: Edith Wharton (1862–1937)
Type of plot: Social criticism
Time of plot: Late nineteenth century
Locale: New York City
First published: 1920

> *Principal characters:*
> NEWLAND ARCHER, a young attorney
> MAY WELLAND, his fiancée
> COUNTESS ELLEN OLENSKA, her cousin

The Story:

Newland Archer, a handsome and eligible young attorney engaged to lovely May Welland, learned that the engagement would be announced at a party to welcome his fiancée's cousin, Countess Ellen Olenska. This reception for Ellen constituted a heroic sacrifice on the part of the many Welland connections, for her marriage to a ne'er-do-well Polish count had not improved her position so far as rigorous and straight-laced New York society was concerned. The fact that she contemplated a divorce action also made her suspect, and, to cap it all, her rather bohemian way of living did not conform to what her family expected of a woman who had made an unsuccessful marriage.

Newland Archer's engagement to May was announced. At the same party, Archer was greatly attracted to Ellen. Before long, with the excuse that he was making the cousin of his betrothed feel at home, he began to send her flowers and call on her. To him she seemed a woman who offered sensitivity, beauty, and the promise of a life quite different from the one that he could expect after his marriage to May.

He found himself defending Ellen when the rest of society was attacking her contemplated divorce action. He did not, however, consider breaking his engagement to May but constantly sought reasons for justifying what was to the rest of his group an excellent union. With Ellen often in his thoughts, May Welland's cool beauty and correct but unexciting personality began to suffer in Archer's estimation.

Although the clan defended her against all outsiders, Ellen was often treated as a pariah. Her family kept check on her, trying to prevent her from indulging in too many bohemianisms, such as her strange desire to rent a house in a socially unacceptable part of town. The women of the clan also recognized her as a dangerous rival, and ruthless Julius Beaufort, whose secret dissipations were known by all, including his wife, paid her marked attention. Archer found himself hating Julius Beaufort very much.

Convincing himself that he was seeing too much of Ellen, Archer went to St. Augustine to visit May, who was vacationing there with her mother and her hypochondriac father. In spite of her cool and conventional welcome and her gentle rebuffs to his wooing, her beauty reawakened in him a kind of affection, and he pleaded with her to advance the date of their wedding. May and her parents refused because their elaborate preparations could not be completed in time.

Archer returned to New York. There, with the aid of the family matriarch, Mrs. Manson Mingott, he achieved his purpose, and the wedding date was advanced. This news came to him in a telegram sent by May to Ellen, which Ellen read to him just as he was attempting to advance the intimacy of their relationship. Archer left Ellen's house and found a similar telegram from May to himself. Telling his sister Janey that the wedding would take place within a month, he suddenly realized that he was now protected against Ellen and himself.

The ornate wedding, the conventional European honeymoon that followed, and May's assumption of the role of the proper wife, soon disillusioned Archer. He realized that he was trapped, that the mores of his society, helped by his own lack of courage, had prepared him, like a smooth ritual, for a rigid and codified life. There was enough intelligence and insight in Archer, however, to make him resent the trap.

On his return to New York, he continued to see Ellen. The uselessness of his work as junior attorney in an ancient law firm, the stale regimen of his social life, and the passive sweetness of May did not satisfy that part of Archer which set him apart from the rest of his clan.

He proposed to Ellen that they go away together, but Ellen, wise and kind, showed him that such an escape would not be a pleasant one, and she indicated that they could love each other only as long as he did not press for a consummation. Archer agreed. He further capitulated when, urged by her family, he advised Ellen, as her attorney and as a relative, not to get a divorce from Count Olenska. She agreed, and Archer again blamed his own cowardice for his action.

The family faced another crisis when Julius Beaufort's firm, built upon a framework of shady financial transactions, failed, ruining him and his duped customers. The blow caused elderly Mrs. Mingott to have a stroke, and the family rallied around her. She summoned Ellen, a favorite of hers, to her side, and Ellen, who had been living in Washington, D.C., returned to the Mingott house to stay. Archer, who had not met Ellen since he advised her against a divorce, began seeing her again, and certain remarks by Archer's male acquaintances along with a strained and martyrlike attitude which May had adopted, indicated to him that his intimacy with Ellen was known among his family and friends. The affair came to an end, however, when Ellen left for Paris, after learning that May was to have a baby. It was obvious to all that May had triumphed, and Archer was treated by his family as a prodigal returned. The rebel was conquered. Archer made his peace with society.

Years passed. Archer dabbled in liberal politics and interested himself in civic reforms. His children, Mary and Dallas, were properly reared. May died when Archer was in his fifties. He lamented her passing with genuine grief. He watched society changing and saw the old conservative order give way, accepting and rationalizing innovations of a younger, more liberal generation.

One day, Archer's son, Dallas, about to be married, telephoned him and proposed a European tour, their last trip together. In Paris, Dallas revealed to his father that he knew all about Ellen Olenska and had arranged to visit her apartment. When they arrived, however, Archer sent his son ahead, to pay his respects, while he remained on a park bench outside. A romantic to the end, incapable of acting in any situation that made demands on his emotional resources, he sat and watched the lights in Ellen's apartment until a servant appeared on the balcony and closed the shutters. Then he walked slowly back to his hotel. The past was the past; the present was secure.

Critical Evaluation:

Edith Wharton's *The Age of Innocence* is probably one of her most successful books because it offers an inside look at a subject the author knew very well, that is, New York society during the 1870's. That was her milieu, and her pen captures the atmosphere of aristocratic New York as its inhabitants move about in their world of subtleties, innuendoes, and strict adherence to the dictates of fashionable society. Wharton describes those years for herself as "safe, guarded, and monotonous." Her only deviation as a young adult consisted in frequent journeys abroad and summers in Newport. Her marriage to Edward Wharton, a prominent Bostonian, assumed the same character as her own early life until it became apparent that he suffered from mental illness and would have to be hospitalized. During World War I, Wharton worked for the allies and received the French Cross of the Legion of Honor for her work with the Red Cross in Paris. Most critics agree that her best years as a novelist were from 1911 to 1921, during which time she produced *Ethan Frome*, a grim New England study, and *The Age of Innocence*, for which she was awarded the Pulitzer Prize.

Wharton's most successful theme (like that of her friend Henry James) was the plight of the young and innocent in a world which was more complicated than that for which they were prepared. Newland Archer and Ellen Olenska found the society of New York intricate and demanding and, as such, to be an impediment to their personal searches for happiness and some degree of freedom. *The Age of Innocence* is a careful blending of a nostalgia for the 1870's with a subtle, but nevertheless inescapable, criticism of its genteel timidities and clever evasions.

With respect to Wharton's style, it can be generalized that she was not a particularly daring writer nor an experimenter in form. Rather, she wrote in a comfortable, fixed, formal style that was closely designed. In some instances, her narrative becomes heavy, and the intricate play and counterplay of the characters' motives can lose all but the most diligent reader. The author's presence is never forgotten and the reader feels her control throughout the story, as the narrative view is quickly established from the beginning. Wharton's characters are portrayed through their actions, and the clear lines of the plot are visible. Since *The Age of Innocence* so carefully fits a historical niche, its scope is limited and its direction narrow. That is not to say that the drama is limited or lacking. On the contrary, in detailing such a small world, the drama is intense, even if it is found beneath a sophisticated, polished surface.

Three figures are projected against the historical background of New York society. First is May Welland, the beautiful betrothed of Newland Archer. May was born and bred in traditions, and she is completely a product of the system she seeks to perpetuate. Newland observes, after their marriage, that May and her mother are so much alike that he sees himself being treated and placated just as Mr. Welland is by his wife and daughter. There is no doubt that May will never surprise Newland "by a new idea, a weakness, a cruelty or an emotion."

Ellen Olenska, on the other hand, has freed herself from the restraints of society by her experiences abroad and through her subsequent separation from her husband, the Polish count. Madame Olenska is not only more cosmopolitan, but she is also a character of more depth and perception than the other women in the novel. She suggests by her presence as well as by her past experiences a tragic and emotionally involved element in the story. Ellen definitely does not conform to the rules of accepted behavior, yet she moves in a cloud of mystery which makes her an intriguing personality to those who observe her, if even only to criticize. As soon as she and Archer are aware of their feelings for each other, Archer tries to convince Ellen, in a halfhearted way, that one cannot purchase freedom at the expense of another. He has given her an idea by which to live and, in so doing, has unknowingly destroyed his one opportunity to find new freedom for himself.

Newland Archer is, in many ways, a typical Wharton masculine figure. He is a man set apart from the people he knows by education, intellect, and feeling, but lacking the initiative and courage to separate himself physically from the securities of the known. The movement of the plot in *The Age of Innocence* is established by the transition from one position to another taken by Archer in his relations with either May or Ellen. Archer's failure to break the barriers of clan convention lead him to an ironic abnegation, for in the last pages of the novel readers see Newland retreating from the opportunity to meet with Ellen—an opportunity his eager son Dallas is quick to arrange.

Dallas is anxious to meet Ellen, for he heard from his mother, shortly before she died, that Archer had given up the thing he had most wanted (namely, Ellen) for her. It is sad to see that Archer, the object of two loves, has never been able to satisfy or be satisfied by either. The tragedy in the novel rests with May, for it is she who appeared to be the most innocent and naïve; yet in the end, she is perhaps the most aware of them all. She has suffered quietly through the years, knowing that her husband's true desires and passions were elsewhere. Dallas' generation observes the whole situation out of context as "prehistoric." He dismisses the affair rather casually, for his contemporaries have lost that blind adherence to social custom that the Archers, Wellands, and the rest knew so well.

The novel is an incisive but oblique attack on the intricate and tyrannous tribal customs of a highly stratified New York Society. Wharton's psychological probing of the meaning and motivation behind the apparent facade of her characters' social behavior shows her to be a true disciple of Henry James. The method is indeed that of James, but Wharton's style is clearer and less involved. Here is a novel, the work of a craftsman for whom form and method are perfectly welded, and the action results inevitably from the natures of the characters themselves. *The Age of Innocence* is a novel of manners which delineates a very small world, yet under the surface, readers see a world of suffering, denial, and patient resignation—a situation which deserves more attention and reflection than one might give at first reading.

ALECK MAURY, SPORTSMAN

Type of work: Novel
Author: Caroline Gordon (1895–1981)
Type of plot: Fictional biography
Time of plot: Late nineteenth and early twentieth centuries
Locale: Virginia, Tennessee, Mississippi, and Missouri
First published: 1934

> *Principal characters:*
> ALECK MAURY, a Southern sportsman
> JAMES MORRIS, his uncle
> VICTORIA, his aunt
> JULIAN, his cousin
> MR. FAYERLEE, the owner of Merry Point
> MRS. FAYERLEE, his wife
> MOLLY FAYERLEE, their daughter and Aleck's wife
> RICHARD and
> SARAH (SALLY), Aleck's and Molly's children
> STEVE, Sarah's husband

The Story:

Aleck Maury's love for hunting and fishing began in childhood. At the age of eight, Aleck went coon hunting with Rafe, a black handyman at the Maury household. Not long after, a mill owner named Jones took the boy fishing and encouraged his lifelong love for that sport. Aleck was always happiest when he was out in the fields. One of five children, he was reared by his oldest sister after his mother died. Until he was ten years old, he was educated at home by his father, who put great stress upon the classics and taught his children nothing else.

At the age of ten, Aleck went to live at Grassdale with his Uncle James and Aunt Victoria Morris and their son, Julian. There, his education was to be broadened under the tutelage of Aunt Victoria, who was a learned woman. Aleck's life at Grassdale was pleasant, centering chiefly around sport.

When Aleck was graduated from the University of Virginia, he had a classical education but no plans for making a living. He tried several jobs. He cleared out a dogwood thicket for a set sum of money; he worked on a construction project on the Missouri River, in the city engineer's office in Seattle, and as a day laborer on a ranch in California. While working at the ranch, he contracted typhoid fever and was sent back east, as far as Kansas City, to stay with some relatives there. At last, through the efforts of his family, Aleck became a tutor at Merry Point, the home of Mr. Fayerlee, near Gloversville, Tennessee.

Aleck, living with the Fayerlees, became the local schoolmaster for the children of most of the landowners in the area. Aleck's first interest, however, was not in the school or the students he taught but in the possibilities for fishing and hunting.

During his stay with the Fayerlees, Aleck fell in love with Molly Fayerlee, and in 1890, they were married. They continued to live with the Fayerlees, and Aleck continued to teach school. During his first year of marriage, Aleck acquired the pup Gyges, a small but thoroughbred bird dog. He trained Gy from a puppy and became greatly attached to him. The next fall, Aleck's son, Richard, was born. Two years later, Sarah, nicknamed Sally, was born. They all continued to live at Merry Point.

When Richard was seven, Aleck was offered the presidency of a small seminary in Mississippi, and over the protestations of the Fayerlee family, the Maurys left Merry Point. On the way, while spending the night in Cairo, Aleck lost Gy. The dog was never heard of again. They continued their journey to Oakland and the seminary. When Aleck arrived, he found that the school was running smoothly under the able direction of Harry Morrow, his young assistant, who was interested in administration rather than teaching. A few months after arriving at Oakland, Aleck acquired an untrained two-year-old pointer named Trecho from his friend, William Mason. Once again Aleck started the slow, arduous training of a good hunting dog.

When Richard was fifteen, Aleck tried to interest him in the joys of his own life, hunting and fishing, but his son, although he was a splendid swimmer and wrestler, had little interest in his father's fondness for field and stream. That summer, Richard, while swimming in the river with a group of his companions, was drowned. The boy had been Molly's favorite and his loss was almost more than she could bear. Aleck thought it would be best for all concerned to leave for different surroundings.

He decided after some correspondence with friends that he would start a school in Gloversville, and the family moved back there. Settled in the small Tennessee town, Aleck found much time for fishing and hunting. He met Colonel Wyndham and from him learned a great deal about casting, flies, and the techniques to be used for catching various fish. Finally, he began to grow tired of the same pools and the same river, and it was with pleasure that he accepted Harry Morrow's offer of a job on the faculty of Rodman College at Poplar Bluff, Missouri, of which Morrow had just been made president.

Aleck's main reason for accepting the position was the possibility it offered for fishing in the Black River. Thus once again, after ten years in Gloversville, the Maury family was on the move to newer fishing grounds. Sally, however, did not accompany them but went to a girls' school in Nashville. The faithful

Trecho was also left behind, for he had been destroyed at the age of twelve because of his rheumatism.

At Rodman, Aleck had only morning classes, a schedule which left him free to fish every afternoon. This pleasant life—teaching in the morning, fishing in the afternoon—continued for seven years. Then Molly died after an emergency operation. Mrs. Fayerlee and Sally arrived too late to see her alive. The three of them took her back to be buried in the family plot at Merry Point.

Aleck returned to Poplar Bluff and continued teaching there for several years, but he at last resigned his position and went to live at Jim Buford's, near Gloversville, where he spent the next two years restocking Jim's lakes with bream and bass. Later, he decided to go to Lake Harris in Florida to try the fishing; but he found it disappointing because of the eel grass, which kept the fish from putting up a fight. About that time, he received a letter from Sally, who had married and gone touring abroad with her husband. The letter informed him that she and her husband were soon to return home and that they hoped to find a quiet place in the country on some good fishing water, where Aleck would go to live with them. Aleck wrote and suggested that they start their search for a house near Elk River.

Four weeks later, he met Sally and Steve at Tullahoma, only to learn that Steve and Sally, who had arrived the day before, had already discovered the place they would like to own. They told him it was the old Potter house, close to the river. When Aleck saw the big, clapboard house, however, all his dreams about a white cottage disappeared, and when he looked at the river, he decided that it would probably be muddy about half the year. Seeing his disappointment, Steve and Sally promised to continue their attempt to find a more ideal house, but at the end of the day's search, they decided that they still liked the old Potter house the best. That night Aleck boarded a bus bound for Caney Fork, the place where he really wanted to live, and he went to stay at a small inn located there. The fishing was always good at Caney Fork.

Critical Evaluation:

Significantly, *Aleck Maury, Sportsman* is dedicated to Ford Madox Ford, one of the most influential literary critics and greatest prose stylists of the twentieth century. Caroline Gordon's narrative is low-keyed and detailed, deliberately avoiding excesses either of syntax or event. An almost obsessive commitment to perfection of tone rules the book; not a word is allowed to appear more vibrant or significant than any other. Above all else, the novel is a masterpiece of *writing*.

From boyhood, Aleck Maury was dedicated to Latin, Greek, and sport, especially hunting and fishing. Life seems to flow amost effortlessly for Aleck, as effortlessly as Caroline Gordon's prose. He is possessed by no powerful passions or erratic impulses. A dedicated, constant love of sport rules his life, taking the place of ambition for wealth or glory or power. His wife even wonders if sportsmanship is more important to him than his family. His love for hunting and fishing, however, is not violent; rather, it is deep and quiet and steady, a part of his being. She cannot be jealous of it any more than she can be jealous of his arms or legs.

As Aleck Maury tells of his life, he frequently pauses to ponder a scene, to examine meticulously a place or moment. "There are times," he says, "in a man's life when every moment seems charged with meaning." This novel is composed primarily of such moments. They are held in suspension while the narrator and reader wait, interested and thoughtful, for the subsequent events to form themselves. Nothing in the book, not marriage or death, not career or rearing of children, happens hurriedly. Always, an even pace is observed as Aleck moves from stream to stream and tramps from hunt to hunt.

ALICE ADAMS

Type of work: Novel
Author: Booth Tarkington (1869–1946)
Type of plot: Social criticism
Time of plot: Early twentieth century
Locale: A small Midwestern town
First published: 1921

>*Principal characters:*
>ALICE ADAMS, a small-town girl
>VIRGIL ADAMS, her father
>MRS. ADAMS, his wife
>WALTER ADAMS, his son
>MILDRED PALMER, Alice's friend
>ARTHUR RUSSELL, the Palmers' relative
>MR. LAMB, of Lamb and Company

The Story:

Alice Adams had been reared in a town in which each person's business was everybody's business, sooner or later. Her father, Virgil Adams, worked for Lamb and Company, a wholesale drug factory in the town, where he also obtained a job for his son Walter. Alice had been one of the town's young smart set while she was in high school, but when the others of the group had gone to college, Alice had remained behind because of economic reasons. As time passed, she felt increasingly alienated. To compensate for a lack of attention, Alice often attracted notice to herself by affected mannerisms.

Alice had been invited to a dance given by Mildred Palmer, who, according to Alice, was her best friend. Walter had also been invited so as to provide her with an escort. Getting Walter to go out with Alice, however, was a process that took all the coaxing and cajoling that Mrs. Adams could muster. On the night of the dance, Alice departed in a made-over formal, carrying a homemade bouquet of wild violets, and with an unwilling escort who was driving a borrowed flivver. The party itself turned out no better than its inauspicious beginning. Alice was very much a wallflower except for the attentions of Frank Dowling, a fat, unpopular boy. Toward the end of the evening, Mildred Palmer introduced Alice to a new young man, Arthur Russell, a distant relative of the Palmers. It was rumored that Mildred and Arthur would become engaged in the near future. Alice asked Arthur to find her brother, whom she had not seen since the second dance. When Arthur found

Walter, the young man was shooting dice with the waiters in the cloakroom; Alice was mortified.

A week later Alice accidentally met Arthur Russell, and he walked home with her. During their walk, Alice learned that Arthur had asked for an introduction to her at the dance. Flattered, Alice built up for herself a background that did not exist. Arthur asked for permission to call on her.

Arthur, however, failed to appear the next evening. Several nights later, after Alice had helped with the dishes, she was sitting on the front porch when Arthur finally came to call. To hold his interest, Alice asked him to promise not to listen to any gossip about her. As time went on, she repeated her fear that someone would talk about her. Arthur could not understand her protestations.

For many years Mrs. Adams had been trying to convince her husband to leave his job at Lamb and Company and go into business for himself. Her idea was that he could start a factory to manufacture glue from a formula he and another young man at Lamb and Company had discovered years before. Meanwhile, the other man had died, and the only people who knew the formula were Mr. Lamb and Mr. Adams. Mr. Lamb had lost interest in the formula. Mr. Adams felt that his wife's scheme was dishonest, and despite her nagging, he refused to do as she wished. Yet, after Mr. Lamb's granddaughter failed to invite Alice to a dinner party she was giving, Mrs. Adams convinced her husband that the true reason was their own poor economic status. In that way she finally won his grudging agreement to her plan.

Without delay, Mr. Adams began to organize his new business. Walter refused to join him because Mr. Adams would not give him three hundred dollars immediately. Mr. Adams needed all his money for his new project. He sent Mr. Lamb a letter of resignation, telling of his intention to start a glue factory. He expected some sort of action or at least an outburst on Mr. Lamb's part when he read the letter, but nothing was forthcoming. He went ahead with his arrangements and began to manufacture his glue.

Alice's mother decided the time had come to invite Arthur to dinner, and Alice agreed with great reluctance. An elaborate meal was prepared; a maid was hired to serve, and Mr. Adams was forced into his dress suit. The dinner, however, was a dismal failure. Everyone, including Arthur, was extremely uncomfortable. Arthur had more reason than the rest for being so, for he had heard Mr. Adam's venture discussed in the most unfavorable light. He had also heard some uncomplimentary remarks about Alice. Before dinner was over, a friend named Charley Lohr came to speak to Mr. Adams. When both her mother and father failed to return to the table, Alice and Arthur went out to the porch. She soon dismissed him, knowing that something had come between them. When she went inside, Charley Lohr informed her that her brother had been caught short in his accounts and had skipped town.

Mr. Adams decided to get a loan from the bank the first thing in the morning in order to pay back what Walter had taken. However, when he went to his factory in the morning, he discovered that the building that had been erected across the street from his was in reality another glue factory, one started by Mr. Lamb. His hopes of obtaining money on his factory were shattered. Then Mr. Lamb rode up to gloat over his retaliation. Mr. Adams angrily accused Mr. Lamb of waiting until Walter got into trouble before announcing his new factory and thereby making Mr. Adams' property practically worthless. He worked himself into such a state that he had a stroke.

Mr. Lamb, feeling sorry for Mr. Adams, offered to buy him out, and Mr. Adams was forced to agree. Now there was no income in the family. Mrs. Adams decided to take in boarders, and Alice finally made up her mind to enroll in Frincke's Business College. She had lost more than Arthur Russell; she had lost her daydreams as well.

Critical Evaluation:

Alice Adams and Booth Tarkington's other masterpiece of Americana, *The Magnificent Ambersons*, together present a surprisingly broad and perceptive picture of small-town life in the first decades of the twentieth century. Because he was writing of people and places he knew intimately, the author brought an unusual understanding and insight to his portrayals. Tarkington's style, deceptively simple, actually is the perfect vehicle for his stories; his prose is clean and supple and does not distract from the vivid characterizations or well-thought-out plots. He was a superior craftsman, and *Alice Adams* is an excellent example of his sensitivity and skill.

The novel hinges on the personality of Alice. Tarkington develops this young girl with amazing insight; her little dreams, her self-delusions, her battles with reality, all are portrayed with a touching honesty and affection. The scene in which Alice, dressed in simple but good taste, attends a party full of pushy, overdressed small-town "society belles" is a pointed commentary on American taste and social standards.

The reader cares deeply about Alice's little humiliations and her attempts to rise beyond the limitations of her station. Her efforts to make her modest home nice and to provide a fine dinner when the young man comes to visit are painfully futile, however well-intentioned. Her little tragedies are the tragedies of everyday life for millions of people and are captured with a deft hand. Many readers will pause and think, "Yes, that's true, that's the way it is." Because many of the efforts and emotions described in the novel are so true to human nature, they do not date any more than those of the Bennett sisters in Jane Austen's *Pride and Prejudice*.

Alice Adams won the Pulitzer Prize for fiction in 1921, and there is no doubt that the novel will endure as an honest and touching picture of real people in genuine struggles with their world.

ALL FALL DOWN

Type of work: Novel
Author: James Leo Herlihy (1927–   )
Type of plot: Social criticism
Time of plot: Late 1950's
Locale: Cleveland, Ohio
First published: 1960

> *Principal characters:*
> CLINTON WILLIAMS, a boy reaching out toward life
> RALPH WILLIAMS, his father
> ANNABEL WILLIAMS, his mother
> BERRY-BERRY, his older brother
> ECHO O'BRIEN, a girl loved by Clinton and destroyed by
>   Berry-berry
> SHIRLEY, a young prostitute

James Branch Cabell once tried to compress the story of all human life into a single, simple image: man embarked upon a journey begun in diapers and completed in a shroud. Yet, this statement, like all sweeping generalities, contains only a part-truth. The route by which man travels from the cradle to the grave is no broad highway but a road with many ups and downs, sudden turnings, and strange byways. To the modern novelist, none of these is more interesting or significant than the downward road to wisdom. In much modern fiction, the beginning of knowledge is the loss of innocence and not a fear of the Lord.

The fable of innocence confronted by evil and gaining a sad kind of wisdom in the encounter is the theme of James Leo Herlihy's novel. The fact that the youthful hero of *All Fall Down* makes a long journey in the geography of his own soul puts him into some rather interesting literary company: Huck Finn on his raft, Holden Caulfield exploring an adult world of hypocrisy and sham, Frankie Addams willing herself into becoming a member of the wedding. Although *All Fall Down* is a book that invites comparisons, to note them is not to say that Herlihy is in any way imitative. Quite the other way around, his ability to present the emotional adventures of youth as a difficult passage between childhood and maturity, and to tell the story as if it had never been written before, is striking proof of his imaginative force and dramatic control.

Clinton Williams, his hero, is a boy as free-wheeling in his character as Holden Caulfield but in a vastly different way. Caulfield is an uncomplicated realist whose quickness of mind enables him to identify pretense wherever he thinks he finds it. Clinton, on the other hand, grows up pursuing an illusion, the glamour that his romantic imagination throws about his older brother, whom Caulfield would have cataloged at once as a phony. When the novel opens, Clinton is fourteen and his brother, Berry-berry, is away "on his travels," begun shortly after his twenty-first birthday. The Williams family has recently moved into a house in a different section of Cleveland. Clinton is afraid that Berry-berry will not be able to find this new house if he should return, and as a gesture of quiet protest he has stayed away from school for fifty-seven consecutive days. In the daytime, he loafs in the Aloha Sweet Shop, recording in his notebooks everything he sees or overhears. At home he eavesdrops on his parents' conversations, which he writes into his journals as well, along with copies of letters he has opened on the sly. During the time he had been skipping school, he filled twenty-five notebooks. His entries— Herlihy gives the reader a fair sampling—are as naïve, funny, boring, and revealing as one might expect. His romantic view of Berry-berry is the first interest of Clinton's life. The second is his tremendous curiosity about people and the nature of experience; hence, his effort to put down everything he knows and learns in order that he may solve some of life's mysteries.

In many ways Clinton is his father's true son. Years before, Ralph Williams had been an active liberal, before he was trapped by marriage and a family. Theoretically he is in business, but he spends most of his time in the cellar with a jigsaw puzzle in front of him and a bottle of bourbon within reach. He has simplified his life to two convictions: that Christ had founded the Socialist Party and that Berry-berry will turn out all right in the end. Mrs. Williams is nervous, querulous, and tearful, constantly wishing for Berry-berry's return without ever realizing that he hates her.

The memory of the absent son is all that holds this strange family together. Ironically, Berry-berry is unworthy of their love or their hopes for his return. A bum, a pimp, and a sadist, he turns up first in one section of the country, then in another, is in jail or out, is either living off one of his women or else calling on his family for money to get him out of his latest escapade. Most of these facts are unknown to Clinton, however, during the time when he is working in an all-night eating place and saving his money against the day when he can join his brother. The opportunity comes when Berry-berry writes, asking his father for two hundred dollars to invest in a shrimping venture in Key Bonita, Florida. Ready to offer the money, Clinton takes a bus to Key Bonita, to find on his arrival that Berry-berry has already skipped town after mauling one of his lady loves. This knowledge comes to Clinton during the night he spends with a prostitute, and the realization of his brother's true nature is almost more than he can stand. He returns home, falls sick, and at one time during his illness contemplates suicide. He is saved when he falls shyly in love with Echo O'Brien, a girl older than he and the daughter of one of his mother's friends, who comes to visit in Cleveland.

Then Berry-berry returns and all is forgotten, or at least forgiven, and the Williamses are reunited by love. As might have been expected, Berry-berry makes a play for Echo O'Brien. His parents hope that the affair will cause Berry-berry to settle down at last. Clinton accepts the fact of Echo's romance with his brother out of gratitude for the atmosphere of family happiness in which he now shares. Berry-berry, however, cannot be reclaimed from the moral rot that infects him. Refusing to accept responsibility for Echo's pregnant condition, he callously discards her, and Echo commits suicide. Clinton at first intends to kill his brother, but in the end, he decides that Berry-berry's knowledge of his own corruption is punishment enough. Berry-berry takes to the road again. Clinton begins writing in his notebooks once more, but now, as he says, he feels that he has grown up.

All Fall Down is a story expertly told, dramatically convincing, and comic in an odd, offbeat sort of way. For his novel's epigraph, Herlihy uses a passage from Sherwood Anderson's *Winesburg, Ohio*, the section telling of people who seize upon some particular truth, try to make it their truth only, and become grotesques as a result. The quotation is relevant to Herlihy's novel for the book is, on one level, a story of grotesques. For a long time the Williamses have lived apart and according to their own concerns. It is not until they make love a shared thing that they really come alive. Also, the use of the grotesque is in keeping with the modern view that its image, anti-romantic and antitragic alike, provides the most effective means of expressing both the irrationality of things and the moral evil that is also the devouring, obsessive evil of modern society, the isolation of the loving and the lonely. Herlihy sees moral isolation as one of the conditions of being, but he does not make it, as some of his contemporaries have done, a reason for fury or despair. His novel ends on a note of hope.

ALL THE KING'S MEN

Type of work: Novel
Author: Robert Penn Warren (1905–   )
Type of plot: Social criticism
Time of plot: Late 1920's and early 1930's
Locale: Southern U.S.A.
First published: 1946

Principal characters:
JACK BURDEN, a journalist and political lackey
WILLIE STARK, a political boss
SADIE BURKE, his mistress
ANNE STANTON, a social worker
ADAM STANTON, her brother
JUDGE IRWIN

The Story:

When Governor Willie Stark tried to intimidate old Judge Irwin of Burden's Landing, the Judge stood firm against the demagogue's threats. As a result, Willie ordered Jack Burden to find some scandal in the Judge's past that could ruin the elderly man.

Jack had met Willie back in 1922, when Willie, the county treasurer, and Lucy Stark, his schoolteacher wife, were fighting against a corrupt building contractor who was constructing the new schoolhouse. Sent by his newspaper, the *Chronicle*, to investigate, Jack found Willie and Lucy both out of jobs but still fighting against graft. Two years later, the fire escape of the school collapsed during a fire drill, and Willie became a hero.

Willie then ran in the Democratic primary race for governor. There were two factions, those of Harrison and MacMurfee. Because it was to be a close election, someone proposed that Willie be used as a dummy candidate to split the rural MacMurfee followers. Tiny Duffy and some other men convinced Willie that he could save the state. By then, Willie had become a lawyer and a politically ambitious man. Jack covered the campaign.

Aiding Willie was Sadie Burke, a clever, energetic woman with political skill. Inadvertently she revealed Harrison's plan to Willie. Crushed and gloomy at this news, Willie rallied his spirits and offered to campaign for MacMurfee, who was elected.

Willie practiced law for a few years until 1930; he then ran for governor with the assistance of Sadie Burke, who became his mistress, and Tiny Duffy, who was Willie's political jackal.

Meanwhile, Jack had quit his job on the *Chronicle*. Reared by a mother who had remarried since Ellis Burden had deserted her, Jack had become a faithless, homeless cynic whose journalism career meant nothing to him as an ideal. He had, in his youth, played with Anne and Adam Stanton. Adam was now a famous surgeon, and Anne, still unmarried, had become a welfare worker.

Jack was in love with Anne, but time had placed a barrier between him and the girl with whom he had fallen in love during the summer after he had come home to Burden's Landing from college. He had been twenty-one then, she seventeen. Jack's youthful cynicism, however, which later took possession of him completely, spoiled him in Anne's eyes.

When Jack went to work for Governor Willie Stark, Jack's mother was deeply pained and Judge Irwin was disgusted, but Jack cared little for their opinions.

By 1933, Willie was on the verge of losing his wife, who could not stand her husband's political maneuvers and his treatment of their son Tom. Willie assured Jack that Lucy knew nothing about Sadie Burke. Lucy remained with Willie through his reelection, in 1934, and then retired to her sister's farm. She appeared with Willie in public only for the sake of his reputation.

Jack began to dig into Judge Irwin's past. Delving into the Judge's financial transactions during the time when he was attorney general under Governor Stanton, Jack learned that a power company had been sued by the government for a large sum. As a bribe to the attorney general, the company fired one of its men to give a highly paid job to Irwin. Later this man, Littlepaugh, committed suicide after writing the facts in a letter to his sister. Still living, Miss Littlepaugh told Jack the story.

The issue of the Willie Stark six-million-dollar hospital demanded use of this scandal which Jack had uncovered. Willie told Jack that he wanted Adam Stanton to head the new hospital. It would, Jack knew, be a ridiculous offer to the aloof and unworldly young doctor, but he made an effort to convince Adam to take the post. Adam flatly refused. A few days later, Anne sent for Jack. She wanted Adam to take the position. Jack showed Anne the documents proving Judge Irwin's acceptance of a bribe and Governor Stanton's attempt to cover up for his friend. Knowing that Adam would want to protect his father's good name, Anne showed the evidence to him. He then said he would head the hospital.

Later, Jack wondered how Anne had known about the plans for the hospital, because neither he nor Adam had told her. Jack's suspicions were confirmed when Sadie Burke, in a torrent of rage, told him that Willie had been betraying her. Jack knew then that Anne Stanton was the cause. Disillusioned, he packed a suitcase and drove to California. This journey to the West and back completed, Jack, his torment under control, went back to work for Willie.

One of MacMurfee's men tried to bribe Adam to use influence in selecting a man named Larson as the builder of the medical center. When Adam, outraged, decided to resign, Anne phoned Jack for the first time since he had learned of her affair with Willie. Anne and Jack decided to get Adam to sign a warrant against the man who had tried to bribe him. Jack also warned Anne that as a witness she would be subject to public scrutiny of her relationship with Willie, but she said she did not care. Jack asked her why she was associating with Willie. She said that after learning about Governor Stanton's dishonesty in the past, she did not care what happened to her. Later, Jack persuaded Adam not to bring suit.

After Willie's political enemy, MacMurfee, tried to blackmail him because of a scandal concerning Tom Stark, Willie ordered Jack to use his knowledge to make Judge Irwin throw his weight against MacMurfee's blackmail attempt. When Jack went to Burden's Landing to confront Judge Irwin with the evidence that Jack had obtained from Miss Littlepaugh, the old man shot himself.

In the excitement following the suicide, Jack's mother told him that he had caused his father's death. Belatedly, Jack discovered the reason for Ellis Burden's desertion. In his will, Judge Irwin left his estate to his son, Jack Burden.

Only one way seemed left to handle MacMurfee. Willie decided to give the building contract for the hospital to MacMurfee's man, Larson, who in turn would suppress the scandal about Tom. Duffy made the arrangements.

Tom Stark was a football hero. One Saturday during a game, his neck was broken. Adam reported that Tom would remain paralyzed. This news had its effect on Willie. He told Duffy that the hospital deal was off. Turning to Lucy once more, he dismissed Sadie Burke and Anne Stanton.

Duffy, driven too far by Willie, telephoned Adam and told him that Anne had been responsible for his appointment. Adam, having known nothing of his sister's relationship with the Governor, went to her apartment to denounce her. Then, in the hall of the state building, Adam shot Willie and was killed immediately afterward by Willie's bodyguard.

Piece by piece, the tangled mess of Jack's life began to take on new meaning. He separated himself from every particle of his past with the exception of two people: his mother, whose devotion to Judge Irwin over all the years had given her a new personality in Jack's eyes, and Anne Stanton, whom he married.

Critical Evaluation:

One of the richest and most powerful of modern American novels is Robert Penn Warren's *All the King's Men*. In its pages the reader can trace a multitude of fascinating subjects ranging from politics to religion, from sociology to philosophy. He can discover an equally wide scope of thematic questions. Arousing, as it does, various responses to its complexities, responses which, for example, praise it as Christian or revile it as nihilistic on exactly the same grounds, the book is generally regarded as the masterpiece of a novelist (*The Cave*, *World Enough and Time*, *Band of Angels*) who is also a respected poet, critic, and professor. Warren, a Kentucky native, has a special affinity for the South, and much of his work suggests the traditions and problems of this region. *All the King's Men*, while exploring issues universal as well as regional, also has an unmistakable Southern flavor in areas more vital than mere setting.

An immediate query regarding this Pulitzer Prize-winning book usually touches on the relationship of Willie Stark and Huey Long. Governor of Louisiana from 1928 to 1931, Long led a career parallel to what Warren designs for Stark and presented a similar powerful and paradoxical personality. The product of a poor background, Long nevertheless became a lawyer at twenty-one after completing the three-year Tulane University course in eight months. Aggressive and determined, at age twenty-four, he sought and won the one state office open at his age—a seat on the Railroad Commission. An unorthodox champion of the little man, Long in his 1924 race for governor was unsuccessful when he tried to remain moderate on the Ku Klux Klan issue. His 1928 try for the office was a triumph, however, and at thirty-five, the outspoken country boy was a governor who almost single-handedly ruled the state. Using patronage as his lever, Long talked the legislature into a thirty-million-dollar bond issue to finance farm roads, hospitals, free school-books, and other programs popular with the poor but infuriating to his opponents. Like Stark, Long soon found himself impeached, charged with bribery, plotting the murder of a senator, misusing state funds, and various other crimes, some of which this strange mixture of demagogue and selfless public servant no doubt committed. Yet his promises and threats kept Long in office when enough senators signed a round robin promising not to convict him no matter what the evidence.

Long's career, which included the unprecedented move of becoming a United States senator while still serving in effect as governor, as well as plans to seek the presidency, was halted by assassination. In a 1935 scene almost re-created in *All the King's Men*, a man stepped from behind a pillar at the capitol and shot once, hitting Long. Felled by sixty-one bullets from Long's bodyguards, the man, Dr. Carl A. Weiss, died within seconds. Thirty hours later, Long, the "Kingfish," was also dead. Weiss's motivations were obscure; speculation said that he was angered when Long's maneuvering cost his father a judgeship.

Despite the overwhelming similarities between Long and Stark, Warren denies that he attempted merely to create a fictional counterpart of a political figure. But, he says, the "line of thinking and feeling" in the book does evolve from the atmosphere of Louisiana he encountered while he was a teacher at Louisiana State University, an atmosphere dominated and directed by Long's tenure as governor.

Central to the book is the primary theme of man's search for knowledge; all other facets are subordinate to and supportive of this theme. Knowledge includes both objective and subjective comprehensions, with the end goal being self-knowledge. "Life is Motion toward Knowledge," readers find in *All the King's Men*. Elsewhere, Warren asserts that the right to knowledge is man's "right to exist, to be himself, to be a man." Man defines himself through knowledge, and the book's pivotal incident demands accumulation of knowledge. Jack, assigned to "dig something up" on the Judge, does indeed uncover the Judge's dishonor, but the information precipitates a far more meaningful understanding.

For each of the characters, it is a lack of knowledge or an incomplete knowledge that constitutes his chief problem, and those who eventually blunder forward do so only when they see what has previously been hidden from them. As the narrator, for example, Jack Burden is allegedly telling Willie Stark's story. Yet the reader senses that as he relates the events, Jack is clarifying their meaning mostly for his own benefit. The product of an aristocratic background, Jack in essence eschews knowledge throughout most of the story, for he exists in a vacuum, refusing to be touched or to feel. At moments of crisis, he seeks oblivion in The Great Sleep or by adhering to a belief in The Great Twitch: "Nobody has any responsibility for anything." He is a man of reflection only until those reflections become troublesome.

Seemingly, Willie is the book's most knowing character. Yet his knowledge is questioned, at first only occasionally, then fully. Unlike Jack, who drops his idealism for inertia, Stark is always a man of action, action based sometimes on only partial knowledge. His innocence, lost by the "knowledge" that he has been betrayed, is replaced by a willingness to use evil if it is necessary for his purposes. He can justify blackmail or protection of a crook on this basis. For a time, Willie maintains and understands the balance between good and evil, but "obsessed with the evil in human nature and with his power to manipulate it," he is drawn completely onto the side of this dark force.

Jack ignores both ideals and the world; Willie ignores the ideals. The third important character is Adam Stanton, who ignores the world. Make good out of evil, says Willie, for the bad is all you have to work with. Horrified by such a philosophy, Adam denies that honor, purity, and justice can commingle with blackness. When his preconceptions of the state of the universe prove false, he repudiates not his ideas but the universe. He is the man of idea untainted by fact or action; thus, his knowledge is also faulty and weak, a situation which leads him to tragedy.

Through his investigation of the Judge, Jack inadvertently stumbles on the greater truth for himself and for the novel. He learns who he is in that he discovers his true father, but more important, he learns what he is as a man: an imperfect being who must accept imperfection in himself and others and lovingly make what he may out of that state. He, like Cass Mastern, learns that men cannot be separated from other men, that no action or idea exists alone, that past, present, and future are entangled in the web. He realizes what Willie initially knew, yet forgot, but reclaimed at the end of the novel. When he tells Jack that all might have been different, Willie implies that his fate might have been different had he remembered that although both good and evil exist and influence each other, they are not the same.

Closely aligned with the knowledge theme is the Humpty Dumpty motif. The title hints at multiple meanings, for on one level, Willie is the King (the boss), and the characters "all the king's men." Yet perhaps greater significance arises if readers see Willie as Humpty, for both fall to their doom and cannot be repaired. In this view, the King is God, and the King's men represent mankind. The fall becomes The Fall because Willie ruins himself by his knowledge of evil unbalanced by a corresponding ability to overcome its effects. Readers may also view Jack as another Humpty, one whose breakage is not irrevocable because his understanding and knowledge of evil ultimately correspond to an appropriate conception of the nature of good.

Warren's literary style is excellent. It is so good that the reader is likely to regret reaching the final pages of the book. From the opening description of Sugar Boy's drive down the country highway until the last pages when Jack Burden realizes his self-destruction and, phoenixlike, rises from the ruins of his past to make a new life with Anne Stanton, the plot is gripping and real.

THE AMBASSADORS

Type of work: Novel
Author: Henry James (1843–1916)
Type of plot: Psychological realism
Time of plot: About 1900
Locale: Paris, France
First published: 1903

Principal characters:
> CHADWICK NEWSOME (CHAD), an American expatriate
> LAMBERT STRETHER, his friend
> MARIA GOSTREY, an acquaintance of Strether
> COMTESSE DE VIONNET, a woman in love with Chadwick
>   Newsome
> MRS. POCOCK, Chadwick's married sister
> MAMIE POCOCK, Mrs. Pocock's husband's sister

The Story:

Lambert Strether was engaged to marry Mrs. Newsome, a widow. Mrs. Newsome had a son, Chadwick, whom she wanted to return home from Paris and take over the family business in Woollett, Massachusetts. She was especially concerned for his future after she had heard that he was seriously involved with a Frenchwoman. In her anxiety, she asked Strether to go to Paris and persuade her son to return to the respectable life she had planned for him.

Strether did not look forward to his task, for Chadwick had ignored all of his mother's written requests to return home. Strether also did not know what hold Chadwick's mistress might have over him or what sort of woman she might be. He strongly suspected that she was a young girl of unsavory reputation. Strether realized, however, that his hopes of marrying Mrs. Newsome depended upon his success in bringing Chad back to America, where his mother could see him married to Mamie Pocock.

Leaving his ship at Liverpool, Strether journeyed across England to London. On the way he met Miss Gostrey, a young woman who was acquainted with some of Strether's American friends, and she promised to aid Strether in getting acquainted with Europe before he left for home again. Strether met another old friend, Mr. Waymarsh, an American lawyer living in England, whom he asked to go with him to Paris.

A few days after arriving in Paris, Strether went to Chad's house. The young man was not in Paris, and he had temporarily given the house over to a friend, Mr. Bilham. Through Bilham, Strether got in touch with Chad at Cannes. Strether was surprised to learn of his whereabouts, for he knew that Chad would not have dared to take an ordinary mistress to such a fashionable resort.

About a week later, Strether, Miss Gostrey, and Waymarsh went to the theater. Between the acts of the play, the door of their box was opened and Chad entered. He was much changed from the adolescent college boy Strether remembered. He was slightly gray, although only twenty-eight years old.

Both Strether and Chad Newsome were pleased to see each other. Over coffee after the theater, the older man told Chad why he had come to Europe. Chad answered that all he asked was an opportunity to be convinced that he should return.

A few days later, Chad took Strether and his friends to a tea where they met Mme and Mlle de Vionnet. The former, who had married a French count, turned out to be an old school friend of Miss Gostrey. Strether was at a loss to understand whether Chad was in love with the comtesse or with her daughter Jeanne. Since the older woman was only a few years the senior of the young man and as beautiful as her daughter, either was possibly the object of his affections.

As the days slipped by, it became apparent to Strether that he himself wanted to stay in Paris. The French city and its life were much calmer and more beautiful than the provincial existence he had known in Woollett, and he began to understand why Chad was unwilling to go back to his mother and the Newsome mills.

Strether learned that Chad was in love with Mme de Vionnet, rather than with her daughter. The comtesse had been separated from her husband for many years, but their position and religion made divorce impossible. Strether, who was often in the company of the Frenchwoman, soon fell under her charm. Miss Gostrey, who had known Mme de Vionnet for many years, had only praise for her and questioned Strether as to the advisability of removing Chad from the woman's continued influence.

One morning Chad announced to Strether that he was ready to return immediately to America. The young man was puzzled when Strether replied that he was not sure it was wise for either of them to return and that it would be wiser for them both to reconsider whether they would not be better off in Paris than in New England.

When Mrs. Newsome, back in America, received word of that decision on the part of her ambassador, she immediately sent the Pococks, her daughter and son-in-law, to Paris along with Mamie Pocock, the girl she hoped her son would marry. They were to bring back both Strether and her son.

Mrs. Newsome's daughter and her relatives did not come to Paris with an obvious ill will. Their attitude seemed to be that Chad and Strether had somehow drifted astray, and it was their duty to set them right. At least that was the attitude of Mrs. Pocock. Her husband, however, was not at all interested in having Chad return, for in the young man's absence, Mr. Pocock controlled the Newsome mills. Mr. Pocock further saw that his visit was probably the last opportunity he would have for a spirited time in the European city, and so he was quite willing to spend his holiday going to theaters and cafés. His younger sister, Mamie, seemed to take little interest in the recall of her supposed fiancé, for she had become interested in Chad's friend, Mr. Bilham.

The more Strether saw of Mme de Vionnet after the arrival of the Pococks, the more he was convinced that the Frenchwoman was both noble and sincere in her attempts to make friends with her lover's family. Mrs. Pocock found it difficult to reconcile Mme de Vionnet's aristocratic background with the fact that she was Chad's mistress.

After several weeks of hints and genteel pleading, the Pococks and Mamie went to Switzerland, leaving Chad to make a decision whether to return to America. As for Mr. Strether, Mrs. Newsome had advised that he be left alone to make his own decision, for the widow wanted to avoid the appearance of having lost her dignity or her sense of propriety.

While the Pococks were gone, Strether and Chad discussed the course they should follow. Chad was uncertain of his attitude toward Mamie Pocock. Strether assured him that the girl was already happy with her new love, Mr. Bilham, who had told Strether that he intended to marry the American girl. His advice, contrary to what he had thought when he had sailed from America, was that Chadwick Newsome should remain in France with the comtesse, despite the fact that the young man could not marry her and would, by remaining in Europe, lose the opportunity to make himself an extremely rich man. Chad decided to take his older friend's counsel.

Waymarsh, who had promised his help in persuading Chad to return to America, was outraged at Strether's changed attitude. Miss Gostrey, however, remained loyal, for she had fallen deeply in love with Strether during their time together in Paris. Strether, however, realizing her feelings, told her that he had to go back to America alone. His object in Europe had been to return Chad Newsome to his mother. Because he had failed in that mission and would never marry Mrs. Newsome, he could not justify to himself marrying another woman whom he had met on a journey financed by the woman he had at one time intended to marry. Only Mme de Vionnet, he felt, could truly appreciate the irony of his position.

Critical Evaluation:

In Henry James's *The Ambassadors*, plot is minimal; the story line consists simply in Mrs. Newsome sending Lambert Strether to Europe to bring home her son, Chad. The important action is psychological rather than physical;

the crucial activities are thought and conversation. The pace of the novel is slow. Events unfold as they do in life: in their own good time.

Because of these qualities, James's work demands certain responses from the reader. He must not expect boisterous action, shocking or violent occurrences, sensational coincidences, quickly mounting suspense, or breathtaking climaxes: these devices have no place in a Henry James novel. Rather, the reader must bring to the work a sensitivity to problems of conscience, an appreciation of the meaning beneath manners, and an awareness of the intricacies of human relationships. Finally, and of the utmost importance, the reader must be patient; the power of a novel like *The Ambassadors* is only revealed quietly and without haste. This is why, perhaps more than any other modern author, James requires rereading—not merely because of the complexity of his style, but because the richly layered texture of his prose contains a multiplicity of meanings, a wealth of subtle shadings.

In *The Ambassadors*, which James considered his masterpiece, this subtlety and complexity is partially the result of his perfection of the technique for handling point of view. Departing from traditional eighteenth and nineteenth century use of the omniscient narrator, James experimented extensively with the limited point of view, exploring the device to discover what advantages it might have over the older method. He found that what was lost in panoramic scope and comprehensiveness, the limited viewpoint more than compensated for in focus, concentration, and intensity. It was the technique perfectly suited to an author whose primary concern was with presenting the thoughts, emotions, and motivations of an intelligent character, with understanding the psychological makeup of a sensitive mind and charting its growth.

The sensitive and intelligent character through whose mind all events in the novel are filtered is Lambert Strether. The reader sees and hears only what Strether sees and hears; all experiences, perceptions, and judgments are his. Strictly adhered to, this device proved too restrictive for James's purpose; therefore, he utilized other characters—called confidants—who enabled him to expand the scope of his narrative without sacrificing advantages inherent in the limited point of view. The basic function of these "listening characters" is to expand and enrich Strether's experience. Miss Gostrey, Little Bilham, Waymarsh, and Miss Barrace—all share with him attitudes and insights arising from their widely diverse backgrounds; they provide him with a wider range of knowledge than he could ever gain from firsthand experience. Maria Gostrey, Strether's primary confidante, illustrates the fact that James's listening characters are deep and memorable personalities in their own right. Miss Gostrey not only listens to Strether, but she also becomes an important figure in the plot, and as she gradually falls in love with Strether, she engages the reader's sympathy as well.

Lambert Strether interacts with and learns from the environment of Paris as well as from the people he meets there; thus, the setting is far more than a mere backdrop against which events in the plot occur. To understand the significance of Paris as the setting, the reader must appreciate the meaning that the author, throughout his fiction, attached to certain places. James was fascinated by what he saw as the underlying differences in the cultures of America and Europe and, in particular, in the opposing values of a booming American factory town such as Woollett and an ancient European capital such as Paris. In these two places, very different qualities are held in esteem. In Woollett, Mrs. Newsome admires practicality, individuality, and enterprise, while in Paris, her son appreciates good food and expensive wine, conversation with a close circle of friends, and leisure time quietly spent. Woollett pursues commercialism, higher social status, and rigid moral codes with untiring vigor; Paris values the beauty of nature, the pleasure of companionship, and an appreciation of the arts with studied simplicity. Thus, the implications of a native of Woollett, such as Lambert Strether, going to Paris at the end of his life are manifold; and it is through his journey that the theme of the novel is played out.

The theme consists of a question of conscience: Should Strether, in his capacity as Mrs. Newsome's ambassador, be faithful to his mission of bringing Chad home, once he no longer believes in that mission? That he ceases to believe is the result of his conversion during his stay in Paris. He is exposed to a side of life that he had not known previously; furthermore, he finds it to be good. As a man of noble nature and sensitive conscience, he cannot ignore or deny, as Sarah Newsome later does, that life in Paris has vastly improved Chad. Ultimately, therefore, he must oppose rather than promote the young man's return. The honesty of this action not only destroys his chance for financial security in marriage to Chad's mother but also prevents him from returning the love of Maria Gostrey. Although Strether's discovery of a different set of values comes too late in life for his own benefit, he at least can save Chad. The lesson he learns is the one he passionately seeks to impart to Little Bilham: "Live all you can; it's a mistake not to. It doesn't so much matter what you do in particular, so long as you have your life. . . . Don't, at any rate, miss things out of stupidity. . . . Live!"

If, in reading *The Ambassadors*, the reader's expectations are for keenness of observation, insight into motivations, comprehension of mental processes, and powerful characterizations, he will not be disappointed. If Henry James demands the effort, concentration, and commitment of his reader, he also— with his depth and breadth of vision and the sheer beauty of his craftsman-ship—repays him a hundredfold.

THE AMERICAN

Type of work: Novel
Author: Henry James (1843–1916)
Type of plot: Psychological realism
Time of plot: Mid-nineteenth century
Locale: Paris, France
First published: 1877

Principal characters:
CHRISTOPHER NEWMAN, an American
MR. TRISTRAM, a friend
MRS. TRISTRAM, his wife
M. NIOCHE, a shopkeeper
MLLE NIOCHE, his daughter
MADAME DE BELLEGARDE, a French aristocrat
CLAIRE DE CINTRÉ, Madame de Bellegarde's daughter
MARQUIS DE BELLEGARDE, Madame de Bellegarde's older son
VALENTIN DE BELLEGARDE, Madame de Bellegarde's younger son
MRS. BREAD, Madame de Bellegarde's servant

The Story:

In 1868, Christopher Newman, a young American millionaire, withdrew from business and sailed for Paris. He wanted to loaf, to develop his aesthetic sense, and to find a wife for himself. One day, as he wandered in the Louvre, he made the acquaintance of Mlle Nioche, a young copyist. She introduced him to her father, an unsuccessful shopkeeper. Newman bought a picture from Mlle Nioche and contracted to take French lessons from her father.

Later, through the French wife of an American friend named Tristram, he met Claire de Cintré, a young widow, daughter of an English mother and a French father. As a young girl, Claire had been married to Monsier de Cintré, an evil old man. He had soon died, leaving Claire with a distaste for marriage. In spite of her attitude, Newman saw in her the woman he wished for his wife. An American businessman, however, was not the person to associate with French aristocracy. On his first call, Newman was kept from entering Claire's house by her elder brother, the Marquis de Bellegarde.

True to his promise, M. Nioche appeared one morning to give Newman his first lesson in French. Newman enjoyed talking to the old man. He learned that Mlle Nioche dominated her father, who lived in fear that she would leave him and become the mistress of some rich man. M. Nioche told Newman that he would shoot his daughter if she did. Newman took pity on the old man and promised him enough money for Mlle Nioche's dowry if she would paint more copies for him.

Newman left Paris and traveled through Europe during the summer. When he returned to Paris in autumn, he learned that the Tristrams had been helpful; the Bellegardes were willing to receive him. One evening, Claire's younger brother, Valentin, called on Newman and the two men found their opposite points of view a basis for friendship. Valentin envied Newman's liberty to do as he pleased; Newman wished himself acceptable to the society in which the Bellegardes moved. After the two men had become good friends, Newman told Valentin that he wished to marry his sister and asked Valentin to plead his cause. Warning Newman that his social position was against him, Valentin promised to help the American as much as he could.

Newman confessed his wish to Claire and asked Madame de Bellegarde, Claire's mother, and the Marquis for permission to be her suitor. The permission was given, grudgingly. The Bellegardes needed money in the family.

Newman went to the Louvre to see how Mlle Nioche was progressing with her copying. There he met Valentin and introduced him to the young lady.

Mrs. Bread, an old English servant of the Bellegardes, assured Newman that he was making progress with his suit. He asked Claire to marry him, and she accepted. Meanwhile, Valentin had challenged another man to a duel in a quarrel over Mlle Nioche. Valentin left for Switzerland with his seconds. The next morning, Newman went to see Claire. Mrs. Bread met him at the door and said that Claire was leaving town. Newman demanded an explanation. He was told that the Bellegardes could not allow a commercial person in the family. When he arrived home, he found a telegram from Valentin stating that he had been badly wounded and asking Newman to come at once to Switzerland.

With this double burden of sorrow, Newman arrived in Switzerland and found Valentin near death. Valentin guessed what his family had done and told Newman that Mrs. Bread knew a family secret. If he could get the secret from her, he could make them return Claire to him. Valentin died the next morning.

Newman attended the funeral. Three days later, he again called on Claire, who told him that she intended to enter a convent. Newman begged her not to take this step. Desperate, he called on the Bellegardes again and told them that he would uncover their secret. Newman arranged to see Mrs. Bread that night. She told him that Madame de Bellegarde had killed her invalid husband because he had opposed Claire's marriage to M. de Cintré. The death had been judged natural, but Mrs. Bread had in her possession a document proving that Madame de Bellegarde had murdered her husband. She gave this paper to Newman.

Mrs. Bread left the employ of the Bellegardes and came to keep house for Newman. She told him that Claire had gone to the convent and refused to see anyone, even her own family. The next Sunday, Newman went to mass at the convent. After the service, he met the Bellegardes walking in the park and showed them a copy of the paper Mrs. Bread had given him.

The next day, the Marquis called on Newman and offered to pay for the document. Newman refused to sell. He offered, however, to accept Claire in exchange for it. The Marquis refused.

Newman found he could not bring himself to reveal the Bellegardes' secret. On the advice of the Tristrams, he traveled through the English countryside and, in a melancholy mood, went to some of the places he had planned to visit on his honeymoon. Then he went to America. Restless, he returned to Paris and learned from Mrs. Tristram that Claire had become a nun.

The next time he went to see Mrs. Tristram, he dropped the secret document on the glowing logs in her fireplace and told her that to expose the Bellegardes now seemed a useless and empty gesture. He intended to leave Paris forever. Mrs. Tristram told him that he probably had not frightened the Bellegardes with his threat, because they knew that they could count on his good nature never to reveal their secret. Newman instinctively looked toward the fireplace. The paper had burned to ashes.

Critical Evaluation:

Christopher Newman of *The American* represents new world culture in conflict with the rigid traditions of the European aristocracy. Newman, a natural aristocrat in his own right, epitomizes the democratic spirit and pragmatic values of a culture in which accomplishment is alone the measure of individual worth. Although Newman suffers from a naïveté which blinds him to the complications of the complex society he encounters in France, he is an essentially moral person whose values ultimately prove superior to those of his detractors.

True to his materialistic background, Newman comes to Paris determined to acquire the best that European culture has to offer. He quickly reveals that he has little instinct for the best in art, and his judgment of people will prove equally inept. His choice of Claire de Cintré is based equally upon his vision of her as his ideal woman and as the ultimate possession to crown his success. His failure to achieve her depends upon his failure to recognize her subordination to the family will and the Bellegarde family's determination not to surrender the aristocratic tradition which is all that remains of their nobility.

Expecting that the Bellegardes will finally sacrifice family tradition to their material interests, Newman enters into a game with rules he never fully understands. His own democratic spirit makes it impossible that he should ever comprehend the almost religious idolatry of family, which characterizes the Bellegardes. As they show their true colors, including criminal responsibility for the death of Claire's father, their "nobility" is shown to be based entirely upon tradition—it has no moral and human equivalent. Newman, on the other hand, rises in the reader's estimation as a natural aristocrat whose moral superiority makes him the real measure of the best in the human condition.

In this novel, Henry James's primary interest is not in the action; his aim is to analyze the various psychological situations created by the events of the plot. The author scrutinizes the inner lives of his characters and writes about them in an urbane and polished style uniquely his own.

AN AMERICAN TRAGEDY

Type of work: Novel
Author: Theodore Dreiser (1871–1945)
Type of plot: Social criticism
Time of plot: Early twentieth century
Locale: Kansas City, Chicago, and Lycurgus, New York
First published: 1925

> *Principal characters:*
> CLYDE GRIFFITHS
> ROBERTA ALDEN, his mistress
> SAMUEL GRIFFITHS, Clyde's wealthy uncle
> SONDRA FINCHLEY, a society girl whom Clyde loves

The Story:

When Clyde Griffiths was still a child, his religious-minded parents took him and his brothers and sisters around the streets of various cities, where they prayed and sang in public. The family was always very poor, but the fundamentalist faith of the Griffiths was their hope and mainstay throughout the storms and troubles of life.

Young Clyde was never religious, however, and he always felt ashamed of the existence his parents were living. As soon as he was old enough to make decisions for himself, he decided to go his own way. At age sixteen, he got a job as a bellboy in a Kansas City hotel. There the salary and the tips he received astonished him. For the first time in his life he had money in his pocket, and he could dress well and enjoy himself. Then a tragedy overwhelmed the family. Clyde's sister ran away, supposedly to be married. Her elopement was a great blow to the parents, but Clyde did not brood over the matter. Life was too pleasant for him; more and more, he enjoyed the luxuries that his job provided. He made friends with the other bellhops and joined them in parties that centered around liquor and women. Clyde soon became familiar with drink and brothels.

One day, he discovered that his sister was back in town. The man with whom she had run away had deserted her, and she was penniless and pregnant. Knowing his sister needed money, Clyde gave his mother a few dollars for her. He promised to give her more; instead, he bought an expensive coat for a girl in the hope that she would yield herself to him. One night, he and his friends went to a party in a car that did not belong to them. Coming back from their outing, they ran over a little girl. In their attempt to escape, they wrecked the car. Clyde fled to Chicago.

In Chicago he got work at the Union League Club, where he eventually met his wealthy uncle, Samuel Griffiths. The uncle, who owned a factory in Lycurgus, New York, took a fancy to Clyde and offered him work in the factory. Clyde went to Lycurgus. There his cousin, Gilbert, resented this cousin from the Middle West. The whole family, with the exception of his uncle, considered Clyde beneath them socially and would not accept him into their circle. Clyde was given a job at the very bottom of the business, but his uncle soon made him a supervisor.

In the meantime, Sondra Finchley, who disliked Gilbert, began to invite Clyde to parties that she and her friends often gave. Her main purpose was to annoy Gilbert. Clyde's growing popularity forced the Griffiths to receive him socially, much to Gilbert's disgust.

In the course of his work at the factory, Clyde met Roberta Alden, with whom he soon fell in love. Since it was forbidden for a supervisor to mix socially with an employee, they had to meet secretly. Clyde attempted to persuade Roberta to give herself to him, but the girl refused. At last, rather than lose him, she consented and became his mistress.

At the same time, Clyde was becoming fascinated by Sondra. He came to love her and hoped to marry her and, thus, acquire the wealth and social position for which he yearned. Gradually, Clyde began breaking dates with Roberta in order to be with Sondra every moment that she could spare him. Roberta began to be suspicious and eventually discovered the truth.

By that time she was pregnant. Clyde went to drug stores for medicine that did not work. He attempted to find a doctor of questionable reputation. Roberta went to see one physician who refused to perform an operation. Clyde and Roberta were both becoming desperate, and Clyde saw his possible marriage to the girl as a dismal ending to all his hopes for a bright future. He told himself that he did not love Roberta, that it was Sondra whom he wished to marry. Roberta asked him to marry her for the sake of her child, saying she would go away afterward, if he wished, so that he could be free of her. Clyde would not agree to her proposal and grew more irritable and worried.

One day he read an item in the newspaper about the accidental drowning of a couple who had gone boating. Slowly a plan began to form in his mind. He told Roberta that he would marry her and persuaded her to accompany him to an isolated lake resort. There, as though accidentally, he lunged toward her. She was hit by his camera and fell into the water. Clyde escaped, confident that her drowning would look like an accident, even though he had planned it all carefully.

He had been clumsy, however, and letters that he and Roberta had written were found. When her condition became known, he was arrested. His uncle obtained an attorney for him. At his trial, the defense built up an elaborate case in his favor. Yet, in spite of his lawyer's efforts, he was found guilty and sentenced to be electrocuted. His mother came to see him and urged him to save his soul. A clergyman finally succeeded in getting Clyde to write a statement—a declaration that he repented of his sins. It is doubtful whether he did. He died in the electric chair, a young man tempted by his desire for luxury and wealth.

Critical Evaluation:

Few readers claim to "like" the works of Theodore Dreiser, for his novels are not ones that charm or delight. Nor are they clever stories that readers explore for their plot. Even his characters are mostly obnoxious beings who fail to appeal in any usual sense. Why then is Dreiser considered by some to be a genius? Why do people read his books at all? The answer lies in a strange paradox: Dreiser's very faults are what attract readers again and again. His stumbling, awkward style, his convoluted philosophies, and his pitiable personages combine to present readers with a world view that, perhaps more successfully than that of any other American writer, conveys the naturalistic atmosphere. Dreiser's books, like the universe he seeks to describe, impress and repel by their very disorder, their mystery, their powerful demands on comfortable assumptions.

All Dreiser's characteristics are most clearly reflected in *An American Tragedy*, the masterpiece of an author who had earlier published three important novels: *Sister Carrie*, *Jennie Gerhardt*, and *The Financier*. In this book, Dreiser the Naturalist asserts the doctrine that man is struggling endlessly to survive in an uncaring world where he is a victim of heredity, environment, and chance which leave him little room for free choice or action. Dreiser's theory of life is basically mechanistic, and for *An American Tragedy*, he invented the term "chemism" to explain the chemical forces that he believed propelled man to act in a certain way. Man, Dreiser said, is a "mechanism, undevised and uncreated and a badly and carelessly driven one at that." Such a poor creature is Clyde Griffiths, the central character of *An American Tragedy*. The book, which is full of scientific imagery, shows readers how Clyde is driven to his final destruction.

Dreiser chooses to concentrate on man's struggle against one particular force: society and its institutions. In each of the novel's three sections, Clyde strives not against a malign God or a malevolent fate but against the unyielding structure of his culture. In other times, men have defined themselves by other touchstones (religion, honor, war), but Clyde can answer his craving for meaning in only one way. For to matter in America means, in the book's terms, to be masterful, to have material goods and status. His America tempts him with its powerful businesses, its glittering social affairs, and its promises that anyone who is deserving can share in these riches. That is a false promise, for the American tragedy is the gap between the country's ideals and its reality.

Doomed to failure in his quest, Clyde, whose story has been called a "parable of our national experience," cannot be blamed for desiring what he sees all about him. Nor can he be criticized for the weaknesses and handicaps that assure his end. Immature and shallow, offering a "Gee" on all occasions, uneducated and poor, Clyde is willing to compromise in any necessary fashion in order to become materially successful. Yet his very lack of moral or intellectual distinction, when coupled with the intensity of his desires, makes him the ideal and innocent representative of a culture where achievement is gauged by such measurements. In the novel, inspired by a 1906 murder case involving Chester Gillette, who killed an inconveniently pregnant girlfriend for reasons much like those in the book, Clyde's attorney calls him a "mental as well as a moral coward—no more and no less," but he later adds that Clyde cannot help this state.

What did create Clyde includes poor parents just as inept as he. Impractical and ineffectual, the Griffiths offer him only their God who, as he can plainly see, has brought them none of the things he (or they) want. Religion is one obstacle Clyde can and does remove when he ignores their protests and responds instead to his environment and inner urgings. His adaptability is exploited in the Arabian Nights atmosphere of the hotels in which he works, places where luxury alone is vital, and kindness and honesty mere trifles. When, in the second part of the novel, Clyde finds himself in Lycurgus, he once again gravitates helplessly toward the surrounding values. Named after the Spartan who initiated that society's rigid rules, Lycurgus is just as tantalizing as the hotels. It is a "walled city" that, as one of the novel's major symbols, allows outsiders to peek at its glories but rarely permits them to enter its gates. Clyde, fascinated and overwhelmed, abandons the simple pleasures he has found with Roberta and attempts to climb its walls.

Whenever Clyde struggles free of his environmental influences, he is frustrated by the accidents and coincidences that haunt him. He unwillingly leaves Kansas City because of the car accident, and he leaves Chicago because of a seemingly happy encounter with his uncle. His chance meeting with Sondra and the mistaken identity developed their relationship, just as Roberta's unplanned pregnancy so rudely obstructed his dreams. Even his murder scheme is derived from a chance newspaper article, and the murder itself is in a sense self-initiated, for Clyde *allows* rather than *forces* Roberta's drowning.

Other characters in the novel are equally victims of the roles in which they find themselves. While many of them are compellingly presented, their main importance is to provide background and stimuli for Clyde. Since he rarely sees them as people but rather as impediments (his family, Roberta) or as exciting objects (Sondra), the reader too is interested in them mostly in this respect, and the book belongs almost entirely to Clyde.

In *An American Tragedy*, Dreiser, a former newspaperman and editor of women's publications, watches his world and its foibles and is moved by men's shared helplessness. He shows readers how useless moral judgment is in solving such dilemmas and insists, as he does in all his works, that all people may expect of one another is compassion for common plights. Although he offers little encouragement, Dreiser does hint that perhaps the human condition may improve. The final scene—"Dusk, of a summer night"—closely resembles the opening. A small boy once again troops reluctantly with a group of street missionaries. Yet Mrs. Griffiths responds to the frustrations of Esta's child as she had never done to Clyde's and gives him money for an ice-cream cone. This child, she promises herself, will be different.

ANTHONY ADVERSE

Type of work: Novel
Author: Hervey Allen (1889–1949)
Type of plot: Picaresque romance
Time of plot: Late eighteenth and early nineteenth centuries
Locale: Western Europe, Africa, and North America
First published: 1933

> *Principal characters:*
> ANTHONY ADVERSE
> MARIA, his mother
> DON LUIS, MARQUIS DA VINCITATA, her husband
> MR. BONNYFEATHER, Anthony's grandfather
> FAITH PALEOLOGUS, Mr. Bonnyfeather's housekeeper
> ANGELA GIUSEPPE, Anthony's mistress
> FLORENCE UDNEY, Anthony's first wife
> DOLORES DE LA FUENTE, Anthony's second wife
> VINCENT NOLTE, Anthony's friend, a banker

The Story:

The pretty young Marquise Maria da Vincitata, daughter of a Scottish merchant of Leghorn, fell in love with young Denis Moore within the year after her marriage and met with him secretly in France while her husband was taking a cure for his gout. Don Luis, the arrogant Marquis da Vincitata, discovering the intrigue, spirited his wife away and killed her gallant, luckless lover when he started out in pursuit. Maria's baby was born high in the Alps. After his wife died during childbirth, Don Luis took the child to Leghorn, where he stealthily deposited the infant at the Convent of Jesus the Child. The only tokens of its parentage were a cape and a statue of the Madonna that had belonged to Maria.

The boy, christened Anthony by the nuns, lived at the convent until he was age ten. Then he was delivered to a prominent merchant of the town, Mr. Bonnyfeather, to become his apprentice.

Bonnyfeather and his housekeeper had no trouble recognizing the cape and the doll as possessions of the merchant's daughter, Maria. Although Anthony was given the surname Adverse and was not told of his relationship to his benefactor, he was carefully educated with the tacit understanding that he would one day inherit the flourishing Bonnyfeather business.

Anthony matured early. Seduced by the housekeeper, Faith Paleologus, he also had a brief affair with the cook's daughter, Angela. He was also

ANTHONY ADVERSE by Hervey Allen. By permission of the author and the publishers, Rinehart & Co., Inc. Copyright, 1933, by Hervey Allen.

attracted to the English consul's daughter, Florence Udney, but was not encouraged by her mother, who was unaware that Anthony had any expectations.

Anticipating the eventual arrival of Napoleon's army in Leghorn, Mr. Bonnyfeather quietly liquidated his business, sent his money abroad, and made plans to retire. He arranged passage for his grandson on the American ship *Wampanoag*, under Captain Jorham. Anthony was to sail to Cuba to collect some money on a long-overdue account.

The *Wampanoag* stopped first at Genoa. There Anthony visited Father Xavier, a Jesuit who had been his guardian at the convent. Mr. Bonnyfeather had given the priest the right to decide whether the time had come to tell Anthony that he was the merchant's heir. It was from the priest's lips that Anthony learned of his origin and prospects.

When the *Wampanoag* reached Havana, Anthony discovered that his creditor, Gallego, was in Africa as a slave trader. With the aid of the captain-general, Don Luis de las Casas, a plan was devised whereby Anthony would sail to Africa as a government agent. There he would impound a cargo of Gallego's slaves, bring them to Cuba for sale, and split the proceeds with the captain-general, thus satisfying the Bonnyfeather debt. Strongly attracted by Don Luis' young relation, Dolores de la Fuente, the young man finally agreed to stay in Africa and to ship several additional cargoes of slaves, for the enrichment of the captain-general and the increase of his own hopes that he might one day marry Dolores.

The trip aboard the *Ariostatica* was a trying one. Father François, a monk who was being shipped to Africa because he had tried to give aid and comfort to the slaves, fell ill of yellow fever and nearly died. Anthony, forced to rule the crew and its captain with an iron hand, was able to put down a mutiny as the ship sailed up the Rio Pongo to the Gallego establishment. There he learned that Gallego had died a few months before, leaving his factor, Ferdinando, in charge.

Anthony took over the trade station and, for three years, shipped cargoes of human freight to Cuba to be sold there. To the sorrow of Father François, he took the half-breed Neleta, Ferdinando's sister, as his mistress. He, however, was not able completely to reconcile himself to trading in human bodies.

While Anthony was absent from the trading station, Father François was captured by a native witch doctor, Mnombibi, and crucified. Upon his return, Anthony found the priest pinioned to his own cross. With the knowledge that Mr. Bonnyfeather was dead and that Captain Bittern of the *Unicorn* was waiting in the Rio Pongo to bear him back to Leghorn, Anthony decided to leave the trading station. He left Neleta behind.

Don Luis, Marquis da Vincitata, arrived in Leghorn at the same time. They were both there on business, the Marquis to close the Casa Bonnyfeather, of which he was landlord, and Anthony to receive the merchant's will from Vincent Nolte, a banker with whom he had been friendly in his youth. Vincent suggested that Anthony take advantage of an offer made by M. Ouvrard, a French financier who was planning to supply the bankrupt Spanish government with French food and money in return for silver from Mexican mines. Anthony was to take charge of the shipments, which would arrive at New Orleans from Vera Cruz, and to reinvest profitably as much of the money as he could. The rest was to be shipped to Florence Udney's husband, David Parish, in Philadelphia, and from there on to Europe.

Traveling to Paris to make arrangements, Vincent and Anthony were waylaid in the Alps by Don Luis, who tried to force their coach over a cliff. His plans were thwarted, however, and his own carriage and coachman plunged into the deep gorge. At the time, Don Luis was traveling with Faith Paleologus, whom he had made his mistress. The two had dismounted to watch the destruction of Anthony and his friend. After their plot failed, they were left to descend the mountain on foot.

In Paris, Anthony met Angela for the first time in many years. She had borne him a son and had become a famous singer and the mistress of Napoleon. She refused to marry Anthony and follow him to America, but she did give him his son. At her entreaty, Anthony left the child with Vincent's childless cousin, Anna.

Anthony's affairs prospered in New Orleans. He was able to invest the silver profitably, to form a bank, and to build a handsome plantation for himself. When David Parish died of heart failure, Anthony married Florence. Their daughter, Maria, was three years old when the plantation house caught fire one night while Anthony was away. His wife and daughter were burned to death.

Burdened by his sorrow, Anthony started west. Captured by a tribe of Indians, he escaped, only to fall into the hands of soldiers from Santa Fé. There he was brought before the governor, Don Luis, and sentenced to go to Mexico City in a prison train. That same day, Don Luis had a stroke and died. Faith, his wife by that time, prepared to return to Spain.

Anthony spent two years in the Hospital of St. Lazaro before Dolores, widow of a wealthy landowner, found him and arranged his release. Later, they married and went to live in the village of San Luz. Dolores bore him two children. All went well until an ax slipped and caught Anthony in the groin while he was felling a tree. He bled to death before he was found.

Many years later, long after the village had been deserted by Dolores and her people, a group of migrants on their way to Santa Fé came to its site. The little Madonna, which Anthony had carried with him through life, still stood in a chapel in the ruins of San Luz. Mary Jorham, the young niece of Captain Jorham, found the image, but she was not allowed to keep it because her parents thought it a heathen idol. Instead, it served as a fine target for a shooting match. It was splintered into a thousand pieces.

Critical Evaluation:

A massive novel of intrigue and romance, heavily spiced with history and action, *Anthony Adverse* was immensely popular when it was first published. All the characters are larger than life, ruled by jealousies, enormous greed, and overwhelming cravings for vengeance; yet thanks to the vitality of the narrative, they never seem merely absurd. Few novels of such size move with such an unrelenting pace. As coaches and horses ceaselessly rush from one part of Europe to another, so the story catapults from one subplot to another. The author is in no hurry to tell his story, but he never risks boring the reader. Although the characters are not analyzed in depth, their motives are always clear. If the book has a flaw, perhaps it is that there is little mystery to the characters, although they are involved *in* mysteries. The obscure corners of the human personality are never explored, but the characters do not suffer from this lack; they are filled with life and are both amusing and memorable. Don Luis, Faith, and Mr. Bonnyfeather are old-fashioned, Dickensian characters, carefully formed of "characteristics" rather than allowed to develop according to the psychological insights of the author.

Nearly one hundred pages pass before the hero of this picaresque novel makes his appearance as a baby, but the scene is set for the intrigues that follow. The novel is intricately constructed, with characters reappearing and long-hidden secrets suddenly changing the course of the action. This attempt to create a modern *Tom Jones* is not entirely unsuccessful. The difficulty is that this book does not speak for its time as Fielding's book did for its time. Ultimately, *Anthony Adverse* is no more than a superior entertainment, well-crafted and enjoyable, but it makes no statement and is a part of no literary tradition.

The precocious and lusty personality of Anthony is the finest part of the book. His spirit of adventure and his determination and cleverness win the reader's admiration, and his vitality holds the reader's interest. As with *Tom Jones*, the hero's destiny is a secret that can be discovered only by unraveling certain clues; and as with Fielding's protagonist, Anthony does not let himself be inhibited by his lack of a definite origin. If the book as a whole is less than the sum of its parts, it is not Anthony's fault; he comes close to being a major literary figure. Angela is perhaps the most intriguing character in the book, and one can easily imagine her rising to become Napoleon's mistress. More of her inner life and emotions are revealed than those of any other character. The novel is also interesting because its various sections represent different types of romantic fiction.

THE APOSTLE

Type of work: Novel
Author: Sholem Asch (1880–1957)
Type of plot: Religious chronicle
Time of plot: Shortly after the Crucifixion
Locale: The Roman Empire
First published: 1943

> *Principal characters:*
> SAUL OF TARSHISH, later known as Paul
> JOSEPH BAR NABA OF CYPRUS, Saul's friend, an early
>   convert
> REB ISTEPHAN, a famous Jewish preacher
> SIMON BAR JONAH, called Peter
> REB JACOB, Joseph's son

The Story:

It was seven weeks after the crucifixion of Yeshua of Nazareth by Pontius Pilate. All the poor of Jerusalem, who had found in Yeshua their Messiah, had gone into hiding; but the word was spreading. Little by little the story was told: of Yeshua who had come back after his death and of the Messiah who had appeared to his disciples. The matter was hotly argued on all sides. The pious Jews could not believe in a Messiah who had been killed; the Messianists devoutly affirmed their faith.

Saul of Tarshish and Joseph bar Naba came upon a street preacher, a rustic Galilean, who told with great conviction of Yeshua's return after he had been entombed. Cries of belief and of repugnance interrupted his talk. Saul himself spoke with great bitterness against this Messiah, for he had no patience with the gentle Yeshua who was hanged.

The agitation rapidly spread. One of the most vigorous upholders of Yeshua was Reb Istephan. He had a gift for moving men's souls, and more and more Jews became persuaded. Joseph bar Naba had known Yeshua in his lifetime, and when Joseph heard Reb Istephan, he was convinced. Joseph became a Messianist. This conversion disgusted Saul, and in sorrow and bitterness, he turned away from his friend Joseph.

Then a dramatic incident took place. Simon, the first of Yeshua's disciples, healed Nehemiah the cripple in the name of the Nazarene. Many were impressed by the cure, but others resented Simon's use of the Messiah's name. As a result, his enemies had their way, and Simon was imprisoned by the High Priest to await trial. Then another miracle happened. Simon and his

---

THE APOSTLE by Sholem Asch. Translated by Maurice Samuel. By permission of the author and the publishers, G. P. Putnam's Sons. Copyright, 1943, by Sholem Asch.

follower Jochanan had been securely locked in a dungeon, but in the morning, they were walking the streets again. It was said that they had passed directly through the stone walls—with the help of Yeshua.

The resentment against the wild Galileans grew among the rulers, while the humble folk followed Simon with trust. The High Priest again brought Simon to trial; but Simon spoke so well in defense of his doctrine that he was freed; and now the tumult increased. The ignorant folk, seeing Simon released, concluded that there was official sanction for the new cult; hence more joined the followers of Yeshua.

Saul was greatly incensed. He believed that the Messiah was yet to come and that the disciples were corrupting Jerusalem. He went to the High Priest and secured an appointment as official spy. In his new job, Saul tracked down the humble Messianists and sentenced them to the lash. Growing in power, Saul the Zealot finally took Reb Istephan prisoner for preaching the new faith. With grim pleasure, Saul led the way to the stoning pit and watched Istephan sink beneath the flung rocks. As he died, the preacher murmured a prayer forgiving his tormentors. Saul was vaguely troubled.

Then the Messianists were much heartened. Yeshua's younger brother, Reb Jacob ben Joseph, came to Jerusalem to head the humble cult, and Saul could do little against this pious and strict Jew. By chance, the High Priest heard of more Messianists in Damascus. Saul volunteered to investigate and hurried to his new field. En route, however, a vision appeared to him and said, "Saul, Saul, why dost thou persecute me?" Saul then recognized Yeshua as his Lord, and as he was commanded, he went on to Damascus, although he was still blinded by the heavenly apparition. A follower of the new religion baptized him and restored his sight. The penitent Saul hurried away from the haunts of man. In all, he waited seven years for his mission.

Finally as he prayed in his mother's house, the call came. Joseph bar Naba asked Saul to go with him to Antioch to strengthen the congregation there. At last Saul was on the way to bring the word of the Messiah to others. He left for Antioch with Joseph and the Greek Titus, Saul's first convert.

Now Simon had founded the church at Antioch among the Greeks. The perplexing question was, could a devout Jew even eat with the Gentiles, let alone accept them into the church? In Jerusalem, Jacob held firmly to the law of the Torah: salvation was only for the circumcised. Simon vacillated. In Jerusalem, he followed Jacob; among the Greeks he accepted Gentiles fully. Joseph had been sent by the elders of Jerusalem to Antioch to apply the stricter rule to the growing Messianic church.

Saul at first met with much suspicion. The Messianists remembered too well Saul the Zealot who had persecuted them. Yet, little by little the apostle won them over. Yeshua appeared to Saul several times, and he was much strengthened in the faith. At last Saul found his true mission in the conviction that he was divinely appointed to bring the word of Yeshua to the Gentiles.

He worked wonders at Antioch and built a strong church there, but his acceptance of Gentiles cost him Joseph's friendship. As a symbol of his new mission, Saul became Paul and began his years of missionary work.

Paul went to all the Gentiles—to Corinth, to Ephesus, to Cyprus. Everywhere, he founded a church, sometimes small but always zealous. Lukas, the Greek physician, went with him much of the time. Lukas was an able minister and a scholar who was writing the life of Yeshua.

The devout Jews in Jerusalem were greatly troubled by this strange preacher who accepted the Gentiles. Finally, they brought him up for trial. Paul escaped only by standing on his rights as a Roman citizen. As such, he could demand a trial before Caesar himself. Paul went to Rome as a captive, but he rejoiced, for he knew the real test of Christianity would be in Rome. Simon was already there, preaching to the orthodox Jews.

The evil Nero made Paul wait in prison for two years without a hearing and, even then, only the intervention of Seneca freed the apostle. For a short time, Simon and Paul worked together, one among the Jews and the other among the Gentiles. They converted many, and the lowly fervently embraced the promise of salvation.

To give himself an outlet for his fancied talents as an architect, Nero burned Rome and planned to rebuild a beautiful city. The crime, however, was too much, even for the Romans. To divert suspicion from himself, Nero blamed the Christians. He arrested thousands of them and, on the appointed day, opened the royal carnage. Jews and Christians, hour after hour, were gored by oxen, torn by tigers, and chewed by crocodiles. At the end of the third day, many Romans could no longer bear the sight, but still Nero sat on. It was so strange: the Christians died well, and with their last breath, they forgave their persecutors.

Simon, only a Jew, was crucified afterward; Paul, born a Roman citizen, was beheaded. Gabelus, the gladiator who had accepted Christianity, went with them to the execution. The deaths of Simon and Paul, however, were in reality the beginning. The martyrdom of the early Christians was the foundation stone of the Christian church.

Critical Evaluation:

The Apostle is the story of Saul of Tarshish, the man who heard a voice while traveling the road to Damascus, and whose whole life was changed as a result. He gave up former ideals, following instead the new religion of the Messiah, and suffering shipwreck, hunger, scourging, imprisonment, and finally death as a result of his faith. The novel is the story of one man's search for the meaning of life, told against the larger backdrop of the story of all the early Christians in their struggles after the crucifixion. As a Jew steeped in the writings of the Old Testament from his youth, Sholem Asch was well qualified to write this powerful and beautiful story. He clearly and vividly traces the Jewish heritage of the Christian faith and shows how the fulfillment of the law of Moses links the Christian and the Jew inextricably.

The characterizations in the novel, especially those of Peter and Paul, are clearly and movingly drawn. Peter—gentle, humble, and devoted—is in sharp contrast to Paul—intense, proud, and overbearing—yet, the two men are brothers in their faith in Jesus and their desire to spread His word to all parts of the Roman empire. Paul is a difficult personality with which to identify— he is fanatical and abrasive by nature. Yet, in the years following his conversion, he becomes more loving and compassionate, as he relinquishes all claim to the pleasures of this life in order to preach the redemptive spirit of love to the outcast Gentiles. Beyond telling the stories of individuals like Peter and Paul, however, Asch chronicles the historic struggle for dominance between the Pharisees, who believed in the resurrection of the soul and a life after death, and the High Priests, or Saducees, who believed only in this life.

In addition to his true-to-life characterizations and his faithful yet vivid rendering into fiction of historical information, Asch is more than competent as a descriptive writer; he creates settings that bring the story alive for the reader. One example is the memorable scene of Paul's landing in Antioch, an idyllic place where oleanders nod gently in the breeze, cypress and laurel trees perfume the air, and meadows thick with poppies, violets, jasmine, and lilies glow triumphantly in the sun. Yet it is a tainted Eden, as Paul discovers when he encounters scenes such as the procession of madly dancing naked priests who slash their own wrists with their teeth to show their devotion to Apolens, the fish-goddess. All this Asch renders with great skill and descriptive power.

No one can read *The Apostle* without learning a great deal about the Judeo-Christian heritage of Western civilization; no reader will finish the novel untouched by the devotion and zealous energy that one man called forth in the hearts of so many people.

THE APPLE OF THE EYE

Type of work: Novel
Author: Glenway Wescott (1901–   )
Type of plot: Regional romance
Time of plot: Twentieth century
Locale: Rural Wisconsin
First published: 1924

> *Principal characters:*
> HANNAH MADOC, a primitive
> JULE BIER, Hannah's lover
> SELMA, Jule's wife
> ROSALIA, Jule's and Selma's daughter
> MIKE, Rosalia's lover
> DAN STRANE, Rosalia's cousin

The Story:

When her drunken father came home one night and swung at her with a broom handle, patient, hard-working Hannah Madoc pushed him off the porch in self-defense. He died a few days later, leaving his daughter orphaned and penniless, and Hannah went to work in Mrs. Boyle's store. There, she waited on customers during the day and served the men liquor in the evening.

One night, Jule Bier saw her behind the store counter. Since the death of his wife and the piling up of debts, old Mr. Bier had struggled to make enough money from his farm to give Jule a chance in life. Cold and calculating, the elder Bier had sent Jule to work as a hired hand on the neighborhood farms. Jule began to court Hannah during long walks at night; he took her to neighborhood dances, and they went for rides in his buggy. Hannah soon tired of the attentions of other men. When Mr. Boyle attempted to make love to her, she quit her job and went to work on a farm near Jule's home.

Old Mr. Bier sent Jule to court Selma Duncan, the oldest daughter of a wealthy farmer. Blindly obeying his father, Jule proposed to the girl and was accepted. Then he realized what he had done. Facing Hannah, he was bewildered by her grief, only half aware of his own.

Leaving the neighborhood of Sheboygan, Hannah went to Fond du Lac, where she became a prostitute and gradually lost her beauty and vitality. At last, Jule went to Fond du Lac to bring his former sweetheart back to her home. Hannah ended her years in bitter sterility, answering a call for help from a neighbor, nursing a sick calf, or taking care of someone's children when their mother became ill. She died, prematurely aged and broken, as

---

the result of a fall.

Jule and Selma had one daughter, Rosalia. Selma's sister, Mrs. Strane, had a son, Dan, who was a boy of fourteen when Rosalia was in her early twenties. Mike, a young man with a keen zest for life, worked on Jule's farm. Because his mother was so tight-lipped and because she tried to instill in him a chastity of ignorance and abstinence, Dan had developed an adolescent feeling of frustration and curiosity. He longed to know what sex was and how it affected people, but at the same time, he was overcome by an inbred feeling of shame. It was Mike who clarified matters for Dan after they became friends. Mike, who believed that life should be full of experience both physical and mental, made life's processes a wonderful thing, not obscene and dirty, as Dan's mother had led the boy to believe. Breaking away from the mother who had been his idol, Dan replaced her with his new friend, Mike. Mike, in love with Rosalia, shared his deeper feelings with his young friend. Dan had grown up.

Mike loved and desired Rosalia, but at first she resisted his lovemaking. One afternoon he seduced her. Rosalia's subsequent tears frightened him, but soon she learned to hide her terror of love. She told Mike that they ought to get married to redeem their sin, but Mike's suggestion that Selma might not approve quieted the frightened girl. Mike was not certain that he wanted to marry Rosalia. When Jule quietly told Mike that he had noticed Rosalia's and Mike's love and that he would not object to the marriage if Mike wanted it, Mike felt trapped. He quit his job with Jule and left the Bier farm.

Dan was inconsolable. Having looked upon his cousin and Mike as perfect lovers, he could not understand why Mike should leave. Rosalia brooded, her sense of guilt increasing after Mike's departure. Although she hid her feelings from her parents, Dan knew enough of her affair with Mike to be curious about Rosalia's feelings; but he could learn nothing from her. Rosalia herself was not as calm as she appeared to be. The punishment for love was a child. She felt a surge of emotion within her, and it seemed permanently a part of her. She concluded that she must be pregnant. It was inevitable; she had sinned and this was to be her harvest. Deserted by her lover/husband, she could not bear to think of her shame. She told some neighbors that she was going to run off to meet Mike, and one night during a snowstorm she left her home.

No one had heard from Rosalia or Mike. Dan and Selma waited through the winter. Once, when Dan went to visit his aunt in Milwaukee, he looked for Mike, but he did not find him. In the spring, a neighbor brought the news to Jule that Rosalia's body had been found in the swamp. Fearing that the news would kill the already ailing Selma, Jule made the neighbor and Dan promise to tell no one about Rosalia's body. They buried the girl in the swamp.

All summer Dan worked on his father's farm. He had begun to hate the memory of Mike ever since he had helped Jule bury the body of Rosalia. A hundred times over, Dan killed Mike in effigy. In the fall Selma died, and Dan went to live with Jule. The kindly, patient man, who had seen so much of life, won Dan's affections.

Jule wanted Dan to tell him all he knew about Rosalia and Mike. The wonderful understanding of the old man impressed his nephew. Mike had done the best he knew how, Jule maintained. In turn, he told Dan about Hannah Madoc. If Hannah had been Rosalia's mother instead of Selma, Jule said, Rosalia would not have been destroyed through fear. Hannah knew how to handle life. Religious people were always trying to make life better than it was, but life should be accepted at its simple, natural values. Dan accepted his uncle's views.

Dan's father had never understood his son. Having completed his high school education, Dan was becoming restless. His father, realizing that Dan was not suited for farm work, suggested that he go to college. With high hopes that he would find more answers to his questions about life, Dan prepared to enter the state university.

Critical Evaluation:
The Apple of the Eye is a novel concerned with sexuality and its impact on human relationships and religious values. Written by a young man, it is a novel filled with lyrical passages and obsessed with the emergence and demands of sex.

The novel is organized in three interrelated sections. The first section, devoted to Hannah Madoc, is by far the most successful. The later sections, more philosophical and autobiographical, filled with long, abstract conversations, are less impressive.

The central question posed by *The Apple of the Eye* is whether a satisfactory and happy life can be achieved within the boundaries of conventional relationships. The story of Hannah Madoc demonstrates that there are a variety of fulfilling lives. She is a woman who violates conventions and who has the courage to defend herself; at the same time, however, she pays a stiff penalty for her passion.

The story of Rosalia and Mike elaborates this idea. Although Dan is initially taken completely by Mike's hedonism, Rosalia's death proves that living for the body alone is dangerous, even fatal. Glenway Wescott stresses this point in his description of Rosalia's decomposed body. Its ugliness has a tremendous moral impact on Dan. Through Dan's evaluation of his own feelings, Wescott suggests that Mike's hedonism and Mrs. Strane's puritanism are each one-sided. Neither offers, by itself, a system of values which is ultimately workable.

The Apple of the Eye does not, finally, offer a system of its own to replace these alternatives. Nevertheless, like other American novels of the 1920's, it does ask significant questions. In an era when old values were being seriously questioned, writers such as Wescott attempted to explore the implications of different systems of values. It was an effort to search for standards by which people could conduct themselves and with which Americans could lead fulfilling lives. This effort, in the case of *The Apple of the Eye*, is certainly worthwhile.

APPOINTMENT IN SAMARRA

Type of work: Novel
Author: John O'Hara (1905–1970)
Type of plot: Naturalism
Time of plot: 1930
Locale: Pennsylvania
First published: 1934

Principal characters:
JULIAN ENGLISH, a car dealer
CAROLINE, his wife
HARRY REILLY, a rich man
AL GRECCO, the bootlegger's handyman

The Story:

Julian English was thirty years old, a congenial seller of cars, and popular with the country club set. He had the right connections with Ed Charney, the local bootlegger, and consequently was always well supplied with liquor. He and Caroline had been married four years. They were both natives of Gibbsville and had an assured social position. They had no children.

Just before Christmas, they went to a party at the country club. As usual, Julian had had too much to drink. He sat idly twirling his highball and listening to Harry Reilly's stories. Harry was a rich Irish Catholic and definitely a social climber. Actually, Julian hated Harry, although Harry had lent him twenty thousand dollars the previous summer to bolster his Cadillac agency. That loan, however, did not give Harry the right to make passes at Caroline, Julian thought darkly.

Harry told stories in paragraphs. He always paused at the right time. Julian kept thinking how fitting it would be if he stopped the stories by throwing his drink in Harry's face. Julian grew bored. On impulse he did throw his drink in Harry's face. A big lump of ice hit Harry in the eye.

On the way home, Julian and Caroline quarreled furiously. Julian accused his wife of infidelity with Harry, among other people. Caroline said that Julian always drank too much and chased women as well. More important, Harry had a mortgage on the car agency and a good deal of influence with the Catholics, and he was a man who could hold a grudge.

Al Grecco was a little man who, as Ed Charney's handyman, had a certain standing in the town. He liked Julian because Julian was the only one of the social set who was really friendly. Al grew up on the wrong side of the tracks. Before he was finally sentenced to a year in prison, he had been arrested several times. When he got out, he worked in a poolroom for a while until his boss died. The widow wanted Al to stay on as manager, but he went to work for Charney. Now he delivered bootleg booze, ran errands, and kept an eye on the torch singer at the Stage Coach, a country inn owned by Charney. Helene Holman, the singer, was Charney's girl, and if she were not carefully watched, she might, out of sheer good-heartedness, extend her favors to other men.

On Christmas Day, Julian woke up with a hangover. As was his custom, he quarreled with the cook. At Caroline's suggestion, he went to Harry Reilly's house to apologize. Although Reilly's sister was sympathetic, she brought down word that Harry would not see him; he had a black eye and was still perturbed.

Julian's father and mother came for Christmas dinner. The father, a staid, successful surgeon, was suspicious of his son. He always looked for evidence of moral weakness in Julian, for his own father had committed suicide after embezzling a fortune. He was afraid that the English inheritance was stained. Dinner was a trying time.

Caroline and Julian had supper at the club. The usual crowd was there. Julian was unmercifully ribbed in the locker room. In a dismal mood, he sat drinking by himself while he waited for a chance to see Father Creedon and ask him to patch up his affair with Harry. The old priest was sympathetic and made light of the incident. After agreeing that Harry was a bore, he promised to send Julian some good Irish whiskey.

Ed Charney was a good family man who spent Christmas Day with his wife and son. He intended to go out to the Stage Coach only in the evening. Then his son became suddenly ill. It looked as if he would have to stay home. Mindful of Helene's weaknesses, he telephoned Al Grecco to go out to the inn to keep watch on her. It was Christmas night, and she would be drinking too much. Al did not care for the assignment, but he dutifully went out to the inn and sat down with Helene.

The country club set began to drift in. Froggy Ogden, who was Caroline's one-armed cousin, was the oldest man there; he seemed to feel a responsibility for Julian, who was still drinking. In a spirit of bravado, Julian danced several times with Helene, even though Al warned him of Charney's anger. Finally, carried away by the music and too many drinks, Julian and Helene left the dance floor. Caroline and Froggy found Julian in a stupor in the back of a sedan and took him home.

The day after Christmas, Caroline went to her mother and announced her intention to divorce Julian. Her mother found it difficult to listen to her daughter; she believed herself above the foibles of the younger generation. Caroline thought herself a heroine in an old-fashioned melodrama. She was determined, however, not to go back to Julian. After meeting him on the street and quarreling with him again, she canceled the big party that they were to have given that very evening.

Al Grecco, as he backed out of the garage with a case of Scotch, had decided to kill Ed Charney. When Charney had phoned him, he had tried to excuse his lack of vigilance: he protested that he had only let Helene dance. Nevertheless, Ed, in a rage, had said some things that Al could not accept.

Determined to look businesslike, Julian went to his office at the automobile agency. He sat importantly at his desk and wrote figures on a piece of scratch paper. The only conclusion he could reach was that he needed more money. One of his salesmen came in to try to lay down the law. He asserted that Julian's difficulties were gossiped about strenuously in the little town of Gibbsville. The offense to Charney was particularly grave: he had been a good friend to the agency and had helped them sell cars to other bootleggers.

Julian left the office in no cheerful mood. He wandered into his club for lunch. Since it was the day after Christmas, the dining room was deserted except for some elderly lawyers and Froggy. Avoiding his wife's cousin, Julian sat down in a far corner of the room. After picking up his plate, Froggy followed him and began to reproach him for his conduct with the torch singer. He told Julian he had always distrusted him and had warned Caroline about his conduct many times. When Froggy invited him outside to fight, Julian refused because he could not hit a one-armed man. Froggy became more insulting, so that the lawyers came to their table to intervene. Julian was intensely angered when they seemed to side with Froggy. Turning quickly, he hit one of the lawyers in the mouth and dislodged his false teeth.

Julian went home and fell asleep. About ten o'clock, a society reporter awoke him when she came to get a story about the canceled party. After several drinks, he tried to seduce her but with no success. As soon as she left, Julian went to the garage, closed the door, and started the motor; his death was pronounced a suicide by the coroner.

Critical Evaluation:

John O'Hara was supreme in the art and craft of the short story. Perhaps because of his newspaper background, he was able to condense a tale to its fundamentals and produce a tightly crafted and powerful short fiction. With his ear for speech and eye for effect, he was able to bring to life in two or three sentences a character from nearly any walk of life. This gift also gave his novels the primary value that they possess, and perhaps this is especially true of his first novel, *Appointment in Samarra*.

One of O'Hara's shortest and best-structured novels, *Appointment in Samarra* is the story of hubris in a modern setting. It takes place in 1930, after the crash of 1929 but before people understood just how bad the Depression was to become. The hero of the novel, Julian English, has status but destroys himself by not living up to it. Julian has two problems: people and alcohol, but both are revealed to be part of his own inner problems, which ultimately ruin him. There is much discussion in the book of who "belongs" and who does not, of which clubs count in Gibbsville, and what preparatory schools and what colleges matter, and where one should be seen or not be seen. The laborer, mobster, and society man all think constantly about how they fit into the social ladder. Julian English thinks about it too much.

An accurate picture of a broad cross section of Gibbsville society is presented in the novel. With the observations of different kinds of people, from the secretary in the automobile agency to the ex-convict working for the gangland boss to the society matron, O'Hara achieved a new kind of fictional reporting, in the best sense of the term. The humor and fast pace of the novel and the clean, sure style give it a surface slickness that is almost misleading, for it is not a superficial novel. There is depth behind the meretricious glitter and hard-boiled sensual flavor. The book's racy language and sexual candor continued the pathbreaking trend begun only a short time before by Ernest Hemingway. The characters are concerned with superficialities, but that does not make them superficial characters. O'Hara is able to capture, especially in his dialogue, the nuances of tone that reveal the hidden depths of his many characters.

Julian English, the central figure of the novel, is the most complex and interesting of the characters. Some individuals seem to burn with a compulsion to self-destruction; Julian English is one of these people. Yet, however drunk he gets, part of his mind warns him when he is about to do something dangerous. Like many intelligent people, he observes himself as he moves through life. Yet, he recklessly plunges ahead, throwing the drink in Harry Reilly's face, dancing and going out to the car with Helene Holman at the roadhouse, getting deliberately drunk so that he will not care what happens. (By the time he quarrels with Froggy Ogden at the club and fights with the lawyers in the dining room, he has given up all hope—he is as contemptuous of himself as he is of them. Rational action has ceased to have any meaning for him.) Julian English is a direct forerunner of the existential heroes of Sartre and Camus a decade later—who were influenced by O'Hara and Hemingway and other writers of the American "hard-boiled" school of writing—as he toys with his fate with an almost objective curiosity. "If I do this," he seems to think, "will I get away with it?" Of course, he knows somewhere deep inside of him that he will not "get away" with it, that nobody ever gets away with anything. He is filled with "tremendous excitement" when he realizes that "he is in for it." Perhaps, as he contemplates his "unknown, well-deserved punishment," he is even slightly masochistic in his longing for pain and destruction.

Julian English's fatalism, and the fatalism that permeates the novel (and gives it its title), seem to be influenced in part by the novels and stories of Hemingway and Fitzgerald, but O'Hara, while lacking the poetic vision and poetic style of Fitzgerald, avoids the hard-boiled prose of Hemingway and adds a poignant ruthlessness of his own. With economy and artistry, O'Hara draws the painful and engrossing portrait of a complex, fascinating, and doomed individual.

An inevitable progression, gaining in momentum like a ball rolling down a steep hill, takes over Julian English's fate until it would take a miracle to halt the inevitable doom that waits for him at the end. As Julian knows, miracles do not happen for people like him. His death is early foreshadowed by the suicide of his grandfather. His own father frequently expresses fears that Julian's character is as weak as that of his grandfather; Julian himself comes to believe in his defective character, and he is doomed by it. This belief numbs him and renders him helpless before the onrush of events.

This novel rises above O'Hara's other long works of fiction because it makes more of an attempt to deal with significant ideas and values. Often, his technique of recording action with the detachment of a photographer fails to establish a moral frame of reference. The reader does not know what the author's attitude toward the characters and events is. But the character of Julian English lifts *Appointment in Samarra* above the author's other novels.

O'Hara always surrounds his dramatic action with great pieces of historical exposition and discussion and long descriptions of styles of the period: the fashions, the horses and clubs, the automobiles, and the other transitory items that date a moment in history. In *Appointment in Samarra*, the precise documentation of social strata lends vividness and realism to the story. O'Hara's accuracy with labels and styles had not yet become the excessive mannerism that weighted down his later novels.

O'Hara was born in 1905 in Pottsville, Pennsylvania, the prototype of the Gibbsville of many of his novels and stories. He had a varied career in journalism as a reporter, critic, and social commentator; later, after his first success as a writer, he became a screenwriter and used much of his Hollywood experience in his fiction. His late work added little to his stature, but his early novels and his stories have shown a remarkable durability.

ARROWSMITH

Type of work: Novel
Author: Sinclair Lewis (1885–1951)
Type of plot: Social criticism
Time of plot: Early twentieth century
Locale: The United States and West Indies
First published: 1925

> *Principal characters:*
> MARTIN ARROWSMITH, a medical scientist
> LEORA, his wife
> DR. MAX GOTTLIEB, a scientist
> GUSTAVE SONDELIUS, a scientist
> TERRY WICKETT, Martin's friend
> JOYCE LANYON, a young widow
> DR. ALMUS PICKERBAUGH, a public health reformer

The Story:

Martin Arrowsmith was the descendant of pioneers in the Ohio wilderness. He grew up in the raw red-brick town of Elk Mills, in the state of Winnemac. A restless, lonely boy, he spent his odd hours in old Doc Vickerson's office. The village practitioner was a widower with no family of his own, and he encouraged Martin's interest in medicine.

At age twenty-one, Martin was a junior preparing for medical school at the University of Winnemac. Continuing on at the medical school, he was most interested in bacteriology, research, and the courses of Professor Max Gottlieb, a noted German scientist. After joining a medical fraternity, he made many lifelong friends. He also fell in love with Madeline Fox, a shallow pseudointellectual who was taking graduate work in English. To the young man from the prairie, Madeline represented culture. They became engaged.

Martin spent many nights in research at the laboratory, and he became the favorite of Professor Gottlieb. One day, Gottlieb sent him to the Zenith City Hospital on an errand. There Martin met an attractive nurse named Leora Tozer. He soon became so interested in Leora that he became engaged to her as well. Thus, young Martin Arrowsmith found himself engaged to two girls at the same time. Unable to choose between them, he asked both Leora and Madeline to lunch with him. When he explained his predicament, Madeline stalked angrily from the dining room and out of his life. Leora remained, finding the situation amusing. Martin felt that his life had really begun.

ARROWSMITH by Sinclair Lewis. By permission of the author and publishers, Harcourt, Brace & Co., Inc. Copyright, 1925, by Harcourt, Brace & Co., Inc.

Through his friendship with Gottlieb, Martin became a student instructor in bacteriology. Leora was called home to North Dakota. Because of Leora's absence, trouble with the dean, and too much whiskey, Martin left school during the Christmas holidays. Traveling like a tramp, he arrived at Wheatsylvania, the town where Leora lived. In spite of the warnings of the dull Tozer family, Martin and Leora were married. Martin went back to Winnemac alone. A married man now, he gave up his work in bacteriology and turned his attention to general study. Later Leora joined him in Mohalis.

Upon completion of his internship, Martin set up an office in Wheatsylvania with money supplied by his wife's family. In the small prairie town, Martin made friends of the wrong sort, according to the Tozers, but he was fairly successful as a physician. He also made a number of enemies. Meanwhile, Martin and Leora moved from the Tozer house to their own home. When Leora's first child was born dead, they knew that they could never have another child.

Martin had again become interested in research. When he heard that the Swedish scientist Gustave Sondelius was to lecture in Minneapolis, Martin went to hear his lecture. In that way, Martin became interested in public health as a means of controlling disease. Back in Wheatsylvania, still under the influence of Sondelius, he became acting head of the Department of Public Health. Because Martin, in his official capacity, found a highly respected seamstress to be a chronic carrier of typhoid and sent her to the county home for isolation, he became generally unpopular. He welcomed the opportunity to join Dr. Almus Pickerbaugh of Nautilus, Iowa, as the Assistant Director of Public Health, at a considerable increase in salary.

In Nautilus, he found Dr. Pickerbaugh to be a public-spirited evangelist with little knowledge of medicine or interest in scientific control of disease. The Director spent his time writing health slogans in doubtful poetic meter, lecturing to clubs, and campaigning for health by means of Better Babies Week, Banish the Booze Week, and Tougher Teeth Week. Martin was gradually drawn under the influence of the flashy, artificial methods used by his superior. Although he tried to devote some time to research, the young doctor found that his job took all of his time. While Dr. Pickerbaugh was campaigning for election to Congress, Martin investigated the most sanitary and efficient dairy of the town. He found that the dairy was spreading disease through a streptococcus infection in the udders of the cows. Against the advice of Dr. Pickerbaugh, Martin closed the dairy and made many enemies for himself. Despite his act, however, he was made Acting Director of Public Health when Dr. Pickerbaugh was elected to Congress.

In his new capacity, Martin hired a competent assistant in order to have more time for research in bacteriology. Largely because he fired a block of tenements infested with tuberculosis, Martin was asked to resign. For the next year, he worked as staff pathologist of the fashionable Rouncefield Clinic in Chicago. Then publication of a scientific paper brought him again to the attention of his old friend and professor, Max Gottlieb, now located at the McGurk Institute in New York. Dr. Arrowsmith was glad to accept the position Gottlieb offered him.

At the McGurk Institute, Martin devoted his whole time to research, with Gottlieb as his constant friend and adviser. He worked on staphylococcus germs, producing first a toxin, then an antitoxin. Under the influence of Gottlieb and Terry Wickett, his colleague at McGurk, Martin discovered the X Principle, a bacterial infection that might prove to be a cure for disease. Although Martin wanted to postpone publication of his discovery until he was absolutely certain of its value, the directors of the institute insisted that he make his results public at once. Before his paper was finished, however, it was learned that the same principle had already been discovered at the Pasteur Institute, where it was called a bacteriophage. After that disappointment, Martin began work on the possibility of preventing and curing bubonic plague with the phage, as the new antitoxin was called.

Meanwhile, Gustave Sondelius had come to the McGurk Institute. He became so interested in Martin's work that he spent most of his time helping his young friend. When a plague broke out on St. Hubert, an island in the West Indies, Martin and Sondelius were asked to go there to help in the fight against the epidemic. Accompanied by Leora, they sailed for the island of St. Hubert. Before leaving, Martin had promised Gottlieb that he would conduct his experiment by deliberately refusing to treat some of the plague cases with phage. In this way, the effects of the treatment could be tabulated against a control group.

The plague spread daily on the tropical island. Sondelius was stricken, and he died. Martin was often away from his laboratory as he traveled between villages. During one of his trips, Leora lighted a half-smoked cigarette that she had found on a table in his laboratory. The tobacco had been saturated with germs from an overturned test tube. Leora died of the plague before Martin's return.

Martin forgot to be the pure scientist. He gave the phage to all who asked for it. Although his assistant continued to take notes to carry on the research, Martin was no longer interested in the results. When the plague began to abate, he went back to New York. There, lonely and unhappy, he married Joyce Lanyon, a wealthy young widow whom he had met on St. Hubert. The marriage, however, was not a success. Joyce demanded more of his time than he was willing to take from research; he felt ill at ease among her rich and fashionable friends. When he was offered the assistant directorship of McGurk Institute, he refused the position. In spite of Joyce's protests, he went off to join his old friend and colleague Terry Wickett at a rural laboratory in Vermont, where they intended to run experiments, searching for a cure for pneumonia. At last, Martin believed, his work—his life—was really beginning.

Critical Evaluation:

In the 1920's, Sinclair Lewis hit his full stride as a novelist—during that time, he wrote *Main Street* (1920), *Babbitt* (1922), *Arrowsmith* (1925), and *Dodsworth* (1929), among other novels—and enjoyed both popular and critical acclaim. His considerable achievement in that decade earned for Lewis the Nobel Prize in Literature in 1930, the first American author to be thus distinguished. Even earlier, *Arrowsmith* was selected for the 1926 Pulitzer Prize for the novel. Lewis, however, objected to one of the criteria for awarding the prize, finding it incompatible with intellectual freedom; he therefore declined to accept. Such political bickering notwithstanding, *Arrowsmith* as a work of art is typical of Lewis' work at the peak of his literary productivity. It contains the fundamental elements of realism and satire that characterize Lewis' style at its best.

In *Arrowsmith*, as in other novels of this period, Lewis' realism is most obviously demonstrated in the generous use of detail. Almost in the fashion of a television documentary, Lewis embellishes the verisimilitude and credibility of his story with fact piled upon fact.

As for satire, the ethical dilemmas of the medical profession still abound: the issues may change, but the controversy endures. Martin Arrowsmith, emotionally wracked by the deaths from bubonic plague of his colleague, Gustave Sondelius, and his wife, Leora, is no less obsessed and no less caught in ethical conflicts than today's practictioner dealing with a victim of cancer. The satiric view emerges from this double vision of life: pursue pure science or save whatever lives can be saved. To a certain extent, the dichotomy is artificial, for such "either/or" simplicity is not characteristic of medical decisions or any other decisions. In practical terms, however, it is very real: a choice between short-term and long-term benefits. Martin Arrowsmith chooses short-term benefits. He provides antitoxin for all, destroying the scientific validity of the tests that were to be conducted. The satiric flavor thus emerges as Martin's obligatory choice between two impossible alternatives.

Still, Martin himself is a somewhat ambiguous character. Are readers to admire him or despise him? Part of the answer will revolve around personal commitments to abstract "good" or immediate practical benefits. One may nonetheless view Dr. Arrowsmith as somewhat profoundly influenced by his mentors and professional colleagues; he does indeed strive for the best his fellows represent. If he falls short, Lewis would have readers believe that Arrowsmith's intentions are nevertheless worthy of respect.

A legitimate question remains, however: Does Professor Max Gottlieb (significantly, translated as "love of God") appear as a secret protagonist in the novel? Does Gottlieb represent the guiding force behind Martin Arrowsmith's actions?

The answer is by no means definitive, but it is evident that Lewis himself was not at all clear on the issue of whether Arrowsmith or Gottlieb should triumph. By presenting a dilemma, rather than trying to solve it, Lewis established himself as a Realist and a satirist, for he depicted an unvarnished human condition and portrayed the hazards of moral choice. His satire of medicine—like his satire of middle-class attitudes (*Babbitt*), of religious evangelism (*Elmer Gantry*), and of middle-class business (*Dodsworth*)—rang, and still rings, true.

AS I LAY DYING

Type of work: Novel
Author: William Faulkner (1897–1962)
Type of plot: Psychological realism
Time of plot: Early twentieth century
Locale: Mississippi
First published: 1930

>   *Principal characters:*
>   ADDIE BUNDREN, a dying old woman
>   ANSE BUNDREN, her husband
>   CASH,
>   DARL,
>   JEWEL, and
>   VARDAMAN, their sons
>   DEWEY DELL, their daughter

The Story:

Addie Bundren was dying. She lay propped up in a bed in the Bundren farmhouse, looking out the window at her son Cash as he built the coffin in which she was to be buried. Obsessed with perfection in carpentry, Cash held up each board for her approval before he nailed it in place. Dewey Dell, Addie's daughter, stood beside the bed, fanning her mother as she lay there in the summer heat. In another room, Anse Bundren, Addie's husband, and two sons, Darl and Jewel, discussed the possibility of the boys making a trip with a wagonload of lumber to earn three dollars for the family. Because Addie's wish was that she be buried in Jefferson, the town where her relatives lay, Anse was afraid the boys might not get back in time to carry her body to the Jefferson graveyard. He finally approved the trip, and Jewel and Darl set out.

Addie died while the two brothers were gone and before Cash could finish the coffin. When it was obvious that she was dying, Dr. Peabody was summoned, but he came too late to help the sick woman. While Dr. Peabody was at the house, Vardaman, the youngest boy, arrived home with a fish he had caught in the river; his mother's death somehow became entangled in his mind with the death of the fish, and because Dr. Peabody was there when she died, Vardaman thought the doctor had killed her.

Meanwhile, a great rainstorm came up. Jewel and Darl, with their load of lumber, were delayed on the road by a broken wagon wheel. Cash kept working through the rain, trying to finish the coffin. At last it was complete, and Addie was placed in it, but the crazed Vardaman, who once had almost smothered in his crib, tried to let his mother out by boring holes through the top of the coffin.

After Jewel and Darl finally got back with the wagon, neighbors gathered at the Bundren house for the funeral service, which was conducted by Whitfield, the minister. Whitfield had once been a lover of Addie's after her marriage, and Jewel, the son whom she seemed to favor, had been fathered by the minister.

Following the service, Anse, his family, and the dead Addie started for Jefferson, normally one hard day's ride away. The rainstorm, however, had so swollen the river that the bridge had been broken and could not be crossed by wagon. After trying another bridge, which had also been washed out, they drove back to an old ford near the first bridge. Three of the family—Anse, Dewey Dell, and Vardaman, with the assistance of Vernon Tull, a neighboring farmer—got across the river on the ruins of the bridge. Then Darl and Cash attempted to drive the wagon across at the obliterated ford, with Jewel leading the way on his spotted horse. This horse was Jewel's one great possession; he had earned the money to purchase it by working all day at the Bundren farm and then by working all night clearing ground for a neighbor. When the wagon was nearly across, a big log floating downstream upset the wagon. As a result, Cash broke his leg and nearly died; the mules were drowned; the coffin fell out, but was dragged to the bank by Jewel; and Cash's carpenter's tools were scattered in the water and had to be recovered one by one.

Anse refused the loan of anyone's mules, insisting that he must own the team that carried Addie to the grave. He went off to bargain for mules and made a trade in which he offered, without Jewel's consent, to give the spotted horse as part payment. When Jewel found out what his father had done, he rode off, apparently abandoning the group. Later it turned out that he had put the spotted horse in the barn of Snopes, who was dickering with Anse. Thus, they got their new mules, and the trip continued.

By the time they arrived in Mottson, a town on the way to Jefferson, Addie had been dead so long that buzzards followed the wagon. In Mottson, they stopped to buy cement to strengthen Cash's broken leg. The police and citizens, whose noses were offended, insisted that the wagon move on, but they bought the cement and treated the leg before they would budge. While they were in the town, Dewey Dell left the wagon, went to a drugstore, and tried to buy medicine that would abort the illegitimate child she carried, for she had become pregnant by a man named Lafe, with whom she had worked on the farm. The druggist refused to sell her the medicine.

Addie Bundren had been dead nine days and was still not buried. The family spent the last night before their arrival in Jefferson at the house of Mr. Gillespie, who allowed them to put the odorous coffin in his barn. During the night, Darl, whom the neighbors had always thought to be the least sane of the Bundrens, set fire to the barn. Jewel rescued the coffin by carrying it out on his back. Anse later turned Darl over to the authorities at Jefferson; they sent him to the asylum in Jackson.

Lacking a spade and shovel to dig Addie's grave, Anse stopped at a house in Jefferson and borrowed these tools. The burial finally took place. Afterward, Dewey Dell again tried to buy medicine at a drugstore. One of the clerks pretended to be a doctor, gave her some innocuous fluid, and told her to come back that night for further treatment. The further treatment took the form of a seduction in the basement of the drugstore.

Cash's broken leg, encased in cement, had by now become so infected that Anse took him to Dr. Peabody, who said Cash might not walk for a year. Before starting on the trip home, Anse bought himself a set of false teeth that he had long needed. He then returned the borrowed tools. When he got back to the wagon, he had acquired not only the new teeth but also a new Mrs. Bundren, the woman who lent him the tools.

Critical Evaluation:

Considered by many contemporary critics the greatest American fiction writer, William Faulkner was awarded the Nobel Prize in Literature in 1949, after a prolific career that included nineteen novels and two volumes of poetry. Although his formal education was limited, Faulkner read prodigiously in the Greek and Roman classics, the Bible, Shakespeare, the English Romantics, Conrad, Joyce, and Eliot. After relatively undistinguished early attempts in poetry and prose, Faulkner was advised by Sherwood Anderson to concentrate on his "own postage stamp of native soil." This led to the saga of Yoknapatawpha County, a partly true regional history (based on Oxford, Mississippi) merging imperceptibly into a coherent myth, that began to unravel with *Sartoris* (1929) and was continued in *The Sound and the Fury* (1929) and *As I Lay Dying* (1930).

In the Yoknapatawpha novels, Faulkner placed himself in the forefront of the avant-garde with his intricate plot organization, his bold experiments in the dislocation of narrative time, and his use of the stream-of-consciousness technique. His stylistic view of time was affected by his sense that past events continue into the present. As he once said, "There is no such thing as *was*; if *was* existed, there would be no grief or sorrow." These stylistic characteristics were undergirded by the development of a complex social structure that enabled Faulkner to explore the inherited guilt of the Southern past, the incapacity of the white aristocracy to cope with modern life, the relations between classes, and the relations between black and white.

Starkly realistic, poignantly symbolic, grotesquely comic, and immensely complicated as an experiment in points of view, *As I Lay Dying* ranks with Faulkner's greatest novels: *The Sound and the Fury*, *Sanctuary* (1931), *Light in August* (1932), and *Absalom, Absalom!* (1936). The relative simplicity of its style, characterized by staccatolike sentences and repetitive dialogue, enhances the tragicomic effect. At the same time, the prosaic quality of the narrative often renders into poetry—as when Dewey Dell becomes the symbol of heedless motherhood by wiping everything on her dress, when Darl sees stars first in the bucket and then in his dipper, when Jewel's horse appears "enclosed by a glittering maze of hooves as by an illusion of wings," when the buzzards accompanying Addie's coffin are juxtaposed suddenly with the sparks that make the stars flow backward for Vardaman, or when Darl, in his visionary fashion, speculates: "It is as though the space between us were time: an irrevocable quality. It is as though time, no longer running straight before us in a diminishing line, now runs parallel between us like a looping string, the distance between the doubling accretion of the thread and not the interval between."

The novel's theme, in the very widest terms, is man's absurdly comic distinction between being and not-being. Peabody describes death as "merely a function of the mind—and that of the ones who suffer the bereavement." The theme is stated most clearly in the single chapter narrated from Addie's viewpoint: "I could just remember how my father used to say that the reason for living was to get ready to stay dead a long time." Addie has long since considered Anse dead, because she realizes that he, like most humans, cannot distinguish between the "thin line" of words that float upward into nothingness and the terrible reality of "doing [that] goes along the earth, clinging to it." Her attitude is expressed tersely and succinctly when she comments, after allusively revealing her affair with Whitfield: "Then I found that I had Jewel. When I waked to remember to discover it, he was two months gone."

Nineteen of the fifty-nine chapters are narrated from Darl's viewpoint, making him the primary persona of the novel. His references to his family's conglomerate madness sets the tone: "In sunset we fall into furious attitudes, dead gestures of dolls." The novel proceeds in a jerky, doll-like movement, as the narration passes through the viewpoints of fifteen different characters, not without occasional retrogression and hiatus. Although Darl might be called the primary narrator, whose voice is most representative of the author's own, he is not the only interesting one. Vardaman, with ten chapters, displays a mentality reminiscent of Benjie's in *The Sound and the Fury*, showing readers the crazy events connected with the burial through the eyes of a confused and simple-minded child. The third chapter from his viewpoint consists of a single sentence: "My mother is a fish." Only three chapters present Anse's viewpoint; but that is enough to show that he is a bizarre combination of his sons' characteristics: Darl's imagination, Vardaman's insanity, Cash's stubborn practicality, and Dewey Dell's earthiness (which also sets her in contrast with the bitterness of Addie's outlook toward sex and motherhood).

As he does in *The Sound and the Fury*, with Jason's chapter, Faulkner achieves his greatest artistic success with the least intrinsically interesting character, Cash. The first chapter (of five) from Cash's viewpoint is an artistic *coup*. Until this point, readers have heard, through many different viewpoints, the steady buzzing of Cash's saw preparing his mother's coffin—a sound that provides the thread of continuity through the first half of the novel. Even through the rain and through the night, Cash will not cease his labor: "Yet the motion of the saw has not faltered, as though it and the arm functioned in a tranquil conviction that rain was an illusion of the mind." Finally, his own voice is heard in chapter 18: "I made it on the bevel." After this statement, Cash proceeds to explain what he means as Faulkner presents the carpenter's methodological mind in a straightforward list: "1. There is more surface for the nails to grip," ending with, "13. It makes a neater job." Cash's second chapter is a nine-line warning to his impatient father and brothers that the coffin "wasn't on a balance" in the wagon. When the tragedy in the river results from their ignoring his warning, Faulkner presents Cash's third chapter in three lines, beginning with, "It wasn't on a balance," and not even mentioning the fact that Cash's leg has been broken. Cash's single-minded craftsmanship and superhuman patience become a reflection of the author's own technique. The final chapter is Cash's.

THE AWKWARD AGE

Type of work: Novel
Author: Henry James (1843–1916)
Type of plot: Social realism
Time of plot: 1890's, presumably
Locale: London and outlying estates
First published: 1899

Principal characters:

FERNANDA BROOKENHAM (MRS. BROOK), the leader of a smart London sct

EDWARD BROOKENHAM, her husband and a government employee

NANDA, their daughter

HAROLD, their son

MR. LONGDON, a more or less elderly gentleman and a former suitor of Mrs. Brook's mother, Lady Julia

GUSTAVUS VANDERBANK (VAN), a member of Mrs. Brook's circle and a government employee

MR. MITCHETT (MITCHY), a wealthy young man who belongs to the circle

THE DUCHESS (JANE), the widow of an Italian duke, also a member of the circle

LITTLE AGGIE, her niece

TISHY GRENDON, a young married woman and a friend of Nanda

CARRIE DONNER, her sister

MR. CASHMORE, Mrs. Donner's lover

LADY FANNY CASHMORE, his wife

LORD PETHERTON, Lady Fanny's brother and Mitchy's friend

The Awkward Age stems from that intensely experimental period at the turn of the century in which Henry James laid the groundwork for the major accomplishments of *The Ambassadors*, *The Wings of the Dove*, and *The Golden Bowl*. Coming as it does between *What Maisie Knew*, in which the point of view is restricted to that of a young girl, and *The Sacred Fount*, in which the point of view is that of a narrator for whom the actions of the other characters are the subject of endless but unconfirmable speculation, *The Awkward Age* is more technically dazzling, and possibly more enigmatic, than either in that James restricts himself almost entirely to dialogue and eschews, except for two or three very brief passages, his customary practice of "going behind," that is, of entering the minds of any of his characters. The effect is rather that of a lengthy closet drama (James admits in the preface that his model has been the *roman dialogué* of the French author Gyp), but a drama surpassing in subtlety, intricacy, and elusiveness anything heretofore written in that genre. With the help only of those few occasions when James renders Nanda's and Vanderbanks' thoughts, and of a hypothetical spectator to whom James attributes hypothetical interpretations of tones of voice and facial expressions, the reader is left to infer, as the characters themselves do, the motivational and situational realities behind the labyrinth of the novel's conversation, or at least to register how the characters' own inferences bring about the events in which they participate.

The central characters of the novel are members of Mrs. Brookenham's "group," a select circle of sophisticated conversationalists for whom innuendo and the immediately perceived hinted nuance have become a style of life. Beyond mere talk—their lives reside so largely in their talk—is the prospect of what will happen to the group's tone and what restraints will be imposed when they are admitted into the drawing room of Mrs. Brook's marriageable but unmarried daughter, Nanda. Into this distinctly "modern" society comes Mr. Longdon, and the novel opens on a lengthy conversation between him and Vanderbank following the occasion of their having spent the evening— Mr. Longdon's first—at Mrs. Brook's. Vanderbank, who presents, it emerges, a remarkably handsome and imposing appearance, but whose means are hardly commensurate with the impression he creates, is taken with the older man who so charmingly contrasts with the tone he is accustomed to, and Mr. Longdon, despite misgivings about that tone—which finds its quintessence in Mrs. Brook—is similarly pleased. Mr. Longdon confides to Van that he has been a suitor to both Van's mother and Mrs. Brook's mother, Lady Julia, and that he has never forgotten his feeling for the latter, from whom her own daughter differs so dramatically. Upon seeing a picture of Nanda, Mr. Longdon exclaims on her similarity to Lady Julia. The conversation ends on Mr. Longdon's revealing that the conversational tone of the evening has indeed shocked him.

The next "act," so to speak (there are ten), presents readers immediately with Mrs. Brook in colloquy with her son Harold, whom she catches in the act of stealing a five-pound note. Mrs. Brook is operating in her family mode, a studied and languorous melancholy quite at odds with her public performances, and her conversation turns on the problem of getting Harold invited to house parties (her son has obviously taken lessons in manipulation from her) and the family's financial straits. With Harold's exit and the entrance of the Duchess, the talk turns to Nanda, who is visiting her married friend Tishy Grendon. The Duchess chides Mrs. Brook for allowing her daughter to mingle with such questionable associates; whereas she, in the European manner, has carefully sheltered her niece, Little Aggie, from any such possible contaminations, has preserved her a perfect little *tabula rasa* until the time of her marriage. She then urges Mrs. Brook to snare Mitchy as a husband for Nanda; she adds that his ugliness and his being the son of a shoemaker render him totally unsatisfactory as a potential mate for Aggie, though she will shortly thereafter instigate a maneuver designed to land him for Aggie. After a brief conversation between Mrs. Brook and her husband, Mitchy and Petherton enter, and it is shown that Petherton is probably the Duchess' lover. Mrs. Brook attributes to Mitchy, despite his outrageous talk, a gentleness and "niceness" lacking in the rest of them, and her comment, sincere or not, will be borne out in the development of the novel. The Duchess reenters, this time with Aggie, and when Carrie Donner's arrival is shortly followed by that of Lady Fanny, the talk turns to the erotic entanglements of the Grendon-Donner-Cashmore set. The Duchess then informs Mitchy that it is Nanda who is her mother's source on the degree of intimacy between Mrs. Donner and Mr. Cashmore.

In the following scene, Mr. Longdon and the reader are confronted for the first time with Nanda, whose resemblance to Lady Julia overwhelms Mr. Longdon. He and Nanda develop an immediate rapport.

Mrs. Brook sounds Van on the subject of Mr. Longdon's fortune and what he may do for Nanda, and in the same dialogue indicates that she is possibly in love with Van.

At a weekend party given by Mitchy, Mr. Longdon urges Nanda to marry, but she rejects Mitchy as impossible and confides to him that she will probably never marry. The Duchess tries to persuade Mr. Longdon to settle on a sum to give Van that will allow him to marry Nanda (thus leaving Mitchy, upon whom Mrs. Brook has designs for Nanda, free for Aggie), who is "as sick as a little cat—with her passion" for him. Mr. Longdon makes his offer to the uncertain Van, who requests time to consider the proposition and refuses to allow his prospective benefactor to name a sum.

In the ensuing conversation, Van reveals Mr. Longdon's generous offer to Mrs. Brook, which that lady—whether merely prophetically or in an attempt to determine his hand—enigmatically hints he will refuse. Mrs. Brook then, against Van's articulated wishes, imparts to Mitchy the information she has just gained and suggests that Van will pass up the chance to propose to Nanda rather than appear to accept a bribe. She has, she says, made her revelation simply in accordance with that principle of openness and honesty, which is so much the note of their society, and the scene concludes with the mutual bestowal of lavish accolade, somewhat undercut by Van's ironic awareness of the prevalent duplicity and the possible mixture of motive for Mrs. Brook's behavior. Nanda enters shortly after the departure of her mother's guests, and Mrs. Brook questions her about her relationship with Mr. Longdon and broaches the possibility and advisability of his adopting the girl.

At Mr. Longdon's, Nanda approaches Mitchy, whom she knows to be in love with her, and urges him, for his own sake and that of Aggie, to marry the Duchess' niece, thus effectually eliminating him as a candidate for her own hand. Mitchy, to gratify Nanda and to enjoy the only proximity of relationship with her now open to him, that of simply being thoroughly together with her on the matter of Aggie, acquiesces to her promptings and reveals his intentions to Van, indicating that the way is now completely open to the latter. Van, however, remains uncommitted and indecisive. The conversation ends rather darkly on the question of what Mr. Longdon will do for Nanda should Van fail to propose.

The climactic scene of the novel occurs several months later at Tishy Grendon's, where all the principal characters are gathered. At this time, Nanda has been Mr. Longdon's guest for several months; Harold has ably distracted Lady Fanny from her design to run off with another gentleman; and Little Aggie, after her marriage, has been divested with a vengeance of her innocence and has taken up with her aunt's lover, Petherton. Mrs. Brook, in a tremendous scene, demands Nanda's return from Mr. Longdon and forces the public exposure of the group, climaxing her performance with the revelation that Nanda has read a scabrous French novel, lent to her by Vanderbank, and has even pronounced it unfit for the presumably far more experienced Tishy to read. The effect is to reveal to Vanderbank the depths of knowledge already open to Nanda, depths in the unveiling of which he has been instrumental but which, with cruel irony, render her an impossible choice for his wife. Mrs. Brook, who knows Van all too well, has eliminated the possibility of losing him to her daughter.

The scene at Tishy Grendon's, however, has served to destroy the solidarity of the group, and it is only after months that Van returns to Mrs. Brook's, supposedly to see Nanda but ultimately avoiding the chance to do so, an avoidance that Mrs. Brook interprets as his finally having given Nanda up. This information she enjoins Mitchy to give Mr. Longdon, for, as she has explained to her remarkably obtuse husband, her purpose in creating the horrid scene at Tishy's had been simply to confirm Mr. Longdon's belief that she and her world were impossible for Nanda and to insure his taking care of the girl.

The final "act" occurs two weeks later, with the overwrought and embarrassed Van making what is presumably his final visit to Nanda. Nanda, however, lets the now awkward young man off easily by assuming the false position herself, and she generously entreats him not to desert her mother, a plea she repeats to Mitchy in her next interview. Finally, there is only Mr. Longdon, and before him she breaks down in the fullness of her suffering. It is Little Aggie whom Vanderbank ought to have married, they agree. Only that innocence could have met his measure, though an innocence capable of becoming its own obverse at the first taste of experience. Even under such a circumstance, however, Mitchy would still have been totally out of the question for her; it has been his fate, as it has been Nanda's, to love only that person for whom he is an impossibility. Nanda's thoughts revolve around the suffering Mitchy as she prepares to be taken away the following day by Mr. Longdon.

Turning as it seems to on the question of a girl's reading a questionable book, *The Awkward Age* may appear to the superficial glance as a period piece, elaborate and elegant, but without the reverberating significance of James's three final masterpieces. To see the novel in this light, however, is to neglect its hard and lucid inquiry into the coexistence of moral vision and the knowledge of a world seemingly its antithesis. Little Aggie is innocent of such knowledge, but her innocence is the merest ignorance of that which she will become. Paradoxically, Nanda's knowledge, the superficial taint as opposed to the inward blight, of the world in which she is so thoroughly implicated, a knowledge that is perhaps instrumental in creating Nanda's moral dimension, renders her unacceptable to Vanderbank. And yet if Nanda's magnanimous vision can exist only in her retreat with Mr. Longdon from the world, there is a sense in which she too, by her pressuring Mitchy into marrying Aggie, has been implicated in the network of selfishness, guilt, and suffering, which is perhaps the inevitable result of the brush of human contact.

Finally, there is the pragmatism of the magnificent Mrs. Brook, the ability to make do in a world where one is unlikely to get what one wants. What Mrs. Brook wants is unquestionably Van. The book leaves the question moot whether they have ever been lovers, though most of the evidence points to the fact that they have not. Her scene at Tishy Grendon's appears from one angle a wanton destruction of her daughter's hopes; yet, given her knowledge of Van's nature (a nature, it must be said, that contact with her has in no small measure formed), her seemingly brutal actions may just as well be motivated, as she explains to Edward, by a desire to provide, no matter how deviously, for a daughter who has no other chance, to ensure for her the opening of an escape from a world that has already left its mark. To acknowledge that the selfish desire to retain Van for herself enters Mrs. Brook's design is to admit the necessary multiplicity of motive inherent in taking any course of human action. Mrs. Brook's motives are decidedly mixed—and her awareness of the fact is part of her limited triumph. She provides the only alternative, if a partially cruel one, to the very different satisfactions offered by renunciation.

BABBITT

Type of work: Novel
Author: Sinclair Lewis (1885–1951)
Type of plot: Social satire
Time of plot: 1920's
Locale: Zenith, a fictional Midwestern town
First published: 1922

Principal characters:
GEORGE F. BABBITT, a middle-aged real-estate broker
MYRA, his wife
TED, their son
VERONA, their daughter
PAUL RIESLING, Babbitt's friend
ZILLA, Paul's shrewish wife

The Story:

George F. Babbitt was proud of his house in Floral Heights, one of the most respectable residential districts in Zenith. Its architecture was standardized; its interior decorations were standardized; its atmosphere was standardized. Therein lay its appeal for Babbitt.

He bustled about in a tile and chromium bathroom during his morning ritual of getting ready for another day. When he went down to breakfast, he was as grumpy as usual. It was expected of him. He read the dull real-estate page of the newspaper to his patient wife, Myra. Then he commented on the weather, grumbled at his son and daughter, gulped his breakfast, and started for his office.

Babbitt was a real-estate broker who knew how to handle business with zip and zowie. Having closed a deal whereby he forced a poor businessman to buy a piece of property at twice its value, he pocketed part of the money and paid the rest to the man who had suggested the enterprise. Proud of his acumen, he picked up the telephone and called his best friend, Paul Riesling, to ask him to lunch.

Paul Riesling should have been a violinist, but he had gone into the tar-roofing business in order to support his shrewish wife, Zilla. Lately, she had made it her practice to infuriate doormen, theater ushers, or taxicab drivers, and then ask Paul to come to her rescue and fight them like a man. Cringing with embarrassment, Paul would pretend he had not noticed the incident. Later, at home, Zilla would accuse him of being a coward and a weakling.

So sad did Paul's affairs seem to Babbitt that he suggested a vacation to

BABBITT by Sinclair Lewis. By permission of the author and publishers, Harcourt, Brace & Co., Inc. Copyright, 1922, by Harcourt, Brace & Co., Inc.

Maine together—away from their wives. Paul was skeptical, but with magnificent assurance, Babbitt promised to arrange the trip. Paul was humbly
grateful.

Back in his office, Babbitt refused a raise for one of his employees. When
he got home, he and his wife decided to give a dinner party, with the arrangements taken bodily from the contents of a woman's magazine, and everything
edible disguised to look like something else.

The party was a great success. Babbitt's friends were exactly like Babbitt.
They all became drunk on prohibition-period gin, were disappointed when
the cocktails ran out, stuffed themselves with food, and went home to nurse
headaches.

Sometime later, Babbitt and Myra paid a call on the Rieslings. Zilla, trying
to enlist their sympathy, berated her husband until he was goaded to fury.
Babbitt finally told Zilla that she was a nagging, jealous, sour, and unwhole-
some wife, and he demanded that she allow Paul to go with him to Maine.
Weeping in self-pity, Zilla consented. Myra sat calmly during the scene, but
later she criticized Babbitt for bullying Paul's wife. Babbitt told her sharply
to mind her own business.

On the train, Babbitt and Paul met numerous businessmen who loudly
agreed with one another that what this country needed was a sound business
administration. They deplored the price of motor cars, textiles, wheat, and
oil; they swore that they had not an ounce of race prejudice; they blamed
Communism and socialism for labor unions that got out of hand. Paul soon
tired of the discussion and went to bed. Babbitt stayed up late, smoking
countless cigars and telling countless stories.

Maine had a soothing effect upon Babbitt. He and Paul fished and hiked
in the quiet of the north woods, and Babbitt began to realize that his life in
Zenith was not all it should be. He promised himself a new outlook on life,
a more simple, less hurried way of living.

Back in Zenith, Babbitt was asked to make a speech at a convention of
real-estate men, which was to be held in Monarch, a nearby city. He wrote
a speech contending that real-estate men should be considered professionals
and called realtors. At the meeting, he declaimed loudly that real estate was
a great profession, that Zenith was God's own country—the best little spot
on earth—and to prove his statements, he quoted countless statistics on water-
ways, textile production, and lumber manufacture. The speech was such a
success that Babbitt instantly won recognition as an orator.

Babbitt was made a precinct leader in the coming election. His duty was
to speak to small labor groups about the inadvisability of voting for Seneca
Doane, a liberal, in favor of a man named Prout, a solid businessman who
represented the conservative element. Babbitt's speeches helped to defeat
Doane. He was very proud of himself for having Vision and Ideals.

On a business trip to Chicago, Babbitt spied Paul Riesling sitting at dinner with a middle-aged and pretty woman. Later, in his hotel room, Babbitt indignantly demanded an explanation for Paul's lack of morality. Paul told Babbitt that he could no longer stand living with Zilla. Babbitt, feeling sorry for his friend, swore that he would keep Paul's secret from Zilla. Privately, Babbitt envied Paul's independence.

Babbitt was made vice-president of the Booster's Club. He was so proud of himself that he bragged loudly when his wife called him at the office. It was a long time before he understood what she was trying to tell him; Paul had shot his wife.

Babbitt's world collapsed about him. Though Zilla was still alive, Paul was in prison. Babbitt began to question his ideas about the power of the dollar. Paul was perhaps the only person Babbitt had ever loved. Myra had long since become a habit, and the children were too full of new ideas to be close to their father. Babbitt felt suddenly alone. He began to criticize the minister's sermons. He no longer visited the Athletic Club and rarely ate lunch with any of his business acquaintances.

One day, the pretty widow Mrs. Judique came to his office and asked him to find her a flat. Babbitt joined her circle of Bohemian friends. He drank more than he had ever drunk in his life. He spent money wildly. Two of the most powerful men in town requested that he join the Good Citizen's League—or else. Babbitt refused to be bullied. For the first time in his life, he was a human being. He actually made friends with his archenemy, Seneca Doane, and discovered that he liked his liberal ideas. He praised Doane publicly. Babbitt's new outlook on life appealed to his children, who at once began to respect him as they never had before. Babbitt, however, became unpopular among his business-boosting friends. When he again refused to join the Good Citizen's League, he was snubbed in the streets. Gradually, Babbitt found that he had no real resources within himself. He was miserable.

When Myra became ill, Babbitt suddenly realized that he loved his colorless wife. He broke with Mrs. Judique and joined the Good Citizen's League. By the time Myra was well again, there was no more active leader in the town of Zenith than George F. Babbitt. Once more he announced his distrust of Seneca Doane. He became the best Booster the club ever had. His last gesture of revolt was private approval of his son's elopement. Outwardly he conformed.

Critical Evaluation:

Zenith, "the Zip City—Zeal, Zest, and Zowie," is Sinclair Lewis' satirical composite picture of the typical progressive American "business city" of the 1920's, and middle-aged, middle-class Midwesterner George F. Babbitt is its average prosperous citizen. Everything about Zenith is modern. A few old buildings, ramshackle witnesses of the city's nineteenth century origins, are embarrassing, discordant notes amid the harmony of newness produced by shining skyscrapers, factories, and railroads. One by one, the old buildings are surrounded and bulldozed. The thrust of all energies in the city is toward growth: one of Zenith's most booming businesses is real estate; one of its favorite occupations is the religious tallying and charting of population increase.

As Lewis presents his characters, however, the reader discovers that the prosperity and growth of Zenith has been inversely proportional to the intellectual bankruptcy and spiritual stagnation of its inhabitants. Because they subscribe to the values of Zenith's culture, which are all based on the "Dollar Ethic," Lewis' characters think in terms of production and consumption, judge people on the grounds of their purchasing power, and seek happiness in the earning and spending of money. This creed of prosperity permeates every aspect of society. It is evident not only in political and economic beliefs (discussion between Babbitt and his friends about government affairs is limited to the monotonous refrain, "What this country needs is a good, sound business administration") but in moral and religious attitudes as well. Thus, Dr. Drew attracts followers to his "Salvation and Five Percent" church with a combined cross-and-dollar-sign approach. Even more sinister is the facility with which the upright Babbitt carries through crooked deals in his real estate business. In one maneuver, he plots with a speculator to force a struggling grocer to buy the store building (which he has been renting for years) at a scalper's price. The money ethic is so elemental to Babbitt's conscience that he honestly feels nothing but delight and pride when the deal is completed; his only regret is that the speculator carries off nine thousand dollars while Babbitt receives a mere four hundred and fifty dollar commission. At the same time, Babbitt—with no inkling of his hypocrisy—discourses on his virtue to his friend Paul Riesling, touting his own integrity while denigrating the morality of his competitors.

The value placed on money also determines Zenith's aesthetic standards. There is no frivolity about the city's architecture; the most important structures are the strictly functional business buildings. Other structures, such as the Athletic Club—where the businessmen go to "relax" and discuss weighty matters of finance—are gaudy, unabashed copies of past styles; the Club's motley conglomeration includes everything from Roman to Gothic to Chinese. The culmination of literary talent in Zenith is the work of Chum Frink, whose daily newspaper lyrics are indistinguishable from his Zeeco car ads. He comes to Babbitt's dinner party fresh from having written a lyric in praise of drinking water instead of poison booze; with bootleg cocktail in hand, he identifies the American genius as the fellow who can run a successful business or the man who writes the Prince Albert Tobacco ads.

Most important, the prosperity ethic is at the heart of social norms in Zenith; it is the basis upon which each citizen judges his individual worth. Lewis' novel includes caricatures of men in every major field of endeavor: Howard Littlefield is the scholar; T. Cholmondeley Frink, the poet; Mike Monday, the popular preacher; Jake Offut, the politician; Vergil Gunch, the industrialist. Yet despite their various professions, these men are identical in their values; they are united in their complacent pride at their own success and in their scorn for those who have not "made it." A man is measured by his income and his possessions. Thus, Babbitt's car is far more than his means of transportation, and his acquisition of gimmicks like the nickel-plated cigar cutter more than mere whim; both car and cigar cutter are affirmations of competence and virility. But the more Babbitt and his peers strive to distinguish themselves through ownership, the more alike they seem. Thus, the men of Zenith, since they are saturated day after day with the demands of the business life and its values, are even more alike than the women, who are not as immersed in the "rat race" as their husbands.

Mercilessly revealing and minutely detailed as the portrait of Zenith is, however, *Babbitt* would not be the excellent novel it is if Lewis had stopped at that. In addition to being an exposé of shallowness, the novel is the chronicle of one man's feeble and half-conscious attempt to break out of a meaningless and sterile existence. In the first half of the book, George Babbitt is the Zenithite *par excellence*; but in the realtor's sporadic bursts of discontent, Lewis plants seeds of the rebellion to come. Babbitt's complacency is occasionally punctured by disturbing questions: Might his wife be right that he bullied Zilla only to strut and show off his strength and virtue? Are his friends really interesting people? Does he really love his wife and enjoy his career? These nagging questions and the pressures in his life finally build sufficient tension to push Babbitt to the unprecedented step of taking a week's vacation in Maine without his wife and children. The trip relieves his tension and dissolves the questions, and he returns to another year in Zenith with renewed vigor and enthusiasm for Boosters, baseball, dinner parties, and real estate.

It takes the personal tragedy of his friend Paul Riesling to really shock Babbitt out of his routine way of life; Paul's shooting of his wife and consequent imprisonment, which occur approximately midway in the novel, shake Babbitt to his foundations. The Babbitt of the first half of the story is a parody; the Babbitt of the second half, a weak and struggling human being. After Paul goes to prison, Babbitt, to all appearances, throws over his whole previous life-style: he drinks, smokes, and curses; he frequents wild parties, befriends the city's bohemian set, adopts radical opinions, and has a love affair. All these things are part of his rebellion against stifling circumstances and his attempt to escape into individuality. The attempt fails because he lacks the inner strength to be independent, and his revolt is ultimately little more than a teapot tempest. Whether preaching the philosophy of the Elks or rebelliously praising the radical politics of Seneca Doane, whether giving a dinner party with his wife or sneaking out to see Mrs. Judique, Babbitt never truly acts on his own.

Thus, by the end of the novel, Babbitt has "returned to the fold," joining the Good Citizen's League and redoubling his zeal in behalf of Zenith Booster activities. But even though Babbitt lacks the strength to break out of his mold, Lewis does not imply that he is unchanged by his experience. On the contrary, Babbitt rediscovers his love for his wife and learns something about himself. The Babbitt at the close of the novel has grown in awareness, even if he has proven himself incapable of essentially changing his life. If he has lost his own individuality, he is still able to hope for better things for his son, Ted, of whose elopement he secretly approves.

BARREN GROUND

Type of work: Novel
Author: Ellen Glasgow (1874–1945)
Type of plot: Social criticism
Time of plot: Late nineteenth and early twentieth centuries
Locale: Rural Virginia
First published: 1925

> Principal characters:
> DORINDA OAKLEY, daughter of a poor white Virginia
> farmer
> JOSIAH and
> RUFUS, her brothers
> JASON GREYLOCK, the last member of an old Virginia
> family
> GENEVA ELLGOOD, later, Jason's wife
> NATHAN PEDLAR, a country farmer and merchant

The Story:

Late one cold winter day, Dorinda Oakley started to walk the four miles between Pedlar's Mill and her home at Old Farm. The land was bleak and desolate under a gray sky, and a few flakes of snow were falling. For almost a year, she had worked in Nathan Pedlar's store, taking the place of his consumptive wife. Her brisk walk carried her swiftly over the rutted roads toward her father's unproductive farm and the dilapidated Oakley house. On the way, she passed Green Acres, the fertile farm of James Ellgood, and the run-down farm of Five Oaks, owned by dissolute old Doctor Greylock, whose son, Jason, had given up his medical studies to take over his father's practice and to care for his drunken father.

As she walked, Dorinda thought of young Jason Greylock. Before she reached Old Farm, Jason overtook her in his buggy. During the ride to her home, she remembered the comment of old Matthew Fairlamb, who had told her that she ought to marry Jason. The young doctor was handsome. He represented something different from the drab, struggling life Dorinda had always known. Her father and mother and her two brothers were all unresponsive and bitter people. Mrs. Oakley suffered from headaches and tried to forget them in a ceaseless activity of work. At Old Farm, supper was followed by prayers and prayers by sleep.

Dorinda continued to see Jason. Taking the money she had been saving to buy a cow, she ordered a pretty dress and a new hat to wear to church on

Easter Sunday. Her Easter finery, however, brought her no happiness. Jason sat in church with the Ellgoods and their daughter, Geneva, and afterward, he went home with them to dinner. Dorinda sat in her bedroom that afternoon and meditated on her unhappiness.

Later, Jason proposed unexpectedly, confessing that he too was lonely and unhappy. He spoke of his attachment to his father that had brought him back to Pedlar's Mill, and he cursed the tenant system, which he said was ruining the South. He and Dorinda planned to be married in the fall. When they met during the hot, dark nights that summer, he kissed her with half-angry, half-hungry violence.

Meanwhile, Geneva Ellgood told her friends that she was engaged to Jason Greylock. Later in September, Jason left for the city to buy surgical instruments. When he was overlong in returning, Dorinda began to worry. At last she visited Aunt Mehitable Green, an old black conjure woman, in the hope Aunt Mehitable would have heard some gossip from the Greylock servants concerning Jason. There Dorinda became ill and learned that she was to have a child. Distressed, she went to Five Oaks and confronted drunken old Dr. Greylock, who told her, as he cackled with sly mirth, that Jason had married Geneva Ellgood in the city. The old man intimated that Jason was white-livered and had been forced into the marriage by the Ellgoods. He added, leering, that Jason and his bride were expected home that night.

On the way home, Dorinda saw, herself unseen, the carriage that brought Jason and Geneva to Five Oaks. Late that night, she went to the Greylock house and attempted to shoot Jason. Frightened, Jason begged for pity and understanding. Despising him for his weakness and falseness, she blundered home through the darkness. Two days later, she packed her suitcase and left home. By accident, she took the northbound train rather than the one to Richmond, and so she changed the course of her life.

Dorinda arrived in New York in October, frightened, friendless, and with no prospects of work. Two weeks later, she fortunately met a kindly middle-aged woman who took her in and gave her the address of a dressmaker who might hire her. On the way to the shop, however, Dorinda was knocked down by a cab. She awoke in a hospital. Dr. Faraday, a surgeon who had seen the accident, saved her life, but she lost her baby. Dr. Faraday hired her to look after his office and children.

Dorinda lived in New York with the Faradays for two years. Then her father had a stroke, and she returned home. Her brother Josiah was married; Mrs. Pedlar was dead. Dorinda had become a woman of self-confidence and poise. She saw Geneva Greylock, who already looked middle-aged, and had only pity for the woman who had married Jason. Her brother Rufus said Jason was drinking heavily and losing all his patients. Five Oaks Farm looked more run-down than ever. Determined to make the Oakley land productive once more, Dorinda borrowed enough money to buy seven cows. She found

Nathan Pedlar helpful in many ways, for he knew good farming methods and gave her advice. When she saw Jason again, she wondered how she could ever have yielded herself to the husk of such a man.

After her father's death, Josiah and his wife Elvira went to live on their own land. Rufus, who hated the farm, planned to go to the city. Before he left the farm, however, Rufus was accused of murdering a neighboring farmer. Dorinda was sure that he had committed the murder, but Mrs. Oakley swore under oath that her son had been at home with her at the time of the shooting. Her lie saved Rufus. Mrs. Oakley's conscience began to torment her because of the lie she had told, and she took to her bed. Her mind broken, she lived in dreams of her youth. When she died in her sleep, Dorinda wept. To her, it seemed that her parents' lives had been futile and wasted.

During the next ten years, Dorinda worked hard. She borrowed more money to improve the farm, and although she had to save and scrimp, she was happy. Geneva Greylock was losing her mind. One day she told Dorinda that she had borne a child but that Jason had killed it and buried it in the garden. Geneva drowned herself the same day that Nathan Pedlar asked Dorinda to marry him.

Together Dorinda and Nathan prospered. She was now thirty-eight and still felt young. John Abner Pedlar, Nathan's crippled son, looked to her for help, and she gave it willingly. Nathan's other children meant less to her, and she was glad when they married and moved away. When Five Oaks was offered for sale, Dorinda and Nathan bought it for six thousand dollars. As Jason signed over the papers to her, Dorinda noticed that he was his dirty, drunken old father all over again.

The next few years Dorinda devoted to restoring Five Oaks. John Abner was still her friend and helper. There were reports that Jason was living in an old house in the pine woods and drinking heavily. Dorinda, busy with her house and dairy farm, had little time for neighborhood gossip.

One day, Nathan took the train to the city to have a tooth pulled and to attend a lawsuit. The train was wrecked, and Nathan was killed while trying to save the lives of the other passengers. He was given a hero's funeral.

The years following Nathan's death were Dorinda's happiest, for as time passed, she realized that she had regained, through her struggle with the land, her own integrity and self-respect.

One day, some hunters found Jason sick and starving in the woods, and her neighbors assumed Dorinda would take him in. Unwillingly, she allowed him to be brought to Old Farm, where she engaged a nurse to look after him. In a few months, Jason died. Many of the people at the funeral came only out of curiosity, and a pompous minister said meaningless things about Jason, whom he had never known. Dorinda felt nothing as she stood beside the grave, for her memories of Jason had outlived her emotions. She sensed that for good or ill, the fervor and fever of her life were ended.

Critical Evaluation:

   Barren Ground is a disturbing novel because it represents the ways life
can be lived under the most harrowing of circumstances. Ellen Glasgow writes
about farmers who are faced with the difficulties of making an unwilling
earth—a wasteland in fact—yield. A few triumph against the odds; some do
their best and barely survive; others give up and die early. All except those
in the last category work exceedingly hard. Glasgow believes, as she says in
the 1933 preface to *Barren Ground*, that "the novel is experience illumined
by imagination." In this novel, she is faithful to her own experience in her
native Virginia, but, as in much of her work, she colors that experience with
a dark imagination that views human life as a constant struggle in which even
the strong do not always survive. Those who do survive must adjust their
idealism to fit reality.

   The main theme of the novel is stated by its main character, Dorinda
Oakley, who thinks that for the majority, life is "barren ground where they
have to struggle to make anything grow." Dorinda has more than the soil of
rural Virginia to make her feel this way. At the age of twenty, she has the
seed of love planted in her heart only to have it uprooted by her lover's
weakness: he marries Geneva Ellgood under the duress of her brothers.
Henceforward, her heart is indeed barren ground where passion is concerned.
Furthermore, Glasgow seems to suggest that Dorinda's life is also barren
ground as far as happiness is concerned. To women, Glasgow writes, "love
and happiness [are] interchangeable terms." After Jason jilts her, Dorinda
spends a lifetime distrusting men and building emotional, mental, physical,
and financial walls in order to protect herself from them. She permits herself
to marry Nathan Pedlar only because she fears loneliness and because he is
submissive to her and is willing to live without any physical intimacy. Dorinda
becomes a cynic about love and marriage, believing that they seldom, if ever,
go together; and even when they do, the love does not endure.

   Dorinda, like the characters of Thomas Hardy novels, is driven by forces
beyond her control, by the "eternal purpose." She feels that the trivial incidents in life are the crucial ones. One of these trivial incidents was Nathan's
train trip, which resulted in his heroic death. That incident

   was apparently as trivial as her meeting with Jason in the road, as the failure
   of her aim when the gun had gone off, as the particular place and moment when
   she had fallen down in Fifth Avenue. These accidents had changed the course
   of her life. Yet none of them could she have foreseen and prevented; and only
   once, she felt, in that hospital in New York, had the accident or the device of
   fortune been in her favour.

Much like Dreiser's Carrie Meeber or Hurstwood, Dorinda is "a straw in the
wind, a leaf on a stream."

Glasgow, however, as she says in her preface, believes that "character is fate," so that the individual destinies of her characters are partly determined by the nature they inherited, by, that is, their blood: destiny is in the genes. The "vein of iron" that keeps Dorinda struggling (and that helps her to succeed) is a product of the "sense" of her great-grandfather, a member of the Southern upper class, and the physical strength of her father, a member of the "poor white" class. Jason fails, like his father had, because of "bad blood." Even though unforeseen events control one's destiny, one's character determines what is done under the unasked-for circumstances.

Archetypally, Dorinda is at first Medea, who falls in love with a Jason who will forsake her for another. But she becomes an Artemis or an Atalanta, the devouring female who remains estranged, physically and psychologically, from the male. (In the last analysis, Glasgow shows that each individual is always isolated from his fellow creatures.) She is also, paradoxically, an Earth Mother, who causes the soil to be productive and who keeps the best cows in the state. Her maternal instinct is satisfied by this bond with the soil as well as by her adoption through marriage of Nathan's children, John Abner in particular.

Although she is never a whole person psychologically, Dorinda does the best she can, given her character and experience. She achieves a wholeness that most never achieve. Though a woman, she farms better than most of the men in her rural community. Her black hair symbolizes her relationship with the earth and combines with its opposite, the sky, in her blue eyes. Her experiences are much like her mother's (an early separation from a lover, a loveless marriage), but she manages to combine her mother's hard-work habits with a contentment—if not a happiness—that her morally repressed mother never had. Jason goes away to New York and comes back to a dying father just as Dorinda is to do. Yet, Jason allows the interminable broomsedge to conquer him. Dorinda does not.

THE BAY OF SILENCE

Type of work: Novel
Author: Eduardo Mallea (1903–   )
Type of plot: Social realism
Time of plot: 1926–1940
Locale: Buenos Aires, London, Paris, Italy, and Brussels
First published: 1940

>   *Principal characters:*
>   MARTÍN TREGUA, the narrator
>   ANSELMI, a fellow law student
>   JIMÉNEZ, an office employee
>   CÉSAR ACEVEDO, a wealthy Argentine
>   BLAGODA, an associate on the magazine *Enough*
>   GLORIA BAMBIL, a librarian

An outstanding Argentine writer, and one of the most important figures in the literature of Latin America, Eduardo Mallea is a skilled technician in fiction and the literary editor of the Buenos Aires *Nación*. Among his experiments, he has written short stories such as *The City Beside the Motionless River* (1933) and essays such as *History of an Argentine Passion* (1937), both seeking, behind the faults and the grandeur of a new country, the basic principles of Argentine life. This theme pervades most of Mallea's writing.

Of the group of young writers who considered individual freedom and man's responsibility, Mallea reveals the greatest power and possesses the greatest technical skill, though his work is sometimes marred by a turgid style. He demonstrated these qualities as early as 1936, with the publication of *Fiesta in November*, an impressionistic portrait of the decadent upper class of the Argentine capital. Into the small talk and the evidences of corruption that reveal the "buyers and the bought" is woven an incident of Fascist violence, presented with complicated technique.

Between paragraphs of the account of an armed patrol dragging a poet out of bed, rushing him off to an open space, and shooting him, is the story of Eugenia Rague and her weak family: the husband trying to conclude an advantageous stock transfer, one daughter undergoing an abortion, and the other exchanging philosophies with an anarchistic poet.

There is more plot and optimism in *The Bay of Silence* (first translated into English in 1944 from the original *La bahía de silencio*). Mallea's belief is that there has been a decline in the moral qualities of Argentine national life. "It was marching along, then the motivating force broke down," is the way he expresses it. Even those only casually acquainted with Argentina can realize how it had deteriorated economically, culturally, and spiritually, even before the era of Perón. This decline is especially noticeable in its theater.

In *The Bay of Silence*, a roomer in a student boardinghouse, the aging Dr. Dervil, expresses his sentiments when he declares that Argentina is a lost nation, still colonial in spirit. He wonders when the healthy but submerged country, which exists because men believe in it, will rise from the depths of ignorance and sloth. Mallea's own hope, like that of the young former law student supposedly writing *The Bay of Silence*, is that the re-creation of Argentina will come from the unspoiled rural areas.

Martín Tregua, who had stopped attending law school because of his disgust with methods of teaching and the unscientific, spiritless faculty, turned to writing. His first project was to give meaning to the life and suffering of the average Argentine in a volume called *The Forty Nights of Juan Argentino*. Then the sight of a lovely woman of his own age, never once mentioned by name but called only "You," inspired Martín to write to her, telling her the story of his life and letting her see her effect upon him. So *The Bay of Silence* comes into being.

The book is divided into three parts. The first, "Youth," covers Martín's life from his birth in Río Negro, through his student days, to his first success as a writer in 1932. Part 2, "The Islands," tells of his trip to Europe. The last section, "The Defeated," brings his life up to 1939. The novel ends as it began, with the narrator's glimpse into a flower shop in Buenos Aires and of the woman he had adored in silence for twelve years.

The story is developed with a wealth of detail. When Martín takes a walk, the streets he traverses and the buildings along the route are named, and the casual actions of unimportant people along the way are fully described. There is very little action in the first part. It is mostly an exchange of ideas about the fundamental problems of the world that the students discuss endlessly in their boardinghouse or pass around the editorial table of the magazine *Enough*, which they have founded with the financial assistance of a wealthy man of the city.

In the course of Martín's European trip, the author contrives to get him into conversations with a Czech munitions millionaire, several Fascist underlings, and a disillusioned surgeon in Brussels. Then he returns, in the final section, to his own country, whose destiny he feels as keenly as his own, to write a sequel to his *Juan Argentino*. This task becomes complicated when he is attracted to a lending librarian named Gloria Bambil, one of many women in his life. Earlier, the unsettled and unsettling Mercedes Miró had been his companion at art exhibits, French theatrical performances, and musicales, circumstances related with many details and references that reveal Mallea's wide acquaintance with contemporary culture.

Because Gloria was unconsciously an Existentialist, Martín must occupy his time by reassuring her, in taking her from the mountains to the seashore in an attempt to give her confidence in herself and her future. Failure in this effort made him one of the many defeated in the final section of the novel.

Meanwhile, Martín Tregua has been finding his way from the uncertainties of youth to the disillusioned wisdom of middle age.

The title is twice explained. Once, in discussing *The Forty Nights of Juan Argentino*, Martín declares that his book is to be a sea, rich and abundant, where there are storms and stresses, and delightful bays of silence, filled with the dreams and sufferings of his people. Again, at the end, he tells the unnamed woman to whom he is writing that she has reached that place at which the angry sea of persecution beats in vain: the place, a bay of silence, where those who have turned their failure into triumph may wait.

A BELL FOR ADANO

Type of work: Novel
Author: John Hersey (1914–   )
Type of plot: Social criticism
Time of plot: 1943
Locale: Adano, Italy
First published: 1944

Principal characters:
MAJOR VICTOR JOPPOLO, the American Military
   Governor of Adano
SERGEANT BORTH, Major Joppolo's subordinate
CAPTAIN PURVIS, the head of the Military Police
GENERAL MARVIN, Commander-in-Chief of the American
   invasion troops and Major Joppolo's superior

The Story:

When the American army invaded Sicily, Major Victor Joppolo was placed in command of Adano. He set up his office in the city hall, rehired the janitor, and investigated the records left by the Fascist mayor, who had fled to the hills.

Soon after his arrival, Major Joppolo summoned the leading citizens of the town and asked them, through Giuseppe, his interpreter, what they considered the most important thing to be done. Some answered that the shortage of food was the most pressing problem. Others insisted that what the town needed most was its bell, which had been removed by the Fascists. The bell, it seemed, had a soothing tone. It also regulated the lives of Adano's residents.

The Major promised every effort to recover the bell. Meanwhile, the problem was to obtain food and to have produce brought into the town. In order that his directives would be understood and carried out, the Major issued proclamations that the town crier, after being silent for so long, hastened to shout in the village.

On Sunday morning, the Major attended mass at one of the churches. There he noticed a blonde girl sitting in front of him. When he later asked Giuseppe about her, the interpreter assumed that the American's interest had nothing to do with official business. Major Joppolo's primary interest, however, was the girl's father, Tomasino, owner of a fishing fleet. He had Giuseppe ask Tomasino if he would come to see him. Tomasino, however, distrustful of authority, would not come to the headquarters. The Major decided to go to Tomasino. He went, followed by practically all the townspeople. The old

Italian was defiant, sure that the Major had come to arrest him. Finally, the Italian was convinced that the Major meant neither to arrest him nor to ask for a cut in the proceeds from the sale of the fish. He agreed to go out with his fishing fleet, despite the danger of mines.

By that time, the Major and his policies had become the subject of much discussion among the people. The Fascist mayor provided them with a great deal of amusement. He had come out of hiding and had been paroled into Sergeant Borth's custody. Every morning the mayor went to Sergeant Borth and publicly confessed a Fascist sin. Giuseppe was astonished to discover that when the Major told him to report for work at seven in the mornings, he meant it. Gargano, the former Fascist policeman, learned that he could no longer force the others to make way for him when they stood in line at the bakery.

While driving through Adano one day, General Marvin found the road blocked by a mule cart. The driver, having had his daily quota of wine, was sleeping peacefully.

When the mule refused to budge, the General ordered the vehicle thrown into the ditch. Reluctantly, the soldiers dumped the cart, mule, and sleeping driver. Swearing furiously, the General drove to the city hall, confronted Major Joppolo, and ordered that the Major forbid the entrance of all carts into Adano.

The next day, a group of townspeople besieged the Major. The carts, they explained, were essential, for they brought food and water into the town. Major Joppolo countermanded the General's order and telephoned Captain Purvis that he would accept full responsibility. Captain Purvis, anxious to keep out of trouble, ordered Lieutenant Trapani to make a memorandum and to send it to General Marvin. The Lieutenant, however, out of regard for Major Joppolo, put the memorandum among Purvis' papers in the hope that the Captain, who rarely looked through his files, would never find it.

Major Joppolo's efforts to restore the bell were not successful, for it had been melted down by the Fascists. However, a young Naval officer, in charge of a nearby station, promised to obtain a ship's bell for him.

In the meantime, Captain Purvis had gone through the papers on his desk and had found the memorandum for General Marvin. He ordered it forwarded at once. Lieutenant Trapani mailed it, but addressed it to the wrong person at headquarters in Algiers. From there, it was forwarded to the General's aide, Colonel Middleton. Every day the Colonel met with General Marvin and went over important communications. Accordingly, he was half-way through Purvis' letter before he realized what it was. He tried to go on to the next letter, but it was too late. The General had heard Major Joppolo's name, and that of Adano, and remembered both.

The bell arrived in Adano. It was touched, prodded, sounded by the experts, and admired by everybody. When it pealed forth, the townspeople

declared that its tone was even better than that of the old bell. The Major
was a hero. To show their appreciation and affection, the townspeople had
him taken to a photographer. From the resulting picture, a local artist painted
his portrait.

At the celebration that night, Sergeant Borth was very, very drunk. He
refused to take orders from Major Joppolo, saying that the Major was no
longer in any position to give orders. Captain Purvis, said the Sergeant, almost
sobbing, had a letter from General Marvin. It ordered Major Joppolo back
to Algiers. The next morning, the Major said goodbye to Borth, who apologized for his conduct of the previous night. The Major asked him to help his
successor make the people happy. As he drove away from the town, he heard
in the distance the tolling of a bell, the new bell for Adano.

Critical Evaluation:

John Hersey's *A Bell for Adano* was popularly regarded as the finest novel
to come out of World War II when it first appeared in 1944. The passing of
time has removed it from this position, but along with *Mr. Roberts* and *Catch
22*, it shows that war was far better represented in humor than melodrama.
The early appeal of the book was found in the light-hearted episodes of life
in a postliberation Sicilian village, Adano, and in the appeal of the character
of the protagonist, Major Joppolo.

To the American public of the postwar period, Joppolo was the embodiment of the father/husband/brother figure who was fighting for democracy in
a strife-torn world. He was what Americans thought they were: young, sensitive, and good. General Marvin, on the other hand, was the embodiment
of a pompous autocrat, thus creating much of the novel's sense of conflict.

Hersey, a war correspondent, was at his best, however, when portraying
the common soldier or farmer—ordinary men who were caught up in the
circumstances of war and were neither all good nor all bad. Early reviewers
admitted that they enjoyed reading the book, but its lack of critical character
analysis and unity has caused it more and more to be regarded as second rate
literature. Most saw it as a dramatized attempt at nonfiction rather than a
novel. Some critics also made mention of the rather "off-color" language of
the soldiers in the book. Though rather mild by later standards, some of the
words in the book were harsh for the reading public of the middle 1940's.
Critics aside, however, it was the American people who made *A Bell for
Adano* a best seller, a hit play on Broadway, and later a popular motion
picture.

BEN-HUR
A Tale of the Christ

Type of work: Novel
Author: Lewis (Lew) Wallace (1827–1905)
Type of plot: Historical romance
Time of plot: At the time of Christ
Locale: Antioch and Jerusalem
First published: 1880

Principal characters:
> BEN-HUR, a Roman-educated Jew
> BALTHASAR, an Egyptian
> SIMONIDES, a Jewish merchant and friend of Ben-Hur
> ESTHER, daughter of Simonides
> IRAS, daughter of Balthasar
> MESSALA, a Roman and an enemy of Ben-Hur

The Story:

In the Roman year 747, three travelers met in the desert, where the Athenian, the Hindu, and the Egyptian had been led by a new bright star shining in the sky. After telling their stories to one another, they journeyed on, seeking the newborn child who was King of the Jews. In Jerusalem, their inquiries aroused the curiosity of King Herod, who asked that they be brought before him. Herod then asked them to let him know if they found the child, for he, too, wished to adore the infant whose birth had been foretold. Arriving at last in Bethlehem, the three men found the newborn child in a stable. Having been warned in a dream of Herod's evil intentions, however, they did not return to tell the king of the child's whereabouts.

At that time, there lived in Jerusalem three members of an old and eminent Jewish family named Hur. The father, who had been dead for some time, had distinguished himself in service to the Roman Empire and had, consequently, received many honors. The son, Ben-Hur, was handsome, and the daughter, Tirzah, was likewise beautiful. Their mother was a fervent nationalist who had implanted in their minds a strong sense of pride in their race and national culture.

When Ben-Hur was still a young man, his friend Messala returned from his studies in Rome. Messala had become arrogant, spiteful, and cruel. As Ben-Hur left Messala's home after their meeting, he was hurt, for he realized that Messala had so changed that their friendship must end.

A few days later, while watching a procession below him in the streets, Ben-Hur accidentally dislodged a piece of tile that fell on the Roman procurator. The Roman believed that the accident was an attempt on his life. Led by Messala, who had pointed out his former friend to the soldiers, the Romans arrested the Hur family and confiscated their property.

Ben-Hur was sent to be a galleyslave. While he was being led away in chains, a young man took pity on him and gave him a drink. One day, while he was rowing at his usual place in the galley, Ben-Hur attracted the attention of Quintus Arrius, a Roman official. Later, during a sea battle, Ben-Hur saved the life of Quintus, who adopted the young Jew as his son. Educated as a Roman citizen, Ben-Hur inherited his foster father's wealth when Quintus died.

Ben-Hur went to Antioch, where he learned that his father's old servant, Simonides, was now a prosperous merchant. In effect, the wealth of Simonides was really the property of the Hur family, for he had been acting as agent for his dead master. Simonides assured himself that Ben-Hur was really the son of his old master and begged that he be allowed to serve the son as well. Ben-Hur was attracted to Simonides' daughter, Esther.

In company with a servant of Simonides, Ben-Hur went to see a famous well on the outskirts of Antioch. There an aged Eygptian was watering his camel, on which sat the most beautiful woman Ben-Hur had ever seen. While he looked, a chariot came charging through the people near the well. Ben-Hur seized the lead horse by the bridle and swerved the chariot aside. The driver was his false friend, Messala. The old Egyptian was Balthasar, one of the wise men who had traveled to Bethlehem. The beautiful girl was his daughter, Iras.

Learning that the arrogant Messala was to race his chariot in the games at Antioch, Ben-Hur wished to defeat and humiliate his old playfellow. He had Simonides and his friends place large wagers on the race, until Messala had staked his whole fortune. The day of the race came. At the turn, Messala suddenly struck with his whip at the horses of the chariot Ben-Hur was driving. Ben-Hur managed to keep his team under control, and then in the last lap around the arena, he drove his chariot so close to Messala's vehicle that the wheels locked. Messala was thrown under his horses and crippled for life. Because Messala had attempted foul play earlier in the race, the judges allowed Ben-Hur to be proclaimed the winner. Messala was ruined.

From Balthasar, Ben-Hur learned that the King of the Jews to whom the Egyptian and his companions had paid homage some years before was not to be the king of a political realm, but of a spiritual one. Simonides, however, convinced Ben-Hur that the promised king would be a real deliverer who would lead the Jews to victory over the Romans.

From Antioch, Ben-Hur went to Jerusalem to search for his mother and sister. There he learned the part Messala had played in the ruin of his family. After his own arrest, his mother and sister had been thrown into prison, and Messala and the procurator had divided the confiscated property between them. Messala knew nothing of the fate of the two women after the procurator had ordered them confined to an underground cell. There they had contracted leprosy. When Pilate, the new procurator, arrived, he had ordered all political prisoners freed and so the two women had been set at liberty. Yet, there was no place for them to go except to the caves outside the city where the lepers were sent to die. A faithful old servant found them and carried food to them daily, under sacred oath never to reveal their names. When Ben-Hur met the old servant, she allowed him to believe that his mother and sister were dead.

Meanwhile, Simonides, acting for Ben-Hur, bought the Hur home. He, Esther, Balthasar, and Iras took possession of it. Ben-Hur himself could visit it only at night and in disguise. He was plotting to overthrow the Roman rule and was recruiting an army to follow the future King of the Jews. He went one day near the place where the lepers usually gathered on the hill beyond the city gates. On the way, he met a young man whom he recognized as the one who had given him a drink of water years before when he was being led away to slavery. The young man was the Nazarene. That day, the old servant had persuaded Tirzah and her mother to show themselves to the Nazarene as he passed. Both were cured, and Ben-Hur saw the two lepers transformed into his mother and sister.

Ben-Hur's attitude toward the King of the Jews was slowly changing. When he witnessed the crucifixion in company with Simonides and old Balthasar, any doubts that he might have had were removed. He was convinced then that Christ's kingdom was a spiritual one. From that day on, he and his family were Christians.

Some years later, in the beautiful villa at Misenum, Ben-Hur's wife, Esther, received a strange visit from Iras, the daughter of Balthasar. Iras told Esther that she had killed Messala for the misery he had brought her. When he learned of the visit, Ben-Hur was sure that on the day of the crucifixion, the day that Balthasar himself had died, Iras had deserted her father for Messala.

Ben-Hur was happy with Esther and their two children. He and Simonides devoted their fortunes to the Christian cause. When Nero began the persecution of the Christians in Rome, it was Ben-Hur who went there to build the catacombs under the city itself, so that those who believed in the Nazarene could worship in safety and peace.

Critical Evaluation:

Lewis Wallace was a man of many vocations; in addition to writing several novels, he was, at one time or another during his life, a soldier, a lawyer, territorial governor of New Mexico, and minister to Turkey. His knowledge of and experience in the military, the law, government, and diplomacy developed in him an appreciation for history which enhanced the historical verisimilitude of his novels. It is that quality of evoking the spirit of the times which, in large part, accounts for the popular success of Wallace's two best novels, *The Fair God* (1873) and *Ben-Hur*. In fact, *Ben-Hur* is one of the all-time best-selling novels in English, having sold more than two million copies.

The book has also been widely translated into several foreign languages.

Like Wallace's other books, *Ben-Hur* is a historical novel in the mainstream of that venerable tradition. Basic elements in the genre include a background of genuine historical events, which Wallace provides in his depictions of Roman decadence counterpointed against the birth of Christianity. Also included are genuine historical figures in minor roles in the narrative, just as Wallace uses King Herod, Balthasar, Pontius Pilate, Nero, and Jesus in cameo parts. The third element is a fictional protagonist whose deeds are not part of the historical record and whose actions and emotions can thus be manipulated at will by the novelist to suit the needs of his tale. Judah Ben-Hur is just such a protagonist. Finally, the central focus of the plot is on events related to the personal and individual concerns of the protagonist, with historical matters relegated to the periphery of the action in the novel or used to highlight— sometimes ironically—the protagonist's role (usually a minor one) in the major affairs of his time. Thus, Wallace devotes most of his attention to the tribulations of the Jewish protagonist Ben-Hur and the perfidies of the Roman antagonist Messala, with historical events forming parentheses, as it were, around the beginning and the end of this central narrative.

It is interesting, moreover, that the final historical note in *Ben-Hur* depicts the protagonist—by then a convert to the Christian cause—as building the Roman catacombs for the sheltering and the protection of persecuted Christians: interesting because *Hur* is the Hebrew word for cave or cavern (*ben* is a Hebrew prefix signifying *son of*). Surely, given Wallace's penchant for accurate details, his choice of a name for his protagonist was neither accidental nor coincidental. The entire novel bears out this view, for in *Ben-Hur* Wallace has produced a novel that vividly demonstrates the classic elements of the historical romance.

BENITO CERENO

Type of work: Novella
Author: Herman Melville (1819–1891)
Type of plot: Adventure romance
Time of plot: 1799
Locale: The harbor of St. Maria, off the coast of Chile, and Lima, Peru
First published: 1856

Principal characters:
AMASA DELANO, an American sea captain
DON BENITO CERENO, a Spanish sea captain
BABO, a black slave

The Story:

Captain Amasa Delano was commander of an American sealer called *Bachelor's Delight*, which was anchored in the harbor of St. Maria, on an island off the coast of southern Chile. While there, he saw a ship apparently in distress, and thinking it carried a party of monks, he set out in a whaleboat to board the vessel and supply it with food and water. When he came aboard, he found that the ship, the *San Dominick*, was a Spanish merchant ship carrying slaves. The crew was parched and moaning; the ship itself was filthy; the sails were rotten. Most deplorable of all, the captain, the young Don Benito Cereno, seemed barely able to stand or to talk coherently. Aloof and indifferent, the Captain seemed ill both physically (he coughed constantly) and mentally. The Captain was attended by Babo, his devoted slave.

Delano sent the whaleboat back to his ship to get additional water, food, and extra sails for the *San Dominick*, while he remained aboard the desolate ship. He tried to talk to Cereno, but the Captain's fainting fits kept interrupting the conversation. The Spaniard seemed reserved and sour, in spite of Delano's attempts to assure the man that he was now out of danger. Delano finally assumed that Cereno was suffering from a severe mental disorder. The Captain did, with great difficulty and after frequent private talks with Babo, manage to explain that the *San Dominick* had been at sea for 190 days. They had, Cereno explained, started out as a well-manned and smart vessel sailing from Buenos Aires to Lima but had encountered several gales around Cape Horn, lost many officers and men, and then had run into dreadful calms and the ravages of plagues and scurvy. Most of the Spanish officers and all the passengers, including the slave owner, Don Alexandro Aranda, had died of fever. Delano, who knew that the weather in recent months had not been as extreme as Cereno described it, simply concluded that the Spanish officers had been incompetent and had not taken the proper precautions against disease. Cereno continually repeated that only the devotion of his slave, Babo, had kept him alive.

Numerous other circumstances on the *San Dominick* began to make the innocent Delano more suspicious. Although everything was in disorder and Cereno was obviously ill, he was dressed perfectly in a clean uniform. Six black men were sitting in the rigging holding hatchets, although Cereno said they were only cleaning them. Two were beating up a Spanish boy, but Cereno explained that this deed was simply a form of sport. The slaves were not in chains; Cereno claimed they were so docile that they did not require chains. This notion pleased the humane Delano, although it also surprised him.

Every two hours, as they awaited the expected wind and the arrival of Delano's whaleboat, a large black in chains was brought before Cereno, who would ask him if he, the Captain, could be forgiven. The man would answer, "No," and be led away. At one point, Delano began to fear that Cereno and Babo were plotting against him, for they moved away from him and whispered together. Cereno then asked Delano about his ship, requesting the number of men and the strength of arms aboard the *Bachelor's Delight*. Delano thought they might be pirates.

Nevertheless, Delano joined Cereno and Babo in Cereno's cabin for dinner. Throughout the meal, Delano alternately gained and lost confidence in Cereno's story. He tried, while discussing a means of getting Cereno new sails, to get Babo to leave the room, but the man and the master were apparently inseparable. After dinner Babo, while shaving his master, cut his cheek slightly despite the warning that had been given. Babo left the room for a second and returned with his own cheek cut in a curious imitation of his master's. Delano thought this episode curious and sinister, but he finally decided that the man was so devoted to Cereno that he had punished himself for inadvertently cutting his master.

At last, Delano's whaleboat returned with more supplies. Delano, about to leave the *San Dominick*, promised to return with new sails the next day. When he invited Cereno to his own boat, he was surprised at the Captain's curt refusal and his failure to escort the visitor to the rail. Delano was offended at the Spaniard's apparent lack of gratitude. As the whaleboat was about to leave, Cereno appeared suddenly at the rail. He expressed his gratitude profusely and then, hastily, jumped into the whaleboat. At first Delano thought that Cereno was about to kill him; then he saw Babo at the rail brandishing a knife. In a flash, he realized that Babo and the other slaves had been holding Cereno a captive. Delano took Cereno back to the *Bachelor's Delight*. Later they pursued the fleeing slaves. The slaves, having no guns, were easily captured by the American ship and brought back to shore.

Cereno later explained that the slaves, having mutinied shortly after the ship set out, had committed horrible atrocities and killed most of the Spaniards. They had murdered the mate, Raneds, for a trifling offense and had committed atrocities on the dead body of Don Alexandro Aranda, whose skeleton they placed on the masthead.

On his arrival in Lima, Don Benito Cereno submitted a long testimony, recounting all the cruelties the slaves had committed. Babo was tried and hanged. Cereno felt enormously grateful to Delano, recalling the strange innocence that had somehow kept the slaves from harming him, when they had the chance, aboard the *San Dominick*.

Don Benito Cereno planned to enter a monastery; however, broken in body and spirit, he died three months after he completed his testimony.

Critical Evaluation:

Originally serialized in *Putnam's Monthly* in 1855, *Benito Cereno* first appeared, slightly revised, in book form as the first story in Herman Melville's *Piazza Tales* in 1856. It was not reprinted until 1924, when interest was being revived in Melville's writings. Since then it has often been praised as not only one of Melville's best fictional works but also one of the finest short novels in American literature. In 1964, Robert Lowell adapted *Benito Cereno* into verse-drama as the third act of his play *The Old Glory*.

Benito Cereno is Melville's version of a true story he had read in Amasa Delano's *Narrative of Voyages and Travels in the Northern and Southern Hemispheres* (1817). Melville freely adapts Delano's account to his own fictional purposes. The court depositions, which make up a considerable part of the latter half of *Benito Cereno*, have been shown to be close to those in Delano's account, though Melville omitted some of the court material. In contrast, the creation of atmosphere, the building of suspense, the development of the three main characters—Delano, Cereno, and Babo—and the extended use of symbolism are among Melville's chief contributions to the original story. Also, the thematically important conversation between Delano and Cereno at the end of *Benito Cereno* was added by Melville.

The remarkable third paragraph of *Benito Cereno* illustrates Melville's careful combining of atmospheric detail, color symbolism, and both dramatic and thematic foreshadowing.

> The morning was one peculiar to that coast. Everything was mute and calm; everything grey. The sea, though undulated into long roods of swells, seemed fixed, and was sleeked at the surface like waved lead that has cooled and set in the smelter's mould. The sky seemed a grey surtout. Flights of troubled grey vapours among which they were mixed, skimmed low and fitfully over the waters, as swallows over meadows before storms. Shadows present, foreshadowing deeper shadows to come.

The description, with its repeated use of *grey* and *seemed*, is important in setting the scene for a story the action of which will be, as seen through Delano's eyes, ambiguous and deceptive until the light of truth suddenly blazes upon the American captain's mind. Until that time, he will be seeing both action and character through a mist. The *grey* is symbolically significant also because Delano's clouded vision will cause him to misjudge both the whites and blacks aboard the *San Dominick*. In the light of the final revelations of the story, the *grey* has a moral symbolism too, perhaps for Melville and surely for the modern reader, since Cereno and Delano are not morally pure white or good, nor is Babo all black or bad. The Spaniard is a slaver and the American appears to condone the trade though he is not a part of it; the slave is certainly justified in seeking an escape from captivity for himself and his fellow blacks, though one cannot justify some of the atrocities consciously committed by Babo and his followers. The closing sentence of this mist-shrouded paragraph—"Shadows present, foreshadowing deeper shadows to come"—not only looks forward to the mystery that so long remains veiled, but it also anticipates the final words of the two captains, words that partly suggest the great difference in their characters. Delano says, "You are saved: what has cast such a shadow upon you?" Cereno replies, "The negro."

In reading *Benito Cereno*, one is caught up in the same mystery that Captain Delano cannot penetrate, and one longs for a final release of the suspense, a solution to the strange puzzle. Melville's hold upon the reader until the flash of illumination in the climax is maintained by his use of Delano's consciousness as the lens through which scene, character, and action are viewed. The revelation is so long delayed because of Delano's being the kind of man he is: ". . . a person of a singularly undistrustful good nature, not liable, except on extraordinary and repeated incentives, and hardly then, to indulge in personal alarms, any way involving the imputation of malign evil in man." His heart is benevolent, but his mind is slow to perceive through the dragging hours from his boarding the *San Dominick* until he is finally shocked into recognition of the truth when Babo prepares to stab Don Benito with the dagger he had concealed in his hair. Delano is alternately repelled by Don Benito's manner or suspicious of his intentions and then inclined to acquit Cereno of seeming rudeness because of his frail health or condemn himself for his suspicions with the excuse that "the poor invalid scarcely knew what he was about."

Just as Melville may have intended to portray Delano as representing a type of American—good-hearted, friendly, and helpful but rather slow-witted and naïve—so he may have delineated Don Benito as emblematic of eighteenth century Spanish aristocracy—proud, enfeebled, and, finally, troubled in conscience over such moral crimes as slave trading. To Delano, he first appears as "a gentlemanly, reserved-looking, and rather young man . . . dressed with singular richness, but bearing plain traces of recent sleepless cares and disquietudes." Later, Don Benito's manner "conveyed a sort of sour and gloomy disdain [which] the American in charity ascribed to the harassing effects of sickness." Further observation leads Delano to conclude that Don Benito's "singular alternations of courtesy and ill-breeding" are the result of either "innocent lunacy, or wicked imposture." He is finally undeceived and apologizes for having suspected villainy in Don Benito toward the end of the danger-filled encounter with the slaves. Delano is lighthearted and eager to dismiss the affair when the danger is over and his suspicions have been erased. Don Benito's mind, however, is of a different cast. He broods on the results in human experience of the confusing of appearance and reality: ". . . you were with me all day," he says to Delano, "stood with me, sat with me, looked at me, ate with me, drank with me, and yet, your last act was to clutch for a monster, not only an innocent man, but the most pitiable of all men. To such degree may malign machinations and deceptions impose. So far may ever the best man err, in judging the conduct of one with the recesses of whose condition he is not acquainted."

The horrors resulting from the slave mutiny and the tensions and terror that followed Delano's kind offer to aid a ship in apparent distress, leave an already ill man a dejected and broken one. The shadow of "the negro" has been cast forever upon him. He retires to the monastery on the symbolically named Mount Agonia and, three months later, is released from his sufferings.

Babo, the third major character in *Benito Cereno*, is unforgettable, one of the first important black characters in American fiction (Mrs. Stowe's Uncle Tom had preceded him by only four years). He is one of the most striking of Melville's "masked" men who appear in his work from beginning to end, hiding their true selves behind the semblance they present to the world. Captain Delano is completely deceived in his first sight of Babo with Don Benito: "By his side stood a black of small stature, in whose rude face, as occasionally, like a shepherd's dog, he mutely turned it up into the Spaniard's, sorrow and affection were equally blended." His attentiveness makes him seem "less a servant than a devoted companion" to Don Benito. Though he speaks little, his few brief speeches suggest the intelligence that enables him to lead the revolt on the *San Dominick*. He is capable of irony when Benito explains that it is to Babo he owes his preservation and that Babo pacified "his more ignorant brethren, when at intervals tempted to murmurings." "Ah, master," he sighs, ". . . what Babo has done was but duty." The remark is as masked as Babo's bowed face, and the American is so completely taken in that, "As master and man stood before him, the black upholding the white, Captain Delano could not but bethink him of the beauty of that relationship which could present such a spectacle of fidelity on the one hand and confidence on the other."

With its many ironies—an aristocratic Spanish slaver captured by his slaves, a murderous black posing as a faithful servant, a naïve American protected from violent death through his own innocence and uncovering villainy by accident—*Benito Cereno* may be read as a magnificently contrived parable of limited, rational, well-ordered man struggling against evil in the social and natural universe and achieving at least a partial victory.

THE BIG SKY

Type of work: Novel
Author: A. B. Guthrie, Jr. (1901–   )
Type of plot: Adventure romance
Time of plot: 1830–1843
Locale: Western United States
First published: 1947

Principal characters:
BOONE CAUDILL, a mountain man
TEAL EYE, his Indian wife
JIM DEAKINS, his friend
DICK SUMMERS, an old hunter
JOURDONNAIS, a keelboat captain
POORDEVIL, a half-witted Blackfoot
ELISHA PEABODY, a Yankee speculator

The Story:

In 1830, Boone Caudill set out alone for St. Louis and the West after a fight with his father. Taking his father's rifle with him, he headed for Louisville to get out of the state before his father could catch him. On the road, he met Jim Deakins, an easy-going redhead, and the two decided to go West together. At Louisville, where the sheriff and Boone's father were waiting for the runaway, he and Jim were separated. Boone escaped by swimming the Ohio River to the Indiana shore.

When Boone was falsely accused of attempted theft and jailed, Jim, who had followed him after their separation, stole the sheriff's keys and released him. Together the boys continued west.

In St. Louis, they signed onto the crew of the keelboat *Mandan*. Most of the crew were French, as was the leader, Jourdonnais. The boat was headed for the country of the Blackfeet with a store of whiskey and other goods to trade for furs. Jourdonnais also had aboard Teal Eye, the young daughter of a Blackfoot chief. She had been separated from her tribe for some time; Jourdonnais hoped to gain the friendship of the Indians by returning the girl to them.

The keelboat moved slowly upstream by means of poles, tow rope, and oars. Boone and Jim found a friend in Dick Summers, the hunter for the *Mandan*, whose job was to scout for Indians and keep the crew supplied with meat. He made Boone and Jim his assistants. Jourdonnais was worried about getting to Blackfoot country before winter, and he worked the crew hard. At last, they passed into the upper river beyond the mouth of the Platte. All the greenhorns, including Boone and Jim, were initiated by being dunked in the river and having their hair shaved off.

At last they were in buffalo country. Summers took Boone with him to get some fresh meat. Attacked by a hunting party of Sioux, the white men escaped unharmed; but Summers expected trouble from the hostile Indians farther along the line. A few days later, the *Mandan* was ambushed by a large Indian war party. Only the swivel gun on the deck of the boat saved the white men from death.

Shortly before the *Mandan* arrived at Fort Union, two men tried to sabotage the cargo. At Fort Union, Jourdonnais accused the American Fur Company trader McKenzie of trying to stop him. McKenzie denied the charge, but he tried to argue Jourdonnais out of continuing upriver and offered to pay double value for *Mandan's* cargo. Jourdonnais refused. At Fort Union, Boone met his Uncle Zeb, an old-time mountain man. He predicted that the days of hunting and trapping in open country were nearly over. Boone and Jim, however, did not believe him.

When the *Mandan* arrived in Blackfoot country, Teal Eye escaped. The crew began to build a fort and trading post. One day, Indians attacked and killed all but the three hunters, Boone, Jim, and Summers.

For seven years these three hunted together, and Summers made real mountain men out of the other two. In the spring of 1837, the three headed for a rendezvous on the Seeds-Kee-Dee River, where they could sell their furs and gamble, drink, and fight with other mountain men. They took with them a half-witted Blackfoot named Poordevil.

At the rendezvous, Boone killed a man who said that he was going to take Poordevil's scalp. Then, after they had had their fill of women and liquor, the three friends left the camp. Summers, however, did not go hunting with them. No longer able to keep up the pace of the mountain men, he went back to settle in Missouri. Boone, Jim, and Poordevil headed up the Yellowstone toward Blackfoot country.

The journey was Boone's idea. He knew that Teal Eye was now a grown woman. Her beauty had remained in his memory all those years; now he wanted her for his squaw. On the way to the Three Forks, Boone stole a Crow horse and took a Crow scalp, two coups that would help him to make friends with the Blackfoot Indians.

They came upon a Blackfoot village ravaged by smallpox, but Boone refused to stop until he was certain that Teal Eye was dead. At last he located her. She was with a small band led by Red Horn, her brother, who sold her to Boone as his squaw.

Life was good to Boone. For five years he lived happily among the Blackfoot Indians with Teal Eye as his wife. Jim lived in the Blackfoot camp also, but he often left for months at a time to go back down the Missouri. He craved companionship, while Boone enjoyed living away from crowds. On one of his trips, Jim met Elisha Peabody, a shrewd Yankee speculating upon the future prosperity of the Oregon Territory, who wanted someone to show him a pass where wagons could cross the mountains. Jim and Boone contracted to show him a suitable pass. Before Boone left, Teal Eye told him that he would have a son when he returned.

The expedition had bad luck. Indians stole all the horses and wounded Jim badly. Then snow fell, destroying all chances to get food. Finally, Boone was able to shoot some mountain goats. Jim recovered from his wound, and the party went ahead on foot. Boone and Jim showed Peabody the way across the mountains and into the Columbia Valley. It was spring when Boone returned to Teal Eye and his son.

The child, born blind, had a tinge of red in his hair. The baby's blindness brought a savage melancholy to Boone. Then some of the old Indians hinted that the red hair showed the child was Jim's baby. Boone laid a trap to catch Jim with Teal Eye. Jim, suspecting nothing, found Teal Eye alone in her lodge; he tried to comfort her about her child's blindness and the ugly mood of her husband. Boone mistook the intent of Jim's conversation. Entering the lodge, he shot Jim in the chest, killing him. He cursed Teal Eye and left the Blackfoot camp. Then he headed back to Kentucky to see his mother before she died.

In Kentucky, he found his brother married and taking care of the farm. Boone grew restless. Slowly it came to him that he had been wrong about Jim and Teal Eye, for he noticed that one of his brother's children had a tinge of red hair. His mother said that there had been red hair in the family. When a neighbor girl insisted that he marry her because he had made love to her, Boone started back to the West. He longed both for freedom and for Teal Eye.

In Missouri, he visited Summers, who now had a wife and a farm. Over their whiskey, Boone revealed to Summers that he had killed Jim. He knew now that he had made a mistake. Everything was spoiled for him—Teal Eye, and all the West. The day of the mountain man was nearly over; farmers were going to Oregon. Without saying goodbye, he stumbled out into the night. Summers could see him weaving along the road for a short distance. Then the darkness swallowed him, and he was gone.

Critical Evaluation:

In the tradition of James Fenimore Cooper's Leatherstocking romances, *The Big Sky* is distinguished among other fine historical novels for its realism and sharp insight into the psychology of the American Western pioneer. Like Cooper's land-adventure fiction, A. B. Guthrie's book treats the clash between two cultures—that of the retreating Indian tribes and of the advancing Yankee frontiersman. As the frontier expands westward, the Indians are forced to surrender their lands, their freedom, and their spiritual heritage. In the unequal struggle, the white pioneer, too, loses a portion of his heritage: a sense of idealism.

The "big sky" of Guthrie's title is the vast open land of the frontier, once teeming with wildlife, but slowly—even within the chronology of the novel, 1830 to 1843—changing, with the slaughter of buffalo, beaver, and other creatures of the forest and plains. In his descriptions of the land, its vegetation, and animals, as well as of the rough frontiersmen, Guthrie has the eye of a naturalist: the smallest detail does not escape his attention. From *The Big Sky* one learns how a trapped beaver expires, its eyes bulging in terror; how deer, elk, and mountain goats survive in the wilderness; how rivermen operate a keelboat; how fur hunters kill and strip game; how mountain men endure the bitter Northern winters. Unlike many other adventure stories treating the western movement, Guthrie's novel is without sentimentality. For the hunters, traders, and marginal farmers of the outlying territories, life is hard and often brutal. In his realism, Guthrie does not gloss over the harsh truths of the time. Trapped in a winter storm without food, Beauchamp becomes a cannibal and devours his dead companion, Zenon. Boone Caudill murders his best friend, Jim Deakins, whom he wrongly suspects of fathering his half-Indian son. The child himself is born blind, an innocent victim of the white man's syphilis. Guthrie's treatment of the Indians is similarly unsentimental. The squaws who mate with the white hunters are described, for the most part, as dirty, complaisant whores; whole tribes, like the Piegans, are wiped out by smallpox; others are reduced to the condition of drunken sops; Poordevil, the Blackfoot who accompanies Boone, Jim, Dick Summers, and the other trappers, is a driveling alcoholic. Thus, to Guthrie, the clash between the two cultures brutalizes both the whites and the native Indians.

In his analysis of the characters' motivation, the author is also a tough-minded realist. His protagonist, Boone, is a violent, headstrong, mostly insensitive man whose redeeming virtue is his loyalty. Throughout most of his adventures, he trusts, with good reason, his longtime friend Jim. Yet at the last, he kills Jim when he fears, mistakenly, that his friend has betrayed him. In a similar vengeful action, he abandons his beloved Indian wife, Teal Eye, when he suspects her of adultery. From these impulsive actions he brings about the ruin of his dreams. Guthrie once wrote that the theme of *The Big Sky* (paraphrasing Oscar Wilde) is that each man detroys the thing he loves best. Nevertheless, Boone's destructive impulse results as much from his early experiences as from his conscious will. Abused by his father, robbed by the clever rascal Jonathan Bedwell, cheated by the law, Boone has come to regard men warily, as objects of his revenge. His passions, too elemental to be curbed by reason, run their course, as in Greek tragedy. In a larger sense, however, his personal defeat is insignificant judged by the greater tragedy of the dwindling American frontier. Although Boone and his fellow frontiersmen love the land, they are at least partly responsible for ravaging it. By 1843, the year when the novel ends, much of the frontier still remained—Oregon, for example; but the pattern for its destruction has already been established. The "big sky," like the mountain men's idealistic ambitions, must henceforth be diminished.

BILLY BUDD, FORETOPMAN

Type of work: Novel
Author: Herman Melville (1819–1891)
Type of plot: Symbolic tragedy
Time of plot: 1797
Locale: Aboard a British man-of-war
First published: 1924

Principal characters:
BILLY BUDD, a young British sailor
CAPTAIN VERE, commanding officer of H.M.S.
Indomitable
CLAGGART, master-at-arms aboard the *Indomitable*

The Story:

In 1797, the British merchant ship *Rights-of-Man*, named after the famous reply of Thomas Paine to Edmund Burke's criticism of the French Revolution, was close to home after a long voyage. As it neared England, the merchant vessel was stopped by a man-of-war, H.M.S. *Indomitable*, and an officer from the warship went aboard the *Rights-of-Man* to impress sailors for military service. This practice was necessary at the time to provide men to work the large number of ships that Britain had at sea for protection against the French.

The captain of the *Rights-of-Man* was relieved to have only one sailor taken from his ship, but he was unhappy because the man was his best sailor, Billy Budd. Billy was what his captain called a peacemaker; because of his strength and good looks, he was a natural leader among the other sailors, and he used his influence to keep them contented and hard at work. Billy Budd seemed utterly without guile, a man who tried to promote the welfare of the merchant ship because he liked peace and was willing to work hard to please his superiors. When informed that he was not to return to England but was to head for duty with the fleet in the Mediterranean Sea, he did not appear disturbed; he liked the sea, and he had no family ties. He was an orphan who had been left as a tiny baby in a basket on the doorstep of a family in Bristol.

As the boat from the warship took him away from the merchant ship, Billy called farewell to the *Rights-of-Man* by name, a deed that greatly embarrassed the naval officer who had impressed him. The remark was unwittingly satirical of the treatment to which Billy was being subjected by the navy.

Once aboard the *Indomitable*, Billy quickly made himself at home with

---

the ship and the men with whom he served in the foretop. Because of his good personality and his willingness to work, he soon made a place for himself with his messmates and also won the regard of the officers under whom he served.

At first, the master-at-arms, a petty officer named Claggart, seemed particularly friendly to Billy, a fortunate circumstance, Billy thought, for the master-at-arms was the equivalent of the chief of police aboard the warship. The young sailor was rather surprised, therefore, when he received reprimands for slight breaches of conduct which were normally overlooked. The reprimands came from the ship's corporals who were Claggart's underlings. Since the reprimands indicated that something was wrong, Billy grew perturbed; he had a deadly fear of being the recipient of a flogging in public. He thought he could never stand such treatment.

Anxious to discover what was wrong, Billy consulted an old sailor, who told him that Claggart was filled with animosity for the young man. The reason for the animosity was not known, and because the old man could give him no reason, Billy refused to believe that the master-at-arms was his enemy. Claggart had taken a deep dislike to Billy Budd on sight, however, and for no reason except a personal antipathy that the young man's appearance had generated. Sly as he was, Claggart kept, or tried to keep, his feelings to himself. He operated through underlings against Billy.

Not long after he had been warned by the old sailor, Billy spilled a bowl of soup in the path of Claggart as he was inspecting the mess. Even then, Claggart smiled and pretended to treat the incident as a joke, for Billy had done the deed accidentally. A few nights later, however, someone awakened Billy and told him to go to a secluded spot in the ship. Billy went and met a sailor who tried to tempt him into joining a mutiny. The incident bothered Billy, who could not understand why anyone had approached him as a possible conspirator. Such activity was not a part of his personality, and he was disgusted to find it in other men.

A few days later, the master-at-arms approached the captain of the ship and reported that he and his men had discovered that a mutiny was being fomented by Billy Budd. Captain Vere, a very fair officer, reminded Claggart of the seriousness of the charge and warned the master-at-arms that bearing false witness in such a case called for the death penalty. Because Claggart persisted in his accusations, Captain Vere ended the interview on deck, a place he thought too public, and ordered the master-at-arms and Billy Budd to his cabin. There Captain Vere commanded Claggart to repeat his accusations. When he did, Billy became emotionally so upset that he was tonguetied. In utter frustration at being unable to reply to the infamous charges, Billy hit the master-at-arms. The petty officer was killed when he fell heavily to the floor.

Captain Vere was filled with consternation, for he, like everyone except the master-at-arms, liked Billy Budd. After the surgeon had pronounced the petty officer dead, the Captain immediately convened a court-martial to try Billy for assaulting and murdering a superior officer. Because England was at war, and because two mutinies had already occurred in the British navy that year, action had to be taken immediately. The Captain could not afford to overlook the offense.

The court-martial, acting under regulations, found Billy Budd guilty and sentenced him to be hanged from a yardarm the following morning. Even under the circumstances of Claggart's death, there was no alternative. The only person who could have testified that the charge of mutiny was false was the man who had been killed.

All the ship's company were dismayed when informed of the sentence. But Billy bore no animosity for the Captain or for the officers who had sentenced him to die. When he was placed beneath the yardarm the following morning, he called out a blessing on Captain Vere, who, he realized, had no other choice in the matter but to hang him. It was quite strange, too, that Billy Budd's calm seemed even to control his corpse. Unlike most hanged men, he never twitched when hauled aloft by the neck. The surgeon's mate, when queried by his messmates, had no answer for this unique behavior.

Some months later, Captain Vere was wounded in action. In the last hours before his death, he was heard to murmur Billy Budd's name over and over again. Nor did the common sailors forget the hanged man. For many years, the yardarm from which he had been hanged was kept track of by sailors, who regarded it almost as reverently as Christians might revere the Cross.

Critical Evaluation:

According to Harrison Hayford and Merton M. Sealts, the editors of *Billy Budd, Sailor*, Herman Melville began the novel in 1886, developed and revised it through several stages, and then left it unpublished when he died in 1891. The Hayford-Sealts text, published in 1962, differs considerably from earlier ones published in 1924 and 1948. Among the noteworthy differences is the change of name for the ship on which the action occurs, from *Indomitable* to *Bellipotent*. The symbolism of the latter name relates it to the emphasis that Melville places in the novel on war, man's involvement in it, and the effects of war on the individual.

That Melville did not wish his readers to mistake the nature or the general intent of his novel is clear in his early warning that Billy "is not presented as a conventional hero" and "that the story in which he is the main figure is no romance." The story itself is extremely simple. A young sailor on a British merchant ship is impressed for service on a British warship. He offers no resistance but accepts his new assignment with good will and attempts to be an ideal sailor. The ship's master-at-arms takes an immediate and unwarranted dislike to the sailor, plots to cause him trouble, and then accuses him to the

captain of having plotted mutiny. The captain summons the sailor, asks him
to defend himself, and sees him strike and accidentally kill his accuser. The
captain imprisons him, convenes a court-martial, condemns him to death,
and has him hanged. This plot is the vehicle for Melville's extended use of
moral symbolism throughout the novel.

Billy Budd, Claggart, and Captain Vere are all clearly symbolic characters,
and Melville brings out the symbolism through information supplied about
their backgrounds, language used to describe them, and authorial comment
of moral, theological, and philosophical import.

Melville employs a double symbolism for Billy: he is both a Christ-figure
and a representation of innocent or Adamic man. Before Billy is removed
from the merchant ship, the Captain explains to the lieutenant from the
warship that Billy has been most useful in quieting the "rat-pit of quarrels"
that formerly infested his forecastle. "Not that he preached to them or said
or did anything in particular; but a virtue went out of him, sugaring the sour
ones." The Captain's words echo Luke, 6:19: "And the whole multitude
sought to touch him: for there went virtue out of him, and healed them all."
When the lieutenant is adamant about Billy's impressment, the captain's last
words to him are: ". . . you are going to take away my peacemaker." Again,
there is no mistaking the reference to the Prince of Peace. In describing Billy
as he appears to the men and officers on the warship, Melville mentions
"something in the mobile expression, and every chance attitude and movement, something suggestive of a mother eminently favored by Love and the
Graces." An officer asks, "Who was your father?" and Billy answers, "God
knows, sir." Though Billy explains that he was told he was a foundling, the
hint has already been given of a divine paternity. Melville drops the Christ
symbolism of Billy until the confrontation with Claggart when Billy, unable
to reply to Captain Vere's request that he defend himself, shows in his face
"an expression which was as a crucifixion to behold." At the hanging, Billy's
last words are, "God bless Captain Vere!" and the reader recalls Christ's
words on the Cross, "Father, forgive them; for they know not what they do."
The symbolism continues with the hanging itself. Captain Vere gives a silent
signal and "At the same moment it chanced that the vapory fleece hanging
low in the East was shot through with a soft glory as of the fleece of the Lamb
of God seen in mystical vision, and simultaneously therewith, watched by the
wedged mass of upturned faces, Billy ascended; and, ascending, took the full
rose of the dawn." In the final chapter, Melville adds that

> The spar from which the foretopman was suspended was for some few years
> kept trace of by the bluejackets. . . . To them a chip from it was as a piece of
> the Cross. . . . They recalled a fresh young image of the Handsome Sailor, that
> face never deformed by a sneer or subtler vile freak of the heart within. This
> impression of him was doubtless deepened by the fact that he was gone, and in
> a measure mysteriously gone.

Even in the verses which close the novel, with Billy's words, "They'll give me a nibble—bit o' biscuit ere I go./ Sure a messmate will reach me the last parting cup," one cannot miss the Last Supper reference.

Yet, though Billy is Christ-like, he belongs to the race of man, and Melville repeatedly employs him as an archetype. His complete innocence is first suggested in Melville's comment that ". . . Billy in many respects was little more than a sort of upright barbarian, much such perhaps as Adam presumably might have been ere the urbane Serpent wriggled himself into his company." Later, Captain Vere thinks of the handsome sailor as one "who in the nude might have posed for a statue of young Adam before the Fall." But innocence will not protect Billy. As Adam's human imperfection led to his fall, so an imperfection in Billy leads to his destruction. In times of stress, Billy stutters or is even speechless and, says Melville, "In this particular Billy was a striking instance that the arch interferer, the envious marplot of Eden, still has more or less to do with every human consignment to this planet of Earth."

The innocence that is his "blinder" causes Billy (or "Baby" as he is called) to fail to see and be on guard against the evil in Claggart, and his "vocal defect" deprives him of speech when he faces his false accuser. He strikes out as instinctively as a cornered animal, and his enemy dies. Billy did not intend to commit murder but, as Captain Vere tells his officers, "The prisoner's deed—with that alone we have to do." Billy does not live in an animal's instinctive world of nature. His life is bound by social law and particularly by naval law in a time of war. As Captain Vere explains, innocent Billy will be acquitted by God at "the last Assizes," but "We proceed under the law of the Mutiny Act." That act demands death for Billy's deed, and he dies in order that discipline may be maintained in the great navy which must protect Britain against her enemies.

As Billy symbolizes innocent man, Claggart represents the spirit of evil, the foe of innocence. There is a mystery in Claggart's enmity toward harmless Billy. For, says Melville, "what can more partake of the mysterious than an antipathy spontaneous and profound such as is evoked in certain exceptional mortals by the mere aspect of some other mortal, however harmless he may be, if not called forth by this very harmlessness itself?" Claggart's evil nature was not acquired, "not engendered by vicious training or corrupting books or licentious living, but born with him and innate." He can recognize the good but is "powerless to be it." His energies are self-destructive; his nature is doomed to "act out to the end the part allotted to it." Although he destroys an innocent man, he must himself be destroyed as well.

As Billy at one extreme is Christ-like and childishly innocent and Claggart at the other is Satanic, Captain Vere represents the kind of officer needed to preserve such an institution as the navy he serves. He is a man of balance, "mindful of the welfare of his men, but never tolerating an infraction of discipline; thoroughly versed in the science of his profession, and intrepid to the verge of temerity, though never injudiciously so." His reading tastes incline toward "books treating of actual men and events . . . history, biography, and unconventional writers like Montaigne, who, free from cant and convention, honestly and in the spirit of common sense philosophize upon realities." More intellectual than his fellow officers, he seems somewhat "pedantic" to them, and Melville hints that, in reporting Vere's long speech to his junior officers of the drumhead court, he has simplified the phrasing of the argument. Yet elsewhere Captain Vere's speech is simple, brief, and direct.

Although Captain Vere is a thoughtful, reserved man, he is not without feeling. Quickly recognizing Billy's inability to speak when he has been ordered to defend himself, he soothingly says, "There is no hurry, my boy. Take your time, take your time." He is even capable of momentary vehemence as when he surprises the surgeon with the outburst, "Struck dead by an angel of God! Yet the angel must hang!" But he quickly regains control. Melville does not report what Captain Vere says to Billy when he informs him privately of the death sentence, though he suggests that Vere may have shown compassion by catching Billy "to his heart, even as Abraham may have caught young Isaac on the brink of resolutely offering him up." Vere is seemingly overcome after Billy's last words, "God bless Captain Vere!" and the echo from the crew, since "either through stoic self-control or a sort of momentary paralysis induced by emotional shock," he stands "rigidly erect as a musket." The final view of a man whose heart balanced his mind is given in the report of Captain Vere's dying words, "Billy Budd, Billy Budd," spoken not in "the accents of remorse." Though capable of fatherly feeling toward an unfortunate young man, he had caused to be carried out a sentence he believed was needed if the strength of order was to be maintained in the turmoil of war.

Although *Billy Budd* has occasionally been read as a veiled attack on the unjust treatment of a hapless man by an impersonal, authoritarian state, a close reading of the novel makes it seem more likely that Melville's intent was to show, especially through Captain Vere, that the protection of a state during a time of war must inevitably involve on occasion the sacrifice of an individual. Melville does include scattered satiric comments on the imperfections of both men and organizations, but his overwhelmingly favorable portrait of Captain Vere as a high-principled and dedicated representative of the state leaves the reader with the final impression that Melville had at last become sadly resigned to the fact that imperfect man living in an imperfect world has no guarantee against suffering an unjust fate. That Billy uncomplainingly accepts his end, even asking God's blessing upon the man who is sending him to death, suggests that Melville too had become reconciled to the eternal coexistence of good and evil in the world.

BLACK VALLEY
A Romance of the Argentine

Type of work: Novel
Author: Hugo Wast (Gustavo Adolfo Martínez Zuviría, 1883–1962)
Type of plot: Regional romance
Time of plot: Early twentieth century
Locale: Córdoba and the hill country of northern Argentina
First published: 1918

>*Principal characters:*
>GRACIÁN PALMA, an orphan
>DON JESÚS DE VISCARRA, his guardian
>MIRRA, Don Jesús' daughter
>FLAVIA, Don Jesús' sister
>DON PABLO CAMARGO, a neighboring landowner and
>   Don Jesús' enemy
>VICTORIA, daughter of Flavia and Don Pablo
>LAZARUS, a creole overseer
>AMOROSO, Flavia's devoted peon
>PICHANA, an old beggar woman

The Story:

Gracián Palma was in his fourteenth year when his father died suddenly, and the boy, already motherless, became the ward of Señor Palma's old and trusted friend, Don Jesús de Viscarra. Gracián had seen Don Jesús only once in his life; he remembered him as a tall, distinguished-looking man whom his father described as the owner of Black Valley—"where the wind roars," his father had added. To Gracián these words seemed to cast an air of mystery about Don Jesús and his home.

Shortly after Señor Palma's death, Don Jesús visited Gracián at the convent school in Córdoba and promised to take him to Black Valley for the summer. On the last day of the term, Don Jesús appeared at the school, and that afternoon, they took a train for Cosquín. From there they traveled by horseback through a wild, hilly countryside that reminded Gracián of fairies and witches. Darkness fell long before they arrived at the ranch house, where Gracián met the other members of Don Jesús' family—his young daughter Mirra and his sister Flavia. While they were at supper, a harsh scream sounded from the darkness outside. Flavia said that the cry had been made by old Pichana. Lazarus, the creole overseer, spoke up to say that he had seen Pichana about a league away on the road to Cosquín. Gracián felt that there was some mystery at Black Valley that he did not understand.

The next morning, Don Jesús left to visit his brother, a rancher in the sierras, and Gracián was free to play with Mirra. While they were eating some roasted corn near a willow grove, the boy saw an old black woman in ragged clothes crouched in the fork of one of the trees. Mirra said that the crone was Pichana, a beggar whom many people believed a witch, but really a harmless old woman. Later the girl pointed out the house of the neighboring landowner. She said that Don Pablo Camargo claimed part of Don Jesús' land and that Flavia was unkind to her because she had once quarreled with Victoria, Don Pablo's daughter. When they returned home, Flavia drew Gracián aside and asked him if he had seen anyone on the Camargo estate.

Because of a boundary dispute, the Camargos and the Viscarras had been enemies for several generations. Don Jesús had been prepared to forget the ancient grudge until Don Pablo met Flavia de Viscarra and fell in love with her. Because of the young man's reputation for wildness and violence, Don Jesús refused to consent to his sister's engagement to his family's enemy, and he had sent her to live with some distant relatives. There she had stayed, nursing her resentment, until Don Jesús' wife died and Flavia came to live at Black Valley as his housekeeper. What Don Jesús did not know, however, was that Flavia had secretly given birth to Don Pablo's child, the little girl Victoria. For a time after her return to Black Valley, Flavia had avoided her former lover, but at last her desire to see her daughter had drawn her to him. When he arrived at their meeting place, Don Pablo would imitate Pichana's wild screech and Flavia would steal out to join him. Although she was deeply disturbed in her own conscience by her deceit, she continued to meet him because she hoped that he would sometime bring Victoria with him. Except for Amoroso, the only resident of Black Valley who knew Flavia's secret was Lazarus, the overseer. In love with Flavia, he spied on her movements and followed her when she left the house to meet Don Pablo.

So matters stood when Gracián came to Black Valley. A few days later, Don Jesús announced that Don Pablo had begun a suit for possession of the disputed land. That night a heavy thunderstorm was brewing. Gracián, unable to sleep, saw Flavia walking in the courtyard. Toward midnight he was awakened by a clap of thunder. Mirra, frightened, came to his room and said that the sound had been a shot. The children discovered that Flavia was not in her room. The next morning, the events seemed like a dream until Gracián and Mirra found one of the watchdogs dead, shot through his throat.

One day Mirra took Gracián to the place of the winds, great caves at the bottom of a river gorge where Pichana's hut stood. A storm came up while they were exploring the caverns through which the wind roared, and they found it impossible to climb out of the canyon. Pichana found the children in the cave in which they had taken refuge and led them back to Don Jesús' house. On another day, Gracián met Victoria, who became angry when she learned that he came from Black Valley.

Gracián returned to school in Córdoba. By the time he came to Black Valley in the spring, Flavia had conceived a plan: Gracián must fall in love with Victoria, marry her, and so restore the girl to her mother. That summer, with the aid of Lazarus, Flavia met Victoria and revealed herself as the child's mother. A short time later, Lazarus began to approach Flavia with bold flattery, and she was forced to reprove him. Consequently, when Don Jesús received a letter accusing Flavia of having secret meetings with Don Pablo, she was sure that Lazarus was the writer. To her dismay, she saw that the handwriting was Don Pablo's.

That winter, Mirra learned Flavia's secret from Pichana. Also, Gracián's uncle, who had been living abroad, returned and wrote to Don Jesús saying that he wanted his nephew to spend the next vacation with him. Mirra grieved because Gracián would not be coming to Black Valley for the summer. The next three years brought more changes. Flavia no longer went to meet Don Pablo, and at times Don Pablo acted like a madman as his love and hatred grew more intense. Lazarus, still in love with Flavia, overstepped at last the bounds of a servant, and Don Jesús discharged him. The creole swore to be revenged. While he waited to ambush Don Jesús on the road from Cosquín, Don Pablo suddenly appeared and shot the master of Black Valley; the lawsuit was finally decided in Don Jesús' favor, and Don Pablo was wild with fury. Don Jesús died after asking that the law not pursue his murderer.

Although the police suspected both Don Pablo and Lazarus, nothing could be proved against either man. Don Pablo moved with Victoria to Cosquín. One day he was seen whitewashing a wall—a peon's work—and people began to say that his mind was affected. Then, wishing to be near her daughter, Flavia also went to Cosquín and secured an appointment as a teacher in the government school. Left alone, Mirra decided to open a school of her own for the children of the district.

Some years passed before Gracián returned from his travels abroad. Bored with life in Córdoba, he went to see Flavia in Cosquín where she was taking care of Don Pablo, now a broken, sad man. There Gracián met Victoria again, and the two fell in love. Gracián, who had never forgotten Mirra, would have broken off the affair with Victoria if Flavia had not talked to him and shamed him. One day he saw Mirra at mass, and all his old affection for her was reborn. Months later, after Flavia had heard that Gracián was staying at Black Valley and that he and Mirra were soon to be married, she went to her niece and begged for her own daughter's happiness and good name. Mirra did not hesitate between duty and love. She sent Gracián back to Victoria, the mother of his unborn child.

Critical Evaluation:

Black Valley—in the original, *Valle negro*—is subtitled "A Romance of the Argentine." The romantic elements of the novel are readily apparent. A story of a primitive way of life and elemental emotions, the action has been staged against a background of wild natural beauty. Hugo Wast's settings are real, as are his people and the way of life he presents. Lacking certain of the didactic elements found in *Stone Desert*, this work reveals to excellent advantage the novelist of character and the painter of landscapes. The plot, although episodic in form, is well ordered, and the story moves forward with increasing emotional and dramatic interest as the writer unfolds the dual theme presented through the ill-fated love of Flavia and Don Pablo and the relationship of spoiled, weak Gracián and strong, devoted Mirra. The style is vigorous, precise, and pure.

It is a fertile work that embodies Wast's basic writing techniques—the use of a clear style, sustained suspense, melodrama, deep interest, and spontaneous sprouting of the story. Wast used Argentine geography in all of his backgrounds and spent most of his life in Santa Fe Province, in Argentina's Far West. *Black Valley* is thus laced with local color, life-style, and personality. Even the title reflects the novel's tone, for this wind-whipped, isolated valley has weird beauty such as hidden caves, wild beasts, wild flowers, and a misty, Nordic beauty. The latter flavor perhaps reflects Wast's political bent, since, after becoming Argentina's Minister of Education shortly before World War II, he was accused of pro-German and anti-Semitic views. In any event, Wast's earlier and prolonged popularity with Argentine readers might have stemmed not only from his nationalism but also from his knack of jerking urban readers out of their stifling settings and, through sublimation, establishing them in rustic beauty and peace.

Black Valley was sneeringly dismissed in a local contest as being beneath consideration but promptly became a best-seller and won a gold medal from the prestigious Spanish Academy, which paid Wast the added honor of including his Argentine idiomatic expressions in its dictionary. Written with slight touches of Alexandre Dumas, *Black Valley* is readable and entertaining. Its characters are not too numerous, nor do they enter and leave the story like shooting stars but steadily grow as a function of the plot. *Black Valley* also reflects Wast's tastes for blending romantic idealism in his imaginative elements with *costumbrista* realism in his observed elements. He almost attains a biblical flavor when describing individual misfortunes. Manias, foolishness, odd notions, and other human failings are lampooned.

Wast was educated by Jesuits just before the end of the nineteenth century. He felt that women were morally superior to men and excoriated cruelty, selfishness, and the flint-hearted rich. Atheism and Communism were attacked in his oceanic literary output, but he also criticized clergymen who lacked spartan qualities. In his novels, large cathedrals are considered inferior to small and humble churches that serve as oases of peace for individuals suffering affliction.

THE BLITHEDALE ROMANCE

Type of work: Novel
Author: Nathaniel Hawthorne (1804–1864)
Type of plot: Psychological romance
Time of plot: Mid-nineteenth century
Locale: Massachusetts
First published: 1852

Principal characters:

MILES COVERDALE, a resident of Blithedale Community
ZENOBIA, a worldly woman
PRISCILLA MOODIE, a simple maiden
HOLLINGSWORTH, beloved of Zenobia and Priscilla
WESTERVELT, an evil conjurer
OLD MOODIE, Priscilla's father

The Story:

As Miles Coverdale prepared to journey to Blithedale, where he was to join in a project in community living, he was accosted by Old Moodie, a seedy ancient who seemed reluctant to state his business. After much mysterious talk about having Coverdale do him a great favor, he changed his mind and shuffled off without telling what it was that he wanted.

It was April, but Coverdale and his companions arrived at Blithedale in a snowstorm. There they were greeted by a woman called Zenobia, a well-known magazine writer. Zenobia was a beautiful, worldly woman of wealth and position. At all times she wore a rare, exotic flower in her hair. Zenobia spent most of her energy fighting for "woman's place in the world."

On the evening of Coverdale's arrival, another of the principals arrived at Blithedale. He was Hollingsworth, a philanthropist and reformer. In fact, philanthropy was to him a never-ceasing effort to reform and change mankind. He brought Priscilla with him, a simple, poorly dressed, bewildered young girl. Priscilla went at once to Zenobia and, falling at the proud woman's feet, never took her eyes from that haughty face. There was no explanation for such behavior. Hollingsworth knew only that he had been approached by Old Moodie and asked to take Priscilla to Blithedale. That was the request Old Moodie had tried to ask of Coverdale, but his courage failed him. Such was the community of Blithedale that the inhabitants made the girl welcome in spite of her strange behavior.

It was soon evident to Coverdale that Hollingsworth's philanthropy had turned inward until that man was on the way to madness. He was convinced that the universe existed only in order for him to reform all criminals and wayward persons. The dream of his life was to construct a large edifice in which he could collect his criminal brothers and teach them to mend their ways before doom overtook them. To Coverdale, he was a bore, but it was obvious that both Zenobia and Priscilla were in love with him. Priscilla blossomed as she reaped the benefits of good food and fresh air, and Zenobia viewed her as a rival with evident but unspoken alarm. Hollingsworth seemed to consider Priscilla his own special charge, and Coverdale feared the looks of thinly veiled hatred he frequently saw Zenobia cast toward the lovely girl. Priscilla, devoted to Zenobia, wanted always to be close to the beautiful woman.

When Old Moodie appeared at Blithedale to inquire of Priscilla, Coverdale tried to persuade him to reveal the reason for his interest in the girl. But the old man slipped away without telling his story.

Shortly after this incident, Professor Westervelt came to Blithedale to inquire about Zenobia and Priscilla. Coverdale saw Westervelt and Zenobia together and was sure that even though Zenobia hated him now, she once had loved and been ruined by this evil man. Coverdale knew that all the misery that he sometimes saw in Zenobia's eyes must surely have come from this man. Coverdale felt also that there was still some bond between them.

After Westervelt's visit, Zenobia was short-tempered and more vehement than usual about the poor lot of women. But she was so much in love with Hollingsworth that even the misery, or perhaps terror, caused by Westervelt did not deter her from literally worshiping at his feet. Hollingsworth, in his egotism, believed that women were placed on earth only to serve men, and so great was Zenobia's passion that she accepted his words without protest, not proclaiming her real thoughts in his presence. It was clear to Coverdale that Hollingsworth intended to use Zenobia's money to build the school for criminals of which he never ceased to talk. When Coverdale refused to join him in this project, Hollingsworth became quite cool in his dealings with Coverdale.

Tiring of the life at Blithedale, Coverdale took a vacation in town. He was greatly surprised when Zenobia, Priscilla, and Westervelt also arrived in the town shortly afterward. He called on the ladies and was disturbed by the tension that was apparent. When he chided Zenobia about Priscilla and Hollingsworth, she warned him not to interfere lest he cause serious trouble. Priscilla obviously did not know why she was there. She told Coverdale that she was like a leaf blown about by the wind. She had no will of her own, only the will of Zenobia. Then Westervelt called for the two women, and the three left Coverdale standing as if they did not know he was there.

Determined to uncover the mystery surrounding the three, Coverdale sought out Old Moodie and pried from him the story of the two girls. Once Moodie had been a wealthy and influential man until, through dishonest business practices, he was ruined. Then, leaving his wife and daughter, Zenobia, he wandered about in poverty and disgrace. His wife died and he married again. To them Priscilla was born, as different from his first child as it was possible to be. Zenobia was beautiful and proud, Priscilla plain and shy. Neighbors thought Priscilla had supernatural powers, but her kindness and her goodness made everyone love her.

Zenobia, after Moodie's disgrace, was reared by his brother; and since Moodie was believed dead, Zenobia, as the next heir, inherited her uncle's wealth. Because she grew up a wild and willful girl, it was whispered that she had made a secret marriage with an unprincipled man. No one, however, knew anything definite. Such were her beauty and wealth that no one criticized her. Moodie called her to his home and, not telling her who he was, cautioned her to be as kind as a sister to Priscilla.

During his vacation, Coverdale chanced upon a magician's show in a nearby village. There he found Hollingsworth in the audience and Westervelt on the stage. Westervelt produced a Veiled Lady, an ethereal creature whom he said he could make do his bidding. At the climax of the act, Hollingsworth arose from the audience and strode to the platform. He called to the Veiled Lady to remove her veil, and as he spoke, Priscilla lifted her veil and fled into the arms of Hollingsworth with a cry of joy and love. She looked like one who had been saved from an evil fate.

Coverdale returned to Blithedale. There he witnessed a terrifying scene between Zenobia, Priscilla, and Hollingsworth. Hollingsworth admitted his love for Priscilla to Zenobia. Zenobia reviled him and warned her sister against the emptiness of his heart. She said she knew at last the complete ego of the man and saw that he had deceived her only to get her fortune for his great project. After the lovers left her, Zenobia sank to the ground and wept, and that night the unhappy woman drowned herself in the river flowing close by. Westervelt came to view her dead body, but his only sorrow seemed to be that he could no longer use Zenobia in his black schemes.

After Zenobia's tragedy, Coverdale left Blithedale. Priscilla and Hollingsworth lived quietly, he giving up his desire to reform other criminals because he felt himself Zenobia's murderer. In his twilight years Coverdale confessed his real interest in these ill-fated people. He had from the first been in love with Priscilla.

Critical Evaluation:

Nathaniel Hawthorne himself explained that *The Blithedale Romance* grew out of his experiences at Brook Farm, that famous but short-lived experiment in communal living indulged in by idealists, reformers, and writers. In the story, however, the setting is incidental to the plot and the characters, all of whom, Hawthorne asserts, are fictitious. There is no attempt to judge the merits or evils of community living, only an effort to show the way in which certain characteristics affect the lives of people thrown together into close associations.

Hawthorne is well-known as an explorer of the darker side of human consciousness. Henry James admired his powers of psychological and moral analysis and maintained that his works gave "glimpses of a great field, of the whole deep mystery of man's soul and conscience." It is true that readers, imagining what lies behind the minister's black veil (in the story so titled) or looking into Ethan Brand's fiery kiln, encounter visions of hellish torment. In *The Blithedale Romance* there is a noticeable distancing from such visions. Evil is in the book, but largely because of calculated effects in plotting and point of view (Miles Coverdale's narration), it seems somewhat removed. The form of the work, romance, provides a filter that softens the impact of the psychological stresses the story records.

Brook Farm itself is ingenuously naïve in the earnestness with which it pursues social and moral welfare; just as the Pilgrims' isolation and religious fanaticism could not save them from the truth of the human heart—a theme Hawthorne sounded most eloquently in *The Scarlet Letter*—so this idyllically isolated settlement provides no haven from the passions animating men and women. The Hollingsworth-Zenobia-Priscilla triangle comes to a drastic head precisely because of the proximity of all the principals. Instead of a social haven, Brook Farm is finally an arena for a tragedy of love.

Miles Coverdale is perhaps the most severely judged character in the novel. His detachment and fear of accepting the consequences of his passions mark his life as wasted. He says as much about himself in the confession that ends the novel. The only thing that saves Miles Coverdale from the fate of a Roger Chillingsworth is that *The Blithedale Romance* is primarily a romance and *The Scarlet Letter* categorically a tragedy.

THE BOSTONIANS

Type of work: Novel
Author: Henry James (1843–1916)
Type of plot: Psychological realism
Time of plot: Early 1870's
Locale: Massachusetts and New York City
First published: 1886

Principal characters:

OLIVE CHANCELLOR, a Back Bay woman of modest
means

MRS. ADELINE LUNA, her sister

BASIL RANSOM, her cousin from Mississippi, who marries
Verena Tarrant

VERENA TARRANT, Olive's protégée and a platform
prodigy

"DOCTOR" SELAH TARRANT, a mesmeric healer and
Verena's father

MRS. TARRANT, the daughter of Boston Abolitionists and
Verena's mother

MISS BIRDSEYE, a veteran of New England reform
movements

DR. PRANCE, a woman doctor attending Miss Birdseye

MRS. FARRINDER, a campaigner for women's rights

MRS. BURRAGE, a New York society hostess

HENRY BURRAGE, her son, a Harvard undergraduate who
courts Verena

The Bostonians is the longest of Henry James's novels in an American setting, and in spite of his later dissatisfaction with its middle section or the high promise given to the unfinished *The Ivory Tower*, it is his most important fictive statement on America. The name and setting of the novel are significant; two other American novels, *Washington Square* and *The Europeans*, are set in New York City and Boston respectively; *The Bostonians* begins in Charles Street and ends in the Music Hall in Boston, but its second half begins in New York, which James always claimed as his native city. James had difficulty selecting the title, but when he had settled on *The Bostonians*, he knew it was an exact description of the contents and of his meaning.

The best commentary on the work is found in James's preface to the New York edition; its significance in James's American canon is discussed by F. O. Matthiessen in his introduction to *The American Novels and Stories of Henry James*. James had several times tried to clarify his famous passage, in his life of Hawthorne, on what America offered and lacked in respect to the novelist. By his experience, James was limited as an American novelist, and *The Bostonians* was his attempt to write on a subject that was at once local and typical, a local manifestation of a national trait. James naturally chose that distinguishing feature of American life, the American woman, whose novelty he had presented in Isabel Archer and other heroines. The locality was the Boston he knew in the early 1870's and the New York he lovingly introduces in the novel. For his purpose, more important than the locale of Boston was its atmosphere of exhausted triumph after abolition and the hectic pursuit of new reform movements, especially that of women's rights. James's general distaste for the reformers if not for their proposals may be sensed in his portraits in the novel.

The "Bostonians" may be variously identified as one, two, or more characters, but the term, used only once, refers to Olive Chancellor and Verena Tarrant. Although James referred to Verena as the "heroine," the true "Bostonian" is Olive, the embodiment of the clash between discrimination and undiscriminating action in Boston of the 1870's. Destined by nature and appearance to be a "New England Nun," she becomes a Boston battler in the very last paragraph of the novel, haranguing a capacity crowd in Boston's largest auditorium in place of Verena, who has in the nick of time been carried away by Basil Ransom to meet her proper destiny as his wife. These three play out an ironic and psychologically penetrating form of the eternal triangle.

James seems to approve Verena's fate, largely because she is unawakened throughout almost the whole novel; she remains a pretty young girl with no mind and of little interest to James. Basil Ransom is a Mississippian trying to revive the family plantation by practicing law in New York; he does not have ideas (until he begins to write reactionary articles) but lives by a code: everyone must do his or her work well in one's appointed station in life. When he tries to express this idea to Verena as they sit in Central Park, she is horrified and fascinated because there is no "Progress" in his code. In the end, however, Basil and Verena pair off as a fairly normal couple. What Mississippi was to make of Verena would have made a superb sequel to this work, but James did not know the South, and treats it simply as the last reservoir of acceptable masculinity from which he plucks his necessary hero.

Olive Chancellor was much more in James's acquaintance. With no other family ties except those to her sister, Mrs. Luna, comfortably settled in Charles Street, she had time, intelligence, taste, and money that she diffused quietly through twenty committees and reform groups. She is the very portrait of a Boston lady; her tragic flaw is to allow her desire for real action to overrule her taste: she falls in love with Verena's sweet stream of humbug as Basil falls in love with Verena's voice. This is not wholly Olive's fault, as is shown by the gallery of Bostonians introduced at the suffragette party in Miss Birdseye's tasteless apartment at the beginning of the novel. The two male Bostonians are a hack journalist and "Doctor" Selah Tarrant, a mesmeric healer and a fake not only to Basil's eyes but also to those of Dr. Prance, a woman doctor who is really active in her role of "new woman" and who has little time for talking about the subject. As the real and fake doctors are contrasted, so is Dr. Prance contrasted with the suffragette campaigner, Mrs. Farrinder, who is not a Bostonian and who is also suspicious of Tarrant and Verena's "inspirational" views. Mrs. Farrinder's weak husband shows what men will amount to and what Basil fights against in the new regime, and Mrs. Farrinder, in thinking that talk will achieve the revolution Dr. Prance quietly demonstrates, shows the possible and probable results of Olive's degeneration.

Also ranged about Olive in contrasting positions are the other three Bostonians. Mrs. Luna is completely worldly and contemptuous of any womanly activity except that of the salon. Equally worldly but totally vulgar is Verena's mother, who urges her daughter to accept Olive's impulsive invitation to visit Boston. Verena's visit ends in her staying with Olive and becoming the latter's protégée instead of "Doctor" Tarrant's prodigy: Olive pays the Tarrants to keep away from Verena.

The last and best of the Bostonians is Miss Birdseye, James's favorite creation in the novel. At the age of eighty, she is still a compulsive reformer in a completely selfless and ineffectual manner that contrasts with the practical Dr. Prance and Mrs. Farrinder, and with the worldly creatures of Boston and New York. She appears only three times in the novel: at the initial party which introduces most of the characters; when she plays the part of destiny in giving Ransom Verena's Cambridge address, under the impression that he is interested in the movement for women's rights; and at Olive's summer cottage, at Marmion, where she dies happily, mistakenly believing that Verena has enlisted Ransom in the cause. She stands for Boston's true nature, which Olive ignores in trying to achieve a triumph through Verena.

In the second part of the novel, Olive compounds her failure of discrimination by accepting the invitation of Mrs. Burrage, a New York society hostess, to show off Verena in New York; Olive thinks she has triumphed in securing Verena's promise not to marry and in diverting young Henry Burrage's attentions from Verena. Olive thus overreaches herself at the same moment and in the same way as Verena: Olive's initial mistake was to invite Ransom to Boston; Verena invites him to the Burrage evening party, partly as a result of his seeking her out in Cambridge. She thinks she is working for the cause, but she is shown as very slowly awakening to her love for Ransom, which precipitates the catastrophe.

Verena is the fulcrum of the plot, and her affection first for Olive, then for Ransom, is reflected in the structure of the novel. The first twenty chapters contain four scenes: Olive's dinner with Basil, Miss Birdseye's party that night, Basil's call on Olive and Verena the next morning, and some months later a tea party at the Tarrants for Olive and, as it turns out, Henry Burrage. This first half of the novel concentrates on Olive's developing affection for Verena. Verena, however, is incapable of decision or action and in the second half of the novel, as Basil Ransom takes the center of the stage, she gradually falls under his influence. Four principal settings are employed: Cambridge, where Ransom visits Verena; New York, the scene of Mrs. Burrage's party and the discussion between Verena and Basil in Central Park; Marmion, where Olive's cottage is the scene of Miss Birdseye's death and Olive's looming defeat in the suit Basil Ransom presses on Verena; and Boston, where in the anteroom of the Music Hall on the evening of Verena's first public appearance, Basil finally defeats Olive and carries off Verena as most of the remaining cast make a final appearance—the Tarrants, the Burrages, the Farrinders.

Throughout the novel, the characteristic devices of James's late middle style are apparent: lengthening paragraphs, alternating direct and indirect colloquy, the use of idiomatic terms to carry nuances of meaning. More obvious, especially in the dramatic close, is the growing dependence on set scenes to show the stages of the drama. Over all these is the play of James's irony and pity directed at the latterday Bostonian, Olive Chancellor, the local representation of a national type and the heroine of this distinctly American tragedy.

THE BRIDGE OF SAN LUIS REY

Type of work: Novel
Author: Thornton Wilder (1897–1975)
Type of plot: Philosophical romance
Time of plot: Early eighteenth century
Locale: Peru
First published: 1927

Principal characters:

BROTHER JUNIPER, a Spanish friar
THE MARQUESA DE MONTEMAYOR, a lonely old woman
PEPITA, her maid
THE ABBESS MADRE MARÍA DEL PILAR, directress of the
    Convent of Santa María Rosa de las Rosas
UNCLE PIO, an actor-manager
LA PÉRICHOLE, an actress
MANUEL, a foundling
ESTEBAN, his brother

The Story:

On Friday, July 20, 1714, the bridge of San Luis Rey, the most famous bridge in Peru, collapsed, hurling five travelers into the deep gorge below. Present at the time of the tragedy was Brother Juniper, who saw in the event a chance to prove, scientifically and accurately, the wisdom of that act of God. He spent all his time investigating the lives of the five who had died, and he published a book showing that God had had a reason to send each one of them to his death at exactly that moment. The book was condemned by the Church authorities, and Brother Juniper was burned at the stake. He had gone too far in explaining God's ways to man. Through a strange quirk of fate, one copy of the book was left undestroyed, and it fell into the hands of the author. From it, and from his own knowledge, he reconstructed the lives of the five persons.

The Marquesa de Montemayor had been an ugly child and was still homely when she grew up. Because of the wealth of her family, she was fortunately able to marry a noble husband, by whom she had a lovely daughter, Doña Clara. As she grew into a beautiful young woman, the Marquesa's daughter became more and more disgusted with her crude and unattractive mother, whose possessive and over-expressive love left Doña Clara cold and uncomfortable. The daughter finally married a man who took her to Spain. Separated from her one joy in life, the Marquesa became more eccentric than before and spent her time writing long letters to her daughter in Spain.

In order to free herself of some of her household cares, the Marquesa went to the Abbess Madre María del Pilar and asked for a girl from the Abbess' school to come and live with her. So Pepita, unhappy that her beloved teacher was sending her away from school, went to live with the Marquesa.

When the Marquesa learned by letter that Doña Clara was to have a child, she was filled with concern. She wore charms, bought candles for the saints, said prayers, and wrote all the advice she could discover to her daughter. As a last gesture, she took Pepita with her to pay a visit to a famous shrine from which she hoped her prayers would surely be heard. On the way, the Marquesa happened to read one of Pepita's letters to her old mistress, the Abbess. From the letter, the Marquesa learned just how heartless she had been in her treatment of the girl, how thoughtless and egotistic. She realized that she had been guilty of the worst kind of love toward her daughter, love that was sterile, self-seeking, and false. Aglow with her new understanding, she wrote a final letter to her daughter, telling her of the change in her heart, asking forgiveness, and showing in wonderful language the change that had come over her. She resolved to change her life, to be kind to Pepita, to her household, to everyone. The next day she and Pepita, while crossing the bridge of San Luis Rey, fell to their deaths.

Esteban and Manuel were twin brothers who had been left as children on the doorstep of the Abbess' school. She had brought them up as well as she could, but the strange relationship between them was such that she could never make them talk much. When the boys were old enough, they left the school and took many kinds of jobs. At last they settled down as scribes, writing letters for the uncultured people of Lima. One day Manuel, called in to write some letters for La Périchole, fell in love with the charming actress. Never before had anything come between the brothers, because they had always been sufficient in themselves. For his brother's sake, Manuel pretended that he cared little for the actress. Shortly afterward, he cut his leg on a piece of metal and became very sick. In his delirium, he let Esteban know that he really was in love with La Périchole. The infection grew worse and Manuel died.

Esteban was unable to do anything for weeks after his brother's death. He could not face life without him. The Abbess finally arranged for him to go on a trip with a sea captain who was about to sail around the world. The captain had lost his only daughter, and the Abbess felt he would understand Esteban's problem and try to help him. Esteban left to go aboard ship, but on the way, he fell with the others when the bridge broke.

Uncle Pio had lived a strange life before he came to Peru. There he had found a young girl singing in a tavern. After years of his coaching and training, she became the most popular actress of the Spanish world. She was called La Périchole, and Uncle Pio's greatest pleasure was to tease her and anger her into giving consistently better performances. All went well until the viceroy took an interest in the vivacious and beautiful young actress. When she became his mistress, she began to feel that the stage was too low for her. After living as a lady and becoming prouder and prouder as time went on, she contracted smallpox. Her beauty was ruined, and she retired to a small farm out of town to live a life of misery over her lost loveliness.

Uncle Pio had a true affection for his former protégée and tried time and again to see her. One night, by a ruse, he got her to talk to him. She refused to let him help her, but she allowed him to take Jaime, her illegitimate son, so that he could be educated as a gentleman. The old man and the young boy set off for Lima. On the way, they came to the bridge and died in the fall when it collapsed.

At the cathedral in Lima, a great service was held for the victims. Everyone considered the incident an example of a true act of God, and many reasons were offered for the various deaths. Some months after the funeral, the Abbess was visited by Doña Clara, the Marquesa's daughter. Doña Clara had finally learned what a wonderful woman her mother had really been. The last letter had taught the cynical daughter all that her mother had so painfully learned. The daughter, too, had learned to see life in a new way. La Périchole also came to see the Abbess. She had given up bemoaning her own lost beauty, and she began a lasting friendship with the Abbess. Nothing could positively be said about the reason for the deaths of those five people on the bridge. Too many events were changed by them; one could not number them all. But the old Abbess believed that the true meaning of the disaster was the lesson of love for those who survived.

Critical Evaluation:

The Bridge of San Luis Rey marked the beginning of a key stage in Thornton Wilder's development and also revealed the essential dimensions of the artistic program he would follow. His first novel, *The Cabala* (1926), had viewed the decadent aristocracy of contemporary Rome through the eyes of a young American student. In the tradition of Henry James and Edith Wharton, the highly autobiographical work suffered by comparison and was not praised by the critics. But *The Bridge of San Luis Rey*, which vividly evoked a forgotten era and a type of society utterly foreign to Wilder's experience, sold three hundred thousand copies in its first year and made its author a celebrity. The description of early eighteenth century Peru was, in Edmund Wilson's estimation, "solid, incandescent, distinct." This success confirmed Wilder's intention to make abundant use of historical materials, and he set his next novel, *The Woman of Andros* (1930), in postclassical Greece. *The Bridge of San Luis Rey* also served notice that a major philosophical and theological writer had entered the literary scene. The engaging simplicity of the book drew its readers toward problems no less recondite than those of the justice of God, the possibility of disinterested love, and the role of memory in human relationships. That Wilder's subsequent works consistently returned to these themes was a surprise to no one, so powerfully had this novel stated them.

The Christianity that inspires and informs *The Bridge of San Luis Rey* is existential and pessimistic. "Only one reader in a thousand notices that I have asserted a denial of the survival of identity after death," Wilder once remarked of the book. He also denies the value of the apologetic task that Brother Juniper undertakes. For even if human reason could "scientifically demonstrate" God's providence—a proposition Wilder rejects—man would inevitably employ this knowledge in a self-aggrandizing manner. The inherent mystery of the divine intention is a check to human pride. And pride is Wilder's overriding concern, especially that pride which cloaks itself in the guise of "unselfish love." If there is providence, Wilder suggests, it most clearly operates as something that exposes the egoistic taint in all love and reveals to the lover his need to be forgiven both by the one he loves and the social community.

Despite the ostensible importance of Brother Juniper, Uncle Pio, and Esteban, only Wilder's female characters develop sufficiently to gain awareness of the meaning of the novel's action. The Marquesa undergoes the clearest transformation. The maternal love that she cultivates so assiduously is neither spontaneous nor generous. Rather, the Marquesa craves her daughter's affection as an antidote to her own insecurity. Her imagination first magnifies the daughter's virtues and prestige; then, to assuage a deep self-loathing, she demands from this "great lady" a meticulous and servile devotion. Although the Marquesa is aware of her manipulative impulses, she is nevertheless powerless to conquer them. She is not aware of how her distorted passion causes misery to those around her. The revelation of Pepita's agonized loneliness shames and humiliates her, but she thereby gains the strength to eliminate the element of tyranny in the love she bears for her daughter.

Because La Périchole (Camila) appears in each of the three tales, she is the novel's most real character. Her satirical attack on the Marquesa becomes ironic when, later on, her own ugliness and avarice also make her the object of gossip and scorn. Like the Marquesa, she does not believe herself to be intrinsically valuable. Yet Uncle Pio, who first treated Camila as something to dominate and take aesthetic delight in, now loves her unconditionally. Her willingness to accept this fact and express her love causes him to suffer and isolates her unnaturally from society. Such a painful yet liberating acceptance is made possible both by Pio's persistence and her love for Jaime. Her grief, and the possibility of disinterested love that it implies, moves her at last to present her disfigured self to society.

Even though her moral insight makes the Abbess the standard against which all in the novel is measured, she too must suffer and grow. Unlike the abstract and detached Brother Juniper, she makes herself vulnerable to the pains that love and service involve. Unlike the Marquesa, she does not demand instant expressions of servile devotion from those who love her. She does, however, yearn to have her work remembered, to gain that (in Wilder's view illusory) immortality which comes to those who labor for great causes. Consequently, she manipulates Pepita much as Uncle Pio manipulates Camila. That Pepita died lonely and forsaken reveals to the Abbess the results of her misguided passion. Her faith undergoes a purification when she confronts the fact that "Even memory is not necessary for love."

The episode of Esteban and Manuel does not fit neatly into the pattern Wilder generally establishes. Some critics have suggested that Wilder here meant to deal with homosexual love. This view is partially refuted by the heterosexual activity of both youths and by Esteban's evident unwillingness to stand between Manuel and Camila. But does Estaban unconsciously attempt to retain possession of his brother, communicating his feelings through the uncanny channels of sympathy that bind these twins? Even if this were so, there remains the fact that Manuel also is unable to conceive of a separation. The tale thus seems to constitute a digression, one which serves to underscore the enormous mystery and intensity of all relationships of love. It is linked to the central thematic pattern by Esteban's deep feelings for the Abbess, which enables him to reach out to another human being despite his tragic sorrow.

For Wilder, it is almost impossible for human beings to live serenely and faithfully knowing that their personalities will neither be remembered by society nor allowed to survive death in a hereafter. This prospect creates an anxiety that pervades all their efforts to love. They persistently use the beloved to prove themselves worthy and immortal. Then to love are added additional, degrading elements. Men never realize, in the Abbess' words, that "the love will have been enough." Wilder's views could have led him to enormous sentimentality, but in truth, *The Bridge of San Luis Rey* is extraordinarily stark. It is sustained only by the single hope that "all those impulses of love return to the love that made them."

BROAD AND ALIEN IS THE WORLD

Type of work: Novel
Author: Ciro Alegría (1909–1967)
Type of plot: Social chronicle
Time of plot: 1912–1926
Locale: Peru
First published: 1941

Principal characters:

ROSENDO MAQUIS, mayor of a community of Indians
DON AMENABAR, the tyrannical owner of a neighboring ranch
BISMARCK RUIZ, a rascally lawyer
CORREA ZAVALA, a lawyer friendly to the Indians
FIERO VASQUEZ, a highwayman friendly to the Indians
BENITO CASTRO, an Indian who had lived away from the village

The Story:

Rosendo Maquis was the mayor of Rumi, a small Indian town in the Peruvian uplands. The village was a communal organization, as it had been for centuries. Its life was peaceful, for the Rumi Indians were an agricultural people. Rosendo's only troubles were personal. Because his wife was dying, he had been sent into the mountains to find herbs to be used in making medicine for the sick woman. On his way back to the village, he saw an evil omen in the passage of a snake across his path. Troubled times, he felt, lay ahead.

That same night, Rosendo's wife died, and her death marked the beginning of many misfortunes for the mayor and his people. A few days later, it became known that Don Amenabar, whose ranch bordered the Indian village, was filing suit to take away the best of the land belonging to Rumi. Rosendo and his selectmen saddled their horses and rode to the nearby town to get a lawyer to defend them. They hired Bismarck Ruiz, a man who had a poor reputation in the town because of his love affair with La Castelaña, a notorious woman of very expensive tastes. In return for a large fee, Bismarck Ruiz promised to win the suit for the Indians.

Life went on as usual in the village during the days before the trial. There was a cattle roundup, to which Don Amenabar sent men to collect the cattle belonging to him. Although he did not pay the grazing fee, and the Indians knew it would be futile to ask it of him, he charged them a high fee to redeem

---

BROAD AND ALIEN IS THE WORLD by Ciro Alegría. Translated by Harriet de Onis. By permission of the publishers, Rinehart & Co., Inc. Copyright, 1941, by Farrar & Rinehart, Inc.

any cattle that accidentally wandered onto his lands. The Indians were also busy building a school, for the commissioner of education of the province had promised them a schoolmaster as soon as they had a hygienic place for the school to convene.

In an effort to learn what Don Amenabar was plotting against them, the Indians sent one of their number to the ranch to sell baskets and woven mats. When Don Amenabar saw the Indian on his ranch, he ordered his overseers to give the unlucky fellow a hundred lashes, a punishment that would have killed many men.

Finally, the case came to court. The Indians felt at first that they would win. Don Amenabar's men had removed the stones marking the community boundaries, but the Indians had returned them. The return, they felt, was indicative of their success. But the case was soon over, thanks to a large number of perjuring witnesses who testified against the Indians by claiming that the people of Rumi had encroached on Don Amenabar's land. Even the judge had received money and preferment from the rancher.

The Indians' lawyer immediately made up a brief for an appeal to a higher court, but Don Amenabar's men, disguised as the followers of Fiero Vasquez, the outlaw, stole the mailbag containing the documents as the mailcarrier passed through a desolate part of the Andes. Don Amenabar did not want the authorities in Lima to hear of the affair because he wished to send his son to the legislature and, eventually, to become a senator himself.

Correa Zavala, a young lawyer fired with zeal for the cause of the Peruvian Indians, took up the villagers' case. It had become clear to the Indians that Bismarck Ruiz was not helping them with all his ability, and they had evidence that he was really in the pay of Don Amenabar. The young lawyer made up a long brief that included many documents from the history of the village. These were sent to the capital with a guard of troops and Indians, for their loss would have made it difficult to prove the village's legal existence as a community.

All was to no avail, however, for at last the day came when the court order, enforced by troops, was delivered to the Indians. They were to leave the most fertile of their lands and move to what was left to them in the higher areas. When one of the village women went to her lover, Fiero Vasquez, the notorious highwayman and bandit, he came with his band of cutthroats to help the Indians drive off the people who were forcing them to leave. Rosendo refused aid from the outlaws because he knew that resistance would have been useless. His point was made when a villager was machine-gunned to death for daring to kill one of Don Amenabar's men with a rock.

Even in the highlands the Indians were not safe from Don Amenabar, who wanted to make them slaves to work a mine that he owned on another piece of property. Because he had resolved never to be satisfied until they were delivered into his hands, his men raided the Indians' cattle herds, even creeping up to the corrals in the village at night. At last, the prize bull of the village disappeared. The Indians found the animal on Don Amenabar's ranch. In spite of the brand, Don Amenabar refused to return the bull and ordered Rosendo off the ranch. That same night the mayor returned, determined to regain the animal for his people. He found the bull, but as he was leading the animal away, he was captured. Taken into town, Rosendo was jailed on a charge of thievery. At his trial, he was found guilty and sentenced to a long term in prison.

While Rosendo was in jail, Fiero Vasquez was captured and placed in the cell with Rosendo. Having plenty of resources to make bribes, the highway-man made arrangements to break out of prison. When he escaped, Rosendo was blamed. The prison guards beat the old man so severely that he died within a few hours.

Not long after the death of Rosendo, a young Indian he had reared came back to the village after an absence of many years. Benito Castro, a soldier and a gaucho, was quickly accepted as a leader by the Indians, who needed the wisdom and aid of someone who had been outside the mountain village. Under Castro's leadership, the people drained swampy meadows and rebuilt their village in a better location in the highlands. Their relative prosperity, however, was short-lived, for Don Amenabar still planned to enslave them or drive them into hiding. At last, a large detachment of troops, augmented by men convinced that the Indians were mutinous against the government, attacked the village. In a long battle with the forces sent against them, the Indians were utterly defeated, their leaders were killed, and the village was destroyed. The few survivors, told by the dying Benito Castro to save them-selves, had no idea where they could go to seek a refuge in that harsh, lawless land.

Critical Evaluation:

Ciro Alegría's panoramic novel mirrors life in the Peruvian Andes early in the twentieth century. Its many themes include defense of the downtrodden, justice against injustice, the tragedy of human life, dishonest lawyers and courts, litigation over land boundaries, suffering, villainy and heroism, and racism.

The novel's power lies in its defense of the abused Indian populace of Rumi. The reader lives with Rumi's people throughout the story and identifies with them. Unforgettable is the noble old leader of Rumi, Rosendo Maquis, and his efforts, ideals, character, misfortunes, and death. Grave and good like the community of Rumi itself, Rosendo incarnates his people, who are idealized by Alegría. The dark night and demise of Rumi itself is another Wagnerian touch ably painted by Alegría, giving the novel an epic reach. Besides its many regionalist qualities, moreover, *Broad and Alien Is the World* (translated into English in 1941 from the original *El mundo es ancho y ajeno*) has a well-developed plot and generally convincing characterization that rank it as one of the better contributions to the literature of *Indianismo*, which defends the Indian peoples of Latin America. The plot reaches a final crescendo with the destruction of Rumi and all that the recently murdered Rosendo stood for; but the noble Rosendo, his wife the pathetic Pascuala, black-clad Fiero Vasquez, and Benito Castro still live and stand out in the reader's memory.

Alegría's style has its virtues. His language is poetic, lively, and colorful. He uses standard Spanish laced with occasional regionalisms, including Quechua words, to good effect. Dialogue is authentic. The reader's interest is captured from the opening sentence, which is "Danger!" The novel is nevertheless unwieldy, structurally chaotic, and betrays a lack of careful planning owing to its hasty composition (it was completed in a matter of months).

Geography is always a silent presence in the novel. At times, it is almost a dominant character, reflecting the fact of the importance of geography in Peru's culture. One thus sees the lofty Andean sierra with its crisp, thin air, its gaunt landscapes, sparse vegetation, and rocky soil, and pastel Rumi with its cobbled, windswept streets and huddled houses. Rumi's people grow potatoes and tend their llamas, but they chew coca to cope with hunger and the cold, and their chests are like those of pouter pigeons since the air has so little oxygen.

Alegría was born and reared on a *hacienda* in the same region that he set his novel. Although his parents were his first teachers, he later credited the whole Peruvian people with having molded him and caused him to understand their grief. An Indian wet nurse cradled him in her arms and taught him to walk; he played as a child with Indian children, and later "saw things that he couldn't forget." In *Broad and Alien Is the World*, thus, Alegría penetrates the Indian mind, revealing the native's feeling for the soil, his poverty, stoicism, dignity, superstition, and occasional lapsing into alcoholism or sexual license. Unfortunately, Alegría ladled out some crude propaganda by lambasting safely unpopular types such as white men, priests, and landowners. These stock, one-dimensional figures are reminiscent of Diego Rivera's murals with their pasty-faced, evil whites, bloated priests, cruel-faced landowners, and clean-cut Indians. Thus, neither Don Amenabar, Bismarck Ruiz, nor the poltroonish priest are convincingly drawn. Alegría reveals unconscious prejudice in this respect, even though his own family owned land and was Nordic-Caucasian in appearance. Thus, as is so often the case in Spanish-American literature, a talented writer produces an inspired and sincerely motivated work but simultaneously betrays the fact that he himself belongs to a privileged social class and has not been as truly a member of the working classes as, say, John Steinbeck, Jack London, or José Villareal.

Nevertheless, one of Alegría's great contributions is his pictorial depiction of rural Peruvian society. One thus sees many social types and their folkways, traditions, mentality, society, and sorrows. In Rumi, readers see the kaleidoscopic results of four centuries of blending between Inca and Spaniard. One of the finest examples is the colorful sketch of Rumi's village meeting, with its touches of imagery wherein bronzed Indian faces mingle with lighter mestizos and an occasional white face, against a background of Inca and Spanish dress, manners, postures, and gestures. The novel is thus a storehouse of all that has happened to Peru, from the days of the mysterious Inca Empire, through the dramatic conquest by the Renaissance men of Spain, and the four ensuing centuries of racial and cultural blending. It is said that all of Alegría's works demonstrate a determination to create an original literature that not only interprets the Peruvian reality but also expresses contemporary Peru's peculiarities. He therefore draws the mestizo, whose heart is rooted to the Peruvian soil and in whose soul exists a harmonious mixture. A mestizo is the central personality in all of Alegría's novels with the possible exception of *Broad and Alien Is the World*, and even in that work, the mestizo, Benito Castro, inherits Rosendo Maquis' role and develops into the most significant personality of the latter part of the novel.

Broad and Alien Is the World is essentially a novel of the high sierra as other Spanish-American novels are novels of the pampa, llanos, desert, jungle, or city. It nevertheless broadens the social and human conflict beyond the boundaries of the community of Rumi to Peru's coast and jungle—nowhere under the Peruvian flag is there a place that is not hostile to the Indian. Benito Castro is regarded as an extremist agitator in Lima; one of Rosendo's sons is blinded by the explosion of a rubber ball in the eastern jungles; Calixto Páucar dies in a mine shaft; other emigrants from Rumi meet misfortune in many parts of the Peruvian Republic, for "broad and alien is the world." Alegría's great achievement, thus, is that his masterpiece has undoubtedly helped to implement reform in favor of the mountain-dwelling Indians and mestizos of Central Peru, for their lot has slowly but surely improved since the day when, while writing a scene for another novel concerning the expulsion of some Indians from their community, Alegría was struck with such force "by an intense gust of ideas and memories" that the inspiration for his masterpiece was born.

This novel won for its author a two-thousand-dollar award offered in 1941 by the Division of Intellectual Co-operation of the Pan-American Union. Although the book and author are Peruvian, the novel was submitted by the Chilean committee. Stephen Vincent Bénet later dramatized part of the novel. When the novel appeared, it was frequently referred to as a South American version of John Steinbeck's *The Grapes of Wrath*. In addition to the sociological elements, the novel is a veritable storehouse of Peruvian lore, giving as it does a detailed picture of the social structure of the Indian community, its innate dignity, its traditions, and its overwhelming tragedy. Alegría was exiled from Peru in 1934 because of his political views.

BROTHER ASS

Type of work: Novel
Author: Eduardo Barrios (1884–1963)
Type of plot: Psychological mysticism
Time of plot: 1920's
Locale: Santiago, Chile
First published: 1922

Principal characters:

BROTHER LÁZARO, the narrator
BROTHER RUFINO, a man who practices cruel self-discipline
THE FATHER GUARDIAN
BROTHER ELIAS, a cruel and cynical man
GRACIA, the girl Lázaro once loved
MARÍA MERCEDES, her younger sister
SEÑORA JUSTINA, their mother

Unamuno, the Spanish philosopher, once declared that Spanish philosophy is based on mysticism. Certainly there is nothing more essentially Castilian than the work of the sixteenth century mystic Santa Teresa, whether one considers its spirit, its doctrine, or its style. Mysticism has been defined as a direct relationship with God or some other unifying principle of life. This merging of the individual consciousness with the Supreme Consciousness was not confined to Spain. Europe had other mystics, like Thomas á Kempis in Germany and Anselm of Canterbury in England, but nowhere were there more practitioners of mysticism than in Spain. The bibliographer Nicolás Antonio in his *Bibliotheca Hispana* lists more than four thousand local mystic writers, including those who studied the relationship of the soul with God and the ascetics who sought the way of virtue and happiness through abnegation, love, and sacrifice.

Among the Spanish mystics were the poets Fray Luis de León and St. John of the Cross, as well as a host of prose writers with Santa Teresa de Jesús and Fray Luis de Granada the most outstanding.

Their speculation took two paths. To some, God was a metaphysical entity existing outside the soul, to be approached in a series of stages. To others, God was everpresent, dwelling within the soul, to be discovered by going deeper into one's own reality.

The beginning of the movement in Spain represented a revolt against the paganism of the Renaissance. It had its sources in Platonism and the Neoplatonism of Plotinus and was spread through the influence of Franciscan and Erasmian doctrines. The Spanish translation in 1568 of a treatise on divine love by the Spanish Jew León Hebreo, *Dialogues of Love*, supplied metaphors and comparisons that were augmented by a terminology borrowed from human love.

The dearth of mystic writers in the New World makes one wonder about the reason, in view of their abundance in Spain. Because of the contemplative nature of mysticism, it is easy to attribute their scarcity to the activity demanded in the settlement of a new continent. Actually, many of the priests in the New World were active in many other lines. Perhaps the intellectual caliber of most of the religious leaders in the early period provides an explanation. They were selected for their ability to tuck up their robes and slog through the trackless jungle to win converts among the illiterate aborigines who would not have understood even the most persuasive of mystical writing. Yet America had many writers, as is proved by the vast quantity of chronicles and travel books. Diego de Hojeda, a Peruvian priest-poet, composed a twelve-book Christian epic, *La cristiada*. However, about the only practicing mystic known was Saint Rosa of Lima, the first American saint. She lived largely withdrawn from the Peruvian world and left no important writing when she died at the age of thirty from the severity of her religious practices.

Brother Ass, by the Chilean Eduardo Barrios, practically the only mystic literary work of Spanish America, springs from many sources. Barrios' other novels mark him as a master of abnormal psychology. One critic noted that he excelled in painting abnormal personalities, not exactly neurotics but, rather, human beings whose emotional nature is overwrought and who end in insanity or spiritual disintegration. That is true of his earliest intensely poetic novel, actually a novelette, *El niño que enloqueció de amor* (*The Boy Who Went Crazy with Love*, or as generally translated, *Sentimental Madness*), which was published in 1915. It purports to be the diary of a ten-year-old boy who falls in love with Angelica, a friend and contemporary of his mother.

For his second long fiction, *Un perdido* (*A Lost Soul*), published in 1917, Barrios chose a Chilean city environment, in which the abnormally sentimental hero—suggested perhaps by Frédéric Moreau in Flaubert's *A Sentimental Education*—spends a life of maladjustment and frustration.

Among his other works are a more realistic novel of life on a nineteenth century Chilean farm, *Gran señor y rajadiablos* (*Great Man and Hell-raiser*), which came out in 1948, and *Los hombres del hombre* (*A Man of Many Aspects*), published two years later, a psychological novel in which each aspect of the protagonist assumes a different name. Different from all of them was his 1922 novel, *El hermano asno* (*Brother Ass*, 1942).

The author was able to vary his themes because he himself was a man of many facets. His father was an officer in the Chilean army during the War of the Pacific, and his mother came from occupied Peru. The child was born in Valparaíso, Chile, but was taken by his mother to Peru shortly after the death of his father. At age fifteen, he was returned to Chile to attend a military school from which he ran away to live his own life as a bookkeeper

for a Chilean nitrate mine, as a rubber worker in Peru, as a weight lifter in
a circus, and as a traveling salesman hawking stoves in Buenos Aires. For a
time, he lived in a Franciscan monastery that gave him local color and inspiration for his greatest novel.

Its title comes from the words of the Italian Saint Francis of Assisi, who
called his body "Brother Ass" and begged its pardon for treating it so harshly
by fasting and scourging. The founder of the Franciscan Order enters the
story again in connection with Brother Rufino's miracle of creating a friendly
feeling between cats and mice, as Saint Francis considered all birds and beasts
fellow creatures.

Brother Ass is supposed to be an autobiography by Brother Lázaro.
According to Barrios, who retells his story, on the first page of the manuscript,
in one corner and written in tiny letters and watery ink, as if the Brother had
wished to whisper them, were three lines from the poetry of a Mexican poet
of mystical tendencies, Amado Nervo, an invocation to the temple of his
dreams, a place of deep silence, not dogma.

A medieval legend of a juggler in the Abbey of Cluny, later retold by
Anatole France as "The Juggler of Notre Dame," has as its chief character
an impoverished juggler who was given shelter in the abbey before Christmas.
Others of the abbey were using their skills to make Christmas gifts for Our
Lady. One wrote a poem, another composed a hymn, one painted a fresco,
and another carved a statue. The juggler, however, had no artistic ability. So
he decided to contribute as best he was able by juggling before her shrine.
When the priests, horror-stricken by such sacrilege, tried to drive him from
the temple, Our Lady descended with a smile from her shrine and wiped the
juggler's brow.

Brother Lázaro of *Brother Ass* was in a similar predicament. He had no
great ability. In fact, he was a failure as a priest. For more than seven years
he had been a member of the Franciscan community without being ordained.
He still felt unworthy to become even a good minor friar. A similar feeling
is frequently described in mystic literature as "the dark night of the soul." In
the approach to God, first to come is a purification of the soul and a feeling
of illumination, followed by increasing love; but poor Brother Lázaro had
discovered only that morning, while accompanying the Father Guardian to a
nearby hospital to hear the confession of a dying man, that he could not
discern the love of God in his fellow monks. Too clearly he saw the flaws of
all of them, especially of Brother Rufino, like himself still unordained. Brother
Rufino's obstacle was his life of penitence that prevented the completion of
his studies; Brother Lázaro's difficulties were worries that his worldly past
made him unfit for religious duties.

Going to the monastery garden to meditate about leaving the Church, he
was interrupted by the appearance of another Franciscan, Brother John,
bursting with news of a miracle. Brother Rufino, seeking as had the founder

of the Order to be a friend of all creatures, had set scraps of food on a plate in his cell. Both cats and mice were sharing it in harmony.

More evidence of his lack of Christian qualities came to Brother Lázaro when he allowed the joking of Brother Elias at his expense to enrage him so greatly that another brother felt impelled to draw him aside with a reminder of the need for brotherly love.

Animal brotherhood can go too far. The monks in the monastery discovered that when the mice were no longer frightened away by their natural enemies, they began devouring the wafers, the wax, and the oil. So, reluctantly, the Father Guardian ordered Brother Rufino to stop putting out food.

So far, *Brother Ass* has been like a medieval legend. Now comes the plotting and complications to make it a story. At the communion, Brother Lázaro was sure he saw Gracia, the cause of his withdrawal from the world when she jilted him eight years earlier. It was not, however, his former sweetheart but her younger sister, María Mercedes. He learned that Gracia had a family now, but the sister, much more beautiful, represented a temptation to the flesh that he had difficulty resisting. He tried to discourage her from coming back to the monastery by refusing to help her see Brother Rufino, now considered a saint and adored by all the children.

Brother Rufino had also seen the lovely girl, and his soul, once filled with a mystical longing for perfection and humility, was tormented almost to madness. He tried to fight temptation by fasting. He became cadaverous. He refused to tell Brother Lázaro his trouble, except to say that it was the vileness of Brother Ass.

The more Brother Rufino tortured his flesh, the greater grew his saintly reputation. Even people from beyond the parish sought him out, imploring prayers and cures.

Eventually, Brother Lázaro mastered his thoughts of María Mercedes and found peace in the monastery despite frequent sight of her and Gracia. Not so Brother Rufino. One day while in his cell, Brother Lázaro heard María Mercedes scream. He saw her rush out of Brother Rufino's cell; she was crying, and her clothes were torn. When he entered, the gaunt Franciscan was moaning that Brother Ass had been too strong for him. A few moments later he died.

The girl brought no charges, but her angry mother arrived as the bells were tolling for the funeral of Brother Rufino. She cried that the dead man had attacked her daughter. That was the moment when Brother Lázaro made to God his supreme gift. He took the accusation upon himself and confessed that he was the guilty one.

Later, he told the truth to Father Provincial, but it was decided that for the prestige of Brother Rufino and for the good of the Order, Brother Lázaro should be the one publicly considered guilty. He would be transferred to a distant province. He agreed to the decision and prayed that God would accept his sacrifice and make of him a good minor Brother of his Order.

Barrios began his literary career with a volume of short stories published in Iquique. Later he turned to the theater, first with a brief dialogue, *Papa and Mama*. Then in 1912 came a satire on government bureaucracy, *Por el decoro* (*For the Good of the Office*); in 1913, he published the first of his fantasies, *Lo que niega la vida* (*What Life Denies*), taking place in the soul rather than in any definite locality; and in 1916, his best play appeared, *Vivir* (*Life*), a psychological tragedy filled with frustrated women. The impossibility of earning a livelihood in Chile's theaters, however, turned him to novel writing, a profession he combined with such occupations as Chile's Minister of Education and Director of the National Library. When he died in Santiago in 1963, in his eightieth year, Barrios was esteemed as the dean of Chilean literature and the man chiefly responsible for the present popularity and high quality of its psychological fiction.

THE BULWARK

Type of work: Novel
Author: Theodore Dreiser (1871–1945)
Type of plot: Social realism
Time of plot: 1890 to the mid-1920's
Locale: Dukla, Pennsylvania; Philadelphia; New York City; and Atlantic City
First published: 1946

Principal characters:

SOLON BARNES, a Quaker banker
BENECIA, his wife
RUFUS BARNES, Solon's father
HANNAH BARNES, Solon's mother
PHOEBE KIMBER, Hannah's sister
CYNTHIA, Solon's sister
RHODA KIMBER and
LAURA KIMBER, Phoebe's daughters
JUSTUS WALLIN, Benecia's father
ISOBEL, the oldest child of Solon and Benecia
ORVILLE, the second child of Solon and Benecia
DOROTHEA, the attractive third child of Solon and Benecia
ETTA, the fourth child of Solon and Benecia
VOLIDA LA PORTE, Etta's friend
HESTER WALLIN, Justus Wallin's sister
WILLARD KANE, an artist and Etta's lover
STEWART, the youngest child of Solon and Benecia
VICTOR BRUGE and
LESTER JENNINGS, Stewart's friends
PSYCHE TANZER, a young girl

The Story:

Rufus Barnes was a farmer and tradesman living near Segookit, Maine. He and his wife, Hannah, were good Quakers. When Hannah's sister, Phoebe Kimber, living in Trenton, New Jersey, lost her husband, she asked Rufus to come to New Jersey to help settle her husband's affairs. Rufus, finding himself the executor of a rather large estate, did a thorough and competent job. In gratitude for his help and in hopes that he would move his family close to her, Phoebe offered Rufus one of her properties, an old, rundown, but elegant house in Dukla, Pennsylvania, just across the Delaware from Trenton. Rufus was willing to restore the house and try to sell it, but Phoebe was eager to give the house to him. At last, Rufus agreed to take the house and move his family to Dukla. He and his wife had the house restored to great taste and beauty.

Rufus and Hannah became somewhat more worldly in Dukla. Rufus went into business, dealing in real estate, but he applied his Quaker principles to his business and helped the poor farmers make their land yield more profit so that he would not have to foreclose. Respected and prosperous, he and his wife still followed their faith and taught it carefully to their two children, Cynthia and Solon.

Solon Barnes cut his leg with an ax. An incompetent doctor bungled the treatment; and for a time, they all feared that the boy might die. But his mother prayed devoutly, and Solon recovered, an event that kept the family strictly loyal to their faith.

Sent to school with their cousins, Laura and Rhoda, Phoebe's children, Cynthia and Solon, began to acquire more polish and knowledge of the world. At school, Solon also met Benecia Wallin, the daughter of a wealthy Quaker. The other children, Cynthia, Laura, Rhoda, and Benecia, were all sent to a Quaker finishing school at Oakwold, but Solon chose to remain at home and help his father in the real-estate business.

Justus Wallin, Benecia's father, was impressed by the Barnes family. He admired the way Rufus and Solon conducted their business; he was impressed with Hannah's faith and her behavior at Quaker meetings. The families became friendly, and Justus asked Rufus and Solon to become the agents for his extensive holdings. Solon and Benecia fell in love. Justus found a job for Solon in his Philadelphia bank and, although Solon had to start at the bottom, it was clear that he had both the talent and the influence to rise quickly to the top. Solon and Benecia were married, to the delight of both families, in a Quaker ceremony.

The years passed. Solon and Benecia were happy and successful. Solon did well at the bank in Philadelphia; Benecia was a quiet, principled, and religious woman. After the death of Solon's parents, Solon and Benecia moved into the house in Dukla. Although Solon occasionally experienced metaphysical doubts, he lived in complete adherence to the moral principles of the Quakers. He became a bulwark of the community, an honest forthright man who did not approve of smoking, drinking, art, music, literature, or dancing. He and Benecia brought up their five children in accordance with these strict Quaker principles.

Each of the children reacted differently to this upbringing. The oldest daughter, Isobel, unattractive and unpopular in school, found it difficult to make friends. She began to read books and decided, against the ideas implanted by her parents, that she wanted to avoid the Quaker finishing school and go to college. Solon managed to compromise and send her to Llewellyn College for Women, a Quaker institution, where she remained to do postgraduate work. Orville, the oldest son, inherited Solon's severity, although not his kindness. Orville became interested in business at an early age, although his materialism was not tempered by any principle deeper than respectability. He married a wealthy socialite and went into her father's pottery business in Trenton. The third child, Dorothea, was the beauty of the family. She had been taken up by her father's cousin Rhoda, who had married a wealthy doctor, one of Benecia's cousins, in the Wallin family. More worldly than the Barnes family, Rhoda gave elegant parties, approved of dancing, and soon had Dorothea married to a wealthy and socially acceptable young man. None of these three children, however, overtly abandoned the Quaker faith or caused their parents serious concern.

The fourth child, Etta, was more interesting. Sensitive, pretty, highly intelligent, she soon began to read forbidden books. She became friendly with a young girl named Volida La Porte, who introduced her to French novels and gave her the idea of studying literature at the University of Wisconsin. When Solon insisted that his daughter attend the Llewellyn College for Women, Etta ran away to a Wisconsin summer session after pawning her mother's jewels to provide the fare. Solon went after her, and the two were reconciled. Etta acknowledged the theft and returned the jewels. In the meantime, old Hester Wallin had died and left Etta, as well as each of her sisters, a small income.

Solon allowed Etta to remain at Wisconsin for the summer session. After she left the university, Etta moved to Greenwich Village to continue her studies. There she met Willard Kane, an artist, and eventually had an affair with him, even though she realized that he had no intention of jeopardizing his artistic career by marriage. The Barnes family knew of the affair—Orville had discovered it—and they highly disapproved.

The youngest child, Stewart, was the wildest of all. He lacked the essential honesty of his brothers and sisters. Spoiled by his cousin Rhoda, who took him up as she had taken up Dorothea, and sent him to a snobbish private school, Stewart was interested only in his conquests of lower-class girls on riotous trips to Atlantic City. With his friends, Bruge and Jennings, Stewart would pick up girls and take them off for the weekend. He often had to steal money from his parents or his brother to finance his escapades. His reckless life was paralleled by wild financial speculations in the business world that increasingly worried Solon. Solon's bank was involved in some questionable activities, but Solon, true to his religious principles, felt he could not pull out of the situation without hurting others who depended on him. Similarly, he could not abandon Stewart.

One weekend, Stewart's friend Bruge gave a young girl, Psyche, some of his mother's "drops" because Psyche had not yielded to Bruge, and he felt the "drops" might make her comply. They did, but they also killed Psyche. The boys, frightened, left her body on the road. The police soon apprehended them and charged all three with rape and murder. Unable to face his family and feeling some vestiges of religious guilt, Stewart killed himself in jail.

The shock of Stewart's suicide caused Benecia to suffer a stroke. Etta left her lover and returned home shortly before her mother's death. She found Solon greatly changed. In his despair, he had lost his severity and no longer felt he had the right to judge others. Realizing that his concern with business and with strict standards had cut him off from the kindness and light at the center of his faith, he had learned to love all things, all creatures of nature. Etta, who often read to him, found herself more and more attracted to the central "Inner Light" of the Quaker belief. Always the most understanding child, she and her father developed a genuine closeness and affection for each other before Solon died of cancer six months later. Etta, left alone and removed from the commercial contemporary world, became the embodiment of essential Quaker principles.

Critical Evaluation:

As the foremost twentieth century American exponent of Naturalism, Theodore Dreiser dramatized in his fiction a view of life that saw man as the victim of a variety of internal and external forces that prevented him from exercising free choice and controlling his destiny. Dreiser believed that all of a person's actions were predetermined by the essential qualities of his temperament, which was itself molded by forces of environment, both natural and social, and by circumstance. He saw nearly all man's problems as arising from the conflict between his natural animal instincts, which were usually suppressed, and the restrictions imposed by artificial social and moral conventions. In particular, in novels such as *The Financier* and *The "Genius,"* he was concerned with the problems posed by life in an industrial, commercial world where natural human desires were all but stifled beneath materialistic ambition and the pursuit of social status. In most of Dreiser's works, including novels such as *Sister Carrie*, *Jennie Gerhardt*, and *An American Tragedy*, this Naturalistic vision is conveyed through an atmosphere of angry, bitter, or fatalistic feelings; but in such a late work as *The Bulwark* (published posthumously), the tone is much more mellow. The Naturalistic underpinnings are there, but their manifestations are markedly softened in comparison to the earlier novels.

In addition to its quieter tone, *The Bulwark* is marked by its relatively small amount of economic and social background and stronger emphasis on individual character motivations; it is an excellent piece of sensitive demography without the statistical accoutrements. The novel tells the story of three generations of the Barnes family, and traces the increasing struggle of its members to reconcile the Quaker ideal of a pious, unselfish life with the demands made by a modern materialistic world. Dreiser depicts all the stages of the change that gradually occurs, from the staunch Quaker patriarch Rufus and his wife Hannah, with their unshakable convictions and their disapproval of dancing, singing, art, literature, and undue wealth, to their young grandchildren, who marry for money and social position, engage in loveless extramarital affairs, pursue business ambitions, and amass wealth.

By the time Solon's youngest son, Stewart, commits suicide in his prison cell, it has become clear to the father that somewhere in the course of his life, he has lost that "Inner Light" which was the essence of his Quaker faith. Solon dies soon after this realization, but Dreiser ends on a more optimistic note than usual: Solon's sensitive daughter Etta, long detached from her family and living with a Greenwich Village artist, returns home to be reconciled with her father. After his death, Etta rediscovers her own identity and the true spirit of Quakerism, which she embraces in place of the values of the contemporary commercial, materialistic world.

THE CABALA

Type of work: Novel
Author: Thornton Wilder (1897–1975)
Type of plot: Fantasy
Time of plot: About 1920
Locale: Rome
First published: 1926

> *Principal characters:*
> SAMUELE, a young American student and writer
> JAMES BLAIR, his friend
> THE DUCHESS D'AQUILANERA, a Cabalist
> MARCANTONIO, her son
> CARDINAL VAINI, a former Chinese missionary
> ASTRÉE-LUCE DE MORFONTAINE, a religious fanatic
> ALIX D'ESPOLI, a Cabalist princess in love with James
>   Blair

The Story:

When Samuele went to Rome with his friend, James Blair, he learned of the existence there of a certain group known as the Cabala, talented and wealthy aristocrats, clever esoterics who had mysterious influence in affairs of Church and State. Blair, a bookish person, was familiar with some of its members, and he introduced his friend into that strange circle of Roman society. Samuele soon became a favorite of the Cabalists.

One of them, the Duchess d'Aquilanera, had a great problem on her mind. Her sixteen-year-old son Marcantonio had had five or six love affairs with various women, and she was disturbed by his unsettled habits. She had arranged a marriage for him, but the wedding would not take place unless Marcantonio changed his ways. She pleaded with Samuele to spend a weekend at her villa and to talk to the boy in an effort to show him the errors of the life he was leading. Samuele refused, thinking the whole matter ridiculous. Then he had a talk with Cardinal Vaini, a friend of the Duchess, who said that Marcantonio had begun his wild career by imitating his older friends. Later his vicious morality had become a habit and, finally, a mania. Samuele was so shocked by the cardinal's description of the boy's character that he finally agreed to go to the villa, as the Duchess had requested.

Marcantonio liked to drive automobiles as fast as possible. He also told Samuele that he wished to train for the Olympics. Samuele, in a passionate outburst, denounced the boy's loose loves. The next day, Marcantonio jumped

THE CABALA by Thornton Wilder. By permission of the author. Copyright, 1926, by Albert & Charles Boni, Inc.

from a balcony and killed himself.

Samuele was shocked and grieved. Yet, he was soon to become involved in the strange conduct of another Cabalist, the Princess Alix d'Espoli. Alix always had the habit of falling in love with men who could not possibly be attracted to her. She had beauty and charm, but little intelligence. To make up for her lack, she cultivated a way of speaking that was interesting and appealing. Although people enjoyed having her at dinner, she accepted few invitations.

One day, she went to visit Samuele and found James Blair in his apartment. Although Blair was rude, she fell in love with him and proceeded to lay siege to his affections. At last she was convinced that she had scored a triumph, for Blair gave her a book that had once been mentioned in casual conversation. She began going to his rooms uninvited. When Blair became upset, Samuele suggested that the only way out was for him to leave Rome. After Blair left on a trip to Spain, Alix proceeded to lose herself in the life of the city. She accepted all sorts of invitations, even asking to be introduced to various people. She seemed happy in a round of pleasure. Samuele hoped that she had forgotten Blair.

A month later, Blair wrote to Samuele, saying that he was returning to Rome. Samuele warned him to stay away, but Blair insisted that his researches into ancient secret societies made his return necessary. One night, both of them went to visit a famous seer who was holding a seance in an old Roman palace. While they were there, a heavily veiled woman came in, rushed to the seer, and implored his help in some matter. Recognizing Alix, Samuele and Blair attempted to leave, but the woman saw them before they could get out of the room. Abruptly and angrily, she went away. Later Samuele heard that she had become interested in the fine arts and that she was studying music. She started on a trip to Greece but returned suddenly without an explanation. Some said that she continued to search for a lover. More and more, she was spoken of in a derogatory manner.

One day in her presence, a Danish archeologist said that he had met Blair. Upon hearing his name, Alix fainted.

Samuele also spent much of his time with Astrée-Luce de Morfontaine, a deeply religious woman. She saw some spiritual meaning in the initials of an American teacher named Irene H. Spencer, and on one occasion, she was deeply offended when someone spoke slightingly of the pelican, because to her the bird was a holy symbol. She had great faith in prayer. One day, the cardinal spoke derisively of prayer, and she broke down. The cardinal said that she had never suffered and that she did not know the meaning of suffering. The woman's faith was badly shaken. She invited the cardinal to her house for a party. During the evening, she accused him of being the devil, took out a pistol, and shot at him. He was not hurt; but a later reconciliation was impossible. The cardinal decided to go back to his mission in China. En route, he caught a fever, died, and was buried at sea.

Before Samuele left Rome, he called on Miss Elizabeth Grier, an American member of the Cabala. From her, he learned at last who the men and women of the Cabala really were. They were the pagan gods of Europe grown old, deities whose brooding ancient wisdom could not save them from the sufferings and follies of ordinary humanity. Miss Grier confused Samuele by stating her belief that he was the new god Mercury, an idea vaguely upsetting to a young American of New England ancestry.

Critical Evaluation:

Practically all Thornton Wilder's work is unusual in one degree or another. *The Cabala*—really a series of sketches held together by locale and a group of people who have something in common—is no exception. Like *The Woman of Andros*, the sister work to *The Cabala*, this novel explores the haunting connections between pagan and Christian states of mind. Wilder was fascinated by the interpenetration in the modern mind of these radically different world views. Ever since the Church fathers "Christianized" the Greek philosophers, and Renaissance artists reinterpreted Christian ideas in pagan forms, Western civilization has been torn by the opposing forces within it. Wilder's fantasy records the inevitably self-destructive effect of trying to live in totally opposite worlds. The soul is literally torn asunder in its impossible yearning for immanence in an alienated world. Marcantonio and Alix are sacrificed to their hedonistic instincts; as "lost" gods, they cannot find worshipers, only tormentors and judges. Like Milton's pagan deities in "On the Morning of Christ's Nativity," they flee the conquering Christ—who is ironically represented in the Puritan Americans, Samuele and James, apostles of modern Christianity.

In *The Woman of Andros*, Wilder directs his pagan heroine toward Christian piety and feeling; that novel records a rite of passage and is full of wonder and awe at the evolution of religious consciousness from pagan to Christian values. *The Cabala*, however, concentrates on the incompleted passage, the unaccommodated pagan consciousness that survives despite the nominal victory of Christianity. Although the bulk of the novel records the pain of the pagan gods in the modern world, the closing speech of Virgil closes on an elegiac and even heroic note. Can we ever stop loving Rome? Can we confront the modern city without the ancient one in our hearts?

CALL IT SLEEP

Type of work: Novel
Author: Henry Roth (1906–   )
Type of plot: Social realism
Time of plot: 1907–1913
Locale: Lower East Side, New York City
First published: 1934

Principal characters:
DAVID SCHEARL, a young Jewish immigrant boy
GENYA SCHEARL, his mother
ALBERT SCHEARL, his father
JOE LUTER, a print shop foreman
BERTHA, Genya's sister and David's aunt
YUSSIE MINK, David's friend
ANNIE MINK, his sister
LEO DUGOVKA, another of David's friends
NATHAN STERNOWITZ, a widower and later Bertha's
husband
POLLY STERNOWITZ and
ESTHER STERNOWITZ, his daughters
RABBI YIDEL PANKOWER, David's teacher

Henry Roth's only novel was first published in 1934, the year that produced F. Scott Fitzgerald's *Tender Is the Night*, Graham Greene's *It's a Battlefield*, John O'Hara's *Appointment in Samarra*, William Saroyan's *The Daring Young Man on the Flying Trapeze*, and Evelyn Waugh's *A Handful of Dust*. The same year saw the publication of forty-three other works considered memorable enough to be listed in the second edition of *Annals of English Literature*. *Call It Sleep* is not listed, nor is the novel or its author referred to in such compendia as Willard Thorp's *American Writing in the Twentieth Century* or Herzberg's *Reader's Encyclopedia of American Literature*.

The novel, however, has survived its early neglect. For *Call It Sleep* is one of those books written in the wrong generation. Just as the poems of Emily Dickinson and the great whale book of Herman Melville waited decades for full appreciation, so Roth's book came to full public attention thirty years after its publication in 1934. One obvious reason for its success in the 1960's was its subject: life in the Jewish ghetto. In the meantime, novelists such as Saul Bellow, Bernard Malamud, and Philip Roth had made the American Jew significant in contemporary literature. It is no wonder that the American public should respond to another book on this popular subject, especially after it has been called one of the most distinguished novels telling of Jewish life in America.

The real achievement of the book, however, derives more from technique than from subject. The chief merits of the novel are its harsh but poetic realism, its remarkable power of vivid evocation, and its technical control. Realism implies a picture of life as it is. The life Roth chooses to portray is that of an Austrian Jewish boy enduring four acutely and painfully formative years in the New York ghettos. Reminiscent of Theodore Dreiser's *Sister Carrie* and of Stephen Crane's *Maggie*, *Call It Sleep* portrays the day-to-day existence of David Schearl with a sophisticated accumulation of sensuous detail. One critic, in fact, believed it must be the noisiest novel ever written, so vivid are the sounds of shouts, groans, whispers, insults, streetcars, clocks, feet tramping, and mouths chewing.

Detail for its own sake does not make literature, however. Roth's success is in the relevance of the detail and in its controlled use to stir and alter emotion in the reader. Aunt Bertha, for example, is a bawdy, loud-mouthed woman who exists as a foil to sensitive, fearful David. Through her, Roth evokes both the truth of David's uncomfortable life and the necessary sympathy that the reader must have if the novel is to come alive.

Call It Sleep is a masterpiece, and to read it is to be astounded at its neglect. It is difficult to think of another writer (Dickens? Wolfe?) who can recall the agonies of childhood with such urgency and immediacy. David Schearl is a child of his race, his time, his environment, but he is all children as well; the reader experiences something close to discomfort as his memory is jogged by the universality of David's search for understanding of, and reconciliation with, the world about him.

David's world is presented mainly through a careful documentation of the boy's consciousness. Roth, in a brilliant stroke, begins with a prologue that creates both the physical and psychological environment with which David will have to struggle. Readers are taken first to a steamer leaving Ellis Island in 1907. Among the immigrants are David, then about two years old, and his mother, Genya. Albert, the father, had come to America earlier, and the family is now to be reunited. In Albert's behavior, however, there is a coldness markedly different from the outspoken joy that pervades other such groups around him. His remarks to his wife and son are contemptuous and accusatory; in a gesture full of shame and pathetic pride, he snatches David's old-country hat and hurls it into the river simply because he does not want his boy to look like an immigrant.

The prologue is wonderfully graphic, but it is also important as a source of basic themes and metaphors. First, it establishes the Schearls as people in an alien culture, a circumstance that colors the whole novel. Secondly, it establishes another and more profound kind of alienation existing between mother and son, on the one hand, and father and son, on the other. Finally, the prologue suggests a metaphor that underlies the entire work: the voyage that David must take into the alien world of complex experience. In this sense, the sheltering arms of Genya are the old world; David is the immigrant in life who must leave their haven and seek his own meanings in the new culture of maturity. It is one of the particular triumphs of *Call It Sleep* that these closely related themes lead readers from the surface of life to the depths of inner experience, and finally into a pattern that lies under the lives of everyone.

The stages of David's three-year voyage shape the four books into which the novel is divided. David is six years old as the narrative begins. His attachment to his mother is profound not only for her but also for the shelter she provides between him and the icy contempt of his father. Critics have pointed out that the mother-son relationship is strongly Oedipal. Irving Howe has had the wisdom also to observe that through David's observation of the placid and beautiful Genya, readers are made to relive a relationship that is profoundly touching to most men, whatever its psychiatric implications.

In sharp contrast is the brilliantly realized character of the father: aloof, suspicious, gullible, and eaten away by a tragic pride. Albert is at war with the world. His great fear, induced partly by an awareness of his own foreignness and partly by some deeper insecurity, is that he will be laughed at, cheated, and made a fool. And so, of course, he is; in an early episode, David's immature but meticulous consciousness records that Albert's foreman, Luter, is flattering Albert only in order to be with Genya.

The first two books are largely concerned with the traumas of David's broadening experience: the Luter episode, a repugnant sexual encounter with a neighborhood girl, and a terrible thrashing by Albert. In the second book, David watches the courting of Aunt Bertha by the laconic Sternowitz and listens in confused fascination to his mother's account of an earlier love affair in Russia. Throughout these chapters, Roth portrays with great skill a young boy's developing awareness of sexuality, particularly his uneasy realization that his mother is also a sexual being.

The third book is centered in the Hebrew school, the *cheder*, where David's intellect is awakened by the Rabbi Yidel Pankower. Pankower is one of the great achievements of the novel, a tragicomic figure of classic proportions. The *cheder* dances to the tunes of his invective. David learns rapidly, but one afternoon, a verse from Isaiah puzzles him: It tells how Isaiah saw the Lord seated upon a throne and was afraid. Then a seraph touched a fiery coal to Isaiah's lips, and he heard God speak. David yearns to ask about that coal but does not get the chance. At home, he asks his mother to explain God. He is brighter than day, she says, and He has all power.

On the first day of Passover there is no school, and David wanders toward the East River. He stares at the river, meditating on God's brightness. The experience is almost a mystical trance, but the dazzling contemplation is broken by three boys who come up and taunt him. They can show him magic if he will go to the car tracks and drop a piece of scrap metal in the groove between the tracks. David does so. Suddenly there is a blinding light. David is terrified. His child's mind connects God's power and light with the electrical flash.

David sometimes does not get along with the rough boys of the neighborhood. One day, he discovers the roof of the flat as a place of refuge. From there, he sees a boy with blond hair flying a kite. Leo Dugovka is confident and carefree, and he has skates. Leo is surprised to learn that David knows nothing about the Cross or the Mother and Child. David desperately wants Leo to like him.

The next day, David goes on a long walk to Aunt Bertha's candy shop to see if she has any skates he can use. The living quarters behind the store are cramped, dark, and filthy. Bertha tells him to get Esther and Polly out of bed while she watches the store.

Aunt Bertha has no skates. David goes to Leo's flat. There he is attracted to a picture of Jesus and to a rosary. Leo is sexually interested in David's two cousins after he hears about them. The next day, Leo promises David the rosary if he will take him to see the girls. Though uncomfortable, David agrees. Leo is successful with Esther, but they are caught in the act by Polly. She tattles.

David is terrified; he will be implicated. At *cheder* in the afternoon, he reads nervously before a visiting rabbi. Bursting into tears, he entangles himself in hysterical lies fabricated out of the secret in his mother's past. He says his mother is dead and that his father was a Gentile organist in Europe.

While the puzzled rabbi goes to clear up matters with the Schearls, Nathan is angrily blaming David for what happened to Esther. The rabbi soon learns that David has lied, but the mention of the organist arouses Albert's suspicion. He accuses his wife of unfaithfulness and believes David to be someone else's child. Genya cannot convince him that he is wrong.

When Bertha and Nathan arrive, David, terrified, runs into the street while his elders argue violently. Images, recollections, and fears spin through his mind. Finding a steel milk-dipper, he desperately decides to produce God again at the car tracks. At first, nothing happens as he inserts the dipper; then, suddenly, he receives a terrific electric shock that knocks him out. The flash draws a crowd of anxious people, but David has not been hurt seriously. Even his father seems slightly relieved that he is all right.

Soon it is night, and he can go to sleep and forget it all. In sleep, all the images of the past—sights, sounds, feelings—become vivid and alive. While life was painful and terrifying, in sleep he triumphs.

A fundamental aspect of Roth's triumph is his mastery of style. The dialect of a slum street is rendered with unshrinking fidelity; the cultural dilemma of the immigrant is touchingly demonstrated in the disparity between David's American street language and the dignified language of his home, representing a translation of the family's native Yiddish. When the reader enters David's stream-of-consciousness, language becomes direct experience, and *Call It Sleep* takes its place beside the great lyrical novels of the century.

It would be tempting to summarize Roth's achievement through comparisons. One could say that as an example of urban Naturalism, *Call It Sleep* rivals the best of Dreiser and Farrell; that in some elements of its stylistic virtuosity, it rivals the work of Joyce; that as a novel of growing up, it must be ranked with *Huckleberry Finn* and *Look Homeward, Angel*. Yet, such comparisons are beside the point. What one most admires about the novel, what must make it survive, is the incomparable richness of its experience recreated in the totality and finality of the work of art.

THE CALL OF THE WILD

Type of work: Novel
Author: Jack London (1876–1916)
Type of plot: Adventure romance
Time of plot: 1897
Locale: Alaska
First published: 1903

Principal characters:
BUCK, a dog
A SPITZ, his enemy
JOHN THORNTON, his friend

The Story:

Buck was the undisputed leader of all the dogs on Judge Miller's estate in California. A crossbreed of St. Bernard and Scottish shepherd, he had inherited the size of the first and the intelligence of the latter. Buck could not know that the lust for gold had hit the human beings of the country and that dogs of his breed were much in demand as sled dogs in the frozen North. Consequently, he was not suspicious when one of the workmen on the estate took him for a walk one night. The man took Buck to the railroad station, where the dog heard the exchange of money. Then a rope was placed around his neck. When he struggled to get loose, the rope was drawn so tight that it shut off his breath, and he lost consciousness.

He recovered in a baggage car. When the train reached Seattle, Washington, Buck tried to break out of his cage while he was being unloaded. A man in a red shirt hit him with a club until he was senseless. After that, Buck knew that he could never win a fight against a club. He retained that knowledge for future use.

Buck was put in a pen with other dogs of his type. Each day, some of the dogs went away with strange men who came with money. One day, Buck was sold. Two French-Canadians bought him and some other dogs and took them on board a ship sailing for Alaska. The men were fair, though harsh, masters, and Buck respected them. Life on the ship was not particularly enjoyable, but it was a paradise compared to that which awaited Buck when the ship reached Alaska. There he found men and dogs to be little more than savages, with no law but the law of force. The dogs fought like wolves, and when one was downed, the pack moved in for the kill. Buck watched one of his shipmates being torn to pieces after he lost a fight, and he never forgot the way one dog in particular, a Spitz, watched sly-eyed as the loser was slashed to ribbons.

The Spitz was Buck's enemy from that time on.

Buck and the other dogs were harnessed to sleds on which the two French-Canadians carried mail to prospectors in remote regions. It was a new kind of life to Buck but not an unpleasant one. The men treated the dogs well, and Buck was intelligent enough to learn quickly those things which made him a good sled dog. He learned to dig under the snow for a warm place to sleep and to keep the traces clear and thus make pulling easier. When he was hungry, he stole food. The instincts of his ancestors came to life in him as the sled went farther and farther north. In some vague manner, he sensed the great cunning of the wolves who had been his ancestors in the wilderness.

Buck's muscles grew firm and taut and his strength greater than ever. Yet, his feet became sore, and he had to have moccasins. Occasionally, one of the dogs died or was killed in a fight, and one female went mad. The dogs no longer worked as a team, and the two men had to be on guard constantly to prevent fights. One day Buck saw his chance; he attacked the Spitz, the lead dog on the sled, and killed him. After that, Buck refused to be harnessed until he was given the lead position. He proved his worth by whipping the rebellious dogs into shape, and he became the best lead dog that the men had ever seen. The sled made record runs, and Buck was soon famous.

When they reached Skaguay, the two French-Canadians had official orders to turn the team over to a Scottish half-breed. The sled was heavier and the weather bad on the trip back to Dawson. At night, Buck lay by the fire and dreamed of his wild ancestors. He seemed to hear a faraway call which was like a wolf's cry.

After two days' rest in Dawson, the team started back over the long trail to Skaguay. The dogs were almost exhausted. Some died and had to be replaced. When the team arrived again in Skaguay, the dogs expected to rest, but three days later, they were sold to two men and a woman who knew nothing about dogs or sledding conditions in the northern wilderness. Buck and the other dogs started out again, so weary that it was an effort to move. Again and again, the gallant dogs stumbled and fell and lay still until the sting of a whip brought them to their feet for a few miles. At last, even Buck gave up. The sled had stopped at the cabin of John Thornton, and when the men and the woman were ready to leave, Buck refused to get up. One of the men beat Buck with a club and would have killed him had not Thornton intervened, knocking the man down and ordering him and his companions to leave. They left Buck with Thornton.

As Thornton nursed Buck back to health, a feeling of love and respect grew between them. When Thornton's partners returned to the cabin, they understood this affection and did not attempt to use Buck for any of their heavy work.

Twice, Buck saved Thornton's life and was glad that he could repay his friend. In Dawson, Buck won more than a thousand dollars for Thornton on a wager, when the dog broke loose a sled carrying a thousand-pound load from the ice. With the money won on the wager, Thornton and his partners went on a gold-hunting expedition. They traveled far into eastern Alaska, where they found a stream yellow with gold.

In his primitive mind, Buck began to see a hairy man who hunted with a club. He heard the howling of the wolves. Sometimes he wandered off for three or four days at a time, but he always went back to Thornton. At one time, he made friends with a wolf that seemed like a brother to Buck.

Once Buck chased and killed a great bull moose. On his way back to the camp, he sensed that something was wrong. He found several dogs lying dead along the trail When he reached the camp, he saw Indians dancing around the bodies of the dogs and Thornton's two partners. He followed Thornton's trail to the river, where he found the body of his friend full of arrows. Buck was filled with such a rage that he attacked the band of Indians, killing some and scattering the others.

His last tie with man broken, he joined his brothers in the wild wolf packs. The Indians thought him a ghost dog, for they seldom saw more than his shadow, so quickly did he move. Had the Indians watched carefully, however, they could have seen him closely. Once each year, Buck returned to the river that held Thornton's body. There the dog stood on the bank and howled, one long, piercing cry that was the tribute of a savage beast to his human friend.

Critical Evaluation:

On its simplest, most superficial and insensitive level, *The Call of the Wild* is just another of Jack London's "dog stories," which also include *White Fang* (1906) and *Jerry of the Islands* (1917). Yet, so cavalier a dismissal of *The Call of the Wild*—usually accompanied by contemptuous allegations that the novel is nothing more than a potboiler—is quite unwarranted. Buck's story has far broader implications than the first, hasty reading may reveal. Admittedly, the book's popular success stems largely from its romantic-adventure qualities, yet there is much more to the novel than mere entertainment.

Jack London led a checkered life and had a checkered career; his experiences and knowledge are reflected in his novels and short stories, particularly his sociopolitical and economic views. At best, London's position could be described as eclectic; at worst, vacillating. He admired Herbert Spencer, Charles Darwin, Karl Marx, and Friedrich Nietzsche simultaneously and without much recognition of the contradictions among them. He embraced socialist causes while espousing Nietzschean "superman" theories. It is thus that Buck—under the presumably civilizing influence of John Thornton—becomes a good socialist; that is, Buck works for the common good rather than for his individual advancement. Bereft of Thornton's guidance when his mentor dies, Buck reverts to the Darwinian survival of the fittest and the Nietzschean superman principles for his own protection.

To be sure, the novel has been faulted for Buck's so-called reversion to the wild. Even the most venerable of critics have praised *White Fang* and *Jerry of the Islands* for depicting savagery under civilized control, while disparaging *The Call of the Wild* as a clarion-call to brute force. Yet, however such critics deplore the Darwinian-Nietzschean point of view, they seem to ignore the realities of the Marxian position: peasants and poor people—like Buck—can work with their kind for mutual benefit; but without a spirit of cooperation and without leadership or guidance, they must fend for themselves, or they will not endure. The cruelties of life are severe for both man and dog; and here, the dog Buck is virtually an allegory for Everyman, in the pristine medieval sense, symbolizing the plight of the oppressed and the downtrodden everywhere in their struggle to maintain life. Whatever his intentions or his convictions, and no matter how skewed, London has portrayed, in *The Call of the Wild*, a vivid picture of the dilemma of the disadvantaged, even though he did so by using a dog as his protagonist.

THE CANNIBAL

Type of work: Novel
Author: John Hawkes (1925–   )
Type of plot: Fantastic allegory
Time of plot: Winter, 1945, and Winter, 1914
Locale: Spitzen-on-the-Dein, a town in Germany
First published: 1949

Principal characters:

MADAME STELLA SNOW, the aristocratic landlady of a
  rooming house
ERNST SNOW, her husband
HERMAN SNOW, his father and the proprietor of a
  Brauhaus
JUTTA, Stella's younger sister and a tenant
SELVAGGIA, Jutta's little girl
JUTTA'S YOUNG SON, unnamed
ZIZENDORF, Jutta's lover, a leader of insurrection, and a
  tenant
A CENSUS-TAKER, Zizendorf's friend and a tenant
THE DUKE, a tenant
HERR STINTZ, a schoolteacher and a tenant
BALAMIR, an escapee from an asylum, living in the
  basement
GERTA, Stella and Jutta's nurse
CROMWELL, an English traitor
LEEVEY, an American soldier
THE MAYOR
MILLER, the pastor
STELLA'S MOTHER AND FATHER

In *The Cannibal*, one of the most accomplished American experimental
novels of the 1940's, John Hawkes makes the town Spitzen-on-the-Dein representative of Germany during the early stages of the Allied occupation after
World War II; it is also the scene of an extended flashback to World War I.
With the collapse of normality in every phase of their daily lives during both
wars, the people of the town move in a nightmare landscape. Even in the
midst of almost total ruin, aristocratic, majestic Madame Stella Snow, who
runs a boardinghouse, feels a sense of community. Most of the major characters are tenants in Stella's house. Stella's sister Jutta, who was about the
age of her little girl, Selvaggia, at the end of the first war, has always lived a
life of rigid restraint, but now, neither man nor woman, she wallows in listless
sexuality with Zizendorf, the leader of the insurrection, while the drunken

Census-Taker watches. The Duke, a brave tank commander during the war, is already in pursuit of Jutta's effeminate son when the novel begins. Resentful of Stella, Jutta fears her family's and the Duke's aristocratic heritage and has no sense of patriotism. The only person Selvaggia fears is Herr Stintz, the one-eyed schoolteacher, who plays a dirge on his tuba every night and who is perversely attracted to her. Balamir, escapee from the local asylum, lives in the basement; the real or imagined son of the Kaiser, he thinks of Stella as the Queen Mother.

Fragmented images of the landscape, past and present, are repeated as haunting motifs throughout the novel. The scenic props of the glorious German past rot in the present: flags and brass band instruments. The architecture is expressive of the Germanic concept of the race's soul: the focus in 1914 is the *Sportswelt Brauhaus* and Stella's ancestral house; in 1945, it is the asylum and Stella's rooming house. The novel begins, repeatedly refers to, and ends with the asylum, situated just outside town. Animals make their lairs in rooms vacated by patients. Balamir and his brother inmates do not realize they are out; they merely move on a landscape that is an objectification of their own private lunacies. The novel is rife with images expressive of the Nordic-Teutonic-Prussian heroic stance and nationalistic tradition; of the relationship between father and son, an exalted notion of family, seen in terms of generations perpetuating ancestral pride; of blustering notions of masculinity; and of the enduring long-suffering of females. The degeneration of the race is manifested in dry, sterile, impotent copulation—promiscuity, prostitution, perversion; infected men and women with shaven heads dance a waltz like zombies in a storehouse on the asylum grounds; Allied parachutists rape women whose vaginas are packed with poison; pregnant women expose themselves to death by freezing, while others suckle children as old as six; German soldiers carry suicidal cyanide capsules. These people struggle to survive in a town where there are no clocks, no postal service, no radios, no newspapers, no fluid for embalming corpses; where all the keys for the machines are welded together; where excrement burns in pits, gas explodes in sewers, typhoid breeds in wells, and flabby rubber rafts, corpses, and fog drift in the canal where the ghosts of British tank soldiers come to drink. Across this landscape creep maimed horses, dry cows, terrified birds, mangy chickens, wild dogs that snarl at train wheels, rabid monkeys, and rats. When ravaging animals are turned loose in a world of violent death, mutilation, and disease, and become assimilated into the human population, people begin to respond to one another in animal terms and resort, finally, to cannibalism. In 1914 and again in 1945, an incredible cold grips the landscape; then a damp air descends, the cold dissolves into a fog, and moonlight reveals things soft with rot and the final acts of horror.

Although his work has been compared with Kafka's, Hawkes's resembles his not at all in technique. Kafka's seemingly unreal world is presented rationally. While Hawkes's images seize the reader and hold him in a tension created by forces of repulsion and abnormal attraction, he deliberately attempts to break the illusion of reality by employing literary elements and devices that act upon one another in such a way that the dream becomes reality, making questions of literary appropriateness irrelevant. Elements of parody, black humor, lyricism, mock sentimentality, farce, and the conscious, controlled use of clichés cause frequent, sudden, and absurd shifts in tone and perspective. Through an eclectic method that is more often expressionistic than impressionistic, Hawkes attempts to project a series of images that reflect the mental climate of an ignobly defeated people whose aspirations were pathologically nationalistic. Hawkes uses a point of view strategy which makes great demands of the reader; if the reader cooperates, he finds himself in the same relation to the author that exists between the novel's victims and victimizers. Obsessed by the past, Zizendorf, editor of the town's defunct newspaper, *The Crooked Zeitung*, is the surrounding narrator. As the present action begins, he is preparing to kill Leevey, the Jewish-American soldier who patrols one third of the nation on a rusty motorcycle as its sole overseer. Zizendorf's monomaniacal purpose is to free his people, rebuild the town, and resuscitate the old nationalistic pride. Thus it is appropriate that all the streams of consciousness, the nighttime reveries and nightmares of the other characters, converge and become assimilated in him. He is the voice, the mind, the collective subconscious of vanquished Germany.

With this device, so expressive of his theme, Hawkes shifts frequently from one character to another—illogically, in view of Zizendorf's limited access to the raw materials of his narrative; but there is a kind of Jungian truth in this technique. The shifts are made without preparation, as thoughts shift erratically in a deranged mind. The reader is into a scene; then, suddenly, he is briefly somewhere else; then he is thrust into yet another character's field of vision. Sometimes the shift is made within a sentence. Though there are few scenes of sustained length, Hawkes will present, after a relatively long scene, a series of brief images, bringing the separate action of each character forward a little, usually with ironic effect.

There is almost none of the sustained stream of consciousness passages one finds in Virginia Woolf or Joyce. Hawkes's characters simply respond to the stimuli the author provides for all their senses. In Hawkes's surreal (but all too real) world, the reader's senses are assaulted by violent odors, ghastly sights, eerie sounds, foul tastes; and he feels the touch of soft rot. The characters are defined in terms of extreme experiences to which they are always subordinate. A relative lack of individualization gives the effect of a single, many-faceted character. Thus, the all-embracive mind of Zizendorf, the Hitlerian temperament reemergent, becomes the reader's own consciousness; to his horror, the reader discovers that it is a consciousness in which values of all kinds are suspended, much the same as in a dream where people commit or witness atrocities upon which they make no judgments. What the reader experiences are extreme moments of bestiality, not as a social creature but as a beast would experience them—purely.

Hawkes uses a technique that is more poetic and cinematic than novelistic. The shifts among points of view are made by a method of juxtaposition or montage. The juxtaposition of poetic images, which are charged with vivid visual components expressive of theme, character, and event, has the effect one experiences when two shots in a motion picture are juxtaposed to create a third dimension of emotion or thematic significance. The rhythm of the camera is, at its best, the rhythm of poetry rather than that of prose. The montage is essentially the method of Eliot's *The Waste Land*, which, along with "The Hollow Men," is one poetic influence upon *The Cannibal*. Eliot's principle of the objective correlative is basic to this novel. Hawkes externalizes the internal neuroses of a people. The method of juxtaposition operates throughout the book, within each section, each scene, and often within each paragraph and sentence, creating a kind of continuity that proceeds according to a logic quite different from that of a conventional novel. Here again the effect of pure vision—of things seen as they are—is apparent. Hawkes's images come to the reader as though from electronic impulses bounced off the moon rather than from an author; with the distance of a film director, he achieves control and restraint in the way he handles images which assail readers as though poured out chaotically by an extremely undisciplined writer. The roving camera eye—going in and out of focus, zooming in like a telephoto lens for a microscopic scrutiny of, for example, the mouth of the dead merchant clotted with cobwebs—is being very coldly guided. A vividly descriptive style which employs all the devices of rhetoric enhances the impact of these images.

There is as little order in the sequence of images as there is in the spread of shrapnel; as though a camera caught it in slow motion, that is what is seen—the explosion of a mine which the reader steps on in Hawkes's field of view. Just as there are lines of force in an explosion that give it a unity, which the victim cares little to imagine, so beneath the apparent chaos of the novel's images and occasional scenes, a pattern of events may be discerned. The novel is in three parts; the present action in 1945 surrounds an extended flashback to events in 1914. This structure emphasizes the oneness of the two wars; and within each chapter the method of juxtaposition conveys a sense of the simultaneity of all events.

If in part 1, Hawkes tries to make the reader feel he is having hallucinations, he deliberately eases him into a rather traditional narrative occurring around 1914. Stella sings in the Sportswelt Brauhaus; Ernst, the son of Herman Snow, the proprietor, falls in love with her. A coward, Ernst resents his father, a virile lover, sportsman, and soldier, who urges him to "join in the chase"; sullenly, bitterly observing the masculine way of the frequenters of the Brauhaus, Ernst, too, wants to earn a place in Valhalla. When Cromwell, a friend of Herman, takes Stella home in a carriage, Ernst desperately runs after them. An English traitor, Cromwell admires the German spirit of nationalism, tradition of heroism, and ideals of conquest; he is eager to see it demonstrated in a prolonged war.

War begins the next day. Hawkes presents the members of Stella's family, including the children's nurse Gerta. The mother dislikes the world she sees, but the ninety-year-old father, a general, who is dying, shouts "War" at breakfast and "Victory" at noon, thinking the war is already over. Women and children, Hawkes shows, are the innocent victims of such insane masculinity: a lone British plane falls in the marketplace, and the mother is killed. Stella nurses the old general, who dies with his plumed helmet on his chest. Already prefigured in the death of Stella's parents, the decline of the German nation is symbolized by the death of the old horse that moves between the lower world of dogs and the upper world of the mountains where Stella and Ernst go on their honeymoon. A parallel to this old horse is the legless, headless statue of a horse in the square, a monument to the heroic past. When Cromwell arrives in the mountains, gleefully reciting the details of the war and praising the German troops, Ernst and Stella return to Stella's house; in her father's room, Ernst is dying of a fever.

A further suggestion of decline is Herman Snow's failure as a soldier and a lover; he encounters Gerta in the wreckage of the Brauhaus where she goes in the course of her promiscuous prowling among soldiers. Hawkes's montage method operates with great rapidity, shuttling back and forth over the ruined town (images of which are a mild foreshadowing of the devastation of World War II) between Gerta and Herman and Stella and Ernst; the strong women take care of the weak men. The role of coincidence in such a world is demonstrated when Gerta brings Herman to the very room where Stella is nursing Ernst. Herman, who had imagined in his own delirium of passing on to Ernst the spirit of love and war, accuses his son of "feigning."

At the conclusion of the 1914 section, Hawkes focuses on Jutta. A student of architecture when the war began, she has gone into a convent and is seriously ill with a fever; she is a victim of the stern love of the mother superior and is violated by the Ober-Lieutenant who is staying overnight at the convent. It is her vision of life that Hawkes would have readers see: not miraculous, yet clear; not right, though undeniable. The perspective on life that circumstances give these people is one divested of a moral dimension; it is simply clear (and by it readers see clearly and are terrified) and undeniable (though under "normal" circumstances one denies it daily to maintain a precarious sanity).

By returning, at the opening of part 3, to Zizendorf where he left him on the embankment of the Autobahn, Hawkes makes his structure comment thematically upon his raw material: the present encloses and carries forward the past. The bizarre parallels of nightmares pervade the novel, merging past and present. While the Duke pursues Jutta's son, Jutta, who has been taking care of the drunken Census-Taker, sleeps; but her little girl, Selvaggia, watches for her brother at the window. Passing through the sleeping mother's room, Herr Stintz finally goes to Selvaggia. Though his single eye is the threatening moon in whose glare all horror occurs, Selvaggia goes with him, and thus, like most Hawkes victims, collaborates in her own violation. He wants the child, who has been protected from the slaughter of the Allied offensive, to witness her father's, Zizendorf's, murder of Leevey; then Stintz intends to inform. While this psychological rape is going on, the Duke corners Jutta's son in a wrecked motion-picture theater, where Stella's son, who returned from the war with only one leg, lives with his wife; Stella's son is flattered by the Duke's visit. Before Zizendorf kills Leevey, Hawkes provides a long flashback to the day when the American colonel and Leevey first came to the town to execute Miller, the pastor who had changed his views during the war. Stintz, out of a motiveless malice, and the Mayor, from fear of the colonel, had cooperated: Zizendorf had been forced to join the firing squad, and it was his bullet that killed the pastor. Miller fell into the frozen canal, where his body thawed and bloated in the fog. It is appropriate that Zizendorf should begin his insurrection by killing a Jew. Hawkes, however, makes Leevey merely a simple soldier who says, "Hi ya, Mac," and wishes he were back in the delicatessen. When Jutta's husband was reported missing in Siberia, Zizendorf took over both Jutta and the editorship; Hawkes connects Zizendorf with the husband by having Jutta, seconds before Zizendorf kills Leevey, reread a letter in which her husband tells of shooting a Russian leader from his horse. After Leevey strikes the log in the road, Hawkes shifts back to the morning of his death when, ironically, he had lain with a vicious German girl who infected him with disease. With the insurrection under way, Hawkes has Stella, the strong woman whom Zizendorf admires, recall the riot in the insane asylum, a riot that began among the monkeys kept for experiments and spread to the psychopaths. Under Stella's leadership, it was the women, bereft of men, who put down the riot. The continuation of this ironic juxtaposition climaxes the book: with the institution of a new government, the insane people who have been at large return to the madhouse. Society's pathological drives are pushed underground once more, while their manifestations are worked out in various guises of normality until the nightmare of history visits again. Childhood fears, in Hawkes's prophetic vision, prove to refer to the childhood of the race which civilization never entirely outgrows.

When the riot began, Stella was strangling a mangy chicken under the gaze of Balamir, who had just escaped from the asylum. As the Duke hacks up the body of Jutta's son with a rusty sword cane as though the child were a fox, furious with himself for his lack of aristocratic finesse, Zizendorf tosses Leevey's body among countless other dead soldiers in the swamp; handbills inciting the people to rise up against the Allies are being printed in the chicken house behind Stella's place; Stella is nursing Balamir, who, ironically, is thinking of himself as the one who will free his people and rebuild the town; learning from Selvaggia of Stintz's betrayal, Zizendorf bludgeons him with the old man's tuba, carts the body to the Mayor's house, and sets fire to it, while the Mayor sleeps fitfully, as he has throughout the novel, afflicted with chronic nightmares of Miller. As Zizendorf goes to sleep with Jutta, Selvaggia, seeing the fire, stays awake with her fears. Stella accepts the Duke's invitation to dinner (she does not know that she will eat the body of her nephew whom she has rejected as having no resemblance to her aristocratic family); a few seconds later, Zizendorf's handbill invites her to kill Americans. Thus, she becomes one of the cannibals of her reverie in 1914. Ironically, the Duke is driven to the extreme act of cannibalism at that very moment when Zizendorf has succeeded (or so he is convinced) in restoring order and well-being; nor does the Duke know that Zizendorf has made him Chancellor; other "qualified" persons have been appointed to positions in the new government. Hawkes's irony asserts that Zizendorf's methods perpetuate and will ultimately reaffirm the kind of atrocity the Duke has committed, for the German (and in a sense all) national ego grows out of the carnage of its past wars. The piecemeal mutilation of Ernst in his bungling duels anticipate the butchering of Jutta's son; Ernst dies clutching one of the Christ figures carved by an old idiot in a shack near the mountain hotel. Men become Christs or cannibals.

The Cannibal is a short novel. It can be experienced in one sitting, just as one can suffer a nightmare in one sleeping. Yet, just as the aura of some nightmares persists throughout the day, this is a nightmare from which the reader, as cannibal, is a long time waking.

CASS TIMBERLANE

Type of work: Novel
Author: Sinclair Lewis (1885–1951)
Type of plot: Social criticism
Time of plot: 1940's
Locale: Grand Republic, Minnesota
First published: 1945

Principal characters:
CASS TIMBERLANE, a district judge
JINNY MARSHLAND TIMBERLANE, his wife
BRADD CRILEY, Jinny's lover

The Story:

After his divorce from his wife, Blanche, Judge Cass Timberlane continued to meet his old friends socially and to hold court in his usual honest and effective manner. It was not until Jinny Marshland appeared in his court as witness in a routine case, however, that Cass once more began to find his life interesting. Because Cass was forty-one and Jinny in her early twenties, he told himself that he was foolish to think of her in a romantic manner. Yet, in spite of his logical reasoning, Cass thought more and more about Jinny; and within a few days of their first meeting, he had arranged to see her again. Dignified Judge Cass Timberlane was falling in love.

He had no smooth romance. His friends thought him stupid to become involved with a young girl of the working class. It seemed strange to Cass that his friends would dare to criticize anyone. For example, there was Dr. Roy Drover, who openly made love to any and every cheap girl he met without bothering to conceal his infidelities from his wife. In the same class were Boone and Queenie Havock, both loud, brassy, and very vulgar; Jay Laverick, rich, lustful, and a drunkard; Bradd Criley, notorious for his affairs with the wives of his best friends. Cass Timberlane's friends were not the only ones opposed to the affair. Jinny's young radical friends thought Cass a stuffy conservative. The only two people who were sympathetic with Cass were Chris Grau, who also wanted to marry him, and Mrs. Higbee, his housekeeper.

What his friends thought of Jinny did not matter; it was what Jinny would think of them that worried Cass at the time of their marriage. After the honeymoon, they lived in his old family home, although Jinny would have preferred a new house in the country club section. They went out seldom, for they were happy enough to stay at home together. It was the first year of the war, and Jinny found work to do in various civic activities. Cass hoped

---

that the work would keep her stimulated. When he noticed that she was beginning to be bored by civic duties, he encouraged her to accept a part in a little theater production. Later, he was sorry that he had encouraged her, for the town began to talk about Jinny and various male members of the cast, particularly Jay Laverick. When Cass spoke to her about the gossip, Jinny accused him of being unreasonably jealous and then apologized. Cass loved her more than ever.

Cass sold some property at an unexpectedly high price and bought the new house that Jinny had desired in the country club district. While waiting for it to be finished, they took a trip to New York. At first, Jinny was enchanted with the size and brightness of the city, but soon she was bored by the unfriendliness of everyone she met until Bradd Criley arrived in New York and took them under his wing. Then Jinny enjoyed herself. Cass was not so happy.

Shortly after they returned home, they learned that Jinny was pregnant; but their happiness was marred by the knowledge that Jinny had diabetes. Roy Drover, her doctor, assured Cass that there was no cause for worry if Jinny followed her diet and got plenty of rest. Because Bradd Criley seemed to amuse her, Cass often invited him to the house.

Jinny went through her delivery safely, but the baby died. For many weeks afterward, she would see no one but Cass. Then she suddenly, for no apparent reason, wanted to have a party almost every night. Cass tried to be patient with her, for he knew that she was still reacting to the death of the baby and also that the restrictions placed on her by her illness were irritating. When his friends once again warned him about allowing Jinny to see so much of Bradd, his patience wore thin; he almost ordered Jinny to stop seeing Bradd, and he told Bradd to stay away from Jinny. Later, Bradd apologized to Cass and the three were friends once more. After Bradd moved to New York, all tension between Jinny and Cass seemed to disappear for a time. Then Jinny grew restless again and began to talk of moving to a larger city. Although Cass prized his judgeship and hated to give it up, he was still willing to do anything for his wife. They took another trip to New York, where Cass hoped to find a partnership in an established law firm. They met Bradd during their visit. Although he trusted his wife, Cass was relieved when Jinny told him that she knew she would not really like living in New York and that she wanted to go home. They left hurriedly, without seeing Bradd again before their departure.

On their first night at home, Jinny told Cass that she loved Bradd and that he had become her lover while she was in New York. When Cass refused to give her a divorce until she had had ample time to consider her own wishes carefully, she went back to New York to stay with Bradd's sister until Cass would free her. For Cass, the town, the house, his friends, and his work were now meaningless. He could think only of Jinny. Then he had a telegram from her. Failing to follow her diet, she was desperately ill, and she wanted Cass. He flew to New York that night. He found Jinny in a coma, but she awakened long enough to ask him to take her home.

After Jinny could be moved, Cass took her to a seashore hotel and then home. He had forgiven her completely, but he warned her that she would have to work hard to win back their friends. They still had to make their own private adjustment. It was not until Bradd returned to Grand Republic that Jinny was able to see him as the charming philanderer that he really was. That night, she went to Cass's room. He received her as if she had never been away.

Critical Evaluation:

Sinclair Lewis' turbulent career was reaching its end by the time he attempted this "novel of husbands and wives," one of the last of his many theme novels. *Cass Timberlane* is not one of Lewis' great works, but it is a good novel, conscientiously thought-out and well crafted. Written in 1945, the novel now has the feeling of a historical novel; its period, as portrayed by Lewis, seems quite as removed as that of the author's earlier novels *Main Street* or *Babbitt*. Perhaps this is partly because Lewis' famous ear was not as sharp as it once had been, and he used already dated slang, and satirized rather tired, well-used subjects. The novel presents a carefully thought-out (although sometimes obvious) dramatic structure. It might not be fair to say that the wheels are always visible as they turn in this novel, but sometimes they creak and groan a bit.

Lewis' technique is to establish a situation and then methodically follow it through the logical unraveling of the plot with few surprises. His satire is broad, not subtle, but often effective; his style of relentless irony is softened with a genuine good humor. Lewis has a sincere fondness for the Middle West about which he is writing and a true affection for his characters. The author does not penetrate very deeply into the minds and souls of his characters, but the people he chooses to write about do not possess complicated inner lives. He deliberately limits himself to the portrayal of certain superficial aspects of life.

Most of the people wandering through these pages are bored, but only half realize it. Lewis, in his etching of the triumphant, arrogant ignorance of many of his characters, achieves the difficult feat of writing interestingly about boredom. To be fair to Lewis, one should judge the novel against the author's intentions, and he did succeed effectively with what he set out to accomplish.

CATCH-22

Type of work: Novel
Author: Joseph Heller (1923–   )
Type of plot: Social satire
Time of plot: 1944
Locale: Pianosa, a mythical island eight miles south of Elba, and Rome,
   Italy
First published: 1961

   Principal characters:
      CAPTAIN JOHN YOSSARIAN, a United States Air Force
         bombardier
      COLONEL CATHCART, the group commander
      MAJOR MAJOR MAJOR, the 256th Squadron commander,
         who was promoted by an I.B.M. machine
      MAJOR _____ DE COVERLEY, the squadron executive
         officer whose first name nobody knows because no one
         has ever dared ask him
      LIEUTENANT MILO MINDBINDER, the mess officer, who
         turns black marketing into big business
      CAPTAIN BLACK, the squadron intelligence officer
      CHIEF WHITE HALFBOAT, an Indian from Oklahoma and
         the assistant intelligence officer
      DOC DANEEKA, the flight surgeon
      CAPTAIN R. O. SHIPMAN, the chaplain
      NURSE SUE ANN DUCKETT
      CLEVINGER,
      ORR,
      HAVERMEYER,
      KID SAMPSON,
      MCWATT,
      AARDVAARK (AARFY),
      HUNGRY JOE,
      DOBBS, and
      NATELY, pilots, bombardiers, and navigators of the 256th
         Squadron
      NATELY'S WHORE, who tries to kill Yossarian
      GENERAL DREEDLE, the wing commander
      GENERAL PECKEM, the commanding officer of Special
         Services
      EX-PFC WINTERGREEN, a goldbrick who controls 27th Air
         Force Headquarters because he sorts, and unofficially
         censors, all the mail

In 1961, the publication of *Catch-22* became an occasion for some rather free-wheeling critical acclaim. Many reviewers called it the best novel out of World War II, and at least one proclaimed it the best American novel out of anywhere in years. "Comic," "horrifying," "Rabelaisian," "exhilarating," "devastating," "rowdy," "cruelly sane," and "compellingly moving" were among the epithets used to describe Joseph Heller's rambunctious first novel. In short, the book got off the ground with all the speed and thrust of jet propulsion.

Some of this acclaim was probably a tribute to the author's daring and prodigality. At a time when most young writers appeared to be so obsessed by the idea of the well-made novel that their books tended to resemble carefully composed mood studies or tone poems, Heller broke all the rules. The energy and imagination he displays are determinants rather than coordinates in fiction. The simple truth is that *Catch-22* is somewhat less and something more than the conventional novel. As a novel, it is turgid, loose-jointed, and always threatening to break out at the seams. As a piece of writing, however, it is an altogether remarkable performance. Ferociously and bawdily funny in parts, banal in spots, fantastically gruesome at times, it achieves a lunatic identity and wild inner logic of its own. The book is what one might expect in a collaboration between Kafka and Krazy Kat, to which have been added dialogue passages by a Hemingwayesque master of speech patterns, some scatological scenes suggested by Henry Miller, hallucinated nonsense out of Lewis Carroll, and some chunks of the most undisciplined writing since Thomas Wolfe. It is not, as some critics have suggested, Mauldin's cartoons in prose or an American version of *The Good Soldier: Schweik*. It is a collage of wartime violence, sex, military snafu, black market dealing, hymns of hate, and guffaws of gutty humor.

The scenes shuttle back and forth between Pianosa, an imaginary Italian island where an Air Force bombing group is sweating out the closing months of World War II, and Rome, where the flyers go on leave to stage latter-day Roman orgies in that city filled with prostitutes. Men who behaved like madmen, as Heller notes, were awarded medals. In a world of madmen at war, the maddest—or the sanest—of all is Captain John Yossarian, a bombardier of the 256th Squadron. Deciding that death in war is a matter of circumstance and having no wish to be victimized by any kind of circumstance, he tries by every means he can think of—malingering, defiance, cowardice, irrational behavior—to get out of the war. That was his resolve after the disastrous raid over Avignon, when Snowden, the radio-gunner, was shot almost in two, splashing his blood and entrails over Yossarian's uniform and teaching the bombardier the cold, simple fact of man's mortality. For some time after that, Yossarian refused to wear any clothes, and when General Dreedle, the wing commander, arrived to award the bombardier a Distinguished Flying Cross for his heroism, military procedure was upset because Yossarian wore no uniform on which to pin the medal. Yossarian's logic of nonparticipation is so simple that everyone thinks him crazy, especially when he insists that "they" are trying to murder him. His insistence gets him into an argument with Clevinger, who is bright and always has an excuse or an explanation for everything. When Clevinger wants to know who Yossarian thinks is trying to murder him, the bombardier says that everyone of "them" is trying. Clevinger says that he has no idea who "they" can be. Yossarian then asks how he knows that "they" are not. Clevinger merely sputters.

Yossarian goes off to the hospital, complaining of a pain in his liver. If he has jaundice, the doctors will discharge him; if not, they will send him back to duty. Yossarian spends some of his time censoring the enlisted men's letters. To some, he signs Washington Irving's name as censor. On others, he crosses out the letter but adds loving messages signed by the chaplain's name. The hospital would have been a good place to stay for the rest of the war if it had not been for a talkative Texan and a patient so cased in bandages that Yossarian wondered at times whether there was a real body inside. When he returns to his squadron, he learns that Colonel Cathcart, the group commander, has raised the number of required missions to fifty. Meanwhile, Clevinger had dipped his plane into a cloud one day and never brought it out again. He and his plane simply vanished, and now he is not around the officers' club any longer to explain what had happened that time.

It is impossible for Yossarian to complete his tour of combat duty because, first, Colonel Cathcart wants to get his picture in *The Saturday Evening Post* and, second, to become a general. Consequently, he continues to increase the number of required missions for his outfit beyond those required by the 27th Air Force Headquarters. By the time he has set the number at eighty, Kraft, McWatt, Kid Sampson, and Nately are dead, Clevinger and Orr have disappeared, the chaplain has been disgraced (the C.I.D. accuses him of the Washington Irving forgeries), Aarfy has committed a brutal murder, Hungry Joe screams in his sleep night after night, and Yossarian is still looking for new ways to stay alive. It is also impossible for him to be sent home on medical relief because of Catch-22. As Doc Daneeka, the medical officer, explains, he can ground anyone who is crazy, but anyone who wants to avoid combat duty is not crazy; so he cannot be grounded. This is Catch-22, the inevitable loophole in the scheme of justice, the self-justification of authority, the irony of eternal circumstance. Catch-22 explains Colonel Cathcart, who continues to raise the number of missions and volunteers his men for every dangerous operation in the Mediterranean theater. He also plans to have prayers during every briefing session but gives up that idea when he learns that officers and enlisted men must pray to the same god. Catch-22 also explains the struggle for power between General Dreedle, who wants a fighting outfit, and General Peckem of Special Services, who wants to see tighter bombing patterns—they look better in aerial photographs—and issues a directive ordering all tents in the Mediterranean theater to be pitched with their fronts facing toward the Washington Monument. It explains Captain Black, the intelligence officer who compels the officers to sign a new loyalty oath each time they get their map cases, flak suits and parachutes, paychecks, haircuts, and meals in the mess. It explains, above all, Lieutenant Milo Mindbinder, the mess officer, who parlays petty blackmarket operations into an international syndicate in which every man, as he says, has a share. By the time he has his organization on a paying basis, he has been elected mayor of half a dozen Italian cities, Vice-Shah of Oran, Caliph of Baghdad, Imam of Damascus, and Sheik of Araby. Once he almost makes a mistake by cornering the market on Egyptian cotton, but after some judicious bribery, he unloads it on the United States government. The climax of his career comes when he rents his fleet of private planes to the Germans and from the Pianosa control tower directs the bombing and strafing of his own outfit. Men of public decency were outraged until Milo opened his books for public inspection and showed the profit he had made. Then everything was all right, for in the writer's strange, mad world, patriotism and profit are indistinguishable; the world lives by Milo's motto, the claim that whatever is good for the syndicate is good for the nation.

Eventually, Yossarian takes off for neutral Sweden, three jumps ahead of the authorities and less than one jump ahead of Nately's whore, who for some reason blames him for her lover's death and tries to kill him, but not before he has spent a night wandering alone through wartime Rome. This portion of the book is appalling in its picture of greed, lust, and brutality. *Catch-22* is a work reaffirming the ancient ties of cruelty and humor in its vision of everything vicious and absurd in our muddled society. Heller seems to say that, in this world, men of good will must either escape from reality or perish and that if this world is sane, then madness alone makes sense. Without being profound, Heller's novel is a work repudiating the world's values and society's behavior.

Despite its obvious flaws, *Catch-22* is brilliant, devastating, and apocalyptic. Since its publication, it has become a pivotal work in the contemporary literature of the absurd, which is sometimes, and somewhat inaptly, called black humor or bitter comedy. It is not, as is the case with novels of World War I, a story of initiation. In theme, fable, and mood, it deals with the simple, grim realities of survival in a world with all values reversed by the violence of war. As such, it is an assault, made in hilarious prose, on the mechanical, institutionalized, homogenized, anesthetized society in which we live. Black humor has as the objects of its guffawing satire the clichés of thought, feeling, and action that color almost every aspect of modern life, from stereotypes of love, home, religion, and death to the Bomb. If Heller's novel has an underlying purpose, it is to be found in the writer's apparent belief that a comic vision of experience and a sense of the outrageously absurd in human affairs provide the only possible stance for the rational man in a world in which the dividing line between graspable reality and wild fantasy has all but disappeared.

CEREMONY IN LONE TREE

Type of work: Novel
Author: Wright Morris (1910–   )
Type of plot: Psychological realism
Time of plot: One day in March, 1957
Locale: Acapulco, Mexico; Lincoln, Nebraska; and Lone Tree, Nebraska
First published: 1960

Principal characters:

GORDON BOYD, a middle-aged writer
DAUGHTER, his girlfriend
WALTER MCKEE, Boyd's boyhood friend and a cattle raiser
GORDON MCKEE, Walter's little grandson
LOIS MCKEE, Walter's wife, once in love with Boyd
TOM SCANLON, Lois' ninety-year-old father
CALVIN MCKEE, Scanlon's great-grandson
ETOILE MOMEYER, Calvin's cousin
MAXINE MOMEYER, Lois' sister
BUD MOMEYER, Maxine's husband, a mailman
LEE ROY MOMEYER, Bud's nephew
CHARLES MUNGER, a pathological killer
JENNINGS, a writer of pulp Westerns

In his first nine novels, Wright Morris processed fragments of a vision that focused on the American land, character, and dream. In *The Field of Vision*, the first novel of a trilogy, these fragments began to cohere. *Ceremony in Lone Tree* is the second novel in the trilogy.

Morris' usual method has three phases: he describes the scene; next, he conducts a roundup of the characters; then, he depicts a kind of ceremony that serves to establish significant relationships and to evoke transient moments of self-knowledge which cause a faint transformation in the characters.

Through a flawed pane of glass in the hotel lobby, old Tom Scanlon gazes upon Lone Tree, Nebraska, a ghost town; his view is to the west over the arid plains; but to the east, the prairie town of Polk prospers. Morris describes "The Scene" in such a way as to suggest his themes and to convey an impression of the spiritual desolation of his characters. The ancestors of the old Western pioneers have now turned eastward again. Having no perspective on the present, Scanlon's point of view is restricted to the wasteland; for the rest of the novel, Morris pushes the old man into the background; during "The Ceremony," he sleeps on a cot behind the stove.

In *Ceremony in Lone Tree*, Morris exhibits most impressively his talent for creating people who illustrate aspects of the American character; if they appear grotesque, they may prove to be similar to the folks next door. In "The Roundup," Morris presents each character in a separate section of his own. Boyd, a self-exiled Nebraska writer, approaches the homeplace from Acapulco, where he has been trying to forget an encounter with his childhood friends, Walter and Lois McKee, at a bullfight in Mexico City. When McKee impulsively invites him to a reunion in honor of Tom Scanlon's ninetieth birthday, Boyd is drawn by perverse nostalgia. To shock the folks back home, he takes with him a woman whom he calls Daughter; audacious, youthful spirit of the present, she sustains him during his journey into the past. Next come the viewpoints of McKee and Lois, who approach Lone Tree from the modern city of Lincoln, Nebraska. McKee has lived his empty life vicariously through Boyd, hoping the hero will fill it with meaning. Lois, the opposite of Daughter, epitomizes the suppression of emotions that make everyone tense and nervous. Characters not presented in *The Field of Vision* appear next. Maxine Momeyer has a difficult life; her daughter, Etoile, is sexually precocious, and her husband, Bud, has never grown up; when he goes off duty as a mailman, he collects bounty on stray cats by shooting them with a bow and arrow. Etoile is in love with her stuttering cousin Calvin, who rejects people in favor of horses. Events in the present occur within the frame of a recent incident that shocked the world: the slaughter of ten people by Charles Munger of Lincoln, while his friend, Lee Roy, Bud's nephew, killed two bullies with his hot rod. Jennings, who writes pulp Westerns, is so intrigued by the mystery of life that he has no life of his own. Boyd wonders whether he is drawn to these people because they are so hopeless or so full of hope.

Because there are nine viewpoints, with twenty-eight shifts, unity could have become a problem for Morris, but it is maintained by a controlling conception, by various patterns of relationship among the characters, and by a consistency of style among the viewpoints—a sophisticated manipulation of the clichés of everyday speech, as filtered through the third person. The tone is comic, but Morris' mingling of the bizarre and the humorous creates a strange atmosphere in which the comedy frightens as it amuses. In the absence of an overt pattern of novelistic action, the relationships among the characters generate suspense and excitement by the controlled development of their many twists and turns, nuances, suppressions, and flare-ups. To common situations, past and present, the characters' differing responses are always active, creating an impressive sense of motion. In ways representative of Morris, character, theme, and motif evolve organically as the novel moves to its climax.

Like a ghost-town motion-picture set, the Lone Tree Hotel inspires the enactment of an outdated drama, the personae of which include Buffalo Bill, Billy the Kid, Santa Claus, Charles Lindbergh, Robin Hood, and Davy Crockett; shifting from one to another, most of the men play roles whose styles were shaped in the American past; less inclined to play roles, the women lament the failure of the men to make something real happen in the present. Nothing is what it seems because the characters are disposed to see anything suggested to them; what is there (fact) is no more vivid than what the mind can project (fiction). In the rhetoric of magic, the effect is that of "now you see it, now you don't." Just as Bud's attic and basement are full of the junk he collects from people on his mail route, each character is a repository of cast-off lives; though Lee Roy can make one smoothly running car out of many wrecked ones, a human may break down if he is a composite of other people with no strong self-nucleus. Boyd is like a carnival barker, talking about freaks who try, in an exaggerated way, to be what they are not.

Trains, cars, bombs, and guns are other outward, material symbols of the American experience and of the personalities of the characters. The plains are like the sea, and everything seems to move like ships over a metaphysical landscape. Experience has blended and blurred fact and fiction, nourishing illusions that aggravate the problem of identity. In Lone Tree, where moonlight illuminates the romance and the nostalgia of the past and real events have an aura of the imaginary, the characters behave as though they are in a motion picture and thus free of responsibility, but they experience disillusionment and nausea in the present. In the foreground, Morris presents a parody of American popular culture, but in the background hovers the image of the atomic bomb; near the end, past fiction and present fact collide in the lives of the characters and either wake them or lull them to sleep.

To Morris, the suppression of emotion is a trait in the American character; emotion is released vicariously in unconscious parodies of violence. By suddenly expressing their suppressed emotions, Lee Roy and Charles Munger exemplify themes that relate less drastically to the other characters. Though the spirit of the times helped make them what they are, their audacity differs from Boyd's, and their violence contrasts with that of the old frontier. In Munger, Morris shows an exaggeration of the nightmare side of the American Dream of success: the boy shoots everybody he encounters in order to be somebody. Fear of themselves and of one another, of Munger and his kind, and of atomic annihilation keep the characters tense, but responsive to the unexpected.

In quiet, "normal," even prudish people, Morris suggests, there is an inherent wildness. Giving in to impulse by word or act, each character has a moment of truth, audacity, love, or imagination in which he tastes wildness and freedom. Smothered in Maxine, sexuality breathes deeply in Etoile. Boyd's presence stimulates each character to reveal himself. The reader follows a spontaneous ceremony in which characters rid themselves of the inessentials of the past, improvising upon new personalities. Before the explosion of the bomb (made up of the convergence of lines of tension among the characters), Boyd clowns and indulges in an outburst against the concealment of true feelings. He is, however, made speechless by the behavior of his old witnesses. Ironically, only Boyd and Scanlon, heroes of the past, fail to act audaciously.

The confrontation of the present with the past is dramatized in the most highly charged of the concentrated moments of which the novel is composed. When Etoile and Calvin roar into the ghost town in a wagon, a dead show dog in back, shot by Bud with his bow and arrow, Boyd's audacity finally affects Lois; she fires her grandfather's Colt .45 as an impulsive act that rouses her from emotional stultification and sets off a beneficial chain reaction among the other characters. Symbolically, she kills her father and the mythic past represented by his father's pistol. Now the past has come full circle. Scanlon's birthday is his death day, but it is also the birth of the present for the others. In the wagon in which he was born, old Scanlon is taken to be buried. Morris, however, does not allow this sensational event to jar the primary focus, which is on character consciousness; he goes back to points before the incident and presents it over again through several other points of view.

Ceremony in Lone Tree is a continuation of Morris' exploration of the male-female conflict. Having waited long enough for the men to break up the routine and monotony of their lives, the women act. From a ceremony of death, they try to salvage something for the living. In control, the women will build on the ruins created by the sleeping males.

The relationship between a hero and his witnesses, developed in most of Morris' previous novels, ends in *Ceremony in Lone Tree*. Boyd has always tried, like America, to be more than he is, prompted by his witnesses who have always hoped for something to live by. Between the promise of the amateur and the performance of the master something more than audacity is demanded. Boyd once attempted to walk on water; later, he wrote a book about the incident. Yet in his audacity there is no longer an element of spontaneity and surprise, for after Boyd squirts a bull with pop in Mexico, McKee can anticipate the hero's antics. At the end, Boyd, trapped in his own childhood (in a sense he never left the plains), is asleep at the feet of Scanlon, dead embodiment of the heroic past, while McKee, the disenchanted witness, holds the reins; as they move over a landscape that was once arid plains, McKee gazes over the green wheat of the present, which promises a future unbeguiled by men like Boyd. The present eludes the hero; only the past has pattern. From childhood, he has, as Lois knows, put the later appreciation before the immediacy of the moment. If the kiss Boyd gave her on the porch thrilled Lois, it was the audacity of his own act that charmed Boyd. Lois senses that Boyd's audacity was camouflage, that he was as much afraid of her as McKee was. She sees that Boyd, McKee, and her father have not grown up. Like America itself, they are still adolescent. Hero Boyd and witness McKee begin to merge, but it is not clear whether the virtues and the faults of the two roles will make an effective blend. Having discovered that it gives off no charge in the present, Boyd is free of the past, but he has as yet no indication of a future.

In the behavior of his characters, Morris depicts a conflict between the American past and present; the future is both promising and ominous. His purpose is to free his characters from the past. Concerned almost entirely with immediate or recent happenings, many seem unaware of their captivity in the distant past. Present and past coexist: a fossil himself, Scanlon recalls the exploration of the Western frontier, while overhead a jet crosses the face of the moon. The past is dead, and the present is dying because America has failed to realize its promise and now lives in fear of fallout.

The real reason for the reunion is to get Calvin and Etoile together. On the landscape where things began and are now coming to an end, perhaps something can begin for the young lovers. Calvin is trapped in Scanlon's past (which is purely imaginary, for he has confused his father's past with his own uneventful one). Etoile, however, lives in her own present, eager to precipitate the future. The new generation transforms the past with new forms of audacity. Etoile is Lois' opposite; with Boyd-like audacity, she frees Calvin from the sexual restraint that has prevailed in the past; because the female seizes the day, Calvin experiences with Etoile what Boyd failed to experience with Lois. In the end, when the past and the present confront each other and explode, it is not clear who gains or loses, but the implication is that the ground is cleared, even though none of the younger generation seems promising material out of which to process a meaningful future.

THE CHAINBEARER
Or, The Littlepage Manuscripts

Type of work: Novel
Author: James Fenimore Cooper (1789–1851)
Type of plot: Historical romance
Time of plot: About 1785
Locale: Upstate New York
First published: 1845

Principal characters:

> MORDAUNT LITTLEPAGE, the narrator, who is a young landowner
> ANDRIES COEJEMANS, an old woodsman and surveyor, called Chainbearer
> URSULA MALBONE, his half sister's orphan daughter, called Dus
> FRANK MALBONE, her half brother
> CORNELIUS LITTLEPAGE and
> ANNEKE LITTLEPAGE, Mordaunt's parents
> KATE, Mordaunt's sister
> TOM BAYARD, Kate's fiancé
> PRISCILLA BAYARD, his sister
> JAAP, Mordaunt's black servant
> SUSQUESUS (TRACKLESS), an Indian friend of the Littlepages
> JASON NEWCOME, the squire at Ravensnest
> AARON TIMBERMAN, a squatter and timberman, called Thousandacres
> LOWINY, his daughter
> TOBIT and
> ZEPHANAIAH, two of his sons
> DIRCK FOLLOCK, Cornelius Littlepage's friend

The Story:

Mordaunt Littlepage, son of Cornelius Littlepage, of Satanstoe, was at Princeton for six years studying for his bachelor of arts degree during most of the Revolutionary War. Upon graduation, he served in his father's battalion at the siege of Yorktown and there met sixty-seven-year-old Captain Andries Coejemans, a skilled woodsman and known as Chainbearer because he carried the forward chain in the surveying work he did as a civilian. Mordaunt attained the rank of captain by the time of Cornwallis' surrender.

Mordaunt formed a strong attachment to the hale old man, and at the close of the war, Chainbearer suggested that Mordaunt meet Dus Malbone, his orphaned niece. The captain thought that she would make a fine wife for his young friend, but Mordaunt, determined to remain unattached, returned home. Chainbearer went back to his civilian occupation, which was considered an ordinary laboring job.

Traveling back to Lilacsbush, Mordaunt and his aged servant, Jaap, were low in funds because by that time the continental currency was practically worthless. On one occasion, they stopped at an inn where Jaap performed and collected plenty of money for their lodging. After stopping at Lilacsbush, Mordaunt and Kate, his youngest sister, rode on to Satanstoe to visit their grandmother. During the ride, Kate told Mordaunt that she hoped to marry Tom Bayard, whom they would meet at Satanstoe, where he was visiting with his sister Priscilla, Kate's good friend. Kate had hoped that Mordaunt would fall in love with Priscilla. Mordaunt's grandmother was also conniving to have him fall in love with Priscilla Bayard.

Mordaunt found that Priscilla, as beautiful and intelligent as his sister had promised, was outspoken in her independence and also free in her opinions, which always found Mordaunt in perfect agreement. Tom, her brother, was rather conservative in his beliefs, but Tom and Mordaunt respected each other. Mordaunt readily gave his consent to his sister's marriage.

After a short time, Mordaunt announced that he was going to travel to Ravensnest, land that his grandfather, Herman Mordaunt, had left him, and that he was to be gone for the entire winter. Before they parted, however, Mordaunt learned that Priscilla was a schoolfriend of Dus, Chainbearer's niece, and had the highest opinion of her. The two discussed the qualities of Dus and Chainbearer, who had been hired to contract for all the surveying work at Ravensnest.

Mordaunt went with Jaap to Ravensnest. It was to be Mordaunt's first visit to the wilderness tract. Jaap had been there several times previously with Mordaunt's father. Chainbearer was already on the ground and surveying the land into small plots for rental. At the Bridge Inn, it was learned that he was working with Dus and her half brother, Frank Malbone. Before reaching Ravensnest, Mordaunt heard a beautiful Indian song sung as he learned later, by Dus, and he met Susquesus, a faithful Indian hunter who had served Mordaunt's father years before. Susquesus was a good friend of old Chainbearer.

Putting on clothes less fitting a gentleman, Mordaunt and the Indian went to Ravensnest village to learn something of the people there. He learned that a town meeting had been called, with Squire Jason Newcome presiding. Newcome, a powerful and highly respected man, prodded the crowd to vote for the erection of a Congregational rather than a Presbyterian church. Mordaunt watched the proceedings with contempt. The men of the town raised the pikepoles of the church with the help of a girl who, Mordaunt later learned, was Dus.

Chainbearer welcomed Mordaunt to Ravensnest and took him to the hut where he lived when he was not surveying. There Mordaunt met Dus formally. She seemed ashamed to meet him and said that she had been working with her uncle; she considered herself below Mordaunt because of her work. Mordaunt convinced her that she was his equal.

Mordaunt made Frank Malbone his agent, replacing Squire Newcome, who had proved himself untrustworthy. This work assured Frank of a good living. Newcome was given a new rental lease to which, it was explained, he had no right other than the liberality of his landlord.

When Chainbearer took Mordaunt to see the land he had surveyed, Dus accompanied them. By that time, Mordaunt had fallen in love with her, as he told her one evening. Dus answered that her affections were tied to another. Mordaunt left the hut and that night slept on the open ground.

The next morning, Mordaunt found Susquesus camped nearby. The Indian brought word that a hidden sawmill was being illegally operated on Littlepage land. Following his guide, Mordaunt came upon Aaron Timberman's sawmill, called Thousandacres. Not knowing that his white visitor was Mordaunt Littlepage, Thousandacres welcomed him. Later, Mordaunt made himself known and was thrown, a prisoner, into the storehouse. Susquesus made his escape, however, and informed Jaap of Mordaunt's capture before returning to aid the prisoner. Captured by several of Thousandacre's sons, the Indian was also imprisoned in the storehouse. Meanwhile, Mordaunt learned that Thousandacres and his sons, Tobit and Zephanaiah, like most squatters, would have nothing to do with the law. Lowiny, the daughter, proved friendly to Mordaunt and did not think that he should be kept a prisoner. From his place of confinement, Mordaunt watched Squire Newcome visit the mill and offer to buy the timber at a lower price than Thousandacres demanded, for, as Newcome insisted, the Littlepages were sure to discover the mill before long. Thousandacres sent Newcome away as soon as possible.

That night, Lowiny came to the storehouse bringing food. The next morning, Chainbearer appeared and, while trying to open the door of the storehouse, was seized and confined with Mordaunt and Susquesus. Dus, hiding nearby, sent Zephanaiah a letter saying that she would not now have him as a husband.

At a family council, Thousandacres tried to bargain with Chainbearer, but the old man refused to be disloyal to the Littlepage family. Thousandacres then threw Chainbearer back into the storehouse, leaving Mordaunt in the house with Lowiny. While her father and brothers were occupied, the girl helped him to escape. Thousandacres, looking for Mordaunt, found him with Dus, who had just confessed her love to him. Returning to the clearing, Dus was held in the house, and Mordaunt was returned to the storehouse.

At another family gathering, to which Mordaunt and Chainbearer were summoned, Thousandacres attempted to coerce Dus into marrying Zephanaiah. Dus refused, however, and Chainbearer became extremely angry at the suggestion. As the angry old man, his arm around Dus, tried to leave the room, someone fired a shot and Chainbearer fell, mortally wounded. Chainbearer, dying on the bed to which he had been carried, said that death was not a bad thing. He told Dus and Mordaunt, who sat by his bedside, that they must follow whatever course their hearts directed, even though he felt that Dus should not marry above her station.

Suddenly, rifle shots sounded outside. Frank Malbone, informed by Jaap of his master's capture, had arrived at the head of a rescuing posse. During the attack, Thousandacres was mortally wounded. His son and the other squatters fled into the forest. Thousandacres was given a respectable burial, and his widow was allowed to remove her personal possessions from the cabin. Lowiny, who had been friendly with Dus, decided to stay with her.

The business of the squatters settled, Chainbearer's body was taken back to Ravensnest for burial. There they found Kate, Tom, and Priscilla Bayard, and Mordaunt's parents, who had come to pay tribute to Chainbearer after receiving news of his death. Chainbearer was buried with simple but sincere dignity and honor.

Dus, introduced to the Littlepages and now convinced that she was their equal, agreed to marry Mordaunt. Lowiny decided to live with them and serve as their maid. Priscilla Bayard found herself attracted to Frank Malbone, and later they decided to get married. Susquesus, amply supplied by the Littlepages, continued to live at Ravensnest. Jaap, who had become the Indian's good friend, decided to stay with him. The two lived happily together for many years.

Squire Newcome continued his knavery. In the end, however, he died poor and in debt. Mordaunt and Dus had a happy marriage, and they had a child within a year. Feeling deeply indebted to Chainbearer for their happiness, the Littlepages erected a monument at his grave. From then on, he was known as Uncle Chainbearer, and his friends always remembered him with affection.

Critical Evaluation:

For his trilogy, The Littlepage Manuscripts, James Fenimore Cooper took his cue from a contemporary controversy which had its roots in the eighteenth century. Centered in north-central New York state, the Anti-Rent movement, as the controversy was called, stemmed from a conflict between the feudal-agrarian practices established by eighteenth century landowners and perpetuated by their heirs, on the one hand, and the democratic-industrial demands of tenants on the other. The issue was joined in the early 1840's when landowners refused tenants' requests to abolish feudal rents required in perpetuity. A tenants' rebellion, the Anti-Rent War, was put down by troops; but in 1846, the new state constitution prohibited landlords from imposing perpetual dues or services when selling or leasing land.

Cooper's trilogy, published in 1845 and 1846 at the culmination of the controversy, traces three generations of a landowning family, the Littlepages, from the eighteenth century Cornelius Littlepage in *Satanstoe*, through Mordaunt Littlepage of *The Chainbearer*, to the nineteenth century Hugh Littlepage of *The Redskins*. The first of these novels focuses on the Littlepage estate at Satanstoe in Westchester County, New York, and the last, on the Littlepage confrontation with Anti-Rent agitators disguised as Indians. The second novel suggests by its title that attention will center on the Dutchman Andries Coejemans, called Chainbearer. The tale, however, is cast in first-person narrative, the story being told by Mordaunt Littlepage.

The limitations of this narrative form are thus the limitations of *The Chainbearer* as a novel. In order to avoid straining the reader's credulity, Littlepage can report only what he has seen, what has been said to him, or what he has read, overheard, or found accidentally; he cannot tell about things he could or should not know, and he cannot read the minds of other characters. Consequently, the very form of the novel mandates that more be revealed about the narrator Mordaunt Littlepage than about the putative protagonist, Chainbearer. The narrator must be fully developed as a character at the expense of other characters' development. Yet, the epic scope of the trilogy is made coherent by its concentration on the Littlepage family, so *The Chainbearer* can hardly be faulted for spotlighting Mordaunt Littlepage.

The advantages of first person narrative offset many of its limitations: the eyewitness account enhances credibility, and the directness of communication creates a high degree of sympathy between narrator and reader. The result, in *The Chainbearer*, is that the reader tends to sympathize with Mordaunt Littlepage and by extension with the position of the landowners against the Anti-Renters. Still, such sympathy is a function of form rather than ideology; ideology, however, affects characterization. For the unreconstructibly romantic Cooper, characters were either noble in mind and beneficent in spirit (Mordaunt Littlepage and Chainbearer, for example) or petty in mind and mean in spirit (particularly Thousandacres), in a stark juxtaposition of good and evil. Despite so simplistic a moral viewpoint—and despite the liabilities inherent in the narrative form—Cooper has nevertheless produced an exciting adventure story worthy of more attention than it has received.

CHILDREN OF GOD

Type of work: Novel
Author: Vardis Fisher (1895–1968)
Type of plot: Historical chronicle
Time of plot: 1820–1890
Locale: New York, Illinois, and Utah
First published: 1939

> Principal characters:
> JOSEPH SMITH, the founder of the Church of Latter-day
>   Saints
> BRIGHAM YOUNG, the leader of the Church after Smith's
>   death
> JOHN TAYLOR, a later leader of the Mormon Church

The Story:

In the early 1820's, a young man in Palmyra, New York, had visions that led him to believe himself a prophet of the Lord. The young man was Joseph Smith and his visions were the basis upon which he built the Church of Jesus Christ of Latter-day Saints, more commonly known as the Mormon Church. In those days, his followers were few, being only his family and a handful of friends.

In March of 1830, the *Book of Mormon* was published. Shortly after it appeared, Joseph Smith ordained his brothers and the men of the Whitmer family as Latter-day Saints. After Joseph was reported to have cast out the personal devil of a man called Newel Knight, word of the miracle spread about the country near Palmyra and many people were converted.

With success came trouble, however, as on one occasion a mob of men almost lynched the new prophet. On another, he was taken to court for trial. He realized that his life was no longer safe in the state of New York.

Joseph's three hundred followers left New York State for Ohio. Meanwhile, Joseph sent two men, one of them Oliver Cowdery, his first convert, to travel beyond the Mississippi River for the purpose of converting the Indians and locating the place where the Saints were to build their Zion. In Ohio, Joseph Smith was again persecuted. One winter night, a mob abducted him from his house and tarred and feathered him. Shortly afterward, Joseph decided to take his flock to Missouri, and he went with a few of his followers to survey the country.

More trouble awaited him when he returned to Ohio. Several of his converts had set themselves up as prophets during his absence. Reports reached him that the people he had left in Missouri were being mobbed. Then one day, two men came to offer their services to Joseph Smith. One was Brigham Young, the other Heber Kimball. Brigham Young was a great help to the Saints' community because he could make men do what he wished, something that Joseph Smith, the mystic, was never able to learn.

While the Saints in Ohio were facing internal strife, the people of the new faith in Missouri were being horsewhipped, murdered, and driven from their homes by mobs. Eventually, Brigham Young was authorized to organize an army to march upon Missouri and rescue the Mormons there. At the last minute, Joseph Smith went with the army as its leader. The expedition was doomed to failure. Cholera and Indians took their toll among the men. They never fought the Missouri mobs.

For the next few years, the Latter-day Saints prospered in Ohio. Joseph Smith and Brigham Young opened a Mormon-operated bank, which failed, along with many others, in the panic of 1837. The loss of their money turned the Latter-day Saints against their leaders as nothing else had done, and Brigham Young and Joseph Smith fled to Missouri for their lives. They were soon joined by three hundred families from Ohio, who remained true to Joseph's religion and prophetic power.

In Missouri, mobs again harassed their settlements. The desperate Latter-day Saints organized a retaliating secret society called the Danites or Destroying Angels. Finally the governor of Missouri ordered all the Mormons to leave the state or be killed. Again, Joseph Smith and his leaders were tried for treason. Through a friendly guard, they escaped execution.

The Latter-day Saints settled next at Nauvoo, in Illinois, where Joseph Smith began the practice of plural marriages in an effort to keep the women in the church, who outnumbered the men, from becoming charity cases or harlots. Joseph himself soon had twenty wives. His first wife, Emma, made him send away all but two.

Joseph Smith never left Illinois. He was killed by a mob when he gave himself up to stand trial for treason a third time. Brigham Young then took over the leadership of the Mormons, not as a prophet, but as a leader. He decided that the only way for the Mormons to find peace was to leave the United States, to seek a place in the far West.

Trudging westward through the snow, three thousand Mormons started out under Young's leadership. Those left behind felt lost without their leader and soon there were fifteen thousand more people following Young westward.

In the spring of 1847, Brigham Young set out from his winter camp for the Rocky Mountains with a hundred and fifty selected men. The others were to follow later. Young had determined to settle south of the salt lake in Utah. By the winter of 1847, seventeen hundred Mormons were already in Utah. When Young learned that the Utah territory had been ceded to the United States by Mexico, he felt that the Mormons would never have a land of their own. The next winter, five thousand of the Mormons lived through a year of intense cold and starvation rations. The third year in Utah brought a new problem to Brigham Young. California gold attracted thousands of rascals and adventurers, many of whom passed through the settlement of the Mormons on their way to the coast. These scoundrels stole from the scanty stores of the settlers and made trouble among the women.

As the years passed, the Latter-day Saints flourished. Brigham Young was elected governor of the Utah Territory. In 1852, he took a bold step when he announced publicly what many people had long known or at least suspected: the practice of polygamy by the leaders of the Mormon Church. The hue and cry against the practice amazed and embittered Young, for he could say truthfully that it had maintained morality in the Mormon settlements.

In 1855, locusts demolished their crops. Many of the Latter-day Saints turned against the practice of polygamy, for in times of famine a man could not secure enough food for his overexpanded family.

Two years later, the Mormons heard that the Federal government had sent an army to deal with them. From their previous experiences, the Mormons knew they could expect little mercy. The territorial governor sent by the president was vigorously defied, and the Mormons threatened to burn Salt Lake City and leave the country a desert as they had found it. Finally, the president sent a pardon to the Mormons.

With General Grant in the White House, the Mormon problem again became a pressing one. Federal prosecutors invoked the antibigamy law and began to imprison Mormon leaders. Then the prosecutors attempted to indict the leaders, including Brigham Young, for murder. Young was never tried, however, for he died of natural causes.

After Young's death, the authorities secured more indictments in the hope that the Mormons would repudiate polygamy. They also moved against the cooperative stores and industries, which had been founded, and attempted to deprive the Mormon Church of all assets in excess of fifty thousand dollars. The sum of those strains was too great. The president of the Mormon Council denounced plural marriages. No longer could the Mormon community hold itself apart in order to continue its existence. The Latter-day Saints and the settlers from the East would live side by side in the new state of Utah.

Critical Evaluation:

It was perhaps inevitable that Vardis Fisher should attempt writing of the saga of the Mormons, for his own parents came from Mormon converts who went West with Joseph Smith. Despite much repetition, this Harper Prize novel of 1939 bursts with great vividness, especially in the mob scenes. The writing of this long novel was an enormous task, but Fisher managed to bring to the book a message of dedication rarely equaled.

Fisher's serviceable prose methodically draws a picture of the origins of the Latter-day Saints and their efforts to overcome prejudice in nineteenth century America. The scale of the narrative is grand, but Fisher does not penetrate to the depths of his characters' personalities or do more than suggest their private torments. Yet he is able through sheer energy to give the reader the feeling of a continent opening up and a people growing and affirming their newly won ambitions and dreams.

The leaders of Mormonism are revealed in their imperfections as well as greatness. The stubborn strengths of Joseph Smith and Brigham Young dominate the story. Whatever the reader feels about the mission or morals of these two men, he comes away from the book with a profound respect for their power of endurance and supreme dedication. The epic of the Mormons is presented here with all the pain and horror of history. One feels that Fisher meant this book to be more than a conventional historical romance.

Fisher tends to overexplain when he should be content to suggest, but the story is so interesting that the book maintains a steady pace as it follows the beginnings of Mormonism to the end of the first half-century of its existence. Perhaps the author was too concerned with appearing impartial to create a first-rate novel.

CHITA
A Memory of Last Island

Type of work: Novel
Author: Lafcadio Hearn (1850–1904)
Type of plot: Exotic romance
Time of plot: Nineteenth century
Locale: Louisiana coastal waters
First published: 1889

Principal characters:
FELIU VIOSCA, a fisherman
CARMEN VIOSCA, his wife
CHITA, a foundling
DR. JULIEN LA BRIERRE, her father

The Story:

Southward from New Orleans one passes settlements of many nationalities and races, Western and Oriental. Beyond lies an archipelago, the islands of which are Grande Pass, Grande Terre, and Barataria. Still to the south lies Grande Isle, a modern bathing resort, the loveliest island in the Gulf of Mexico. Last Island, forty miles west of Grande Isle, is now desolate, but at an earlier time it was the most popular of the group and a fashionable resort. The hotel there was a two-story timber structure with many apartments, a dining room, and a ballroom. One night the sea destroyed it.

On the northwest side of each island are signs of the incessant influence of the wind and sea, for the trees all bend away from the water. All along the Gulf coast, and on the island beaches, are the ruins of hurricanes, skeletons of toppled buildings, and broken tree trunks. The land itself is being eaten away.

The innocent beauty of summer on these islands is impossible to express. Years ago, Last Island was immersed in the azure light of a typical July. It was an unusually lovely summer and the breathless charm of the season lingered on. One afternoon, the ocean began to stir and great waves started to hurl themselves over the beaches, giving warning on Last Island that a hurricane was brewing. The wind, beginning to blow, continued for a few days to stir the water. A steamer, the *Star*, due that day, was not expected to arrive.

Captain Abraham Smith, an American, knew the sea, and he knew his ship. Sensing that he might be needed, he had sailed for Last Island. As he approached, he saw the storm rising. He ordered the excess weight of the *Star* tossed overboard to help her ride out the storm. On the island, however, the guests at the hotel continued to dance until they noticed water at their feet, and the building began to be buffeted by the waves. Captain Smith spent the night rescuing as many as he could. Buildings were ripped apart, the shores were lashed by wind and wave, lakes and rivers overflowed, and by daybreak countless corpses floated on the stormy sea.

When the hurricane subsided, scavengers came to claim whatever plunder could be salvaged from the ruins and from the bodies of the dead.

On a tiny volcanic island lived Feliu Viosca, a fisherman, and his wife Carmen. On the night of the terrible storm, Carmen was awakened by the noise. Afraid, she aroused her husband, whose calmness comforted her, and he ordered her to return to sleep. In her dreams, her dead child, dark-eyed Conchita, came to her.

The next day the fishermen, gathered at the shore, stood watching the wreckage and the bodies floating past. A flash of yellow caught Feliu's eye. In a moment, he had stripped and was swimming out toward a child, still alive, clinging to her drowned mother. Feliu managed to rescue the baby and swim back to shore.

The half-drowned child was taken to Carmen, whose skillful hands and maternal instincts nursed the little girl into a warm, sound sleep; there was hope she would survive. Her yellow hair had saved her, for it was the flash of sun on her tresses that had caught Feliu's eye.

Captain Harris, of New Orleans, along with several other men, was sailing up and down the coast in search of missing persons, dead or still alive after the storm. Ten days after the rescue of the girl, Harris came to Viosca's wharf. Hardly able to communicate with the men, Feliu told them the story of his heroism but cautioned them that if they wished to question the child, they must proceed gently, since she was still not fully recovered from shock.

The child's Creole dialect was not comprehensible to anyone there until Laroussel, a Creole, began to question her. In her broken speech, she told him that her Creole name was Zouzoune, her real one Lili. Her mother was called Adele and her father Julien. Nothing more could be determined. Realizing that the child's relatives might never be found, Harris decided to leave her with Feliu and Carmen, who promised to give her excellent care. Laroussel gave the little girl a trinket that had caught her eye. Although other searching parties stopped to see Feliu's waif, the child's identity remained a mystery. Meanwhile, near another island, a pair of bodies drifting in the sea had been identified as those of Dr. Julien La Brierre and his wife Adele. The doctor had survived, however; six months later, he was in New Orleans looking at his own epitaph and that of his wife.

Dr. La Brierre had grown up in New Orleans. In maturity, to please his father, he had studied medicine in Paris. After his return to New Orleans, he had fallen in love and had been wounded in a duel with a rival named Laroussel. Following the death of his father and mother, Julien had married Adele, and their child Zouzoune was born.

On the lonely island, the small child, now called Chita, had become a member of the Viosca family. Gradually, she adapted herself to the ways of her foster parents.

Years later, Dr. La Brierre was practicing in New Orleans, a lonely and kindly physician. One year, an elderly patient of his, named Edwards, went to Viosca's Point, which Captain Harris had recommended for the sick man's recovery. While there, Edwards suffered a stroke. Hurriedly summoned, Dr. La Brierre arrived too late to help his patient.

Before the doctor could set out for home, he too became ill. Carmen nursed him. In the vague consciousness that accompanied his malady, the doctor saw Chita, whose resemblance to his dead wife greatly excited him. In his delirium, he called out to Zouzoune and Adele, while Carmen tried to calm him.

Reliving the horror of the hurricane that had taken Adele and Zouzoune from him, the sick man died.

Critical Evaluation:

Despite its graphic rendering of a devastating hurricane, *Chita* is not a Naturalistic novel with a storm for its "hero." Although Lafcadio Hearn was attracted by Herbert Spencer's evolutionary philosophy and read Darwin avidly, his destiny was not to join the rising school of American Naturalism descending from Crane and Norris to Dreiser. Hearn followed that other great trend in late nineteenth century literature—aestheticism. His kindred spirits were Keats, Walter Pater, and Oscar Wilde. He was a pursuer of beauty and a painter with words. Shortly after completing *Chita*, Hearn left for Japan and eventually became the most important literary interpreter of Japan's aesthetic culture to the English-speaking world.

  Chita's sentimental plot—the lost child and her chance reunion with a dying father—is designed to arouse human emotions that will correspond in intensity to the turbulence of the storm. It is the dynamic impressionism of the storm itself that fascinates Hearn: after the deceptive calm of summer come the roaring breakers; the storm swirls houses and ships and creates an incredible magnitude of refuse in its wake. Endless wreckage and bodies are strewn everywhere—including the foundling, Chita.

The child is fished out of all this dying waste like a creature returned from the dead. Her rescue has all the aura of a miracle to the simple Vioscas, who see the child as sent "by the Virgin." At the end of the story, La Brierre's fevered imagination once more re-creates the chaotic horror of the storm, more impressionistic than ever because its setting is now an agonized brain. Once again, a miracle is performed: the lost child is tossed up by the seething wreckage of La Brierre's tortured memories. She is there both in his mind and in actuality. The blurring of the two realities makes for the perfect impressionistic ending. The novel opens with the calm hues of a summery Renoir and closes with the brilliant frenzy of a Monet.

COLOR OF DARKNESS
Eleven Stories and a Novella

Type of work: Short stories
Author: James Purdy (1923–   )
First published: 1957

Color of Darkness is James Purdy's first book. It is a collection of eleven short stories and a novella, throughout which ordinary human experiences are purposely exaggerated so that a covert truth may find expression.

He has since written novels, more short stories, and plays. But it is a writer's first book that serves as a signpost to the road of his intention. It points the way to his personal arena; the piece of ground that he has cleared away and marked out as his own. It betokens the sort of problem with which he shall concern himself, and the types of people. In Purdy's case, it indicates a penchant for unusual and often bizarre situations that his characters seem hardly to notice. The outlandish is handled with nonchalance, and the mundane contains the outlandish.

Each story, like a candle, would guide readers through the darkness, but some burn more and others less intensely. In the more skillful stories, "Sound of Talking," "Cutting Edge," and the title story, "Color of Darkness," readers are inescapably confronted with one of their own hidden human secrets: contact with one another makes people the helpless victims of ambivalence. The life-long lesson that there is no hate, *must* be no hate, for dear ones forces people to conceal the truth that they only sometimes acknowledge, and with which everyone secretly sympathizes. In *Color of Darkness*, Purdy tries courageously to explore that hidden passageway and to shine his light on the unreasoning, frightening ambivalence which, in all its frustrating, infuriating shame, permits a child to brutalize his pet and then to hug it lovingly and tearfully.

It is "Sound of Talking," probably the best of his stories, in which Purdy demonstrates how surely he can implicate his reader. A woman is talking to her husband in the kitchen. Paralyzed, the man is in a wheelchair; and he is in pain. Readers know about the man, Vergil, because they have access to Mrs. Farebrother's thoughts, and she knows him very well. She counters his steady flow of bilious expletives with a loquacity designed to distract him from his pain. By the time the reader realizes that the deceptively innocent kitchen is really Mrs. Farebrother's wheelchair and that she is irrevocably locked into her husband's ebbing life, he has already witnessed and sympathized with her impotent flutterings of chatter. By allowing oneself to welcome her to the fire, one must recognize, when it reveals itself, that her ambivalence is a reflection of one's own. The reader also needs respite from the responsibility of caring for a helpless fellow being.

It is small wonder that her instincts bring her to admire a bird; and a bird that not only can fly but can talk as well. The raven that called her into the seed store keeps readers focused upon that one point of concentration, Mrs. Farebrother's paralytic ambivalence, so that all seemingly independent strands of thought or conversation are ultimately seen as a careful release from this single spool.

The woman first speaks of desire: she would like a bird, a raven. As she describes to her paraplegic husband the events which led up to that desire, she remembers her former attraction to a boy who was called the raven, and that the bird talks of someone who is dead. Both thoughts are seen to be repetitions of her nighttime speculations. In the dark, in her need, she can safely wish Vergil dead, but during the daylight hours, when such thoughts have scurried to their hiding place, she must sheathe herself in solicitous redress. This has been her life's condition since Vergil's release from the hospital long before.

The raven, this raven, is a perfect solution. It would amuse her husband, she hopes, and signify the achievement of a mutual desire; both will have decided to have the bird. But there is more to be profited, which is known to the reader by implication. The bird's presence would give brazen, corporeal expression to her more timid, ambivalent thoughts. Vergil's refusal to accept any responsibility for the pet, however, eliminates all possibility of their ever sharing a desire again. The story ends with this realization, and both continue to manipulate their wheelchairs.

For the reader, having sympathized with Mrs. Farebrother, there is a recognition that her love-hate ambivalence is an exaggeration of something familiar.

Also familiar is the situation in the title story, "Color of Darkness," which concludes uncomfortably, like a long unfulfilled desire nakedly exposed. The faintly dreamlike quality that suffuses this story may be attributed to the pensive nature of the father who is preoccupied with the exploration of his identity. He is out of touch with the people around him and is the victim of his inappropriate responses to them. Purdy designates him "the father" which is a most suitable epithet in its paradoxical implications. He is, indeed, the actual father of the boy, Baxter, for which he will be punished, but he has long ago delegated his parental responsibilities to his housekeeper-"mother," Mrs. Zilke. It is she who at the conclusion of the story has learned with the reader that the boy is already corrupted, that he knows the ways of the world and is a sinister member of the community. From its hiding place within the half truth of love and affection expressed in the boy's snuggling close and suddenly and surprisingly kissing his father, leaps forth the other half to complete the truth, his protestations of hate, culminating with a kick in the groin and an obscene word for that same bewildered father. Baxter allows himself to expose his ambivalence because his father is weak. Purdy seems to recognize in human beings an animal aversion to weakness and sickness that leads to brutality.

Most people handle their ambivalence more gracefully but must recognize that an intensification of the circumstances which evoke such unwelcome feelings could weaken the check on their manifestations. So, Purdy has intensified and exaggerated to denote a truth, and the reader must identify his own properly.

In the novella "63: Dream Palace" and in the story "Why Can't They Tell You Why?", the truth that Purdy overstates remains hidden in the exaggeration. It is hidden because the distortion allows readers to deny its relevance to themselves. What have we to do with a boy who murders the brother he loves in an abandoned house, or with a mother who drives her son into a hysterical state, apparently beyond recall? Readers may sense the horror of it, the disgust of it, but those "abnormalities" are the acts of distant relatives. There is a saving aura of unreality here for the reader; a third person; a dreamlike quality through which we may escape our responsibility of recognition.

The novella's exposition would have readers believe that Fenton Riddleway, a boy who is possessed of what Freud calls brutal egotism, is extremely important to the interlocutors, Grainger and Parkhearst. Their intimacy and boredom, conveyed by what feebly attempts to pass for provocative conversation, suggest that the boy is the subject of frequent discussion and considerable thought. The story's energy is dispersed among the lives of Parkhearst, Grainger, and Fenton, settling finally on the Fenton fragment.

The boy has neither charm nor grace; he demonstrates no wit, nor is he particularly intelligent. His interests are personal, and his learning understandably little. In fact, the most interesting thing about him is the situation in which he finds himself. He is unfamiliar with the city in which he is stranded and is waiting for someone to guide him from the abandoned house to which he was directed. His ability to fascinate seems locked with him within the story, and the reader must accept Fenton, if he will, as the protagonist of a homosexual daydream. Fenton fails to make the reader dream, however; he is inordinately cruel to his brother Claire, and he abuses everyone whose interest in him indicates a weakness. Those who are willing to indulge his predatory nature resemble some flat-toothed creatures who happily embrace the beautiful tiger. Physical beauty is the quality that Fenton possesses, and those who meet him once may never recover from the encounter.

The novella insists that the handsome boy brings havoc to all who seek him out. Why he is so sought, so valuable a possession, cannot be understood easily. The victims' willingness, therefore, to be oppressed, and to share oppression with their friends—Parkhearst brings the tormentor to Grainger and Bruno brings him to Hayden—seems to be an indulgence in homosexual fantasy. This, however, is not the nightmare of a Kafka story that well might be the daylight experience of a nighttime adventure; it is more as though the reader were eavesdropping on someone else's fantasy. The novella fails to ensnare, finally, because Fenton fails to charm without being seen. It is impossible to believe casual reports of a Medusa.

A collection of eleven short stories and a novella, however, is no mean first step for a writer, and if his foot comes down shakily sometimes, that fact does not blur some of the fine, clear prints.

THE CONFIDENCE MAN
His Masquerade

Type of work: Novel
Author: Herman Melville (1819–1891)
Type of plot: Social satire
Time of plot: Nineteenth century
Locale: Mississippi River
First published: 1857

Principal characters:
    THE CONFIDENCE MAN
    CHARLES NOBLE, a talkative passenger
    MR. ROBERTS, a merchant
    PITCH, a frontiersman
    MARK WINSOME, a mystic
    EGBERT, his disciple

The Story:

Aboard the steamboat *Fidele*, in dock at St. Louis, a group of passengers stood reading a placard that offered a reward for the capture of an impostor from the East—a confidence man. A deaf-mute beggar joined the group and began displaying a slate on which he wrote several mottoes praising the virtue of charity. Jeered at by the crowd, the deaf-mute lay down and slept on the forecastle as the steamboat pulled out for New Orleans.

A short time later, Black Guinea, a crippled black, appeared on deck to beg for pennies, which he skillfully caught in his mouth. A man with a wooden leg broke up this cruel game by loudly accusing the man of fraud, but Black Guinea protested his innocence and, in reply to an Episcopal clergyman's request for references, described several persons on the boat, all of whom, along with Black Guinea himself and the deaf-mute as well, were one and the same man—the confidence man. After the clergyman left to find one of these references, only a kindly country merchant gave Black Guinea alms, an act which had unfortunate consequences, since he dropped one of his business cards while he was fishing in his pocket for a coin.

To this merchant, Mr. Roberts by name, the impostor introduced himself as John Ringman. Pretending that he had met Mr. Roberts six years earlier, on a business matter, Ringman won his confidence and talked him out of a sum of money. To repay Mr. Roberts, Ringman gave him a tip on some valuable stock that could be bought aboard ship from the president of the Black Rapids Coal Company.

Next, Ringman accosted a college student who was reading Tacitus. Before Ringman could make a pitch for money, the student left in embarrassment at a lecture Ringman was delivering on the decadence of Tacitus.

The confidence man appeared next as a solicitor of funds for the Seminole Widow and Orphan Society. In this disguise, he was recognized as one of the Black Guinea's references by the Episcopal clergyman. The clergyman gave his alms for Black Guinea and was also prevailed upon to contribute to the Seminole Fund. In the same disguise, the impostor gulled a widow and a gentleman into donating to the fund. Somewhat reluctantly, the gentleman also contributed to a plan for the worldwide consolidation of all charities.

Disguised as Mr. Truman, the president of the Black Rapids Coal Company, the impostor met the student again. Ironically, since he prided himself on his cynicism and circumspection, the student insisted on buying some stock, despite the impostor's feigned reluctance to sell. The good merchant, Mr. Roberts, was also pleased to purchase some of the shares that his friend Ringman had recommended. During the conversation that followed this transaction, Mr. Roberts happened to mention the presence of a sickly old miser aboard ship and thus informed the confidence man of another victim.

The confidence man succeeded in gulling the miser twice: once by selling him some of the bogus stock and once, posing as an herb doctor, by selling him a supply of Omni-Balsamic Reinvigorator, guaranteed, if taken with confidence, to cure a consumptive cough.

A Missouri frontiersman's scorn for herbs and natural healing transformed the herb doctor into a representative of an employment agency, the Philosophical Intelligence Office. This Missourian, named Pitch, had resolved to purchase machinery to work his farm rather than rely on another boy, having had thirty-five unpleasant experiences with as many boys. Through brilliantly specious rhetoric, the impostor persuaded him to hire still another boy.

The impostor appeared to Pitch once more, this time disguised as Francis Goodman, a friendly world traveler and cosmopolitan. Pitch, however, brooding over his own gullibility, was in no mood for fellowship. After trying unsuccessfully to dispel Pitch's misanthropic melancholia, the cosmopolitan moved on in search of more susceptible prey.

He was accosted by Charles Noble, a garrulous passenger who, having overheard the colloquy with Pitch, was reminded of another bitter frontiersman: Colonel John Moredock, a notorious Indian hater. Goodman being agreeable, Noble proceeded to narrate a long tale of Moredock's vendetta against Indians and to expound the philosophy of Indian-hating.

The confidence man was appalled by such a misanthropic tale. Finding that Noble shared his feeling, Goodman agreed to split a bottle of port with him. Over their port, the two found that they shared a high regard for wine, but their incipient friendship was strained by Goodman's suspicion that Noble was trying to get him drunk. Cordiality and noble sentiments prevailed, however, until Goodman asked Noble to prove his professed confidence in mankind by lending him fifty dollars. This startling request produced such a violent reaction that the friendship would have ended then and there had not Goodman pretended that he had been joking. Confidence restored, Goodman told the story of Charlemont, an aristocrat of singularly peculiar behavior, as a prelude to another request for a loan. Before Goodman could make his appeal, Noble abruptly retired.

A passenger who had been watching the two men warned Goodman to beware of Noble's companionship. Goodman had difficulty in extracting a comprehensible reason for this warning because the passenger turned out to be Mark Winsome, an articulate mystic philosopher. Finally, Winsome stated clearly that Noble was a confidence man. Of course, the real confidence man expressed incredulity, whereupon Winsome withdrew, leaving behind a disciple, a young man named Egbert, to explain the Winsome mystic philosophy, which was, in effect, quite practical.

To explore the philosophy on a practical level, Goodman suggested that Egbert use it to answer a hypothetical request for a loan. Steadfastly and consistently, Egbert rejected the plea and finally told a long story to illustrate the folly, the tragedy, of loans between friends. Disgusted by such complete cynicism, the confidence man retreated.

Still in the guise of the cosmopolitan, he visited the ship's barber shop. There he succeeded in cheating the barber out of the price of a shave but failed, ultimately, in persuading the barber to extend credit to his customers.

Later that night, in the gentleman's sleeping cabin, the confidence man found only one person still awake, an old man reading the Bible. Though he mouthed pious sentiments attesting his faith in mankind and God, the old man eagerly bought a traveler's lock and a money belt from a child peddler and accepted a counterfeit detector as a premium. Commenting that the two of them put equal trust in man and God, the confidence man led the old gentleman, who was now carrying a life preserver, off to bed.

Critical Evaluation:

The white-clad mute and Black Guinea symbolize the cosmic forces that Herman Melville dramatizes in *The Confidence Man*. While it is uncertain whether one or both of these figures are manifestations of the Confidence Man, they clearly represent the Christian appeal to love and charity at one extreme, and the power of the diabolic that preys upon human weakness and gullibility at the other. Melville generalizes the *Fidele*'s passengers to represent "that multiform pilgrim species, man," so the Mississippi River setting has universal was well as particularly American implications. Finally, the barber's "No Trust" sign ironically suggests the prevailing attitude of the world in which the action takes place.

In the confrontations between the Confidence Man and his victims, the inappropriateness of the Christian values of faith, hope, and charity are explored. The con man, in his various guises, is actually able to elicit far more trust than the barber's sign would suggest is possible, but he does so only to victimize those with whom he succeeds. At the opposite extreme from those who trust are the misanthropes who, though immune from the devil's wiles, are in their mistrust and isolation as far from the Christian ideal as those who are gulled. The most ironic examples of the extremes of attitude are Winsome and his disciple Egbert, who provide a fine theoretical case for brotherly love but offer an equally compelling pragmatic argument against helping a fellow man.

The encounter with the Bible-reading old man at the end of the novel seems to represent Melville's final commentary on the practical impossibility of a world based on Christian principles. In spite of his ostentatious display of religion, the old man is hopelessly insecure and an easy victim. As the world is plunged into darkness, readers sense the final triumph of evil.

THE CONJURE WOMAN

Type of work: Novel
Author: Charles Waddell Chesnutt (1858–1932)
Type of plot: Regional romance
Time of plot: Post-Civil War
Locale: North Carolina
First published: 1899

> *Principal characters:*
> THE NARRATOR
> ANNIE, his wife
> UNCLE JULIUS, his black coachman
> AUNT PEGGY, the conjure woman

The Story:

When the Narrator's wife began to suffer ill effects from the severe Great Lakes climate, he began to look around for a suitable place to take her. He had been engaged in grape culture in Ohio, and when he learned of a small North Carolina town that seemed to offer what he needed in climate and suitable land, he decided to buy an old, dilapidated plantation and settle there. An untended vineyard was already on the property; with a little care and expense, the vines would flourish once more.

On the day that he took his wife, Annie, to look at the plantation, they happened upon an ancient black who called himself Uncle Julius. He advised them not to buy the plantation because it was goophered. Realizing they did not know that anything goophered was bewitched (conjured), the old man asked permission to tell them the story of the vineyard.

Many years before the war, when Uncle Julius was still a slave, the plantation owner had made many thousands of dollars from the grapes. Because the master could never keep the slaves from eating the rich grapes and stealing the wine made from them, he conceived the idea of having Aunt Peggy, a conjure woman living nearby, put a goopher on the vines. She made one that said that any black eating the grapes would die within a year. Most of the slaves stayed away from the grapes, but a few tried them in spite of the conjure, and they all died. When a new slave came to the plantation, no one remembered to tell him about the conjure, and he ate some of the grapes. So that he would not die, Aunt Peggy made him a counter-goopher. Then a strange thing happened. Every year, as the grapes ripened, this slave became so young and sprightly that he could do the work of several men, but in the

---

fall, when the vines died, he withered and faded. This strange action went on for several years, until the master hit upon the idea of selling the slave every spring when he was strong and buying him back cheaply in the fall. By this transaction, he made money each year.

One year, the master hired an expert to prune his vines, but the expert cut them out too deeply and the vines were ruined. Soon afterward, the slave who had bloomed and withered with the vines also died. Some said he died of old age, but Uncle Julius knew that it was the goopher that finally overcame him. Uncle Julius advised strongly against buying the land because the conjure was still on.

The Narrator bought the plantation, however, and it prospered. Later, he learned that Uncle Julius had been living in a cabin on the place and sold the grapes. He always suspected that the story was told to prevent ruination of the old man's business. He gave Uncle Julius employment as a coachman, and so the former slave was well cared for.

At another time, Annie wanted a new kitchen, and her husband decided to tear down an old schoolhouse on the place and use the lumber from it for the new building. Uncle Julius advised him against the plan. Strangely enough, that schoolhouse was goophered, too. The story was that a slave called Sandy was borrowed by others so often that his woman was afraid they would be separated forever. She was a conjure woman, and so she turned him into a tree. Each night she would turn him back into a man, and they would slip into her cabin until morning, when she would again change him into a tree. One day, the woman was sent away from the plantation before she could change Sandy back into a man. While she was away, the master had the tree that was Sandy cut down to build a new kitchen. The slaves had a hard time felling the tree, which twisted and turned and tried to break loose from the chains. At last, they got it to the sawmill. Later the house was built, but it was never much used. The slaves refused to work there because at night they could hear moaning and groaning, as if someone were in great pain. Only Sandy's woman, when she returned, would stay in the building, and she, poor girl, went out of her mind.

Uncle Julius advised against using goophered lumber for the new kitchen. It also seemed that Uncle Julius needed the old schoolhouse for his church meetings. The goopher would not bother the worshipers; in fact, the preaching would help Sandy's roaming spirit. There was nothing for the wife and her husband to do but buy new lumber for her kitchen. No one would want to use goophered wood.

When the Narrator was about to buy a mule to use in cultivating some land, Uncle Julius warned him against mules because most of them were conjured. Uncle Julius did, however, know of a horse for sale. After his employer bought the horse, which died within three months, Uncle Julius appeared in a new suit he had been admiring for some time.

One day, when Annie felt depressed and listless, Uncle Julius told her and her husband about Becky, a slave traded for a horse. Taken away from her child, she grieved terribly. Aunt Peggy, the conjure woman, turned the baby into a hummingbird so that he could fly down to his mother and be near her and soothe her. Later the conjure woman arranged to have Becky and her baby reunited. But Uncle Julius knew that she would never have had all that trouble if she had owned the hindfoot of a rabbit to protect her from harm. The story seemed to cheer Annie, and her husband was not surprised later to find Uncle Julius' rabbit's foot among her things.

When the Narrator prepared to clear a piece of land, Uncle Julius warned him that the land was goophered and told him a harrowing tale about a slave turned into a gray wolf and tricked into killing his own wife, who had been changed into a cat. Although the gray wolf was said to haunt the patch of land, it did not seem to bother a bee tree from which Uncle Julius gathered wild honey.

One day, Annie's sister Mabel and her fiancé quarreled bitterly. Uncle Julius had another story for them about Chloe, a slave who ruined her life because she was jealous. Chloe listened to a no-account rival and believed his story that her lover was meeting another woman. When she learned that she had lost her lover because she allowed her jealousy to trick her, she sorrowed and died. Even the conjure woman could not help her. Mabel listened to the story and then ran to her fiancé, who just happened to be close to the spot where Julius had stopped their carriage. Later on, the young man seemed to develop a special fondness for Uncle Julius. After the wedding, he tried to hire the old man into his service, but Uncle Julius remained faithful to his employers. He thought they needed his advice and help.

Critical Evaluation:

Less a full-dress novel than a collection of loosely connected tales presented against a unifying background of post-bellum Southern life, *The Conjure Woman* nevertheless preserves a relatively inaccessible and easily overlooked portion of American social and literary history. Well reviewed upon publication, the book became a best-seller in Cleveland, where the author was a practicing lawyer. Interestingly, Charles Waddell Chesnutt deemed it necessary to conceal his racial identity: at no point do the context or the stately, mannered prose indicate that the writer is a black man. Only in rendering Uncle Julius McAdoo's tales does Chesnutt have a chance to display his considerable skill with the now-defunct Gullah Afro-American dialect.

Some of these stories, in the author's words, "are quaintly humorous; others wildly extravagant, revealing the Oriental cast of the negro's imagination; while others . . . disclose many a tragic incident of the darker side of slavery." They remind readers too of the Uncle Remus stories, although those tend to be more avuncular and amusing than Chesnutt's tales; both sets of tales recall the treasury of Afro-American folklore replete with bird and animal stories, tales of witches and spells, spirits and haunts, horrors, wonders, protests, and scares.

The stories in *The Conjure Woman* are valuable for their graphic and touching portrayal of plantation life in the old days, as well as for what William Dean Howells praised as "a wild, indigenous poetry, the creation of a sincere and original imagination." The stories are, in addition, laced with a light and amusing irony. It is worth noting that Uncle Julius' white auditors are inevitably manipulated—usually successfully, sometimes not—by the devices of their simple black storyteller. Chesnutt's triumph, however, is that in the final analysis, the reader is left, through these tales, with an increased appreciation of man's human stature and dignity.

A CONNECTICUT YANKEE IN KING ARTHUR'S COURT

Type of work: Novel
Author: Mark Twain (Samuel L. Clemens, 1835–1910)
Type of plot: Social satire
Time of plot: Sixth century
Locale: England
First published: 1889

> *Principal characters:*
> THE CONNECTICUT YANKEE, the Boss
> CLARENCE, a page
> KING ARTHUR
> SANDY, wife of the Boss
> MERLIN, a magician

The Story:

Struck on the head during a quarrel in a New England arms factory, a skilled mechanic awoke to find himself being prodded by the spear of an armored knight on horseback. The knight was Sir Kay of King Arthur's Round Table and the time was June, A.D. 528, in Merrie England, as a foppish young page named Clarence informed the incredulous Yankee, when his captor took him back to white-towered Camelot. The Yankee remembered that there had been a total eclipse of the sun on June 21, 528. If the eclipse took place, he was indeed a lost traveler in time turned backward to the days of chivalry.

At Camelot, the Yankee listened to King Arthur's knights as they bragged of their mighty exploits. The magician, Merlin, told again of Arthur's coming. Finally, Sir Kay told of his encounter with the Yankee, and Merlin advised that the prisoner be thrown into a dungeon to await burning at the stake on June 21.

In prison, the Yankee thought about the coming eclipse. Merlin, he told Clarence, was a humbug, and he sent the boy to the court with a message that on the day of his death, the sun would darken and the kingdom would be destroyed. The eclipse came, and at the right time, for the Yankee was about to be burned when the sky began to dim. Awed, the king ordered the prisoner released. The people shouted that he was a greater magician than Merlin.

The court demanded another display of his powers. With the help of Clarence, the Yankee mined Merlin's tower with some crude explosives he

A CONNECTICUT YANKEE IN KING ARTHUR'S COURT by Mark Twain. Published by Harper & Brothers.

had made and then told everyone he would cause the tower to crumble and fall. When the explosion occurred, the Yankee was assured of his place as the new court magician. Merlin was thrown into prison.

The lack of mechanical devices in King Arthur's castle bothered the ingenious New Englander, and the illiteracy of the people hurt his American pride in education. He decided to make the commoners more than slaves to the nobility. He had a title of his own by this time, for the people called him the Boss. As the Boss, he intended to modernize the kingdom.

His first act was to set up schools in small communities throughout the country. He had to work in secret because he feared the interference of the Church. He trained workmen in mechanical arts. Believing that a nation needed a free press, he instructed Clarence in the art of journalism. He had telephone wires stretched between hamlets, haphazardly, however, because there were no maps by which to be guided.

When Sir Sagramor challenged the Boss to a duel, the court decided that he should go upon some knightly quest to prepare himself for the encounter. His mission was to help a young girl named Alisande, whose story he could not get straight. With many misgivings, he put on a burdensome coat of mail and on his heavy charger started off with Sandy, as he called her. Sandy was a talkative companion who told endless tall tales as they traveled through the land. Along the way, the Boss marveled at the pitiable state of the people under the feudal system. Whenever he found a man of unusual spirit, he sent him back to Clarence in Camelot, to be taught reading, writing, and a useful trade. He visited the dungeons of the castles at which he stayed and released prisoners unjustly held by their grim masters.

In the Valley of Holiness, he found another opportunity to prove his magic skill. There a sacred well had gone dry because, according to legend, some sin had been committed. When he arrived, Merlin, now released from prison, was attempting magic to make the spring flow. With a great deal of pomp and flourish, the Boss repaired a leak in the masonry at the bottom of the well. As the well filled, Merlin went home in shame.

By chance, the Boss came upon one of his telephone installations in a cave nearby. He talked to Clarence, who told him that King Arthur was on his way to the Valley of Holiness to see the flowing spring. He returned to the spring to find a fake magician assuring the gaping pilgrims that he could tell what anyone was doing at that moment. The Boss asked him about King Arthur. The magician said that he was asleep in his bed at Camelot. The Boss grandly predicted that the king was on his way to the Valley of Holiness. When the king did arrive, the people were again awed by the Boss's magic.

Anxious that King Arthur be convinced of the sufferings of his people, the Boss suggested that he and the king disguise themselves as commoners and travel as pilgrims through the country. The Boss knew that Arthur was not to blame for his own social doctrines; he was a victim of his place in society. On their journey, the king proved to be courageous and kind.

Misfortune soon overtook them. They were seized by an earl and sold as slaves, because they were unable to prove themselves free men. The slaves were taken to London, where the Boss picked the lock that held him and escaped. The rest of the slaves were ordered to be hanged after his escape. The Boss, however, located one of his telephones and called Clarence in Camelot, ordering him to send Sir Lancelot and an army of knights to London to save their king from hanging.

The Boss came back to Camelot in glory, but not for long. He still had to fight a duel with Sir Sagramor—in reality a battle between Merlin and the Boss. Merlin professed to cover Sir Sagramor with an invisible shield, but the credulous knight was invisible to no one but himself. The Boss wore no armor, and so, on the field of the tournament, he was able to dodge the charging knight until Sir Sagramor grew tired. Then the Boss lassoed him and pulled him from his horse. When Sir Sagramor returned once again to the field, Merlin stole the Boss's lasso. There was no alternative; the Boss shot Sir Sagramor with his gun. Then he challenged all the knights of the Round Table. He had only twelve shots in his two revolvers, but fortunately, when he had killed nine of the charging knights, the line wavered and gave up.

Three years passed. By this time, the Boss had married Sandy, and they had a little girl. He and Clarence were planning to declare a republic after the death of Arthur, for the sixth-century kingdom was now a nineteenth century land with schools, trains, factories, newspapers, the telephone and the telegraph. Although the code of chivalry had been abolished, the knights still insisted on wearing their armor. Then little Hello-Central, the Boss's daughter, became ill, and he and Sandy took the child to the seashore for recuperation. On their return, the Boss found Camelot in a shambles. Only Clarence remained to tell him the story. There had been a battle between King Arthur and Sir Lancelot over Queen Guinevere. The king was dead, and by interdict, the Church had destroyed the work of the Boss. Clarence and the Boss built a fortress surrounded by an electrically charged barrier. In a battle with the surviving chivalry of England, the Boss was stabbed. When an old woman came to the fortress from the enemy lines and offered to nurse him, no one recognized her as Merlin. The magician cast a spell on the Boss and declared that he would sleep for thirteen hundred years. And, indeed, the Yankee did awake once more in the nineteenth century.

Critical Evaluation:

A Connecticut Yankee in King Arthur's Court should have offered Mark Twain one of his best opportunities to attack the repressive and antidemocratic forces which he saw in post-Civil War America as well as in sixth century England. That the attack becomes in large part an exposé of the very system Twain sought to vindicate reveals as much the deep division in Twain's own nature as any problem inherent in the material itself. Ironically, though, much of the interest the work holds for contemporary readers is based upon the complications resulting from Twain's inability to set up a neat conflict between the forces of progress and those of repression. Hank Morgan's visit to King Arthur's court unveils not only the greed and superstition Twain associates with the aristocracy and the established Church, but also it reveals some of the weaknesses in man himself which enable these oppressive parasites to exist, and it finally comes to the realization that the industrial Utopia that Hank tries to establish in old England is nothing more than a hopeless dream.

As a character, Hank Morgan is, in many respects, a worthy successor to his predecessor, Huckleberry Finn. Like Huck, Hank is representative of the common people, and, at his best, he asserts the ideal qualities Twain associates with those who escape the corruption of hereditary wealth and power and the conditioning of tradition. Unlike Huck, however, who was largely an observer powerless to change the system, Hank is given the opportunity to make his values the basis of a Utopian society. While Huck saw the threat of being "civilized" as an infringement on his individuality and freedom, Hank is, in his own way, fully "civilized" according to the standards of the world he represents. The pragmatic wit that enabled Huck Finn to survive against all odds becomes for Hank the basis of his rise in the industrial system to a position of authority and success. He fully accepts the nineteenth century doctrines of laissez-faire capitalism, progress, and technology as being expressive of the best social and human principles. Hank represents Twain's vision of technological man as a new social ideal: the greatest product of the greatest society.

Twain's choice of Arthur's court as the testing ground for Hank's ideas was not accidental. Most immediately, he was offended by Matthew Arnold's attacks upon the American glorification of the common man and the Englishman's view of America as a kind of cultural desert. Thus, in attacking the golden age of chivalry, Twain simultaneously sought to expose English history, culture, and traditions of aristocratic privilege. At the same time, Twain associates the age of Arthur with the sorts of romantic attitudes he had exposed in *Huckleberry Finn* as the ruin of the American South. Making his spokesman, Hank Morgan, a product of that society Arnold deplored, Twain mounts a two-pronged attack against Arnold's Europeanism and sophistication and, in his own view, the dangerously reactionary attitudes that asserted the superiority of the "romantic" past over the present.

What begins for Hank, with his prediction of the moment of the eclipse, a simple expedient for survival, quickly becomes open war between Merlin and the Church and the Machine Age represented by the Yankee. Hank sees himself as a Promethean bringer of new knowledge and a new order to the oppressed masses of old England. Hank's humanitarian values are pitted against the selfishness and greed of the aristocracy and the Church, and his reason challenges their superstition. Based upon his own and Twain's view of technological man as the apex of human development, Hank naturally assumes that he is the rightful ruler of the world. Twain, as well as Hank, seems to assume that because he takes up the cause of the oppressed people against their oppressors, he necessarily has, in whatever he does, a moral superiority to those he fights against. Neither Hank nor Twain seems to give consideration to the question of ends and means.

It is particularly ironic that Hank, ostensibly the bringer of light to this benighted people, should rely no less than his archenemy Merlin upon the power of superstition to gain ascendancy over the masses. From the moment he discovers the profound effect that his prediction of the eclipse has upon the audience, Hank begins to challenge Merlin to ever greater miracles. Such episodes as the destruction of Merlin's tower or the restoring of the Holy Well represent Hank's use of technology to create fear and awe like that Merlin has commanded heretofore. Thus, recognizing that man is essentially base and weak, Hank, like Merlin, maintains his power through exploitation of ignorance and gullibility.

It is man rather than technology that finally fails Hank. With the exception of the fifty-two young men who have never been exposed to the teachings of the Church, the society Hank has constructed through his technology reverts to its former state the minute his guard is relaxed. Men are, as Hank perceives them, no more than conditioned animals, and all his modern miracles cannot change that fact. In the end, Hank's technology fails him and his companions. His dream of progress has become a nightmare—a sacrifice to the very ignorance it would replace. Promethean Hank Morgan, the bringer of light and knowledge, finally only vindicates Twain's pessimistic view of human nature.

The ending of *A Connecticut Yankee in King Arthur's Court* is as bleak as anything Twain was ever to write. The scenes of Hank's Utopia destroyed by perverse human nature, the destruction unleashed by the power of technology, and, finally, the prospect of Hank's forces being overcome by the pollution of the bodies piled in their trenches are frightening to contemplate. Twain, having apparently set out to affirm the nineteenth century doctrine of progress, finally comes full circle to suggest that something permanent within human nature makes such dreams hopeless. Clearly, there is here an anticipation of the later Twain who, having lost hope in the human potential of his Huck Finn, would become a misanthropic voice crying out against the "damned human race."

THE COPPERHEAD

Type of work: Novel
Author: Harold Frederic (1856–1898)
Type of plot: Regional romance
Time of plot: 1860's
Locale: Four Corners, New York
First published: 1893

> Principal characters:
> ABNER BEECH, a farmer
> HURLEY, his hired man
> JEFF, his son
> ESTHER HAGADORN, Jeff's sweetheart
> JEE HAGADORN, a cooper and Esther's father
> NI HAGADORN, his son
> JIMMY, an orphan

The Story:

Abner Beech was a stalwart, shaggy man, who had often been supervisor of his district. Jimmy, who was an orphan, went to live with him when he was six or seven years old. Abner was a town leader, a great reader, and he owned more books than most people did in Dearborn County, located in Northern New York State.

For some reason, Abner Beech violently hated the Abolitionists. The first Abolitionist in Dearborn County, as far as Jimmy knew, was old Jee Hagadorn, but now nearly everyone except Abner Beech shared the old man's sentiments. Because the anti-Abolitionists were attacked from the pulpit every Sunday at church meeting, Abner and Jimmy finally stopped going to church. Then someone spread the rumor that Abner's milk had not been accepted at the communal cheese factory because he had put water into it. At that time, Abner's household became real outcasts in Four Corners.

One day in August, Abner came home early from the field. He was furious because he learned that Jeff, his only son, had been seen walking with Esther Hagadorn, the daughter of his enemy. Abner sent Jimmy to call Jeff home. When Jimmy found Jeff and Esther, the young man gave the boy his fishing pole and told him to tell Abner that he was going to Tecumseh to enlist in the Union Army. When Jimmy relayed Jeff's message to their parents, they took the news calmly. They had already guessed his intention, for on that same day, an entire group of boys from the area had gone off to enlist.

Abner's hired man also enlisted, and Abner hired an Irish widower, Hurley, who had been doing odd jobs in the neighborhood. Hurley was also an anti-Abolitionist, the only one in the area besides Abner. It was understood in Abner's household that Jeff's name should never be mentioned, and Abner refused to show regret over the departure of his only son.

In late September, Hurley and Jimmy went to Octavius to buy some butter firkins; Abner refused to buy firkins from Jee Hagadorn, who lived close by. In Octavius, Hurley and Jimmy learned of the terrible battle at Antietam, in which a number of the boys from Dearborn County had taken part. Hurley got into a fight when some of the citizens taunted him for being a Copperhead, a Northerner who sympathized with the Southern cause in the Civil War.

On the way home from Octavius, Jimmy went to see Jee Hagadorn. Jimmy found Esther there, worrying about Jeff. Jee came home elated because Lincoln had signed the Emancipation Proclamation.

A fortnight later, the Beech household learned that Jeff Beech and Byron Truax had been reported missing after a battle in the South.

The work on the farm continued. Warner Pitts, Abner's former hired man, came home on furlough as an officer. A hero to the townspeople, one day he called Abner a Copperhead. Ni Hagadorn, Jee's son, did not like Warner Pitts, and so he went to Abner's house to tell him that he was going south to try to find Jeff. Abner refused, however, to give Ni any money to help him on his journey.

The local citizens were beginning to feel that the North was not carrying on the war as vigorously as they expected. On election day, November 4, Jimmy accompanied Abner and Hurley to the polls. Abner voted proudly, but the inspector said that Hurley's naturalization papers were not in order and that he could not vote. When a fight started, another inspector then said that Hurley could vote. A few days later, it was learned that the Abolitionists had lost in that congressional district. Abner was overjoyed, believing that this defeat would lead to peace and an end of what he considered murder. To celebrate, Janey, one of the hired girls, made a big bonfire.

The next day, Jimmy was in bed with a cold. To the amazement of everyone, Esther Hagadorn came in and asked to speak to Abner. When Abner came home, he was civil to Esther and asked her to stay to supper. Esther said that there was a rumor to the effect that Copperheads were spreading clothes that had smallpox in them and that the local citizens were fearful and angry. She said that Abner's bonfire to celebrate the voting results had made them even angrier and that they were planning to come for Abner that night. Esther then accepted Abner's invitation to remain and have supper with them.

The townspeople arrived to tar and feather Abner and Hurley and to ride them on a rail. Abner, however, stood firm, a loaded shotgun on his arm. Suddenly, Jimmy realized that the house was afire. He fainted.

Jimmy regained consciousness later that night. It was snowing, and the house had been completely burned. With some of the furniture that they were able to rescue, Abner and his wife, M'rye, had improvised a home in the cold barn. Esther, still with them, had regained the friendship of M'rye, since they were both able to talk about Jeff again.

Jimmy, unable to sleep that night, overheard Esther talking to Abner. Abner said that he believed that the townspeople had started a fire for the tarring and feathering and that, because of the strong wind, his house had caught fire accidentally. Esther said that Abner was really liked and respected by the townspeople but that they could not be expected to behave reasonably because so many husbands and sons were now involved in the war.

At that point, Jee Hagadorn arrived in search of his daughter. Abner pulled off Jee's wet boots and gave him some warm socks. They had breakfast in near silence. Suddenly, Ni Hagadorn appeared. He told M'rye that Jeff had been only slightly hurt and was due home any day. M'rye suddenly ran out of the barn, where she found Jeff returned from the war after having lost his left arm.

While everyone was welcoming Jeff and offering condolences, an unexpected visitor arrived. He was Squire Avery, who wanted, on behalf of the townspeople, to apologize for the events of the previous night. Hoping to let bygones be bygones, he asked Abner to send milk to the cheese factory again. He also wanted to have a house-raising bee for Abner's new house and to lend him money if he needed it. Abner, filled with the spirit of forgiveness, said that all of these kindnesses were nearly worth the house burning. He and M'rye expressed the hope that Jeff and Esther would marry.

Critical Evaluation:

A Copperhead was a Northerner who sympathized with the South during the Civil War. The integrity of Abner Beech, the Copperhead of the title, and the pressures upon him, are the subjects of the novel. Beyond the main theme and plot, however, is the impact of the events on the young narrator, Jimmy, and how they change him. Jimmy matures during the course of the novel, as he learns that human motivation is not as simple or obvious as it might appear. The importance of public opinion and its power stand over the book like a shadow. In those days of intense and bitter political convictions and violent tempers, the gossip at the general store and post office could lead to disastrous consequences. Jimmy sees all of this and, young though he is, understands the significance of it. In a simple, unpretentious narrative, he conveys this to the reader.

Technically, the novel is an impressive achievement, a first person narration told by a character who does not participate in the main action, and yet a book with great sweep and dramatic power. The novel is perfectly designed and flows effortlessly from beginning to end, building to a dramatic climax and then settling into a brief denouement. The tone is controlled, with no sense of hysteria or undue passion, although the book deals with irrational and hotheaded individuals. Harold Frederic has maintained such an even tone that perhaps the narrative might even seem too dispassionate. Certainly, he leaves the conclusions of the story to the reader.

In its modest way, this novel is as perfect as *Ethan Frome* and *The Great Gatsby*. In less than two hundred pages, it encompasses a world and finally transcends it. Frederic is writing about honor and morality in this story of the civilian side of the Civil War and about the beauty of ordinary things in a violent world. Although Harold Frederic deplores the irrationality of society in time of stress, the true significance of the theme lies in the thought that it is impossible properly to judge, much less condemn, a man for his political views unless one comes to understand the personal motivations of the man himself. The local descriptions are vivid, and a sense of realism is carried by the heavily flavored dialects and regional locutions of the farmers who live in the community of Four Corners.

A COUNTRY DOCTOR

Type of work: Novel
Author: Sarah Orne Jewett (1849–1909)
Type of plot: Regional romance
Time of plot: Mid-nineteenth century
Locale: Oldfields, Maine
First published: 1884

Principal characters:
NAN PRINCE, a student of medicine
MRS. THACHER, her grandmother
DR. LESLIE, her guardian
MISS NANCY PRINCE, her aunt

The Story:

One cold winter night while Mrs. Thacher and two of her neighbors were sitting around the stove and gossiping about neighborhood activities, they were interrupted by a noise at the door. Adeline Thacher Prince had fallen on the doorstep. In her arms she held her infant daughter, Nan. Dr. Leslie was sent for at once, but by the next day, Adeline was dead. According to her wishes, Dr. Leslie became the little child's guardian, though she lived with her maternal grandmother.

Nan's mother had left home to go to work in a textile mill in Lowell. There she had fallen in love with a young man from Dunport, Maine, and after a short courtship, she had married him. The marriage had been far from happy. Adeline had inherited a wild, rebellious tendency, and it was whispered in Dunport that she had eventually started to drink. Furthermore, Adeline resented the strong opposition of her husband's family to the marriage, and, in particular, the views of her husband's sister, Miss Nancy Prince. After Adeline's husband died, she tried for a time to support both herself and the child. When she could do so no longer, she trudged back to Oldfields to die in her mother's home.

Nan seemed to exhibit some of her mother's traits, for she was mischievous and inclined to pleasure. Her grandmother often thought her a trial, but to Dr. Leslie she was something quite different. One day, Nan retrieved a fallen bird with a fractured leg and applied a splint, as she had seen Dr. Leslie do to his patients. The doctor began to wonder if Nan had not inherited some tendency toward medicine as her father had. He did not insist that she go to school. He thought that the training she received in the woods and the fields was far more beneficial than any she would obtain in the schoolroom.

When Mrs. Thacher died, Nan went to live with Dr. Leslie. There was a great feeling of affection between the two. Nan, who continued to go out on calls with the doctor, exhibited much interest in his work. The time came at last for her to be sent to boarding school. At first, she was shy and rather backward in her studies, but after awhile, she made admirable progress. She would have been completely satisfied with her life if she had not wondered, from time to time, about the mysterious aunt of whom she had heard only rumors. Mrs. Thacher had never explained anything of the girl's family background to her, and Nan had conjured up the figure of a wealthy aristocratic relative who would one day send for her. Miss Prince, who had inherited a large estate, regularly sent money to Dr. Leslie to provide for Nan's upkeep. The doctor never touched a penny of it. When Adeline had died, Miss Prince had asked for custody of the child, but Mrs. Thacher and Dr. Leslie had refused her request.

When Nan grew older, she told Dr. Leslie of her desire to study medicine. Although the doctor was aware of the difficulties she would face, he approved heartily of her interest. Yet, the town of Oldfields did not, and many were shocked at the idea of a woman doctor. Nan continued her studies in the doctor's books, however, and acted as his nurse. She was to continue that training at a medical school in a nearby city.

When the time came for her to leave Oldfields, Nan wrote a brief note to her aunt, Miss Prince, and asked if she might visit her father's sister. Miss Prince, although she feared that Nan might be like her mother, consented to receive her niece. On Nan's arrival in Dunport, Miss Prince, genuinely pleased with her, helped Nan to make friends and openly acknowledged her young relative. Yet, when Nan expressed her wish to study medicine, everyone was shocked, even Miss Prince, who in a large measure blamed Dr. Leslie for Nan's unladylike desire for a professional career. Nan, although made unhappy by her aunt's objections, remained adamant.

Her aunt and her friends, however, sought to lead her astray from her work. Miss Prince had a favorite friend, young George Gerry, to whom she intended leaving her money. When Nan grew fond of George, everyone hoped that they would marry. One day, during an outing, Nan and George stopped at a farmhouse, and Nan treated a farmer who had thrown his arm out of joint. Sometime later, George asked Nan to marry him. She refused, both because she wanted to become a doctor and because she was afraid that her inherited characteristics might cause her to be a bad wife.

At last, she told her aunt that she would have to return to Oldfields. On her arrival, the doctor, who had been apprehensive that Nan might have been influenced by Miss Prince and her money, was pleasantly surprised. She was the same Nan she had been before, and all the more ambitious for a successful medical career.

Nan went away to study. When she returned, Dr. Leslie was older and needed more help in his practice. Nan settled down in Oldfields and slowly the community accepted her. Before many years passed, she had succeeded Dr. Leslie in the affections of the men and women of the village.

Critical Evaluation:

A Country Doctor is a novel of development rather than plot. With sensitivity and insight, Sarah Orne Jewett traces the growth and awakening of an intelligent young girl. Nan Prince has more imagination and energy than the village people are accustomed to seeing in a young girl. They like her but do not quite approve of her; they wonder what will become of such a fanciful, harum-scarum female who does not act as a girl ought to act and do what is expected of her. "I don't mean to be discontented," she says, but it is clear that she has a will of her own. Nan is taught that she owes something to the world besides following her own selfish plans; duty to society is early instilled into her by the doctor, who feels that Nan is not the kind of girl who is likely to marry: she is too independent and self-reliant.

The difficulties Nan encounters because she wants to be a doctor are explored in detail. People tell Nan that a woman's place is in the home, but she insists that since any man who aspires to be a doctor is helped, so should she be. God would not have given her talents equal to those of a man if she were not meant to use them, she tells her aunt. Her family tries to marry her off, but she resists and dedicates herself entirely to her career.

Another theme mentioned in this book and elaborated in nearly all of Jewett's books is that of the old people taking their lifetime's store of local social history and tradition with them when they die. Jewett saw that this valuable source should be tapped and somehow saved for posterity. Perhaps, she suggests, the country doctors could record the memories of their old patients, rather than let them perish.

No American writer had a better ear than Jewett for the speech patterns of her people, for their selection of words and phrases, the rhythms and cadences of their conversation, and their humor. Jewett never satirizes her characters but presents them with both affection and objectivity. She recognizes the flaws in these unsophisticated, work-hardened people, but she forgives them, and in *A Country Doctor*, she shows how a strong and intelligent person such as Nan can rise from among these people and shine with all the stubborn virtues of the native American tradition.

THE COUNTRY OF THE POINTED FIRS

Type of work: Novel
Author: Sarah Orne Jewett (1849–1909)
Type of plot: Regional romance
Time of plot: Late nineteenth century
Locale: Maine seacoast
First published: 1896

Principal characters:
MRS. TODD, a New England herbalist
MRS. BLACKETT, her mother
WILLIAM, her brother
THE BOARDER, a writer
ESTHER, William's sweetheart
MRS. HIGHT, Esther's mother

The Story:

A woman writer came one summer to Dunnet Landing, a Maine seacoast town, to find seclusion for her work. She boarded with Mrs. Almira Todd, a friendly widow and the local herb doctor. Besides having a garden full of herbs, Mrs. Todd often roamed far afield for rarer specimens. The boarder sometimes took care of Mrs. Todd's sales of herbs and birch beer when Mrs. Todd was away.

At last, the boarder realized that she must get to work on her book and give up the society of Mrs. Todd in the daytime. The boarder found the village schoolhouse a quiet place for her writing, and she spent most of her days there. One morning, she was surprised to have a visit from old Captain Littlepage, a retired seaman who seldom left his house. For a time he spoke seriously of the great English poets. When he saw that the boarder did not laugh at him, he launched upon a long narrative. It seemed that he had been shipwrecked upon a small island and had met there another sailor who had been to the North Pole. He told Captain Littlepage of a town of ghosts he had discovered. It was Captain Littlepage's theory that, in this town, souls awaited their passage into the next world. The old man's narrative stopped suddenly as his mind returned to the present. The boarder helped him home and told no one about his strange story.

On another day, Mrs. Todd took her boarder out to Green Island, where Mrs. Todd's mother lived. Mrs. Blackett was more than eighty years old, her daughter was past sixty. Mrs. Blackett still did her own work and kept house

---

for her son William, who was past fifty. William was a bashful man, but he found a friend to his liking in the boarder. Mrs. Todd and the boarder gathered some herbs before they left the island, and Mrs. Todd showed her the spot offshore where her husband had gone down in his boat.

Mrs. Fosdick came to visit Mrs. Todd. The two ladies and the boarder often spent their evenings together. One night, Mrs. Todd told of her husband's cousin Joanna, who had lived on Shell-heap Island. Disappointed in love, Joanna went to live alone on the tiny island. Passing fishermen often left presents on the shore, but no one ever visited her. Finally, Mrs. Todd and the minister went to see her, for the minister was worried about the state of Joanna's soul. They found Joanna living comfortably but simply. Satisfied with her lonely life, she could not be induced to return to the mainland. Joanna lived out her life on the island and was buried there.

Late in August, Mrs. Todd took her boarder and Mrs. Blackett to the Bowden family reunion. They hired a carriage and drove far inland to the family seat. All the Bowdens for miles around came to the reunion, and Mrs. Blackett was one of the privileged guests because of her age. For once, Mrs. Todd forgot her herbs and spent the entire day in the enjoyment of the society of her friends. William had not come to the gathering because of his bashfulness. Mrs. Blackett treasured every moment of the day, for she knew it was one of the last reunions she would attend.

One day, the boarder stood on the shore below Dunnet Landing. There she met Mr. Tilley, one of the oldest fishermen in the village. Mr. Tilley was reserved toward strangers, but he had at last accepted the boarder as a friend, and he invited her to visit him that afternoon. When the boarder arrived, he was knitting some socks. The two friends sat in the kitchen while Mr. Tilley told the boarder about his wife. She had died eight years before, but her husband had never got over his sorrow. He kept the house just as she had left it. Proudly he showed the boarder the seldom-used parlor and Mrs. Tilley's set of china. She left the cottage feeling the loneliness that surrounded the old fisherman.

When the clear, cool autumn came, it was time for the boarder to leave. Mrs. Todd helped her pack and get her belongings down on the wharf for the steamer. Mrs. Todd took her leave of the boarder before she left the house. From the deck of the steamer, the boarder watched Dunnet Landing fade into the distance. She recalled a day of the past summer when William had come to the mainland. He was going trout fishing in an inland stream. Self-consciously, he asked the boarder to go with him. They caught no fish, but William took her afterward to see Mrs. Hight and her daughter Esther. The boarder stayed to talk to Mrs. Hight, while William went out to speak to Esther, who supported her aged and crippled mother by tending sheep. As William and the boarder left, she realized that William and Esther were lovers.

When the boarder returned to Dunnet Landing in the spring, Mrs. Todd told her that Mrs. Hight had recently died and that Esther and William were to be married immediately. He was to come to the mainland the next day if the weather proved good.

Early in the morning, Mrs. Todd was up to watch for a sail from Green Island. Finally, she saw it approaching. Then neighbors began to drop in to inquire why William was coming to the mainland. After the ceremony, William and Esther stopped for a moment at Mrs. Todd's house before returning to the island. Mrs. Todd and the boarder accompanied the pair to the landing to see them off. The older woman expressed no emotion at the leavetaking; but as she and the boarder returned to the house, they walked holding hands all the way.

Critical Evaluation:

Willa Cather, when asked to name three American novels "deserving of a long, long life," selected *The Country of the Pointed Firs* to share this honor with *The Scarlet Letter* and *The Adventures of Huckleberry Finn*. One of Sarah Orne Jewett's last works, and probably her highest achievement, the novel is a moving and wise chronicle, unquestionably a genuine and great work of art. The gentle, thoughtful narrative flows with a precision of description worthy of Flaubert or Turgenev. The apparently effortless and ever graceful prose is the work of a master craftsman and a refined and gifted sensibility. The work is rich in symbols that arise naturally from the world about which the author is writing. Perhaps the dominant symbol is that of the great army of pointed firs, darkly cloaked and "standing as if they wait to embark."

The theme of balance is fundamental to the book, as much a part of it as the carefully structured narrative and perfectly poised sentences. Why, for example, does the major character, Mrs. Todd, choose to live in this tiny community? To keep the world balance true, suggests the author, to offset some other, unknown existence. There is always a reason, if one but knows it. Hand in hand with the theme of balance moves that of solitude. Paths are trodden to the shrines of solitude the world over, writes the narrator, whether it be the island of Miss Joanna or the island of Mrs. Todd's mother, or the caves of the saints of the past. The old sea captain's story of the "Waiting Place," the strange, twilight land hovering by the North Pole, again suggests this theme. Perhaps solitude serves humanity as a kind of purgatory, a way station of the soul on its way to paradise. It can be fearful, this uncharted, inner space, but it must be encountered to achieve our full humanity. The ship that carried Captain Littlepage to this land was not accidentally named "Minerva."

The characterizations in *The Country of the Pointed Firs* are among the finest in American literature. Mrs. Todd is perhaps the glory of the book, a creation worthy of Dickens. She might belong to any age, as the narrator says, "like an idyl of Theocritus"; but with her potions and herbs, her Puritan ancestors probably would have burned her as a witch. She is an unlikely classic heroine, yet the narrator cannot resist some flattering comparisons. Mrs. Todd is likened to a grand and architectural caryatid and compared to Antigone standing alone on the Theban plain. But it is her language, her way with the Old Maine way of speaking, that breathes life into her bulky figure. One can *taste* the salty old expressions as they roll off her tongue.

The past of the whalers, so recently behind the characters, is ever present in the book. Indeed, the past is important on many levels to the characters in the novel. Mrs. Fosdick remarks: "Conversations got to have some root in the past, or else you've got to explain every remark you make." The rule might be said to apply to all civilized social intercourse. People with no respect for the past are left isolated and hopeless. In the world of Sarah Orne Jewett, the present and past mutually enrich each other, and mortals wise enough to accept this are the benefactors.

The Country of the Pointed Firs is a treasure of wisdom and a lesson in the writing of pure, unaffected prose as the highest art. The individuals who stalk through its pages are loners, but they are not unhappy or unloving. Sara Orne Jewett has realized that "in the life of each of us . . . there is a place remote and islanded, and given to endless regret and secret happiness; we are each the uncompanioned hermit and recluse of an hour or a day." When she writes about her isolated New Englanders on their saltwashed islands, she is writing about all of us, about all of humanity.

THE CREAM OF THE JEST

Type of work: Novel
Author: James Branch Cabell (1879–1958)
Type of plot: Satiric fantasy
Time of plot: Twentieth century
Locale: Virginia
First published: 1917

    Principal characters:
     FELIX KENNASTON, an author
     KATHLEEN KENNASTON, his wife
     RICHARD HARROWBY, his neighbor
     ETTARRE, a woman in his novel and his dreams

The Story:

Felix Kennaston told his neighbor, Richard Harrowby, about his dreams. In writing his novels, Kennaston had created a world much different from the ordinary world of the Virginia countryside, and his dreams contained similar elements of the romantic and the marvelous. To Harrowby, the whole thing seemed indecent, for Harrowby was a conventional, unimaginative gentleman farmer, who had made his money in soaps and beauty aids.

Kennaston was writing a novel called *The Audit at Storisende*, and in his dreams, he identified himself with a character named Horvendile, who was looking for the elusive and highly improbable creature, the ideal woman. In Ettarre, his heroine, Kennaston felt he had found her. Much of his plot centered on a broken round medallion bearing mysterious symbols, a medallion he called the sigil of Scoteia.

One afternoon, Kennaston, walking in his garden, stooped to pick up a little piece of shining metal, apparently a broken half of a small disc, and casually dropped it into his pocket. Later, while looking over some books in his library, he thought of the little piece of metal in his pocket. He brought it out and laid it where the light of the lamp fell upon it. At once, he seemed to be talking with Ettarre, who explained that he had picked up half the broken sigil of Scoteia and that it had brought him back to her imagined world of romance and dream. As he reached out to touch her, she disappeared, and Kennaston found himself sitting again in his library.

Kennaston's novel was published as *The Men Who Loved Allison*, a title that his publisher assured him would bring better sales. When several readers, shocked by what they called indecency in the novel, wrote indignant letters to the newspapers, the book became a best-seller. Mrs. Kennaston, who made it a point never to read her husband's books, enjoyed his success. She treated Kennaston with polite boredom.

Strange things happened to Kennaston. One day at a luncheon, a famous man took him aside and asked him whether he bred white pigeons. This question puzzled Kennaston, as did the little mirror the man held in his hand. At another time, he saw an ugly old woman who told him that there was no price of admission to her world but that one paid upon leaving. Several times he talked to Ettarre in his dreams.

One day, Kennaston received an invitation to call on a prelate who had come to Lichfield to attend the bishop's funeral. The prelate praised Kennaston's book. He spoke of pigeons, too, and mentioned how useful he found his little mirror. Kennaston was frankly puzzled. He returned to his dreamland, where, as Horvendile, he experienced almost every passion and emotion known to man; and always, as he reached out to touch Ettarre, the dream would come to an end.

Kennaston read widely in philosophy and the classics, and he began to question the reason for his own existence. He came to the conclusion that the present moment was all that was real—that the past and future had no part in the reality of today. As a man of letters, he became interested in the artistry of creation and decided that God must have been happy over his creation of the character of Christ. Probably because of his interest in God as an artist, Kennaston was confirmed in the country church nearby. This act on his part increased his stature among the people of the neighborhood. They even elected him to the vestry.

One day, Kennaston went to the station to meet his wife's train. While he was waiting, a woman with whom he had once been in love came up to him and started to talk. She was about to go back to her home in St. Louis. They recalled the past, and as she left him to get on her train, he had a moment in which he identified her with Ettarre. His remark to his wife about her, however, was that she was not keeping her good looks as she grew older. What haunted him, however, was that the woman had drawn from her purse a medallion resembling the sigil of Scoteia.

Kennaston—as Horvendile—dreamed of being in many parts of the world in many eras; and one of the mysteries was that he was always a young man of about twenty-five. He was at Queen Elizabeth's court; he was at Whitehall with Cromwell; he was at the French court of Louis XIV; he was among the aristocrats about to be beheaded during the French Revolution; and always beside him was Ettarre, whose contact would bring his dreams to an end.

One afternoon he found, quite by accident, the missing piece of the sigil of Scoteia in his wife's bathroom. After securing the other piece, he put them together on his wife's dressing table and began speculating about the relation of his wife to Ettarre. He hoped that her discovery of the entire sigil would express to her what he had never been able to convey. Yet, she paid no attention to it, and their life continued its banal rounds. Eleven months later, Mrs. Kennaston died in her sleep without ever having discussed the sigil or its significance with her husband. After her death, he showed Harrowby the two halves of the sigil, by which he had almost made his dreams come true. Far from being a magic emblem, the pieces proved to be merely the broken top of a cold cream jar. It was the final disillusionment for Kennaston, who was at last compelled to give up romantic, youthful dreaming for the realities of middle age.

Critical Evaluation:

In 1929, James Branch Cabell collected into one eighteen-volume series all his works dealing with the fictional land of Poictesme and its legendary hero, Dom Manuel. Poictesme—the name probably derived from a combination of Angouleme and Potiers—is an imaginary province in southern France; Cabell traces its history from 1234 to 1750 and describes in detail its social customs, legal procedures, sexual mores, and legendary background. Two of the eighteen books in this Storisende Edition, however, are not set in Poictesme: these are *The Rivet in Grandfather's Neck* (1915) and *The Cream of the Jest*. Both novels are included in the series because they treat the same themes as the Dom Manuel stories: both are concerned with ideals of chivalric love and with the same values found in mythical Poictesme.

The Cream of the Jest is set in the American South, in the town of Lichfield in Virginia; its hero, Felix Kennaston, is an author who, like Cabell, has created a romantic land of fantasy in his novels. When the humdrum life of the Virginia countryside becomes too dull for his imaginative spirit, he escapes to his land of dreams, identifying with his hero, Horvendile; through the character of Horvendile, he enjoys romantic adventures and feeds on the noble and beautiful ideals of chivalry in the manner of a Don Quixote. Cabell uses Kennaston's fantasies to weave an allegorical tale, charged at once with romanticism and realism, symbolism and irony. Through Kennaston's search for the perfect woman, which ends in his discovery that the elusive Ettarre is actually his boring and unimaginative wife, Cabell dramatizes his ironic and romantic comic vision of life.

Cabell's vision is that of a man who has looked deeply into life and found it wanting; he is profoundly discontented with what he has observed. As a remedy, he finds consolation in his great ambition—"to write perfectly of beautiful happenings." He creates fantasies in exquisite language, inspired by his vision of a land of joy and love, a land untroubled by sorrow, frustration, and regret. In *The Cream of the Jest*, Felix Kennaston's career as a dreamer parallels the lives of all men, who turn irresistibly to clouds, romance, and mystery to atone for the boredom or pain of their everyday lives. The gentle irony of Cabell's vision is that he not only sees the dreariness and monotony of human life and understands the saving, soothing value of dreams, but admits with objective clarity and insight that dreams are impotent and a little childish. He knows more than anyone else the necessity and beauty of romance, at the same time that he accepts the reality of life, no matter how far it falls short of his mind's imaginings.

THE CRISIS

Type of work: Novel
Author: Winston Churchill (1871–1947)
Type of plot: Historical romance
Time of plot: Civil War period
Locale: Missouri and Virginia
First published: 1901

>   *Principal characters:*
>   STEPHEN BRICE, a young lawyer from Boston
>   VIRGINIA CARVEL, his sweetheart
>   CLARENCE COLFAX, Brice's rival for Virginia Carvel
>   JUDGE WHIPPLE, Brice's employer and friend
>   COLONEL CARVEL, Virginia's father
>   ABRAHAM LINCOLN

The Story:

In 1858, Stephen Brice emigrated from Boston to St. Louis with his widowed mother. He went to accept the offer of Judge Whipple, his father's friend, who had promised Stephen an opportunity to enter his law firm. A personable young man, Stephen Brice found favor among the people of St. Louis, including Colonel Carvel, and the colonel's daughter, Virginia. Stephen promptly fell in love with Virginia Carvel. He was not encouraged by the girl at first because he was a New Englander.

One day, Judge Whipple sent Stephen to Springfield, Illinois, with a message for the man who was running for senator against Stephen A. Douglas. When Stephen Brice finally found his man, Abraham Lincoln, he was in time to hear the famous Freeport debate between Lincoln and Douglas. Lincoln made a deep impression on Stephen, who went back to St. Louis a confirmed Republican, as Judge Whipple had hoped. Feeling that Stephen would some day be a great politician, the judge had sent him to Lincoln to catch some of Lincoln's idealism and practical politics.

Convinced by Lincoln that no country could exist half-slave and half-free, Stephen Brice became active in Missouri politics on behalf of the Republicans, a dangerous course to take in St. Louis because of the many Southerners living in the city. His antislavery views soon alienated Stephen from the girl he wanted to marry, who then promised to marry Stephen's rival, her cousin and fellow Southerner, Clarence Colfax.

Lincoln lost the election for the senate, but in doing so won for himself the presidency of the United States in 1860. During both campaigns, Stephen

Brice worked for the Republican party. An able orator, he became known as a rising young lawyer of exceptional abilities.

The guns at Fort Sumter reverberated loudly in St. Louis in 1861. The city was divided into two factions, proslavery Southerners and antislavery Northerners. Friends of long standing no longer spoke to one another, and members of the same family found themselves at odds over the question of which side Missouri should favor, the Union or the Confederacy. It was a trying time for Stephen Brice. Because of his widowed mother and his political activities, he was unable to join the army. Judge Whipple convinced him that, for the time being, he could do more for his country as a civilian. It was hard for the young man to believe the judge when all of Stephen's friends and acquaintances were going about the city in uniform.

When war was declared, Missouri had a little campaign of its own, for the state militia, under the direction of the governor, tried to seize the state. This attempt was defeated by the prompt action of Federal forces in capturing the militia training camp without firing a shot. A spectator at that minor engagement, Stephen made the acquaintance of a former army officer named Sherman and of another shambling man who claimed he should be given a regiment. The young officers laughed at him; his name was Ulysses S. Grant.

Among those captured when Federal troops overcame the Missouri militia was Clarence Colfax, Stephen's rival. Clarence refused to give his oath and go on parole, and he soon escaped from prison and disappeared into the South. Virginia Carvel thought him more of a hero than ever.

Because communications with the South and the Southwest had been cut by the Union armies, Colonel Carvel went bankrupt. He and his daughter aided Southern sympathizers attempting to join the Confederate Army. At last, the colonel himself felt that it was his duty to leave St. Louis and take an active part in the hostilities.

The war continued, putting the lie to those optimists who had prophesied that hostilities would end in a few months. By the time of the battle at Vicksburg, Stephen had become a lieutenant in the Union Army. He distinguished himself in that battle and came once more to the attention of Sherman. When the city fell, Stephen found Clarence Colfax, now a lieutenant-colonel in the Confederate Army. The Southerner had received a severe wound. To save Clarence's life, Stephen arranged for him to be sent to St. Louis on a hospital ship. Stephen knew that he was probably sending his rival back to marry Virginia Carvel. Young Colfax realized what Stephen had done and told Virginia as much while he was convalescing in St. Louis. The girl vowed that she would never marry a Yankee, even if Colfax were killed.

Judge Whipple had fallen ill, and he was nursed by Virginia and by Stephen's mother. While the judge was sinking fast, Colonel Carvel appeared. At the risk of his life, he had come through the lines in civilian clothes to see his daughter and his old friend. There was a strange meeting at Judge Whipple's deathbed. Clarence Colfax, Colonel Carvel, and Stephen Brice were all there. They had all risked their lives, for the Confederates could have been arrested as spies, and Stephen, because he was with them, could have been convicted of treason. That night, Virginia realized that she was in love with Stephen.

After the judge's death, Stephen returned to the army. Ordered to General Sherman's staff, he accompanied the general on the march through Georgia. At the battle of Bentonville, Stephen again met Clarence Colfax, who had been captured by Union soldiers while in civilian clothes and brought to Sherman's headquarters as a spy. Once again, Stephen interceded with Sherman and saved the Southerner's life. Soon afterward, Stephen, promoted to the rank of major, was sent by Sherman with some dispatches to General Grant at City Point, Virginia. Stephen recognized Grant as the man he had seen at the engagement of the militia camp back in St. Louis.

During the conference with the general, an officer appeared to summon Stephen to meet another old acquaintance, Abraham Lincoln. The president, like Grant, wished to hear Stephen's first-hand account of the march through Georgia to the sea. When Stephen asked for a pardon for Clarence Colfax, Lincoln said he would consider the matter. Stephen went with Lincoln to Richmond for an inspection of that city after it had fallen to Grant's armies.

Virginia Carvel, not knowing of Stephen's intercession on behalf of Clarence Colfax, traveled to Washington to ask Lincoln for a pardon. She gained an audience with the president, during which she met Stephen once again. Lincoln granted them the pardon, saying that with the war soon to end, the time to show clemency had come. He left Virginia and Stephen alone when he hurried to keep another appointment. The young people had realized during their talk with Lincoln that there was much to be forgiven and forgotten by both sides in the struggle that was drawing to a close. The emotion of the moment overcame their reticence at last, and they declared their love for each other. They were married the following day.

After the wedding, they went to visit Virginia's ancestral home in Annapolis. A few days later, word came to them that Lincoln had died from an assassin's bullet.

Critical Evaluation:

Judged on the basis of his later novels dealing with problems such as class relationships and divorce, Winston Churchill must be considered outmoded in his attitudes and ideas. His own conservative and wealthy background biased him in favor of genteel, romantic, or impractical solutions to tough modern questions, although his thought was often enhanced by its sincerity and moral seriousness. As a historical novelist, however, his reputation is secure; his early works about events in the Revolutionary and Civil wars are excellent examples of vivid historical fiction. One of the most popular of these novels was *The Crisis*, a novel about people whose loves, loyalties, and friendships are threatened by the divisive influences of the Civil War.

Churchill's choice of the city of St. Louis as the setting for the novel's action is crucial, since that city was a crossroads between North and South when hostilities began. St. Louis had its old established families who had emigrated both from Northern and Southern states, and after 1861, the city suffered a painful division in popular sentiment between sympathizers of the Union and the Confederate causes. At one point in the narrative, Clarence Colfax is taken prisoner by Federal troops for his involvement in the Missouri militia's attempt to seize the state. St. Louis is thus the ideal setting in which to play out characters' conflicting personal beliefs and emotions against a backdrop of factual political and social history. Families that had been friends for decades cease to speak to one another, and when Missouri is finally established on the Union side, the city becomes dangerous for its own families of Southern background who have lived there for years.

Likewise, central to the plot is the love relationship of Stephen Brice and Virginia Carvel, which is threatened by the war; Stephen becomes a Union Army lieutenant, while Virginia, whose father is a Colonel in the Confederate Army, vows that she will never marry a Yankee. The two are reconciled in a dramatic scene in Abraham Lincoln's office, where Virginia has come to beg for a pardon for her old suitor, Clarence Colfax, unaware that Stephen has already interceded with the president on his rival's behalf. The believable portraits of Lincoln, General Grant, General Sherman, and other historical figures are feats in themselves; and the successful fusing within a single story of personal, everyday happenings with events and characters of great historical import makes *The Crisis* succeed where so many novels of this type have failed.

CUDJO'S CAVE

Type of work: Novel
Author: John Townsend Trowbridge (1827–1916)
Type of plot: Historical romance
Time of plot: 1861
Locale: Tennessee
First published: 1863

Principal characters:

PENN HAPGOOD, a Quaker schoolmaster
MR. VILLARS, a blind clergyman
VIRGINIA and
SALINA, his daughters
LYSANDER SPROWL, Salina's estranged husband
AUGUSTUS BLYTHEWOOD, a planter
MR. STACKRIDGE, a Unionist farmer
CARL, a German boy and friend of Penn
OLD TOBY, a freed slave
CUDJO and
POMP, runaway slaves
SILAS ROPES, a bully

The Story:

In 1861, Penn Hapgood, a young Quaker, was the schoolmaster in the small Tennessee town of Curryville. Because he made no effort to conceal his antislavery convictions, he was unpopular among the hotheaded Seccessionists of the community. The Unionists, on the other hand, had offered him a commission in the militia unit that they were secretly organizing. Penn refused the commission offered him on the grounds of his religious faith.

His unpopularity grew after he aided Dan Pepperill, a poor white, flogged and ridden on a rail because he had befriended a whipped slave. Penn's friend, a kindly young German named Carl, offered him a pistol to use in self-defense if he were attacked, but the schoolmaster saw no need to arm himself. A short time later, a party of ruffians seized Penn and tarred and feathered him. Carl, unable to save his friend, searched for some Union sympathizers to defend Penn, but by the time the rescue party arrived at the schoolhouse, the young teacher was not to be found. It was learned, however, that he had gone to his boardinghouse, where his landlady, Mrs. Sprowl, had refused to let him in. She had acted on the orders of Silas Ropes, the leader of the mob.

Penn had found shelter in the home of a blind clergyman, Mr. Villars. The minister's household was made up of his two daughters, Virginia and Salina, old Toby, a freed slave, and Carl, the young German. Old Toby and Farmer Stackridge, a staunch Unionist, tended to Penn and put him to bed in the clergyman's home. While he was still resting, Augustus Blythewood, a planter in love with Virginia, appeared at the house. Although she was little attracted to her suitor, Virginia entertained him graciously in order to conceal the fact that the fugitive was hidden nearby. Another caller was Lysander Sprowl, the son of Penn's landlady. Salina, the older sister, and young Sprowl were married, but they had separated some time before.

Sprowl, having learned Penn's whereabouts, promised to lead the villagers to the schoolmaster's hiding place. The aroused townspeople accused Mr. Villars of hiding an Abolitionist. While they were threatening the old man, Penn disappeared from the house under mysterious circumstances.

A mob, aroused by Blythewood, seized old Toby and prepared to flog him in an effort to learn Penn's whereabouts. Carl managed to cut Toby's bonds before the mob could carry out its threat. Toby, escaping, ran into Blythewood and recognized him. The planter then called off the mob and went to the minister's house, where he pretended great indignation at what had happened.

Penn, meanwhile, was safe in Cudjo's Cave, a hideout known only to runaway slaves. Having heard the angry townspeople threatening Mr. Villars, he had in his half-delirious condition fled into an adjoining field before he fainted. When he came to, he found himself beside a fire in a cavern, with Cudjo and Pomp, two escaped slaves, ministering to his wants. They had befriended Penn because of the help he had given Pepperill several weeks before. Pomp, in particular, was a magnificent old fellow, almost heroic in his dignity and spirit. Both slaves had suffered at the hands of Blythewood and Ropes, the town bully. Through the two, Penn sent word to Mr. Villars that he was safe. The clergyman sent Penn's clothes and food to the hiders.

When he was able to travel, Penn decided to set out for the North. Near Curryville, he fell into the hands of a small detachment of Confederate soldiers. Convicted at a drumhead trial, he was sentenced to be hanged unless he joined the army. He refused. Carl, who had helped his friend before, volunteered to enlist in Penn's place. Set free, Penn was again in danger from a group of townspeople led by Ropes and Sprowl, but with the aid of Farmer Stackridge, he managed to elude his pursuers. Blythewood, hearing of his escape, was furious that Penn had slipped through his fingers.

Penn did not go far, however, for he was unwilling to leave the Villars family without protection. His fears were justified. When he returned secretly to the minister's home, he learned that Mr. Villars had been seized and carried off to prison. Penn himself was captured a short time later, and among his fellow prisoners, he found the blind clergyman. Because Carl was one of the soldiers detailed to guard them, he and the minister were able to make their escape. Stackridge was guiding them to a place of safety in the mountains when they were again captured. As the soldiers were about to run their bayonets through Penn, one of their number dropped dead. The others ran away. Pomp and Cudjo appeared and led the fugitives to Cudjo's Cave.

Augustus Blythewood proposed to Virginia Villars, but she, realizing his dislike for Penn, would have nothing to do with the young planter. Meanwhile, Stackridge and a party of his Unionist friends were skirmishing with the Confederate soldiers in the woods nearby. Virginia, while searching for Penn, was captured by a Confederate soldier, but she was relieved when she discovered that her captor was Carl. Before the young German could lead her out of the forest, set afire by the skirmishers, he himself was captured by Ropes's men. After she had climbed to a rocky ledge, the fire having cut off her escape on both sides, she was rescued from her predicament by Penn and Cudjo, who led her to the cave. That night, rain put out the forest fire. In the morning, old Toby appeared at the cave. He was overjoyed to discover that his mistress and her father were both safe.

Lysander Sprowl, in the meantime, had taken possession of Mr. Villars' house and forced Salina to serve him there. When Toby returned with a note to tell Salina that her sister and her father were safe, he tried to deceive Sprowl as to the fate of the fugitives, but Salina, who still loved her worthless husband, incautiously showed him Virginia's note. Sprowl brutally ordered Toby flogged in order to learn where Mr. Villars and Penn were hidden. Angered by Sprowl's cruelty, Salina set fire to her father's house and, under cover of the confusion, helped old Toby to make his escape.

Sprowl, encountering Carl, demanded that the young German lead him to the cave. Carl pretended to agree, but along the way, he managed to hit the bully over the head with a stone. While Sprowl was still unconscious, Carl dragged him to the cave, where he was securely bound. Meanwhile, old Toby and Salina made their way to the cave, and they arrived about the time Carl appeared with the wounded Sprowl. Pomp had also led to the cave the band of Unionists guided by Stackridge. They prepared to turn their quarters into an underground fortress.

Before long, a party led by Silas Ropes discovered the location of the cave. He and his men guarded the entrance in the hope of starving the occupants into submission.

Salina, ever changeable, loosened Sprowl's bonds so that he was able to escape. He went at once to the troops under Blythewood and arranged to have a squad of men sent to attack the cave. When Sprowl, at the head of the attacking force, reached the entrance of the cave, he found it defended by his wife. She fired at her husband, wounding him fatally, and was herself bayoneted by one of the Confederate soldiers. Virginia and her father were captured and taken before Blythewood.

The planter again pleaded his suit with Virginia, but she received his offers with contempt. While they argued, apart from the camp, Pomp suddenly appeared and told his former master that any sudden move would mean his death. Carl and Penn were covering Blythewood with their guns, and he was taken a prisoner to the cave. There Pomp compelled his former master to sign a safe conduct pass for the defenders and an order for the attackers to cease the fight.

Under safe conduct, the defenders left the cave. Mr. Villars, Virginia, Penn, and Pomp set out for Ohio. They left the body of Salina behind them in the cave, as well as those of Cudjo and Ropes, who had killed each other during an earlier attack. Pomp returned long enough to free Blythewood before joining his friends on their way to safety.

Penn and Carl went from Ohio to Pennsylvania, where they enlisted in the same regiment. Pomp served the Union as a scout. In many battles of the war, Penn did heroic service, earning for himself the nickname of "The Fighting Quaker."

Critical Evaluation:

Written during the Civil War, *Cudjo's Cave* mingles elements of propaganda with its historical setting and romantic theme. Because the novel displays deep sincerity, however, and a considerable degree of literary skill, it has enjoyed a popularity outlasting by many years the political issues which gave it birth. The book presents clearly and forcefully the problem of the rural population in Tennessee during that difficult time of decision at the beginning of the Civil War period. In that particular time and place the problem was peculiarly acute because Tennessee was a border state and its citizens had many reasons for indecision when faced by the realities of conflict between North and South. John Townsend Trowbridge, working close to actual history, dramatized effectively the guerrilla warfare fought among the people of Tennessee and Kentucky.

At times, the plot comes close to melodrama, but the narrative strength and the skill of many characterizations manages to raise the action to a higher level. The villains in the tale are the least convincing characters; most of the time, they are no more than sketches, without depth or subtlety. No doubt many men committed such vile acts, but the reader is given no insight into their deeper instincts or motivations. Another flaw in the book is the dialogue, which is at times stilted and unrealistic. In particular, Old Toby's black dialect and Carl's German accent are both unconvincing, falling perilously close to stereotypes. Cudjo's speech and actions occasionally slip into stereotypical patterns as well.

Pomp, however, is a character at once noble and believable. Although on the surface he seems almost too perfect to be true, the reader comes to feel an affection for this extraordinary black man. The author penetrates Pomp's personality and creates in him one of the two best characters in the novel. Penn Hapgood, the Quaker schoolmaster, is the other character who lifts the book above the ordinary. The Abolitionist Penn is shown to be an idealist of subtle feelings and courage, a man willing to risk his life for what he believes. His speeches against the system combine propaganda with genuine emotion.

He shows his wisdom when he declares that "education alone makes men free" and acknowledges that many white men might be considered slaves. Pomp's testimony to the joys of freedom, however precarious, is a moving and powerful statement. Throughout the long novel, Penn and Pomp stir the reader's interest and sympathies.

THE CUSTOM OF THE COUNTRY

Type of work: Novel
Author: Edith Wharton (1862–1937)
Type of plot: Social criticism
Time of plot: Late nineteenth century
Locale: New York and Paris
First published: 1913

Principal characters:
UNDINE SPRAGG, a predatory woman
ELMER MOFFATT, her first husband
RALPH MARVELL, Undine's second husband
PAUL, Undine and Ralph Marvell's son
RAYMOND DE CHELLES, her third husband
PETER VAN DEGEN, her lover
ABNER E. SPRAGG, her father

The Story:

Undine Spragg, who came from Apex City with her parents, had been in New York for two years without being accepted in society. Her opportunity came at last when she was invited to a dinner given by Laura Fairford, whose brother, Ralph Marvell, had taken an interest in her.

Ralph, although his family was prominently established in social circles, had little money. Moreover, he was an independent thinker who disliked the superficiality of important New York figures like Peter Van Degen, the wealthy husband of Ralph's cousin, Clare Dagonet, with whom Ralph had once been in love.

About two months after their meeting, Undine became engaged to Ralph. One night, they went to see a play. Undine was shocked to find herself sitting next to Elmer Moffatt, a figure in her past whom she did not want to acknowledge in public. She promised to meet him privately in Central Park the next day. When they met, Moffatt, a bluntly spoken vulgarian, told Undine that she must help him in his business deals after she married Ralph.

Moffatt also went to see Undine's father and asked him to join in a business deal. Moffatt threatened to publicly reveal Undine's past if Mr. Spragg refused to cooperate.

Ralph and Undine were married, and Ralph was happy until he realized that Undine cared less for his company than for the social world. Mr. Spragg, having made the business deal with Moffatt, had thus been able to give Undine a big wedding. Ralph soon began to realize the ruthlessness of Undine's desire

---

for money. Her unhappiness and resentment were increased when she learned that she was pregnant.

In the next several years, Moffatt became a significant financial figure in New York. Ralph, in an attempt to support Undine's extravagance, went to work in a business to which he was ill-suited. Undine, meanwhile, kept up a busy schedule of social engagements. She had also accepted some expensive gifts from Peter Van Degen, who was romantically interested in her, before Peter left to spend the season in Europe.

One day, Undine saw Moffatt, who wanted to meet Ralph in order to make a disreputable business deal. The business deal succeeded, and Undine went to Paris to meet Peter. Before long, she had spent all of her money. She then met the Comte Raymond de Chelles, a French aristocrat whom she thought of marrying. In the face of this competition, Peter frankly told Undine of his desire for her and said that if she would stay with him, he could give her everything she wanted. At this point, Undine received a telegram announcing that Ralph was critically ill with pneumonia and asking her to return to New York immediately. Undine decided to stay in Paris.

Ralph recovered and, after four years of marriage to Undine, returned to the Dagonet household with his son Paul. For Paul's sake, he began to work hard at the office and on a novel that he had begun.

Undine, after an uncontested divorce from Ralph, lived with Peter Van Degen for two months. Peter, however, was disillusioned when he learned that Undine had not gone to see Ralph when he was critically ill; he left her without getting the promised divorce from his wife Clare.

Ralph, meanwhile, was concerned only with his son and his book. Then he learned that Undine was engaged to Comte Raymond de Chelles and badly needed money to have her marriage to Ralph annulled by the Church. Undine agreed to waive her rights to the boy if Ralph would send her one hundred thousand dollars to pay for her annulment. Ralph borrowed half of the needed sum and went to Moffatt to make another business deal. As Undine's deadline approached, with the deal not yet concluded, Ralph went to see Moffatt, who told him that the matter was going more slowly than expected and that it would take a year to materialize. Moffatt told Ralph that he himself was once married to Undine, back in Apex City, but that Undine's parents had forced the young couple to get a divorce. After hearing this story, Ralph went home and committed suicide.

Undine, now in possession of her son, married Raymond de Chelles. She was very happy in Paris, even though Raymond was strict about her social life. After three months, they moved to the family estate at Saint Désert to live quietly and modestly. When Raymond began to ignore her, Undine became bored and resentful of her husband's family for not making allowances for her customary extravagance.

One day, she invited a dealer from Paris to appraise some of the priceless

Chelles tapestries. When the dealer arrived, the prospective American buyer with him turned out to be Moffatt, now one of the richest men in New York. Over the next several weeks, Undine saw a great deal of her former husband. When the time came for Moffatt to return to New York, Undine invited him to have an affair with her. Moffatt told her that he wanted marriage or nothing.

Undine went to Reno, where she divorced Raymond and married Moffatt on the same day. Moffatt gave Undine everything she wanted, but she realized that in many personal ways he compared unfavorably with her other husbands. The Moffatts settled in a mansion in Paris to satisfy Undine's social ambitions and her husband's taste for worldly display. When Undine learned that an old society acquaintance, Jim Driscoll, had been appointed ambassador to England, she decided that she would like to be the wife of an ambassador. Moffatt told her bluntly that that was the one thing she could never have because she was a divorced woman. Still dissatisfied, Undine was certain that the one thing she was destined to be was an ambassador's wife.

Critical Evaluation:

The Custom of the Country, one of Edith Wharton's most successful novels, was published midway through her productive 1905 to 1920 period, which culminated in a Pulitzer Prize. The novel reflects not only her overwhelming concern with American cultural inadequacies and her contempt for the values of the newly moneyed and growing middle class, in which she resembles her contemporary, Henry James, but also her interest in the issue of women's role in society.

By the time Wharton wrote *The Custom of the Country*, the way had been paved by writers such as Theodore Dreiser and Robert Grant for the portrayal of self-serving, cold-blooded, and unsympathetic heroines. The battle that was fought at the turn of the century between those who insisted on realistic female characters and those who still clung to traditional idealized representations of women had, by 1913, definitely been decided in favor of the realists. Thus, the public had been sufficiently conditioned to accept a heroine like Undine Spragg, who is the epitome of amoral materialism. Through her character, Wharton is able to deal with both the cultural issue and the women's issue simultaneously, since Undine has been molded into her present ugly form by the forces of the grasping, unprincipled, and uncultured new commercial class. She is vain, crude, and opportunistic; she is intellectually, aesthetically, and spiritually empty.

The problem in the novel is that Wharton cannot bring herself to absolve Undine of guilt for becoming what society has made of her—in fact, the author increasingly despises her heroine. Unable to remain objective toward her creation, Wharton allows Undine to become an inhuman abstraction; in so doing, she sacrifices the chance to subordinate individual characterization to a broader indictment of social conditions, as she did so successfully in *The*

House of Mirth. The novel is thus marred not only by her loss of objectivity toward the heroine but also toward some of her minor characters; Wharton is less harsh than she might otherwise have been in her judgment of such characters as Abner Spragg and his wife, simply because their vulgarity is never permitted to triumph as is Undine's. The deeper reason for the author's intolerance of Undine Spragg, however, lies in the fact that her sin of vulgarity is further compounded by pretentiousness and lack of self-understanding—to Wharton, the worst sin of all.

DAISY MILLER
A Study

Type of work: Novelette
Author: Henry James (1843–1916)
Type of plot: Psychological realism
Time of plot: Mid-nineteenth century
Locale: Vevey, Switzerland, and Rome
First published: 1879

> Principal characters:
> DAISY MILLER, an American tourist
> WINTERBOURNE, an American expatriate
> GIOVANELLI, Daisy's Italian suitor

The Story:

Winterbourne was a young American who had lived in Europe for quite a while. He spent a great deal of time at Vevey, which was a favorite spot of his aunt, Mrs. Costello. One day, while he was loitering outside the hotel, he was attracted by a young woman who appeared to be related to Randolph Miller, a young American boy with whom he had been talking. After a while, the young woman exchanged a few words with him. Her name was Daisy Miller. The boy was her brother, and they were in Vevey with their mother. They came from Schenectady, Winterbourne learned, and they intended to go next to Italy. Randolph insisted that he wanted to go home. Winterbourne learned that Daisy hoped to visit the Castle of Chillon. He promised to take her there, for he was quite familiar with the old castle.

Winterbourne asked his aunt, Mrs. Costello, to meet Daisy. Mrs. Costello, however, would not agree because she thought the Millers were common. That evening, Daisy and Winterbourne planned to go out on the lake, much to the horror of Eugenio, the Millers' traveling companion, who was more like a member of the family than a courier. At the last moment, Daisy changed her mind about the night excursion. A few days later, Winterbourne and Daisy visited the Castle of Chillon. The outing confirmed Mrs. Costello's opinion that Daisy was uncultured and unsophisticated.

Winterbourne made plans to go to Italy. When he arrived, he went directly to the home of Mrs. Walker, an American whom he had met in Geneva. There he met Daisy and Randolph. Daisy reproved him for not having called to see her. Winterbourne replied that she was unkind, as he had just arrived on the train. Daisy asked Mrs. Walker's permission to bring an Italian friend, Mr. Giovanelli, to a party that Mrs. Walker was about to give. Mrs. Walker agreed. Then Daisy said that she and the Italian were going for a walk. Mrs. Walker was shocked, as young unmarried women did not walk the streets of Rome with Italians. Daisy suggested that there would be no objection if

Winterbourne would go with her to the spot where she was to meet the Italian and then walk with them.

Winterbourne and Daisy set out and eventually found Giovanelli. They walked together for a while. Then Mrs. Walker's carriage drew alongside the strollers. She beckoned to Winterbourne and implored him to persuade Daisy to enter her carriage. She told him that Daisy had been ruining her reputation by such behavior; she had become familiar with Italians and was quite heedless of the scandal she was causing. Mrs. Walker said she would never speak to Winterbourne again if he did not ask Daisy to get into the carriage at once. Daisy, refusing the requests of Mrs. Walker and Winterbourne, continued her walk with the Italian.

Mrs. Walker was determined to snub Daisy at the party. When Winterbourne arrived, Daisy had not made her appearance. Mrs. Miller arrived more than an hour before Daisy appeared with Giovanelli. Mrs. Walker had a moment of weakness and greeted them politely; but, as Daisy came to say goodnight, Mrs. Walker turned her back upon her. From that time on, Daisy and Giovanelli found all doors shut to them. Winterbourne saw her occasionally, but she was always with the Italian. Everyone thought they were having an affair. When Winterbourne asked her if she were engaged, Daisy said that she was not.

One night, despite the danger from malarial fever, Giovanelli took Daisy to the Colosseum. Winterbourne, encountering them in the ancient arena, reproached the Italian for his thoughtlessness. Giovanelli said that Daisy had insisted upon viewing the ruins by moonlight. Within a few days, Daisy was dangerously ill. During her illness, she sent word to Winterbourne that she had never been engaged to Giovanelli. A week later, she was dead.

As they stood beside Daisy's grave in the Protestant cemetery in Rome, Giovanelli told Winterbourne that Daisy would never have married her Italian suitor, even if she had lived. Then Winterbourne realized that he himself had loved Daisy without knowing his own feelings and that he could have married her had he acted differently. He reasoned, too late, that he had lived in Europe too long and that he had forgotten the freedom of American manners and the complexity of the American character.

Critical Evaluation:

In *Daisy Miller*, Henry James represents the conflicts between American innocence and independence and the rigid social conventions characteristic of the American colony in Rome. While Daisy deliberately flaunts convention by her unorthodox behavior, Mrs. Costello and Mrs. Walker make appearance their only basis for moral judgment. Winterbourne, troubled by the ambiguity in Daisy's character, seeks some objective basis for making a judgment.

Daisy realizes that the other Americans have no interest in her as an individual. Living in a world of moral judgments based entirely upon social conventions, they are only concerned about preserving the appearance of morality through "proper" behavior. Determined to be accepted on more meaningful grounds than these, Daisy asserts those freedoms that she would be allowed in America but that are clearly out of place in Rome. Confident in her own innocence, she refuses to conform to the restrictions her compatriots would place upon her.

Innocence and crudity are the terms characterizing Daisy, and these conflicting qualities are the source of Winterbourne's confusion about her. He, like his aunt and Mrs. Walker, has a tendency to make judgments on the basis of superficial appearances. Daisy, however, seems innocent to him in spite of her unconventional behavior, and he cannot fit her into a neat category as he would like. Discovering Daisy in a seemingly compromising position with Giovanelli in the Colosseum, however, gives Winterbourne the evidence he needs, and with some relief, he declares Daisy morally corrupt. In so doing, he places himself solidly among the other Americans who, like himself, have lived too long abroad to appreciate the real innocence that underlies Daisy's seeming moral laxity. Too late, Winterbourne realizes at the graveside that his formulation of Daisy has been unjust.

THE DAMNATION OF THERON WARE

Type of work: Novel
Author: Harold Frederic (1856–1898)
Type of plot: Social criticism
Time of plot: 1890's
Locale: New York State
First published: 1896

Principal characters:

THERON WARE, a young Methodist minister
ALICE WARE, his wife
FATHER FORBES, a Catholic priest
CELIA MADDEN, a rich young Irish-Catholic girl
DR. LEDSMAR, Father Forbes's friend
MR. GORRINGE, a trustee of Theron's church

The Story:

Theron Ware had gone to the annual statewide meeting of the Methodist Episcopal Church with great expectation of being appointed to the large church in Tecumseh. He was greatly disappointed, therefore, when he was sent to Octavius, a small rural community.

To the minister and his wife, the town and its citizens did not appear formidable at first, but a hint of what was to come occurred the first morning after their arrival. A boy who delivered milk to Mrs. Ware informed her that he could not deliver milk on Sunday because the trustees of the church would object. Shortly afterward, the trustees told the new minister that his sermons were too dignified and that Mrs. Ware's Sunday bonnet was far too elaborate for a minister's wife. Theron and his wife were depressed. Unhappy in his new charge, Theron decided to write a book about Abraham.

One day, Theron assisted an injured Irish-Catholic workman and went home with him to see what help he might give. At the man's deathbed, Theron observed the parish priest and a pretty young redhead, Celia Madden, who assisted him. Upon their acquaintance, the minister was surprised to find that his earlier hostility to Catholics and the Irish was foolish. These people were more cultured than he, as he learned a few evenings later when he went to the priest for some advice in connection with his proposed book.

At the priest's home, he met Dr. Ledsmar, a retired physician interested in biblical research. Both the priest and the doctor knew a great deal about the actual culture of Abraham and his people. They tried to be tactful, but the young minister quickly saw how wrong he had been to think himself ready to write a religious book on any topic; all he knew was the little he had been taught at his Methodist Seminary.

Upon leaving Father Forbes and the doctor, Theron walked past the Catholic church. Hearing music within, he entered to find Celia Madden at the organ. Later, he walked home with her and discovered that she was interested in literature and art as well as music. Once again that evening, Theron was made to realize how little he actually knew. He went home with the feeling that his own small world was not a very cultured one.

Three months later, there was a revival at Theron's church. Mr. and Mrs. Soulsby, two professional exhorters, arrived to lead a week of meetings which were designed to pay off the church debt and put fervor into its members. The Wares, who entertained the Soulsbys, were surprised to find that the revival leaders were very much like insurance salesmen, employing similar tactics. During the revival week, Theron was nonplussed to discover what he thought were the beginnings of an affair between his wife and one of the trustees of his church, Mr. Gorringe.

In a long talk with Mrs. Soulsby, Theron told her that he had almost decided to give up the Methodist ministry because of the shallowness he had discovered in his people and in his church. Mrs. Soulsby pointed out to him that Methodists were no worse than anyone else in the way of hypocrisy and that all they lacked was an external discipline. She also reminded him that he was incapable of making a living because he lacked any worldly training.

Theron's life was further complicated when he realized that he was beginning to fall in love with Celia Madden. Because of her interest in music, he had asked her advice in buying a piano for his home, and she had, unknown to him, paid part of the bill for the instrument. He also found time to call on Dr. Ledsmar, whose peculiar views on the early church interested him. He disgusted the old doctor, however, with his insinuations of an affair between Father Forbes and Celia.

In September, the Methodists of Octavius had a camp meeting. Its fervor did not appeal to Theron, after his more intellectual religious reading and his discussions with Celia and Father Forbes, and he went off quietly by himself. In the woods, he came upon a picnic given by Father Forbes's church. At the picnic, he met Celia and had a long talk with her, kissed her, and told her of his unhappiness in his double bondage to church and wife.

Soon afterward, he alienated Celia by telling her that he was afraid of scandal if he were seen talking with her. He also offended Father Forbes by reports that Dr. Ledsmar had spoken slightingly of Celia. The priest told his housekeeper that he was no longer at home to Theron Ware.

One day, Theron openly confronted his wife with his suspicions about her and Mr. Gorringe. She denied the charges, but her very denial seemed to speak against her in her husband's mind. In his unhappiness, he went to see Celia. She was not at home, but her brother, who was dying slowly of tuberculosis, saw him. With the license of the dying, he said that when Theron arrived in Octavius he had the face of an angel, full of innocence, but that in the eight months the minister had spent in the little town, his face had taken on a look of deceit and cunning. Celia's brother continued by warning the minister that he should stay among his own people, that it was bad for him to tear himself from the support which Methodism had given him.

Leaving the Madden home, Theron learned that Celia was going to New York City. It occurred to him that Father Forbes was also going to the city that evening and perhaps they were traveling together. He went home and told his wife that urgent business called him to Albany; then he went to the station and boarded the train unseen. In New York, he saw the priest and Celia meet, and he followed them to a hotel. After the priest had left the hotel, he went upstairs and knocked at Celia's door. She told him that she was busy and did not wish to see him, adding that she had noticed him following her earlier in the journey. While he pleaded with her, Father Forbes came in with some other gentlemen and informed Theron that they had come to New York to get another brother of Celia out of a bad scrape.

Dismissed, Theron stumbled down the stairs. A few days later, he arrived at the Soulsby house at dawn. He told an incoherent story of having tried to commit suicide, of stealing money from the church at Octavius, and of wandering alone about the city for hours while he tried to drink himself to death.

The Soulsbys took him in and sent for his wife. He was ill for months. After his recovery, both he and his wife realized that he was never meant for the ministry. Through the Soulsbys, Theron was finally able to make a new start in a real-estate office in Seattle. Theron knew he would make a successful real-estate agent; or, if that failed, he could try politics. There was still time enough for him to be in Congress before he was forty.

Critical Evaluation:

In the nineteenth century and the early twentieth century, a great deal of religious debunking took place in American literature, both journalistic and imaginative, fueled—at least in part—by the muckraking temperament of the times. Contributions ranged from Nathaniel Hawthorne's "The Minister's Black Veil" (1836) and *The Scarlet Letter* (1850) to Sinclair Lewis' *Elmer Gantry* (1927). Harold Frederic's *The Damnation of Theron Ware* added another example to the debate, and a debate it was. Clerical ethics and integrity as well as those of institutionalized religion are still hotly contested. Thus, Frederic's novel was meaningful in its own time and still has contemporary relevance.

From this unique position, the novel takes on a significance not usually accorded it by critical consensus, for the book has generally been viewed as a one-of-a-kind indictment of religious hypocrisy rather than as an element in the mainstream of a literary trend. Theron Ware's confusions, for example, were and are viewed in inappropriate nineteenth century terms of self-denial and sacrifice. The emotional problems of Theron Ware have thus been wrongly analyzed: the Reverend Mr. Ware, so the conventional interpretation goes, is simply trying to assert his latent creativity by attempting to write a book and expand his cultural horizons. This interpretation notwithstanding, Ware does not succeed, although his attempts cost him his ministry, alienate his friends, and threaten his marriage. Yet, questions remain: Why did Theron Ware fail? And, why was Theron Ware damned?

First of all, Ware's extraordinary immaturity, engendered largely by the narrowness of his religious upbringing and his ministerial training, left him unequipped to cope with the realities of life. Second, Ware's understanding of sexuality is, at best, adolescent, for he cannot see beyond the virgin or whore dichotomy, and hence he is unable to develop a mature relationship with any woman—Alice, Celia, or Mrs. Soulsby. Third, Ware has virtually no insight into himself. He knows nothing of his capabilities, his needs, or his desires; indeed, he seems at times, unaware of his own existence. Consequently, Theron Ware is an emotional cripple, blocked from meaningful relationships with himself, with women, and with society at large, including its cultural heritage. That religious training should prove so emotionally debilitating is a severe damnation of such training. Yet the person thus afflicted is equally damned but in another, more profound way. For Theron Ware shows at the end of the book, even with the opportunity for a new career in real estate, no more promise of succeeding than he showed at the beginning.

DARK LAUGHTER

Type of work: Novel
Author: Sherwood Anderson (1876–1941)
Type of plot: Psychological realism
Time of plot: 1920's
Locale: Old Harbor, Indiana
First published: 1925

> *Principal characters:*
> BRUCE DUDLEY, formerly John Stockton, a Chicago
>   reporter
> SPONGE MARTIN, a workman close to the grass roots
> FRED GREY, owner of an automobile wheel factory
> ALINE, his wife

The Story:

Bruce Dudley's name was not Bruce Dudley at all. It was John Stockton, but he had grown tired of being John Stockton, reporter on a Chicago paper, married to Bernice who worked on the same paper and who wrote magazine stories on the side. She thought him flighty, and he admitted it. He wanted adventure. He wanted to go down the Mississippi as Huckleberry Finn had done. He wanted to go back to Old Harbor, the river town in Indiana where he had spent his childhood. So, with less than three hundred dollars, he left Chicago, Bernice, and his job on the paper. He picked up the name Bruce Dudley from two store signs in an Illinois town. After his trip to New Orleans, he went to Old Harbor and got a job varnishing automobile wheels in the Grey Wheel Company.

Sponge Martin worked in the same room with Bruce. Sponge, a wiry old fellow with a black mustache, lived a simple, elemental life. That was the reason, perhaps, why Bruce liked him so much. Sometimes when the nights were fair and the fish were biting, Sponge and his wife took sandwiches and some moonshine whiskey and went down to the river. They fished for a while and got drunk, and then Sponge's wife made him feel like a young man again. Bruce wished he could be as happy and carefree as Sponge.

When Bruce was making his way down the Mississippi and when he stayed for five months in an old house in New Orleans—that was before he came to Old Harbor—he watched the blacks and listened to their songs and laughter. It seemed to him that they lived as simply as children and were happy, laughing their dark laughter.

Aline, the wife of Fred Grey, who owned the Grey Wheel Company, saw Bruce Dudley walking out the factory door one evening as she sat in her car waiting for Fred. She did not know who he was, but she remembered another man to whom she had felt attracted in the same way. It happened in Paris after the war. She had seen the man at Rose Frank's apartment, and she had wanted him. Then she had married Fred, who was recovering from the shock of the war. Although he was not what she wished for, somehow she had married him.

One evening, Bruce Dudley passed by the Grey home as Aline stood in the yard. He stopped and looked first at the house and then at Aline. Neither spoke, but something passed between them. They had found each other.

Aline, who had advertised for a gardener, hired Bruce after turning down several applicants. Bruce had quit his job at the factory shortly before he saw her advertisement. When Bruce began to work for her, the two maintained some reserve, but each was determined to have the other. Bruce and Aline carried on many imaginary conversations. Fred apparently resented Bruce's presence about the grounds, but he said nothing to the man. When he questioned his wife, he learned that she knew nothing of Bruce except that he was a good worker.

As Aline watched her husband leave for the factory each morning, she wondered how much he knew. She thought a great deal about her own life and about life in general. Her husband was no lover. Few women nowadays had true lovers. Modern civilization told one what he could not have. One belittled what he could not possess. Because one did not have love, one made fun of it, was skeptical of it, and besmirched it. The little play of the two men and the woman went on silently. Two black women who worked in Aline's house watched the proceedings. From time to time they laughed, and their dark laughter seemed mocking. White folks were queer. They made life so involved, whereas black people took what they wanted—simply, openly, happily.

One day in June, after Fred had gone to march in a veterans' parade and the servants had gone to watch the parade, Aline and Bruce were left alone. She sat and watched him work in the garden. Finally, he looked at her, and he followed her into the house through a door she purposely left open. Before Fred returned, Bruce had left the house. He disappeared from Old Harbor. Two months later, Aline told Fred she was going to have a child.

As Fred came home one evening in the early fall, he saw his wife and Bruce together in the garden. Aline calmly called to him and announced that the child she was expecting was not his. She and Bruce had waited, she went on, so that she might let him know they were leaving. Fred pleaded with her to stay, knowing she was hurting herself, but they walked away with Bruce carrying two heavy bags.

Fred told himself, as he stood with his revolver in his hand a few minutes later, that he could not dispassionately let another man walk away with his wife. His mind was filled with confused anger, and for a moment, he thought of killing himself. Then he followed the pair along the river road. He was determined to kill Bruce; but, he lost them in the darkness. In a blind fury, he shot at the river. On the way back to his house, he stopped to sit on a log. The revolver fell to the ground, and he sat crying like a child for a long time.

After Fred had returned to his home and gone to bed, he tried to laugh at what had happened. He could not. Outside in the road, he heard a sudden burst of laughter. It was the younger of the two black servants who worked in the Grey home. She cried out loudly that she had known it all the time, and again there came a burst of laughter—dark laughter.

Critical Evaluation:

Dark Laughter is an interesting, serious novel that emerged from the aftermath of World War I. Sherwood Anderson's novel reflects the literary and stylistic devices pioneered in the era following that war.

World War I meant, for writers, artists, and thinkers, the end of intellectual, scientific, political, moral, and psychological certainties. Before the outbreak of war, intellectuals considered Western culture the finest flowering and the highest expression of human civilization. The outbreak of the war, its barbarism and the duration and intensity of its savagery, unprecedented in human history, shattered that belief. Scientific discoveries shook hitherto unquestioned assumptions about the Newtonian universe. Marx's theories and the Russian Revolution undermined confidence in social classes and political systems. Freud, by elaborating a theory of an active unconscious and an unconscious life, destroyed the idea that man was a given, known quantity.

All of these developments form the context for "literary modernism," a movement in literature in which accepted patterns of characterization, sequence, and symbols were altered radically. It is in this context that Anderson's *Dark Laughter* can be understood best. *Dark Laughter* is a novel that tries both to formulate a criticism of the old values (made disreputable by the war) and, at the same time, to set forth new values by which men can live.

Given this disillusionment *and* hope, it is appropriate that Anderson establishes two dramatic poles in the novel: one embodies a natural, honest, sincere relationship to life; the other (embodying the old, prewar values) represents an artificial, mechanical, and dishonest approach.

Fred Grey and Bernice Stockton are characters leading superficial and distant lives. Grey, who imagines himself sensitive, cultured, and generous, is actually a morally coarse, suspicious, and tightfisted factory owner. He is, above all, separated from the realities of life by his economic position and his inner sterility.

Bernice Stockton, the wife that Bruce Dudley fled, is a variation of the same type. Her "specialty" is literature, but from hints of the story she is writing—a precious, unreal thing—her characters and plot only reflect her own superficial romanticism rather than the actual conditions of life. She is a member of an "in group" of writers and intellectuals, and Anderson indicates that this membership is more important to her than infusing her art with truth.

Standing in opposition to these characters are Bruce Dudley, Sponge Martin, and, to an extent, Aline Grey. For Anderson, these people represent the new, hopeful values that have come to life after the trauma of war. Sponge Martin (and his wife), for example, have a genuine connection to real life. Their sexual life is natural and unaffected; they have few pretensions; they are generous and simple. Dudley himself, the central character in the novel, is a writer more interested in the truth than in "word slinging." Leaving Bernice was a rejection of her literary pretensions. Falling in love with Aline, and fathering her child, meant answering the deeper, underlying currents in life.

For Aline, who vacillated between these poles, the marriage to Grey represented a confused surrender to the conventional life. Running away with Dudley meant coming to terms with life as it is—not as it exists in the decadent literary circles of postwar France, in the romantic fantasies of her adolescence, or in the expected routines of upper-middle-class life in the United States.

It is also clear that, just as Anderson is criticizing an outworn and mechanical value system, he is also criticizing an earlier literary tradition. Does literature come to terms with the natural, primitive side of life? Does it seek out the unconscious and explore it? Does it portray the uncertainties and difficulties of life? If the answer to these questions is yes, then Anderson approves; but if literary tradition only discusses the superficial and agreeable aspects of life, then Anderson heartily disapproves. Thus, as literature, Anderson hopes *Dark Laughter* both supports and represents a new literary tradition that corresponds to the new postwar values.

Anderson himself said that the literary quality of *Dark Laughter* was influenced by James Joyce, and it is true that Anderson uses a number of modernist techniques: sections of narrative broken into fragments; parts of poems scattered through the text; subjective, semi-stream-of-consciousness narration; and switches in point of view. Anderson, however, does not have Joyce's verbal facility, depth of allusion, grammatical mastery, or density of detail.

The techniques of *Dark Laughter* probably reflect the more general literary climate of the 1920's rather than Joyce's specific influence. In a period of intellectual uncertainty, when old beliefs were brought into question, prose style itself assumed a fragmented, subjective, and somewhat disjointed character.

At the same time, *Dark Laughter* also displays certain negative features of the American literary climate of the 1920's. One of these negative qualities, perhaps the most visible, is the racist aspect of many of Anderson's passages. For example, the title of the novel, *Dark Laughter*, refers to the natural, honest pole that Anderson supports. Yet, associated with this naturalness are the "primitive," "uncivilized," and "amoral" qualities that Anderson links to black people. In fact, *Dark Laughter* refers to the laughter of black maids in the Grey household when they learn of Aline's adultery.

Such prejudices, commonplace in the era in which *Dark Laughter* was written, need not overshadow the major intent of the book. *Dark Laughter* expresses an important opposition of ideas in modernist literary terms; the reader is asked to choose between real life and superficial life; and, in that sense, Anderson has presented the reader with a profound moral choice.

DAVID HARUM

Type of work: Novel
Author: Edward Noyes Westcott (1846–1898)
Type of plot: Regional romance
Time of plot: Late nineteenth century
Locale: Upstate New York
First published: 1898

Principal characters:
> DAVID HARUM, a banker and horse trader
> JOHN LENOX, Harum's assistant
> MARY BLAKE, John's sweetheart
> POLLY BIXBEE, Harum's widowed sister

The Story:

John Lenox was the son of a well-to-do businessman in New York. After college, he lived for several years in Europe at his father's expense. He was twenty-six years old when he returned to America, without having done anything which fitted him to earn a living.

John returned to find that his father's business was failing rapidly and that he would soon have to make a living for himself. His father found a place for him with a New York law firm, but reading law proved uncongenial. When his father died, John left the firm. Then, through an old friend of his father, John became assistant to the owner of a small bank in Homeville, New York.

David Harum, the owner of the bank, was a crusty old man who enjoyed his reputation as a skinflint. What most of the townspeople did not know was that he was quite a philanthropist in his own way but preferred to cover up his charity and good deeds with gruff words. Harum's one vice was horse trading. His sister, who kept house for him, firmly believed that he would rather trade horses than eat or sleep. Moreover, he usually came out ahead in any swapping deal.

David Harum was well pleased with the appearance of his new assistant, John Lenox; and when John took hold of his duties better than any other clerk in the bank had ever done, David Harum began to think seriously of looking after the young man's future. Harum felt that John should have an opportunity to better himself, but he wanted first to be certain that he was not mistaken in judging the young man's character. He set out to discover what he wanted to know in a peculiar way. He let John live uncomfortably in a broken-down hotel for several months to ascertain his fortitude. He also gave John several chances to be dishonest by practices that a sharp trader like Harum might be expected to approve. John's straightforward dealings won Harum's respect and approval. He casually gave John five ten-dollar gold pieces and asked him to move into a room in Harum's own large house with him and his sister, Polly.

John had begun to discover that Harum was not the selfish and crusty old man that he appeared. He knew that Harum had called in a widow whose mortgage was overdue and had torn up the paper because the woman's husband had at one time taken Harum to the circus when the banker was a little boy without a cent to his name. Even Harum's horse trading was different when one came to know him. As John Lenox discovered, Harum only let people cheat themselves. If someone professed to know all about horses, Harum used the trade to teach him a lesson, but if a tyro professed his ignorance of the animals, Harum was sure to give him a fair exchange. He was a living example of the proverb that propounds shrewdly that it is impossible to cheat an honest man and, the corollary, that it is almost impossible not to cheat a dishonest one.

John Lenox's life in Homeville was restricted, and he was thrown much on his own resources. He secured a piano for himself and played in the evenings or read from a small collection of books that he had saved from his father's library. His only real friends were David Harum and Harum's sister, Polly, both old enough to be John's parents. He spent many pleasant hours in Harum's company. They would often take Harum's horses out for a drive, during which the loquacious banker would regale the young man with stories of horse trading, of the foibles of the people in the community, or of Harum's early life when he had run away from home to work along the Erie Canal. On one of these rides, Harum learned that John was in love with an heiress he had met in Europe. John felt that he could not ask her to marry him until he had proved himself a success.

Soon afterward, Harum gave John an opportunity to make a large amount of money. Harum had a tip on a corner in pork on the Chicago market. Harum and John bought several thousand barrels of pork and sold them at a huge profit. This deal was the first step Harum took to make John financially independent.

John's second year in Homeville was more eventful. By that time, he had been accepted as a member of the community and had made friends both in the town and among the wealthy people who came to Homeville during the summer months. Meanwhile, Harum revealed to his sister his plan to retire from active work in the bank and to make John his partner. He also revealed to her that John had a tract of land in Pennsylvania that everyone had considered worthless but that was likely to produce oil. Harum, in his younger days, had spent some time in the Pennsylvania oil fields, and like most small-town bankers of the time, he knew something about a great many financial activities. What he did not reveal to his sister was that he also planned to leave his estate to John, for, excepting Polly, he had no relatives.

By the end of his third year in Harum's bank, John had made enough money through market operations to make himself independent, and he could have left the bank and the town for New York City if he had cared to do so. When the banker broached the subject to him, John admitted that two years before, the prospect of returning to the city would have been welcome. Now he had come to like Homeville and had no desire to leave the home of David Harum and his sister. That was exactly what Harum wanted to hear. He told John that he was to become a partner in the bank. Harum also told him that a company wanted to lease his Pennsylvania land for the purpose of drilling for oil.

Then John fell ill, and his doctor sent him on a Mediterranean cruise. While aboard ship, John met Mary Blake, the young heiress with whom he had fallen in love several years before. At first John thought, because of an error in the ship's passenger list, that Mary Blake was already married. One moonlit night, on a mountain overlooking the bay at Naples, Mary informed John of his mistake and promised to marry him, and a few days later, Harum was overjoyed to receive a cable announcing John's marriage. Harum wired back the good news that drilling had begun on the property in Pennsylvania.

John and Mary returned to the United States several months later. They settled in Homeville, and John took over the bank. Then David Harum was free to spend the rest of his days driving about the countryside and swapping horses.

Critical Evaluation:

David Harum grew directly from Edward Noyes Westcott's experiences both with the people and the customs of Upstate New York and with a type of small-town American banker. *David Harum* is so convincingly rooted in northeastern rural America that it stands as a good example of American "local color" fiction that developed and flourished in the United States during the last half of the nineteenth century. Although local color as a literary movement contains diverse and often contradictory elements, the main energies of its writers were devoted to sketching regional geography, customs, and dialects; it developed partly as a counter to the "American novel" or attempted to capture the whole "American" experience in one work.

What is especially interesting in *David Harum* is Harum himself. Westcott has succeeded in uncovering, with generous detail, the moral and psychological forces, and the central impulses as well as the crotchets, of a small-town banker in Upstate New York. Harum's incessant horse trading, his Yankee sense, and above all, his pragmatism form the central interest of the novel. On the one hand, Harum looks out for himself and so embodies that shrewd, self-interested outlook so characteristic of his type; on the other hand, Westcott has been careful to modify this selfishness with Harum's quiet charity and rough-hewn sense of economic justice. Thus, David Harum stands as both a regional type and as an example of a certain economic morality. He is a banker, but he is also a good man.

The weakness in the novel is the plot concerning Lenox and his sweetheart. This plot, which takes the story too far from its central interest, both geographically and morally, seems both sentimental and contrived. Actually, the difficulty Westcott experienced in sustaining a purely regional narrative, as well as his sentimentality, are weaknesses common among the local colorists.

DEATH COMES FOR THE ARCHBISHOP

Type of work: Novel
Author: Willa Cather (1873–1947)
Type of plot: Historical chronicle
Time of plot: Last half of the nineteenth century
Locale: New Mexico and Arizona
First published: 1927

Principal characters:

> FATHER JEAN MARIE LATOUR, Vicar Apostolic of New
>   Mexico
> FATHER JOSEPH VAILLANT, his friend and a missionary
>   priest
> KIT CARSON, a frontier scout
> JACINTO, an Indian guide

The Story:

In 1851, Father Jean Marie Latour reached Santa Fé, where he was to become Vicar Apostolic of New Mexico. His journey from the shores of Lake Ontario had been long and arduous. He had lost his belongings in a shipwreck at Galveston and had suffered painful injury in a wagon accident at San Antonio.

Upon Father Latour's arrival, in company with his good friend Father Joseph Vaillant, the Mexican priests refused to recognize his authority. He had no choice but to ride three thousand miles into Mexico to secure the necessary papers from the Bishop of Durango.

On the road, he lost his way in an arid landscape of red hills and gaunt junipers. His thirst became a vertigo of mind and senses, and he could blot out his own agony only by repeating the cry of the Saviour on the Cross. As he was about to give up all hope, he saw a tree growing in the shape of a cross. A short time later, he arrived in the Mexican settlement called Agua Secreta (hidden water). Stopping at the home of Benito, Bishop Latour first performed the marriage ceremonies and then baptized all the children.

At Durango, he received the necessary documents and started the long trip back to Santa Fé. Meanwhile, Father Vaillant had won over the inhabitants from enmity to amity and had set up the Episcopal residence in an old adobe house. On the first morning after his return to Santa Fé, the Bishop heard the unexpected sound of a bell ringing the Angelus. Father Vaillant told him that he had found the bell, bearing the date 1356, in the basement of old San Miguel Church.

On a missionary journey to Albuquerque in March, Father Vaillant acquired a handsome cream-colored mule as a gift and another just like it for his bishop. These mules, Contento and Angelica, faithfully served the men for many years.

On another such trip, the two priests were riding together on their mules. Caught in a sleet storm, they stopped at the rude shack of the American Buck Scales. His Mexican wife warned the travelers by gestures that their lives were in danger, and they rode on to Mora without spending the night. The next morning, the Mexican woman appeared in town. She told them that her husband had already murdered and robbed four travelers and that he had killed her three babies. The result was that Scales was brought to justice, and his wife, Magdalena, was sent to the home of Kit Carson, the famous frontier scout. From that time on, Kit Carson was a valuable friend of the Bishop and his Vicar. Magdalena later became the housekeeper and manager for the kitchens of the Sisters of Loretto.

During his first year at Santa Fé, the Bishop was called to a meeting of the Plenary Council at Baltimore. On the return journey, he brought back with him five nuns sent to establish the school of Our Lady of Light. Next, Bishop Latour, attended by the Indian Jacinto as his guide, spent some time visiting his own vicarate. Padre Gallegos, whom he visited at Albuquerque, acted more like a professional gambler than a priest, but because he was very popular with the natives, Bishop Latour did not remove him at that time. At last, he arrived at his destination, the top of the mesa at Acoma, the end of his long journey. On that trip he heard the legend of Fray Baltazar, killed during an uprising of the Acoma Indians.

A month after the Bishop's visit, he suspended Padre Gallegos and put Father Vaillant in charge of the parish at Albuquerque. On a trip to the Pecos Mountains, the Vicar fell ill with an attack of the black measles. The Bishop, hearing of his illness, set out to nurse his friend. Jacinto again served as guide on the cold, snowy trip. When Bishop Latour reached his friend's bedside, he found that Kit Carson had arrived before him. As soon as the sick man could sit in the saddle, Carson and the Bishop took him back to Santa Fé.

Bishop Latour decided to investigate the parish of Taos, where the powerful old priest Antonio José Martinez was the ruler of both spiritual and temporal matters. The following year, the Bishop was called to Rome. When he returned, he brought with him four young priests from the Seminary of Montferrand and a Spanish priest to replace Padre Martinez at Taos.

Bishop Latour had one great ambition; he wanted to build a cathedral in Santa Fé. In that project, he was assisted by the rich Mexican *rancheros*, but to the greatest extent by his good friend Don Antonio Olivares. When Don Antonio died, his will stated that his estate was left to his wife and daughter during their lives, and after their deaths, to the Church. Don Antonio's brothers contested the will on the grounds that the daughter, Señorita Inez, was too old to be Doña Isabella's daughter, and the Bishop and his Vicar had to persuade the vain, coquettish widow to swear to her true age of fifty-three, rather than the forty-two years she claimed. Thus, the money was saved for Don Antonio's family and, eventually, the Church.

Father Vaillant was sent to Tucson, but after several years, Bishop Latour decided to recall him to Santa Fé. When he arrived, the Bishop showed him the stone for building the cathedral. About that time, Bishop Latour received a letter from the Bishop of Leavenworth. Because of the discovery of gold near Pike's Peak, he asked to have a priest sent there from Father Latour's diocese. Father Vaillant was the obvious choice.

Father Vaillant spent the rest of his life doing good works in Colorado, though he did return to Santa Fé with the Papal Emissary when Bishop Latour was made an archbishop. Father Vaillant became the first Bishop of Colorado. He died there after years of service, and Archbishop Latour attended his impressive funeral services.

After the death of his friend, Father Latour retired to a modest country estate near Santa Fé. He had dreamed during all his missionary years of the time when he could retire to his own fertile green Auvergne in France, but in the end, he decided that he could not leave the land of his labors for his faith. Memories of the journeys he and Father Vaillant had made over thousands of miles of desert country became the meaning of his later years. Bernard Ducrot, a young Seminarian from France, became like a son to him.

When Father Latour knew that his time had come to die, he asked to be taken into town to spend his last days near the cathedral. On the last day of his life, the church was filled with people who came to pray for him, as word that he was dying spread through the town. He died in the still twilight, and the cathedral bell, tolling in the early darkness, carried the news to the waiting countryside that, at last, death had come for Father Latour.

Critical Evaluation:

When writing of her great predecessor and teacher, Sarah Orne Jewett, Willa Cather expressed her own belief that the quality that gives a work of literature greatness is the "voice" of the author, the sincere, unadorned, and unique vision of a writer coming to grips with his material. If any one characteristic can be said to dominate the writings of Cather, it is a true and moving sincerity. She never tried to twist her subject matter to suit a preconceived purpose, and she resisted the temptation to dress up her homely material. She gave herself absolutely to her chosen material, and the result was a series of books both truthful and rich with intimations of the destiny of the American continent. By digging into the roots of her material, she found the greater meanings and expressed them with a deceptive simplicity. Her vision and craftsmanship were seldom more successful than in *Death Comes for the Archbishop.* So completely did Cather merge her "voice" with her material, that some critics have felt that the book is almost too polished, without the sense of struggle necessary in a truly great novel. This, in fact, indicates the magnitude of the author's achievement and the brilliance of her technical skill. *Death Comes for the Archbishop* resonates with the unspoken beliefs of the author and the resolved conflicts that went into its construction. On the surface, it is cleanly wrought and simple, but it is a more complicated and profound book than it appears at first reading. Cather learned well from her early inspiration, Sarah Orne Jewett, the secret of artless art and of craftsmanship that disarms by its very simplicity but that is based in a highly sophisticated intelligence.

   Death Comes for the Archbishop is a novel reaffirming the greatness of the American past. This chronicle of the Catholic Southwest is a story, beautifully told, which re-creates in the lives of Bishop Latour and Father Vaillant, his vicar, the historical careers of Bishop Lamy and Father Macheboeuf, two devout and noble missionary priests in the Vicarate of New Mexico during the second half of the nineteenth century. The novel lives in its bright glimpses of the past, stories that cut backward into time so that the action is not always upon the same level. Tales and legends that go beyond the period of American occupation into three centuries of Spanish colonial history and back to the primitive tribal life of the Hopi, the Navajo, and the vanished cliff-dwellers break this chronicle at many points and give the effect of density and variety to a work which recaptures so completely the spirit and movement of the pioneer West.

   It is true that this novel is an epic and a regional history, but much more than either, it is a tale of personal isolation, of one man's life reduced to the painful weariness of his own sensitivities. Father Latour is a hero in the most profound sense of the word, at times almost a romantic hero, with his virtues of courage and determination, but he is also a very modern protagonist with his doubts and inner conflicts and his philosophical nature. His personality is held up in startling contrast to that of his friend and vicar, Father Vaillant, a more simple, although no less good, individual. Cather's austere style perfectly captures the scholarly asperity and urbane religious devotion that compose Father Latour's character; and always in this book, the reader is aware of a sense of the dignity of human life, as exemplified in the person of this individual. Cather was not afraid to draw a good man, a man who could stand above others because of his deeds and because of his innate quality. The novel must stand or fall on this character, and it stands superbly.

   Although this book is based on a true sequence of events, it is not a novel of plot. It is a chronicle and a character study and perhaps, more specifically, an interplay of environment and character. Throughout the book, the reader is aware of the reaction of men to the land, and of one man to the land he has chosen. Subtly and deeply, the author suggests that the soul of man is profoundly altered by the soul of the land, and Cather never doubts for a moment that the land does possess a soul or that this soul can transform a human being in complex and important ways. Cather was fascinated by the way the rough landscape of the Southwest, when reduced to its essences, seemed to take human beings and reduce them to their essences. She abandoned traditional Realism in this book, turning toward the directness of Symbolism. With stark pictures and vivid styles, she created an imaginary world rooted in Realism but transcending Realism. The rigid economy with which the book is written forces it to stand with a unique power in the reader's mind long after his reading. Further, the personality of Bishop Latour stands as the greatest symbol, like a wind-swept crag or precipice in the vast New Mexico landscape, suggesting the nobility of the human spirit, despite the inner conflicts against which it must struggle.

The descriptions of place set the emotional tone of the novel. The quality of life is intimately related to the landscape, and the accounts of the journeys and the efforts to survive despite the unfriendliness of the barren land, all help to create an odd warmth and almost surreal passion in the narrative. The personalities of Bishop Latour and Father Vaillant establish a definite emotional relationship with the country, and if the other characters in the book are less vividly realized as individuals, perhaps it is because they do not seem to have this relationship with the land. Some of them have become part of the land, worn down by the elements like the rocks and riverbeds, and others have no relationship to it at all; none of them, however, is involved in the intense love-hate relationship with the land with which the two main characters struggle for so many years.

Although the chronology of the book encompasses many years, the novel is essentially static, a series of rich images and thoughtful movements highlighted and captured as by a camera. This quality of the narrative is not a fault; it is a fact of Cather's style. The frozen moments of contemplation and the glimpses into Father Latour's inner world and spiritual loneliness are the moments that give the book its greatness. Despite the presence of Kit Carson, the novel is not an adventure story any more than it is merely the account of a pair of churchmen attempting to establish their church in a difficult new terrain. The cathedral becomes the most important symbol in the final part of the book, representing the earthly successes of a man dedicated to nonworldly ambitions. This conflict between the earthly and the spiritual is at the heart of Bishop Latour's personality and at the heart of the book. The reader understands, at the end, when the bell tolls for Father Latour, that the temptations were never very deep and the good man's victory was greater than he ever knew. The author does not spell out her meaning, but the emotional impact of her narrative brings it home to the reader.

A DEATH IN THE FAMILY

Type of work: Novel
Author: James Agee (1909–1955)
Type of plot: Psychological realism
Time of plot: 1915
Locale: Knoxville, Tennessee
First published: 1957

> *Principal characters:*
> RUFUS FOLLET, a six-year-old boy
> MARY FOLLET, his mother
> JAY FOLLET, his father
> CATHERINE, his small sister
> JOEL LYNCH, Mary Follet's father
> CATHERINE LYNCH, his wife
> AMELIA and
> ANDREW LYNCH, Mary's sister and brother
> HANNAH LYNCH, Joel's spinster sister
> RALPH FOLLET, Jay's brother

Perhaps the most significant aspect of *A Death in the Family* is the fact that it restored a world of feeling and moral value to American fiction. A Pulitzer Prize winner in 1957, it is a novel about love that is neither adult lust nor adolescent groping and about death as an inescapable part of the human condition, universal and therefore to be borne. In a very real but almost old-fashioned sense, the book is a celebration of these two great mysteries of experience. At a time when most writers choose to treat love as a process of glandular secretions and death as a meaningless commonplace of violence, nothing in this novel reveals the originality and power of James Agee more than his ability to suggest the atmosphere of wonder and awe that once surrounded man's awareness of his being and his mortality.

The essential difference found between Agee and the leading specialists in primitivism and violence goes even deeper. *A Death in the Family* is a novel of compassion almost overwhelming in its sensitivity, a circumstance not entirely accounted for by its autobiographical theme and the writer's obvious attempt to get at the meaning of the central experience in his own life, the death of his father forty-odd years before. He is not dealing with that form of compassion which has left its mark on much recent fiction, the subverted sentimentality of a growing concern for the alcoholic, the inarticulate brute, the lonely spinster, the inadequate male, the lost child, the homosexual, the bum—all the misfits and outcasts of society. His compassion is for simple, decent people of ordinary lives—the very "ordinariness" of his material is one of the notable features of the novel—in a time of loss and grief. These are matters that he presents with a feeling of shared sorrow and sympathy for what is most personal and yet most general in the human situation.

Agee's sense of experience shared presupposes a universe of social continuity and moral order, not a world in which the values of the moment must be salvaged from the spectacle of fragmented, isolated lives within a disordered society, but one in which the human effort, in spite of its accumulation of grief, hunger, and waste, becomes meaningful and worthwhile when judged by community values and the idea of man's moral responsibility to man. As a serious writer, Agee was interested in the nature of good and evil; in his novel, death, the complement of life, is the chink in the armor that gives a small boy his first awareness of evil and threatens with the shock of loss a family in which the ties of kinship have been fulfilled by love. That he was able to shape on a purely domestic level a fable of compelling tenderness and compassionate insight, or to achieve within this framework his effects of lyricism, meditative speculation, and drama, is proof that Agee's death lost to American letters one of the resourceful and authentic talents of his generation.

Behind this novel, however, lay years of preparation and apprentice work in a variety of media within the fairly short span of his writing career. He was born in Knoxville, the setting of *A Death in the Family*, in 1909, and he died of a heart attack in a New York taxicab in 1955. After schooling at Exeter and Harvard, he had joined the staff of *Fortune* in 1932. His first book was *Permit Me Voyage*, a collection of poems published in the Yale Younger Poets Series in 1934. This verse was rather conventional in form, romantic in its display of strong personal feeling. As poetry written in a period of technical experiment and at a time when writers were expected to carry banners in the picket lines of the class war, the book, like *A Death in the Family*, seemed strangely old-fashioned. (Archibald MacLeish's somewhat ambiguous comment was that Agee had not assumed a "position.") Later, out of an assignment to write a documentary report on the sharecropping system in the South, he produced one of the most original but least *read* books of its decade, *Let Us Now Praise Famous Men*, a curious blend of narrative, social history, satire, and philosophy. It is in many ways a youthful book but an impressive one in its praise of the American earth and its rage against the exploiters of the land and its workers. As a social document, the book is still eloquent and moving, even though the first impression is likely to be one of tremendous power of language under poor control. Still later, he wrote about motion pictures for *The Nation*, critiques which have become the classics of their kind, and reviewed books for *Time*. In 1948, he gave up journalism to devote himself to *A Death in the Family*, but he was constantly being diverted to other tasks: articles for *Life*; scenarios for *The Quiet One*, *The African Queen*, *Face to Face*, *The Bride Comes to Yellow Sky*, *The Night of the Hunter*; a documentary on the life of Lincoln for television; and the novella, *The Morning Watch*, published in 1950.

Although Agee came late to fiction, his admirers saw in *The Morning Watch* a moving study of adolescent confusion against the background of a boys' school, promise of the major work of which he was capable. *A Death in the Family* almost fulfills that promise. When Agee died in 1955, his novel was virtually complete except for the tying in of loose ends and the final polishing. In preparing the manuscript for publication, the editors have inserted as thematic interludes several episodes not directly related to the time scheme of the novel and have added as a prologue the sketch titled "Knoxville: Summer 1915," which had been written some years before. It is safe to say that if Agee had lived, he would have given his book greater structural unity and might have recast in more dramatic form several sections which remain static in effect. It is doubtful, however, if he could have improved upon the rich contrasts of texture conveyed in characterization, mood, and scene, or refined to greater precision the beautiful clarity of his style.

As an introductory piece, "Knoxville: Summer 1915" creates the mood of affectionate reminiscence within which the novel is embodied. It is a twilight study of a summer evening when children play around the corner lampposts and men in shirt sleeves sprinkle their lawns after supper. Later, crickets chirp in the early dark which seems filled with stars as a small boy lies with his father, mother, uncle, and aunt on quilts that have been spread on the grass in the back yard. This is the enchanted world of childhood as it appeared to young Rufus Follet: safe, warm, secure, a world of protection and understanding and love.

Rufus and his younger sister Catherine are asleep when the telephone rings, summoning his father to the country, where his Grandfather Follet has been taken suddenly ill. The ties of family relationships—intimate, trivial, amusing, tender—are evoked as Jay Follet prepares to start out before daybreak and his wife Mary gets up to cook his breakfast. Because he expects to be back in time for supper, he leaves without waking the children. They are asleep the next night when the telephone rings again and a stranger's voice tells Mary that her husband has been in an accident; on the way back from the country, the steering mechanism of his car had broken, and Jay, thrown clear when the car left the road, had been killed instantly. This, in outline, is the story of *A Death in the Family*, but not its whole substance. More important is the effect of death on the people involved. To Mary, it brings the realization that death happens to many people and is very common. In her distress, she turns to her faith for consolation. To Rufus, his father's death is not the maturing experience it will eventually become but only another baffling circumstance among the mysteries of his young life, like his nightmares, his mother's command that he must never mention the color of a black nursemaid's skin, the memory of a visit made a short time before to see his withered old great-great-grandmother in the country, or the reason why older boys ask him his name and then break into laughter and run away. Yet he knows that the event gives him some importance that he had never known before: slowly, to himself, he repeats the fact that his father is dead. Catherine is too young to understand her loss or her mother's sorrow. Beyond these characters is the widening circle of family: Grandfather Lynch, the agnostic; deaf Grandmother Lynch; Great-aunt Hannah, a tower of strength; Andrew, the sharp-tongued artist uncle, and his sister Amelia; weak, drunken Uncle Ralph Follet, the undertaker, who asks to prepare his own brother's body for burial. These people give the novel its texture, establishing the world in which adults and children confront the fact of death while trying to understand its meaning in terms of grief and love.

The novel contains memorable passages in which deep feeling is combined with power and precision of language, as in the account of the relationship between father and son unfolded as Jay and Rufus walk slowly home after seeing a Charlie Chaplin film, in the scene in which Great-aunt Hannah and Rufus go shopping and he wears down an adult's reasonable firmness with his small boy's persistence over the purchase of a loud-checked cap, in the moment when the mourning family seems to sense the dead man's presence in the house, and in the scene in which young Rufus, eager to display his new cap, runs to his parents' bedroom and sees that his father is not there. Instead, he finds his mother propped up on two pillows, looking as if she were sick or tired.

James Agee began as a poet, and he never lost a poet's eye for the telling detail or the poet's ear. *A Death in the Family* contains passages that, even out of context, show the true quality of a writer to whom literature was a total job of action and feeling, of sights and sounds, of image and meaning, of language and mood. The book is not a perfect novel, perhaps not even a major work, but in the universality of its theme and the compassion that it invokes, it uncovers a world of feeling in which all may share. This is more than the truth-telling for which the Realist strives; it is truth itself.

THE DEATH OF ARTEMIO CRUZ

Type of work: Novel
Author: Carlos Fuentes (1928–   )
Type of plot: Social commentary
Time of plot: 1889–1959
Locale: Mexico
First published: 1962

Principal characters:
ARTEMIO CRUZ, a dying tycoon
CATALINA, his wife
LORENZO, his son, who was killed in the Spanish Civil War
TERESA, his daughter
GLORIA, his granddaughter
GERARDO, his son-in-law
DON GAMALIEL BERNAL, his father-in-law
GONZAO BERNAL, a young lawyer executed by Villistas
FATHER PÁEZ, a priest
REGINA, a dead woman Artemio had loved
LILIA and
LAURA, Artemio's mistresses
PADILLA, Artemio's secretary
LUNERO, a mulatto peon

To the thinking Mexican, the Revolution of 1910 is the great and inescapable fact in his country's destiny and his own personal identity. A second conquest of the land and the past, it was the climax of four centuries of turbulent history and the adumbration of all that has happened since. The revolution did more than topple the paternal dictatorship of Porfirio Díaz; it tore a nation apart by fratricidal strife and then put it together again in a strange new way that continues to disturb and puzzle its citizens. It swept away lingering remnants of colonialism, brought into being a revolutionary oligarchy still in power, created a new middle class, moved Mexico ahead into the twentieth century, and helped to shape a literature both ancestral and prophetic in its pictures of a sad and violent land.

In some ways, this situation is comparable to the aftermath of the Civil War in the United States, where Americans are still trying to see their own fraternal conflict in perspectives of cause and consequence. Among Southerners, especially, readers find a sense of the uniqueness of the regional experience, a response to events viewed imaginatively as a national tragedy. A somewhat similar spirit prevails in certain areas of Mexican life, but on a greater scale, complicated by a growing belief that the revolution has failed and that the real revolution is still to come. In fact, the Mexican intellectual today is often self-conscious in much the same manner that Faulkner and writers of his generation were self-conscious: obsessed by feeling for place, burdened by the past, uneasy in the new society, seeking to reclaim old values lost in the process of change in their stories and poems. Feeling that history has isolated him in his own particular moment in time, the parochialism of the revolution, the Mexican writer often turns inward to create a literature that veers between moods of fury and outrage and the poetry of nocturnal silence. He lives, to borrow a phrase from the poet Octavio Paz, in a "labyrinth of solitude." It was José Luis Cuevas, the avant-garde painter, who first used the term "Cactus Curtain" in protest against the isolation of the Mexican artist. In an earlier novel, *Where the Air Is Clear*, Carlos Fuentes said that it is impossible to explain Mexico. Instead, the artist believes in it with anger and a feeling of outrage, with passion, and with a sense of alienation.

This statement carries the reader a long way toward an understanding of Fuentes' fiction. It is clear that he has rejected Mexican life as it is constituted today, but at the same time, he uses it in his novels to test his sensuous powers and dramatic vigor. The country he writes about is not the land that tourists see or a land of tradition; it is the country of art, a place and people transformed by compelling imagination into something rich, strange, and meaningful. This is one reason for his restless experiments with technique, the broken narrative structures, the shifting points of view, his lovely, solemn hymns to landscapes and time, the interior monologues by which he tries to probe the national conscience as well as the consciousness of his people. If he has not yet assimilated in his own writing the influences he has absorbed from such varied figures as Proust, Joyce, Faulkner, Dos Passos, and Wolfe, he has nevertheless put his borrowings to brilliant use in catching the tempo of Mexican life in its present stage of uncertainty and indirection.

Although his methods may vary in his discontinuity of form and the labyrinthine turnings of his style, his theme remains constant, for his novels are studies in the responsibility that power, knowingly or unknowingly, brings and the corruption that almost necessarily accompanies power. He began with *Where the Air Is Clear*, a novel set against the background of Mexico City. There the extremes of poverty and wealth allowed a study in breadth of what has happened on all levels of society after the Revolution failed to fulfill its promises. Central to Fuentes' theme is Federico Robles, once an ardent revolutionary but now a driving power in the country's political and financial life. His rise in the world, through treachery, bribery, ruthless exploitation, and the corruption of better men, has made him many enemies. The novel tells the story of his fall. Yet, more than one man's ruin is involved in the panoramic picture presented. Behind the events of the story, the failed revolution throws long shadows into the present, the realization of wasted effort, of lives lost to no purpose, of high aims given over to meaningless deeds of sensuality, folly, and outrage. Robles is what he is, as can be seen at the end, because others in their selfishness and pride have assisted in his rise. Now they hate him because they see in him an enlarged image of themselves. *Where the Air Is Clear* is saved from becoming an ideological polemic by its roots that reach toward much that is flawed and gross in the human condition.

Fuentes tells much the same story in *The Good Conscience*, although in that novel his concern is with a family, grandfather, father, and son, rather than a single individual. The setting is Guanajuato, where the oldest of the Ceballos, a dry-goods merchant, laid the foundation of a family fortune. Representative of the new middle class, the materialistic, ambitious Ceballos men marry for position, play a cynical political game for security, and carry on their shady business deals for gain. Society accepts them; the State protects them; the Church sustains them. The writer's picture of chicanery and corruption is magnificent up to a point; but the book breaks abruptly in the middle to present in Jaime Ceballo, the youngest of the family, a story of adolescent confusion and rebellion. Torn between the self-seeking practices of his family and the teachings of the Church, he attempts to follow the example of Christ, fails, and falls back on radicalism as the only alternative to the greed, lust for power, and hypocrisy of his class. The ending is unconvincing after the ironical, somber overtones orchestrated through the earlier sections of the novel. The reader feels that the writer's own Marxist beliefs rather than the logic of character and experience dictated an ending, which seems more contrived than real.

The Death of Artemio Cruz (first translated into English in 1964 from the original *La muerta de Artemio Cruz*) is more limited in its presentation of this theme than Fuentes' previous work. True, the book is flawed by his bewildering cross-chronology, the points of view constantly shifting and intermingling, and his varied stylistic effects. In the end, however, the novel rises above its faults in its compelling picture of one man's life and the relation of that life to all the years of disorder and change that have conditioned the course of Mexican history from the beginning of the century to the present day. Again, this central figure is a force in the land, a millionaire who has climbed to his position of wealth and power by violence, blackmail, bribery, and brutal exploitation of the workers. Like Federico Robles, he is a former revolutionist who stands for the Mexican past as well as its present. (The robber bands who represented the extreme of the revolutionary effort, Fuentes seems to say, have now been replaced by the robber barons of modern finance and politics.) On the wall of his office, a map shows the extent of his holdings: a newspaper, mines, timber, hotels, foreign stocks and bonds, and, not shown, money on deposit in English, Swiss, and United States banks.

Artemio Cruz is on his deathbed when the novel opens. Stricken by a gastric attack after his return from a business trip to Hermosillo on April 9, 1959, he lies in his mansion in a fashionable section of Mexico City, the moral corruption of his life as much a stench in his nostrils as the processes of decay already at work in his body. An officious priest tries to administer the last sacrament in spite of his protests; Cruz had abandoned the church years before. Doctors subject him to the indignity of their instruments as they examine his body. In the background are his estranged wife and the daughter who despises him. Although they pretend concern for the dying man, their greatest anxiety is the whereabouts of his will, and he refuses to tell them. His only hold on reality is a tape recording, an account of business deals and proposed transactions, played by his secretary, Padilla. While these people jostle about his bed, Artemio Cruz drifts between past and present, not in any coherent order but in a series of flashbacks tracing the course that has brought him to his present state.

Thus, he is seen in 1919 as an ambitious young veteran of the Revolution arriving at the home of the Bernal family in Perales. Ostensibly he is there to bring to a bereaved father and sister an account of Gonzalo Bernal's death before a Villista firing squad and yet, in reality, to insinuate himself into the confidence of the old *haciendado*, marry his daughter, and get possession of the Bernal estates. His wife, Catalina, however, never fully realizes that Artemio had really fallen in love with her; influenced by Father Páez, the family priest, she believes that her marriage bought her father's security and her own at the cost of her soul, and she hates herself for the passion to which Artemio moves her at night. In the end, the two despise each other, and she blames him when their son, whom he has removed from her control, is killed while fighting in the Spanish Civil War. Before Catalina there was Regina, the camp follower he also loved, taken hostage by Villa's troops and hanged. After her death, there were other women: Lilia, the young mistress he took on a holiday in Acapulco and who betrayed him there, and Laura, who later married someone else. Artemio's adventures, however, are not all with women. Readers see him ruining his neighbors at Perales and getting possession of their lands, using bribery and blackmail to buy his first election as a deputy, giving his lavish parties where the guests who mocked him behind his back were not supposed to bore him with their conversation, negotiating big deals, ruining competitors, and all the while preparing himself for the loneliness and desolation he feels when his time comes to die. Close to the end of the novel, Fuentes presents two episodes that throw light on the later years of Artemio's career. One is the story of his capture by a Villista troop. Sentenced to death, he decides to give information to the enemy. Although he later kills the officer to whom he had promised betrayal, he had at least been guilty by intent. Some justification for his deed is given in the words of Gonzalo Bernal, the disillusioned idealist who nevertheless goes bravely to his death. Bernal declares that once a revolution has been corrupted by those who act only to live well, to rise in the world, the battles may still be fought and won, but the Revolution without compromise has been lost to the ambitious and the mediocre. The last episode tells how it all began. Artemio Cruz was born on the *petate*, the mat symbolic of the peon's condition, the son of a decayed landowner and a half-caste girl. His only friend during his early years is Lunero, a mulatto who serves the needs of Artemio's half-crazed old grandmother and his lazy, drunken uncle. After the boy accidentally shoots his uncle, he runs away to Veracruz. There, as readers learn indirectly, a schoolmaster tutors Artemio and prepares him for the part he is to play in the Revolution before he loses his ideals and makes the choice of betrayal and rejection that leads him to the corrupting use of power in other men's lives and his own. Fuentes' meaning in this final episode seems clear. The Revolution, in the end, was betrayed by the common people who had made it.

The character of Artemio Cruz is handled with a considerable degree of subtlety and skill. Fuentes does not gloss over his cynicism, opportunism, or brutal ruthlessness. Yet, he is saved from becoming a monster of pure abstraction and calculation by his relationships with the three people who mean most in his life: Lunero, the devoted mulatto for whose sake he committed a murder; Regina, the girl killed by Villistas; and his son, Lorenzo. Through the novel, like a refrain, runs a reference to the time just before Lorenzo went off to fight in the Spanish war when father and son took a morning ride toward the sea. By the end of the novel, Artemio's story fulfills all that it promised to a young boy, one man's journey with no real beginning or end in time, promises of love, solitude, violence, power, friendship, disillusionment, corruption, forgetfulness, innocence, and delight. There is also in this story the realization of how, at the end, a man's death is joined to his beginning.

To get his story told, Fuentes employs three voices. The first is the obvious third person, used to present in dramatic form the events of Artemio's life as they are pieced together in past time. The second is the "I" of the present as the old man lies dying, shrinks from the decay of his body, and takes fitful account of what is going on around him. The third is a vatic presence never identified—conscience? consciousness?—addressing Artemio as "you." This, perhaps, is the unrealized Artemio, the man he might have been. He is a lover of the land that the real Artemio Cruz robbed and raped, the product of history, or the re-created moral conscience of the revolution. He speaks in metaphors, poetry, and prophecy about history and time, places and people, because they belong to the beautiful but sad and tragic land of his birth.

The Death of Artemio Cruz is a divided book, terse yet chaotic, passionate, and ironic. Too much has been made, undoubtedly, of Carlos Fuentes as one of Mexico's angry young men. In spite of his Marxist beliefs, he is essentially a Romantic. He is also the possessor of an exuberant, powerful, and very contemporary talent. Aside from the surface effects of undisciplined but compelling style, the writing of Fuentes comes through in a clear, unhackneyed fashion, even in translation.

THE DEATH SHIP

Type of work: Novel
Author: B. Traven (Berick Traven Torsvan, 1900–1969)
Type of plot: Proletarian
Time of plot: 1920's
Locale: Belgium, Holland, France, Spain, and the Mediterranean Sea
First published: 1926

> *Principal characters:*
> GERARD "PIPPIP" GALES, a young American sailor
> STANISLAV, a Polish sailor and Gerard's friend

Based on the author's own experiences, written when he was about twenty-four, *The Death Ship* (first translated into English in 1934 from the original *Das Totenschiff*) is unique, apparently free of direct influences, just as B. Traven is in some ways unlike any other writer. The book may be classified as a proletarian novel, written in the style of tough-guy fiction. Its thesis, however, is not as doctrinaire, as deliberately worked out as that of a proletarian novel, nor is its style as conscious as that of a tough-guy novel.

For Gerard Gales, the young American narrator, stranded in Antwerp when his ship returns to New Orleans without him, the passport has displaced the sun as the center of the universe. Unable to prove his citizenship, he is a man without a country, and his physical presence is no official proof of his birth. Like Kafka's K. in *The Trial*, he moves through a labyrinth of bureaucracy; officials empowered to dispense passports, certificates, sailors-books, receipts, affidavits, seals, and licenses conduct the inquisition of the modern age. The war for liberty and democracy has produced a Europe in which to be hungry is human, to lack a passport is inhuman—unless you are rich.

A victim of nationalism, moving among fading echoes of speeches on international brotherhood, Gerard is an individualist. Immigration officials conspire to smuggle him from Belgium into Holland, then back into Belgium, then into France, where he is jailed for riding a train without a ticket and later sentenced to be shot as a suspected spy. Ironically, when he senses the universal animosity toward Americans and pretends to be a German, he is treated royally. In Spain, he is left entirely alone. A people politically oppressed, the Spanish seem freer than other men, and Gerard loves them. The peasants, however, are so good to him that he feels useless and hates himself; he senses the error in a Communist state where the individual is denied the privilege of taking his own risks. Because he is a sailor without a ship and because he wants to return to his girl, Gerard signs aboard *The Yorikke*.

If he once thought that the world consisted of deckhands and men who made paint, he descends now into a sailor's hell as drag man in a stokehold. Its name obscured on the bow, *The Yorikke*, too, appears to lack a proper birth certificate; but though she seems ashamed of her name, Gerard exhibits a kind of nationalism himself when he withholds his true name and country and signs on as an Egyptian; no American would sail on such a ship, and he realizes that, despite its many faults, he loves his country and is wretchedly homesick. *The Yorikke* resembles no ship he has ever seen; she appears to be insane. A model death ship, she has no life jackets. A death ship is so called because her owners have decided to scuttle her for the insurance. The crew, desperate men called "deads," at the end of their tether when they come aboard, do not know when the ship will go down. The sea, Gerard imagines, will probably eructate the diseased ship for fear of infection. No supplies—spoons, coffee cups, blankets—are provided; the men repeatedly steal a single bar of soap from one another until it has been through every filthy hand; conditions are worse than in a concentration camp. The only thing in ample supply is work, and if a man tries to collect overtime on a ship pathologically committed to profits, he may find himself in a black hold with rats that would terrify a cat. Traven conveys a vivid sense of what "she" means as pronoun for a ship; Gerard constantly describes *The Yorikke* in very intimate and telling female terms.

Gerard admires his mysterious captain whose intelligence sets him apart from the old-style pirate. He takes care of his men, and they would rather sink with the ship than inform the authorities that she is carrying contraband for the Riffs. *The Yorikke* crew is the filthiest Gerard has ever seen; the men wear bizarre rigs and rags. Some appear to have been shanghaied off the gallows. In the towns, other sailors shun them; men, women, and children fear them; and the police, afraid they may leave the town in ashes, follow them.

The filthiest member of the black gang is the drag man, who must perform extra and loathsome chores. Work is at the center of this novel—the struggle to get it and, under extreme conditions, the horror and ultimate beauty of it. Delight in conveying an inside view is a characteristic of tough-guy literature. Gerard gives all the details of various work routines. One of the most horrific passages in literature is Traven's description of putting back fallen grate bars while the boiler is white hot. After his first bout at what becomes a daily task, Gerard declares that he is free, unbound, above the gods; he can do what he wishes and curse the gods, because no hell could be greater torture.

Gerard resurrects the freshness of the cliché that men become like machines. He feels like a gladiator for Caesar's fight-to-the-death spectacles. Bravery on the battlefield is nothing when compared to the bravery of men who do certain work to keep civilization afloat. No flag drapes the bodies of casualties; they go like garbage over the fantail. On a death ship, no laws keep a man in line; each worker is crucially necessary, and work is a common bond. With no sense of heroics, Gerard helps save two men and is himself saved. His true countrymen, he discovers, are those workers who are scalded and scorched at the same furnace with him; he does not desert because his friend Stanislav would then have to work alone. Though Traven appears to show how men grow accustomed to misery and filth, he insists that nobody really gets used to them; one simply loses the capacity to feel and becomes hard-boiled. Few fictive descriptions of the life, the hopes, the illusions and attitudes of the doomed sailor, his qualities of ingenuity, improvisation, and audacity are as complete as Traven's.

Ironically, just as Gerard, despite his misery, learns to live and laugh on the ship, he senses *The Yorikke*'s imminent doom. A further irony comes when Gerard and Stanislav are shanghaied from *The Yorikke* to serve on the new but disastrously slow *Empress of Madagascar*, which is to be scuttled in a few days. The *Empress*, however, kills her plotting captain and stands like a tower between the rocks before she sinks. Stanislav eats like a shipowner before he drowns. He and Gerard are safely tied to a piece of wreckage, but Stanislav has a hallucination in which he sees *The Yorikke* leaving the dock. Wanting to go with her, he detaches himself and slips into the sea. Not yet rescued, Gerard pays his respects to his comrade in the last lines of the novel.

The style of the story—rough, garrulous, and full of completely justified profanity—sounds translated, but it is consistent with Gerard's semiliterate immigrant background. Though these qualities become wearisome in three hundred pages, the sheer energy of the telling achieves a special eloquence. Traven is overly fascinated by the way words come about; Gerard indulges in figurative rhetoric; many of his wisecracks seem lame, probably because his slang is dated. Humor, wit, and comedy are interwoven quite naturally among the darks of Traven's narrative. The style provides an amplification of theme through the play of language. Although Traven does not set up satirical situations, his diction and metaphorical pretenses create a satirical distortion in the telling of such episodes as those involving bureaucracy.

No plot or story line as such holds the novel together; narratively, it seems split in half, but the handling of theme, the picaresque looseness, and the personality of the narrator create an appropriate effect to the material. The static quality is relieved by sudden transitions and by the frequent use of tales and anecdotes, as in *The Treasure of the Sierra Madre*. Gerard is a storyteller who never tires of retelling a tale. The consulate scenes are repetitious; readers get variations on the same routine, though speeded up and foreshortened sometimes; and toward the end, Stanislav tells Gerard a story about himself that closely resembles Gerard's earlier experiences. Gerard is especially fond of ridiculing popular fiction and film versions of the seafaring life; the difference between living and listening to an experience is discussed in the beginning and at the end. Gerard tells his general story the way a sailor would, commenting with joking metaphors and reflecting constantly on the meaning of events. The reader is visualized as a captive audience for a man who has at last found a way to speak without interruption on various social, political, and economic conditions. The novel has some poignant moments, too, but, as is typical of the tough-guy novel, sentimentality occasionally intrudes.

Gerard and Stanislav are not to be associated with the victims of recent literature. They are more victims of the nature of things than of conditions that can be reformed. Gerard may gripe with every breath he takes, but he does not whine. He proudly insists that he can do work any man can do, anywhere. He contemptuously refuses to bow to circumstance. He refuses to blame the shipowners; having failed to take his fate in his own hands by jumping ship, he has no right to refuse to be a slave. He can only hope that he will be resurrected from the "deads" by his own will and fortitude. He knows that for the courageous man who survives the ordeal of *The Yorikke*, anything is possible. By going to the bottom of agony in his daily task of replacing grate bars, Gerard comes out with a kind of peace, aware of his place in a universe that now has meaning for the slightest thing. This earned romanticism enables him to see beauty in the conventionally ugly.

Although Gerard covers, directly to the reader and in dialogue, almost every grievance of the laborer of the first twenty-five years of this century, he is not interested in easy working conditions and fringe benefits. Repeatedly, he preaches the gospel of hard work, not because work is good for the soul, which seems less involved than muscle, but because it is good for man the animal. Unlike proletarian writers, Traven achieves a kind of mystique about work. One thinks of Albert Camus' Sisyphus: for his disobedience, Sisyphus was condemned to the futile task of rolling a huge rock to the top of a mountain, after which it rolled back down to the plain. Camus likened this labor to that of the proletariat. Unintentionally, perhaps, Traven has translated Sisyphus' mythic task into existential reality. The intentions of the novel are uncertain; but at moments, it appears to be an allegory about the laboring class. Working unseen at sea, deep in the black hole of an ash pit, these men, who were never born, in a sense, who are without a country, go to their deaths on a ship that does not exist officially. Gerard constantly speaks of the ship metaphorically as being more than five thousand years old. The flag is so dirty that it could represent any country and thus represents all. Many nationalities are represented among the crew; each nameless person is called, ironically, by the name of the country that he claims but that has denied his existence.

DEEPHAVEN

Type of work: Tales
Author: Sarah Orne Jewett (1849–1909)
Type of plot: Regional romance
Time of plot: Nineteenth century
Locale: Maine seacoast
First published: 1877

> *Principal characters:*
> HELEN DENIS, the narrator
> KATE LANCASTER, her friend
> THE CAREWS and
> THE LORIMERS, Deephaven's society
> MRS. KEW, the wife of the lighthouse keeper
> CAPTAIN LANT,
> CAPTAIN SANDS, and
> DANNY, Maine seamen
> MRS. BONNY, an elderly eccentric
> MISS CHAUNCEY, an elegant woman

The Story:

Kate Lancaster's grandaunt, Katherine Brandon, had died, leaving to Kate's mother a charming old house and the family estate, including wharf rights, at Deephaven, a quaint sea town that had known better days. Since Kate's family was scattering for the summer, she asked Helen Denis, a friend, to spend the season with her in the old house on the Maine coast. They took two maids with them who came from that part of New England, and they left Boston without regret.

Riding with them in the stagecoach from the railway station was a large, weather-beaten but good-natured woman who turned out to be Mrs. Kew, the wife of the lighthouse keeper. She was a keenly observant person but so warmhearted that the girls knew that she meant her invitation to visit the Light, and by the end of the summer, they knew that wherever she was, there was always a home and a heart for them.

Grandaunt Brandon's house was a sedate and imposing one, full of furnishings brought home by generations of seagoing ancestors. Its closets were filled with china, and its walls were covered by family portraits. The girls rummaged the place from cellar to attic until they felt that they knew Katherine Brandon as well as if she were still alive. Then they started to learn their way around the shore, out to the lighthouse, through the town, and out into the country.

People who had known Katherine Brandon and Kate's mother felt themselves the girls' friends by inheritance, and the girls were never lonely. Those people had held Katherine Brandon in great respect and with fond admiration. The girls tried to do nothing to hurt the Brandon name. Through Widow Jim Patton, they realized that Kate's aunt had been a thoughtful, generous soul, who remembered in her will her less fortunate neighbors.

To the girls, it seemed as though the clocks had stopped long ago in Deephaven and that the people continued repeating whatever they had been doing at that time in the past. Even their faces looked like those of colonial times. The people attached a great deal of importance to the tone of their society, handed down from the fabulous times of Governor Chantrey, a rich shipowner and an East India merchant. Now there were few descendants of the old families left; these were treated almost with reverence by the others. Even the simple fishermen felt an unreasoning pride in living in Deephaven. There were no foreigners, and there were no industries to draw people in from out of town.

The Carews and the Lorimers, old friends of Katherine Brandon, became friends of Kate and Helen. Mr. Dick Carew had been an East India merchant. Mr. Lorimer was the minister. The ladies were of the old order, inordinately proud of their mementos of the old days and always happy to tell reminiscences of earlier times.

Naturally, in a seacoast town, there were also sailors, all of whom were called captain by the time they reached a certain age. When attacks of rheumatism did not keep them home, they gathered on the wharves. Huddled close together, for many had grown deaf, they repeated the tales of their distant voyages. The girls noticed that silence fell when anyone approached the group, but on one occasion they hid close by to hear the old men's yarns.

Singly the old mariners were pleased to have a new audience, and before long, Kate and Helen were friendly with many of the old men. While some of them told stories of marine superstitions and adventures, others told supernatural tales that they swore were true. Captain Lent related the story of Peletiah Daw, to whom he had been bound out in his youth. Old Peletiah put more store by his wild nephew Ben than he did by his own sons. One night, when Peletiah was old and feeble, he cried out and begged his sons to cut down Ben, whom he had seen hanging from a yardarm. The sons thought their father was delirious, but a short time later, a sailor came to tell them that Ben had died of a fever. Peletiah called the man a liar, but the sailor held to his story before the women. Outside, he told the sons that Ben had been hanged from the yardarm, just as the old man had said, and on the day Peletiah had cried out.

Kate and Helen came to know Danny, a silent, weather-beaten fisherman who spent most of his time cleaning fish but who told them shyly about a pet cat he owned. Another good friend was Captain Sands, who kept in a warehouse all the souvenirs of his sea voyages that his wife refused to have cluttering her house.

When they took Mrs. Kew with them to a circus in nearby Denby, they all had a hilarious time, although the circus turned out to be a droopy and dispirited performance. Their high spirits were dampened for a while when Mrs. Kew recognized the fat lady as a girl who had once been her neighbor in Vermont.

The girls learned to know people all over the countryside as far as their horses would carry them. The person they liked best was Mrs. Bonny, who they thought looked so wild and unconventional that they always felt they were talking to a good-natured Indian.

One family along the coast was so forlorn that the thought of them preyed on the girls' minds all summer. Neither the father nor the mother had health, and there were several little children with whom they had made friends. Early in the fall, Kate and Helen went back along the coast to see them. Receiving no answer, they were standing undecided at the door when some neighbors came up to say that the mother had died a short time before. The father, after drinking heavily, was now lying dead, and the children had been parceled out as best they could be. Not daring to go to the funeral, the girls watched it from a distance. They felt that their everyday world was very close to the boundary of death.

Still closer to that boundary was Miss Chauncey of East Parish, a town even smaller and more forgotten than Deephaven. She was an aristocratic and splendid-looking old lady who had been mildly insane but harmless for years. Hers had been a rich and happy childhood until her father lost his fortune during the embargo early in the century. It was said that a sailor to whom he had broken a promise cursed her father and his family. One brother killed himself, another died insane. Miss Chauncey herself had been so ill that her guardian sold all her household goods to pay her hospital bills. Suddenly she became well, her mind unclouded. No one had told her that her house furnishings had been sold. Her shock at seeing the bare house unbalanced her mind again, but she remained harmless. She refused to leave the house, and she never seemed to realize that it was bleak and empty. She was still an elegant woman, possessed of unusual worldly advantages; she lived, however, without seeing the poverty of her surroundings. Although she had no idea of time, she always knew when Sunday came. She read the Bible beautifully. Faith sustained her.

By fall, Kate and Helen had become so attached to their friends in Deephaven that they postponed their return to Boston as long as possible. Helen thought that, though they might never return, they would always remember their completely happy summer in that old-fashioned village.

Critical Evaluation:

The provincial characters in *Deephaven* (Jewett's first collection of tales) do not yet possess the universality that they would acquire in Sarah Orne

Jewett's latest stories and novels; but the author acutely observes this small fishing village, clearly defining its social gradations and representative types. Equally well detailed are the varieties of "fashion" adopted by the inhabitants of Deephaven. Yet it is the people themselves—their faces, their speech, and their lives—that the reader best remembers.

Life in Deephaven moves slowly, so that even the details of common existence assume importance and become leisurely and pleasant activities. The narrator details with obvious relish the housekeeping routine and the quiet day-to-day village life. Always, a gentle humor pervades the book.

Memories constitute much of *Deephaven*'s narrative. The old sailors, their widows, village spinsters, old bachelors, everyone seems to live at least half of his or her life recollecting the past; and the "ancient mariners" of the village are the heroes, if the book has any. Sometimes they romanticize the past, sometimes they view it clearly, but always it is present before them, as real as the ever-changing bay and the tides. The ships remembered by the old skippers assume vivid personalities. The rich history of bygone days is preserved by the people who lived it. Jewett saw history as basically the story of human beings and the events of their lives. This vision dominates and shapes *Deephaven*.

The whalers and seafaring men and their families have had more contact with the world than most villagers and are not as narrow-minded as many small-town people. They possess more than folk wisdom; along with trinkets from foreign ports, they have picked up an awareness of the larger issues that face humanity. Sarah Orne Jewett especially loved and respected these people.

THE DEERSLAYER
Or, The First War-Path, a Tale

Type of work: Novel
Author: James Fenimore Cooper (1789–1851)
Type of plot: Historical romance
Time of plot: 1740
Locale: Northern New York State
First published: 1841

Principal characters:

NATTY BUMPPO, a woodsman called Deerslayer by the Delawares
HURRY HARRY, a frontier scout
CHINGACHGOOK, Deerslayer's Indian friend
THOMAS HUTTER, owner of the lake
JUDITH HUTTER, a girl Thomas Hutter claims as his daughter
HETTY HUTTER, Judith's sister
WAH-TA!-WAH, Chingachgook's beloved

The Story:

Natty Bumppo, a young woodsman known as Deerslayer, and Hurry Harry traveled to the shores of Lake Glimmerglass together. It was a dangerous journey, for the French and their Iroquois allies were on the warpath. Deerslayer was planning to meet his friend Chingachgook, the young Delaware chief, so that they might go against the Iroquois. Hurry Harry was on his way to the lake to warn Thomas Hutter and his daughters that hostile Indians were raiding along the frontier. Harry was accustomed to hunt and trap with Hutter during the summer, and he was an admirer of Hutter's elder daughter, the spirited Judith.

Hutter and his daughters lived in a cabin built on piles in the middle of the lake. Hutter had also built a great, scowlike vessel, known among frontiersmen as the ark, on which he traveled from one shore of the lake to the other on his hunting and trapping expeditions. On their arrival at the lake, the two found a hidden canoe. Having paddled out to the cabin and found it deserted, they proceeded down the lake and came upon the ark anchored in a secluded outlet. Hutter had already learned of the Indian raiders. The party decided to take refuge in the cabin, where they could be attacked only over the water. The men managed to maneuver the ark out of the narrow outlet and sail it to the cabin. They had one narrow escape. As the ark was clearing the outlet, six Indians tried to board the boat by dropping from the overhanging limbs of a tree. Each missed and fell into the water.

Under cover of darkness, Hutter, Deerslayer, and Hurry Harry took the canoe and paddled to shore to get Hutter's two remaining canoes hidden there. They found the canoes and, on their way back to the ark, sighted a party of Indians camped under some trees. While Deerslayer waited in a canoe offshore, the other two men attacked the Iroquois camp in an attempt to obtain scalps, for which they could receive bounties. They were captured. Deerslayer, knowing that he was powerless to help them, lay down to sleep in the canoe until morning.

When Deerslayer awoke, he saw that one of the canoes had drifted close to shore. To rescue it, he was forced to shoot an Indian, the first man he had ever killed.

Returning to the fort with his prizes, Deerslayer told the girls of their father's fate. It was agreed that they should delay any attempt at rescue until the arrival of Chingachgook, whom Deerslayer was to meet that night.

Under cover of darkness, the party went in the ark and met Chingachgook at the spot where the river joined the lake. Back in the cabin, Deerslayer explained that the Delaware had come to the lake to rescue his sweetheart, Wah-ta!-Wah, who had been stolen by the Iroquois. Suddenly, they discovered that Hetty Hutter had disappeared. The girl, who was somewhat feeble-minded, had cast off in one of the canoes with the intention of going to the Indian camp to rescue her father and Hurry Harry.

The next morning, Wah-ta!-Wah came upon Hetty wandering in the forest. She took the white girl to the Iroquois camp. Because the Indians believed deranged persons were protected by the Great Spirit, she suffered no harm.

It was Deerslayer's idea to ransom the prisoners with some rich brocades and carved ivory that he and Judith found in Tom Hutter's chest. Its contents had been known only to Hutter and the simpleminded Hetty, but in this emergency, Judith did not hesitate to open the coffer. Meanwhile, a young Iroquois had rowed Hetty back to the cabin on a raft. Deerslayer told him that the party in the cabin would give two ivory chessmen for the release of the captives. He was unable to drive quite the bargain he had planned. In the end, four chessmen were exchanged for the men, who were returned that night.

Hetty brought a message from Wah-ta!-Wah. Chingachgook was to meet the Indian girl at a particular place on the shore when the evening star rose above the hemlocks that night. Hurry Harry and Tom Hutter were still determined to obtain scalps. When night closed in, Hurry Harry, Hutter, and Chingachgook reconnoitered the camp. To their disappointment, they found it deserted and the Indians camped on the beach, at the spot where Wah-ta!-Wah was to wait for Chingachgook.

While Hutter and Harry slept, the Delaware and Deerslayer attempted to keep the rendezvous. Unfortunately, the girl was under such close watch that it was impossible for her to leave the camp. The two men entered the camp and boldly rescued her from her captors. Deerslayer, who remained at their rear to cover their escape, was taken prisoner.

When Judith heard from Chingachgook of Deerslayer's capture, she rowed Hetty ashore to learn what had become of the woodsman. Once more, Hetty walked unharmed among the superstitious savages. Deerslayer assured her there was nothing she could do to help and that he must await the Iroquois' pleasure. She left to return to Judith.

As the girls paddled about, trying to find the ark in the darkness, they heard the report of a gun. Torches on shore showed them that an Indian girl had been mortally wounded by a shot from the ark. Soon the lights went out. Paddling to the center of the lake, they tried to get what rest they could before morning came.

When daylight returned, Hutter headed the ark toward the cabin once more. Missing his daughters, he had concluded that the cabin would be the most likely meeting place. Hutter and Harry were the first to leave the ark to go into the cabin. There the Iroquois, who had come aboard in rafts under cover of darkness, were waiting in ambush. Harry managed to escape into the water, where he was saved by Chingachgook. Judith and Hetty came to the ark in their canoe. After the savages had gone ashore, those on the ark went to the cabin. They found Hutter lying dead. That evening, he was buried in the lake. Hurry Harry took advantage of the occasion to propose to Judith, but she refused him.

Shortly afterward, they were surprised to see Deerslayer paddling toward the ark. He had been given temporary liberty in order to bargain with the fugitives. The Iroquois sent word that Chingachgook would be allowed to return to his own people if Wah-ta!-Wah and Judith became brides of Iroquois warriors. Hetty, they promised, would go unharmed because of her mental condition. Although Deerslayer's life was to be the penalty for refusal, these terms were declined.

Deerslayer did not have to return to his captors until the next day, and that evening he and Judith examined carefully the contents of her father's chest. To the girl's wonder, she found letters indicating that Hutter had not been her real father, but a former buccaneer whom her mother had married when her first husband deserted her. Saddened by this knowledge, Judith no longer wished to live at the lake. She intimated slyly to Deerslayer that she loved him, only to find that he considered her above him in education and intelligence.

When Deerslayer returned to the Iroquois the next day, he was put to torture with hatchets. Hetty, Judith, and Wah-ta!-Wah came to the camp and attempted to intercede for him, but to no avail. Suddenly, Chingachgook bounded in and cut his friend's bonds. Deerslayer's release was the signal for the regiment from the nearest fort to attack, for Hurry Harry had gone to summon help during the night.

The Iroquois were routed. Hetty was mortally wounded during the battle.

The next day, she was buried in the lake beside her parents. Judith joined the soldiers returning to the fort. Deerslayer departed for the Delaware camp with Chingachgook and his bride.

Fifteen years later, Deerslayer, Chingachgook, and the latter's young son, Uncas, revisited the lake. Wah-ta!-Wah was long since dead, and, though the hunter inquired at the fort about Judith Hutter, he could find no one who knew her. Rumor was that a former member of the garrison, then living in England on his paternal estates, was influenced by a woman of rare beauty who was not his wife. The ark and the cabin in the lake were falling into decay.

Critical Evaluation:

The Deerslayer is the fifth and last published of the Leatherstocking Tales; when the entire series was republished in 1850, it became the first. Having written two books about Leatherstocking in middle age and two picturing him in his declining years, James Fenimore Cooper turned back to young Natty Bumppo before he had gained fame among the Indians as Hawkeye or Long Rifle. In *The Deerslayer*, Natty is the idealized "natural man."

Deerslayer is initiated into warfare when he first kills a fellow man—in self-defense—and then comforts his dying foe, who confers upon him the new name, Hawkeye, which honors him as a fighter. He also learns of some of the evil in the world through his acquaintance with Thomas Hutter and Hurry Harry who kill Indians—including women and children—for profit only. Cooper's idealization of Indian character is brought out partly through what he himself writes about Indians and partly through what Natty says of them.

The common theme that ties the Leatherstocking Tales together is the protagonist. Although he is known by different names in the various novels, he is identified throughout the series by his qualities as a brave and honorable hero. As a character, he is developed from youth to old age. He is a loner and an individualist and has moral and ethical concerns about the environment. He commands a strong integrity in dealing with other human beings, treating both friends and enemies with courtesy and respect. Ultimately, he follows his own simple moral scheme and demonstrates unwavering dedication to the principle of self-reliance. *The Deerslayer* is one of two Leatherstocking Tales (the other was *The Pathfinder*) that Mark Twain chose to mock amusingly but rather unjustly in his "Fenimore Cooper's Literary Offenses." The defects of plot, characterization, and style are easily seen by modern readers, but the romance is a far better book than Twain's comments would lead one to believe. Some critics have seen it as perhaps the best of the five tales. Cooper in his 1850 preface said *The Pathfinder* and *The Deerslayer* were "probably the two most worthy of an enlightened and cultivated reader's notice."

DELTA WEDDING

Type of work: Novel
Author: Eudora Welty (1909–   )
Type of plot: Regional realism
Time of plot: Early 1920's
Locale: Mississippi
First published: 1946

Principal characters:

> LAURA McRAVEN, a cousin to the Fairchilds
> DABNEY FAIRCHILD, a bride-to-be
> ELLEN, her mother
> BATTLE, her father
> SHELLEY, her sister
> GEORGE FAIRCHILD, her uncle
> ROBBIE, George's wife
> TROY FLAVIN, a plantation manager

The Story:

Nine-year-old Laura McRaven made her first journey alone from Jackson to the Delta to visit her dead mother's people, the Fairchilds. One of her cousins, Dabney Fairchild, was to be married, and Laura's chief regret was that she could not be in the wedding party because of her mother's recent death. She remembered Shellmound, the Fairchild plantation, and knew that she would have a wonderful time with her exciting cousins and aunts. The Fairchilds were people to whom things happened, exciting, unforgettable things.

At Shellmound, Laura found most of the family assembled for the wedding. Although children her age were her companions, she was also aware of the doings of the grownups. It was obvious that the family was not happy about Dabney's marriage. Her husband-to-be was Troy Flavin, the manager of the plantation, whose inferior social position was the main mark against him. Uncle Battle, Dabney's father, was most of all reluctant to let one of his family go from him, but he could not bring himself to say anything to Dabney, not even that he would miss her. Laura found this fact about her cousins to be very strange. They seldom talked as a united family, but they always acted as one.

There were so many members of the family that it was hard for Laura to keep them straight. Uncle Battle's wife was Aunt Ellen, and their oldest daughter was Shelley, who was going to be a nun. Again the whole family disapproved of her plan, but there was seldom any attempt to get her to change her mind. The obvious favorite was Uncle George, Battle's brother. Uncle George had also married beneath him. He and his wife, Robbie, lived in Memphis, where everyone knew poor Uncle George could never be happy.

When George arrived for the wedding festivities, he was alone and miserable. Robbie had left him, and he had come down alone to see his family. Not wanting to make Dabney unhappy, they did not tell her of Robbie's desertion. The children and the aunts and grandaunts were not told either, although one by one they began to suspect that something was wrong. Ellen could have killed Robbie for making George unhappy, but she kept her feelings to herself except when she was alone with Battle, her husband.

Robbie's anger at her husband began on the afternoon of a family outing. George had risked his life to save one of the cousins, a feebleminded child caught in the path of a train as they crossed a railroad trestle. After that incident, Robbie was never the same with George. She seemed to want him to prove that he loved her more than he loved his family.

Probably Shelley understood the family best. She knew that they had built a wall against the outside world, but she suspected that they were more lonely than self-sufficient. Most people took the family as a group, loving or hating them all together. Only Uncle George seemed to take them one by one, loving and understanding each as an individual. Shelley thought that this was why they all loved Uncle George so much.

Dabney seemed to wish for more than she had in her love for Troy. Sometimes she felt left out, as if she were trying to find a lighted window but found only darkness. She loved Troy, but she wanted to feel even more a part of him. She also wished that her family would try to keep her with them; she wanted to make certain of their love.

Preparations for the wedding created a flurry. The dresses had been ordered from Memphis, and when some of the gowns failed to arrive, there was the usual hubbub among the women, a concern that the men could not appreciate. One of the children fell sick at the last minute, so that Laura was made one of the wedding party after all. Troy's mother sent some beautiful handmade quilts from her mountain shack. Troy felt proud, but the Fairchilds were even more self-consciously and unwillingly ashamed of his background.

After their wedding, Dabney and Troy would live at Marmion, an estate owned by the family. Dabney rode over to see the house. Looking at the stately buildings and the beautiful old trees, she knew that best of all she would love being inside it, looking out on the rest of the world. That was what she wanted the most, to be inside where she was a part of the light and warmth. That was what marriage must give her.

All the time, unknown to any of the family but Shelley, Robbie was not far away. She had come after George in hopes that he was looking for her. What had almost defeated Robbie was the fear that she had not married

George but the whole Fairchild family. It was that fear which had made her angry at the affair on the railroad trestle. Wanting desperately to come first with George, she knew instinctively that he could never set her apart or above the family. Contrite and humble, she went to Shellmound. The fact that George was not even there at the moment hurt her even more, for she wanted very much for him to be miserable without her. He was, but it was not the Fairchild way to let anyone see his true feelings.

Robbie probably hit the secret of the family when she said that the Fairchilds loved each other because, in so doing, they were really loving themselves. That fact was not quite true in George's case. He was the different one. Because of his gentleness and his ability to love people as individuals, he let Robbie see his love for her without ever saying the words she had longed to hear.

The wedding was almost an anticlimax, a calm scene following gusty storms of feeling. Troy and Dabney took only a short trip, for Troy was needed to superintend the plantation. While they were gone, Battle worked the hands hard to get Marmion ready for them. Dabney was anxious to move in, but the move was not so necessary after her marriage as it had seemed before; she no longer felt left out of Troy's life. She thought her life before had been like seeing a beautiful river between high banks, with no way to get down. Now she had found the way, and she was at peace. Indeed, the whole family seemed to have righted itself.

When Aunt Ellen asked Laura to live with them at Shellmound, her being wanted by the Fairchilds seemed too wonderful to believe. Laura knew that she would go back to her father, but still feeling that she really belonged to the Fairchilds seemed like a beautiful dream. She clung briefly to Aunt Ellen, as if to hold close that wonderful moment of belonging.

Critical Evaluation:

Eudora Welty has created in Shellmound, the home of the Fairchild family in *Delta Wedding*, a world set apart from the rest of Southern plantation society of the 1920's. Shellmound is a haven, isolated from the mainstream of Southern life and unaffected by extremes of grief and suffering: there is no racial tension, no poverty, no war or natural catastrophe, no sense of alienation and instability generated by contact with modern urban society, and no severe moral deficiencies in the characters that would preclude natural human happiness. The Fairchild estate is thus the perfect stage upon which to play out a drama about the growth of every type of love, from romantic to filial to platonic.

The main focus of the book, therefore, is on the nature of the numerous members of the Fairchild clan and on their relationships. Welty shows how the men are different from the women, how the "insiders" are different from those who have married into the family, how each person relates to the others, and how each person grows individually and privately. In order to explore these various aspects, the author utilizes different narrative voices, thus enabling the reader to view the characters from different perspectives. Aunt Tempe, for example, provides the older generation's point of view; she believes that Delta women have inherited traits that cannot be learned by outsiders, traits that enable them subtly to control their men and the plantations. At the young end of the spectrum is nine-year-old Laura, who comes to live at Shellmound temporarily after her mother's death; she provides the child's viewpoint of events during the hectic wedding preparations. The most objective, wise, and clearsighted outlook, however, is provided by Aunt Ellen. As an "outsider" (she married Battle Fairchild), she not only sees the situation more accurately than her more involved and subjective relatives but also brings to her judgment insights from the world beyond the plantation.

What distinguishes the Fairchilds most is their simultaneous independence from and reliance upon one another; each person is at once intensely caught up in family concerns and fiercely private and separate. The only member who transcends the insular closeness of the circle to achieve a more universal outlook on life is Uncle George; able to feel and see beyond the limitations of life at Shellmound, he is nevertheless tied to the Fairchilds in his heart. Through the family's constant attempts to study and understand George, and through George's emotional involvement in events at the estate, Welty reveals a group of people at once selfishly exclusive and warmly affectionate, tender, loving, and devoted.

DODSWORTH

Type of work: Novel
Author: Sinclair Lewis (1885–1951)
Type of plot: Social criticism
Time of plot: 1920's
Locale: The United States and Europe
First published: 1929

Principal characters:
SAM DODSWORTH, an American manufacturer
FRAN DODSWORTH, his wife
KURT OBERSDORF, Fran's lover
EDITH CORTRIGHT, Sam's friend and later his fiancée
CLYDE LOCKERT, Fran's admirer
EMILY, the Dodsworths' daughter
BRENT, the Dodsworths' son

The Story:

In 1903, Sam Dodsworth married Fran Voelker whom he had met at the Canoe Club while he was assistant superintendent at the Zenith Locomotive works. Five years after their marriage, Sam became vice-president and general manager of production for the Revelation Automobile Company. By 1925, the Dodsworths had two children, Emily, about to be married, and Brent, in school at Yale. When Sam sold his factory to the Unit Automotive Company, they decided to go to Europe for a leisurely vacation, a second honeymoon.

The first night out on the S.S. *Ultima*, Major Clyde Lockert seated himself at Sam's table in the smoking room. Lockert, who said he was growing cocoa in British Guiana, quickly became friends with Fran Dodsworth, and while Sam looked on like an indulgent parent, he squired her about, censuring and selecting the new friends she made. He continued to see the Dodsworths after they arrived in London.

Fran was snobbishly pleased when he took them to visit his cousins, Lord and Lady Herndon. Between them, Fran and Lockert made Sam feel almost like an outsider. He was a failure at the dinner party the Herndons gave, for he was unable to discuss cricket or polo, and he had no opinions about the Russian situation.

One evening, Hurd, manager of the London branch of the Revelation Motor Company, invited Sam to a gathering, along with about thirty representatives of American firms. Sam was surprised to learn that few of them wanted to go back to the United States except, perhaps, for a visit. They all preferred the leisureliness and the freedom from imposed moral restraint, which their adopted land afforded. These arguments made Sam see Europe in a different light.

When he returned to the hotel, he found Fran in tears. Lockert had taken her out that evening and, on their return, had tried to make love to her. Fran, ashamed of the situation in which she had placed herself and sure that Lockert would be laughing at her, asked that they leave for France as soon as possible. They started four days later.

France was a new experience for Sam Dodsworth. When Fran was willing to go sightseeing, he was able to see Paris and observe its people. When she chose to be fashionable and take tea at the Crillon with other American tourists, he was less fortunate. The more he saw, however, the more convinced Sam became that he could not understand Frenchmen. In the back of his mind, he was afraid that his inability to accept foreign ways, and Fran's willingness to adopt them, would finally drive them apart. He felt lonely for his old friend Tubby Pearson, president of the Zenith bank.

Before long, Fran had many friends among expatriate Americans of the international set. With her constant visits to dressmakers and her portrait painter, her outings with the leisured young men who escorted her and her friends, she and Sam saw less and less of each other. When he went home for his college class reunion that summer, he left Fran to take a villa with one of her new friends. He was to join her again in the fall, so that they might go on to the Orient together.

Back in New York, Sam felt, at first, as if he had become a stranger to the life of noise and hurry which he had previously taken for granted. Nor was he interested in the newest model Revelation that had been, quite competently, developed without his aid. He discovered also that he and his son no longer shared common ground. Brent was planning to sell bonds. The newly married Emily, her father observed, was the very capable manager of her own home and needed no assistance. Even Sam's best friend, Tubby Pearson, had gone on without him to new poker-playing and golfing companions.

At first, his letters from Fran were lively and happy. Then she quarreled with the friend who shared her villa over one of their escorts, Arnold Israel, a Jew. Sam grew increasingly anxious as he realized that the man was trailing Fran from one resort to another and that their relationship was becoming increasingly more intimate. He made sailing reservations and cabled his wife to meet him in Paris.

Sam had no difficulty discovering that his wife had been unfaithful to him; she admitted as much during their stormy reunion in Paris. With the threat that he would divorce her for adultery if she did not agree to drop Israel, he forced her to leave for Spain with him the following day.

The Dodsworths wandered across Spain into Italy and, finally, on to Germany and Berlin, and Sam had ample time to observe his wife. Increasingly he noted her self-centeredness, her pretentiousness, and his pity for her restlessness made him fonder of her.

At the home of the Biedners, Fran's cousins in Berlin, the Dodsworths met Kurt Obersdorf, a ruined Austrian nobleman. Kurt took them to places of interest in Berlin and became Fran's dancing companion.

When the news came that the Dodsworths were grandparents, for Emily now had a boy, they did not sail for home. In fact, they did not tell their friends of the baby's birth because Fran feared that, as a grandmother, she would seem old and faded to them. When Sam went to Paris to welcome Tubby Pearson and his wife, abroad for the first time, Fran remained in Berlin.

Sam and Tubby enjoyed themselves in Paris. Then Sam, driven by a longing to see his wife, flew back to Berlin. That night, Fran announced that she and Kurt had decided to marry and that she wanted a divorce. Sam agreed, on the condition that she wait a month before starting proceedings.

Sadly, Dodsworth left for Paris and later went on to Italy. While he was sitting on the piazza in Venice and reading one of Fran's letters, he saw Edith Cortright, a widow whom the Dodsworths had met during their earlier trip to Italy. Mrs. Cortright invited Sam home to tea with her, and on his second visit, he told her about his separation from Fran.

Sam spent most of the summer with Edith and her Italian friends. He began to gain a new self-confidence when he found that he was liked and respected by these new acquaintances, who admired him and were satisfied with him as he was. He grew to love Edith, and they decided to return to America together. Then Sam received a letter from Fran telling him that she had dropped divorce proceedings because Kurt's mother objected to his marriage with a divorced American.

Without saying good-bye to Edith, Sam rejoined Fran, homeward bound. He tried patiently to share her unhappiness and loneliness; but before long, Fran became her old self, implying that Sam had been at fault for the failure of their marriage, and flirting with a young polo player aboard ship. After breakfast, one morning, Sam sent a wireless to Edith, making arrangements to meet her in Venice. When the boat docked in New York, Sam left his wife forever. Three days later, he sailed again to Italy and Edith Cortright.

Critical Evaluation:

Sinclair Lewis was born a member of the American middle class, and his novels suggest that he both loved and detested his own kind, a crucial fact in understanding the unevenness of his satirical portraits. Alfred Kazin (*On Native Grounds*) views Lewis with Sherwood Anderson as New Realists—post-World War I reporters freed by the war into a struggle for "freedom of conduct" in middle America. Both writers, liberating forces in American literature of the 1920's, made "transcriptions of average expcrience," some-times reproducing it and sometimes parodying it, but always participating in the native culture if primarily to reveal its shortcomings. Thus, a typical Lewis novel, domestic satire, affords a mixture of scorn and compassion for its characters. To read his work in its own time was to see oneself or one's neighbor and to marvel at the likeness. He became immensely popular with such readers, an irony when one realizes that his ostensible intention was to expose the provincial, materialistic, bigoted, go-getters whom Mencken tagged the "booboisie."

Although Lewis published more than twenty novels, a play, short stories, and sketches between 1914 and his death in 1951, his reputation as an artist now rests on four novels of the 1920's. *Main Street* (1920), *Babbitt* (1922), *Arrowsmith* (1925), and *Dodsworth* (1929). The protagonists of the "big four" continue to generate interest and empathy because Lewis' feeling for the characters as human beings overrode his abiding skepticism. These characters are memorable, and they are living individuals whose natures and problems transcend Dickensian caricature and the topical.

Dodsworth, whose working title was "Exile," was written in Europe, where Lewis had journeyed in the aftermath of his ruined marriage. While there he found or imagined that he found a culture superior to that of America's half-educated, anti-intellectual boosters. Lewis' strong if troubled vision of middle-America appears to have come from a deep sense of his own inferiority (a chronic state documented in Vincent Sheean's *Dorothy and Red*, an account of the courtship and marriage of Lewis and Dorothy Thompson). Although he was the first American to receive the Nobel Prize in Literature, he later remarked that it ruined him; he could not "live up to it." This sense of native inferiority and resulting attempts to gain self-respect and love are duplicated in Sam Dodsworth's experiences in Europe. Lewis blends autobiography with fiction in a well-controlled third-person narrative technique in *Dodsworth*, focusing primarily on the protagonist, creating a fully realistic account of Sam's travels by simultaneously documenting the journeys and reasserting Dodsworth's value as a human being.

Lewis sees Dodsworth idealistically, for the most part, but so skillfully that the romantic and nostalgic are veiled by the realistic surface of events. Sam is the post-Victorian embodiment of American virtue. He is essentially honest, doggedly willing to remain open to new experience, boyish in his sincere if awed appreciation of femininity and womanliness but reluctant to be hen-pecked forever. His almost monkish physical courtship of Edith Cortright entails only kissing her hands. He is reserved, well-mannered, admirably dignified for an American, even while clutching his Baedeker. By contrast, most other American male characters are inferior if not nefarious. Arnold Israel engages in questionable financial pursuits, is sensual, and is more Euro-pean than the Europeans. Tub Pearson is the perennial adolescent whose idea of humor is to address French waiters as "Goosepeppy" and to ask for fricassee of birds' nests. Brent, the Dodsworths' son, decides to live by selling bonds, hoping to reach the "hundred and fifty thousand a year class."

Most significant in the characterization of Dodsworth, however, is his devotion to a work ethic of substance which proves to be his salvation. Sam slowly but persistently weighs his values against those of older cultures: England, France, Italy, Spain, and Germany. Europeans know wine, history, women, politics, and are not afraid of things theoretical, even socialism. Therefore, they can just "be"; that is, they can rest in the self-confidence inherent in their familial and cultural heritage. Americans, however, Sam dimly realizes, are born apostles and practitioners of technology. They must "do." Forces beyond their knowledge and control harness their dreams and energies. Their destiny is to build more and better autos, plumbing, and electrical appliances. Sam and Edith decide to return to Zenith to work but not on what Sam calls "kitchy banalities."

Lewis uses architecture as the symbol of Dodsworth's new life and work. In Europe, Sam, becoming absorbed in architecture, observes and sketches bridges, towers, and doorways. He is impressed by their lines, their strength, their beauty, but he recognizes that they are European. So rather than return to Zenith to build a phony pastiche of villas and chalets in the San Souci development, Sam and Edith talk of building homes for Americans, native to the soil and spirit. Optimistically, Edith cries that the American skyscraper is the only new thing in architecture since the Gothic cathedral. Working together, their future promises a sharp contrast to that of the pitiful Fran, to whom all culture was interesting as "social adornment."

Occasionally, Lewis abandons the detached third-person narrative technique to speak directly to the reader, to regale with satirical comments about travelers in general, or with a series of descriptions of American tourists complete with names in the comedy of humors tradition. Evident also are some forced metaphors, a few poorly integrated references to "morality hounds" in America or to the absurdities of Prohibition. Yet Lewis endows the novel with great power, basically by making Sam Dodsworth a sympathetic, authentic American whose life matters, after all, to him and to the reader.

DON SEGUNDO SOMBRA
Shadows on the Pampas

Type of work: Novel
Author: Ricardo Güiraldes (1886–1927)
Type of plot: Regional romance
Time of plot: Late nineteenth century
Locale: Argentina
First published: 1926

> Principal characters:
> DON SEGUNDO SOMBRA, a gaucho
> FABIO, a young waif
> DON LEANDRO GALVÁN, a rancher
> PEDRO BARRALES, a gaucho
> PAULA, a pretty young woman and beloved of Fabio

The Story:

Fabio was a young lad who lived with his two maiden aunts in a small Argentine village. He disliked his aunts, who felt, in their turn, that he was simply a bother. He was not sure that the two women were truly his relatives, for they paid him little heed as long as he gave them no trouble. Don Fabio Cáceres, a rancher, occasionally came to see the boy and took him into the country for a day, but the man ceased coming when Fabio was about eleven years old.

Fabio grew up to be a cheeky youngster who showed off for the worst element of the town. He knew all the gossip and spent most of his time hanging about the saloons; no one seemed to care that he never went to school. The village loafers hinted that he was an illegitimate, unwanted child. At best, he seemed destined to be a ne'er-do-well who carried a chip on his shoulder in defiance of the rest of the world.

One night, a gaucho rode into the town as Fabio was going home from fishing. The man impressed the boy instantly, and a little later, Fabio earned the gaucho's interest by warning him of an ambush laid by a knife-wielding bully. The kind words spoken by the gaucho, Don Segundo, went to the boy's heart, and Fabio immediately decided to follow the man when he left town. Gathering together his meager possessions, which fortunately included a saddle and two ponies, Fabio went quietly away without telling anyone where he was going, in order to escape his hated aunts. He rode to the ranch belonging to Don Leandro Galván, where he knew Don Segundo was going to spend a few days breaking wild horses.

DON SEGUNDO SOMBRA by Ricardo Güiraldes. Translated by Harriet de Onis. By permission of the publishers, Rinehart & Co., Inc. Copyright, 1935, by Farrar & Rinehart, Inc.

When he arrived, the boy applied for work and was accepted. By the time Don Segundo was ready to leave the ranch on a cattle drive, Fabio had convinced Don Leandro and Don Segundo that he was a willing worker, and they let Fabio go with the other gauchos on half pay. At the end of the drive, Fabio was well along in his apprenticeship as a gaucho.

For five years, Fabio continued under the tutelage of Don Segundo. Traveling from ranch to ranch, they worked for a number of landowners. From the older man, Fabio learned to care for himself and his horses, to work cattle under various conditions, to live courageously, to get along with all kinds of people, and to have a good time singing songs, dancing, and telling stories. It was more than a way of making a living that the man passed on to the boy; it was an entire culture, a culture as old as the cattle industry and in some respects even older, going back as it did to the culture of Spain.

There were many incidents in their wanderings, including a time when Fabio won a large number of pesos by picking the winning bird in a cockfight when everyone else bet against the bird. That happened in the town of Navarro, a town which remained a lucky place in young Fabio's mind. He remembered also a long drive with cattle to a ranch on the seashore. There Fabio found a country he detested and a young woman he loved, as well as a great store of bad luck. He had picked up quite a respectable string of horses, the tools of the gaucho's trade, and he was very proud of them. In working the cattle at the seashore ranch, however, two of the horses were injured, much to the young gaucho's dismay. One of them was badly gored by a bull, and when Fabio came across the bull one evening while exploring with another young man, he vowed to break its neck. He lassoed the beast and broke its neck with the shock, but in doing so, he injured himself severely, breaking several bones.

While Fabio remained at the ranch convalescing from his injuries, he fell in love, he thought, with Paula, a pretty young girl who lived on the place. Unfortunately, she led him on while she also led on the rather stupid son of the rancher. The other lad took advantage of Fabio's crippled arm and attacked him with a knife. Fabio, not wanting to injure the owner's son, to fight over a woman, or to violate the father's hospitality, avoided the other fellow's thrusts until they became deadly. Then with a quick thrust, Fabio slashed the boy's forehead slightly, quickly taking the will to fight out of him. Paula, over whom the fight began, rebuked the crippled Fabio. Disgusted at her and at himself, Fabio, crippled as he was, mounted his horse and rode away to rejoin Don Segundo, who was working at a nearby ranch until Fabio could be ready to travel.

Don Segundo and Fabio happened into a small village on a day when people had gathered from miles around to race horses. Fabio bet and lost a hundred pesos, then another hundred, and finally the third and last hundred he possessed. Still not satisfied that he was a hopeless loser, he gambled five of his horses and lost them as well. He came out of the afternoon's activity a sad young man.

He and Don Segundo were hired to trail a herd of cattle from a ranch near the village to the city to be butchered. It was a long, hard drive, even for experienced gauchos. It was made even more difficult for Fabio by the fact that he had only three horses, for the animals soon became fatigued from the work of carrying him and working the cattle on the road. When the herd stopped to rest one afternoon, Fabio decided to see if he could somehow get another horse or two.

While looking about, he found Pedro Barrales, a gaucho who had traveled with him and Don Segundo several times before. Pedro Barrales had a letter addressed to Señor Fabio Cáceres, a letter which he gave to Fabio. The lad looked blankly at the letter, not believing it was addressed to him, for he thought he had no surname. Don Segundo opened the letter to find that the maiden aunts had been truly Fabio's relatives and that Don Fabio Cáceres who had visited him at his aunt's home was really his father, from whom he had inherited a fortune and a large, well-stocked ranch. The news saddened Fabio because he saw that it would take him away from the life he loved. He was angered, too, because he had been left so long under the impression that he should be ashamed of his parentage.

Acting upon the good advice of Don Segundo, Fabio returned to his native town, however, and from there to the ranch where he had begun work under Don Leandro Galván, who had now become his guardian. When Don Segundo agreed to remain with him for three years on his own ranch, Fabio was willing to settle down. Yet, the three years passed all too swiftly, and at the end of that time, Fabio was exceedingly sad when Don Segundo, answering the gaucho's call to wander, rode away.

Critical Evaluation:

Don Segundo Sombra: Shadows on the Pampas has been called the South American counterpart of *Huckleberry Finn*: Like the hero of Mark Twain's novel, Fabio wanders on his own through youth in a new country, giving the author a chance not only to tell a story but also to present a vivid and varied documentary of details about the people, the customs, and the countryside. In Argentina, the book was immediately popular. It and the earlier gaucho epic *Martín Fierro* are the best narratives dealing with the gaucho, the South American cowboy. The hero of Ricardo Güiraldes' novel was drawn from a real-life gaucho whom the author had known and loved in his own childhood on his father's ranch, La Portena, in the province of Buenos Aires. The novel reflects a pastoral form of life that has all but disappeared in Argentina, and the story will probably fascinate later generations much as Owen Wister's picturesque narrative of the North American cowboy in *The Virginian* has caught the fancy of postfrontier readers.

This novel is considered the classic novel of the gaucho. It has the clean lines of Hemingway's *The Old Man and the Sea*, for Don Segundo Sombra, the patriarchal old gaucho, and Fabio, the boy, are thrown into relief as they ride across the billowing pampa. Don Segundo is introduced into the novel dramatically for, when first seen by the boy, he looms enormously, a giant and almost overwhelming horseman. When Don Segundo rides off at the novel's end, only the pampa and the sky are seen as he disappears, shadowlike, into the distance.

A touch of the American motion picture *Shane* is present in the friendship between the boy and the mature man, and the hero worship of the former for the latter. It is almost a fantastic example of youth forming an image of the ideal that it wishes to reach, and at the same time, finding an example of this ideal upon which it can concentrate its attention and imitation.

Another theme is the passing of a breed, as represented by Don Segundo, the last of the true gauchos. Freedom is still another theme: the wild wandering of the duo across the pampa; the freedom, now disappearing, once enjoyed by the dying gaucho; the gradual smothering of such freedom by civilization. *Don Segundo Sombra* is simultaneously set late in the day of the gaucho's traditional frontier enemy, the wild Indian tribes, who have already been pushed up against the setting sun, into the Andean foothills. Thus, while entertaining, the novel has various social and historical messages.

Güiraldes made unusual use of water imagery. The pampa itself is almost presented as an ocean of land, the reflecting sky being an overhead ocean. Ponds and streams add other touches of water imagery, while Don Segundo and Fabio even reach the Atlantic Ocean itself once and stare raptly at it. Life itself is symbolized by water, for life flows like water, as does the novel's action.

Adventure and travel give another element, in this case Quixotesque. The two riders wander at will, like Don Quixote and Sancho Panza, satiating the human yen to travel and see what lies over the horizon. This appeal to wanderlust is so intense that it has a strong mystic touch. The novel is realistic and true to life, but it can almost be classified as a romance of chivalry, since it exalts the virtues of Don Segundo and his adventures with Fabio in the field of struggle of a gaucho's daily labor and in battle against the inclemencies of weather and nature.

The vocabulary has many Argentinisms, some of colonial vintage brought down centuries before from Jesuit mission lands in Paraguay, but is never difficult. The plot develops serenely to a logical climax; the novel's style is good but not distinctive; the few characters are well done or deliberately shaded out so as not to distract from the protagonist, Don Segundo, and his young companion, Fabio. The reader thus identifies easily with both.

Güiraldes' use of nature is not equal in some respects to that of, say, Louis L'Amour, but it is blended so well into the narration that one can almost hear the rustle of leaves in the trees, the murmuring of the streams, and even the sound of the wind. There is some use of colors and tints—the green ombú trees, the colors of the steers and horses, while gaucho lore is presented extensively and authentically without any touch of "drug-store gauchoism." In general, relatively little of the milk of human kindness or warmth is presented, for Fabio is very much alone in a cold world until he meets Don Segundo.

As genres, the gaucho novel and poetry are extensive. They are important not only because of their intrinsic worth as genuine, regional products of the American hemisphere, but also because they have tinged other aspects of Argentine literature, even the theater and essay. This is true in Argentina itself—where the core, pampa heartland insinuates itself into other geographical regions of the country—and in "The Purple Land" of Uruguay and the undulating pampa of southern Brazil. In the latter area, another gaucho literature exists in Portuguese, forming a natural component to the gaucho genre, produced in the River Plate world and its collateral systems, such as the Uruguay, Paraná, and Paraguay.

DOÑA BÁRBARA

Type of work: Novel
Author: Rómulo Gallegos (1884–1969)
Type of plot: Regional romance
Time of plot: Early twentieth century
Locale: Arauca Valley, Venezuela
First published: 1929

> *Principal characters:*
> DOÑA BÁRBARA, a beautiful, unscrupulous mestiza
> SANTOS LUZARDO, the owner of the Altamira ranch
> MARISELA, the illegitimate daughter of Doña Bárbara and Lorenzo Barquero
> ANTONIO, a cowboy at the Altamira ranch
> THE WIZARD, a rascally henchman of Doña Bárbara
> SEÑOR DANGER, an American squatter on the Altamira ranch
> DON BALBINO, the treacherous overseer at the Altamira ranch

The Story:

The Altamira ranch was a vast estate in the wildest section of the Arauca River basin of Venezuela, a ranch that had been established early in the history of the cattle business of that South American country. Late in the nineteenth century, however, it had been divided into two parts by the joint heirs of one of the owners. One part retained the old name and went to the male heir of the Luzardo family. The other part, going to a daughter who had married a Barquero, took its name from the new owner. As the years went by, the two families carried on a feud that killed most of the men on both sides. In the years of the Spanish-American War, the owner of Altamira and his elder son quarreled; the father killed the son and then starved himself to death. Doña Luzardo took her only remaining son and went to Caracas to rear him in a more civilized atmosphere.

Years went by, and finally the son, Santos Luzardo, decided to sell the ranch, which had been allowed to deteriorate to almost nothing under irresponsible overseers. In order to set a price upon his property, he went into the back country to see it for himself. On his arrival, he found that the neighboring ranch of the Barqueros had fallen into the hands of Doña Bárbara, a mestiza who had been the mistress of the real owner before she ran him off his own property. Doña Bárbara was in the process of taking over Altamira ranch with the help of several henchmen, including Don Balbino, the overseer of Altamira ranch. Santos decided to keep the ranch and try to make it a prosperous business, if he could only keep it out of Doña Bárbara's hands.

To help him, Santos had a handful of loyal cowboys who had known him as a child, including Antonio, a cowboy who had been his playmate years before. Santos Luzardo's first move was to end the feud between himself and the Barqueros. He found Lorenzo Barquero living in a cabin in a swamp, the only land his mistress had not taken from him. After making his peace with Lorenzo and his illegitimate daughter Marisela, Santos took them to live at Altamira ranch. Marisela was as beautiful as her mother, Doña Bárbara, and Santos wished to retrieve her from barbarity.

Most of the cattle had been stolen from Altamira ranch, until only about a hundred head were left. Nevertheless, Antonio, the loyal cowboy, had seen to it that many hundreds more had been allowed to stray into wild country in order to save them from the depredations of Doña Bárbara and Señor Danger, an American who had begun as a squatter and who was carving his own ranch out of Altamira land. Don Balbino, the treacherous overseer, was immediately discharged. Since he had been working for Doña Bárbara and was her lover, he sought the mestiza's protection.

Santos, who had been trained as a lawyer, decided first to try a legal means of repossessing part of his ranch. He went to the local magistrate and, through his knowledge of the law, forced that official to call in Doña Bárbara and Señor Danger. They were told to permit a roundup of his cattle and to help him, since their herds were intermingled with those from Altamira. They were also told to take action with respect to fences. Danger had to build fences, for according to the law, he had too few cattle to let them run wild. Doña Bárbara was to help build a boundary fence between her ranch and Altamira. Surprisingly, she took the decisions with good grace. Her henchmen were completely surprised, for previously she had ridden roughshod over all opposition. The answer lay in the fact that she was secretly in love with Santos Luzardo, and she thought she could command his love and his property by her beauty.

As weeks of deadening ranch routine passed, Santos was glad that he had brought Marisela to his house, for his efforts to teach her culture kept him from losing touch with civilization. Although his interest in her was only that of a friend and tutor, Marisela had fallen in love with the rancher.

Along the Arauca River, there were thousands of herons. When the birds were moulting, the people of Altamira went out to collect the plumes and to gather fifty pounds of the valuable feathers, which were sent with two of the cowboys to market. Santos intended to use the money from the sale to fence his boundaries. On their way to market, the cowboys were murdered and the feathers stolen. Their loss and the failure of the authorities to track down the culprit caused a great change in Santos. He determined to take the law into his own hands and to match violence with violence when he found it necessary.

His first act was to have three of Doña Bárbara's henchmen captured and sent to prison, for they had long been wanted for a number of crimes. A short time later, he received word from Doña Bárbara, who was pulled in two ways by her love for him and by her wish for power, that he would find in a certain canyon the thief who had taken the feathers. Santos went in the night and killed the Wizard, Doña Bárbara's most trusted and bloodthirsty henchman. Meanwhile, Don Balbino, the treacherous overseer who had been in charge of Altamira and who had been Doña Bárbara's lover, became distasteful to her. She had him killed after discovering that it was he who had stolen the feathers. To aid Santos, she threw the blame on Don Balbino for killing the Wizard.

Recovering the feathers, Doña Bárbara went to town to sell them for Santos. At the same time, she had documents made out to transfer the disputed lands to their rightful owner. When she returned to her ranch, she found that her people had deserted her; they could not understand why she had turned on her trusted killers. Doña Bárbara rode immediately to Altamira, where she found Santos talking to Marisela, whose father had recently died. Because the girl's love for Santos showed plainly on her face, Doña Bárbara, unseen, drew her revolver to kill her daughter. Her own love for Santos prevented the deed, however, and she rode away without revealing her presence.

Doña Bárbara was not heard from again. The next day, a large envelope was delivered to Santos. In it, he found a sheaf of documents giving back the property that had been stolen from him, and others transferring the Barquero ranch to Doña Bárbara's daughter Marisela. Shortly afterward, Santos and Marisela were married, and thus the two ranches that had been separated for many years were once again joined under one owner.

Critical Evaluation:

Doña Bárbara is *the* novel of the *llanos*. In it is painted the llanos, or tropical grassland bordering the Orinoco River, in the center of Venezuela, a republic almost as large as America's Southwest. Next to the llanos itself, the ranchwoman Doña Bárbara is the most clearly etched character, symbolizing barbarism, for she is a wild, dreadful, beautiful half-breed from beyond the remotest tributaries of the Orinoco. Her very name reeks of barbarism. Opposed to her is Santos Luzardo, who symbolizes the civilizing energy that is trying to penetrate the llanos' savagery and tame it.

Rómulo Gallegos uses symbols for barbarism, such as the great *tolvaneras*, or whirlwinds, which periodically flay the llanos. There are also rampaging herds of horses and steers; a midnight-black stallion as savage as Satan but tamed by Santos Luzardo; the power of flowing rivers and currents; a fire that scorches the plains, leaving blackened embers in its hellish path; and, evoking the violent spirit of the llanos, the llanero horsemen who almost destroy the tendrils of civilization that come within reach. Gallegos does bring in beauty such as flowers, sunset tints, breezes, white clouds, rains, the pink herons, and other delicacies, but, ever lurking wraithlike in the background is the malaria that had earlier nearly depopulated the llanos, causing its historical decline (the llanos had once supplied the cavalry that had filled General Simón Bolívar's revolutionary army's ranks, giving it victory over Spain's Royalist armies during Venezuela's War of Independence from Spain).

Gallegos also uses some standard characterizations, however, that are not overdone: the llanero, or cowboy; the boatmen of the Arauca River; a stock military official; ranch owners; and the itinerant Syrian peddlers, both rascally and otherwise. Some of Gallegos' sociological types are presented as clearly as if they inhabited an animated museum. Possibly his only near-caricature is Mister Danger, a one-dimensional villain who overrepresents the alleged Yankee rascality that is the compulsive whipping boy of so many Spanish-American novelists.

Gallegos' plot is logically developed. Coupled with worthy subject matter and knowledge of his fellow Venezuelans, it produces a near-masterpiece. Human cruelty is not overdrawn, realism is almost never lacking, and there are few distortions, but—as a city dweller and intellectual, belonging to a professional class not noted for dirtying its hands with physical toil—Gallegos did not give an in-depth study of the llanos' lowest social types. The novel is thus limited at times by an unconscious social prejudice, and the author's perception of the llaneros' religious views, psychology, or superstitions is superficial. Human suffering is not presented feelingly, and introspection is generally lacking. Yet, most of the characters do live and are not likely to be forgotten by the reader, for they develop and change subtly but gradually. The reader thus lives with them through the pages of *Doña Bárbara* and with their llanos grasslands.

The basic themes of *Doña Bárbara* are universal ones. Civilization against barbarism is about as dominant a theme as in Domingo Sarmiento's *Facundo* (the noted masterpiece of Argentine literature). Also present are such themes as man against nature, female against male, cruelty against kindness, justice against oppression, and freedom against bureaucratic government. Nowhere in *Doña Bárbara*, however, is it suggested that hard work and thrift, such as practiced not only by Horatio Alger but also by, say, Japanese, Germans, Jews, Mormons, or even Venezuela's Syrian peddlers, could alleviate the llanos' poverty.

Doña Bárbara is rich in Venezuelan expressions, idioms, and flavor of speech, but its vocabulary is not difficult. Gallegos' style moves effortlessly along and reader interest is not sacrificed by excess words or structural disorganization. The plot also moves briskly and is never clouded by deviant subplots or excessive complexity, yet even discerning readers cannot anticipate events, including the climax with its curiously passive finale for Doña Bárbara, the violent woman of the barbaric Venezuelan plains. From the first page, violence hangs over the story like a Sword of Damocles or a nightmare. It either lurks in the background, like a boa constrictor coiled in the llanos grass, or it erupts like a llanos fire.

Doña Bárbara, like various other Venezuelan novels, exposed and spotlighted national ills. Realistic reform could have come earlier to Venezuela, aided by such revelatory writings, but it was slow even when Gallegos himself became president. Gallegos was apparently not strong enough or perhaps lacked enough political horse sense to accomplish what was accomplished in the nineteenth century by Argentina's two literary presidents, Bartolomé Mitre and Domingo Sarmiento, who were men of action as well as of the pen. As a genre, the novel remains, nevertheless, the most important literary tool not only in Venezuela but also in all Latin America. Being the broadest and least restricted literary form, and mirroring social ills, it is a supple tool in the hands of would-be reformers, such as Rómulo Gallegos, who are brave enough to risk political persecution for their writings.

DRAGON SEED

Type of work: Novel
Author: Pearl S. Buck (1892–1973)
Type of plot: Social chronicle
Time of plot: World War II
Locale: China
First published: 1942

Principal characters:
> LING TAN, a Chinese farmer
> LING SAO, his wife
> LAO TA,
> LAO ER,
> LAO SAN and
> PANSIAO, their children
> ORCHID, Lao Ta's wife
> JADE, Lao Er's wife
> WU LIEN, Ling Tan's son-in-law
> MAYLI, a mission teacher

The Story:

Ling Tan's family all lived together in his ancestral home. Besides Ling Tan and his wife, Ling Sao, there were three sons, Lao Ta, Lao Er, and Lao San, and a daughter, Pansiao. Lao Ta and his wife Orchid had two children. Lao Er and his wife Jade as yet had none.

Jade was a strange woman who cared little for the old rules and customs governing Chinese wives. Her free manners and frank tongue were an embarrassment to Lao Er, for the men chided him about it. Then, too, he felt as if he did not really understand his wife. One evening, after they had both heard how the Japanese had begun war in the north, they unburdened their hearts to each other, and Lao Er accepted the fact that he was married to a woman who was not like the others. He promised to go to the city and buy her a book so that she could learn what was happening in the world.

While Lao Er was in the city, he visited Wu Lien, a merchant who had married his older sister. Some Chinese students destroyed the Japanese merchandise that Wu Lien had for sale and branded him as a traitor. When Ling Sao heard this bad news, she, too, went to the city. Wu Lien was sick with worry over what had happened to him; he had also heard that the Japanese had landed on the coast nearby and were pushing inland. Ling Sao comforted him as well as she could and returned home.

The next morning, Ling Tan was working in his fields when he saw Japanese aircraft approaching to bomb the city. He and the other farmers watched the planes, curious and unafraid. That night Wu Lien came to his father-in-law's house seeking refuge, for his shop had been hit by a bomb. Only then did Ling Tan's family learn the meaning of what had happened that day.

The next day, Ling Tan and Lao San went to the city, where they were caught in the second air raid. Gravely, Ling Tan asked his family how they were going to resist this enemy. Lao Er and Jade said that they must go westward into the hills, for Jade was now expecting a child. The rest of the family decided to stay and hold the ancestral land at all costs.

Streams of refugees passed along the road toward the west, and Lao Er and Jade joined a group of students who were moving their school inland. Lao Er promised to send word when the baby was born. Other students passed through the village and stopped to tell of the atrocities of the Japanese, but the simple farmers could not believe the stories they heard. After a month or so, Ling Tan and his family could hear the roar of the Japanese guns as they approached the city. Chinese soldiers deserted to the hills, leaving the inhabitants at the mercy of the enemy. For a few days after the city was taken, all was peaceful. Then some Japanese marched to the village and demanded wine and women. Ling Tan hid his family in the fields. The soldiers discovered Wu Lien's mother, who was too old and fat to flee. When they found no other women, they attacked her and killed her. Then they wrecked the house and left.

Since he knew now that no woman was safe from the Japanese, Ling Tan put all of the women of his family with the white missionary lady in the city. The men remained at the farm, except for Wu Lien. He returned to his shop in the city and advertised for Japanese business.

Meanwhile, the soldiers came again to Ling Tan's house in search of women. When they found none, they attacked Lao San, the youngest son. Humiliated and filled with hatred, the boy left to join the hill people who were fighting the Japanese.

Wu Lien ingratiated himself with the conquerors and was appointed to a job in the new city government. He took his family from the mission and moved into spacious quarters provided by the Japanese.

Orchid grew bored in the mission. She thought that the city was quiet now and nothing could happen to her. One day she went for a walk. Five soldiers captured her and killed her while they satisfied their lust. When her body was returned to the mission, Ling Sao sent for Ling Tan and Lao Ta. She could no longer stay in the city. She returned to the farm with Ling Tan, Lao Ta, and the two children of Orchid and Lao Ta. Pansiao was sent westward to a mission school in the hills, where she would be safe.

A message from Lao Er announced that Jade had a son. Ling Tan sent for Lao Er and his family to come and help with the farm. Lao Er obeyed the summons, for he could be useful as a messenger between the village and the guerrilla warriors in the hills. He and Jade made a secret cavern under the house where they could store arms for the villagers. Meanwhile, the children of Lao Ta died of flux and fever. Despondent, he left for the hills to join Lao San. Ling Tan worked his farm as best he could and held back as much grain from the enemy as he dared.

Lao San and Lao Ta returned from the hills with rifles to hide in the secret cavern. Whenever there were no witnesses, the farmers killed Japanese soldiers and secretly buried them. Jade succeeded in poisoning many Japanese leaders at a great feast in the city. A cousin of Ling Tan went to the city and stole a radio from Wu Lien. Afterward, he was able to report to the people the progress of the war. The people took heart from the knowledge that there were others fighting the Japanese.

Lao San had become a ruthless killer and Ling Tan thought that he needed a spirited wife to tame him. Jade wrote to Pansiao, asking her to find a wife for Lao San among the girls at the mission. Pansiao told one of her teachers, the daughter of a Chinese ambassador, about her brother. This girl, Mayli, traveled to see Lao San for herself. The young people fell in love at first sight, but Mayli returned to the hills to wait for Lao San to come after her. Lao Ta also returned home with a new wife. Ling Tan's house was full again, for Jade gave birth to twin boys.

The hardships continued. Losing all hope of conquering the Japanese, Ling Tan began to brood. Then one day, Lao Er took the old man to the city to hear the news from the hidden radio. They heard that England and the United States were now fighting on their side. Ling Tan wept for joy. Perhaps some day there would be an end to the war. Once again there was hope.

Critical Evaluation:

Pearl S. Buck's novel *Dragon Seed* was written during the early part of World War II, which partially accounts for its views on the Sino-Japanese conflict of the late 1930's. Buck, the daughter of American missionaries, was reared in China, although she was born in the United States. Many of her works are about China, and she came to have a great affinity for these people. *The Good Earth*, her greatest novel, was written in 1936 about China, and became the major factor in leading her to the Nobel Prize for Literature in 1938. *Dragon Seed*, though similar in scope, never demonstrates the power of that great first work. It provides a colorful background to the Chinese people during the Japanese occupation of China prior to World War II, but the story is not a profound one.

The basic plot involves the common people's struggle against the oppression of a tyrannical regime. This is a typical war-oriented story line and one that can only rise above the commonplace if it has good characterization and excellent writing. Buck's characters are real, which is the saving grace of the book, and her writing style is lucid; thus, readers accepted *Dragon Seed* with fervor, and it was a nationwide best-seller. However, the book is seriously limited by its polemical topicality, which borders on the propagandistic. It has not survived the test of time as has her earlier work *The Good Earth*.

Much of *Dragon Seed*, particularly near the end when great hopes are raised after the announcement that the United States has entered the war on the side of China, is an expression of wartime patriotism and, as such, limits the lasting value of the book. One excellent aspect of the book, however, is the characterization of Ling Sao, the female protagonist. Her strong will was atypical for a woman from China, at least in popular fiction. Traditionally, Chinese women have been portrayed as silent, subservient creatures. This is not the case in the books of Pearl Buck, however, where females are usually the stronger and therefore deeper characters.

DRUMS

Type of work: Novel
Author: James Boyd (1888–1944)
Type of plot: Historical romance
Time of plot: American Revolution
Locale: North Carolina and London
First published: 1925

Principal characters:

SQUIRE FRASER, a North Carolina planter
MRS. FRASER, his wife
JOHN FRASER, their son
SIR NAT DUKINFIELD, a sportsman
CAPTAIN TENNANT, Collector of the Port at Edenton
EVE TENNANT, his daughter
WYLIE JONES, a plantation owner
PAUL JONES, a sailor
SALLY MERRILLEE, a neighbor of the Frasers

The Story:

John Fraser lived with his mother and father in the backwoods of North Carolina. Squire Fraser, a strict but kind Scotsman, was determined that his son should have a gentleman's education, and so he sent John to the coastal town of Edenton to be tutored by Dr. Clapton, an English clergyman.

While there, John made many friends. Sir Nat Dukinfield, a young rake, asked John to go riding with him one afternoon. They parted close friends. Through Dr. Clapton, John met Captain Tennant, the Collector of the Port at Edenton. Captain Tennant took John home with him and introduced him to Eve, his daughter, who overwhelmed John and embarrassed him with her coquettish manners. Captain Flood, a riverboat skipper, was another of his friends. The old man taught him some sea lore and, on his trips up and down the river, acted as a messenger between John and his parents.

John went often to visit Captain Tennant and Eve. One evening, two other gentlemen arrived at their house, Mr. Hewes, a shipbuilder, and Mr. Battle, a young lawyer. A bitter argument began among the gentlemen over the new tax on tea. Autumn came, and Squire Fraser sent for John to come home for a short vacation. Captain Flood took John up the river to Halifax. There he stayed overnight at the plantation of Wylie Jones, a rich young landowner.

After three years of schooling from Dr. Clapton, John became a young provincial gentleman. The only cloud on his horizon was the report of troubles

---

with the British in Boston. Many people were angry; some predicted violence. John thrust dark thoughts aside, however, for tomorrow was the day of the races. Sir Nat was to match his horse against a thoroughbred from Virginia. Everyone seemed to be excited over the holiday except Mr. Hewes, Mr. Battle, and Wylie Jones. The three sat apart at a table in the tavern and talked seriously among themselves while the rest of the company sang songs. At last, Wylie Jones rose and announced that the ministers in Parliament had requested the king to declare the American Colonies in a state of rebellion.

The next day, John rode to the races with Sir Nat; Eve was going with fat Master Hal Cherry, a repulsive but rich boy. Sir Nat's horse was in perfect condition; his jockey, who had been drunk the night before, was not. He lost the first heat to the horse from Virginia. Then Sir Nat turned to John and asked him to ride. John rode the next two heats and won both of them. His friends celebrated the victory he had won for North Carolina.

Spring came. Sir Nat, putting no stock in rumors of war with the Colonies, volunteered for the English cavalry; he wanted to fight the French. The day after Sir Nat left for England, John learned of the battle fought at Lexington.

Squire Fraser sent a letter to his son with instructions to come home at once if British authority were overthrown at Edenton. John went to say good-bye to Captain Tennant and Eve, and then, following his father's instructions, he took leave of Dr. Clapton and went up the river with Wylie Jones. At Wylie's plantation, he met Paul Jones, an adventurous seaman who had taken Wylie's last name. Mr. Battle, Paul Jones, and Wylie discussed a naval war against the British. They urged John to decide soon which side he would take. He rode sadly home from Wylie's, but he brightened when he met Sally Merrillee, an old playmate. He suddenly decided that he liked her backwoods manners, so different from those of Eve Tennant. Later, a company of militia camped on the Merrillee property, and the officers were billeted in Sally's house. John became angry at Sally's attentions to the militia officers and ceased courting her. Finally, Squire Fraser sent John to England to put the family money in a safe bank. John was happy at a chance for an honorable escape from his problem. When he went to say good-bye to Sally, however, she had only contempt for him. Her brother had gone with the militia.

In London, John became the clerk of an importing firm and again met Eve and Captain Tennant. He received a letter from Wylie Jones, who asked him to deliver some money to Paul Jones's mother in Scotland. John was staying at an inn on the Scottish coast the night American sailors made a shore raid. Suddenly homesick for America, he went back with them to their ship. The captain was Paul Jones. Grateful for the favor that John had done for him in Scotland, he signed John on as a crew member.

After a naval engagement, the ship anchored in the French harbor of Brest. Then came long months of waiting while Paul Jones tried to get a larger ship from the French. Sir Nat arrived from England to visit John. One evening, the two became involved in a tavern brawl, and Sir Nat was killed. At last, Paul Jones obtained another ship, the *Bonhomme Richard*.

The ship put to sea with a motley crew and captured several British merchant vessels. Then, in a running fight with the Baltic Fleet, John was wounded in the left elbow. No longer fit for active duty and still feverish from his wound, he sailed home to North Carolina on a Dutch ship. As soon as his arm had healed, he volunteered in the militia, but they wanted no stiff-armed men. He helped Sally's mother on her farm. Sally had gone north to nurse her brother, who had smallpox. Mr. Merrillee had been killed in the war.

When Sally returned, John went to call on her. Yet, when he tried to tell her that he loved her, she wept. Thinking she was rejecting his love, he left disconsolately. He volunteered again for the militia and was accepted. In a skirmish with British troops, he was wounded a second time.

His arm now useless, John spent his days sitting on the front porch. One day, Sally's mother came to call on him and scolded him for neglecting her daughter. Sally was in love with him; he had mistaken her reason for crying. John suddenly felt much better. He felt better still when his father heard that the British were retreating. As he sat on the porch, General Greene's victorious army passed along the road. John stumbled down to the fence and raised his stiff arm in an Indian salute as the last man of the rear guard came to the crest of a hill. The distant soldier, silhouetted against the sunset, raised his rifle over his head in answer. The war was over. In a few days, he would be strong enough to visit Sally.

Critical Evaluation:

At a time when major American novelists like Hemingway and Fitzgerald were involved in expatriate experience for its test of character and enlargement of their social and artistic consciousness, James Boyd sought similar enrichment closer to home. Upon publication in 1925, *Drums* was hailed as one of the finest novels written about the American Revolution; it launched Boyd, who had been a moderately successful short-story writer, on a major career as a historical novelist. *Marching On* (1927), another war novel (this time about the Civil War in the South), was followed by *The Long Hunt* (1930), *Roll River* (1935), and *Bitter Creek* (1939). The later novels continued to explore the evolving American character.

In many ways, *Drums* is a conventional historical romance: a morally sound young hero weathers the temptation of superficial but charming aristocrats, lovers, and friends and discovers his democratic soul in the heat of battle. His bravery in the battle between the *Bonhomme Richard* and the *Serapis* recalls the fictional treatment of the same fight in Melville's *Israel Potter* and is the kind of ordeal by fire that American youths have endured from Crane to Hemingway.

Boyd was trying to do more than simply write a traditional historical novel with the usual trappings of adventure and romance. He wanted to suggest some of the things that went into the making of the American Revolution itself. John Fraser's assuming of the American cause is the psychological and moral equivalent of the emergence of what Boyd felt was the American identity. The indifference of the English aristocrats to the dying vagabond, and Sir Nat's coming to the defense of American honor despite his basic social detachment, are the kind of examples that gradually educate John Fraser to the strong emotional response to the democratic army that marches across the horizon at the end of the novel.

DRUMS ALONG THE MOHAWK

Type of work: Novel
Author: Walter D. Edmonds (1903–   )
Type of plot: Historical chronicle
Time of plot: 1775–1783
Locale: The Mohawk Valley
First published: 1936

Principal characters:

GILBERT MARTIN, a young pioneer
MAGDELANA BORST MARTIN (LANA), his wife
MARK DEMOOTH, a captain of the militia
JOHN WOLFF, a Tory
BLUE BACK, a friendly Oneida Indian
MRS. MCKLENNAR, Captain Barnabas McKlennar's widow
JOSEPH BRANT, an Indian chief
GENERAL BENEDICT ARNOLD
NANCY SCHUYLER, Mrs. Demooth's maid
JURRY MCLONIS, a Tory
HON YOST, Nancy's brother

The Story:

Magdelana Borst, the oldest of five daughters, married Gilbert Martin and together they started off from her home at Fox's Mill to settle farther west in their home at Deerfield. The time was July, 1776, and the spirit of the revolution had reached into the Mohawk Valley, where settlers who sided with the rebels had already formed a company of militia commanded by Mark Demooth. Soon after he came to his new home, Gil had to report for muster day. Some Indians had been seen in the vicinity. Also, the militia had decided to investigate the home of John Wolff, suspected of being a king's man. Finding evidence that a spy had been hidden on the Wolff farm, they arrested John Wolff, convicted him of aiding the British, and sent him to the Newgate Prison at Simsbury Mines.

A few months after their arrival at Deerfield, Gil decided to organize a logrolling to clear his land for farming. The Weavers, the Realls, and Clem Coppernol all came to help with the work. When they were about half finished, Blue Back, a friendly Oneida Indian, came to warn them that a raiding party of Seneca Indians and whites was in the valley. The settlers immediately scattered for home to collect the few movable belongings, which they might save, and then drove to Fort Schuyler. Lana, who was pregnant, lost her baby as a result of the wild ride to the fort. The enemy destroyed the Deerfield settlement. All the houses and fields were burned; Gil's cow was killed; and Mrs. Wolff, who had refused to take refuge with the people who had sent her husband to prison, was reported missing. Gil and Lana rented a one-room cabin in which to live through the winter. With spring coming and needing a job to support himself and Lana, Gil became the hired man of Mrs. McKlennar, a widow. The pay was forty-five dollars a year plus the use of a two-room house and their food.

General Herkimer tried to obtain a pledge of neutrality from the Indian chief, Joseph Brant, but was unsuccessful. At the end of the summer, word came that the combined forces of the British and Indians, commanded by General St. Leger, were moving down from Canada to attack the valley. The militia was called up, and they set out westward to encounter this army. The attack by the militia, however, was badly timed, and the party was ambushed. Of nearly six hundred and fifty men, only two hundred and fifty survived. The survivors returned in scattered groups. Gil received a bullet wound in the arm. General Herkimer, seriously injured in the leg, died from his wounds.

After the death of General Herkimer, General Benedict Arnold was sent out to reorganize the army and lead it in another attack—this time against General St. Leger's camp.

When Nancy Schuyler, Mrs. Demooth's maid, heard that her brother, Hon Yost, was in the neighborhood with a group of Tories, she decided to sneak out to see him. On the way, she met another Tory, Jurry McLonis, who seduced her. Before she was able to see Hon, the American militia broke up the band. Hon was arrested but was later released when he agreed to go back to the British camp and spread false reports of American strength. As a result of her meeting with Jurry McLonis, Nancy became pregnant. About the same time, John Wolff escaped from the prison at Simsbury Mines and made his way to Canada to join Butler and to look for his wife.

The following spring brought with it General Butler's destructives, raiding parties that would swoop down to burn and pillage small settlements or farms. Mrs. Demooth tormented Nancy constantly because of her condition and one night frightened the girl so completely that Nancy, in terror, packed a few of her belongings in a shawl and ran away. Her only idea was to try to get to Niagara and find her brother Hon, but she had not gone far before labor pains overtook her, and she bore her child beside a stream. An Indian found her there and took her with him as his wife. Lana had her child in May. The destruction by the raiding parties continued all through that summer, and the harvest was small. Mrs. McKlennar's stone house was not burned, but there was barely enough food for her household that winter. In the spring, Colonel Van Schaick came to the settlement with an army, and the militia headed west once again, this time to strike against the Onondaga towns.

Lana had her second child the following August. Because of the lack of food during the winter, she was still weak from nursing her first boy, Gilly, and after the birth of her second boy, it took her a long time to recover. The next winter they all had enough to eat, but the cold was severe. During that winter, Mrs. McKlennar aged greatly and kept mostly to her bed. The destructives continued their raids through the next spring and summer. The men never went out to their fields alone; they worked in groups with armed guards. One day, after all the men had gone to the fort, Lana took the two boys for a walk and then sat down at the edge of a clearing and fell asleep. When she awoke, Gilly was gone. Two Indians were near the house. She put the baby, Joey, into a hiding place and then searched for Gilly. She found him at last, and the two of them also crawled into the hiding place. Meanwhile, the two Indians had entered the house and set it on fire. Overwhelmed by Mrs. McKlennar's righteous indignation, they carried out her bed for her. They fled when men, seeing the smoke, came hurrying from the fort. Gil and the two scouts, Adam Helmer and Joe Boleo, built a cabin to house them all during the coming winter.

With the spring thaws, a flood inundated the valley. As the waters receded, Marinus Willett came into the Mohawk Valley with his army, with orders to track down and destroy the British forces under General Butler. Butler's army was already having a difficult time, for British food supplies were running out and tracking wolves killed all stragglers. The militia finally caught up with Butler, harassed his army for several miles, killed Butler, and scattered the routed army in the wilderness. The Mohawk Valley was saved.

Three years later, the war over, Gil and Lana went back to their farm at Deerfield. They now had a baby girl, and Lana and Gil felt content with their hard-won security, their home, their children, and each other.

Critical Evaluation:

During the 1930's, the historical novel became extremely popular. Most of them followed the same pattern: they were long, had many characters, were full of action and realistic detail, and usually ended happily. *Drums Along the Mohawk* has all of these qualities, but it is one of the best of the genre. In 1936, it was on the best-seller list. Walter D. Edmonds, in his author's note, defends the genre, noting that the life presented is not a bygone picture, for the parallel is too close to the reader's own. The valley people faced repercussions of poverty and starvation and were plagued by unfulfilled promises and the inevitable red tape of a central government that could not understand local problems. Thus, the valley farmers, in the typically American tradition, learned to fight for themselves and for the land they had worked so hard to wrench from the wilderness and could not abandon.

Contrary to the patriotic myth, the war was not a glorious fight for freedom for all American soldiers. Many fought only because it was necessary to protect their families. They never thought of the American troops in the

South and East; that was too remote, while the ever-present threat of instant disaster was too near. When Captain Demooth says to Gil, "Who gives a damn for the Stamp Tax?" Gil admits that it had not bothered him and asks the key question of most of the farmers: "Why do we have to go and fight the British at all?" The attitude of many of the men conscripted for the militia is "Damn the militia! I need to roof my barn." Yet, as the attacks upon the small settlements begin, they realize that they must band together and fight.

At times, the Western settlers wonder which side is the enemy. Denied food, munitions, and the protection of regular troops by the government at Albany, their seed grain commandeered and their fences burned for firewood, the settlers of German Flats become extremely bitter at the indifferent treatment they receive. When the widowed Mrs. Reall, with her many children, tries to collect her husband's back pay, she is denied because he is not marked dead on the paymaster's list. Even though Colonel Bellinger swears that he saw Reall killed and scalped, the money is withheld. The only alternative she is given is to file a claim before the auditor-general, which must then be passed by an act of Congress. In the meantime, the family must either starve or rely on the charity of others who cannot really afford to help. They find that the Continental currency is practically worthless, but the climax of the colonists' disillusionment with the Congress comes when the residents receive huge tax bills for land that has been abandoned, buildings that have burned, and stock that has been killed. The incredulous settlers realize that the tax list is the one formerly used by the king.

The bestiality of what war does to men dominates the book. As the Indian raids become more ghastly, the Continentals grow more brutal. Scalps are taken by both Indian and white, and the atrocities and mutilations committed by both sides become increasingly barbarous.

Yet, in spite of the ever-present atmosphere of horror, fear, and death, Edmonds also presents the forces of life. There is fierce energy in the characters in spite of their hardships. This is seen most clearly in the character of Lana, who, though weakened by starvation, work, and fear, manages to bear and care for her two boys. There is a mystery about her as she nurses and cares for her babies. Although she deeply loves Gil, with the birth of the first child, she becomes mother first. Even the rough scout Joe Boleo senses the maternal mystery she exudes. There is also beauty in life itself as seen in the human body and in reproduction. The pregnant Nancy becomes more beautiful as she carries her illegitimate child, and the marriage of young John Weaver to Mary Reall begins another generation when Mary becomes pregnant.

Edmonds' style is free flowing, and he has an excellent ear for natural folk speech. As omniscient narrator, he goes deeply into the minds of the main characters and captures their reactions to the many events going on about them. All of the main characters have individuality and the gift of life.

The praise that is often given the novel is for the realism that Edmonds achieves by minute detail; however, this is also a weakness. His accounts of the many battles and raids become repetitious, for in the interest of historical truth, he does not want to eliminate anything. Thus, the action becomes blurred because there are so many similar accounts.

Structurally, the book is well handled with the exception of the last chapter, "Lana," which occurs three years after the preceding one. It appears to have been tacked on simply to tie up a few loose ends and to give the story a happy ending. In a book that has proceeded slowly season by season for five years, the three-year interval startles the reader.

The theme of the novel is the strength of the men who will endure anything to achieve the American Dream. Through their own efforts, they hope to earn their land, houses, animals, and the material things necessary to make life easier and more beautiful for themselves and particularly for their children. Lana and Gil begin their marriage with a cow, a few pieces of furniture, and Lana's most valued possession—a peacock feather that, with its mysterious beauty, symbolizes the beauty of the dream. All of this is lost in the war; but in the last chapter, Gil realizes his ambitions. He is farming his own land, he has built a new house, and he owns a yoke of oxen. Lana has her two boys, a baby daughter, security, and even the now battered but still gorgeous peacock feather which the Indian Blue Back returns to her. She is supremely content and secure as she tells herself, "We've got this place. . . . We've got the children. We've got each other. Nobody can take those things away. Not any more."

THE EAGLE AND THE SERPENT

Type of work: Novel
Author: Martín Luis Guzmán (1887–   )
Type of plot: Autobiographical chronicle
Time of plot: 1913–1915
Locale: Mexico and the United States
First published: 1928

> *Principal characters:*
> THE NARRATOR
> FRANCISCO VILLA, a revolutionist and commander of the
> "Division of the North"
> VENUSTIANO CARRANZA, the supreme chief of the
> Constitutionalist Army

The Mexican Revolution, perhaps the only military movement that radically changed the position of a Latin American country after achieving its independence from Spain, affected the Mexican writers of those days in different ways. Some remained indifferent; others defended its motives and facts; a few engaged themselves actively in its vicissitudes. To no one can be attributed greater and more direct participation than that of Martín Luis Guzmán. Executor, witness, chronicler, interpreter, critic, novelist, he embraced all the possible angles of relationship with the Mexican Revolution. For this reason, his work about the movement is the closest, most objective, and penetrating of all the literary productions written upon the subject.

Guzmán authored three books—at the same time biography, history, and novel—about the Revolution: *El aguila y la serpiente* (*The Eagle and the Serpent*, 1930), *La sombra del caudillo*, and *Memorias de Pancho Villa* (*Memoirs of Pancho Villa*). Of these, the nearest to a work of the creative imagination is the first, published in fascicles in 1926 and as a book in 1928.

The reasons why Guzmán titled his book in such a way may be found in the origins of Mexican nationality. The Aztecs, the main indigenous ancestors of Mexico, had as a legendary core of their nomadic period the belief that they should found their capital city in a spot where they would find an eagle, devouring a serpent, perched upon a nopal. Guzmán took these images and turned them into symbols for his book, to show the bipolarity of Mexican history, in constant conflict between repentant passions and an ascension of the spirit.

There is no better source to know the genesis and spirit of this book than the speech pronounced by the author at the time of his reception as a member of the Mexican Academy of the Language. Son of his time and his country, Guzmán declared that from his earliest childhood, he was accustomed to beauty from having lived in Tacubaya, one of the most charming suburbs of

Mexico City, near the Chapultepec Castle, scene of many decisive moments in Mexican history, and that this same environment imposed on him a feeling for history in all its grandeur. Some years later, when he embraced the cause of the Revolution, he had at his disposal raw historical material of the first quality, out of which he took the subject for his most representative books.

For a long time, Guzmán hesitated to write about the Revolution. On one side, he had been the witness of ruthless crimes, usurpations, disloyalties; on another, he had seen in many participants of that movement a great spirit of service, purity of intention, and patriotic goals. This knowledge finally moved him to write about the Revolution, to transform into literary values those violent deeds against the dictatorship of Porfirio Díaz. He finally decided to embody what he had seen or done. He thought that if the chief leaders of the Revolution had not been as faulty as they were, the Revolution would not have been what it became.

To understand some pages of this book, the reader must take into account the fact that the revolutionary movement was not born from a set of ideas but erupted from instinctive forces, submitted to oppression for many centuries.

El aguila y la serpiente, a work that brings together literature and history, truth and fiction, is divided into two parts: "Esperanzas Revolucionarias" ("Revolutionary Hopes") and "En la Hora del Triunfo" ("At the Hour of the Triumph"). In the first part, consisting of seven books, Guzmán tells of his revolutionary adventures during the period preceding the peak of the fighting. In the second section, also of seven books, he tells of deeds that occurred during the most turbulent years of the conflict.

The book opens when Guzmán, apparently the narrator of most of the work because of its strong autobiographical structure, escapes from Victoriano Huerta's usurping government and sets sail, incognito, in flight from Veracruz to the United States, with the intention of reaching the northern Mexican states of Sonora or Coahuila and helping Venustiano Carranza in his fight against Huerta. Aboard ship, he meets four Mexicans, one of them a physician who shares his political views. They establish relations with a beautiful American woman who turns out to be a spy of the Huerta government. When this fact becomes known to Guzmán and his associates, the physician, in order to get rid of her, pretends ardent love for the lady and proposes that they marry in Havana, the next stop on the voyage. The trick fails because the ship delays its departure in that port, after landing the Mexicans and the beautiful secret agent. Again aboard ship, the revolutionaries are afraid of being imprisoned upon their arrival in New York. Then the physician feigns intent to kill the spy, but the woman does not appear at any place when they go ashore. The reader grows perplexed over the fate of the woman, but the author does not add to what has already been told.

Guzmán, unable to carry out his plan to contact Carranza, returns to Mexico City. Yet his enthusiasm for the Revolution causes him to embark again for Havana and later for New Orleans. After traveling to San Antonio, Texas, he meets there José Vasconcelos, a writer and the only great minister produced by the Revolution, according to Guzmán. Finally, in Ciudad Juárez, the author meets Pancho Villa, who is for him the chief hero of the Revolution. The encounter is not as dramatic as could be expected, but an intimate, deep impression about Villa will remain with the writer. Later, he is introduced to Venustiano Carranza, first chief of the Constitutionalist Army; the first ideological collision with him ensues because Carranza had the viewpoint that good will is the primary virtue in leading men; Guzmán believed in technique. The author met another revolutionary leader, Alvaro Obregón, whom he considers an impostor. Gradually, Guzmán realizes that sooner or later deep disagreement will arise among the fighters. He thinks that at the very bottom everything could be reduced to the eternal dispute of the Mexicans who are always looking for power and the accomplishment of personal ambitions instead of great, disinterested aspirations.

A good number of episodes are intermingled in this part of the work. Perhaps they are the most interesting and representative material in the novel. Among them, "A Night in Culiacán," "The Murdering Spider," "A Race in the Darkness," and "The Feast of the Bullets" emerge as masterpieces of suspense and narrative vigor. This part of the work ends when the author is again in Ciudad Juárez, under the influence of Villa, after a journey to New York.

The second part of the novel deals with the triumph of the Revolution as a group, but the schism between the leaders of the movement is inevitable, chiefly between Villa and Carranza. Guzmán joins Villa because he thinks that, in spite of the revolutionist's instinctiveness and moral blindness, he is the only possible leader who can give a democratic and impersonal character to the Revolution, in contrast to Carranza, who is too prone to oligarchy. The author arrives again at Veracruz, taken by American soldiers, and finally makes his way to Mexico City. Guzmán exultantly writes now the most lyric pages he has ever composed. The sight of the city and the volcanoes, the inhalation of the thin air of the plateau, the bath of clarity, the perfect adequation of person and environment were some of the unforgettable impressions of the "rebel who returned," as Guzmán calls himself. He goes again to Chihuahua, meets Villa anew, and gets the impression that the legendary warrior could never exist if there were not a gun in the world. Villa and his pistol were a single thing; from his gun, all of his friendships and enmities were born. To combat now against Carranza, the writer goes to Mexico City again. For him, Carranzaism is synonymous with ambition, lack of ideals, systematic corruption, and theft. Imprisoned by Carranza's orders, he is sent to Matamoros, but the Convention of Aguascalientes, a meeting of revolutionists in which was decided the way to future action of the movement, sets him free. Having been appointed Minister of War by President Roque González Garza, Guzmán rejects the post and is threatened with the penitentiary; but he escapes and goes to see Villa, who has been estranged by the Convention of Aguascalientes. The writer, caught between loyalty to the Convention and friendship toward Villa, expatriates himself to the United States.

EAST OF EDEN

Type of work: Novel
Author: John Steinbeck (1902–1968)
Type of plot: Regional chronicle
Time of plot: 1865–1918
Locale: California
First published: 1952

> *Principal characters:*
> ADAM TRASK, a settler in the Salinas Valley
> CATHY AMES, later Adam's wife
> CALEB and
> ARON TRASK, their twin sons
> CHARLES TRASK, Adam's half brother
> SAMUEL HAMILTON, a neighbor of the Trasks
> LEE, Adam's Chinese servant
> ABRA BACON, Aron's fiancée

The Story:

The soil of the Salinas Valley in California is rich, although the foothills around it are poor, and its life shrivels during the long dry spells. The Irish-born Hamiltons, arriving after American settlers had displaced the Mexicans, settled on the barren hillside. There Sam Hamilton, full of talk, glory, and improvident inventions, and Liza, his dourly religious wife, brought up their nine children.

In Connecticut, Adam Trask and his half brother Charles grew up, mutually affectionate in spite of the differences in their natures. Adam was gentle and good; Charles, roughly handsome with a streak of wild violence. After Adam's mother had committed suicide, his father had married a docile woman who gave birth to Charles. Adam loved his stepmother but hated his father, a rigid disciplinarian whose fanatic militarism had begun with a fictitious account of his own war career and whose dream was to have a son in the army. To fulfill his dream, he chose Adam, who could gain the greater strength that comes from the conquest of weakness as Charles could not. Charles, however, whose passionate love for his father went continually unnoticed, could not understand this final rejection of himself. In violent despair, he beat Adam almost to death.

Adam served in the cavalry for five years. Then, although he hated regimentation and violence, he reenlisted, for he could neither accept help from his father, who had become an important figure in Washington, nor return to the farm Charles now ran alone. Afterward, he wandered through the West and the South, served time for vagrancy, and finally came home to find his father dead and himself and Charles rich. In the years that followed, he and Charles lived together, although their bickering and inbred solitude drove Adam to periodic wanderings. Feeling that their life was one of pointless industry, he talked of moving west but did not.

Meanwhile, Cathy Ames was growing up in Massachusetts. She was a monster, born unable to comprehend goodness but with a sublimely innocent face and a consummate knowledge of how to manipulate or deceive people to serve her own ends. After a thwarted attempt to leave home, she burned her house, killing her parents and leaving evidence to indicate that she had been murdered. She then became the mistress of a man who ran a string of brothels and used his insatiable love for her to torment him. When he realized her true nature, he took her to a deserted spot and beat her savagely. Near death, she crawled to the nearest house—the Trasks'—where Adam and Charles cared for her. Adam found her innocent and beautiful; Charles, who had a knowledge of evil through himself, recognized the evil in her and wanted her to leave. Cathy, needing temporary protection, enticed Adam into marrying her, but on their wedding night, she gave him a sleeping draught and went to Charles.

Feeling that Charles disapproved of Cathy, Adam decided to carry out his dream of going west. He was so transfigured by his happiness that he did not take Cathy's protests seriously; as his ideal of love and purity, she could not disagree. Adam bought a ranch in the richest part of the Salinas Valley and worked hard to ready it for his wife and the child she expected. Cathy hated her pregnancy, but she knew that she had to wait calmly to get back to the life she wanted. After giving birth to twin boys, she waited a week; she then shot Adam, wounding him, and walked out.

Changing her name to Kate, Cathy went to work in a Salinas brothel. Her beauty and seeming goodness endeared her to the proprietress, Faye, and Kate gradually assumed control of the establishment. After Faye made a will leaving Kate her money and property, Kate slyly engineered Faye's death. Making her establishment one which aroused and purveyed to sadistic tastes, she became legendary and rich.

Adam was like a dead man for a year after his wife left him, unable to work his land or even to name his sons. Finally, Sam Hamilton woke him by deliberately angering him, and Sam, Adam, and Lee, the Chinese servant and a wise and good man, named the boys Caleb and Aron. As the men talked of the story of Cain and Abel, Lee concluded that rejection terrifies a child most and leads to guilt and revenge. Later, after much study, Lee discovered the true meaning of the Hebrew word *timshel* (thou mayest) and understood that the story meant in part that man can always choose to conquer evil.

Sam, grown old, knew that he would soon die. Before he left his ranch, he told Adam of Kate and her cruel, destructive business. Adam, disbelieving in her very existence, visited her and suddenly knew her as she really was. Though she tried to taunt him, telling him that Charles was the true father of his sons, and to seduce him, he left her a free and curiously exultant man. Yet he could not tell his sons that their mother was not dead.

Caleb and Aron were growing up very differently. Aron was golden haired and automatically inspired love, yet he remained single-minded and unyielding; Caleb was dark and clever, a feared and respected leader left much alone. When Adam moved to town, where the schools were better, Aron fell in love with Abra Bacon. Abra told Aron that his mother was still alive, but he could not believe her because to do so would have destroyed his faith in his father and thus in everything.

About this time, Adam had the idea of shipping lettuce packed in ice to New York, but the venture failed. Aron was ashamed of his father for failing publicly. Caleb vowed to return the lost money to his father.

As they faced the problems of growing into men, Aron became smugly religious, which was disturbing to Abra because she felt unable to live up to his idealistic image of her. Caleb alternated between wild impulses and guilt. Learning that Kate was his mother, he began following her until she, noticing him, invited him to her house. As he talked to her, he knew with relief that he was not like her; she felt his knowledge and hated him. Kate herself, obsessed by the fear that one of the old girls had discovered Faye's murder, plotted ways to destroy this menace. Although Caleb could accept Kate's existence, he knew that Aron could not. To get the boy away from Salinas, Caleb talked him into finishing high school in three years and beginning college. Adam, knowing nothing of Caleb's true feelings, was extravagantly proud of Aron.

World War I began. Caleb went into the bean business with Will Hamilton and made a fortune because of food shortages. With growing excitement, he planned an elaborate presentation to his father of the money once lost in the lettuce enterprise. First he tried to persuade Aron, who seemed indifferent to his father's love, not to leave college. Caleb presented his money to Adam, only to have it rejected in anger because Adam's idealistic nature could not accept money made as profit from the war. He wanted Caleb's achievements to be like his brother's. In a black mood of revenge, Caleb took Aron to meet his mother. After her sons' visit, Kate, who was not disturbed by those she could hurt as she was by someone like Caleb, made a will leaving everything to Aron. Then, overburdened by age, illness, and suspicion, she committed suicide.

Unable to face his new knowledge of his parents' past, Aron joined the army and went to France. Adam did not recover from the shock of his leaving. Abra turned to Caleb, admitting that she loved him rather than Aron, whose romantic stubbornness kept him from facing reality. When the news of Aron's death arrived, Adam had another stroke. As he lay dying, Caleb, unable to bear his guilt any longer, told his father of his responsibility for Aron's enlisting and thus his death. Lee begged Adam to forgive his son. Adam weakly raised his hand in benediction and, whispering the Hebrew word *timshel*, died.

Critical Evaluation:

The expressed concern of *East of Eden* is philosophical—the nature of the conflict between good and evil. In this conflict, love and the acceptance or rejection it brings to the individual play an important role, yet one has always the opportunity to choose the good. In this freedom lies man's glory. The book's defects stem from the author's somewhat foggy and sentimental presentation of its philosophy and his tendency to manipulate or oversimplify characters and events for symbolic purposes.

In most of his other works, John Steinbeck was concerned with social issues from a realistic or a naturalistic point of view, portraying human travail with relentless accuracy through an intensive examination of a short time span. In *East of Eden*, however, Steinbeck departs from his customary literary style to write an epic portrait which ranges less intensively over a much broader time span of about seventy years. Although depictions of characters and events are really no less vivid than in his other novels, Steinbeck's *East of Eden* is certainly less structured, a looser novel than his dedicated readers had come to expect. Thus, despite some quite explicit sex scenes, disappointed reader expectation accounts in large measure for the failure of *East of Eden* to win immediate popular or critical acclaim. It simply was not what people had come to expect of Steinbeck.

The novel is, however, respectable if not brilliant. In fact, it is, in many ways, a historical romance in its panoramic sweep of significant history overlaid with specific human problems. The story ranges from the Civil War to World War I, from the East Coast to the West Coast, over several generations of two families. It displays all of the conventional elements of historical romance. Genuinely historical events and people provide the backdrop, even the shaping forces that mold the fictional characters' lives and determine their destiny. These characters thus appear to have only partial control over their lives, at best; and external factors consequently determine, to a large extent, what they must cope with in order to survive. They appear to be buffeted mercilessly by fate.

However, Steinbeck's philosophical commitment to free will aborts the naturalistically logical conclusion. As a result, both Charles and Adam Trask appear to select freely their own paths in life, the former indulging fantasies of evil and the latter choosing to disregard everyone's evil inclinations, including his own. So, too, is Cathy made to seem capable of choice and responsible for it. Likewise, the other major characters are depicted as having the capacity for moral choice and for living with the consequences. Yet it is just this aspect of *East of Eden* that flies in the face of the reader's expectations of "typical" Steinbeck and flies in the face of both logic and reality. Finally, it is Steinbeck's own ambivalence about free will and determinism that constitutes the major weakness in *East of Eden*. For whatever readers or Steinbeck believe about a historical/biblical Garden of Eden, neither readers nor Steinbeck believe that a Garden of Eden exists now—east or west—even in the Salinas Valley.

THE EDGE OF THE STORM

Type of work: Novel
Author: Agustín Yáñez (1904–   )
Type of plot: Social criticism
Time of plot: Spring, 1909–spring, 1910
Locale: Near Guadalajara, Mexico
First published: 1947

> *Principal characters:*
> DON DIONISIO, the parish priest
> MARÍA and
> MARTA, his nieces
> PADRE ISLAS and
> PADRE REYES, assistant priests
> DAMIÁN LIMÓN, a young man who had been to the
>   United States
> MICAELA RODRÍGUEZ, a spoiled girl
> VICTORIA, a young widow, visiting from Guadalajara
> GABRIEL, a young man reared by Don Dionisio
> LUIS GONZAGA PÉREZ, a seminary student
> MERCEDES TOLEDO, another young girl
> LUCAS MACÍAS, a soothsayer

Al filo del agua (*The Edge of the Storm*, 1963) is a Spanish phrase with two meanings, one literal, the other figurative. Literally, it signifies the moment that the rain begins. However, it is in its figurative sense that it takes on meaning as the title of this book: the imminence of something that is about to happen. The event about to take place was brought on by a growing dissatisfaction with the political situation and the unnaturalness of the environment imposed by the Church as reflected by life in a small town in Mexico.

In 1910, Porfirio Díaz had been dictator of Mexico for more than thirty years. He had ruled with an iron hand and only recently had the dream of political freedom and social improvement begun to filter through to the many semi-isolated towns of Mexico. The same few families had always been the social leaders and political bosses in the communities and Díaz' thirty-odd years of rule had done nothing to lessen this stranglehold or to improve the lot of the common man. Education was nonexistent except for the privileged few, and superstition was rampant.

Another force that held the people in its grip was the Church, a circumstance especially true in rural areas where the long arm of Juarez' 1859 Reform Laws seldom reached. These laws had greatly reduced the political power of the Church, and such things as processions and public religious festivities were forbidden. In the small towns, however, with the ever-present threat of arrest hanging over their heads, the priests often continued their regular clerical activities in spite of the law.

Agustín Yáñez has painted against this background a series of character studies portraying the effects of a narrow and rigid, as well as dull and conventional, life on people of different ages, with varying degrees of education and exposure to outside influences. (These influences, being outside ones and therefore bad, make up a long and varied list and include such things as Free Masonry, bright clothing, strangers, uncensored writings, fun, spiritualists, people who had been to the United States; the list could go on and on.) Yáñez creates a sense of monotonous semigloom with the sure hand of an artist who has experienced this kind of life himself at one time or another. The fictitious, but very typical, town in which the action takes place is set in the state of Jalisco, of which the author is a native.

Each morning the church bells in this town call the people out of their beds as early as four o'clock to begin another dreary, quiet, prayerful day. Life is very serious. The women wear dark somber colors and do not leave the house except to go to church or to do necessary errands. There is no visiting except in the case of extreme illness or a death in the house of a neighbor. There is little laughter, dancing, or singing. Strangers and strangeness are not only suspect but already condemned. Nonconformity, even in small things, starts tongues wagging. At the end of each unvarying day, the church bells send the people to bed, an act that for many means the onset of sleepless hours or wrestling with guilty consciences and with wondering when and in what form God's wrath will be brought down upon their heads.

With this daily pattern providing the atmosphere, broken only by funerals, special fiesta days, and an occasional scandal, the action in the story begins as the people are preparing for their Lenten and Easter activities. The panorama of people and events proceeds on through the year, displaying the special religious days of June, the expected deaths, illnesses, and bad luck of August, the celebration of patriotic holidays in September, the scandalous prank of the students home for vacation in November, the Christmas season with its festivities, and continues on into the New Year, at which time the people are awaiting the appearance of Halley's Comet. This event is being anticipated so intently by Lucas Macías, the soothsayer, that the rest of the people do well to prepare for trouble, for Lucas has from the start associated the appearance of this comet with the stepping onto the scene of Francisco Madero, the man who is to lead the revolution against the tyranny of Díaz.

The person who can most nearly be described as the main character is Don Dionisio, the stern and upright but just and compassionate parish priest. He alone touches in some way upon the lives of all the other characters in the book. His main ecclesiastical help comes from two assistant priests who present a vivid contrast to each other, one, Padre Reyes, being liberal and forward-looking, the other, Padre Islas, narrow and conservative beyond belief. Although Padre Reyes is much more likable, it is Padre Islas, scurrying along the street from church to home so as to avoid meeting his parishioners on a personal basis, who wields more influence on the lives of the townspeople, for it is he who directs the organization to which all the unmarried girls belong. Into their minds he instills the urgent need to stay pure by remaining single, and he imbues them with a sense of guilt for even thinking wholesome thoughts connected with the opposite sex. This narrow man will never use the chapel of the Holy Family but always the chapel of the Virgin Mary, and Padre Reyes, the other assistant, is not above teasing him by asking if he thinks María and Juan will make a nice couple, or if he is aware that Mercedes is just about ready to make someone a good wife. These questions are calculated to enrage Padre Islas. Padre Reyes, with his modern ideas about such things as life insurance—too far removed from the imaginations of the people to be noticed—is largely ignored, while Padre Islas is revered as a saint beyond the temptations and afflictions of ordinary man. Great is the disillusionment when the good Father Islas is found collapsed on the floor of the church in a fit of epilepsy, which results in his having to be removed permanently from the priesthood. The archbishop had chosen wisely when Don Dionisio was made head priest, with the authority for making final decisions, for he approaches the problems of his parishioners with the best elements of the philosophies of his two assistants—an urgent sense of responsibility for their souls accompanied by a forgiving and understanding heart.

Two other personalities who present a study in contrasts are María and Marta, the orphaned nieces of Don Dionisio, who has reared them since they were very small. At the time the story begins, they are in their twenties, unmarried, and on the verge of taking opposite paths in life. Marta, the contented, with her love for children, her work in the hospital, and other gentle occupations, is the ideal end product of the social and religious forces at work in her environment. María, the rebellious, who has always read forbidden literature (*The Three Musketeers* and newspapers from the capital) behind her uncle's back, and who finally runs away with a woman of very questionable reputation to follow the revolutionary army, is a creature of reaction against this unnatural environment.

What happened to María happens, with variations, to nearly all the young people who have had contact in any way with the outside world. Luis Gonzaga Pérez, a young and talented seminary student, is unable to reconcile his inhibitions concerning the opposite sex with his natural desires, and at the end of the novel, he is drawing lewd pictures on the walls of his room in an insane asylum.

Damián Limón, the young son of a fairly prosperous landowner, leaves home, like the prodigal son, and goes to the United States to work. Upon his return home, when criticized for going to such a sinful place where Mexicans are treated like dogs, he counters by stating that at least they are paid in money instead of in promises as in Mexico. Damián becomes scandalously involved in a flagrant love affair and kills the girl, after having just caused his father to have a fatal heart attack over an argument about his father's will. A corrupt political boss has a disgracefully light sentence placed upon him, and at the end of the story, he rides away to join the ranks of the revolutionaries.

The parents of Micaela Rodríguez, a spoiled only child, make the mistake of taking her to Mexico City for a few months. There she sees the parties, pretty clothes, and merriment of the capital's young people. Never again is she satisfied to stay in her dreary hometown and, failing to force her parents to move away to a livelier place, she threatens vengeance on the environment that binds her and shocks the town to its roots with her shameless flirting and indecent dress. She ends up being stabbed by a jealous lover but dies forgiving him and putting the blame for her death on her own actions.

Doubt seems to be the villain that causes the downfall of these unfortunate young people. They have tasted of the world, compared it with their narrow surroundings, and found them wanting. Being few in number, these unlucky ones have fallen under the weight of a relentless social system that will tolerate no questioning.

The time is near at hand, however, when many doubters will join together with enough force to make a crack in this teetering wall of hypocrisy, a crack that will become ever wider as education and enlightenment seep through. It is in this thought that the essence of the title *The Edge of the Storm* is captured.

Agustín Yáñez has given the reader an unprejudiced and intricately detailed view of life in a Mexican town shortly after the turn of the century. The purpose of the book is not a call to arms to reform but to present an understanding, not necessarily sympathetic, and touching story.

ELMER GANTRY

Type of work: Novel
Author: Sinclair Lewis (1885–1951)
Type of plot: Social criticism
Time of plot: 1915–1925
Locale: Midwest America
First published: 1927

Principal characters:

ELMER GANTRY, a minister

JIM LEFFERTS, Elmer's companion in rowdiness during his days at Terwillinger College

JUDSON ROBERTS, a former football star and state secretary of the Y.M.C.A.

FRANK SHALLARD, a minister and Elmer's chief antagonist

EDDIE FISLINGER, a minister and distant admirer of Gantry, constantly hoping to convert him during college, theological school, and in life

MRS. GANTRY, Elmer's mother

WALLACE UMSTEAD, the Director of Physical Culture at Mizpah Theological Seminary

HORACE CARP, one of the High Churchmen in the seminary

HARRY ZENZ, the seminary iconoclast

JACOB TROSPER, D.D., Ph.D., LL.D., and Dean of Mizpah Theological Seminary

LULU BAINS, Elmer's mistress

AD LOCUST, a traveling salesman for the Pequot Farm Implement Company

SHARON FALCONER, a woman evangelist

CECIL AYLSTON, Sharon Falconer's assistant

ART NICHOLS, the cornet and French horn player in Sharon Falconer's three-piece orchestra

MRS. EVANS RIDDLE, an evangelist and a New Thought leader

CLEO BENHAM GANTRY, Elmer's wife

T. J. RIGGS, a rich associate of Elmer in Zenith

HETTIE DOWLER, another of Elmer's mistresses

OSCAR DOWLER, Hettie's husband and companion in trying to trap Elmer

Sinclair Lewis wrote *Elmer Gantry* at the height of his fame, in the middle of the remarkable decade of the 1920's that began for Lewis with *Main Street* and ended with *Dodsworth* and that saw not only *Babbitt* and *Arrowsmith* but also their author's refusal of a Pulitzer Prize that had been awarded to him. Yet curiously, *Elmer Gantry* gives readers a first hint of the waning of Lewis' powers. Before this novel, Lewis had served a long apprenticeship and had achieved great success. From 1915 to 1920, he wrote fifty short stories and five novels, trying out his themes and characterizations, sketching out his satiric portraits of various types; not the least among these were religious types, though the climax of that kind of portraiture was not to come until *Elmer Gantry* appeared in 1927.

Main Street burst upon the world in 1920, the result of several years Lewis spent perfecting his method of research to establish the realistic foundation upon which his satires were to rest. His book was a sensational best-seller, and apparently it occurred to Lewis that he could repeat his success if he would only, in a programmatic way, turn his satiric eye upon the various aspects of American life in sequence. After his exposure of the village, he next chose Zenith, a middle-sized city, and George F. Babbitt, a middle-class businessman. Then he applied his attention (now in collaboration with Dr. Paul de Kruif) to medicine, public health, and medical experimentation. Other projects flashed through his mind and were rejected, until he at last found a challenging project he could eagerly work upon, the ministry; and he began to consider how he could assemble ideas, plot, character, and especially background for what would later become *Elmer Gantry*. Undertaking an exposure of hypocrisy in religion was a formidable and dangerous task, but Lewis felt confidently ready for it. In *Babbitt*, he had written of Mike Monday, the evangelist; Mrs. Opal Emerson Mudge, leader of the New Thought League; and the Reverend John Jennison Drew, author of *The Manly Man's Religion*.

Following his usual method of research, he sought expert advice to provide the background for his novel. Acquainted with a minister in Kansas City, he went there to find some of his material. He gathered a weekly "seminar" of local pastors of many faiths and sects; after luncheon, there might be a session on "The Holy Spirit," with Lewis challenging, pressing, arguing, and thus absorbing material. Gradually, characters and plot took shape. Elmer Gantry was to be Lewis' most extravagant faker, a salesman of religion with no real knowledge of theology and no scruples or morals, a stupid man who would exploit his parishioners as he climbed to success from village to town to city, a seducer of women, and a man of greed.

Elmer Gantry, captain of the football team at Terwillinger College, was known as "Hell-cat" to his classmates and especially to his roommate, a drinking and carousing friend, Jim Lefferts. Then something happened to convert Gantry from being the heathen that he was; he was taken up with the moment. He had met Judson Roberts, a former football star who had a following among members of the "manly" set. Gantry's mother had been urging him to give his soul to God, and so at a prayer meeting, Elmer was swept up and converted with a mob of other "saved" people, while his mother, Judson Roberts, and his disbelieving classmates looked on. From that point on, Lewis exposed Gantry's cheap education, revealed his mistaken, temporary, and even fraudulent initial religious impulses, surrounded him with religionists of neither character nor morality, carried him through several near-catastrophes, only to allow Gantry to recover and rise further still.

Gantry was ordained a minister at Mizpah Theological Seminary. During his time there, he was sent to the town Schoenheim with an assistant, Frank Shallard. Shallard, noting Gantry's questionable motives toward Lulu Bains, a deacon's daughter, reproached Elmer and threatened to take the matter to Dean Trosper. Gantry caught Shallard off guard and reminded him that his faith was shaky and that if Dean Trosper were to know of this, it would end Shallard's career at the seminary. When Shallard realized that someone else was aware of this problem, he left the post at Schoenheim and devoted his time to added study. In Lewis' effort to contrast Gantry with some men of good will and genuine religiosity, his imagination and understanding failed him, and no true opponent, no convincing expression of what religion could mean or be, emerges from the book. Frank Shallard, Elmer's chief antagonist, remains only a shadowy character; finally, his doubts get the best of him, and he leaves the ministry in order to put his Christian principles into practice— and he is painfully defeated.

Gantry's troubles with Lulu Bains had just begun; she informed him that they must get married, and thus Gantry was forced into announcing his betrothal to her. He finally managed to get Lulu involved with an innocent but willing bystander, and in this way, he was able to break the engagement.

Gantry left Schoenheim, supposedly heartbroken, and was sent to a new post in Monarch. On his way to preach the Sunday sermon, he met Ad Locust, a traveling salesman for the Pequot Farm Implement Company. When Gantry became too drunk to show up at the church, he was fired from the seminary, even though he remained an ordained Baptist minister. Elmer then took a job with the Pequot Farm Implement Company and worked for them for two years. While in Sautersville, Nebraska, he met Sharon Falconer, a woman evangelist. He followed her and eventually became her assistant and lover. Everything went well for Gantry until the opening of Sharon's Waters of Jordan Tabernacle, which burned, killing a large number of the attending worshipers and Sharon.

Gantry then took up with Mrs. Evans Riddle, but he was kicked out of her group when she discovered that he was stealing from the collection. He then moved to a Methodist pastorate after teaching his own school of thought for a brief time. At this post, he married Cleo Benham. After several successful charges in larger churches, Gantry was given a large church in New York. Gantry had not lived a pious life even after his marriage, and he became involved with his secretary, Mrs. Hettie Dowler. Those who opposed him used this opportunity to get back at him for his hellfire and brimstone sermons in which he spared no one. The newspapers got wind of the scandal and printed it, but T. J. Riggs saved Gantry from ruin. Gantry swore he would never again desire another woman, but as he knelt to pray because of the congregation's faith in him, he noticed at the same time the ankles of a new and attractive choir member.

Lewis has shown a large gallery of ministerial frauds, such as Mrs. Riddle, the New Thought leader who taught classes in Concentration, Prosperity, Love, Metaphysics, Oriental Mysticism, and the Fourth Dimension, as well as how to keep one's husband. Another example is Judson Roberts, the state secretary of the Y.M.C.A., a young giant with curly hair and a booming voice that he used to bring in the big fellows.

Lewis gave much of his attention to his portrait of Sharon Falconer, the beautiful and somewhat mad female evangelist who preaches in a majestic temple, then leads Gantry to her retreat in the hills where she allows herself to be seduced on an altar she has built to such pagan goddesses as Astarte. Sharon says that she has visions and confesses that she hates little vices like smoking and swearing but loves big ones like lust and murder. Yet from some confused notions about God, Sharon derives sufficient strength to stand at the pulpit in her burning tabernacle and attempt to quell the panic of the mob of her parishioners, while Gantry knocks aside dozens of helpless people and is able to escape. Into such scenes as these, and into the final episode in which Gantry narrowly is saved from entrapment in the old badger game, Lewis poured all his vitality. What critics have missed, and what seems to suggest the first waning of Lewis' powers, is the lack of any real opposition, referred to before. In Gantry himself, there seems to be no decency, and therefore, there are no alternatives contending in his soul. In the "good" characters, there is insufficient understanding and fortitude, and they neither supply important alternatives nor force Gantry to any choices. In this book, Lewis displayed his virtuosity as a satirist, but he also indulged it and failed to find for it any opposition in positive values. Thus, as a satirist of American life, he was by now really beginning to repeat himself, and it turned out to be essentially true (though not without some occasional exceptions) that he was to go on for about twenty-five years looking here and there for aspects of American life to expose, exploiting as best he could his earlier brilliance at recording the clichés of life and language but not advancing to any new understanding either for himself or for his readers. Meanwhile, the world moved on. If he was right that there was hypocrisy and corruption in the religious practices of America, his portrait was also incomplete in not showing some of the glimmer that would begin to be fanned into the light of leadership that religion is trying to provide in the crises of today.

THE END OF THE ROAD

Type of work: Novel
Author: John Barth (1930–   )
Type of plot: Existentialism
Time of plot: 1951–1955
Locale: Wicomico, Maryland
First published: 1958

> Principal characters:
> JACOB HORNER, a teacher of English and the narrator
> JOE MORGAN, a teacher of history
> RENNIE MORGAN, his wife
> PEGGY RANKIN, a teacher of English
> THE DOCTOR, a doubtful M.D.

The End of the Road begins ambiguously with some doubt as to the narrator's, Jacob Horner's, existence. He tells readers that he became a teacher of English at Wicomico State Teachers College on the advice of the Doctor, never given a name, who operates a Remobilization Farm for the treatment of functional paralysis. Between this doubtful beginning and the nonending, John Barth examines the problems of existence and identity that began with his first novel, *The Floating Opera.*

Read on a literal level, the story is a rather banal love triangle involving Jacob, Joe Morgan, and Joe's wife. Read on a serious abstract-ethical level, it becomes the setting for a duel of opposing points of view, both concerned with the problems of Nihilism.

Jacob meets the Doctor in a railroad station, where he has come after finishing his oral examination for his master's degree. In trying to decide where to go for a vacation, he has been overcome by paralysis. He is unable to make a choice. No one destination seems better than another; his will to do anything at all is paralyzed. The Doctor takes him to his Remobilization Farm near Wicomico and begins a series of therapy sessions designed to avoid situations involving complicated choices, the point being to make some choice, any choice, in order to keep moving, so that he would not fall into immobility again.

Mythotherapy, based on the Existentialist premises that existence precedes essence, and that man is free not only to choose his essence but also to change it at will, is the chief therapy prescribed for Jacob. It is a process of assigning a role to himself and carrying it out logically. It is essentially a mask to protect the ego.

At the college, Jacob becomes acquainted with Joe Morgan and his wife Rennie. The relationship quickly develops into a love triangle, but one in which the responsibility is shared equally by all three. Here, as elsewhere,

Barth gives readers no chance to make any judgments, to fasten onto any solid ethical ground. *The End of the Road* is a short novel with the characters sketched and filled in quickly, with very little background or examination of motivational processes.

Jacob's *modus operandi* is mythotherapy. Joe's is one of Ethical Positivism; he has a set of consistent, relative values that he is trying to impress on Rennie. It is around Rennie that the action centers. While teaching Jacob to ride horseback, she tells him of her meeting with Joe and their subsequent relationship and marriage. Until she met Joe, she had no philosophy of her own, and she willingly erased her own personality to adopt that of her husband. She is still unsure of herself and not quite at ease with her adopted role. Later on, she comes to see Jacob as Satan, tempting her to abandon her assumed personality. She sees him as inconsistent, as having nothing but ever-changing masks, donning one after the other as the situation demands. Following logically, she sees Joe as a god: consistent, moral, and logically right. Over the battleground of Rennie, Jacob and Joe fight out their opposing points of view: Jacob with the shifting inconsistencies and limited goals of Existentialism, Joe with his relative ethical values that deny any absolutes.

After Rennie and Jacob commit adultery, Barth abandons any consideration of Rennie and concentrates on the relationship between Jacob and Joe. The adultery had happened almost casually, while Joe was away. The seeds had been planted for it when Jacob and Rennie, peeking in on Joe after one of their rides, watched him making faces at himself in the mirror and engaging in a series of disgusting sex activities. Rennie is shattered; her god has his inconsistencies, too.

Rennie tells Joe of her infidelity, and he confronts Jacob with it. Instead of behaving like an outraged husband, Joe tries to find the reasons behind the deed. All Jacob can say is that he does not know why it happened. Joe's search for causes goes far beyond the point of believability so that one is forced to view it in abstract terms. Here, as elsewhere, Barth carries action to an extreme and exaggerated point until it becomes parody.

Jacob's relationship with Peggy Rankin is a parody of Joe's and Rennie's relationship. Both fail: Joe's because it is too intellectualized and Jacob's because it is too physical. Barth implies a middle way, one would assume, but he never says so directly. In fact, Barth provides no absolutes, but merely presents a set of actions. He seems to suggest that human involvement is the answer to the problems posed by Nihilism.

Upon Joe's urging, Rennie visits Jacob several more times. She tells him that she does not know whether she hates or loves Jacob, but she wants to find out. When both Rennie and Joe visit Jacob one evening, it is to tell him that Rennie is pregnant and that they do not know whose child it is. All she knows is that she will commit suicide if she cannot have an abortion. This situation drives Jacob to his hour of concern. Through a series of lies, impersonations, and gall, he convinces one of the local doctors to give Rennie something to make her abort. When he tells Rennie what he has done and that she must give a false name and story, she refuses. She would rather shoot herself than lie. Jacob, by his imperfect realization of his role and his readiness to assume all the responsibility, has become fully involved, but his commitment is the very thing that the Doctor had told him he must avoid. Joe also has failed in his personal absolutism by turning to Jacob for an answer.

In desperation, Jacob goes to the Doctor and asks him to perform an abortion. The Doctor finally agrees on the condition that Jacob will give him all his money and go with him to a new location in Pennsylvania. Jacob agrees and brings Rennie to the Remobilization Farm. While on the operating table, Rennie dies.

Jacob is afraid that Joe will inform the police. Several days later, he receives a telephone call from Joe, who tells him that he has taken care of everything. Joe and his convictions have suffered a mortal blow. He is lost and desperate. He turns to Jacob for an explanation, but Jacob has nothing to offer. Both positions, Moral Nihilism and Ethical Positivism, have been wrecked in their encounter with reality. Joe is left to reconstruct his life. Jacob returns to the Doctor because he is not yet ready to assume the responsibilities of life.

The End of the Road is a bitter commentary on the plight of man. Barth, in his examination of Nihilism, has given no answers. There are no moments of high good humor, as in *The Sot-Weed Factor*, only an unrelieved pessimism. On the surface, the novel is akin to the Theater of the Absurd in its insistence on telling only the observable actions of a story. John Barth points no morals and draws no conclusions but only shows that Nihilism, in its several guises, is not an end in itself.

THE ENORMOUS ROOM

Type of work: Novel
Author: E. E. Cummings (1894–1962)
Type of plot: Autobiographical fiction
Time of plot: 1917
Locale: France
First published: 1922

> *Principal characters:*
> E. E. CUMMINGS, an American ambulance driver
> W. S. B., his American friend
> APOLLYON, head of the French prison
> ROCKYFELLER,
> THE WANDERER,
> ZOO-LOO,
> SURPLICE, and
> JEAN LE NÈGRE, fellow prisoners

The Story:

E. E. Cummings and his friend, B., were unhappy as members of the Norton-Harjes Ambulance Service, a unit sent by Americans to aid the French during World War I. One day, they were arrested by French military police. From hints dropped during an investigation, Cummings gathered that B. had written some letters suspected by the censor. Because they were good friends, both men were held for questioning. They never found out exactly what they were suspected of doing. On one occasion, Cummings was asked whether he hated the Germans. He replied that he did not, that he simply loved the French very much. The investigating official could not understand how one could love the French and not hate Germans. Finally, Cummings and B. were separated and sent to different prisons. As time went by, Cummings was questioned again and again and moved from one spot to another, always under strict guard.

Late one night, he was taken to a prison in the little provincial town of Macé. There, he was thrown into a huge darkened room, given a straw mattress, and told to go to sleep. In the darkness, he counted at least thirty voices speaking eleven different languages. Early the next morning, he was told that B., his friend, was in the same room. The two men were happy to see each other again. B. told him that the prisoners in the room were all suspected of being spies, some only because they spoke no French.

That morning, he learned the routine of the prison. The enormous room

was lined with mattresses down each side, with a few windows to let in light
at one end. It smelled of stale tobacco and sweat. Some of the men in the
room were insane; most of them were afraid they might become so. To all
of them, life consisted of following dull prison routine. At five-thirty in the
morning, someone went down to the kitchen under guard and brought back
a bucket of sour, cold coffee. After coffee, the prisoners drew lots to see who
would clear the room, sweep the floors, and collect the trash. At seven-thirty,
they were allowed to walk for two hours in a small, walled-in courtyard. Then
came the first meal of the day, followed by another walk in the garden. At
four, they had supper. At eight, they were locked in the enormous room for
the night.

There was little entertainment except fighting and conversation. Some of
the men spent their time trying to catch sight of women kept in another part
of the prison. Cummings began to accustom himself to the enormous room
and to make friends among the various inmates. One of the first of these was
Count Bragard, a Belgian painter who specialized in portraits of horses. The
Count was a perfect gentleman, even in prison, and always looked neat and
suave. He and Cummings discussed painting and the arts as if they were at
a polite party. Before Cummings left, the Count began to act strangely. He
withdrew from his old friends. He was losing his mind.

One day Cummings was taken to see the head of the prison, a gross man
he called Apollyon, named after the devil in *Pilgrim's Progress*. Apollyon
had no interest in the prisoners as long as they made as little trouble as
possible for him. He questioned Cummings for a considerable time in an
effort to learn why the American was there, a circumstance over which the
American himself often wondered.

When new inmates arrived in the room, everyone looked them over with
anticipation, some to find a man with money he could lend, some to find a
fellow countryman, and some to find a friend. One day a very fat, rosy-
cheeked man joined the group. He had been a successful manager of a disreputable house. Because he had a large sum of money with him, he was
nicknamed Rockyfeller. He hired a strong man to act as his bodyguard.
Nobody liked him, for he bought special privileges from the guards.

During his stay in the room, Cummings met three men, very different from
one another, whose personal qualities were such that they made life seem
meaningful to him. He called them the Delectable Mountains, after the mountains Christian found in *Pilgrim's Progress*. The first was the Wanderer, whose
wife and three little children were in the women's ward of the prison. He was
a strong man, simple in his emotions and feelings. Cummings liked to talk
with him about his problems. One of the Wanderer's children, a little boy,
sometimes came to the enormous room to visit his father. His pranks and
games both bothered and amused the men. The Wanderer treated his son
with love and the deepest kind of understanding. Until he was sent away, he

remained Cummings' best friend.

The second Delectable Mountain was called Zoo-loo, a Polish farmer who could speak neither French nor English, but who could communicate by signs. In a short time, he and Cummings knew all about each other. Zoo-loo had a knack for hiding money, and despite the fact that the head of the prison had him searched from head to toe, and all his belongings searched, he always seemed able to produce a twenty franc note from his left ear or the back of his neck. His kindnesses to Cummings and B. were innumerable.

The third Delectable Mountain was an amazing little man named Surplice. Everything astonished him. When Cummings had some candy or cheese, Surplice was sure to come over to his cot and ask questions about it in a shy manner. His curiosity and friendly conversation made everything seem more important and interesting than it really was.

One morning, Jean Le Nègre was brought to the enormous room, a gigantic, simple-minded black whom Cummings was to remember as the finest of his fellow prisoners. Jean was given to practical jokes and tall tales; he had been arrested for impersonating an English officer and had been sent to the prison for psychopathic observation. Because of his powerful body, the women prisoners called their approval and admiration when he walked in the courtyard. His favorite was Lulu, who smuggled money and a lace handkerchief to him. When she was sent to another prison, Jean was disconsolate. When one of the prisoners pulled at Lulu's handkerchief, Jean handled him roughly. A scuffle followed. The guards came, and Jean was taken away for punishment. Calls from the women prisoners aroused him so that he attacked the guards and sent them flying until he was quieted and bound by a fellow prisoner whom he trusted. After that experience, Jean grew quiet and shy.

Just before Cummings was released, B. was sent away. Jean Le Nègre tried to cheer Cummings with his funny stories and exaggerated lies, but without much success. Cummings was afraid B. might never get free from the prisons of France, a groundless fear as he learned later. He left the enormous room knowing that in it he had learned the degradation, nobility, and endurance of human nature.

Critical Evaluation:

The Enormous Room tells of more than three uncomfortable months in prison; it tells of the outrage and terror and hope and fear of men caught in the mesh of wartime government. E. E. Cummings wanted to tell of the strange and amazing things he had learned about people while in prison. In reading the book, one gets to know not only the author and his friend B., but all the inmates of the enormous room. Each is a study of some human quality. Abounding with sharply drawn scenes and portraits, the novel is compelling in its vivid detail. The book is not so much a study of the stupidity and brutality of war as it is a quietly passionate vindication of Man.

The book reveals the disillusionment and cynicism characteristic of the writers who emerged after World War I, and Cummings' particular hatred of systems that threaten individualism and freedom. The human capacity to keep feeling alive in a dehumanizing world is Cummings' basic theme. As in his poetry, he seeks to present his characters through their own particular idioms. Though showing the influence of Fielding, Dickens, and (especially) Bunyan, Cummings' highly autobiographical novel is new both in content and technique.

Chapters entitled "I Begin a Pilgrimage," "A Pilgrim's Progress," "Apollyon," and "An Approach to the Delectable Mountains" make clear parallels between the journey of Bunyan's Pilgrim to salvation and Cummings' own metaphorical journey. From the moment of his arrest, Cummings finds himself in the power of an insecure authority administered by a mindless bureaucracy. Intolerant of the smallest deviation from its norms, the French government— ironically representative of the "democracy" the war was fought to preserve— imprisons all nonconformists, derelicts, and misfits who come to its attention. Ironically, the enormous room holds no real traitors, spies, or enemies of the state.

Supreme among the inmates of the prison are those characters Cummings calls the "Delectable Mountains." Though they are widely diverse types, Cummings seems to find in them a wonderful capacity for feeling which sets them apart from their peers. Thus, these Delectable Mountains in particular come to symbolize for Cummings the beauty and honesty of human emotion in contrast to the unfeeling, mindless, and cruel institution. Through his pilgrimage, Cummings comes to believe in the indomitable ability of men to preserve the best of their humanity even in the face of dehumanizing oppression. The novel ends with a bright ray of sunshine, symbolizing Cummings' hope for a future founded upon man's best rather than his worst qualities.

EPITAPH OF A SMALL WINNER

Type of work: Novel
Author: Joaquim Maria Machado de Assis (1839–1908)
Type of plot: Philosophical realism
Time of plot: 1805–1869
Locale: Rio de Janeiro, Brazil
First published: 1881

> *Principal characters:*
> BRAZ CUBAS, a wealthy, cultured Brazilian
> MARCELLA, his first mistress
> VIRGILIA, his fiancée and later his mistress
> LOBO NEVES, Virgilia's husband
> QUINCAS BORBA, a philosopher and pickpocket

The Story:

Braz Cubas, a wealthy Brazilian, died of pneumonia in his sixty-fifth year. After his death, he decided to write his autobiography, to while away a part of eternity and to give mankind some record of his life.

Braz was born in 1805. His childhood was an easy one, for his father was extremely wealthy and indulgent, only pretending to be severe with his child for the sake of appearances. One of the earliest experiences the boy remembered was the elation of the Brazilians over the defeat of Napoleon, an occasion marked in his memory by the gift of a small sword. The sword was the most important aspect of the occasion, and Braz remarked that each person has his own "sword" that makes occasions important.

As a child, Braz Cubas did not like school. In his seventeenth year, he had his first love affair with a courtesan named Marcella. Trying to please his mistress, Braz spent all the money he could borrow from his mother, and then gave promissory notes to fall due on the day he inherited his father's estate. His father, learning of the affair, paid off his son's debts and shipped him off to a university in Spain. At first, Braz hoped to take Marcella with him. She refused to go.

Graduated from the university and awarded a degree, Braz admitted that he knew very little. He then took advantage of his father's liberality and wealth and spent several years traveling about Europe. Called back to Rio de Janeiro by news that his mother was dying of cancer, he arrived home in time to see her before she died. After her death, he went into retirement, remaining in seclusion until his father came to him with plans for a marriage and a seat in the Brazilian legislative body. After some vacillation, Braz decided to obey his father's wishes. The reason for his hesitation was a love affair with a rather beautiful girl. His discovery that she was lame, however, turned him away from her. On his return to social life, he learned that the young woman his father had picked out for him, a girl named Virgilia, had position, wealth, and beauty. It was through her father's influence that the elder Cubas expected his son to get ahead politically. Unfortunately for the schemes of both father and son, Virgilia met Lobo Neves, a young man with more ambition and greater prospects. She decided to marry him, a decision that ended, at least temporarily, prospects of a political career for Braz.

Disappointed and disgruntled with life, he accidentally met Marcella, his former mistress. He found her greatly changed, for smallpox had destroyed her beauty. After losing her looks, she had left her earlier profession to become the keeper of a small jewelry shop.

Disappointment over his son's failure to win Virgilia was too much for his father, who died shortly afterward. There was a great to-do after the father's death, for Braz's brother-in-law turned out to be an avaricious man who wanted his wife, Braz's sister, to have as much of the estate as possible. Braz accepted calmly the selfish and unfortunate aspect of human nature thus revealed, and agreed, for his sister's sake, to be reconciled with his greedy brother-in-law.

Not very long after his father's death, Braz learned from Virgilia's brother that Virgilia and her husband were returning to Rio de Janeiro. Braz was pleased; he was still in love with her. A few days after the return of Virgilia and her husband, he met them at a ball. Virgilia and Braz danced several waltzes together and fell more deeply in love than they had ever been while Braz was courting her. They continued to meet, and before long, Virgilia became his mistress.

One day, Braz found a package in which were several bundles of banknotes. He kept the money and later used it to establish a trust fund for Doña Placida, a former servant of Virgilia's family, who maintained the house in which Virgilia and Braz kept their assignations. They managed for several years to keep their affair a secret, so that Braz could be a guest in Virgilia's home as well. In fact, he and Lobo Neves were good friends.

One day, Braz met Quincas Borba, an old schoolmate who had been reduced to begging. The man took some money from Braz and, as he discovered later, also stole his watch. That night, Braz suggested to Virgilia that they run away. She refused to do so. They had a lover's quarrel, followed by a tender scene of repentance.

A short time later, Lobo Neves was offered the governorship of a province, and he suggested that Braz accompany him as his secretary. The situation was inviting to the two lovers, but they knew that in the smaller provincial capital their secret could not long be hidden. Their problems were unexpectedly solved when superstitious Neves refused the government post because the document appointing him was dated on the thirteenth of the month.

The love affair continued until Virgilia became pregnant. Neither of the lovers doubted that Braz was the father of the child, and he acted very much like a husband who expected to be presented with his firstborn. The child, not carried the full term, died at birth, much to the sorrow of Virgilia and Braz, and of the husband as well, who thought the child was his.

One day, Braz received a letter from Quincas Borba, the begging schoolmate who had stolen his watch. Having improved his finances, the beggar had become a philosopher, a self-styled Humanist. Borba's ideas fascinated Braz, who had always fancied himself an intellectual and a literary man. He was also pleased when Borba sent him a watch as good as the one he had stolen. Braz spent a great deal of time with Borba, for Neves had become suspicious of the relationship between his wife and her lover, and the two were discreet enough to stay away from each other for a time.

At last, Virgilia and her husband left Rio de Janeiro after Neves received another political appointment. For a time, Braz felt like a widower. Lonely, he turned to public life. Defeated for office, he then became the publisher of an opposition newspaper, but his venture was not successful. He also fell in love and finally decided to get married. Once more, he was disappointed, for his fiancée died during an epidemic.

The years passed rather uneventfully. Braz grew older, and so did his friends. Not many weeks after the death of Quincas Borba, who had become a close companion, Braz fell ill of pneumonia. One visitor during his last illness was Virgilia, whose husband had died, but even her presence was not enough to keep Braz from slipping into delirium. In his dying moments, he cast up the accounts of his life and decided that in the game of life he was the winner by only a small margin, in that he had brought no one else into the world to suffer the misery of life.

Critical Evaluation:

Joaquim Maria Machado de Assis' ancestry is slightly mysterious. His father was supposedly a "son of free mulattos" and a housepainter, and his mother an impoverished white washerwoman, but these versions of his background are open to question. Although John Nist, for example, wrote that Machado de Assis left the slums of Rio de Janeiro to found Brazil's Academy of Letters, after having conquered Brazil with the greatest outpouring of literary talent in that country's history, some persons question the tradition that he grew up in poverty in Rio's slums. While little is known of Machado de Assis until he reached fifteen years of age, he is known to have had only a primary-level education. It is also known that a French bakeshop owner taught him French and that he was an autodidact, acquiring his impressive culture by educating himself. Even though rather finely featured, he was spindly legged, myopic, rachitic, a stammerer, endured alarming epileptic seizures, and suffered intestinal disorders. He was Caucasian in features, but his African blood was an added problem for him in nineteenth century Brazil. His white wife's brothers strongly opposed her marriage to Machado de Assis on racial grounds.

Machado de Assis has been awarded a unique place in Brazilian literature and is considered its most singular eminence. Brazilians have called him their sphinx, their enigma, their myth. His writings, including *Epitaph of a Small Winner*, have been contradictorily labeled brilliant, dry, rich, colorless, or ironic, refined, intuitive, pure, correct, limpid, balanced, boring, and elegant. Some Brazilians smell the scent of Brazilianism exuding from his pages or a literary nativism so strong as to comprise a natural emanation. Yet Pedro Calmon wrote that he did not seem Brazilian, and his works were once described as being psychologically French. Besides *Epitaph of a Small Winner* (in Portuguese as *Memórias pósthumas de Braz Cubas*), many of his novels and other works have been translated into English. Literary critics commonly eulogize him for stylistic purity, perfect linguistic knowledge, and a great inner richness. It was once said that he knew well all the secrets of the art of writing and that his intuitive insight into man's intimate peculiarities was remarkable.

As is evident in *Epitaph of a Small Winner* and the three novels that chronologically followed it, Machado de Assis became steadily more disillusioned with human beings. It is said that these novels, plus his masterpiece, *Dom Casmurro*, published twenty-eight years after *Epitaph of a Small Winner*, supply the most convincing evidence for his ever-continuing disillusionment. In any event, each of Machado de Assis' most celebrated novels paints a wasted human life.

His disenchantment with human beings became universal, and his soul was ever more strained by inner turmoil. He liked to expose human egotism and believed that all nature revealed man's idiocy, that everything in the universe resented what it was and pined to be something else. He came to view man as always bouncing, ball-like, until his passions destroyed him. Sometimes compared to William Somerset Maugham for his inferiority complex, Machado de Assis deliberately withheld information about his personal life and hinted that it had little to do with his writing. In *Epitaph of a Small Winner*, however, Machado de Assis puts into Braz Cubas' mouth the statement that although many European novelists had made tours of one or more countries, he, Braz Cubas, had made a tour of life. In this tour, added Braz Cubas, he had seen assininity, human evil, and the sorry vanity of all matter.

Machado de Assis strove for thirty years to master the art of narration. *Epitaph of a Small Winner* as well as his other early works give a hint of the development to come, for he always experimented with his storytelling skills. He usually used short sentences, brief chapters, and deliberately interrupted narrative. He was eventually credited with brilliant manipulation of language and haunting character analysis through skilled use of symbols and metaphors. Machado de Assis has also been likened to a hard rock miner delving into the earth to seek man's infernal image. He cautioned his readers to scrutinize his lines for an interlocking pattern that integrated the various parts. He tinged names of characters with significance and color and derived inspiration from Shakespeare. He withdrew from the Romanticist movement that was literarily dominant during his youth and became a Realist. In 1907, shortly before his death, he noted that thirty years' time had separated two editions of one of his works and that these thirty years illustrated the difference in composition and temper of his writing.

Machado de Assis rarely left his native Rio de Janeiro, entwined in its granite mountains and curving bay, and he never journeyed far when he did. He remained an autodidact in ideas and cultural values to the end of his life. He died as he lived, loathing the idea of being either a bore, spectacle, or hypocrite. As he was dying, attended by Brazil's most famous writers of the day, he wanted to call a priest but then reflected that it would be hypocritical.

In any event, it can be said that despite Machado de Assis' celebrated pessimism and bleak insight into human nature, none of his novels alleges that it is impossible to view the world in a more cheerful light than he did; they merely state that it would be difficult.

ETHAN FROME

Type of work: Novel
Author: Edith Wharton (1862–1937)
Type of plot: Domestic tragedy
Time of plot: Late nineteenth century
Locale: Starkfield, Massachusetts
First published: 1911
>   *Principal characters:*
>   ETHAN FROME, a New England farmer
>   ZENOBIA FROME (ZEENA), his wife
>   MATTIE SILVER, Zeena's cousin

The Story:

Ethan Frome was twenty-one years old when he married Zenobia Pierce, a distant cousin who nursed his sick mother during her last illness. It was a wedding without love. Zenobia, called Zeena, had no home of her own, and Ethan was lonely. So they were married. Yet, Zeena's talkativeness, which had been pleasing to Ethan during his mother's illness, quickly subsided, and within a year of their marriage, Zeena developed the sickliness that was to plague her husband all her life. Ethan became increasingly dissatisfied with his life. He was an intelligent and ambitious young man who had hoped to become an engineer or a chemist. He soon, however, found himself chained to a wife he detested and a farm he could not sell.

The arrival of Mattie Silver brightened the gloomy house considerably. Mattie, Zeena's cousin, had come to Starkfield partly because she had no other place to go and partly because Zeena felt in need of a companion around the house. Ethan saw in Mattie's goodness and beauty every fine quality that Zeena lacked.

When Zeena suggested that Ethan help Mattie find a husband, he began to realize how much he was attracted to the girl. When he went to a church social to bring Mattie home and saw her dancing with the son of a rich Irish grocer, he realized that he was jealous of his rival and in love with Mattie. On his way home with her, Ethan felt his love for Mattie more than ever, for on that occasion as on others, she flattered him by asking him questions on astronomy. His dreams of happiness were short-lived, however, for when he reached home, Zeena was her nagging, sour self. The contrast between Zeena and Mattie impressed him more and more.

One day, Ethan returned from his morning's work to find Zeena dressed in her traveling clothes. She was going to visit a new doctor in nearby Bettsbridge. Ordinarily, Ethan would have objected to the journey because of the expensive remedies that Zeena was in the habit of buying on her trips to town. On this occasion, however, he was overjoyed at the news of Zeena's proposed departure, for he realized that he and Mattie would have the house to themselves overnight.

With Zeena out of the way, Ethan again became a changed man. Later in the evening, before supper, Ethan and Mattie sat quietly before the fire, just as Ethan imagined happily married couples would do. During supper, the cat broke Zeena's favorite pickle dish, which Mattie had used to brighten up the table. In spite of the accident, they spent the rest of the evening happily. They talked about going sledding together, and Ethan told shyly—and perhaps wistfully—that he had seen Ruth Varnum and Ned Hale, a young engaged couple, stealing a kiss earlier in the evening.

In the morning Ethan was happy, but not because of anything out of the ordinary the night before. In fact, when he went to bed, he remembered sadly that he had not so much as touched Mattie's fingertips or looked into her eyes. He was happy because he could imagine what a wonderful life he could have if he were married to Mattie. He got glue to mend the pickle dish, but Zeena's unexpected return prevented him from repairing it. His spirits were further dampened when Zeena told him that the Bettsbridge doctor considered her quite sick. He had advised her to get a girl to relieve her of all household duties, a stronger girl than Mattie. She had already engaged the new girl. Ethan was dumbfounded by this development. In her insistence that Mattie be sent away, Zeena gave the first real hint that she may have been aware of gossip about her husband and Mattie.

When Ethan told Mattie of Zeena's decision, the girl was as crestfallen as Ethan. Zeena interrupted their lamentations, however, by coming downstairs for something to eat. After supper, she required stomach powders to relieve a case of heartburn. In getting the powders, which she had hidden in a spot supposedly unknown to Mattie, Zeena discovered the broken pickle dish, which had been carefully reassembled in order to give the appearance of being unbroken. Having detected the deception and learned that Mattie was responsible for the broken dish, Zeena called Mattie insulting names and showed plainly that the girl would be sent away at the earliest possible moment.

Faced with the certainty of Mattie's departure, Ethan thought of running away with her. But his poverty, as well as his sense of responsibility to Zeena, offered no solution to his problem, only greater despair. On the morning Mattie was to leave Starkfield, Ethan, against the wishes of his wife, insisted on driving Mattie to the station. The thought of parting was unbearable to both. They decided to take the sleigh ride that Ethan had promised Mattie the night before. Down the hill they went, narrowly missing a large elm tree at the bottom. Mattie, who had told Ethan that she would rather die than leave him, begged until Ethan agreed to take her down the hill a second time and run the sled into the elm at the bottom of the slope; but they failed to hit the tree with force sufficient to kill them. The death they sought became a living death, for in the accident Mattie suffered a permanent spine injury and Ethan an incurable lameness. The person who received Mattie into her home, who waited on her, and who cooked for Ethan was—Zeena.

Critical Evaluation:

Ethan Frome is a compact novelette that etches with acid the existential tragedy of misspent lives and talent gone awry. In it, Edith Wharton depicts Ethan Frome and Mattie Silver as intelligent and fundamentally decent human beings whose souls—and finally, whose bodies—are crushed by meaningless but inexorable social conventions, represented by Zeena Frome.

Ethan, in particular, reflects Wharton's view that twentieth century America has repudiated the fine nineteenth century values which Wharton cherishes so deeply, for Ethan stands for all those bygone qualities that she admires. He has a good mind, commendable ambition, and strong integrity. A twentieth century Ethan might, for example, think of killing Zeena—and possibly even attempt it—but Wharton's nineteenth century man, living in an inhospitable twentieth century, is instead slowly destroyed by a society that has no use for him or his anachronistic values. In the end, he is tended by Zeena, who takes care of him much as a museum curator takes care of ancient artifacts entrusted to him.

Although *Ethan Frome* is unusual in the large corpus of Wharton's work for its revelations about the author's bitterness toward what she views as the shallowness of modern industrial society, it is by no means unique. Wharton earlier treated a similar theme in *The House of Mirth* (1905), a novel frequently paired with *Ethan Frome* for purposes of comparison; and indeed, the likenesses are there. Like Ethan, for instance, Lily Bart in *The House of Mirth* is meant for a better life than she has, but in her pursuit of what she clearly deserves, she is subjected to calumny, deceit, and fraud, which finally drive her to a fatal overdose of sedatives. These two simple tragedies stand out from Wharton's other work, which concerned itself largely with complex sociomoral conflicts, but they are certainly not inferior, despite their apparently anomalous position. In fact, *Ethan Frome* is considered by many to be Wharton's finest work.

A FABLE

Type of work: Novel
Author: William Faulkner (1897–1962)
Type of plot: Religious allegory
Time of plot: 1918
Locale: Western Front in France
First published: 1954

> *Principal characters:*
> THE CORPORAL
> THE MARSHAL, Commander-in-Chief of the Allied Armies
> in France
> GENERAL GRAGNON, the French Division Commander
> THE QUARTERMASTER GENERAL, the Marshal's former
> fellow student
> THE RUNNER, a former officer, in sympathy with the
> Corporal's aims
> THE REVEREND TOBE SUTTERFIELD, a black American
> preacher
> THE CORPORAL'S WIFE
> MARTHE, the Corporal's younger half sister
> MARYA, the Corporal's feeble-minded half sister
> DAVID LEVINE, a British flight officer
> POLCHEK, a soldier in the Corporal's squad
> PIERRE BOUC, another soldier in the Corporal's squad
> BUCHWALD, an American soldier

The Story:

On a Monday in May, 1918, a most unusual event took place on a battlefield in France where French and German troops faced one another after four years of trench warfare. At dawn, the regiment under the command of General Gragnon refused to attack. Another unbelievable event occurred when the Germans, who were expected to take advantage of the mutiny, did not move either. At noon, the whole sector of the front stopped firing and soon the rest of the front came to a standstill. Division Commander Gragnon requested execution of all three thousand mutineers; he also demanded his own arrest.

On Wednesday, the lorries carrying the mutinous regiment arrived at headquarters in Chaulnesmont, where the dishonor brought on the town aroused the people to noisy demonstration. Relatives and friends of the mutineers knew that a corporal and his squad of twelve, moving in a mysterious way behind the lines, had succeeded in spreading their ideas about peace on earth and good will toward men among the troops. Four of the thirteen men were not Frenchmen by birth; among those only the Corporal spoke French, and he was the object of the crowd's fury.

This situation created uncertainty among the Allied generals because a war ended by mutiny was not reconcilable with military principles. To clarify the confusion, a conference took place to which a German general was invited, and an agreement was reached for continuation of the war.

To young Flight Officer David Levine, the unsuspected pause in war meant tragedy. Determined to find glory in battle but realizing that he might miss his opportunity, he committed suicide. To another soldier, the Runner, the truce at the front was a welcome sign. A former officer, he had rejected submissive principles and abuse of authority by superiors, and he had been returned to the ranks. Having heard about the Corporal from the Reverend Tobe Sutterfield, an American black preacher who had arrived under unexplainable circumstances in France, the Runner tried to show once again the power of the Corporal's ideas. He forced a sentry, who profiteered by collecting fees for life insurance among the soldiers, to leave the trenches and join a British battalion in a peaceful walk toward the German line. When they showed their empty hands, the Germans also came unarmed to meet the French. A sudden artillery barrage by French and German guns killed the sentry and crippled the Runner.

The man to decide the fate of the mutineers was the Commander-in-Chief of the Allied Armies, an aged French Marshal. The orphaned son of a prominent family, he had attended France's St. Cyr. There his unselfish attitude combined with his devotion to studies had made him an outstanding and beloved student. Especially attracted to him was the man who was now his Quartermaster General. After leaving school, the Marshal had been stationed in the Sahara, where he incurred blood-guilt by sacrificing a brutal legionnaire to tribal justice. Later, he spent several years in a Tibetan monastery. In the Middle East, he had met a married woman with two daughters. This affair resulted in the birth of a son in a stable at Christmas. The mother died in childbirth, and Marthe, one of the daughters, cared for the boy. When World War I broke out, the Marshal became the Allied commander and the hope of France.

The mutinous troops were kept in a former factory building while awaiting trial. The Marshal, not surprised by the court proceedings, seemed to anticipate all answers. Marthe and Marya, the Corporal's half sisters, and his wife arrived in Chaulnesmont and, in an interview with the Marshal, revealed that the Corporal was his son. Marthe had married a French farmer, Dumont, and the boy had grown up on her farm. Soon after the outbreak of war, he had enlisted in the army and received a medal for bravery in action. He had married a former prostitute from Marseilles. Again, the old Marshal was not surprised and seemed to know every detail.

On Thursday, a meal was served to the squad during which it became known that soldier Polchek had betrayed the Corporal. Another soldier, Pierre Bouc, denied his leader thrice. After the meal, the Corporal was called away to meet the Marshal. On a hill overlooking the town, the Marshal tried to explain the futility of his son's martyrdom. When he promised a secret ocean passage to escape the death penalty, the Corporal refused the offer. Later the Marshal made a last attempt to influence his son with the help of an army priest. Recognizing his own unworthiness before the humble Corporal, the priest committed suicide. On the same evening, General Gragnon was executed by an American soldier named Buchwald.

On Friday, the Corporal was tied to a post between two criminals. Shot, he fell into a coil of barbed wire that lacerated his head. The Corporal's body and his medal were buried on the Dumont farm near St. Mihiel. After the burial, a sudden artillery barrage plowed the earth, leaving no trace of the Corporal's grave.

After the war, a unit was sent to reclaim a body to be placed in the Unknown Soldier's tomb under the Arc de Triomphe in Paris. As a reward, they were promised brandy. Near Verdun, they obtained a body and drank the brandy. While they were guarding the coffin, an old woman approached. Having lost her mind because her son had not returned from the war, she had sold her farm in order to search for him. Knowing about the mission of the soldiers, she wanted to look at the body. Convinced that the dead soldier was her son, she offered all her money for the corpse; the soldiers accepted and bought more brandy with the money. They secured another body from a field adjoining the Dumont farm. Thus, the body of the Corporal reached Paris. Four years later, the Runner visited the Dumont farm and picked up the medal.

Six years later, the Marshal's body was carried to the Arc de Triomphe, with dignitaries of the Western world following the coffin on foot to pay their respects to the dead leader. As soon as the eulogy started, a cripple made his way through the crowd. It was the Runner, who threw the Corporal's medal at the caisson before an angry mob closed in and attacked him. Rescued by the police, he was dragged into a side street, where a few curious onlookers gathered around the injured cripple. While he lay in the gutter, a man resembling the old Quartermaster General stepped forward to comfort the Runner, who declared that he would never die.

Critical Evaluation:

A Fable is probably the most ambitious, though not the most successful, work of one of the twentieth century's most ambitious novelists. By juxtaposing elements of the Passion of Christ against a story of trench mutiny in World War I, William Faulkner attempts to combine two very different types of narrative: an allegorical "fable" based upon parallels between the events of his story and those of the original "myth" as well as a realistic narrative of war, politics, and personal relationships.

Most of the similarities to Christ's life and death are obvious. The Corporal, who was born in a stable and is thirty-three years old, leads a mutinous group of twelve followers, and the events surrounding his capture and execution suggest the Passion: one disciple betrays him for money, another denies him three times; the followers have a "Last Supper"; the Corporal is executed between two thieves in a manner that suggests Christ's crucifixion; he acquires a crown of thorns; he is mourned by women who resemble Mary Magdalene and Mary; and his body vanishes three days after burial. It is necessary, however, to remember that *A Fable* is *not* the Passion retold in modern dress. Faulkner does not simply update or interpret Christian myth: he *uses* it. Therefore, any attempt to come to terms with *A Fable* must consider the unique, personal vision that Faulkner presents in his book.

Some critics have faulted the novel on the grounds that the Corporal's personality is insufficiently developed. It is true that he is not strongly individualized, but to present the character in greater detail would risk either the creation of a purely symbolic figure or one too humanized to maintain the Christ parallel. Instead, the Corporal remains a silent, mysterious embodiment of man's spiritual side; the concrete presentation of his "meaning" is entrusted to other characters. The most important thing is that, for all the biblical allusions, the Corporal is not the chosen Son of God, but is definitely a son of man—specifically of the Marshal—and the thematic center of the novel is dramatized in the conflict between the Corporal and his father-Marshal antagonist.

In the novel's most powerful and important scene, the final confrontation between the two men, the Marshal defines their basic natures as

> two articulations . . . not so much to defend as to test two inimical conditions which . . . must contend and one of them—perish: I champion of the mundane earth . . . while you champion of an esoteric realm of man's baseless and his infinite capacity—no passion—for unfact.

Thus, *A Fable* is not really about man's relationship to God, or even to society, but to himself. Each of these men stands for one aspect of the human personality, and the conflict between them can be seen in several ways: son versus father, youth versus age, idealist versus realist, common man versus authority, heart versus mind. In short, the major conflict of the book is, in the words of Faulkner's Nobel Prize speech, "the human heart in conflict with itself"— man's basic dualism: the major theme of Faulkner's late fiction.

However, if the Corporal remains the shadowy incarnation of man's spiritual side, the Marshal, both in his symbolic and his realistic functions, is a much more vivid and complicated character. On the literal level, it is he, as the supreme commander of the Allied Armies in France, who masterminds the successful military counterstrategy; symbolically, as the primary representative of secular power, the Marshal represents everything in human society that denies personal autonomy and spiritual freedom to man.

Any attempt to pin down the Marshal's symbolic antecedents more precisely is very difficult. At times he suggests Satan, at times Pilate or Caesar, or simply military authority, but in the central confrontation scene, his role seems to most closely resemble that of the "Grand Inquisitor," who appears in the greatest of earlier "Second Coming" fictions, Ivan Karamazov's parable in Fyodor Dostoyevski's *The Brothers Karamazov*.

Like the Grand Inquisitor, the Marshal faces a Christ surrogate who poses a threat to the established order. Likewise, the Marshal makes an offer to his antagonist of life and freedom in return for betrayal, which he knows in advance will be refused. The Marshal's background also resembles the Inquisitor's in that he, too, began life with a spiritual quest by renouncing the world in favor of the desert and the mountains. Like the Inquisitor—and Christ— the Marshal was tempted and, like the Inquisitor—*but unlike Christ*—he accepted the temptations and the view of life they represented in return for temporal power.

Thus, although he knows and understands man's duality, the Marshal rejects the spiritual and creative side of man and accepts him only as a mundane, earthbound creature who needs security and control rather than individual freedom and spiritual fulfillment. Further, on the practical level, he commits himself to the human institution that fixes and formalizes this view of man. Like the Inquisitor, the Marshal justifies his actions on the grounds that they are what man needs and wants. He taunts his opponent with the notion that he, not the Corporal, is the true believer in man: "after the last ding dong of doom has rung and died there will still be one sound more; his voice, planning still to build something higher and faster and louder. . . . I don't fear man, I do better: I respect and admire him. . . . Because man and his folly—they will prevail."

These words echo the Nobel Prize speech but differ in one important respect from the novelist's own; in the address, Faulkner went on to add: "He is immortal, not because he alone among creatures has an inexhaustible voice, but because he has a soul, a spirit capable of compassion and sacrifice and endurance." This statement defines the essence of the conflict between the Marshal and the Corporal and their visions.

If the Marshal's view of mankind is correct, then the military hierarchy, the rituals and institutions it supports, and the war itself are things man creates for himself and needs for survival. The Corporal's mutiny is, therefore, not only foolish, but even destructive to man's well-being. On the other hand, if the Corporal's vision is true, such things are artificial, malevolent restraints on man's potential. The mutiny in this context becomes a necessary act in the struggle to cast off the life-denying lies and organizations imposed on him and to fulfill his own human and spiritual capacities by taking control of his own destiny. Because the immediate secular power belongs to the Marshal, the earthbound view seems to win, but the question Faulkner raises is whether the impact of the Corporal's actions and martyrdom does not postulate the ultimate triumph of the spiritual vision.

To answer that question, Faulkner attempts to work out the implications of the Corporal's ethic in the actions of several other characters and especially in the attempt of the English Runner to foment a second and wider mutiny. Here lies the primary critical problem of the book: Do these secondary actions establish and elaborate the novel's main thrust, or do they obscure and finally bury it?

Although he borrows Christian symbolism, Faulkner is clearly not presenting a conventionally religious message. He affirms the human spirit, but his attitude toward its ultimate fate is ambiguous. If the Corporal dies a heroic martyr, the other witnesses to the human spirit—the English Runner, the Sentry, the Reverend Sutterfield, the Quartermaster General—suffer dubious or ignominious fates and even the Corporal's death has no clear effect beyond stimulating the Runner's Quixotic gestures. Faulkner postulates *hope* and *faith* as vital elements in man's fulfillment, but they are presented as ends in themselves; it is unclear as to what man should hope *for* or have faith *in*.

It seems likely that Faulkner began to write *A Fable* with a number of abstract concepts in mind rather than a special set of human experiences. In his best works, however, the meanings grow out of the concrete situations; in *A Fable*, he tries to impose his meanings on his characters' actions. Consequently, the novel is not completely satisfying on either the realistic or the symbolic level.

Yet, even with these problems, *A Fable* is a powerful reading experience. If it fails to fulfill completely Faulkner's most ambitious intentions, it does present separate characters and scenes that are powerful and memorable, and if all of Faulkner's concepts are not completely clear, his dramatization of man's basic duality is stimulating and provocative.

THE FALL OF THE HOUSE OF USHER

Type of work: Short story
Author: Edgar Allan Poe (1809–1849)
Type of plot: Gothic romance
Time of plot: Nineteenth century
Locale: The House of Usher
First published: 1839

  Principal characters:
  RODERICK USHER, a madman
  MADELINE, his sister
  THE NARRATOR, a visitor

The Story:

As the visitor approached the House of Usher, he was forewarned by the appearance of the old mansion. The fall weather was dull and dreary, the countryside shady and gloomy, and the old house seemed to fit perfectly into the desolate surroundings. The windows looked like vacant eyes staring out over the bleak landscape.

The visitor had come to the House of Usher in response to a written plea from his boyhood friend, Roderick Usher. The letter had told of an illness of body and mind suffered by the last heir in the ancient line of Usher, and although the letter had strangely filled him with dread, the visitor had felt that he must go to his former friend. The Usher family, unlike most, had left only a direct line of descent, and perhaps it was for this reason that the family itself and the house had become one—the House of Usher.

As he approached closer, the house appeared even more formidable to the visitor. The stone was discolored and covered with fungi. The building gave the impression of decay, yet the masonry had not fallen. A barely discernible crack extended in a zigzag line from the roof to the foundation, but otherwise there were no visible breaks in the structure.

The visitor entered the house, gave his things to a servant, and proceeded through several dark passages to the study of the master. There he was stunned at the appearance of his old friend. In Usher's cadaverous face, eyes were liquid and lips pallid. His weblike hair was untrimmed and floated over his brow. All in all, he was a depressing figure. In manner, he was even more morbid. He was afflicted with great sensitivity and strange fear. There were only a few sounds, a few odors, a few foods, and a few textures in clothing that did not fill him with terror. In fact, he was haunted incessantly by unnamed fears.

Even more strangely, he was imbued with the thought that the house itself exerted great influence over his morale and that it had obtained influence over his spirit. Usher's moodiness was heightened by the approaching death of his sister, Lady Madeline. His only living relative, she was wasting away from a strange malady that baffled the doctors. Often the disease revealed its cataleptic nature. The visitor saw her only once, on the night of his arrival. Then she passed through the room without speaking, and her appearance filled him with awe and foreboding.

For several days, the visitor attempted to cheer the sick master of Usher and restore him to health, but it seemed, rather, that the hypochondria suffered by Usher affected his friend. More and more, the morbid surroundings and the ramblings of Usher's sick mind preyed upon his visitor. More and more, Usher held that the house itself had molded his spirit and that of his ancestors. The visitor was helpless to dispel this morbid fear and was in danger of subscribing to it himself, so powerful was the influence of the gloomy old mansion.

One day, Usher informed his friend that Madeline was no more. It was his intention to bury her in one of the vaults under the house for a period of two weeks. The strangeness of her malady, he said, demanded the precaution of not placing her immediately in the exposed family burial plot. The two men took the encoffined body into the burial vault beneath the house and deposited it upon a trestle. Turning back the lid of the coffin, they took one last look at the lady, and the visitor remarked on the similarity of appearance between her and her brother. Then Usher told him that they were twins and that their natures had been singularly alike. The man then closed the lid, screwed it down securely, and ascended to the upper rooms.

A noticeable change now took possession of Usher. He paced the floors with unusual vigor. He became more pallid, while his eyes glowed with even greater wildness. His voice was little more than a quaver, and his words were utterances of extreme fear. He seemed to have a ghastly secret that he could not share. More and more, the visitor felt that Usher's superstitious beliefs about the malignant influence of the house were true. He could not sleep, and his body began to tremble almost as unreasonably as Usher's.

One night, during a severe storm, the visitor heard low and unrecognizable sounds that filled him with terror. Dressing, he had begun to pace the floor of his apartment when he heard a soft knock at his door. Usher entered, carrying a lamp. His manner was hysterical and his eyes those of a madman. When he threw the window open to the storm, they were lifted almost off their feet by the intensity of the wind. Usher seemed to see something horrible in the night, and the visitor picked up the first book that came to hand and tried to calm his friend by reading. The story was that of Ethelred and Sir Launcelot, and as he read, the visitor seemed to hear the echo of a cracking and ripping sound described in the story. Later, he heard a rasping and grating, of what he knew not. Usher sat facing the door, as if in a trance. His head and his body rocked from side to side in a gentle motion. He murmured some sort of gibberish, as if he were not aware of his friend's presence.

At last, his ravings became intelligible. He muttered at first but spoke louder and louder until he reached a scream. Madeline was alive. He had buried Madeline alive. For days, he had heard her feebly trying to lift the coffin lid. Now she had escaped her tomb and was coming in search of him. At that pronouncement, the door of the room swung back and on the threshold stood the shrouded Lady Madeline of Usher. There was blood on her clothing and evidence of superhuman struggle. She ran to her terrified brother, and the two fell to the floor in death.

The visitor fled from the house in terror. He gazed back as he ran and saw the house of horror split asunder in a zigzag manner, down the line of the crack he had seen as he first looked upon the old mansion. There was a loud noise, like the sound of many waters, and the pond at its base received all that was left of the ruined House of Usher.

Critical Evaluation:

A full century and a quarter after his death, Edgar Allan Poe probably remains, both in his life and his work, America's most controversial writer. Numerous biographical and critical studies have not succeeded in rectifying the initially distorted "myth" of Poe, promulgated by his hostile first biographer, as a self-destructive, alcoholic, almost demoniac creature. Even today, after much serious research and analysis, the "true" Poe remains enigmatic and elusive. The same is true of his works. Experts as important and varied as D. H. Lawrence, Henry James, T. S. Eliot, Charles Baudelaire, and Aldous Huxley have differed greatly in assessing their merits, with opinions ranging from extravagant eulogy to total dismissal. And no work of his has excited more diverse opinion or been given more conflicting analyses than his short story "The Fall of the House of Usher."

The problem is that there are many completely different, yet seemingly "valid," interpretations of the tale; contradictory readings that can "explain" all of the story's numerous ambiguities. And yet, obviously, as one prominent Poe critic has lamented, "they cannot all be right." Is there any way of choosing between these views or of synthesizing the best of them into a single one? Perhaps the task is not impossible if two important facts about the author are remembered: he was an adroit, conscious craftsman and critic who worked out his ideas with mathematical precision, and yet he was essentially a lyric poet.

These diverse readings can be divided roughly into three primary types: natural or psychological, supernatural, and symbolic. In the first approach, the analysis has usually focused on the "unreliable" narrator as he chronicles Roderick Usher's descent into madness. As an artist, intellectual, and introvert, Usher has become so lopsided that his prolonged isolation, coupled with the sickness of his sister, has driven him to the edge of madness; along with the narrator, the reader sees him go over the edge. Or perhaps the tale is simply a detective story minus a detective; Usher manipulates the narrator into helping him murder Madeline and then goes insane from the emotional strain. The crucial "fantastic" elements in the story—Madeline's return from the tomb and the collapse of the house into the tarn—are "logically" explained in terms of the narrator's mounting hysteria, the resulting hallucination, and the natural destructiveness of the storm.

According to the second general view, the actions of the characters can be explained only by postulating a supernatural agency: The Usher "curse" is working itself out; the house is possessed and is destroying the occupants; Roderick is a demon drawing vitality from his sister until, as a Nemesis figure, she returns to punish him; Madeline is a vampire claiming her victim.

In the third view, the story is seen as an allegory: Roderick as intellect is suppressing sensuality (Madeline) until it revolts; Madeline is a Mother figure who returns from the grave to punish Usher-Poe for deserting her and for having incest desires; Roderick is the artist who must destroy himself in order to create; the entire story is a symbolic enactment of the Apocalypse according to Poe.

Both as a critic and a writer, Poe was thoroughly aware of the machinery of the Gothic Romance, and "The Fall of the House of Usher" is a veritable catalog of devices from the genre—the haunted mansion, the artistic hero-villain, the twins motif, suggestions of vampirism—and all of the physical paraphernalia—dank crypts, violent electrical storms. It does not follow, however, that because Poe utilizes the conventions of the form, he is also holding himself to the substance of them. It is precisely because he does not commit himself exclusively to either a rational, supernatural, or symbolic reading of the tale that he is able to provoke emotional reactions by indirection and implication that would be impossible if he fixed his meaning more precisely. The technique is essentially that of the lyric poet who uses the power of image, atmosphere, and suggestion to evoke emotions and to produce the desired single effect on the reader—which was Poe's stated aim as a short-story writer.

"I feel that the period will sooner or later arrive," says Roderick Usher, "when I must abandon life and reason together, in some struggle with the grim phantasm, FEAR." Thus, Poe underscores "fear" as the central emotion he wishes to provoke, and the story can best be discussed in terms of how he develops this response.

The tale divides into five distinct parts: first, the description of the house and the background of the narrator's relationship to Usher; second, his meeting with Roderick Usher that ends with his glimpse of Lady Madeline; third, the survey of Usher's art, that is, music, painting, the recitation of the poem "The Haunted Palace," Roderick's theory of "sentience," and the description of the library; fourth, Madeline's "death" and entombment; and fifth, her return from the crypt counterpointed against the narrator's reading of "The

Mad Trist" story which culminates in the death of the twins, the narrator's flight, and the collapse of the house into the tarn. Each of these phases not only furthers the plot line, but also intensifies the emotions provoked in the reader by means of the narrator's progressive hysteria and the growing distortion of the atmosphere.

The narrator is quickly characterized as a skeptic, who attempts to explain everything rationally, but who is, at the same time, quite susceptible to unexplained anxieties and undefined premonitions. His first glimpse of the Usher mansion provokes "a sense of unsufferable gloom." As he describes it, the house resembles a giant face or skull with "eye-like windows" and hairlike "minute fungi" that almost seem to hold the decayed building together, as well as a "barely perceptible fissure" that threatens to rip it apart. He is even more horrified when he looks into the tarn (a small, stagnant lake in front of the house) and sees the house's inverted reflection in the black water. Thus, in the first paragraph of the tale, readers are introduced to three crucial elements: the subjective reactions of the narrator, which begin with this furtive, general uneasiness and will end in complete hysteria; the central image of a huge, dead, decaying object that is, paradoxically, very alive; and the first of many reflections or doubles that reinforce and intensify the atmosphere and implications of the story.

When the narrator meets his old friend Roderick Usher, the other side of the death-life paradox is suggested. Whereas the dead objects seem "alive," the "live" things seem dead. All the peripheral characters—the two servants, the doctor, the "living" Madeline—are shadows. Roderick, with his "cadaverous" complexion, "large, liquid and luminous eyes," "thin and very pallid" lips, and "hair of more than web-like softness," seems more zombie than human. Moreover, his description mirrors that of the house's exterior: his eyes are like the windows; his hair resembles the fungi.

Roderick does, however, have a definable personality. For all of the spectral hints, Poe never abandons the possibility that Roderick's character and fate can be explained naturally. Although Usher's behavior is violent and erratic, perhaps manic-depressive by modern clinical standards, tenuous rationalizations are provided for everything he does.

Nor does Roderick's role as an artist resolve the questions about his character. The extended catalog of his artistic activities may seem digressive in terms of Poe's strict single-effect theory, but it is, in fact, the necessary preparation for the story's harrowing finale. Each of Roderick's artistic ventures conforms to both his realistic personality and the otherworldliness of the situation; they can either signal his descent into psychosis or his ineffectual attempts to understand and withstand the incursion of supernatural forces. His dirges suggest death; his abstract painting of a vaultlike structure previews Madeline's interment. When he recites "The Haunted Palace" poem, he is either metaphorically recounting his own fall into madness, or he is, literally, talking about "haunting." Roderick's statements about the sentience of all vegetable things—that is, the conscious life in all inanimate matter—brings a notion that has previously been latent in the reader's mind to the surface. Finally, Roderick's exotic library, made up almost entirely of books about supernatural journeys, suggests either a perversely narrow and bizarre taste or an attempt to acquire the knowledge needed to defend against demoniac intruders.

Nevertheless, for all of the mounting intensity of suggestion and atmosphere, the actual story does not begin until almost two-thirds of the narrative has been completed. When Roderick announces that Lady Madeline "is no more," the story quickens. It is at this point that the narrator notices the "striking similitude between the brother and sister" and so emphasizes the "twin theme," the most important reflection or double in the tale. As they entomb her, the narrator takes note of the "mockery of a faint blush upon the bosom and the face." Does this suggest a trace of life and implicate Roderick, consciously or unconsciously, in her murder? Or, does it hint at an "undead" specter who, knowing that she will return from the grave, mocks the attempt to inter her?

Nowhere is the value of indirection in the maximizing of suspense more evident than in the last sequence of the story. Having established the literary context of the narrative, Poe then counterpoints the reading of a rather trite medieval romance against Madeline's actual return from the crypt. At the simplest level, "The Mad Trist" tale is a suspense-building device that magnifies the reader's excitement as he awaits Madeline's certain reappearance. Thematically, it suggests a parallel—either straight or ironic, depending on the reader's interpretation—between the knight Ethelred's quest and Madeline's return from the tomb. Reinforced by the violent storm, the narrator's frenzy, and Usher's violence, Madeline's return, her mutually fatal embrace of her brother, the narrator's flight, and the disintegration of the house itself, all fuse into a shattering final effect, which is all that Poe claimed he wanted, and a provocative insight into—what? The collapse of a sick mind? The inevitable self-destruction of the hyperintroverted artistic temperament? The final end of aristocratic inbreeding? Or incest? Or vampirism? Or the end of the world?

Although the meaning of "The Fall of the House of Usher" remains elusive, the experience of the story is powerful, disturbing, and lasting. And that, in the final analysis, is where the greatness lies and why it must be considered one of the finest short stories of its kind ever written.

A FAREWELL TO ARMS

Type of work: Novel
Author: Ernest Hemingway (1899–1961)
Type of plot: Impressionistic realism
Time of plot: World War I
Locale: Northern Italy and Switzerland
First published: 1929

Principal characters:
FREDERIC HENRY, an American serving with an Italian
ambulance unit
CATHERINE BARKLEY, an English nurse

The Story:

Lieutenant Frederic Henry was a young American attached to an Italian ambulance unit on the Italian Front. An offense was soon to begin, and when Henry returned to the Front from leave, he learned from his friend, Lieutenant Rinaldi, that a group of British nurses had arrived in his absence to set up a British hospital unit. Rinaldi introduced him to Nurse Catherine Barkley.

Between ambulance trips to evacuation posts at the Front, Henry called on Miss Barkley. He liked the frank young English girl in a casual sort of way, but he was not in love with her. Before he left for the Front to stand by for an attack, she gave him a St. Anthony medal.

At the Front, as Henry and some Italian ambulance drivers were eating in a dugout, an Austrian projectile exploded over them. Henry, badly wounded in the legs, was taken to a field hospital. Later, he was moved to a hospital in Milan.

Before the doctor was able to see Henry in Milan, the nurse prohibited his drinking wine, but he bribed a porter to bring him a supply which he kept hidden behind his bed. Catherine Barkley came to the hospital, and Henry knew that he was in love with her. The doctors told Henry that he would have to lie in bed six months before they could operate on his knee. Henry insisted on seeing another doctor, who said that the operation could be performed the next day. Meanwhile, Catherine managed to be with Henry constantly.

After his operation, Henry convalesced in Milan with Catherine Barkley as his attendant. Together they dined in out-of-the-way restaurants, and together they rode about the countryside in a carriage. Henry was restless and lonely at nights and Catherine often came to his hospital room.

Summer passed into autumn. Henry's wound had healed, and he was due to take convalescent leave in October. He and Catherine planned to spend the leave together, but he came down with jaundice before he could leave the hospital. The head nurse accused him of bringing on the jaundice by drink, in order to avoid being sent back to the Front. Before he left for the Front, Henry and Catherine stayed together in a hotel room; already she had disclosed to him that she was pregnant.

Henry returned to the Front with orders to load his three ambulances with hospital equipment and go south into the Po valley. Morale was at a low ebb. Rinaldi admired the job that had been done on the knee and observed that Henry acted like a married man. War weariness was all-pervasive. At the Front, the Italians, having learned that German divisions had reinforced the Austrians, began their terrible retreat from Caporetto. Henry drove one of the ambulances loaded with hospital supplies. During the retreat south, the ambulance was held up several times by wagons, guns, and trucks which extended in stalled lines for miles. Henry picked up two straggling Italian sergeants. During the night, the retreat was halted in the rain for hours.

At daybreak, Henry cut out of the long line and drove across country in an attempt to reach Udine by side roads. The ambulance got stuck in a muddy side road. The sergeants decided to leave, but Henry asked them to help dislodge the car from the mud. They refused and ran. Henry shot and wounded one; the other escaped across the fields. An Italian ambulance corpsman with Henry shot the wounded sergeant through the back of the head. Henry and his three comrades struck out on foot for Udine. On a bridge, Henry saw a German staff car with German bicycle troops crossing another bridge over the same stream. Within sight of Udine, one of Henry's group was killed by an Italian sniper. The others hid in a barn until it seemed safe to circle around Udine and join the mainstream of the retreat toward the Tagliamento River.

By that time, the Italian army was nothing but a frantic mob. Soldiers were throwing down their arms and officers were cutting insignia of rank from their sleeves. At the end of a long wooden bridge across the Tagliamento, military carabiniere were seizing all officers, giving them drumhead trials, and executing them by the riverbank. Henry was detained, but in the dark of night he broke free, plunged into the river, and escaped on a log. He crossed the Venetian plain on foot, then jumped aboard a freight train and rode to Milan, where he went to the hospital in which he had been a patient. There he learned that the English nurses had gone to Stresa.

During the retreat from Caporetto, Henry had made his farewell to arms. He borrowed civilian clothes from an American friend in Milan and went by train to Stresa, where he met Catherine, who was on leave. The bartender of the hotel in which Henry was staying warned Henry that authorities were planning to arrest him for desertion the next morning; he offered his boat by means of which Henry and Catherine could escape to Switzerland. Henry rowed all night. By morning, his hands were so raw that he could barely stand to touch the oars. Over his protests, Catherine took a turn at the rowing. They reached Switzerland safely and were arrested. Henry told the police that he was a sportsman who enjoyed rowing and that he had come to Switzerland for the winter sports. The valid passports and the ample funds that Henry and Catherine possessed saved them from serious trouble with the authorities.

During the rest of the fall and winter, the couple stayed at an inn outside Montreux. They discussed marriage, but Catherine would not be married while she was pregnant. They hiked, read, and talked about what they would do together after the war.

When the time for Catherine's confinement approached, she and Henry went to Lausanne to be near a hospital. They planned to return to Montreux in the spring. At the hospital, Catherine's pains caused the doctor to use an anaesthetic on her. After hours of suffering, she delivered a dead baby. The nurse sent Henry out to get something to eat. When he went back to the hospital, he learned that Catherine had had a hemorrhage. He went into the room and stayed with her until she died. There was nothing he could do, no one he could talk to, no place he could go. Catherine was dead. He left the hospital and walked back to his hotel in the dark. It was raining.

Critical Evaluation:

Ernest Hemingway once referred to *A Farewell to Arms* as his *Romeo and Juliet*. Without insisting on a qualitative comparison, several parallels are obvious. Both works are about "star-crossed" lovers; both show erotic flirtations that rapidly develop into serious, intense, mature love affairs; and both describe the romances against a backdrop of social and political turmoil. Whether *A Farewell to Arms* finally qualifies as tragic is a matter of personal opinion, but it certainly represents, for Hemingway, an attempt to broaden his concerns from the aimless tragicomic problems of the expatriates in *The Sun Also Rises* (1926) to the fundamental question of life's meaning in the face of human mortality.

Frederic Henry begins the affair as a routine wartime seduction, "a game, like bridge, in which you said things instead of playing cards." He feels mildly guilty, especially after learning about Catherine's vulnerability because of the loss of her lover in combat, but he still foresees no complications from the temporary arrangement. It is not until he is wounded and sent to her hospital in Milan that their affair deepens into love—and from that point on, they struggle to free themselves in order to realize it. Yet they are constantly thwarted, first by the impersonal bureaucracy of the military effort, then by the physical separation imposed by the war itself, and, finally, by the biological "accident" that kills Catherine at the point where their "separate peace" at last seems possible.

As Henry's love for Catherine grows, his disillusionment with the war also increases. From the beginning of the book, Henry views the military efforts with ironic detachment, but there is no suggestion that, prior to his meeting with her, he has had any deep reservations about his involvement. Hemingway's attitude toward war was always an ambiguous one. He questioned the rationales for fighting them and the slogans offered in their defense. Like Henry, he felt that "abstract words such as glory, honor, courage, or hallow were obscene." For the individual, however, war could be the necessary test. Facing imminent death in combat, one either demonstrated "grace under pressure" and did the "one right thing" or one did not; one either emerged from the experience as a whole person with self-knowledge and control, or one came out of it lost and broken.

There is little heroism in this war as Henry describes it. The hero's disengagement from the fighting is made most vivid in the extended "retreat from Caporetto," generally considered one of the great sequences in modern fiction. The retreat begins in an orderly, disciplined, military manner. Yet as it progresses, authority breaks down, emotions of self-preservation supersede loyalties, and the neat military procession gradually turns into a panicking mob. Henry is caught up in the momentum and carried along with the group in spite of his attempts to keep personal control and fidelity to the small band of survivors he travels with. Upon reaching the Tagliamento River, Henry is seized, along with all other identifiable officers, and held for execution. After he escapes by leaping into the river—an act of ritual purification as well as physical survival—he feels that his trial has freed him from any and all further loyalty to the Allied cause.

Henry then rejoins Catherine, and they complete the escape together. In Switzerland, they seem lucky and free at last. Up in the mountains, they hike, ski, make love, prepare for the baby, and plan for their postwar life together. Yet even in their most idyllic times, there are ominous hints; they worry about the baby; Catherine jokes about her narrow hips; she becomes frightened by a dream of herself "dead in the rain."

Throughout the novel, Hemingway associates the plains and rain with death, disease, and sorrow; the mountains and the snow with life, health, and happiness. Catherine and Frederic are safe and happy in the mountains, but it is impossible to remain there indefinitely. Eventually everyone must return to the plains. When Catherine and Henry descend to the city, it is, in fact, raining, and she does, in fact, die.

Like that of Romeo and Juliet, the love between Catherine and Henry is not destroyed by any moral defect in their own characters. Henry muses that Catherine's fate is the price paid for the good nights in Milan, but such a price is absurdly excessive. Nor, strictly speaking, is the war responsible for their fate, any more than the Montague-Capulet feud directly provokes the deaths of Shakespeare's lovers. Yet the war and the feud provide the backdrop of violence and the accumulation of pressures that coerce the lovers into actions which contribute to their doom. Yet, in the final analysis, both couples are defeated by bad luck—the illness that prevents the friar from delivering Juliet's note to Romeo, the accident of Catherine's anatomy that prevents normal childbearing. Thus, both couples are "star-crossed." But if a "purpose" can be vaguely ascertained in Shakespeare's version—the feud is ended by the tragedy—there is no metaphysical justification for Catherine's death; it is, in her own words, "a dirty trick"—and nothing more.

Hemingway does not insist that the old religious meanings are completely invalid but only that they do not work for his people. Henry would like to visit with the priest in his mountain village, but he cannot bring himself to do it. His friend Rinaldi, a combat surgeon, proclaims atheism, hedonism, and work as the only available meanings. Count Greffi, an old billiard player Henry meets in Switzerland, offers good taste, cynicism, and the fact of a long, pleasant life. Catherine and Henry have each other: "You are my religion," she tells him.

All of these things fail in the end. Religion is only for others, patriotism is a sham, hedonism becomes boring, culture is a temporary distraction, work finally fails (the operation on Catherine was "successful"), even love cannot last (Catherine dies; they both know, although they will not admit it, that the memory of it will fade).

All that remains is a stoic acceptance of the above facts with dignity and without bitterness. Life, like war, is absurd. Henry survives because he is lucky; Catherine dies because she is unlucky. There is no guarantee that the luck ever balances out and, since everyone ultimately dies, it probably does not matter. What does matter is the courage, dignity, and style with which one accepts these facts as a basis for life, and, more important, in the face of death.

THE FATHERS

Type of work: Novel
Author: Allen Tate (1899–1979)
Type of plot: Social history
Time of plot: 1860–1861
Locale: Northern Virginia and Georgetown
First published: 1938

Principal characters:

LACY GORE BUCHAN, the narrator
MAJOR LEWIS BUCHAN, his father
SEMMES BUCHAN, his older brother, killed by George
  Posey
SUSAN BUCHAN POSEY, his sister
GEORGE POSEY, his brother-in-law
JANE POSEY, George's sister, who is loved by Lacy and
  Semmes
YELLOW JIM, George's mulatto half brother

Allen Tate had the misfortune to have *The Fathers* published two years after *Gone with the Wind* appeared, with the result that his novel soon became a literary derelict bobbing in the backwash of Margaret Mitchell's overwhelming popular success. Consequently, the reappearance of Tate's book in a slightly revised version twenty-two years later was an event of considerable importance. *The Fathers*, as *Gone with the Wind* does not, provides an occasion for defining the idea of the South and for critical reflection on the moral significance Tate was able to extract from his social scene and his historical perspective. That the novel failed to evoke any such response is shown by the reviews written at the time.

Reading these reviews today is an illuminating experience, as much for what they do not say as for what they do. The critics were, on the whole, sympathetic toward the book and generous in their comments, but one takes away the impression that many had not read it carefully and almost none understood the writer's intention. Many readers saw it only as a moving story of one family's tragic collapse during the Civil War; certainly this reading testifies to the richness of the narrative if to nothing else. Others thought that Tate was dramatizing within a family unit the fatal clash of two social orders that the traditional society of the South symbolized by Major Buchan and the industrial society of the North represented by George Posey, the Major's son-in-law. This conflict was viewed in all its dramatic tensions and implications, but with a feeling on the part of the reviewers that Tate had failed to prove the superiority of the Buchans' ancestral code over George Posey's antitraditional conduct. It is possible to read *The Fathers* in this way, just as one can read much of Faulkner in a similar fashion, but to do so is to miss the point, so to speak, of a novel remarkable for its realistic detail, thematic extensions of symbolic reference, moral intensity, and passionate, historical sense of life.

Briefly, *The Fathers* presents a philosophical view of society and history within a framework of particular events. It is only natural that these events should center upon the Civil War, for to the Southern writer concerned with the life or culture of his region, the war is the image of violence dividing its past and present. It is no longer enough to know what that conflict did; it is also necessary to know what it meant. For this purpose, the Civil War provides a vast controlling image that gives meaning to the facts of the regional experience, not only to the structure of Southern society but also to the code of morality on which it was based.

Before *The Fathers* appeared, Tate had already defined his position on the South in a series of essays written between 1930 and 1936. In one of these, "Religion and the Old South," he outlined his theory of history in terms of the Long View and the Short View. Within the perspective of the latter, all history reduces to a variety and confusion of images out of which it is possible for readers to make choices in reconstructing the scene or the period. The opposed view sees history as idea or concept, not as an account of the particular lives of particular men in a contemporaneous setting that often bewildered them, but as a record of events without accident, contingency, or personal involvement and thus the worldview, the destroyer of tradition.

Tate's own choice between these two processes of historical vision and thinking is as apparent in his fiction as in his poetry. The reviewers who found no real meaning in his novel were looking at history as an abstract concept of principles and causes. *The Fathers* incorporates the Short View.

The novel is spacious in outline, as any work must be which attempts to contain within its limits the picture of a whole society, and beautifully selective in attention to the detail with which people and places are described, habits of speech and manners are recorded, and the impressions made by events upon the mind of the narrator are carefully noted. Tate achieves his organizational effect, the configuration of theme and structure, by his skillful management of a special point of view. The person telling the story is Lacy Buchan, who as an old man is looking back on events that had happened almost a half century before. As a story retrieved in memory, the novel moves simultaneously on two levels: one, the plane of action conveying with all immediacy the impact of events upon the consciousness of a young boy whose reactions to experience are direct and sensuous; the other, the plane of reflection on which the man, now old, looks back on those happenings and contemplates meanings unperceived at the time of his boyhood. The ease with which Tate moves from past to present and back, setting up a relevant interplay between some event and its significance in retrospect, all the while causing the narrative to expand, its values to join and grow into one another, becomes one of the major triumphs of the novel. What is presented is a deep concern with historical processes and moral issues, but it is all done simply, without resort to the self-conscious or the portentous in association or image. The older Lacy reflects that only in memory and symbol can knowledge of the past be preserved, never in the feelings of the time.

Through all of Lacy Buchan's reflections runs the question of evil, but the problems of sin, responsibility, and guilt remain shadowy and unresolved. He wonders why life cannot change without entangling many lives; why the inno- cent, for example, lose their innocence and become violent or evil, thus causing change. He reflects that just as man needs to recognize the innate aspect of evil in human nature, there is also need to face that same evil, symbolized by darkness and imaged by man alone.

The image at the center of *The Fathers* is the family, the social unit that, with all its widespread connections of kinship, was the foundation of Southern society. The story tells how the Buchan family of Fairfax County, Virginia, is weakened and disrupted by the fierce energies of George Posey, the son- in-law for whom all life—because he cannot recognize, or submit to, the authority that tradition imposes—becomes impulse and motion. In later years, Lacy always thinks of him as a horseman galloping over an abyss, a man of courage and generosity and charm, but doomed because his reckless and irresponsible deeds menaced himself as well as family unity and social order.

Lacy reflects that the Poseys possessed more refinement than the Buchans but were less civilized. This difference is emphasized at the beginning of the novel when Major Buchan, at the time of his wife's funeral, plays the role of the gracious host and not the bereaved husband; he is merely upholding the accepted code of good manners. In much the same way, he leaves his place in his wife's funeral procession to take the hand of Mrs. Buchan's black maid and draw her, immediately behind the coffin, into the line of mourners. George Posey, on the other hand, orders his horse saddled and rides away, unable to face the idea of death. Another trait which he displays is a heartless disregard for others, as when he sells his mulatto half brother in order to buy a blood mare, an act that involves the Buchans and Poseys in a family catas- trophe even more devastating than the disunion caused by the Civil War. Before the end of the novel, he has destroyed the Buchans' agrarian economy, killed his brother-in-law Semmes, driven his wife mad, brought about his sister's ruin, and caused his father-in-law's death.

It is important to note that George Posey is neither a villain by nature nor a symbol of Northern capitalism assaulting Southern tradition. He stands for that element in Southern life which was wild and undisciplined from the beginning, just as Semmes Buchan's weakness and John Langdon's violence were a part of the tradition as well. In Tate's view, apparently, the old order was already corrupted from within before the Civil War destroyed it from without. (This is Faulkner's belief as well.) Whether that way of life truly satisfied the needs of the men who created it is a matter of relative unimportance. What is important is the fact that the traditional order established sanctions and defined virtues and obligations by which, for a time, men could assume the social and moral responsibilities of their humanity; it set up a concept of truth that made the human effort seem worthwhile. Major Buchan recognizes these sanctions and obligations and acts accordingly, but George Posey does not; therefore, he corrupts or destroys all who come in contact with him.

This is the meaning of the episode in which Lacy Buchan, semidelirious with fever, imagines that he and his dead grandfather are sitting on a pile of fence rails while the old man retells the myth of Jason and Medea. The scene is poetically conceived and morally instructive. Jason's fate, the old man says, was to secure the Golden Fleece or attempt some impossible feat, at the same time becoming involved with the humanity of others whom, in the end, he betrayed not through his intention but through his nature. The old man says that George Posey never really intends to commit evil; his flaw is the lack of will to do good. Thus the only expectancy possible for him is loneliness and the grave.

The Fathers is a novel in which the private life of the family and the public life of action converge upon a decisive moment in history, the outbreak of the Civil War. Its importance as fiction is its power to illuminate, through realistic detail and symbolic extension, the meaning of the past and the shape of the future.

FICCIONES

Type of work: Short stories
Author: Jorge Luis Borges (1899–   )
First published: 1944

Since 1961, when he shared the Prix Formentor with Samuel Beckett, Jorge Luis Borges' English and American reputations have been steadily growing, as witnessed in 1962 by the publication in the United States of two books: *Ficciones*, a translation of short stories that Borges published first in one volume in Spanish in 1945; and *Labyrinths*, a translation of selections from five volumes, including *Ficciones*, of his short stories, parables, and essays.

Early criticism of his work fell back feebly on comparisons with Kafka's, consequently involving the critics unnecessarily in the old so-called problem. As Eliseo Vivas has remarked, however, the Kafka problem arises from the confused demands made by his readers and not from any unusual difficulty inherent in Kafka's works. The same might very well be said of Borges, whose works on a superficial level, so much resemble Kafka's: their apparent difficulty disappears as soon as one can simplify himself to the point of appreciating the significance of mere plot. Borges once claimed, indeed, that the basic devices of all fantastic literature were only four in number: the work within a work, the intrusion of dream upon reality, the voyage in time, and the double. These devices become for Borges, as for Kafka, both technique and theme, form and content.

The most important technique-theme in *Ficciones* is the device of the work within a work, which Borges uses, although with considerable variation, in more than half of the seventeen stories in the volume. Such stories as "The Approach to Al-Mu'tasim," "Pierre Menard, Author of *Don Quixote*," and "An Examination of the Work of Herbert Quain," for example, actually take the form of literary criticisms or appreciations. In all three stories, references to well-known writers in footnotes and text supply a counterpoint of presumptive reality to the basic fantasy of the rest of the text, a fantasy that in turn is directed, by the accumulation of circumstantial detail, at proving not only the existence but also the literary worth of unwritten works by nonexistent authors. Borges believes, in fact, that no writer can be original, that writing is essentially the manipulation of archetypal counters, that literary achievement must lie more in the outlining of possible directions for these manipulations than in the actual production of a work. The nonexistent works therefore described within his own works attain—at the very least from the mere circumstantiality of Borges' sustained allusions to them—a level of reality, a solidity worthy perhaps only of masterpieces. This solidity reflects, inevitably, upon Borges' own works, giving them the fanciful strength and substance of so many Baroque monuments. There is no need in these works for things as ephemeral as characters.

An inheritor of Hispanic tradition, Borges is quite at home with the Baroque, and it has been demonstrated that his style is in effect a modern version of the Latinized Baroque *stil coupé*. He writes, that is, with a kind of jagged preciousness that the translators of *Ficciones* have often been at perhaps unwarranted pains to make smooth, a preciousness that, closely examined, reveals links not only with the Spanish of Quevedo but also with the English of Browne, Gibbon, Poe, and Chesterton. Nor does Borges deny these influences, holding as he does that there is no such thing as originality and that his use of obvious sources can only make those sources themselves, in the light of the new context he gives them, richer.

Particularly devoted to Chesterton, Borges has given the creator of Father Brown a role in Hispanic literary history that far surpasses any he might have played hitherto in English, by basing works like "The Garden of Forking Paths," "The Form of the Sword," "Theme of the Traitor and Hero," "Death and the Compass," and "The Sect of the Phoenix," for example, upon the particular conventions so skillfully employed in Chesterton's detective stories. All five of these fictions center around the solution of a problem: in "The Garden of the Forking Paths," perhaps the most striking of the group, one finds the solution to a puzzle in military history also supplying the solution to an inverted puzzle in crime, while "The Form of the Sword" and "Theme of the Traitor and Hero" provide intricate problems of curiously reversed identity. "Death and the Compass" stands as almost a parody of the classic detective form. "The Sect of the Phoenix" establishes an atmosphere of conspiracy that is dissipated, suddenly and surprisingly, only in the last sentence.

The image of the labyrinth, that archetype of all puzzles and problems, occurs again and again in *Ficciones*, as if it represented in some ultimate form the ideal of Borges' art. In "Tlön, Uqbar, Orbis Tertius," "The Babylon Lottery," and "The Library of Babel," one finds Borges constructing whole societies upon the basis of labyrinthine principles, erecting complete social designs out of chance, choice, trial, and error. If these societies seem to represent Borges' vision of man in relation to himself, however, stories like "Funes, the Memorious," "The Secret Miracle," and "The South" give readers Borges' vision of man in relation to the only ultimate gauge he has of the universe outside himself—time. The heroes of all three stories triumph over time, achieving an immortality by the supreme exercise of those faculties that would mark them out ordinarily as being mortally human: memory and the imagination. In his short lifetime, Funes lives the imaginative life of thousands of other men, while Hladik and Dahlmann, the heroes of "The Secret Miracle" and "The South," bestow upon themselves the power both to postpone fatality and to welcome it in the end, as a part of an aesthetic order they themselves have created. They *are* the human mind.

It is memory and imagination, as well, that make Jorge Borges a great writer. He has, as someone has remarked, read all the books, with everything he read feeding the Minotaur of his mind. Like Vladimir Nabokov, with whom his attitudes, theories, and practices have a great deal in common, he was compelled to wait a long time for some sort of adequate literary recognition, perhaps because he, too, is so unabashedly an intellectual.

THE FIELD OF VISION

Type of work: Novel
Author: Wright Morris (1910–   )
Type of plot: Impressionistic realism
Time of plot: Christmas, 1956
Locale: Mexico City, Mexico, and Lone Tree, Nebraska
First published: 1956

> *Principal characters:*
> GORDON BOYD, a middle-aged writer
> WALTER J. MCKEE, Boyd's boyhood friend and a cattle
> breeder
> LOIS MCKEE, Walter's wife, once in love with Boyd
> TOM SCANLON, Lois' ninety-year-old father
> DR. LEOPOLD LEHMANN, an Austrian amateur
> psychologist and Boyd's friend
> GORDON MCKEE, McKee's grandson
> PAULA KAHLER, a male transvestite, Lehmann's patient

In *The Territory Ahead*, a critical book, Wright Morris discusses a particularly American dilemma: the writer's nostalgic immersion to the point of
immolation in an overflowing reservoir of raw material. In most of the nine
novels before *The Field of Vision*, Morris processed fragments of his own
material, searching for a conception that would enable him to achieve the
kind of control and coherence he saw in F. Scott Fitzgerald's *The Great Gatsby*.

In a deliberate act of rediscovery, he took a fresh look at recognizable
American artifacts, archetypal American experiences—the young romantic's
nomadic wandering away from and nostalgic return to the home place—and
presented some of the most authentic Americana of the 1940's. Like Faulkner,
he explored his own special province, the Nebraska plains where the fertile
prairie grass fades into the arid regions. His vision was seriocomic, and his
style made imaginative use of Midwestern speech patterns. *The Field of Vision*
is Morris' first major attempt to get the fragments of his raw material into
focus, to compress into expressive metaphors his conception of American
Land, Dream, and Character.

If both the author and the artist hero of his early novels have become
immersed in a nostalgia, unsettled by nausea, and thus need some distance
from Lone Tree, Nebraska, what better vantage point than the Mexico City
bull ring? An external experience has no significance, neither in life nor in
literature, Morris believes, until by a deliberate act of consciousness it becomes
an internal event. Morris' arrangement of this event is skillfully crafted.

Quite by chance, Gordon Boyd, a failed bohemian writer, encounters
Walter J. McKee, his boyhood friend, in the lobby of a hotel in Mexico City.

To shock them, he takes the folks from back home to the bullfight. Seating his characters at the ring, Morris confines the present action to the duration of the bullfight; but in memory, forty years of the past are conjured up. He enters the minds of five of the characters: Boyd; McKee; his wife, Lois; Tom Scanlon, Lois' father; and Dr. Lehmann, Boyd's analyst. Using the third-person point of view, Morris focuses certain external events through each of these characters one after the other in a sequence that he repeats five times. Some common focal point, seen from contrasting angles, provides transition from one character's mind to another's. Morris does not go into the minds of two other characters: Paula Kahler, who is traveling with Boyd and Lehmann; and little Gordon, McKee's grandson. Each of the personae provides Morris with a different perspective from which to view the American character.

In the excitement of the accidental reunion and of the bullfight, the characters are charged with the past and the immediate present. The phases of the bullfight and the presence of the others stimulate each character to recall an event in the past in such a way that it is possible for him to experience a shock of recognition in the present. The bullfight ritual, with its artistic, spiritual, and brutally physical dimensions, and the technique of shifting points of view provide Morris with a controlling framework that enables him to shuttle back and forth, weaving a tapestry of collective consciousness in which time present and time past form a design. Thus, the reader witnesses a double ceremony. As the torero and his bull move toward the moment of truth, each character comes closer to the horns of his private dilemma. To make the moment of truth possible, the torero must risk being gored; the human mind confronting itself runs a similar risk.

There is also a contrast between the action in the ring and the events enacted in the theater of the mind. The events of the past are simple and cliché; Morris manipulates the clichés of mass culture and language as a witty and humorous function of style working toward insight. McKee, Lois, and Boyd share (though each in the isolation of his own mind) the incident on the front porch in Lone Tree when Boyd kissed Lois, McKee's fiancée, and swept her off her feet. Neither Gordon Boyd nor McKee knows that Lois got up that night from her cot on the back porch and, sleepwalking, unlatched the screen to admit her dream lover, Boyd; in the midst of her dream, the cot collapsed. The hero's failure to appear in the flesh persuaded Lois to marry McKee, but she named her firstborn Gordon, who named his own son Gordon.

In another act of audacity, Boyd attempted to "walk on water" at the sand pit outside town; until Boyd went down, McKee believed the hero would succeed. He witnessed a similar bungled act of audacity when Boyd ran onto the field to get a foul ball autographed by Ty Cobb; Boyd dropped the ball but ripped a pocket from Cobb's pants. In the present, parallel audacious gestures are made: for example, a Mexican boy climbs into the bullfight arena to make the archetypal amateur's confrontation with the bull that has just gored the professional toreador.

In their childhood, Boyd was the hero and McKee was his major witness. He responded to the promise of greatness in Boyd. As opposites, Boyd and McKee are attracted to each other. They illustrate a dichotomy in the American character, two dimensions of the American dream: the man of action and the dreamer, the artist and the businessman, the power of fiction and the authority of fact. At Lone Tree, the land itself, fertile to the east and sterile to the west, exhibits these contrasts.

Through the hero-witness relationship, Morris depicts an element in the American character that frustrates the attempt to realize the dream in a land of promise: the audacity that bewitches rather than transforms both the doer and his observer. To accomplish his limited goals, McKee, like Sancho Panza, must believe that Boyd (Don Quixote) is capable of success somewhere in the realm of possibilities. In *Ceremony in Lone Tree*, however, McKee will escape captivity in the hero-witness relationship, though to no great purpose.

In his youthful enthusiasm, McKee extended this relationship to include Lois, whose own response added a sexual dimension. When Boyd failed to follow up on the kiss, Lois (Dulcinea) saw that his foolishness would not end in wisdom. Concluding that most males are hopeless, her father included, she began to suppress her emotions. Ironically, Boyd now regards her as a typical example of the frigid Midwestern housewife. In Mexico, she almost bolts from her situation with a tourist, but he also is a man of mere gestures.

In the American experience, gesture is not often enough followed by the consummate act. Audacious Columbus, too, walked on water, but reached the wrong shore; Americans have domesticated a continent but are homeless. The audacious frontier hero survives in men like Boyd: the boy who once attempted the impossible has become the middle-aged clown who becalms a raging bull by squirting Pepsi Cola into its mouth. With that gesture, Boyd touches bottom. Aware that each of the adults has failed in his own way, ways McKee's grandson may imitate, Boyd makes a desperate attempt to pass the hero's charge on to his namesake, little Gordon. Flinging the boy's phony coonskin cap into the bullring where the beast lies slain by a professional, Boyd lets the boy down into the ring to retrieve his cap and to take the risk that may transform the amateur into the disciplined man.

Observing the hero-witness relationship between Tom Scanlon and little Gordon, Boyd gets perspective on himself. The old man tells the boy tales of a bygone era of audacity. A fossilized victim of the past, Scanlon is reminded by the gored torero's cry for water of the pioneer trek his father led across the arid plains. His father, Tim, lying on a bed in a back room of the Lone Tree Hotel, so bemused Tom with stories of the great age of adventure that Tom now believes, in his senility, that it was he who went through the inferno of the desert and witnessed the cannibalism of the survivors upon those who perished. The witness has become the hero and both are defunct. Trapped himself in Ty Cobb's pocket, which he still carries as a talisman, Boyd knows that the spirit represented by such emblems of the past, including Gordon's coonskin cap, must be repeatedly resurrected in acts of transformation.

A different reflection of each character is offered by every other in the crazy house of mirrors that only Morris, with the complicity of the reader, can focus. As the link between the reader and the characters, Dr. Lehmann, an amateur student of life, is able to view at some distance the triangular Boyd-McKee-Lois relationship. McKee and Lois can see the similarity of the bullring to the porch, the sandpit, the ballpark, and the stage where Boyd's play, depicting those symbolic moments of the past, was performed: but while reality imposes correspondences upon the mind, keeping it moving over the surface of things, man must will the achievement of insights and concepts. Thus, Lehmann seeks connections. He interprets Boyd's dilemma in terms of Paula Kahler's. Having tasted the ashes of success, Boyd tries to make a success of failure—a typical American enterprise. Unable to cope with human nature, Paula changed her own, from male to female, from a crippling compassion for people to a safer sympathy for insects and animals. Lehmann discerns the way a self-ventriloquism deceives us in our realization of the dummy in ourselves.

Morris demonstrates Lucifer's perception: "The mind is its own place, and in itself/ Can make a Heav'n of Hell, a Hell of Heav'n." Thus, at the bullring, McKee and Lois are able to see only what they brought with them from Nebraska. The human dilemma is posed in this way: just as no two people see the same bullfight, despite its element of artistic order, no two characters share the same field of vision. Though they may arrive at similar moments of insight, people communicate in terms of clichés, while the real drama, when it occurs, is an almost unbroken soliloquy. To each character, all the others appear to be mad Hamlets.

These missed connections are at once pathetic, because they foster lives of quiet desperation, and comic, because most of the characters are fools who persist in their folly to a dead end. Morris merely juxtaposes the elements that make perception possible, and while the characters themselves usually miss the connection, the reader is in a position to make it. Morris' art is resolved in the response of the reader, but it is as inaccessible to the inattentive reader as the moment of perception is to the purblind character. Lehmann, however, knows that the accidents and coincidences of a life essentially without design can be patterned by a conscious act of imagination; and he sees the pathos of the human inability to realize those rare moments of truth, those epiphanies. He sees, as does Boyd less clearly, that in such structured experiences man transcends impermanence (as in the bullfight ritual) and enters, if only momentarily, the realm of permanence.

THE FIELDS

Type of work: Novel
Author: Conrad Richter (1890–1968)
Type of plot: Regional romance
Time of plot: Early nineteenth century
Locale: Northwest Territory, later Ohio
First published: 1946

Principal characters:

SAYWARD WHEELER, a woods woman
PORTIUS, her husband
GENNY SCURRAH, her sister
WYITT LUCKETT, her brother
RESOLVE,
GUERDON,
KINZIE,
SULIE,
HULDAH,
SOOTH,
LIBBY,
DEZIA, and
MERCY, her children
JAKE TENCH, a white runner
MISTRESS BARTRAM, a schoolteacher
JUDAH MACWHIRTER, a neighbor

The Story:

Portius Wheeler's family had written from Boston to the trader at the post near Sayward's cabin to inquire about the woodsy girl Portius was living with. Sayward told the trader to write back that she was a woods girl, all right, and she could not read or write, that she had married Portius legally even if the ceremony had taken place while Portius was drunk, but that she was not keeping him from returning to the Bay State because she had not known that his family had written Portius to come home. She said Portius could have gone back if he had had a mind to, but since he wanted to remain she was staying with him.

Genny helped Sayward when the Wheelers' first boy was born. At that time, Portius had gone on business to the territory seat. He was away for days. Knowing he was no woodsman, Sayward remembered stories of Indian atrocities along the trace. When he finally came home, he would not look at his son, but in his powerful voice told Sayward that the Chillicothe convention had ratified the constitution. Now they lived in Ohio State. He warmed so to his subject of politics and government in the wilderness that he scared the baby, who yelled until Portius had to look at his son. It was a question of who was the more scared, father or child. Sayward thought Portius should get used to children because she intended to fill the cabin with them.

The handiest meeting place the neighbors had when a circuit rider came around was a sawmill, open to the sky and hemmed in by trees, but Sayward felt that the Lord knew it was His place when folks gathered there. Genny felt His presence too as she sang the hymns, with her beautiful voice reaching out farther than any other. Sayward could not believe it was Genny singing; that was the first time Genny had sung since her husband, Louie Scurrah, went off to the English lakes with her sister Achsa. Portius, a disbeliever, refused to go to the meeting, but Sayward took her son with her and had him christened Resolve.

Sayward had three boys and a girl by the time their township was formed. On Old Christmas, Portius asked everybody in the settlement to come to his cabin to make out a taxing list. That was what Sayward liked, a lot of people in the house, particularly in winter when a body was not apt to see neighbors often. They made a party of it. By the time the men worked out the taxing list, everybody realized that their township was a reality.

Sayward named her first girl for her lost sister Sulie. Sayward's Sulie was the liveliest and brightest child she had ever seen, but she never forgot the tokens she had had before Sulie was born. Resolve thought he had seen a strange little black boy, all dressed in white, peeking in the window. The day before Sulie was born, Resolve saw his first black man, a new hired man in the settlement. He could not stop talking about Caesar's color. When her blonde baby girl came, Sayward could only sigh with relief. Sulie was burned to death when she was about three years old. Resolve, seeing her charred body in the coffin, pulled at his mother's skirts to show her that it was not their Sulie lying there but the black boy who had peeked in the window.

The farmers complained so much about night dogs and other wild animals getting their stock that they banded together for one big hunt. Men, closing in from four sides, chased the animals down into a low place called the Sinks. There they fired on the beasts until nothing moved. Wyitt, with a new rifle much like Louie's, joined in the hunt. Later on, he realized that there would be no more game left in the woods, and he decided to follow his father and head west. He hated not saying good-bye to Sayward, but he was afraid she might keep him on the farm if he did.

The winter Sayward had five children living and one dead followed a cold summer when the crops could not grow. No one had enough meal to last. Portius took Resolve with him into Kentucky when a number of the men from the settlement went there to get meal on credit. The men were gone so long that Sayward had no food left for the children. Weak because she had fed the young ones instead of herself, she went out and shot a turkey, though she could barely hold the gun. Resolve did not come back with Portius. He had broken his leg and had to stay in Kentucky.

The next time the circuit rider came around, the sawmill had been deserted and sprouts had grown up to stand between the meeting folk and the preacher. Sayward gave a piece of land, near the burying ground where Jary and Sulie lay, for a meeting house. When the men built it, she could see it from her doorstep.

The day Resolve came home, he went with his father to Judah Mac-Whirter's. Jude had been wolf-bitten by a slobbering night dog that he caught in his cattle pen. Three weeks later, his fits had begun. Between times he was rational and wanted Portius to help him make a will. The night Resolve was there, Jude had to be tied to his bed because his fits were coming faster. Resolve never forgot Jude's dying after begging someone to kill him before he hurt anyone he loved.

Portius and the children wanted Sayward to sell her place and move to the new town upriver, but she could not leave her fields. Instead, she persuaded Portius to start a school, primarily because Resolve wanted so much to learn that he deliberately broke his leg again to have time to read. Portius kept school for a year until his law practice in Tateville grew so large that he spent a good deal of time there. About that time, Sayward decided that seven living children were enough and she was not sleeping with Portius.

The children heard that Portius was seeing the new lady schoolteacher who had taken over his school, but they could not tell Sayward. When Mistress Bartram hurriedly married Jake Tench, Sayward insisted upon going to the wedding because she felt sorry for a girl who had to get married and who was obviously not marrying her child's father. Genny told Sayward that folks were saying Portius was the father.

She worked out her feeling of shame without saying anything to Portius. When Sayward's baby Mercy was small, Jake had a celebration for his keelboat, the first built in the township. Sayward, hating to face Jake's wife with the baby that filled the gap between Dezia and Mercy, could not stay home. She had heard that Jake's wife seldom left her cabin, but she was surprised not to find her at Jake's party.

Riding down the river on the keelboat, Sayward realized that a real town was springing up along the river. Now her children no longer deviled her about moving to Tateville, and Portius, after making a fine speech in honor of Jake's industry, was solicitous of her comfort on the boat ride.

Critical Evaluation:

The second novel in Conrad Richter's trilogy, *The Fields* expresses how progress is made in the Ohio pioneer settlement in the cultivation of farmland that had been dense forest; in the maturing of Sayward, emotionally and mentally; and in the growth of the Wheeler family and the settlement near their cabin. The making of a settlement and town from wilderness is Richter's recurrent theme, and he has researched pioneer life thoroughly so that his descriptions are accurate. Sayward's remembrances of the forest land and her comparisons of it to the new settlement add a vivid and personal touch to the historical account of the town's evolution.

Character development is as important in this novel as in *The Trees*. The personalities of Sayward's children are described primarily through Sayward's inner thoughts as she compares each one to Portius, to one of her brothers or sisters, or to herself. She begins to see how family and community circumstances together shape the characters of children

In the community Portius represents education, sharp wit, and political awareness. He is the humorist and the proponent of progress In his own sly way, Portius ridicules the church, the people's ignorance, the sawmill, and sometimes even his own wife. His views add a new perspective to the events surrounding community expansion.

The marriage relationship between Sayward and Portius is based on mutual respect for the other's skills and intelligence. Each has an independent streak: Sayward reveals hers in stubbornness when her principles are threatened; Portius displays his physically by leaving home occasionally. He also manifests his independence in an episode of adultery, which results in the strongest conflict Sayward has had in her marriage. Without benefit of counsel, Sayward works out an understanding of Portius and of her own feelings that preserves her marriage and self-respect. This is one example of the many situations in this pioneer family that require strength, humility, and acceptance of circumstances. These situations help give the novel its warmth, realism, and vitality.

FIESTA IN NOVEMBER

Type of work: Novel
Author: Eduardo Mallea (1903–   )
Type of plot: Social criticism
Time of plot: Mid-1930's
Locale: Buenos Aires, Argentina
First published: 1938

> *Principal characters:*
> EUGENIA RAGUE, a society leader born in England
> GEORGE RAGUE, her wealthy husband
> MARTA, their bored daughter
> BRENDA, their younger daughter
> SEÑOR RAÍCES, an Argentine financier
> LINTAS, an artist
> AN UNNAMED POET, a political victim

The Story:

The book opens with the underlying plot in italics. A young unnamed poet was writing a poem on love on a scrap of paper. The time was eleven o'clock at night. Suddenly a violent, protracted rapping sounded on the door. As he went to answer the pounding, he took with him a piece of bread. Opening the door, he was confronted by the leader of a patrol of armed men in dirty uniforms. The leader stated that they had come for him.

The main story begins at eight o'clock on a warm springlike evening in November. Eugenia Rague had come down the stairs for a final inspection of the setting for her fiesta. English by birth but Argentine by adoption, she dominated her aristocratic surroundings as Cardinal Wolsey, whose portrait adorned her salon, had dominated his. There passed through her head the memory of the lack of respect shown her by Lord Burglay and Lady Gower during her visit to London. Yet now she had to concentrate on her guests about to arrive.

Others in the house were reacting differently to the hot evening. In another room, her husband, George, was trying to concentrate on acquiring culture through a phonograph record, but he kept thinking of how he could persuade Señor Raíces, after dinner, to sign a profitable stock purchase. Should delays result, he might lose everything. Intruding into these thoughts came those of his treadmill life, his wife's incessant pressure, and his own desire to relax and perhaps to dream. The arrival of the butler with the afternoon mail interrupted and infuriated him. Then it was time for him to prepare for the party. Marta, the older daughter, lay naked on her bed, wondering why she had spurned a highborn lover.

At nine, the lights were turned on, the orchestra tuned up, and the first guests arrived, the elite of Argentine society. Their conversation was frivolous: the latest scandalous behavior of some politician, the proposal to exterminate the unimportant lower class. The reception, with its empty conversation and the broken phrases from the more serious exchange of ideas revealed the waste of these people's lives.

Meanwhile, Marta made her entrance, prepared for a boring and perhaps detestable evening among unexciting people she had fully comprehended several years earlier. Several young men brought her drinks, and her father welcomed her assistance in his social duties. When Raíces appeared, Rague gave the signal to proceed to the dining room.

In perplexity, the poet questioned the armed men, asking what they could possibly want with him.

At the reception the painter, Lintas, rushed in, late as usual, but in time for the chilled consommé. As he drank it, he became attracted to Marta. Her sudden smile showed her reaction to him, but a pseudophilosophic discussion prevented any words. Lintas noticed her distraught expression when her mother mentioned the fact that Brenda was not there. Only Marta knew of the appeal from Brenda to come immediately to give her assistance. While dismissing her curiosity about the identity of the man across the table from her, she tried to imagine what help her sister could need.

(At this point, Mallea devotes considerable space to the inner thoughts of his main characters, passages shot through by allusions to Ruskin, Pater, Hardy, and others.)

After the meal, dancing began in the garden. Lintas found himself dancing with Marta as though they were enemies. Later, more friendly, they discussed some of his paintings. Then she remembered Brenda and without a word of explanation she left.

Meanwhile, the leader of the patrol began to lose patience. His men glared at the young man who was wasting their time. They prepared to march their prisoner away.

Marta's flight took her to a shabby house and into a stench-filled room where she found Brenda recovering from an abortion. Brenda needed her sister's help to conceal her situation from her parents and to supply additional money for the operation, which had cost more than the previous one. Marta left the house and headed for home.

At the fiesta, no one had noticed Marta's absence. Rague and Raíces were discussing stock, and Raíces was trying to explain why he did not want to rush into the transaction. Eugenia Rague had maneuvered Lintas into visiting her art gallery to pass judgment on some new purchases. Amid a group of interested guests, he pronounced them fakes. Lintas knew that he had created a conflict because Eugenia would have preferred a comfortable lie to the unpleasant truth. Marta, returning as Lintas was leaving the fiesta, offered to take him home.

Through the door, the poet saw a fighting cock belonging to a neighbor. He tried to imagine what was going to happen to him. He was suddenly frightened.

In the car, Marta felt impelled to talk. She protested against the sterility of the civilized universe and the difficulty people find in trying to communicate. When they reached his home, he invited her in. The screams of a neighboring woman started him on the story of his life. Poverty had engendered in him a hatred for people like her. He told her of a gang of ruffians who had beaten up an old bookseller because he was foreign and was selling "subversive books." It was his widow who had screamed. This atrocity, making him feel for the first time involved in mankind, had increased his loathing for the governing class that permitted such crimes to go unpunished. They continued their discussion during a walk at dawn through the woods. As she left, they realized that neither had convinced the other of their beliefs.

The prisoner asked for permission to get his hat. What he really wanted was time.

Marta hated to go home. Brenda would be in a troubled sleep; her father would be snoring, and her mother would be sneaking down to the kitchen for a snack. Marta knew that in other parts of the world vigils more painful than hers were going on. She now realized that her trouble was a hatred of herself because of an unsatisfied yearning for something. Suddenly, the thought came to her that she, who had always been served, ought to serve others. She paused at a church, but it offered no promise of relief. She stopped next at a coffee shop. Though sensing herself out of place among the customers, eventually she began to feel a comprehension of them and a oneness with them all. She went home. In her room, she took stock of herself. She felt a resemblance to her country with its variety and abundance. Before she fell asleep, she decided that a true change from the horrors of life must come from the tormented people themselves.

The final pages complete the subplot whose parts have been inserted. The poet's cousin had already been arrested and shot, and his family had been denied permission to bury him. The poet joined the patrol, protesting, but the only reply was rifle butts in his face. When they reached a deserted house and an open space, he tried to run. The patrol fired after him. He fell to the ground and blood soaked the piece of bread he dropped. One of the men turned over the body to make sure the poet was dead. The patrol, leaving him lying on the ground, walked away, loathing one another.

Critical Evaluation:

In a graceful style, rich with vivid, precise images, neither pretentious nor overly decorated, Eduardo Mallea tells the moving story of two people struggling to communicate with each other while lost in the midst of a shallow, violent world. Although the painter Lintas and Marta Rague are the two most sympathetic characters in this short novel, both are held back by their pride from the honesty and openness that would liberate them and enable them to achieve an authentic relationship. They are the only individuals in *Fiesta en noviembre* (*Fiesta in November*, 1942) who even care about moral concerns, except for the poet, unnamed and doomed, whose brief story alternates like an almost subliminal theme with the main body of the story, illuminating and commenting upon it.

The two fiestas, one social, the other of blood, are linked thematically by Lintas' account to Marta of the fatal beating of a Jewish bookdealer in Buenos Aires by a group of Argentine Fascists. An undercurrent of violence also lies behind the conversation and actions of the guests in the house of Marta's mother, Eugenia Rague. The fragments of the condemned poet's story are in italics, suggesting that in spite of its shorter length, this narrative is the more important of the two.

The opening arrest of the poet could be that of Joseph K in *The Trial*. There are more than casual similarities between the work of Kafka and this novel. The contrast between the scene with the poet and the luxurious setting of Eugenia Rague's home is shocking. Eugenia's is a vain, acquisitive character. Her only passions are for her collection of objects from the past and for power. "Power is power," she thinks, "and damn all the rest." She detests sentiment and everything connected with it, so it is not surprising that she is completely alienated from her two daughters. Her husband George, despite his wealth, feels no fulfillment or peace.

A sultry, perfumed lushness pervades the novel, the heat of summer and passion—and of violence. Objects seem to have lives of their own. The opening picture of the dinner party is a devastating glimpse of empty lives and futile social ritual. The characters are struggling with an inner tyranny, a psychic trap more terrible than the cruelty of society, if they only realized it. "All art," thinks Lintas, "is a great and terrible demand for response." Indeed, this unusual novel demands a response from the reader.

Lintas appears on the scene like a breath of fresh air in the stale world of the Rague mansion. Mr. and Mrs. Rague and their guests would be lost without their ceremonies, but Lintas deliberately walks over their carefully plotted maneuvers. Marta and Lintas recognize each other from the beginning as two of a kind—exiles in a world they detest. Marta, at age twenty-seven, still is filled with a passionate curiosity, still is eager to experience life. Human beings, she reflects, only seek their own private ends, only hope to satisfy their appetites. Marta hates the pretense of society, the constant betrayal of her own nature. A dream—unknown but tragic—burns in the depths of her spirit, stifled by daily compromises.

Mirrors and windows and polished surfaces constantly reflect faces, oblique views of people, staring eyes. The reflected images seem more real than many of the actual figures and faces. Mallea seems to be asking, what *is* the reality and what is false?

Brenda Rague, Marta's sister, is having an abortion while her mother's fiesta is in progress. This revelation causes Marta to think in a new way about their lives, and her meeting with Lintas continues to stimulate her chain of thoughts. Lintas himself was made suddenly aware by the episode of the brutal beating of the bookseller. Are there social castes, they ask, or only moral castes? Where is the moral answer? The word *serve* appears to Marta as she walks down the empty city streets before dawn. What does it mean? Could it be the answer for her? She realizes that each individual must, in his own way, be heroic, walk alone, bravely, honestly, into his fate.

The inner dramas of the novel are not resolved. They move from climax to climax, cumulatively, charged with great lyric tension. Seemingly insignificant individual lives are transformed by Mallea into the very essence of the human condition. *Fiesta in November* is an extraordinary novel by a great author. It is a book that haunts the reader, as Mallea intended, for the questions that it raises are not easily answered.

Mallea's view of life is religious and moral. His works often suggest the European Existentialists, although most of his writing anticipated their novels and dramas. He was descended from an old Creole family and attended an English school in Bahía Blanca, where the majority of his classmates were the sons of immigrants. (He has never lost sight of the fact that Argentina is a melting pot.) At the age of thirteen, he moved to Buenos Aires with his family. The city was a revelation for the withdrawn adolescent. His first published stories won immediate attention, and he eventually became an acclaimed public figure. In the 1930's and 1940's, he was director of some of the most influential literary publications in Latin America. He was a steadfast opponent of the Perón regime. After the revolution that overthrew the Perón dictatorship, he was named ambassador to UNESCO in Paris. Subsequently, he returned to private life to devote himself exclusively to writing. He has lectured in Europe and the United States.

Fiesta in November and other novels and stories such as *All Green Shall Perish* and *Chaves* have established Mallea as one of Latin America's greatest writers and one of the outstanding prose stylists and moral spokesmen in the world. His works are great art because they are born out of an intense experience of life; they convey vividly this experience to the reader.

THE FINANCIER

Type of work: Novel
Author: Theodore Dreiser (1871–1945)
Type of plot: Naturalism
Time of plot: About 1850 to 1874
Locale: Philadelphia
First published: 1912

Principal characters:
  FRANK A. COWPERWOOD, the financier
  LILLIAN SEMPLE COWPERWOOD, his wife
  EDWARD BUTLER, a contractor and politician
  AILEEN BUTLER, his daughter
  HENRY COWPERWOOD, Frank's father

The Story:

From his very early years, Frank Cowperwood was interested in only one thing—making money. When he was still in his teens, he made his first successful business transaction. While passing by an auction sale, he successfully bid for a lot of Java coffee, which he sold to a grocer at a profit of one hundred percent. His family marveled at Frank's ability and his wealthy uncle, Seneca Davis, encouraged him to go into business as soon as possible.

Through several well-paying positions and shrewd speculation, Frank acquired enough money to open his own brokerage house. Within a short time, he was immensely successful, one of the most enterprising young financiers in Philadelphia.

One day he met Lillian Semple, the wife of a business associate. About a year later, her husband died, and Frank married the widow. By that time, he had accumulated a large fortune, and he was familiar with local and state politicians, among them Edward Butler, who had risen from being a mere collector of garbage to a leading position in local politics. Through Butler, Frank met many other influential people as his business and popularity increased.

Frank and Lillian had several children, but the youngsters did not particularly interest him. Rather, his sole interest was his business. His father, Henry Cowperwood, finally became president of the bank in which he was employed. Both Cowperwoods built expensive houses and furnished them luxuriously. Frank bought fine paintings and other rare objects of art.

His home life was not satisfactory. Lillian was older, more passive than

---

he, and her beauty had almost disappeared. By contrast, Edward Butler's daughter Aileen was tremendously appealing. She was young, beautiful, and high-spirited. Frank fell in love with her, and in spite of her strong religious training, she became his mistress. He rented a house where they met and furnished it with the paintings and statues he had bought.

Though Frank had become one of the financial powers in Philadelphia, he had to plan and scheme continually in order to thwart more powerful monopolists. He managed to acquire large sums from the state treasury through local politicians. The city treasurer, Stener, proved amenable in many ways, and he and Frank became involved in many shady transactions. Frank bought shares in railroads and local streetcar properties.

After the great Chicago fire, some of Frank's investments were in a perilous state. He went to friends and associates and urged them to stand together in order to avoid losses. So widespread were the effects of the fire, however, that the manipulations of the city politicians were certain to be discovered on the eve of an election. Something had to be done to satisfy indignant reform groups who would demand action when they discovered what had occurred.

In the meantime, someone had sent an anonymous note to Edward Butler, telling him that Frank and Aileen were living together. When Frank went to Butler, the contractor refused to help him, and Frank knew that somehow he had discovered his relationship with Aileen. Butler, who had become his enemy, urged the other politicians to make Frank a scapegoat for their dishonest dealings.

As a result, Frank and Stener, the city treasurer, were indicted on charges of embezzlement and grand larceny. Ruined financially, Frank pleaded not guilty, but the jury convicted both him and Stener. He appealed and posted bail to avoid jail. The appeal was denied, although the judges were not united in their decision. As soon as the appeal had been denied, the sheriff was supposed to take Frank to jail until he should be sentenced; but the sheriff was bribed, and Frank had a few more days of freedom. His property was sold to pay his debts. His father resigned his position at the bank.

Frank and Aileen had given up the house where they formerly met. Their meetings now took place at a house in another part of town. Determined to put an end to the affair, Butler and Pinkerton detectives entered the house and confronted the couple. Butler tried various schemes to make Aileen leave Philadelphia, but all failed after Aileen learned that her father had hired detectives to trail her.

Frank was sentenced to four years and nine months in the penitentiary. Aileen remained faithful to him. When Lillian went to visit him, Frank asked her for a divorce. She refused.

After Edward Butler died, Frank's friends managed to get him a parole. At the end of thirteen months in jail, he was freed in March, 1873. Through

Wingate, a friend and business associate, he had succeeded in rebuilding his business. He had a bachelor apartment where Aileen visited him. Though he was ostensibly still living with his wife, all of the town had long ago known of his relationship with Aileen.

In September, 1873, the panic came. Frank, who had bought stocks cheaply, made a fortune. Several months later, he went with Aileen to Chicago, where he planned to reestablish himself. Lillian got a divorce but remained friendly with the Cowperwood family. She lived luxuriously; Frank, to buy his own freedom, had provided handsomely for her and the children.

Critical Evaluation:

Two symbolic passages concerning sea predators, one early in the novel and one at the conclusion, provide important clues to understanding Theodore Dreiser's theme in *The Financier*. As a boy, Frank Cowperwood stoically observes an unequal contest in a large fish tank between a lobster and a squid. The lobster, certain of victory, bides his time and slowly devours the defenseless squid. In the context of Dreiser's social metaphor, the strong destroy the weak, whether with sudden terrible force or gradually, relentlessly, like the lobster sporting with his prey. The final symbolic passage, crudely added as an epilogue to the novel, treats the *Mycteroperca Bonaci* (or black grouper) which, chameleonlike, changes its colors to avoid danger or to strike out at a weaker adversary. From Dreiser's point of view, the *Mycteroperca Bonaci* represents an element of "subtlety, chicanery, trickery" that is also part of the human condition. The fish is no more responsible, in a Godless universe, for its trickery than man—the social animal—is morally responsible for using deception as a means of power. Cowperwood's rise to wealth and influence, an ascent that is determined by the laws of Social Darwinism, will be continued by the author in *The Titan* (1914), as will the story of his socially conditioned fall from power. In *The Financier*, Dreiser details, with a Naturalistic concern for inductive evidence, the causes both for Cowperwood's success and his eventual failure, just as a scientist might describe the behavior of a fish in an aquarium.

However, unlike a true scientist who observes phenomena objectively and dispassionately, Dreiser views the activities of his hero from the bias of his socialistic philosophy. From that bias Cowperwood, the ruthless financier, ought to serve as an object lesson on the corruption of the capitalistic system. Yet Dreiser, in spite of the Marxist Determinism at the center of his economic philosophy, obviously admires Cowperwood as a man, if not as a social creature. He sympathizes with his hero's single-minded ambition to succeed; his contempt for intellectual inferiors; his violent sexual passions; his stubborn, egoistical will. Although Dreiser's early view of Cowperwood may have been satirical, he treats him ultimately as a Nietzschean superman, advanced beyond the conventional feelings of petty morality, beyond remorse, pity, or loyalty—

except for Aileen Butler, whose iron will and courage matches his own. Yet, even in Cowperwood's love for Aileen, there is a measure of selfishness instead of romantic idealism: quite simply, she satisfies his needs. Unlike many of the protagonists of Dreiser's other novels—Carrie Meeber, Jennie Gerhardt, Clyde Griffiths, Eugene Witla—Frank Cowperwood is a strong, magnetic, self-assured character, in the author's symbolism more the predatory lobster than the pitiful squid. Because Dreiser's attitude toward Cowperwood is ambivalent—he admires the man but is contemptuous of his capitalistic endeavors—the message of the novel is correspondingly ambiguous. How can one despise an economic system that gives its chief rewards to those like Cowperwood, who are the most adept competitors in the survival-of-the-fittest social ethic?

Other weaknesses besides its ambiguous theme will trouble readers of *The Financier*. Never a master of prose style, Dreiser often describes Lillian as "lymphatic" when he probably means "phlegmatic." Also, he describes "sensuously lymphatic" women who "dwelt" in a brothel. When Alfred Semple, Lillian's first husband, comes to an "untimely" death, Dreiser writes that the man's passing is "dramatic in a dull way." Shortly before Frank marries Lillian, his world is "of roseate hue." Later, Dreiser mentions that in Frank's North Front Street house some "pleasing appropriately colored rugs covered the floor." Much later in the novel, Aileen writes a letter to her father that Dreiser describes as a "defiant screed," although the word *screed* seems hardly correct. These and many other lapses in diction and rhetoric damage the novel. Worse still, Dreiser breaks into the narrative, often with ludicrous effect, at times to converse with the reader and at other times, to expound his philosophy of life. Yet in the major scenes, Dreiser—as he commonly succeeds in his important fiction—sustains a sense of realism with powerful, honest emotion. The author is at his best in analyzing Cowperwood's tangled love affair with Aileen. The trial scene is masterly; so are the prison scenes. Without sentimentality, Dreiser touches life. In spite of its ambiguous theme and its many stylistic weaknesses, *The Financier* is a novel of massive integrity that still has force to move the reader's emotions.

THE FLIES

Type of work: Novel
Author: Mariano Azuela (1873–1952)
Type of plot: Social criticism
Time of plot: April, 1915
Locale: Mexico
First published: 1918

> *Principal characters:*
> MARTA REYES-TÉLLEZ, a refugee
> MATILDE, her eldest daughter
> ROSITA, her younger daughter
> RUBÉN, her son
> QUIÑONES, a schoolmate of Rubén
> DONACIANO RIOS, a prosecuting attorney
> RODOLFO BOCANEGRA, a politician
> NEFTALÍ SANCHO PEREDO DE LA GARZA, a poet
> DON SINFOROSO, a former colonel of the Federal Army
> SEÑOR RUBALCABA, a schoolmaster
> GENERAL MALACARA
> MORALITOS, a government clerk
> THE DOCTOR
> THE DORADOS, troops of Villa's bodyguard
> FRANCISCO "PANCHO" VILLA, General of the Northern
> Division of the Revolutionary Army

During the Mexican Revolution, Mariano Azuela served in the medical corps of Francisco "Pancho" Villa's army. In this peripheral position, he had an opportunity to observe the effects of the war upon every type of person. After Villa's defeat in 1915, Dr. Azuela escaped to El Paso, where he recorded recollections of the Revolution in poignant but frequently humorous sketches and novels. *Los de abajo* (*The Underdogs*) is considered his masterpiece. *Los moscas* (*The Flies*, 1956), a much shorter work written two years after *The Underdogs*, shows less biting criticism, less dismal skepticism, and more good-natured understanding of the author's troubled people.

Dr. Azuela joined Villa's forces with the hope of replacing the octogenarian dictator, Don Porfirio Diaz, with the young idealist, Francisco Madero, whom he believed to be the savior of Mexico. Madero, however, proved to be a tragic disappointment. His mismanagement, poor judgment, and ineffectual personality could not establish the looked-for democratic government based upon brotherly love and mutual trust. Those principles that had attracted Dr. Azuela to the Revolution were trampled asunder fifteen months after Madero, backed by Villa and others, entered Mexico City. Then General Victoriano

Huerta seized the government, and President Madero was shot. The next five years were filled with bloody battles in which the various leaders of the Revolution, including Villa, fought for supremacy. Villa reached his peak of power in the winter of 1914, when he and his generals occupied Mexico City and outraged the citizens with their lurid conduct. A powerful and well-regarded general, Alvero Obregon, disillusioned with Villa, pronounced Governor Carranza of Coahuila "First Chief of the Revolution" and drove Villa's forces out of the city. Villa retreated with his army to Irapuato and then to Sonora, where he was completely defeated the following summer.

Dr. Azuela's story begins in a railway station in Mexico City as multitudes of panic-stricken citizens who had thrown their lot with Villa are now trying to escape the city before Carranza's ferocious Indian troops arrive to take over the government. The station is full of puffing trains ready to carry the fugitives to safety. Among them, Marta Reyes-Téllez, the widow of a government employee of long standing, is trying to find her children and secure a place for herself in one of the coaches. She frantically seeks help from Señor Rios and General Malacara, whom she believes to be influential. The missing children are finally discovered in a hospital car where their mother and would-be friends join them.

The Doctor in charge regards the pompous family sourly but is unable to keep them out. Throughout the night and following day, the Doctor remains the one sensible and calm person among the cowards and opportunists who are revealed to the reader in brief descriptive passages and in their conversations. It is easy to imagine that the Doctor of *The Flies* is Dr. Azuela himself, sketching a remarkable gallery of characters drawn from his personal experience after the fall of Pancho Villa.

The Reyes-Téllez family forms the central focus of the action in *The Flies*, for their presence serves as a unifying element in this episodic work. They are the first people singled out of the crowd in the railway station and the last to act before the story ends. Perhaps, too, they are the most totally repugnant of a mob of unsavory characters, for they alone have not a trace of intelligence or good humor about them. Marta, the mother, has obviously sacrificed her virtue for security among the political butchers and bandits, as Rubén, the ne'er-do-well son, intimates when he calls attention to the resemblance between his sister Rosita and the governor. No wonder, Rubén comments cynically, the governor had been good to the family.

In Irapuato, Rubén chases down an old acquaintance familiar with members of the new government who may be able to secure the family once more. Rubén betrays the fellow into the hands of the police without a second thought the moment betrayal appears to be to his advantage.

Matilde is a silly, shallow girl who reveals her true nature when her pet canary is killed in the confusion of escape; her reaction is an example of adolescent emotional experimentation. She savors her grief by indulging in screams of profound agony of which not even she knew she was capable.

Rosita, sin's seed, follows her mother's example. At a very young age, she is using her body to attract men in high places, hoping to be able to use them to her family's advantage.

The crass materialism of the Reyes-Téllez women surpasses all humanity in the closing pages of the book. They push Rubén off the train as it leaves Irapuato carrying them to safety. The foolish boy is deserted with worthless Villa currency and instructions to find a place for the family in the new regime by using Quiñones, the very friend whom Rubén had betrayed.

Azuela's gallery may contain too many characters to be a completely successful one in so few pages. However, if many individuals are static types, such as the Doctor, Rubén, and his family, others are charming caricatures.

The action proceeds through fourteen short chapters, each complete within itself and containing the revelation of at least one individual. The characters are associated by accident. Panic flings them together and fear keeps them together; but in spite of the seriousness of their life or death situation and their moral degeneracy, Azuela has endowed many of them with delightful eccentricities that produce a comic effect. In some cases, this effect is achieved by the old device of using ironic names and then playing with the meaning. General Malacara (bad-face, or unpleasant-look), for example, is ridiculed by the ironic placing of his name directly after a description of his unfailingly good-natured smile. The humor in this wordplay is not lost in translation to the fortunate reader who understands the Spanish name.

A tribute to Azuela's ability to create a pathetic character is the portrait of Don Sinforoso, the arrogant, boastful former federal colonel. In public, he threatens to kill an impudent young soldier, but when fate brings him face to face with the boy alone, he is caught literally with his pants down and reveals himself as a blustery old coward. His days of glory long behind him, he cuts a foolish figure in his efforts to recapture the power and dash of his youth. His name, Sinforoso, is significant; "sin" meaning "without," and "foroso" sounding enough like the Spanish "fuerzo" meaning "strength" or "power" to suggest the Spanish equivalent of "Mr. Powerless," humorous in view of his boastful, militant surface personality, and ironic when contrasted with his inner nature.

Another character, although a minor one, deserves mention as an example of Azuela's narrative technique through character revelation. Chapter 11 is ostensibly devoted to a council of war, held among Señor Rios, Colonel Sinforoso, the General, and Señor Rubalcaba, the schoolmaster. Señor Rubalcaba's personal thoughts during the council become increasingly more and more important, indicating the impossibility of disinterested group concern. A decision must be made as to whether the crowd should wait for General Villa at Irapuato or run to safety at once to some place farther from the capital. In the midst of exaggerated and heated debate, the schoolmaster absently meditates upon the loss of his love, Aurora, meaning "dawn." Again the name is played upon. It is not so easy to cast off the comfortable habit of a woman's company, he muses, particularly since his potbelly and attacks of gout make the likelihood of replacing her very remote. Here the decision being made, which is said to be of inestimable importance, is actually nothing more than the framework in which the author's real concern, that of satirizing the self-centered interests of the common Mexican during the Revolution, may be realized.

An outstanding comic character is Moralitos (little morals), a bloated, grotesque little monkey who runs about the car, flushed and wide-eyed with excitement, spreading rumors of certain destruction, and stepping on everybody. True to the indication of character suggested in his name, Moralitos is a great moralizer. Early in the book his ironic, ranting protestations of sincerity, honesty, and loyalty to the cause on behalf of the refugees provokes an apology from the Doctor which explains the theme of the novel. Speaking of the crowd, the flies that buzz frantically about the sources of power and wealth in the capital, he admits that they are no worse than they have to be. They are models of virtue when their bodily needs are satisfied; they are not to be blamed if their morality is inspired by their bellies.

The precarious existence of these people is threatened by every rumor. They have played amateur politics through three regimes and are in the process of throwing in with whoever wins control of the government. Their problem is one of timing. They must turn their allegiance at precisely the right moment in order to fall in line for the best position in the new government. They are nervous, insincere people who twitch and fawn before every face on the political horizon, but with the possible exception of the Reyes-Téllez family, they are not evil.

The message of *The Flies* is a bitter one that reflects Azuela's personal disillusionment with the war. The story mirrors a fundamental irony of glorious causes, the great dichotomy between political ideology and social reality. Each man sees the Revolution through eyes of self-interest and acts accordingly. Although the human animal may be unable to rise above his hunger pang, he is not a total loss. The author seems to understand and sympathize with human weakness; he points to faults, but he does not blame.

Azuela's prose style in *The Flies* is journalistic in its direct simplicity. He relates the events in the station, on the train, and in Irapuato as they occur, in plain language suitable to his characters. The choppy, fragmentary dialogue is well suited to suggest the jerky movement of the train and the nervousness of the fugitives. While the author's language is not poetic in general, there is a central metaphor that runs through the work, enriching and unifying it. That image appears as a brief glimpse of a cock with flaming plumage, his head held high, his wings outstretched, perched upon a dunghill. A clear picture of pride and arrogance supported by a "dunghill" of past offenses, this representation in animal form is flashed in the train window to indicate the false pride rampant within the hospital car. Carrying out the image in explaining her family's incredible and unfounded snobbery, Matilde refers to her family's plumes which can cross a bog and never show a spot.

The final chapter presents an abrupt change. The town of Irapuato has been evacuated and the now familiar hospital car of assorted fools has departed. Pancho Villa's official train arrives a moment later, almost exactly twenty-four hours after the story began. He is no longer the man in power. Silence now, not madly cheering throngs, greets him. The sun, says Azuela, died forever with Villa's retreat. The night murmurs that Mexico is saved; but on the horizon, the moon looks down, laughing.

The latest swarm of flies is now buzzing about Carranza. So it goes—a new government, a new swarm.

FOGO MORTO

Type of work: Novel
Author: José Lins do Rêgo (1901–1957)
Type of plot: Regional realism
Time of plot: 1848–1900
Locale: Paraíba, Brazil
First published: 1943

> *Principal characters:*
> JOSÉ AMARO, a crippled, embittered saddlemaker
> SINHA, his wife
> COLONEL JOSÉ PAULINO, owner of Santa Clara plantation
> COLONEL LULA, owner of Santa Fe plantation
> CAPTAIN VICTORINO CARNEIRO DA CUNHA, a humane lawyer
> LIEUTENANT MAURICIO
> SILVINO, a bandit

Fogo morto (dead fires), the tenth novel by José Lins do Rêgo, marks his return to the themes of his original Sugar Cane Cycle, after four weak experiments in other fields. The author, descendant of an aristocratic planter family settled for years in Northeast Brazil, was educated for the law, but friendship with Brazil's great sociologist Gilberto Freyre showed him the rich literary inspiration in Brazil's *ingenhos*, or sugar centers, and turned him to fiction writing. Beginning with the novel *Plantation Boy*, Lins do Rêgo went on with *Daffy Boy*, *Black Boy*, *Richard*, *Old Plantation*, and *The Sugar Refinery*, all dealing with the same characters. In 1943, after four lesser novels based on other themes, came *Fogo morto*, his masterpiece, in which some of the characters from the earlier novels reappear. The novel is marked by improved technique, a greater use of dialogue, less morbidity, and better character portrayal.

Some critics see in Victorino, the penniless, abused lawyer, a Brazilian Don Quixote, sure of what is right, hating bandits, cruel soldiers, and haughty plantation owners alike, and fighting all injustice, regardless of the cost to him. Like the Spanish don, Victorino was an aristocrat, related by blood to many of the important families of the region, but censuring their use of power because of his feeling for the common man. There is also a parallel with Don Quixote in the way Victorino was first ridiculed and then admired.

The main character, the crippled and ugly saddlemaker José Amaro, was a failure who tried to hide his sense of inferiority and cowardice behind a biting tongue and a scornful attitude toward everybody. He insisted that nobody owned him, or, as he expressed it more vividly, that nobody could scream at him. His only friends were the kindly black hunter Leandro, who occasionally left part of his bag at José's door, and white Victorino, sunk so low that even the *moleques*, the black boys, mocked him in the streets, calling after him "Papa Rabo."

José's attitude toward the bandit, Captain António Silvino, arose from the admiration of a coward for a man daring enough to brave the power of the plantation owners. The imagination of the saddlemaker built Silvino into a kind of Robin Hood, siding with the poor against the grasping landlords, especially at the moment when the bandit attacked the town of Pilar and sacked the strongbox of the prefect, Quinca Napoleon. Afterward, he invited the villagers to pillage the house. José was grateful because the bandit came to his defense when he was ordered evicted from the house his father and he had occupied for half a century. However, Silvino's threats of interference stiffened the determination of José's landlord.

Not until the end was José disillusioned and the bandit's self-interest revealed. Attracted by rumors that Colonel Lula still possessed the gold inherited from his father-in-law, Silvino came after it, threatening torture unless the hiding place was revealed. In reality, the wealth was not at the plantation. Lula, vanquished by circumstances and about to abandon his estate for the big city, had sent the money ahead. An attack of convulsions momentarily saved the landowner from torture; the protests of Victorino brought him further respite; but it was the arrival of Colonel Paulino that drove off the bandit. Until he realized Silvino's cruelty, José Amaro made sandals for him and his men, spied on his pursuers for him, and even got food and provisions to him when Lieutenant Mauricio and his soldiers were on his trail.

José's feelings toward the wealthy plantation owners were determined by their attitude toward him. The novelist introduces two of them as representative of the landed gentry of the nineteenth century in northeastern Brazil, men who derived their titles from their social and political positions.

With Colonel José Paulino, whose family had long owned the Santa Clara plantation, José Amaro was continually at odds because, as the wealthy man rode past the saddlemaker's house in his family carriage, he would only nod condescendingly. At the beginning of the novel, when Laurentino, the house painter, paused to talk on a May afternoon, while on his way to help the colonel beautify his manor house for the wedding of his daughter, José from his doorway said angrily that he would never work for a man he hated as much as he hated Colonel Paulino.

His attitude toward the other big sugar planter, Colonel Lula César de Holanda Chacón, supposedly modeled on a cousin of the author's grandfather, was less bitter. He finally agreed to go to the Santa Fe plantation to repair the family carriage, whose history is related in the second part of the novel.

During the Revolution of 1848, Captain Tomás Cabra de Malo arrived with his cattle, his slaves, and his family in Parahyba (or Paraíba). He took possession of the Santa Fe plantation, adjoining Santa Clara, bought additional land from the Indians, and planted cotton. About then, a penniless cousin, Lula, turned up and began courting the plantation owner's daughter.

Having won the captain's permission, Lula took her away on a honeymoon from which they returned with a pretentious carriage, practically useless in that roadless region. The rest of Lula's progress, as told in *Fogo morto*, makes him anything but admirable. At Captain Tomás' death, he fought the widow for control until her death. Then, in complete possession of the plantation and sugar refinery, he revealed his avaricious and cruel nature. José overlooked the past of his landlord, however, because Lula occasionally exchanged a word with him.

José's family is introduced early in the story. When Laurentino stopped to talk, the saddlemaker invited him for supper with his wife and their thirty-year-old daughter. The woman had never married because she insisted that she did not want to, but she nearly drove the old man frantic because she spent her days weeping. Eventually, in his exasperation, he beat her until he dropped unconscious; from that time on, his wife thought only of ways to get herself and her daughter safely away. José had no other children. Lacking a son to carry on at his death, he had no incentive to enlarge his leather business or attract new customers.

Lins do Rêgo continually makes thrifty use of minor episodes, not only to carry forward the story, but to reveal character. For example, while working at Colonel Lula's plantation, José revealed his trait of showing contempt for those he tried to impress; and by his actions, he so roused the enmity of Floripes, the Santa Fe overseer, that from then on he worked against José and hastened his tragedy. It was Floripes' lie, the report that José had promised aid to Victorino's candidate against the politician backed by Lula, that persuaded the landowner that his tenant was ungrateful, and so José was ordered to leave the cabin occupied by his family for many years.

The kindness of the hunter in leaving a rabbit at José's door revealed the old man's nausea at the sight of blood, while the blood started a rumor that José was a werewolf. This rumor was crystallized into belief when he was found unconscious beside the river, where, in reality, he had collapsed trying to warn the bandits of the coming of soldiers.

In telling the story, Lins do Rêgo divides his narrative into three parts, with the second one, "The Santa Fe Plantation," a flashback of half a century, covering the rise to power of Lula.

When Isabel, daughter of Emperor Pedro, freed Brazil's last slaves in 1888, Lula was left without anyone to run the plantation or the refinery, for his slaves were quick to get away from a master who used to beat them until he fell down in convulsions. In contrast, Colonel Paulino's field hands, who had been treated kindly, stayed on even after the liberation, and so he was able to lend his cousin by marriage enough laborers to help with the work. Still, the hearth fires of Santa Fe burned lower, and the plantation was doomed.

Neighbors brought suits against Lula that were settled only because Colonel Paulino intervened; and Lula could find no one willing to marry his daughter.

José's fortunes also declined. Disillusioned about the outlaws, he found the soldiers of Lieutenant Mauricio even more cruel. Coming to protect the villagers, Lieutenant Mauricio beat blind Torcuato as a spy, arrested José, and mistreated Victorino, who had won the admiration of his fellow citizens by facing the domineering officer with a writ of habeas corpus in order to free the saddlemaker.

Freedom was meaningless now to old José. His family had left him, and he had no friends. He committed suicide in his empty house, where his friend, Pajarito, found his body. Two cycles had ended. When Pajarito looked out the window, smoke was billowing from the chimneys of the Santa Clara sugar refinery, but he saw no activity at Santa Fe—where the fires were dead.

THE FOLKS

Type of work: Novel
Author: Ruth Suckow (1892-1960)
Type of plot: Regional realism
Time of plot: From 1910, approximately, to the early 1930's
Locale: Belmond, Iowa; Greenwich Village; and California
First published: 1934

> *Principal characters:*
> FRED FERGUSON, a banker in Belmond, and
> ANNIE FERGUSON, his wife, "the folks"
> CARL FERGUSON, their oldest child, a teacher
> MARGARET FERGUSON (Margot), their older daughter
> DOROTHY FERGUSON (Dot), their younger daughter
> BENJAMIN FERGUSON (Bunny), their youngest child
> LILLIAN WHITE, Carl's wife, born and bred in Belmond
> BRUCE WILLIAMS, Margaret's lover, a New York
>   businessman
> JESSE WOODWARD, Dorothy's husband and a bridge coach
> CHARLOTTE BUKOWSKA, Benjamin's wife
> ELLA and
> BEN GARDNER, Fred's sister and brother-in-law

Ruth Suckow is a regional writer by the double achievement of her Iowa stories and her critical thinking about regionalism itself. The two come together in *The Folks* to transcend literally and metaphorically the borders of one state and present a detailed record of one family which in its aspects of saga and allegory stands for all families. The novel presents with honesty and realism the virtues and vices of small-town America.

Suckow's neat scheme of father, mother, two girls, and two boys gives her the six parts of the novel, arranged in alternating long and short lengths. Each of the short parts is lyrical in tone, presenting a static but attractive picture of small-town and family life in the first and third parts, and a more somber view of American life in the fifth part, which, however, achieves a minor resolution of faith in the country as a whole in its conclusion. The alternating longer sections deal with the specific problems of the provincial boy, the provincial girl, and finally of the transformation of the Fergusons into "the folks." The novel explores the fullest meaning of that term by facing up to the difficulties of small-town existence in early twentieth century America, and it makes its point by using the four children to show four different problems, leaving Fred and Annie Ferguson to re-achieve small-town tranquility if they can at the close of the book. That Suckow convinces readers that they can and do achieve it is the triumph of the novel.

The one problem in the structure of the novel stems from the careful balancing of old and young "folks" and of Belmond and the U.S.A. The first and last parts show how Annie and Fred begin as Mr. and Mrs. Ferguson and end as "the folks." To this end, one follows not their lives but those of the four children in the four intervening parts. Each story fades away at the conclusion of the section as the child breaks away from home. None of the parts has as satisfactory an ending as that of "the folks," but each of the four stories contains ideas that could be developed into a full novel for each child. Such a technical problem is impossible to solve within the limits even of a long novel like *The Folks* unless one is prepared, as in the case of William Faulkner, to add a note about their careers as an epilogue. This device seems unnecessary here, for the merit of Suckow's handling of the family is that it is realistic. Every family has its rise and fall; the happiest are those growing clans that do have their own "home place" and "folks" to return to when they must

Part 1, "The Old Folks," opens early in the morning of a fine September day, the shimmering Indian summer atmosphere that fascinated Henry James and Katherine Mansfield and seemed to hold true among the best families anywhere in the calm that preceded World War I. Suckow, like Henry James and Katherine Mansfield, can sense that trouble is brewing. The Presbyterian Fergusons must support their dwindling church and their ailing "old folks." The interaction of family and town is most obvious in part 3, "The Loveliest Time of the Year," a description of Dorothy's marriage to Jesse, the incredibly handsome boy from out of town. The lyricism of the first part is again present, but a note of stern realism is now creeping in: the young folks begin well but end badly.

The deceptively small concerns of daily living and the restrained style, concealing as they do at first glance the human implications of the accumulated events, are probably the reasons for dismissing *The Folks* as a regional Midwest novel. In fact, its setting is America from Greenwich Village to Los Angeles, and its cast is composed of Americans from many walks of life, from several different racial stocks, and over a spectrum of generations from Western pioneer to newly arrived immigrant.

The historical spectrum is analyzed in the story of Carl; the geographical and social scope is covered in the stories of Dorothy and Margaret; the racial picture is completed by Benjamin, nicknamed Bunny.

In part 5, "The Youngest," Fred and Annie Ferguson have seen all their children leave home and are now awaiting the return of Benjamin from college for the summer vacation. Aunt Ella and Uncle Ben Gardner, the salt of the earth or the provincial of the provincials, have retired from the Ferguson farm and live miserably in town. Benjamin arrives with Charlotte Bukowska, whose parents were European peasants, just as Ben and Ella are peasants in the United States. Charlotte, however, is also the new immigrant, as the

Fergusons were years before.

The overwhelming problem of small-town life in America may be summarized from this novel as the decision whether to stay in the town of one's birth and eventually turn into "the old folks," or to go out into the world. In *The Folks*, Carl and Margaret make their departures from the Ferguson nest but eventually return to make their peace with Belmond. Their crises come early in their lives. The crisis in the life of "the folks" comes in late middle age, after the departure of Benjamin with Charlotte.

In a passionate scene with Fred, Annie reproaches him for all the failures concealed beneath the Belmond façade of "the fortunate Fergusons"; none of the four children has married modestly and settled quietly in Belmond, as Fred and Annie did. What is wrong with the children, with their parents? Then Annie realizes she has always been a stranger in Belmond, in the Ferguson clan, and when Fred announces his retirement from the bank, the two decide to leave Belmond for a trip West in order to escape the harsh Iowa winter.

The time is the 1930's, or possibly the late 1920's, when hard times are beginning to be felt: the small-town aristocracy has collapsed in decadence; the young have fled to the city or gone West. When the Fergusons leave the bank, the church, the home place, and Belmond, it looks as if the town will collapse. During their journey, however, all the Fergusons find is discontent and restlessness in Annie's sister Louie, in old Mrs. Spencer, once a neighbor in Belmond, and most of all in "the greater Iowa winter picnic," a gathering of exiles that causes "the folks" to reject the false and superficial pleasures of California and return to Belmond. The news from home is bad; the rival bank has failed and its president, Belmond's first citizen, has fled town. Worse is at hand when they get back. This is where they belong, and they have their home to come back to. With the reunion of Belmond and the Fergusons, and the reconciliation of Fred and Annie to each other, they have become "the old folks," and their house the "home place" of the Fergusons. The story of the Belmond Fergusons ends in the tranquility with which it began.

For both Carl and Margaret, this resolution is particularly necessary, though each uses it in different ways. Part 2, "The Good Son," covers about fifteen years in the life of Carl, the oldest of the younger Fergusons; he and Margaret, the older daughter, are treated at much fuller length than are Dorothy and Ben, the younger children, and the experiences of Carl and Margaret together summarize the life of the young provincial.

Part 4, "The Other Girl," is the longest in the novel and probably the autobiographical core of the whole book. Margaret is the provincial girl in full revolt, as is generally the situation of the girl on whom the small-town mores bear severely. It is a familiar situation, from *Anne of Green Gables* to *The Rainbow*, from Olive Schreiner to Doris Lessing, and Margaret eventually fights herself free of "the folks." The second chapter of part 4, titled "Basement Apartment," describes Margaret's life and acquaintances in Greenwich Village, an animated and witty portrait of un-Belmond-like characters who, it turns out, are all in flight from a Belmond of their own. When Margaret's own rebellion ends, the way is clear for a younger generation to occupy easily the positions she fought for.

The merits of both staying in Belmond and leaving it are thus shown to be complementary, as they were in Suckow's life. The chief virtue of *The Folks* is that it shows how this struggle to achieve harmony takes place in the old as well as the young, and that both are right.

A FOOL'S ERRAND

Type of work: Novel
Author: Albion W. Tourgée (1838–1905)
Type of plot: Polemical realism
Time of plot: 1865–1877
Locale: Rockford County in a Southern state
First published: 1879

Principal characters:
> COMFORT SERVOSSE (THE FOOL), a former Yankee soldier
> METTA SERVOSSE, his wife
> LILY SERVOSSE, their only child
> NATHANIEL HYMAN, the county attorney
> JERRY HUNT, an old black church leader
> MELVILLE GURNEY, a former Klan member and the suitor of Lily

The Story:

In 1861, Comfort Servosse went off to the Civil War as a volunteer. This, in retrospect, was his first action as an idealistic "fool." At age twenty-seven, he gave up a thriving Michigan law practice and a comfortable home. He considered it his duty to help fight against the wrong of slavery.

When the war ended, he was a colonel. He came back home to his wife Metta and daughter Lily. His war exertions had worn him out. Seeking a genial climate and not wanting to rebuild his law practice, he decided to move to the South and begin life afresh. Now that slavery was destroyed, the South was sure to flourish and become the pleasantest part of the country.

He bought the Warrington estate, a place Servosse had admired while stationed nearby. It was dilapidated, and the six hundred acres of land were worn out; but the price was cheap.

Located six miles from Verdenton, a small town, Warrington proved both a challenge and reward. The Servosses made extensive repairs. They found the countryside charming. The people seemed congenial. For Thanksgiving dinner, they invited six Northern girls who taught at a new blacks' school. The country judge, Squire Hyman, paid a visit soon thereafter and gave friendly notice that local residents disapproved of the teachers. Colonel Servosse sarcastically replied that his dinner guests were his own affair. The Verdenton newspaper labeled him a fanatical Abolitionist.

Undaunted, Servosse established a Sunday school for the blacks. He also cut up most of his estate into ten- and twenty-acre plots to sell to blacks, so that they could become self-sufficient property owners. The Servosses hoped the foolish prejudice of the townspeople would pass.

One summer day, an outdoor political meeting took place. There was a debate over the right of blacks to testify in court. Servosse attended only out of curiosity, but the people saw him and forced him to speak. His ideas were not secret, but he had never before intruded them on anyone. Now he publicly told the Southerners to give political rights to literate, property-owning blacks before the nation lost its patience. It was a bold and unpopular opinion.

Riding home, he encountered old Jerry Hunt, a black, who warned him that some angry white men were planning to ambush and whip him because of his speech. Servosse turned the tables on the conspirators, one of whom was injured. He reached home safely.

The next day, three blacks were accused of murdering the injured man, Savage, although his body had not been found. They were indicted by Judge Hyman and threatened with lynching; but Servosse stood up and said that Savage was alive and at Warrington. The charges were dropped. Soon thereafter, Squire Hyman, more open-minded than his neighbors, called on Servosse to talk. He admitted that perhaps the North had not really been vindictive. The war had occurred because neither side had understood the other.

Such talk was useless, however, and Servosse's speech had marked him as an Abolitionist and agitator. Blacks were beaten. After Servosse received an illiterate threatening letter, he bought arms and ammunition for his family and his black tenants and watched the town grow more hostile.

Christmas, 1866, came and went. At a black prayer meeting, the Servosses observed Jerry Hunt undergoing a mystical experience.

Meanwhile, the child Lily was growing and displaying marked intelligence. It seemed for the young girl that no local friendships, except with blacks, could ever be established.

Servosse lent support to the local Union League. He saw it as a training school in political responsibility for the freedmen. To his neighbors, it was a league of carpetbaggers and blacks united against the defeated Southern whites.

A constitutional convention was soon to meet. Servosse was unaware that people considered him the leader of the local Unionist sentiment. Attending the meeting of Unionists to nominate delegates, he found himself chosen. He issued a frank statement of his principles, and from that day he was ostracized in the region where he had hoped to make his home. The first point on his statement said: "Equal civil and political rights to all men."

Immediately Servosse received letters from the radical Republicans in the Senate. They demanded speedy reconstruction of the state government under the freed blacks and the Southern Unionists. Servosse argued that this measure would only keep the nation further divided because the government would be incompetent and the former white leaders would again rebel. Yet the "Wise Men" of the Senate got their way. Servosse viewed the future with great dismay.

In the winter of 1868–1869, his prediction of unrest was fulfilled. Bob Martin, a black, came to Warrington one day and told of a visitation the night before by thirty black-gowned horsemen. They had whipped Martin, abused his wife and daughter, and killed his infant. Local law officers said nothing could be done about the Klan. Letters to the colonel told of Klan atrocities all over the state; local incidents continued.

Now the white residents of the county, attempting to regain political control, held a mass meeting at the courthouse. John Walters, one of the outspoken Unionists of the county, attended the meeting to take notes. He did not return home. The next morning, his body was found in a courthouse office. Later a black servant told Servosse that the men who had threatened Walters and then killed him were respectable citizens of the community. News of this crime was all that Uncle Jerry Hunt could take. At a black prayer meeting, he suddenly stopped the service, told the details of the crime, and named the kidnapers. The following Saturday, several hundred Klansmen lynched him on the courthouse lawn. Again, the mob was made up of respectable citizens.

When Servosse wrote a letter asking for federal intervention in the terror-ridden county, his request was denied; the principle of states' rights and local government had to be maintained. The reign of terror went on. The Klan was the law, and through it, the Old South now triumphed. Meanwhile the North deluded itself, thinking Reconstruction was complete and effective.

As the years passed, Lily Servosse grew to womanhood. Melville Gurney, the son of a Confederate general, was torn between Lily and his father's stern principles. One day, while her father was in another part of the county with District Attorney Denton, a warning message came to Lily. The Klan was to intercept Judge Denton on his way home and burn him to death on a railroad trestle. Riding desperately to warn the two men, Lily happened upon a Klan rendezvous at a crossroads. In hurrying away, she encountered one of their lookouts and fired a shot at him. It was Melville Gurney.

After warning her father and the judge, she returned home with them. Melville's friend Burleson came along also, and publicly repudiated the Klan, making it easier for Melville to do the same, and thus hopefully to win Lily. For Melville had recognized Lily and had covered for her while she escaped. Burleson's defection was the first of many. The Klan was no longer necessary. The state legislatures issued general pardons for all their heinous crimes.

By 1877, the feeble Reconstruction governments had thus fallen completely into the hands of the old secessionists. It was as Comfort Servosse had predicted. Looking back over the years, he began to understand, if not approve of, the Southern point of view. He saw the Southern genius for leadership reassert itself. He had had his fill of politics. With his neighbors once again running things to their satisfaction, they became more friendly. Reversal to the old status quo of the years before the war had been inevitable.

Melville Gurney, pursuing his courtship, won Colonel Servosse's approval of this. Because Melville's father remained opposed, Lily refused Gurney until his father should approve. Mr. Gurney was on the verge of relenting when Comfort Servosse decided to close up Warrington. Lily would go North to study, and the Colonel would attend to other business affairs. Melville Gurney followed her north.

One day Colonel Servosse visited Dr. Martin, the retired president of his college. For the last time, he surveyed his difficult years in the South. The struggle between North and South had only just begun, he told Dr. Martin sadly, and it had been a fool's errand to try to rebuild the South in the image of the North. Just as matters were before the war, the South would soon dominate and control the nation. Her people were united, and they were born rulers. Like the Israelites, the blacks needed a prophet to arise and bring them out of slavery. The nation would have to educate the black and the poor white, and the power of states' rights would have to be crushed. All would be the work of generations.

Colonel Servosse returned briefly to Warrington after a year, intending a brief stay before taking up a managerial post in Central America. He died at Warrington of yellow fever. Before his death, he wrote his own epitaph and called himself a "Fool."

Critical Evaluation:

In almost all literature dealing with the Reconstruction period in the South following the end of the American Civil War, the carpetbagger is depicted as a villain motivated by greed, vengeance, and opportunism. Albion Tourgée's novel *A Fool's Errand* is the exception; its plot revolves around the career of an idealistic humanitarian Northerner, Comfort Servosse, a retired Union soldier who buys land in the South after the war for the sole purpose of devoting himself to helping the blacks build their future. In its general outline, the plot is modeled on the postwar career of Tourgée himself, whose experiences closely paralleled those of his protagonist.

Ironically, both the strengths and the weaknesses of *A Fool's Errand* arise, in large part, from the fiery zeal and desire to impart the message that inspired it. Tourgée is at his best when he is simply narrating a gripping tale of terror and suspense. Yet the truly powerful narrative is constantly interrupted by the author, who uses the old device of letters to insert discussions of history, eulogies in praise of black people, or diatribes against the South. Likewise, the earnestness of Tourgée's message inspires him to write some of the most realistic and horrifying scenes of mob violence in Southern fiction and to depict with great effectiveness scenes of rabble-rousing and lynching, of conspiracy, secret meetings, and the inner workings of the Ku Klux Klan. At the same time, however, the author presents a one-sided view of the total Southern situation through his omission of equally important facts concerning the corruption and shortsightedness of many Northerners involved in the Reconstruction government. Similarly, the realism that Tourgée achieves in describing the brutality of the Klansmen breaks down when he comes to write the love story of a Northern girl who redeems her Southern lover from his wrong ideas. The same novel that is starkly real and objective in some portions suffers from sentimentality and nearly miraculous turns of plot in others.

The chief merit of *A Fool's Errand* lies, however, not in its plot construction or scenario, but in its astute appraisal of the total failure of Reconstruction politics. Servosse himself is a pure and noble idealist, but he comes to realize that the Northern system of which he is a part is misguided and blind, and that the program it enforces is doomed to failure. The only solution to the Southern problem, Tourgée concludes, must come not from politics, but from mass education: "Let the Nation educate the colored man and the poor-white *because* the Nation held them in bondage, and is responsible for their education; educate the voter *because* the Nation cannot afford that he should be ignorant."

FOR WHOM THE BELL TOLLS

Type of work: Novel
Author: Ernest Hemingway (1899–1961)
Type of plot: Impressionistic realism
Time of plot: 1937
Locale: Spain
First published: 1940

Principal characters:

ROBERT JORDAN, an American fighting with the Spanish
　Loyalists
PABLO, a guerrilla leader
PILAR, his wife
MARIA, the beloved of Jordan
ANSELMO, another guerrilla

The Story:

At first, nothing was important but the bridge, neither his life nor the imminent danger of his death—just the bridge. Robert Jordan was a young American teacher who was in Spain fighting with the Loyalist guerrillas. His present and most important mission was to blow up a bridge that would be of great strategic importance during a Loyalist offensive three days hence. Jordan was behind the Fascist lines, with orders to make contact with Pablo, the leader of a guerrilla band, and with his wife Pilar, who was the strongest figure among the partisans. While Pablo was a weak and drunken braggart, Pilar was strong and trustworthy. She was a swarthy, raw-boned woman, vulgar and outspoken, but she was so fiercely devoted to the Loyalist cause that Jordan knew she would carry out her part of the mission regardless of her personal danger.

The plan was for Jordan to study the bridge from all angles and then to make final plans for its destruction at the proper moment. Jordan had blown up many bridges and three trains, but this was the first time that everything must be done on a split-second schedule. Pablo and Pilar were to assist Jordan in any way they could, even in rounding up other bands of guerrillas if Jordan needed them to accomplish his mission.

At the cave hideout of Pablo and Pilar, Jordan met a beautiful young girl named Maria, who had escaped from the Fascists. Maria had been subjected to every possible indignity that a woman could suffer. She had been starved, tortured, and raped, and she felt unclean. At the camp, Jordan also met Anselmo, a loyal old man who would follow orders regardless of his personal safety. Anselmo hated having to kill but, if he were so ordered, faithful Anselmo would do so.

Jordan loved the brutally shrewd, desperate, loyal guerrillas, for he knew that their cruelties against the Fascists stemmed from poverty and ignorance. But he abhored the Fascists' cruelty, for the Fascists came largely from the wealthy, ambitious people of Spain. Maria's story of her suffering at their hands filled him with such hatred that he could have killed a thousand of them, even though he, like Anselmo, hated to kill.

The first night he spent at the guerrilla camp destroyed his cold approach to the mission before him, for he fell deeply in love with Maria. She came to his sleeping bag that night, and although they talked little, he knew after she left that he was no longer ready to die. He told Maria that one day they would be married, but he was afraid of the future—and fear was dangerous for a man on an important mission.

Jordan made many sketches of the bridge and laid his plans carefully. There his work was almost ruined by Pablo's treachery. On the night before the blowing up of the bridge, Pablo deserted after stealing and destroying the explosives and the detonators hidden in Jordan's pack. Pablo returned, repentant, on the morning of the mission, but the damage had been done. The loss of the detonators and the explosives meant that Jordan and his helper would have to blow the bridge with hand grenades, a much more dangerous method. Pablo had tried to redeem himself by bringing another small guerrilla band and their horses with him. Although Jordan despised Pablo by that time, he forgave him, as did Pilar.

At the bridge, Jordan worked quickly and carefully. Each person had a specific job to do, and each did his work well. First Jordan and Anselmo had to kill the sentries, a job Anselmo hated. Pablo and his guerrillas attacked the Fascist lines approaching the bridge, to prevent their crossing before the bridge was demolished. Jordan had been ordered to blow up the bridge at the beginning of a Loyalist bombing attack over the Fascist lines. When he heard the thudding explosions of the bombs, he pulled the pins and the bridge shot high into the air. Jordan got to cover safely, but Anselmo was killed by a steel fragment from the bridge. As Jordan looked at the old man and realized that he might be alive if Pablo had not stolen the detonators, he wanted to kill Pablo. Yet he knew that his duty was otherwise, and he ran to the designated meeting place of the fugitive guerrillas.

There he found Pablo, Pilar, Maria, and the two remaining gypsy partisans. Pablo, herding the extra horses, said that all the other guerrillas had been killed. Jordan knew that Pablo had ruthlessly killed the other men so that he could get their horses. When he confronted Pablo with this knowledge, Pablo admitted the slaughter, but shrugged his great shoulders and said that the men had not been of his band.

The problem now was to cross a road that could be swept by Fascist gunfire, the road that led to safety. Jordan knew that the first two people would have the best chance, since probably they could cross before the Fascists were alerted. Because Pablo knew the road to safety, Jordan put him on the first horse. Maria was second, for Jordan was determined that she should be saved before the others. Pilar was to go next, then the two remaining guerrillas, and last of all Jordan. The first four crossed safely, but Jordan's horse, wounded by Fascist bullets, fell on Jordan's leg. The others dragged him across the road and out of the line of fire, but he knew that he could not go on; he was too badly injured to ride a horse. Pablo and Pilar understood, but Maria begged to stay with him. Jordan told Pilar to take Maria away when he gave the signal, and then he talked to the girl he loved so much. He told her that she must go on, that as long as she lived, he lived also. But when the time came, she had to be put on her horse and led away.

Jordan, settling down to wait for the approaching Fascist troops, propped himself against a tree, with his submachine gun across his knees. As he waited, he thought over the events that had brought him to that place. He knew that what he had done was right, but that his side might not win for many years. He knew, too, that if the common people kept trying, kept dying, someday they would win. He hoped they would be prepared when that day came, that they would no longer want to kill and torture, but would struggle for peace and for good as they were now struggling for freedom. He felt at the end that his own part in the struggle had not been in vain. As he saw the first Fascist officer approaching, Robert Jordan smiled. He was ready.

Critical Evaluation:

In 1940, Ernest Hemingway published *For Whom the Bell Tolls* to wide critical and public acclaim. The novel became an immediate best-seller, erasing his somewhat flawed performance in *To Have and Have Not* (1937). During the 1930's, Hemingway enjoyed a decade of personal publicity that put most American authors in his shade. These were the years of his African safari which produced *Green Hills of Africa* (1935) and his *Esquire* column (1933–1936). Wherever he went, he was news. In 1940, he was divorced by his second wife, Pauline Pfeiffer, and then married Martha Gellhorn. He set fishing records at Bimini in marlin tournaments. He hunted in Wyoming and fished at Key West where he bought a home. In 1937, when the Spanish Civil War broke out, Hemingway went to Spain as a correspondent with a passionate devotion to the Spain of his early years. Not content merely to report the war, he became actively involved with the Loyalist Army in its fight against Franco and the generals. He wrote the script for the propaganda film *The Spanish Earth* (1937), which was shown at the White House at a presidential dinner. The proceeds of the film were used to buy ambulances for the Loyalists. In 1939, with the war a lost cause, Hemingway wrote *For Whom the Bell Tolls* just as World War II was beginning to destroy Europe.

In order to understand Hemingway's motive in writing *For Whom the Bell Tolls*, it is necessary to know the essence of the quotation from John Donne, from which Hemingway took his theme ". . . any mans death diminishes me, because I am involved in Mankinde; And therefore never send to know for whom the bell tolls; It tolls for thee." Hemingway wanted his readers to feel that what happened to the Loyalists in Spain in 1937 was a part of that crisis of the modern world in which everyone shares.

Even more than in *A Farewell to Arms*, Hemingway here has focused the conflict of war on a single man. Like Frederic Henry, Robert Jordan is an American in a European country fighting for a cause that is not his by birth. Henry, however, just happened to be in Italy when World War I broke out; he had no ideological commitment to the war. Robert Jordan has come to Spain because he believes in the Loyalist cause. Although the Loyalists have Communist backing, Jordan is not a Communist. He believes in the land and the people, and ultimately this belief costs him his life. Jordan's death is an affirmation. One need only compare it with the earlier novels to see this novel as a clear political statement of what a man must do under pressure.

For Whom the Bell Tolls is a circular novel. It begins with Robert Jordan belly-down on a pine forest in Spain observing a bridge he has been assigned to destroy. At the conclusion, Jordan is once again belly-down against the Spanish earth; this time snow covers the pine needles, and he has a broken leg. He is carefully sighting on an enemy officer approaching on horseback, and "he could feel his heart beating against the pine needle floor of the forest." Between the opening and closing paragraphs, two hundred thousand words have passed covering a time period of only seventy hours. At the center of all the action and meditation is the bridge. It is the focal point of the conflict to which the reader and the characters are drawn back again and again.

In what was his longest novel to that point, Hemingway forged a tightly unified plot: a single place, a single action, and a brief time—the old Greek unities. Jordan's military action takes on other epic qualities associated with the Greeks. His sacrifice is not unlike that of Leonidas at the crucial pass or Thermopylae, during the Persian Wars. There, too, heroic action was required to defend an entry point, and there, too, the leader died in an action that proved futile in military terms but became a standard measure of courage and commitment.

Abandoning somewhat the terse, clipped style of his earlier novels, Hemingway makes effective use of flashbacks to delineate the major characters. Earlier central characters seemed to exist without a past. Yet if Robert Jordan's death was to "diminish mankind," then the reader had to know more about him. This character development takes place almost within suspended time. Jordan and Maria try to condense an entire life into those seventy hours. The reader is never allowed to forget time altogether, for the days move, light changes, meals are eaten, and snow falls. Everything moves toward the time when the bridge must be blown, but this time frame is significant only to Jordan and the gypsy group. It has little reference to the rest of the world. Life, love, and death are compressed into those seventy hours, and the novel becomes a compact cycle suspended in time.

The novel has more fully developed characters than the earlier Hemingway novels. In the gypsy camp, each person becomes important. Pilar is often cited as one of Hemingway's better female characters, just as Maria is often criticized as being unbelievable. However, Maria's psychological scars are carefully developed. She has been raped by the Fascists and has seen her parents and village butchered. She is just as mentally unstable as were Brett Ashley and Catherine Barkley. Jordan, too, is a wounded man. He lives with the suicide of his father and the killing of his fellow dynamiter. The love of Jordan and Maria makes each of them whole again.

The bridge is destroyed on schedule, but, through no fault of Jordan's, its destruction is meaningless in military terms. Seen in the context of the military and political absurdities, Jordan's courage and death were wasted. However, the bridge was more important for its effect upon the group. It gave them a purpose and a focal point; it forged them into a unity, a whole. They can take pride in their accomplishment in spite of its cost. Life is ultimately a defeat no matter how it is lived; what gives defeat meaning is the courage that a man is capable of forging in the face of death's certainty. One man's death does diminish the group, for they are involved together. Jordan's loss is balanced by the purpose he has given to the group.

Just as the mountains are no longer a safe place from the Fascists with their airplanes, Hemingway seems to be saying that no man and no place are any longer safe. It is no longer possible to make a separate peace as Frederic Henry did with his war. When Fascist violence is loose in the world, a man must take a stand. Jordan does not believe in the Communist ideology that supports the Loyalists, but he does believe in the earth and its people. He is essentially the nonpolitical man caught in a political conflict that he cannot avoid. He does the best he can with the weapons available to him.

FRANNY AND ZOOEY

Type of work: Novel
Author: J. D. Salinger (1919–   )
Type of plot: Social satire
Time of plot: November, 1955
Locale: Primarily New York City
First published: 1961

> *Principal characters:*
> FRANNY GLASS, a sensitive college English major and
>   actress
> LANE COUTELL, her pseudointellectual boyfriend
> ZOOEY GLASS, her brother and an abrasive television
>   actor
> BUDDY GLASS, her oldest brother and a writer
> BESSIE GLASS, her compassionate mother

Franny and Zooey is J. D. Salinger's third book, coming ten years after his novel of adolescence, *The Catcher in the Rye*, was received with acclaim, and eight years after *Nine Stories* further demonstrated his compassion for the sensitive and disturbed, his fine sense of satiric humor, his penchant for discursive first-person narration, and his growing interest in spiritual salvation in the modern world. The two episodes presented are parts of a larger design still in its developing stage; and the characters named in the title are sister and brother, members of a family with whom Salinger has dealt for some time, both before and after his notable success and pursuit of privacy combined to make him a celebrated contemporary American writer.

Franny and Zooey are the children of Les and Bessie Gallagher Glass, former vaudevillians (Jewish and Irish, respectively) and long-time residents of Manhattan. Franny is a college girl and Zooey is a successful twenty-five-year-old television actor; together they are the youngest children of a family that once numbered five boys and two girls. Like the rest (most of whom were child quiz program performers), they are prodigies. More than that, she is beautiful and he is saved from being dazzlingly handsome only by a slightly protruding ear. Despite these advantages, Zooey has an ulcer, Franny has an incipient nervous breakdown, and both have a sense of profound dissatisfaction with the world, with men, and with themselves. Franny's difficulties, which are the more severe, form the central concern of the book. They are set forth first in her arrival for an Ivy League football game and in what proves to be a disastrous and abortive weekend. Her date, Lane Coutell, epitomizes the self-centered pseudointellectual qualities that have caused her to become hypersensitive to those around her, to withdraw from drama and allied activities, and to seek grace and sustenance in the "Jesus Prayer" (from a devotional book called *The Way of a Pilgrim*) consisting of the phrase, "Lord Jesus Christ, have mercy on me." It is ineffectual, however, as she repeats it at the end of the segment bearing her name, while recovering from a fainting spell in the restaurant to which Lane had taken her for lunch.

The Zooey section, set on the following Monday in November of 1955 in the Glasses' New York apartment, begins to reveal the fundamental causes of both breakdown and ulcer. The early education of Franny and Zooey had been supervised by the eldest children: Seymour, a Ph.D. in his teens who had committed suicide in 1948 at the age of thirty-one, and Buddy, a self-alleged neurotic serving as writer-in-residence at a girls' junior college and as narrator of the "Zooey" section. It had been a program designed to inculcate religious and philosophical knowledge before that of the other disciplines conventionally studied by children. The texts were not only the Testaments but also the Upanishads, the Diamond Sutra, the writings of Zen and Mahayana Buddhism, of Laotse and Sri Ramakrishna, of Eckhart and Kierkegaard. Zooey tells Franny that their training has turned them into freaks at an early age, with their standards freakish as well—like the Tattooed Lady who wanted everyone else to look like her. Franny's discontent is objectified in her cry that she is sick and tired of ego—always ego—her own and everyone's. As she sees its manifestations in Lane Coutell and her professors, so Zooey sees them in his television associates. Exhorting her, and then telephoning her (on Buddy's telephone in Seymour's old room) with his voice disguised as Buddy's, he tries to show her that detachment is the one thing that matters in religious affairs. Finally, as he restores some measure of her self-confidence and emphasizes the need to give love to others, she achieves a kind of peace resembling the *satori* of Zen and drifts into sleep.

The first section of Salinger's book is much the better done of the two. Here he is in control of his material and presents it economically. The second section, however—even granting that it is spoken in the voice of Buddy Glass, brother of the principals, and intimately concerned with their problems—is by contrast prolix and diffuse, at its worst arch and even cute. It demonstrates the consequences of forgetting Henry James's dictum often repeated to himself: dramatize, always dramatize. When Buddy Glass does render action, it takes the form of conversation—between Zooey and Franny or Zooey and his mother—as in a sixty-eight page passage (surely the longest in modern literature set in a bathroom) between the latter two. James's great contemporary, Joseph Conrad, wrote that the novelist's primary task was above all to make his reader see. As if striving doubly hard for concrete visual effects in what he argues is not a mystical story or even one mystifying in a religious sense, Salinger includes much description, but it is description that often, unhappily, takes the form of a lengthy catalog of the contents of the bathroom medicine chest, Bessie Glass's kimono pockets, the furnishings of the living room, or the aphorisms inscribed on the inside of the door of Buddy's room—

two pages' worth being quoted in the text. This looseness of form is also seen in the use of a long footnote and two letters (the letter being, like the diary excerpt, a favorite Salinger device), one of which covers twelve pages.

Early in "Zooey," Buddy writes that the work is not so much a story as a homemade movie in prose, and that Bessie, Zooey, and Franny have advised against making it public. One wishes their misgivings had led the author to edit or reshoot some of his "footage." The long letter that Zooey rereads is described by its sender, Buddy, as being seemingly unending, self-indulgent, opinionated, repetitious, patronizing, and even embarrassing. It is also, he adds, surfeited with affection. All of the latter comment—and much of the former—applies to "Zooey."

This novel is the strangest—one might almost say obsessive—embodiment thus far of Salinger's interest in the individual's quest for spiritual advancement. What the work needs, unrealized in *Raise High the Roof Beam, Carpenters and Seymour: An Introduction*, is assimilation of the impact upon his particular sensibility of this subject matter to an extent which will again make possible the subtle control and command that mark his best work in *The Catcher in the Rye* and several of the tales in *Nine Stories*.

THE FRUIT OF THE TREE

Type of work: Novel
Author: Edith Wharton (1862–1937)
Type of plot: Social criticism
Time of plot: Late nineteenth century
Locale: The United States
First published: 1907

> Principal characters:
> JOHN AMHERST, an assistant mill manager
> BESSY WESTMORE, his first wife and owner of the mills
> JUSTINE BRENT, his second wife
> MR LANGHOPE, Bessy's father
> DR. WYANT, Justine's former suitor

The Story:

When Justine Brent, a nurse who was visiting Mrs. Harry Dressel at Hanaford, volunteered to care for Dillon, an operator who had been injured at Westmore Mills, she was approached by John Amherst, the assistant manager of the mills. Amherst deplored the miserable living and working conditions of the mill workers and, since Dillon's accident had been the result of these conditions, he wanted to use his case to show the need for improvement to Bessy Westmore, the newly widowed owner of the mills who was due to make an inspection tour the following day.

The next day, Amherst conducted Bessy Westmore through the mills. Bessy, touched by Dillon's case, decided to stay at Hanaford for a while. She recalled that she and Justine had attended school together before Justine's parents had lost their wealth.

Bessy and Amherst made plans to improve the living conditions of the workers, and this association finally led to their marriage. Amherst, hoping to make Westmore Mills a model of humanitarianism, was disillusioned to learn that Bessy was not willing to sacrifice the time or the money to accomplish this end.

Some time later, Justine came to Lynbrook, the Amherst country house, to be a companion to Bessy, who was not feeling well. Amherst, meanwhile, spent most of his time at the mills in Hanaford.

Bessy, to compensate for Amherst's long absences, began to entertain lavishly, at the same time confiding her bitterness and loneliness to Justine. Later, Amherst decided to manage a friend's cotton mill in the South.

Justine wrote to Amherst saying that Bessy needed him. Amherst replied that he would not return and, in a postscript, asked her not to permit Bessy to ride a particularly spirited horse they owned. Bessy, learning of his request, later took the horse out into the frost-covered countryside. There Bessy suffered an accident that seriously injured her spinal cord. She was taken home and looked after by Dr. Wyant, a local doctor whose proposal Justine had refused some time before. A surgeon and various other consultants were also summoned. Bessy remained paralyzed after an operation; Justine knew that the sick woman would never recover.

By this time, Amherst was on a business trip into a remote part of South America, and Bessy's father was in Europe.

One day, while Justine was caring for her alone, Bessy regained enough consciousness from her opiate state to plead with Justine to relieve her pain. Justine, convinced that she was doing the right thing, later gave Bessy an overdose of morphine. When Dr. Wyant came into the room, Justine told him that Bessy was dead. Dr. Wyant seemed to sense what had happened.

A year and a half later, Amherst was back at the Westmore Mills. Bessy had left half her fortune to Cicely, her daughter by her first marriage, and the other half to Amherst. He lived at Hanaford and continued his plans of reconstruction.

In the meantime, Justine was taking care of Cicely and an intimate friendship developed between the two. Later, when she went to visit Mrs. Dressel in Hanaford, Justine met Amherst again, a romance developed between them, and they were married. Cicely went to live with her grandfather. Justine took an active part in Amherst's work.

Dr. Wyant, who had left Lynwood and married, now needed money, and he came to Justine and threatened to expose her mercy killing of Bessy unless she arranged to have Amherst write him a letter of recommendation to Mr. Langhope, who could give him a responsible hospital post. Justine, realizing that Dr. Wyant had become a narcotics addict, could not in her conscience arrange a recommendation for him. When she went out of the room, Amherst came in. Learning that Dr. Wyant was in financial straits, Amherst wrote him a letter of recommendation in gratitude for his services to Bessy. On her return, Justine told her husband that Dr. Wyant was not qualified for the hospital post. Dr. Wyant, in retaliation, charged Justine with the mercy killing and left.

Intellectually, Amherst approved of Justine. Emotionally, he was horrified at what she had done. Their relationship became strained.

When Dr. Wyant was appointed to the hospital post, Amherst remembered the letter of recommendation. He knew that if Mr. Langhope were told about Dr. Wyant's addiction to narcotics, the doctor would in turn disclose Justine's crime. Amherst told Justine that if Mr. Langhope thought that she had been in love with Amherst when she killed Bessy, he and Justine would have to give up the mills, go away, and start a new life. Justine secretly went to New

York to see Mr. Langhope and told him the truth about Dr. Wyant and herself. She then promised to disappear if Mr. Langhope would continue on his former terms with Amherst. Mr. Langhope agreed.

Justine, returning to Hanaford, told Amherst that Mr. Langhope had taken the news very well. In the course of the following months, Amherst's horror of Justine's crime caused their relationship to deteriorate even more. At last, Justine went to Michigan to resume her nursing career, thus fulfilling her promise to Mr. Langhope.

A year later, Cicely became ill. Mr. Langhope, realizing that she needed Justine's love, asked Justine to come back to Amherst so that she could be close to Cicely. When Amherst learned why Justine had left him, he felt love for her and remorse for his attitude. They continued, however, to feel somewhat estranged.

About a year later, Amherst, speaking at the dedication of the mill workers' new recreational center, gave a stirring tribute to Bessy who, he said, had drawn up the plans herself. Justine realized that Amherst was referring to the plans for a gymnasium that Bessy had intended for her own pleasure at Lynbrook, in open defiance of Amherst's wishes. Although angry, Justine kept Bessy's secret.

As they left the dedication, Amherst told Justine how good he felt over improved conditions at the mill. They walked away hand in hand.

Critical Evaluation:

The Fruit of the Tree, Edith Wharton's only novel of reform, is concerned with the fundamental differences, financial as well as social, between the lower and upper classes, and with the squalid factory conditions of the late 1800's. The focus of the novel is the cloth mill and the posture each character assumes concerning it. The issue unites and subsequently divides John and Bessy Amherst as they struggle to cope with their opposing ideals.

Wharton portrays both of these characters as unaware of their blind spots. John Amherst's social commitment is maintained at the expense of his other relationships and is untempered by sensitivity to his wife's needs. She, in turn, is whimsical and bored by the continuous unpleasant intrusion of the factory's problems into their life; sacrifice is unknown to her. At the same time, for John to give in to Bessy's life-style would necessitate for him the end to a meaningful existence. Wharton succeeds in setting these characters in the most elemental and crucial way, each against the other.

The third major character, Justine, is Bessy's friend and comforter and Amherst's confessor. Although no longer having family or wealth, she has the genteel manner of the rich plus the sensitivity and humility developed by her commitment to nursing. Those attributes that divide Bessy and John Amherst are united in Justine. She is a person who is aware of the power of money but who does not assume, as John does, that it can mend the problems of society or that it will create a humanistic environment. Wharton has created in Justine a rounded human being who participates sensitively in the human drama. Justine and John share what Bessy does not comprehend, a sense of commitment.

In this novel, Wharton has treated two of the major issues of her age: the problem of class and the effects of industrialization. She precedes Theodore Dreiser in the novel of reform, and she concerns herself with those issues typically avoided by her class.

GABRIELA, CLOVE AND CINNAMON

Type of work: Novel
Author: Jorge Amado (1912–   )
Type of plot: Social criticism
Time of plot: 1925–1926
Locale: Ilhéus, Bahia, Brazil
First published: 1958

> *Principal characters:*
> GABRIELA, a beautiful young mulatto
> NACIB SAAD, the Syrian-born proprietor of the Vesuvius Bar
> MUNDINHO FALCÃO, a young cacao exporter and rising political reformer
> COLONEL RAMIRO BASTOS, the rugged old political boss of Ilhéus
> COLONEL MANUEL OF THE JAGUARS, a planter from the outlands
> COLONEL JESUÍNO MENDONÇA, a cuckold
> COLONEL AMÂNCIO LEAL, a former bandit chief
> COLONEL MELK TAVARES
> MALVINA TAVARES, his young daughter
> PROFESSOR JOSUÉ, a young teacher
> TONICO BASTOS, the most elegant man in Ilhéus and a ladykiller
> COLONEL CARIOLANO RIBEIRO, a wealthy plantation owner
> GLORIA, his mistress
> FATHER BASÍLIO CERGUEIRA, a worldly priest
> JOAO FULGÊNCIO, a good-natured skeptic
> QUINQUANA and
> FLORZINHA DOS REIS, the spinster sisters of an old Ilhéan family
> DONA ARMINDA, Nacib Saad's neighbor and a widow

According to Gilberto Freyre, the internationally respected Brazilian historian and social philosopher, Jorge Amado is perhaps the only Brazilian writer of any importance allied with the Communist Party. Winner of a Stalin Prize and a former resident of Communist Czechoslovakia, this great novelist has served as a Communist representative in the Brazilian government. Reputedly disenchanted by the events of 1956, however, Amado has never been a mere "red intellectual"; and in *Gabriela, cravo e canela* (*Gabriela, Clove and Cinnamon*, 1962) his peculiarly robust, humane, pure kind of

Marxist thought lies deeply buried in an even more humane, more robust, purer art.

The setting of the novel, for example, is perfectly suited to a retelling of that myth by which Karl Marx organized his vision of history. In the middle 1920's of this century, the Brazilian provinces were still suffering under the political, social, and economic dominance of the *coroneis*. These "colonels," who ran the local organization of both major political parties unchallenged, who dictated at whim all manners and morals, and who possessed and held, often by violence, the huge estates that supplied the money upon which all provincial life depended, were the direct administrators of what can only be recognized as a feudal society. Like the planters and cattle barons of North America, they ruled vast territories through a complicated system of allegiances built upon favors, kinship, and the naked use of power. In the country around Ilhéus, a seacoast town in the province of Bahia, the grip of the colonels, given sinews by a boom in the international market for cacao, had remained anachronistically strong. Amado's novel is basically concerned with the breaking of that grip and the change from a feudal order, as represented by these colonels, to a new bourgeois order, as represented by Mundinho Falcão, a rich, energetic, progress-minded young man from Rio.

Unlike most of the colonels, who are self-made men, Falcão is the son of an illustrious family whose influence extends easily upward into the highest reaches of the national government. He has exiled himself from the high life of Rio de Janeiro for three reasons: to make his own fortune, to forget a girl, and to accomplish needed social reforms. As the book opens, however, one of the colonels has just murdered his wife and her lover; and if the fact that she had a lover at all reveals some cracks in the old order, the further implication that the colonel will not be punished under the unwritten law indicates that, for the time being at least, it still survives as an effective force.

Meanwhile, Nacib Saad, a fat, gentle Brazilian from Syria and the owner of the Vesuvius Bar, has just lost his cook, whose appetizers and tidbits had largely accounted for his considerable success. Fortunately for him, however, a continuing drought in the backlands has brought a steady stream of homeless migrants to Ilhéus looking for work; and just as Nacib was becoming desperate, he discovers among them Gabriela, whose cinnamon-colored skin and scent of clove enhance equal talents for cooking food and making love. As a girl of the people, Gabriela represents a way of life that is both older and more essentially Brazilian than any of the ways represented by either the colonels or Mundinho Falcão. She embodies the idea of *convivência*—of varied and mingling races and classes mutually dissolving and living together in harmony and absolute democracy—that is at once a Brazilian tradition and a Brazilian ideal.

While Mundinho Falcão deliberately operates upon the body of society, rechanneling its old systems into new ones, Gabriela unconsciously operates

upon its soul. Every man in town adores her and few of the women, surprisingly enough, are jealous. When election time arrives, the colonels find
their influence whittled away to the vanishing point; and in a last attempt to
save their ascendancy, the more reactionary of them attempt to arrange the
assassination of a powerful political chief who has defected to Falcão. The
killing fails, and Falcão's forces of reform are swept into office, not without
his privately acknowledging, however, that even this reform is only temporary
and must lead to even greater changes. The nature of the changes still to
come, one sees, resides in the musky clove and dusky cinnamon of the beautiful mulatto.

Nacib Saad's attempt to transform Gabriela into a married, respectably
shod, and housebroken little *bourgeoise* merely ends in the discovery that her
love is as naturally democratic as her ancestry: she has slept with any man in
Ilhéus lucky enough to be handsome. As her husband, poor Nacib is shocked,
but not for long. Gabriela still loves him, and he learns, too, in the course
of a short estrangement that was disastrous for the business of the Vesuvius
Bar, that he likewise still loves her. Wild and free, this mulatto girl is as
unregimentable as she is desirable, as indomitable as she is beautiful. At the
novel's end, she finds herself, though no longer his unhappy wife, once again
established as Nacib's happy cook and mistress. All other factions, too, the
colonels' and Falcão's, are reunited in freedom to celebrate new prosperity
and progress for Ilhéus, and the colonel who had shot his wife is sent, as
testimony to a new reign of law, to prison.

Here is Amado's version of Marxist myth. It is Marx, however, with a
considerable difference. Brazil, the writer seems to have recognized, is not
a nineteenth century Germany or England; neither is it a twentieth century
Russia or Czechoslovakia. If Brazil needs a revolution, says Amado—and
even conservatives like Gilberto Freyre agree that it does—let it be not a
puritanical affair, with brigades of workers shouldering picks and marching
under banners, but rather a revolution in the vein of Rabelais, with freedom
and harmony as its goals, and *Fay ce que vouldras* as its motto. What Amado
wants, in the end, are social changes that will confer upon everyone the
freedom of a Gabriela; and it is his passionate desire for this freedom that
makes *Gabriela, Clove and Cinnamon* so superior to the blind exigencies of
any party line. In fable and atmosphere, the novel is a work of robust humanity, sensuous purity, and ultimate universality.

THE "GENIUS"

Type of work: Novel
Author: Theodore Dreiser (1871–1945)
Type of plot: Naturalism
Time of plot: 1889–1914
Locale: Alexandria, Illinois, Chicago, and New York
First published: 1915

> *Principal characters:*
> EUGENE WITLA, an artist, the "genius"
> THOMAS WITLA, his father and a sewing machine agent
> SYLVIA and
> MYRTLE WITLA, his sisters
> STELLA APPLETON, Eugene's first love
> ANGELA BLUE, a schoolteacher and later Eugene's wife
> MARGARET DUFF, a laundry worker and Eugene's first
>   mistress
> RUBY KENNY, an artist's model
> MIRIAM FINCH, a sculptress in New York
> CHRISTINA CHANNING, a singer in New York
> M. ANATOLE CHARLES, an art dealer
> FRIEDA ROTH, a young girl in Alexandria
> CARLOTTA WILSON, a gambler's wife and Eugene's
>   mistress
> DANIEL SUMMERFIELD, head of an advertising agency
> OBADIAH KALVIN, head of a publishing company
> MARSHALL P. COLFAX, a publisher
> FLORENCE J. WHITE, Eugene's associate and enemy
> MRS. EMILY DALE, a wealthy socialite friend of Eugene
> SUZANNE, her daughter
> MRS. JOHNS, a Christian Science practitioner

The Story:

   Eugene Witla, a sensitive seventeen-year-old boy, lived with his parents and his two sisters in Alexandria, Illinois. Eugene had little idea of what he wanted to do, although his aspirations were vaguely artistic. His father, a sewing machine agent and a respectable member of the middle class, got him a job setting type for the local newspaper. His first enthusiasm was for a local girl named Stella Appleton, but even this affair did not keep Eugene, unhappy in his restlessness, from leaving the small town and going to Chicago to seek his fortune.

When he first went to Chicago, Eugene supported himself by moving stoves, driving a laundry wagon, and collecting for a furniture company. While at the laundry, he met the passionate young Margaret Duff and began his first real love affair. About this time, he also met, through mutual friends, a schoolteacher named Angela Blue, a fair-haired beauty who represented everything fine and elegant to impressionable young Eugene.

Eugene began attending art classes at night at the Chicago Art Institute. There he demonstrated some talent, particularly in his class in life drawing, for he seemed to have a special sensitivity in conveying the beauty of the human form. While at the Art Institute, he met a model, Ruby Kenny, and she soon became his mistress. Yet Ruby, like Margaret, was from the lower classes and made her charms easily available to men. Eugene finally left them both, preferring the finer and more fragile beauty of Angela. Engaged to the young teacher, he left Chicago to seek his artistic fortune in the wider world of New York.

In New York, Eugene painted powerful and realistic pictures of what he saw in the city, and began, from time to time, to sell a few of his paintings. After several years, he became moderately successful. Some of the women he met, like Miriam Finch and Christina Channing, began to educate him in the well-read and knowledgeable polish of the New York artistic world. Christina became his mistress for a short time; that sophisticated affair somewhat baffled Eugene, and in spite of his new polish and elegance, he still remembered Angela. Returning to the Middle West to visit her, he seduced her and then, feeling his responsibility, married her and took her back to New York. Angela felt that all her dreams of happiness had been fulfilled.

Eugene's work impressed M. Anatole Charles, manager of a distinguished firm of art dealers in New York. M. Charles held an exhibit which, a great success, marked Eugene as a powerful and rising young artist. Full of enthusiasm, he and Angela went to Paris. The show held when he returned was less successful; people felt that his work in Paris had not been fresh or unusual. While in Paris, Eugene had also begun to suffer a vague malaise, a lack of energy and purpose. He did not, at that time, realize that his marriage was causing his uneasy and restless feeling.

Eugene and Angela returned to Alexandria for an inexpensive rest. While there, Eugene met eighteen-year-old Frieda Roth and found her attractive. Since he was twenty-nine by this time, Frieda represented a renewed interest in youth and beauty. Angela was able to stop this relationship before it advanced further than a few kisses stolen under the trees. Afterward, Eugene and Angela left Alexandria and stayed at several resorts until their money ran out. Angela then returned to her parents, while Eugene returned to New York to reestablish his reputation as an artist.

Eugene, still restless, found himself unable to paint, and he took a job doing manual labor for the railroad in a town near New York. While there, he met and had a passionate affair with his landlady's married daughter, Carlotta Wilson. Again Angela heard of the affair and came to reclaim Eugene. They decided to try to start again in New York.

Eugene worked for a newspaper and then as art director for an advertising agency. His boss there, Daniel Summerfield, was a tyrant who broke his promises and failed to pay Eugene adequately. Eugene left for another job with the advertising department of the *North American Weekly*, under the directorship of Obadiah Kalvin. Successful there, he moved to Philadelphia to accept a twenty-five-thousand-dollar job as head of advertising for all books and publications directed by Marshall P. Colfax. When Eugene was made a vice president, the other vice president, Florence J. White, felt that Eugene's job and salary were unnecessary. White was jealous of Eugene and the two became enemies.

Eugene became greatly successful, both financially and socially. His marriage was hollow, but both he and Angela seemed to accept the situation and to cope with it fairly well. Although Eugene had money enough to retire, his financial success had bred in him a desire for greater financial success, and he had lost the will to paint. His artistic lassitude was matched by the emotional emptiness of his marriage.

About this time, Eugene met Mrs. Emily Dale, a rich socialite. They exchanged visits and became friendly. One day, Mrs. Dale brought Suzanne, her eighteen-year-old daughter, to tea. Eugene fell in love with Suzanne at first sight, and all the yearning of his search for beauty returned. Soon Eugene and Suzanne were meeting, and they confessed their love for each other. Brought up a cultured and sophisticated young woman, Suzanne was willing to become Eugene's mistress. Filled with romantic ideas about becoming an artist's mistress, she insisted, however, on telling her mother of her plans, for she thought that her mother would surely approve; but Mrs. Dale did not approve. Angela, when she discovered the affair, decided that the only way to hold Eugene was to have a baby, despite the fact that doctors had warned her against having children. Angela, who had become a Christian Scientist, believed that her firm faith and will would permit her to have the child. Mrs. Dale took her daughter to Canada to get her away from Eugene. When he tried to follow Suzanne to Canada, Mrs. Dale, through Florence J. White and the threat of scandal to the firm, was able to have him fired from his job. Eugene, having lost both his job and Suzanne, returned to comfort Angela during her ordeal.

After Angela died giving birth to a daughter, also named Angela, Eugene had his sister Myrtle come East to help him make a home for the child. For a time, in his desolation, Eugene began to read Christian Science, but he failed to find comfort or salvation in its message.

When Eugene and Suzanne met by accident on the street two years later, they were each too self-conscious to acknowledge the existence of the other. Living sanely with his daughter and Myrtle and her husband, Eugene began to paint again. He had several shows, was sponsored again by M. Charles, and became a popular and fairly successful artist. He began to weave romantic dreams around his daughter, Angela, thinking of the time when she would grow up and they could search for beauty together. In spite of his new awareness of man's inability to control his fate, of the delusions that belief in beauty or belief in Christian Science represented, Eugene's emotional impulse toward beauty was still strong enough to keep him fashioning impossible dreams for himself and his daughter.

Critical Evaluation:

The "Genius" is generally conceded to be the weakest of Theodore Dreiser's major novels, but critical opinion differs over whether it is a magnificent failure or simply a big, bad book. The usual reason given for its relative impotence is that Dreiser was too subjectively involved with the material to objectify his feelings and clarify his ideas about his artistic protagonist, Eugene Witla. Although all of Dreiser's writings contain many transcriptions of direct experience, *The "Genius"* chronicles traumatic events that were recent personal history. Witla's career as an artist closely parallels Dreiser's own— impoverished youth, odd jobs, modest artistic success, nervous breakdown, restoration, financial success, monetary and professional collapse, and, finally, serious artistic endeavors. More important, in terms of Dreiser's emotional identification with the story, is the fact that Witla's marriage to Angela Blue and all of its consequent disappointments, frustrations, hostilities, and psychic damage is a thinly disguised rendering of his own drawn out, agonized marriage to Sallie White.

If the extreme subjectivity of *The "Genius"* hurts it artistically, it also makes the book a vital document to anyone interested in Dreiser's life and works. The novel is basically about the tensions among three fundamental elements: the urge to artistic creation, the unbridled sexual drive, and the corrupting influence of material success. For all of the complexity, inconsistency, redundancy, and confusion of *The "Genius,"* at the center—and the thing that gives the novel its redeeming strength—is Eugene Witla's prolonged and agonized attempt to reconcile these three diverse, powerful, and contending forces.

In the opening segment of the book, Eugene is introduced to creative activity and sexuality at almost the same time. His artistic impulses, like Dreiser's, are to portray life as realistically and graphically as possible. His vision of women, however, is idealistic: the perfect woman is beautiful, sensual, and "always eighteen." Thus, his sexual impulses are intensified by the fact that he seeks an impossibility and, becoming increasingly frustrated, is driven from woman to woman in an effort to find that ideal—which gets progressively farther away as he ages.

This is made more complicated and painful by his foolish marriage to Angela Blue, the one woman for whom he feels, at best, a lukewarm sexual attraction. Initially, Angela represents America's small-town, conservative, hypocritical morality, especially in sexual matters. Her narrowness, provinciality, possessiveness, and domineering attitude toward Eugene frustrate both his artistic development and his personal fulfillment. Later, as he begins to drift to other women, Angela becomes fiercely aggressive sexually in an attempt to save the marriage. Then, in the novel's most absurd hypothesis, Dreiser ascribes Eugene's nervous breakdown to this "excessive" sexual activity provoked by Angela.

Angela is also blamed for Eugene's turn from artistic creativity to crass commercialism. At her prompting, Witla puts his painting aside and becomes an advertising executive. Thus, a curious alliance of sex, materialism, and middle-class morality combine to suppress temporarily Eugene's creativity, and his return to serious painting results not from any repudiation of materialism but is the consequence, once again, of his rampant sexual adventuring. Witla's affair with eighteen-year-old Suzanne Dale, the daughter of a rich and powerful socialite, costs him his job, his fortune, and his social standing and forces him back to the easel where he quickly—much too quickly—regains all of his creative powers.

Dreiser demonstrates that even the strong-willed and talented are ultimately buffeted by forces over which they have little control. Despite his remarkable abilities and powerful drive, Witla allows major decisions—to be an artist, to marry, to become a businessman, to return to painting—to be made for him by outside circumstances and internal impulses over which he has little conscious control. At the end of the book, there are hopeful hints—his painting, his "forgiveness" of Angela, his feelings for his daughter—but the final image is that of an aged and unreconciled artist who feels neither personal satisfaction nor social identification nor even a conviction that his own life and art have real value and meaning.

GEORGIA SCENES
Characters, Incidents, &c., in the
First Half Century of the Republic

Type of work: Short stories and sketches
Author: Augustus Baldwin Longstreet (1790–1870)
Type of plot: Social history
Time of plot: 1780–1830
Locale: Georgia
First published: 1835

It was an auspicious moment for American literature when the presses of the *Augusta State Rights Sentinel* issued a collection of pieces that had appeared in that newspaper, for this book, born in obscurity, was *Georgia Scenes, Characters, Incidents, &c., in the First Half Century of the Republic* by "A Native Georgian." The author was not a professional man of letters but rather one of those wonderfully versatile gentlemen who flourished in nineteenth century America. Lawyer, judge, politician, Methodist minister, newspaper publisher, and educator (at various times president of Emory College, Centenary College, the University of Mississippi, and the University of South Carolina), Augustus Baldwin Longstreet was ideally suited to the task of writing an informal social history of the southwestern frontier. An educated man (Yale), but no scholar, his activities brought him into personal contact with the whole range of men and manners in the growing country. Although *Georgia Scenes* now enjoys a position as a minor classic, it appealed to its own times as a new and exciting vein of writing. Edgar Allan Poe heralded it as an "omen of better days for the literature of the South," and the reading public called for twelve editions by 1894.

Georgia Scenes is significant on several counts. It is a pioneer work of Realism and one of the milestones in the local-color movement. Longstreet's careful use of dialect foreshadows a whole school of writing that reached a culmination of sorts with Joel Chandler Harris' Uncle Remus tales. As a humorist, Longstreet is intimately connected with the great tradition of rough-and-tumble frontier humorists. In this category, he is a real precursor of Mark Twain, and there is much in *Georgia Scenes* that would not be out of place in *Huckleberry Finn.* Finally, Longstreet wrote with satirical intent, and an argument can be made for his claim to a position among the forerunners of the revolt from the village movement.

Although he was not a literary theorist, Longstreet seems to have worked out a rough theory of Realism. It would be folly to consider *Georgia Scenes* an accidental combination of lucky hits. The preface to the first edition shows that the author's aim was to record accurately the details of the life he had observed:

They [the sketches] consist of nothing more than fanciful *combinations* of *real* incidents or characters. . . . Some of the sketches are as literally true as the frailties of memory would allow them to be. . . . The reader will find in the object of the sketches an apology for the minuteness of detail into which some of them run, and for the introduction of some things into them which would have been excluded were they merely the creations of fancy.

Longstreet, however, was a reporter with a purpose; he applied Realism as the handmaiden of social criticism. Like *The Spectator*, which he appears to have admired, Longstreet exposes the follies and vulgarities of his time for the purpose of reforming men and manners. A number of the sketches close with didactic tags. Yet the author was too much of "A Native Georgian" to advocate replacing good American social norms with foreign modes. He wishes to see a standard of natural, unaffected American manners prevail. Rarely, if ever, does Longstreet miss an opportunity to ridicule or scorn European manners or even imported culture. On the subject of greetings between women he remarks: "The custom of kissing, as practised in these days by the *amiables*, is borrowed from the French, and by them from *Judas*." The whole of a rather thin sketch, "The Song," is devoted to the horrors of Continental music and the absurdity of American girls who study it.

The nineteen sketches of *Georgia Scenes* are roughly divided into two groups—those dealing chiefly with men and those that deal with women. In their original periodical publication, the sketches appeared as two series signed with two pseudonyms. These general categories do not circumscribe the material. A whole world of rural and urban life is packed into the fairly slim volume: brawls, shooting matches, horse races, balls, inns, old wives, young bloods, country schools, high society, and blacks. As Longstreet noted in his preface, there is an abundance of detail, but it is not intrusive, for these are not tightly plotted stories. The term *sketches* describes them perfectly: generally brief descriptive pieces that excel at catching atmosphere, very much like the form of Washington Irving's *Sketch Book* pieces.

The two best-known and most frequently anthologized sketches in *Georgia Scenes* are concerned with the cruder aspects of rural life. In "The Horse-Swap," a professional trader called the "Yellow Blossom" is outduped while trying to pass off a horse with a terrible sore under the saddle. In this sketch, Longstreet shows a sympathy for animals that is completely characteristic of the volume. Not only does he pity the suffering of dumb beasts, but he also sees that savage treatment of animals brutalizes the human beings who inflict it. There is probably nothing else in American literature, before Jack London, quite like "The Fight." In the story, two bully-boys who have always avoided an encounter are pushed into a brawl by a disagreement between their wives. During the course of the knock-down-drag-out fight, an ear, a finger, part of a nose, and part of a cheek are bitten off. A minor character in "The Fight" is of considerable interest. Ransy Sniffle is a diseased runt whose greatest delight is starting fights between other people. The brutality of fights is also scored in "Georgia Theatrics," which shows a man rehearsing all the parts in a bloody fight.

Although Longstreet never uses blacks as leading characters, he takes great pains to transcribe their speech, and in this respect, he was ahead of his time. The practical joker of "The Character of a Native Georgian" asks a black woman to sell him half a live chicken, and she protests: "Name o' God! what sort o' chance got to clean chicken in de market-house! Whay de water for scall um and wash um? . . . Ech-ech! Fedder fly all ober de buckera-man meat, he come bang me fo' true. No, massa, I mighty sorry for your wife, but I no cutty chicken open." Longstreet is equally careful to reproduce the dialect of backwoods whites. In "A Sage Conversation," he records the talk of three old women sitting by the fire: "Indeed, I have a great leanin' to sweats of verbs, in all ailments sich as colds, and rheumaty pains, and pleurisies, and sich; they're wonderful good." This interest in colloquial speech is closely associated with the author's interest in folk customs, as can be seen in "The Turn Out," which describes the custom of giving pupils a holiday if they can turn out (barricade out) the teacher.

Longstreet's crusade against the barbarity of rural sports is most evident in "The Gander Pulling" and "The Turf." In the latter, a black jockey is killed, and the comment Longstreet puts into the mouth of a woman spectator is worthy of Mark Twain at his bitterest: "I declare, had it not been for that little accident, the sport would have been delightful."

One sketch in *Georgia Scenes* is not by Longstreet. "The Militia Company Drill," by Oliver Hillhouse Prince, gives an account of a wildly undisciplined muster. It is as good as the other pieces and merits inclusion in the volume.

After Longstreet mounted the ladder of respectability, he came to feel that *Georgia Scenes* was an undignified work. Though he continued to write, he wrote nothing else that has survived; only one book gives him a literary eminence he probably never expected.

GETTYSBURG

Type of work: Short stories
Author: Elsie Singmaster (Mrs. E. S. Lewars, 1879–1958)
Type of plot: Historical chronicle and regional realism
Time of plot: 1863–1913
Locale: Gettysburg, Pennsylvania
First published: 1913

> *Principal characters:*
> MARY BOWMAN, a widow whose husband died during the
>   battle
> YOUNG PARSONS, a recruit from Gettysburg
> COLONEL FRANK HASKELL, a member of the Thirty-sixth
>   Wisconsin Infantry
> GUNNER ADAM CRISWELL, a blind veteran
> FREDERICK DAGGETT, a military substitute
> GRANDFATHER MYERS, an aged veteran

The Story:

Mary Bowman, scraping lint for wound-dressings, found it difficult to keep her mind on her work. Close by, her three small children played that they were General Early and his ragged Confederate troops, who had passed through Gettysburg several days before. The day before, Union soldiers had marched into town and headed toward Chambersburg. Mary Bowman was glad that the village was not to see fighting and thankful that her husband was with Hooker's unengaged forces. She had dreamed, however, of marching men in the night. Suddenly uneasy, she went to her front door. Hannah Casey, a neighbor, came from her garden across the street. While they stood talking, a soldier rode by and warned them to take shelter. The Army of Northern Virginia was advancing from the north, the Army of the Potomac from the south. The women looked at each other in dismay as a cannon roared threateningly from the ridge west of town.

For months, young Parsons had dreamed of fields filled with dead men. Sometimes he wanted to run away. Marching along the dusty road from Taneytown, he suddenly realized that the army was moving toward Gettysburg, where he had been born. Firing sounded in the distance. As his company marched that night past the cemetery where his father was buried, he could stand the thought of death and battle no longer. Turning, he ran blindly through the darkness to his mother's farmhouse. Finding the door locked, he entered through a window and crept upstairs to his own bed. He awoke in late afternoon, to find the house empty and his mother nowhere about. Looking from a window, he saw men in blue and other men in gray skirmishing outside. His fears forgotten, he began to fire on the Confederates. All that afternoon, he and the Union soldiers held the strategic ground around the Parsons house, where, toward evening, his friends carried him with a bullet wound in his throat. Lying on the kitchen floor, he saw his mother as she came from the cellar where she had hidden herself when the firing began. On Parsons' face was a look of peace; he had come home.

Near a clump of trees, on the third day of the battle, Colonel Frank Haskell waited in a stone-fenced field. Around him were long lines of infantry, re-formed since yesterday's fighting. A mile away, on the opposite ridge, Lee's men also waited. The cannonading began. Smoke drifted across the field. Men fell, but still the Union lines waited. The bombardment ended with heavy, ominous silence. Then, through the smoke, the Confederate ranks appeared, eighteen thousand men, a rolling sea of gray. Shells, shrapnel, and canister failed to stop them. When the Union lines began to waver, the young officer drew his sword and urged his men back. The troops were fighting hand to hand as the smoke closed down. Then the Confederate charge broke. By a clump of trees behind a stone wall, Pickett's charge ended in defeat.

Although she had been forewarned, Mary Bowman was startled by the sound of reveille on the morning of November 19, 1863. The night before, a train from Washington had brought President Lincoln to Gettysburg for the dedication of a cemetery for the dead soldiers. Out there on the battlefield, among the unknown dead, lay Mary Bowman's husband, for whom she had looked in vain. Sad and embittered by her loss, she went to the ceremony only because the judge, a kindly man concerned for her welfare, insisted that she take her children. She heard little that the orator of the day said, for her mind was on the wounded she had nursed, on the grim debris of the battle she had uncovered in her search. As she turned to leave, someone said that the President was about to speak. Abraham Lincoln, lank and sad-faced, spoke only a few words, but, hearing them, Mary Bowman took heart. It was as if he were telling her to be of good comfort, that her duty was to the living as well as the dead.

The explosion that cost Gunner Adam Criswell his eyesight on the second day of the battle had not disabled him. A vigorous old man, he returned to Gettysburg with his friend, Carolus Depew, in September, 1910, for the dedication of the great monument containing the names of all Pennsylvania soldiers who had fought in the battle. While Carolus looked for his own name, a boy read to the blind man the names of those in Criswell's battery. The townspeople had opened their homes to the old soldiers; Criswell and Depew stayed with Professor James and his wife. Another guest was a pompous general who took credit for the plan to inscribe the veterans' names on the monument. The next day, Criswell went to the exercises with Mrs. James. Afterward, the general offered to find the blind man's name on the memorial tablets. Then Criswell told them what he himself already knew. His name had been overlooked.

Frederick Daggett had fought as a substitute. The other man had promised him a thousand dollars, but the money had never been paid. All Gettysburg, knowing Daggett as a drunkard and braggart, laughed at his foolish story. Congressman Ellison Brant, arriving in Gettysburg on the eve of Memorial Day, was unable to find accommodations or a guide until Daggett offered his services. Brant, impatient and demanding, was dissatisfied with the old man's efforts and tried to pay him off contemptuously in the crowded lobby of the Keystone Hotel. Before all the people there, Daggett demanded his thousand dollars, for he had recognized Brant as the man who had cheated him years before. The politician reached for his checkbook before he realized that his gesture was an admission of his guilt. Hurriedly he wrote the check. Daggett took it and deliberately tore the slip of paper in two. Ragged and disreputable, he could always boast that he had thrown away a thousand dollars.

Grandfather Myers, an invalid who was home after Chancellorsville, had watched the Confederates retreating through rain and mud from Gettysburg. Ever since, he had regretted the illness that had kept him from offering food or comfort to the tired, defeated men. He himself was an old man when the state militia held a summer encampment on the battlefield. His son, daughter-in-law, and grandchildren went to see the review, but Grandfather Myers stayed at home because there was no room for him in the buggy. That afternoon, he dressed himself in his blue uniform. He was sitting on the front porch when a detachment of the National Guard came marching in on maneuvers. To the old man, they were Lee's soldiers in retreat, their uniforms yellow with dust instead of tattered and rainsoaked. When they asked for water, he could only nod smilingly. At last, he had given Lee's men something. He could die content.

Although Mary Bowman lived to see the fiftieth anniversary of the battle, she never talked of those days. But she remembered all of her life her husband, lost on that battlefield, the voice of Abraham Lincoln, and most vividly of all, the figure of General Early, as she had seen him riding by on his white horse, the spectral leader of a stumbling, ghostly host on that rain-muffled retreat toward Hagerstown.

Critical Evaluation:

Elsie Singmaster was a regional historical novelist whose fiction, both juvenile and adult, was devoted to presenting a realistic picture of two phases of American life: the quiet and isolated rural communities of German descent in Pennsylvania, where she grew up; and the scenes of crucial battles during

America's Revolutionary and Civil Wars. As sources for novels and short stories dealing with the latter, the author relied on personal conversations with people who had lived through the Civil War, as well as on her own experience with the land and its geography. Singmaster made her home, from 1915 until her death, in Gettysburg, on a site overlooking Seminary Ridge, a pivotal landmark in her stories.

Gettysburg, a series of nine short stories, was the author's first published book and one of her finest. Chronologically, the stories fall into three groups: those set immediately prior to the battle; those depicting the Confederate retreat; and those concerning the reminiscences, told generations later, of people who were there. A unifying thread is provided in the character of Mary Bowman, who witnesses the inception of the battle, loses her husband in the fighting, cares for the wounded, hears Abraham Lincoln's dedication of the battleground three days later, and lives to see the fiftieth anniversary of the event. All the stories have a remarkable ring of truth about them; the reader senses immediately that the characters are based on real people who experienced the famous battle at firsthand, rather than on mere historical data.

Singmaster's style reflects her Pennsylvania German background in its economical prose and in its simple, straightforward language. Her handling of dialogue is particularly effective in establishing verisimilitude, while it allows her to probe deeply into the hopes and fears of persons involved in situations of intense emotional stress. Battle scenes are never presented directly but rather recalled through the minds of soldiers, mothers, wives, and friends; the sense of irreparable loss brought on by war is omnipresent. Not only are the people drawn convincingly, but also the land is brought vividly before the reader's eyes through descriptions that bear the mark of the author's personal involvement with the place.

GIANTS IN THE EARTH

Type of work: Novel
Author: O. E. Rölvaag (1876–1931)
Type of plot: Regional romance
Time of plot: Late nineteenth century
Locale: The Dakotas
First published: 1924–1925
> *Principal characters:*
> PER HANSA, a Norwegian settler
> BERET, his wife
> OLE,
> ANNA MARIE,
> HANS KRISTIAN, and
> PEDER VICTORIOUS, their children

The Story:

Per Hansa moved all his family and his possessions from Minnesota into the Dakota territory. His family consisted of his wife, Beret, and three children, Ole, Anna Marie, and Hans Kristian. Beret was fearful and sad, for she had been uprooted too often and the prairie country through which they traveled seemed bleak, lonely, and savage.

Per Hansa staked out his claim near the family of Hans Olsa at Spring Creek. Then Beret announced that she was carrying another child. Money was scarce. Per Hansa faced overwhelming odds and thoughts of the great risks he was taking kept him awake long after Beret and the children slept. Being something of a poet, Per Hansa thought at times that the land spoke to him, and he often watched and listened and forgot to keep to his work as he cleared his land and built his house. He labored from before dawn until after dark during those long, northern summer days.

When Indians came and drove away the settlers' cows, only Per Hansa had the courage to follow after them. Only he had the sense to doctor a sick Indian. Beret mistrusted his wisdom for foolishness and there were harsh words between them. The grateful Indian gave Per Hansa a pony. Then Per Hansa went on a buying expedition and returned with many needed supplies and, what was more, news of coming settlers.

The next summer, Per Hansa discovered claim stakes that bore Irish names. The stakes were on his neighbor's land; the homesteaders had settled where others had already filed claim. Secretly he removed the stakes and burned them, but not before Beret realized what he was doing. She began to worry

---

over her husband's deed. Per Hansa sold some potatoes to people traveling through and awoke the slumbering jealousy of his neighbors.

In midsummer, more people arrived, the settlers who had set out the stakes that Per Hansa had burned. They called the Norwegians claim jumpers, but after a fight, they took up other land nearby. Per Hansa managed to sell some of his goods to them. That fall, more Norwegians came. The little community was thriving. Beret, however, depressed by the open spaces and her fear that her husband had done a bad thing, brewed a dark remorse within herself. Day by day, she brooded over her lonely life, and she covered her window at night because of her nameless fears. At least Per Hansa, on his infrequent trips around to different settlements, met other people.

When winter came, Per Hansa rested. He could sleep long hours while the winds blew outside, but his wife worried and fretted. He began to quarrel with her. Soon, however, he noticed that his neighbors were suffering hardship and privation. The unmarried young men who had settled near the Hansas were planning to desert the settlement. It required all his ability to convince them to stay and to face the desolate, bitter winter to its end.

The settlers began to talk of a school that would move from house to house so that the parents might learn English along with the children.

During the winter, Per Hansa became lost in a blizzard and only his tremendous strength and courage saw him and his oxen safely through the storm to the Trönders' settlement. The following day, forgetting how Beret must be worrying about him, he stayed on and cut a load of wood to take back home with him.

His next expedition was to bargain with the Indians for furs. He suffered greatly from exposure and lost two toes through frostbite.

When spring came, Per Hansa could not wait to get into his fields to plant his wheat. His friends thought he was planting too early; and so it seemed, for snow fell the next day and freezing weather set in. Determined not to lose heart, Per Hansa decided to plant potatoes in place of the wheat. Beret took to her Bible, convinced that evil was working its way into their lives. Then, unexpectedly, their wheat came up.

Another couple arrived. They were exhausted with travel, the wife saddened by the death of her son on the prairie. Per Hansa and Beret took them in. When they moved on, greater despondency seized Beret. She felt some doom was working its way closer and closer to her life.

That summer, grasshoppers destroyed much of the grain. Most of Per Hansa's crop was saved, but Beret took his good fortune only as a sign that the underground trolls, or evil spirits, were planning greater ruin for her and her husband.

In the following years, the scourge of the grasshoppers returned. Many of the settlers were ruined. Some starved. Some went mad. One summer, a traveling Norwegian minister took up residence with them to plan a religious service for the whole community. His coming worked a change in Per Hansa's household. Per Hansa took courage from it and consolation, but the reveries in Beret's mind grew deeper and stranger. Because it was the largest house in the district, the minister held a communion service in Per Hansa's cabin. Disconnected parts of the service floated all that week in Beret's head. Her mind was filled with strange fancies. She began to think of Peder Victorious, her youngest child, who was born on the prairie, as a savior who would work their salvation.

As the autumn came on, the great plains seemed hungry for the blood and strength of those who had come to conquer it.

That winter, Hans Olsa froze his legs and one hand. In spite of all that Per Hansa and the others did for their neighbor, Hans Olsa grew weaker. Beret stood beside him, predicting that he had not long to live. She put into the sick man's mind the idea to send for the minister. Per Hansa thought that Hans Olsa was weak in calling for a minister and that the way to throw off illness was to get out of bed and go to work. He had never spared himself nor had he spared his sons. He was the man to go for the minister, but this time, he was unwilling to set out on a long winter journey. Hans Olsa was a good man; he did not need a minister to help him die. The weather itself was threatening; however, Per Hansa reconsidered. His sons were digging a tunnel through snow to the pigsty. Inside, his wife was preparing a meal for him. They watched as he took down his skis and prepared to make the journey for the sake of his dying friend. He did not look back at his house or speak farewell to Beret as he started out.

So Per Hansa, on his errand of mercy, walked into the snowstorm. There death overtook him.

Critical Evaluation:

Ole Rölvaag was born in the Helgoland district of Norway and lived there until he was twenty years of age. He attended school irregularly; his ambition to become a poet, once broached in the family circle, brought a discouraging barrage of ridicule. At age fourteen, he left school entirely and went out with the Lofoten fishing fleet. He seemed destined to pursue this hard vocation all his life, and the prospect brought him little contentment. Though considered by his family as too stupid to learn, he read voraciously, both Norwegian and foreign authors. His reading gave him a view of the possibilities of life that made the existence to which he was bound seem intolerably circumscribed. When he had been a fisherman for five years, something occurred that forced him to a decision. The master of his boat, whom he greatly admired, offered to stake him to a boat of his own. Rölvaag realized that if he accepted the offer, he would never be anything but a fisherman, so he declined it and emigrated to America.

For three years he farmed for an uncle in South Dakota; then at the age of twenty-three, with great trepidation, he entered a preparatory school in Canton, South Dakota. Six years later, he was graduated *cum laude* from St. Olaf College. After a year of postgraduate study in Oslo, he took the chair of Norwegian literature at St. Olaf, which he held until his death.

By the time Rölvaag began work on *Giants in the Earth*, at age forty-seven, he had already written five novels, of which four had been published. All were written in Norwegian, published in Minneapolis, and read exclusively by the Norwegian-speaking population of the Midwest. All the works deal with aspects of the Norwegian settlement and appealed strongly to an audience of immigrants. *Giants in the Earth* is actually an English translation of two novels previously written in Norwegian: *I de dage* and *Riket grundlægges*. This novel and its sequel, *Peder Victorious*, spring from a European artistic tradition but treat matters utterly American. They are perhaps unique in both American and foreign literatures.

The European and specifically Norwegian elements that distinguish *Giants in the Earth* are its orientation toward the psychology rather than the adventures of its characters, and its strain of Nordic pessimism. The characters of Beret and Per Hansa illustrate two complementary facets in the psychology of the Norwegian settlers. In Per Hansa, the desire to own and work his own land, to "found a new kingdom," seems to feed on the hazards he encounters. The brute resistance of the soil, the violence of the weather, the plagues of grasshoppers, the danger from Indians, the dispute over the claim-stakes only spur him on to greater feats of daring, endurance, and ingenuity. Every victory over misfortune makes him feel more lucky and fuels his dream of a prosperous freehold for himself and his children. Freed from the cramped spaces and conventions of an old culture, he embraces the necessities of the new life joyfully, trusting in his instinct for the fitness of things to help him establish a new order. Beret, on the other hand, takes no joy in pioneer life and is instead deeply disturbed at having to leave an established way of life to confront the vast, unpeopled plains. Uprooted, she feels morally cast adrift, as if her ethical sense, indeed her very identity, were attached to some physical place. Beret sees Per Hansa's exultant adaptability to pioneer life as evidence of the family's reversion to savagery. For a man to shelter with his livestock, to change his name or give his child a strange name, to parley with Indians, to christen in the absence of a minister indicate to her a failure of conscience, a giving up of the hallmarks of civilization.

Yet she, like Per, has brought her worst troubles with her from home. Her growing despondency about Per's and her neighbor's spiritual condition springs from her own sense of sin in having borne Ole out of wedlock. She sees herself as the deserving object of divine retribution; in her deranged state, she takes every escape from disaster as a sign that God has marked her for some still more awful punishment. The very openness that thrills Per Hansa with its endless potentialities fills her with dread: "Here, far off in the great stillness, where there was nothing to hide behind—here the punishment would fall!" Per, bearing her in his heart, is drawn down in the vortex of her despair.

Ironically, it is only after Beret regains her courage and her faith through religious ministration and ceases to expect calamity from minute to minute, that Per Hansa dies. It even seems as if she sends him out to die. From an aesthetic point of view, however, his death is necessary to the work itself. For all of its realism and modernity of tone, *Giants in the Earth* is a saga, and as sagas must, it ends with the death of heroes. Per Hansa and Hans Olsa are heroes of epic stature, and like the heroes of old legend, they complement each other's virtues. They have loved each other from their youth, and in their prime, their strength and wit combine to carve a new home out of the wilderness. Like Beowulf braving the dragon, they sacrifice themselves in a last great struggle with the prairie before it succumbs to the plow and the fence. Thus "the great plain drinks the blood of Christian men and is satisfied." The deaths of Hans Olsa and Per Hansa signal the passing of the time of legend, when giants walked the earth, and one man could do the work of ten; they signal as well the beginning of a more comfortable time of clapboard houses and coffee hot and plentiful and of heroes of a wholly different kind.

THE GILDED AGE
A Tale of Today

Type of work: Novel
Authors: Mark Twain (Samuel L. Clemens, 1835–1910) and Charles
  Dudley Warner (1829–1900)
Type of plot: Social satire
Time of plot: Nineteenth century
Locale: The United States
First published: 1873

Principal characters:
  WASHINGTON HAWKINS, a young Westerner
  LAURA HAWKINS, his adopted sister
  COLONEL BERIAH SELLERS, an improvident optimist
  PHILIP STERLING, a young engineer
  HARRY BRIERLY, his friend
  SENATOR DILWORTHY, a member of Congress
  RUTH BOLTON, a Quaker

The Story:

Squire Hawkins of Obedstown, Tennessee, received a letter from Colonel Beriah Sellers asking Hawkins to come to Missouri with his wife Nancy and their two children, Emily and George Washington. Moved by the Colonel's eloquent account of opportunities to be found in the new territory, the family traveled West. On the journey, they stopped at a house where a young child was mourning the death of his mother. Taking compassion on the orphan, Hawkins offered to adopt him. His name was Henry Clay.

The travelers boarded the *Boreas*, a steamboat headed up the Mississippi. In a race with a rival, the two boats collided, causing a fire on the other steamboat and killing or injuring scores of passengers. In the confusion, Hawkins found a stray child, Laura, whose parents apparently had died in the fire. The Hawkinses, although now burdened with four children, took hope in the promise of Tennessee lands that they still owned.

After a tiresome journey, they reached their new home, a log cabin surrounded by a dozen or so other ramshackle dwellings. There Colonel Sellers helped the Hawkinses start their new life. Yet Squire Hawkins did not prosper as he had hoped; before long, his affairs became hopelessly involved.

Ten years later, Colonel Sellers was living in Hawkeye, a town some distance away. Squire Hawkins, by that time, was impoverished. Clay had gone off to find work, and Laura, now a beautiful young girl, volunteered to do so. Washington and Emily could not decide what to do. Clay brought money to the destitute family and paid Washington's stagecoach fare to Hawkeye, where he found Colonel Sellers as poorly off as the Hawkins family. Colonel

Sellers, however, was a magnificent talker. His fireless stove became a secret invention, his meager dinner a feast, his barren house a mansion, and under the spell of his words, Washington's dismal prospects were changed to prospects of a glowing future. Colonel Sellers spoke confidentially of private deals with New York bankers and the Rothschilds. He confided that he was working on a patent medicine which would bring him a fortune.

Colonel Sellers took Washington to the real estate office of General Boswell. It was arranged that the young man should live with the Boswells while working for the General. Before long, he fell in love with Boswell's daughter Louise.

Squire Hawkins died, leaving his family only the lands in Tennessee. Among his papers, Laura found some letters from a Major Lackland, who apparently had come across a man believed to be Laura's father. Before Hawkins could get in touch with the man, he had disappeared. Laura's doubtful parentage made her an object of scorn in the region.

Two young New Yorkers, Philip Sterling and Harry Brierly, set out for Missouri to work as construction engineers for a railroad company. In St. Louis, they met Colonel Sellers, who entertained them with boasts about his investments and treated them to drinks and cigars. When he showed embarrassment at having lost his money, Philip relieved him by paying the bill.

In Philadelphia, Ruth Bolton, the daughter of Eli and Margaret Bolton, both Quakers, received a letter from Philip. Rebelling against the rules of the Friends, she told her parents that she wanted to do something different, perhaps study medicine.

Colonel Sellers continued to befriend the two young men in St. Louis. He went so far as to suggest that the railroad should be built through Stone's Landing, a small village not along the route planned for the road. Like the Colonel, Harry was a man of imagination. When their money ran out, Harry and Philip went to an engineer's camp near Hawkeye, and the Colonel joined them to plan the city to be built there.

Philip and Harry arrived in Hawkeye eight years after the death of Squire Hawkins. The Civil War had been fought; the Hawkinses were still supported by Clay, and Laura had become a beauty. During the war, she had married a Colonel Selby, who, already married, had deserted her when his regiment was transferred. After that calamity, she turned her eye upon Harry Brierly, who fell in love with her.

When Senator Dilworthy went to Hawkeye to investigate Colonel Sellers' petition for funds to improve the area, the Senator met Washington Hawkins. Thinking Washington a fine young man, the Senator hired him as a secretary. Laura charmed Senator Dilworthy to such an extent that he invited her to visit his family in Washington.

Ruth Bolton was in school at Fallkill, where she stayed with a family named Montague. On their way to New York, Philip and Harry stopped to see her.

Philip was disappointed in the manner in which Ruth accepted him. Alice Montague was kinder to him; Ruth seemed too attentive to Harry. In Washington, Harry saw the appropriation for Stone's Landing passed by Congress. When the New York office sent no money with which to pay the workers at Stone's Landing, Harry went to New York to investigate. Speculation was everywhere; even Mr. Bolton decided to buy some land near the railroad in Pennsylvania. Unfortunately, Harry learned that the cost of obtaining the Congressional appropriation had been so high that there was no money left to pay for the work at Stone's Landing.

Hired by Mr. Bolton, Philip went to develop the natural resources of a tract of land in Ilium, Pennsylvania. He became a frequent visitor at the Boltons'.

Senator Dilworthy invited Laura to come to Washington, where she immediately became a belle—much to Harry Brierly's consternation. Many people believed her an heiress. The Senator attempted to use her influence in getting congressmen to vote in favor of a bill in which he was interested. At a party, Laura saw Colonel Selby, who had come to Washington to claim reimbursement for some cotton destroyed during the war. When the former lovers met, Laura knew that she still loved Selby and the two began to be seen about town together. When he left Washington, Laura followed him to a New York hotel, where she shot him.

The opening of the Ilium coal mine found Philip and Harry hard at work. Before they had located the main vein, however, Mr. Bolton went bankrupt and surrendered all his property to his creditors, and Philip was able to buy the Ilium tract. Ruth, graduated from medical school, had gone to work in a Philadelphia hospital. Harry was in New York, a witness at Laura's murder trial. Philip, hoping to read law in the squire's office, visited the Montagues in Fallkill. Mr. Montague, seeing value in Philip's mine, offered to finance a further excavation.

Laura's trial attracted much attention. Claiming that she was insane, her lawyer tried to show that her mind had been deranged from the time she lost her parents in the riverboat fire.

Senator Dilworthy's bill, a measure to establish a university for blacks on the Hawkins land in Tennessee, had been for some time in committee. Washington Hawkins and Colonel Sellers expected to make a fortune when the bill passed. Then Dilworthy, up for reelection, attempted to buy votes and was exposed, and his bill was defeated on the floor of the Senate. Washington and Sellers were crestfallen.

Laura was acquitted of the murder charge. Penniless, she tried to begin a lecture tour, but on her first appearance, she found only an empty auditorium. On the streets, she was attacked by angry citizens and driven home to a cold room, where she died of grief.

Philip finally found coal in his shaft, but his elation subsided when a telegram from the Boltons told him that Ruth was gravely ill. He hurried to her bedside, where his presence helped to hasten her recovery.

Critical Evaluation:

Satire was Mark Twain's forte, and in this novel, his wit finds a wide range. In fact, he and his coauthor planned to attack almost every aspect of contemporary society. The weakness in the story lies in its coauthorship; it hangs in uncertain balance between sober reality and sheer hilarity, with no clear demarcation between the two attitudes. Twain's contribution can easily be recognized by readers familiar with the humorist's style. Diffused in its effects, the novel does contain one memorable element, the unforgettable character of Beriah Sellers.

Editor-critic E. L. Godkin described America during the 1870's as a "chromo civilization." Reflecting on the slovenly reality beneath the gaudy exterior of society, Twain dubbed the era the Gilded Age. In this period, society had become more fluid, and many of those individuals of humble origins made it to the top by proclaiming their achievements to the world in boisterous tones, by wearing extravagant apparel, and by living in grotesque mansions. That treacherous and not always successful path from rags to riches fascinated Mark Twain and Charles Dudley Warner. The cost of attaining a pew in the church of the newly rich, while portrayed in a humorous and touching style, was their primary concern.

A crude frontier spirit invaded the realm of the genteel. Twain had seen this phase of the economic process work itself out and felt that its real victims were the environment and American traditions, ideals, and common sense. Washington was swarming with scoundrels, coal mine operators were scarring the once beautiful frontier, and people were selling themselves to the highest bidders. The characters in this novel were pulled from the life of a nation suffering from moral bankruptcy.

Twain especially hated graft, and to get to the root of this evil, he attacked the sacred cows of his generation: organized religion, government, political parties, and flashy entrepreneurs. Colonel Sellers represented all that was naïve and forgivable in that age, and Senator Dilworthy the opposite. In true patriotic spirit, Sellers believed that prosperity would come from a congressional bill, but Dilworthy typified the unscrupulous residents of Capitol Hill.

The satire of this book was not appreciated at the time; people did not want to be ridiculed. When Twain wrote what his audience wanted to read, his fame increased; yet Twain, himself a product of the Gilded Age, would never be free of the cynicism that surfaced in this book.

THE GLASS KEY

Type of work: Novel
Author: Dashiell Hammett (1894–1961)
Type of plot: Mystery romance
Time of plot: 1930's
Locale: New York area
First published: 1931

Principal characters:

> NED BEAUMONT, a gambler and amateur detective
> PAUL MADVIG, his friend and the city's political boss
> SENATOR HENRY, Madvig's candidate for reelection
> JANET HENRY, his daughter
> SHAD O'RORY, Madvig's rival
> OPAL MADVIG, Madvig's daughter
> BERNIE DESPAIN, a gambler owing Ned money

The Story:

Ned Beaumont reported to his friend, Paul Madvig, the political boss of the city, that he had found the dead body of Taylor Henry in the street. Taylor was the son of Senator Henry, Madvig's candidate for reelection. When Madvig failed to show much interest, Ned told his story to the police. The next day, he went to collect from Bernie Despain the 3,250 dollars that he had won on a horse race and found that Bernie had vanished, leaving behind twelve hundred dollars worth of Taylor's I.O.U.'s. Ned had himself appointed special investigator in the district attorney's office so that he could work on Taylor Henry's case. What he really wanted to do was to find Bernie and get his money.

His first step was to get the help of Madvig's daughter Opal, who had been meeting Taylor secretly. Ned had found no hat on Taylor the night of the murder. Opal got one for him from the room she and Taylor had rented. Then Ned went to New York to a speakeasy that Bernie frequented. Bernie came in accompanied by a burly bodyguard who, when Ned asked for his money, struck Ned a terrific blow. With the help of Jack Rumsen, a private detective, Ned trailed Bernie from the hotel where he was staying to a brown-stone house on Forty-ninth Street. There he told Bernie that he had planted Taylor's hat behind a sofa cushion in Bernie's hotel room and would leave it there for the police to find if Bernie did not pay him the money. Bernie paid off.

Back from New York, Ned went to see Farr, the district attorney. Farr

---

showed Ned an envelope enclosing paper on which were typed three questions implicating Madvig in Taylor's murder. Meanwhile, Madvig had decided to have the police close down several speakeasies belonging to Shad O'Rory, gangster and ward boss. O'Rory reopened the Dog House, where Ned went to get information. O'Rory had him tortured for several days. Finally he escaped. He was taken to a hospital.

There he had many callers, including Madvig and Janet Henry, Taylor's sister. Opal Madvig went to tell Ned she was sure her father had killed Taylor. Ned assured her that he did not believe Madvig had committed the murder. Partly recovered, he left the hospital against orders.

Shortly afterward, Ned and Madvig dined with Senator Henry and his daughter Janet. Ned made Janet admit that she secretly hated Madvig, who was in love with her.

Ned went to see Madvig and told him that even his henchmen were beginning to betray him because they thought he had committed the murder. Madvig admitted Taylor had followed him out of the Henry house that night, that they had quarreled, and that he killed Taylor with a brown, knobby cane which Taylor had been carrying. Madvig claimed that he had then carried the cane away under his coat and burned it. Ned later asked Janet to look for the cane. She said it was with some others in the hall of their home. She also told him of a dream in which she and Ned had found a house with a banquet spread inside; they had to unlock the door and let out a great many snakes before they could go in to enjoy the food.

Ned went next to Farr's office and signed an affidavit telling of Madvig's confession. Then he went to a bar where he found Jeff, O'Rory's bodyguard. In a private room upstairs, he accused Jeff of a gangster killing planned by O'Rory. O'Rory walked in on them, and in the ensuing quarrel, Jeff strangled O'Rory. Ned had a waiter call the police to the scene.

Ned went to the Madvig home, where Madvig's mother said that Madvig was nowhere to be found and that Opal had unsuccessfully attempted to commit suicide. The next morning, Ned went to Senator Henry's house and told the Senator that Madvig had confessed. It was all Janet and Ned could do to keep the Senator from rushing out to kill Madvig. The Senator asked Janet to leave him alone with Ned. Ned told him that Janet hated Madvig. The Senator insisted he was not going to permit the murderer of his son to go unpunished. Then Ned accused Senator Henry of killing Taylor, of wanting to kill Madvig so that he would not testify against him, and of caring more for his own reelection than for the life of his son. The Senator confessed that he had interfered in a street quarrel between Taylor and Madvig and had asked the political boss to leave him with his son. Madvig had done so after giving him the cane that Madvig had taken away from Taylor. The Senator, angry with his son because of the quarrel he had forced upon Madvig, had angrily struck Taylor with the cane and killed him. He had then carried home the cane. After hearing the old man's confession, Ned refused to leave him alone because he feared the Senator would kill himself before the police arrived.

The next day, Janet begged Ned to let her go with him to New York. She said the key to the house in her dream had been of glass and had shattered just as they opened the door because they had had to force the lock. When Madvig came in, he learned that he had lost Janet and that she was going away with Ned Beaumont.

Critical Evaluation:

The Glass Key was Dashiell Hammett's personal favorite among his novels and may well be, in the words of critic-novelist Julian Symons, "the peak of Hammett's achievement, which is to say, the peak of the crime writer's art in the twentieth century."

Although Ned Beaumont has much in common with Hammett's other "hard-boiled" heroes, Sam Spade and Continental Op, he is not only a professional detective hired to solve a crime but also a man involuntarily thrust into the center of a violent and puzzling situation. The fate of his employer and best friend, Paul Madvig—and ultimately of himself—is dependent on his ability to solve the murder of Henry Taylor. Beaumont's search for the murderer becomes, moreover, not only a problem in detection but also an exploration of the social mores and political forces operative in the America of 1931. As Ned pursues his quest, he also comes to understand his own relationship to that social and political system.

Hammett's picture of big-city politics has little to do with electoral niceties. Favors are bought and sold. Survival and power go to the fittest; that is, to those most willing and able to manipulate the power factions as they vie to maintain and expand their own self-interests. Paul Madvig is no more honest than his rival Shad O'Rory, only a bit more adroit and likeable. Holding on to power is a matter of keeping a delicate balance of contending factions; the slightest mistake can topple one from the pinnacle all the way down. Those not at the center of the struggle, from District Attorney Farr down to the bartender at the speakeasy where O'Rory is murdered, are loyal only to themselves and switch sides at the slightest indication that power relationships are changing. Thus, to everyone except his sister Janet, the murder of Henry Taylor matters only as a dangerous variable in this struggle for political dominance. The most "respectable" member of the establishment, old Senator Henry, turns out to be the most corrupt. He kills his own son in a fit of temper and is willing to kill again to keep the truth concealed.

Ned Beaumont accepts and even participates in this system of institutionalized corruption. His loyalty to Paul, Janet, and the "job" he has to do, however, suggests another possible morality in the book based on personal relationships rather than on adherence to particular institutions or abstract principles. Although Beaumont fights with Madvig, leaves him at one point, and finally goes off with his girl, he maintains a dogged loyalty to his boss and friend throughout the book, even in the face of nearly fatal tortures and beatings. If the system is corrupt, Hammett seems to be saying, it is still possible for a man to retain his moral integrity by holding fast to his own sense of self, his personal code, and those commitments, to self and others, that are the product of that code.

The book ends on an optimistic note. Ned and Janet are about to leave together. Paul accepts the new arrangement with equanimity and promises to use his expertise and power to do a "housecleaning." This final optimism is unconvincing, and the image of the American Dream that remains in the mind is that of Janet's dream which gives the book its title: a delicious banquet apparently free for the taking, but guarded by hidden snakes that swarm over the unwary who dare to unlock the door with a glass key.

GO DOWN, MOSES

Type of work: Novel
Author: William Faulkner (1897–1962)
Type of plot: Psychological realism
Time of plot: 1830's to about 1940
Locale: The Mississippi Delta
First published: 1942

> *Principal characters:*
>> LUCIUS QUINTUS CAROTHERS MCCASLIN (CAROTHERS), the founder of the McCaslin clan
>> THEOPHILUS MCCASLIN (UNCLE BUCK) and
>> AMODEUS MCCASLIN (UNCLE BUDDY), his twin sons
>> SOPHONSIBA (SIBBEY) BEAUCHAMP, Uncle Buck's wife
>> ISAAC (IKE) MCCASLIN, the son of Buck and Sibbey
>> CAROTHERS MCCASLIN EDMONDS (CASS), the grandson of Carothers' daughter and an Edmonds
>> ZACHARY EDMONDS, Cass's son
>> CAROTHERS MCCASLIN EDMONDS (ROTH), Cass's grandson
>> EUNICE, the slave and mistress of Carothers McCaslin, who drowned herself
>> TOMASINA (TOMEY), the daughter of Carothers and Eunice
>> TERREL (TURL, OR TOMEY'S TURL), the grandson of Carothers and Eunice and the son of Carothers and Tomey
>> TENNIE BEAUCHAMP, the slave of Sophonsiba and her brother Hubert Beauchamp
>> LUCAS BEAUCHAMP, one of the three surviving children of Turl and Tennie
>> MOLLIE, Lucas' wife
>> THE GIRL OF "GO DOWN, MOSES," the granddaughter of Lucas' brother James
>> SAMUEL BEAUCHAMP, the grandson of Lucas and Mollie
>> IKKEMOTUBBE, the Indian chief who sold the land to Carothers McCaslin
>> SAM FATHERS, Ikkemotubbe's illegitimate son and the last survivor of the Indian tribe

Though usually discussed as a novel, *Go Down, Moses* is both a collection of seven short stories, written and published independently, which together form a sharply detailed picture of a small region in the Mississippi Delta, and

an outrageously confusing tale of the McCaslin clan. The book recapitulates
the story of the American South and reaffirms the biblical views of human
history.

"Was," which foreshadows the cruelty and injustice of later generations,
and shows man treating his brother like a piece of property and gambling
over human happiness, is one of the funniest stories that William Faulkner
wrote. It opens with a pack of hounds racing through the house after a fox.
·A central pun of the book, "race" is the theme of the first story, which takes
the form of outrageous rural comedy. Buck and Buddy, twin sons of Carothers
McCaslin, chase their slave and half brother, Tomey's Turl; Turl is after his
sweetheart, Tennie, a slave of Hubert and his sister Sophonsiba Beauchamp;
and Sophonsiba, called Sibbey, the only woman in the whole countryside, is
after Buck. Buck and Buddy must catch Turl before he catches Tennie or
else Sibbey will bring Turl home, stay for a visit, and may catch Buck. When
Buck arrives at Warwick, the dilapidated Beauchamp plantation that Sibbey
fashions after an English estate, he is tricked into staying the night and tricked
again into climbing into a bed that contains the mistress of Warwick. When
he is caught by the smiling Hubert, a poker game ensues to settle once and
for all whether Sibbey gets Buck, whether Turl gets Tennie, and who will
buy the other slave in either event. Buddy comes to the rescue and forces
Hubert's hand with a possible straight over three threes. Buck is free, Turl
gets Tennie, and Hubert must buy Turl. The ending is happy, but when the
hounds break into the house once again in pursuit of the fox, readers sense
that the race is not over. And indeed it is not; Sibbey gets Buck, Ike is born,
and an estate is established that will perpetuate a system of cruelty and
injustice.

The story is set in a mythical past, when a man could ride for days without
having to meet a woman, and when in a lifetime he did not have to dodge
but one. Further, the characters are innocent. Buck and Buddy may have
owned slaves, but they quartered the slaves in the mansion and themselves
in the shack. They may have locked the front door every night after putting
the slaves in, but they never checked the back door which became an exit as
soon as the lock was turned. They may have chased a slave and half brother
with dogs, and they may have gambled over wedlock; but these were forms
or games as silly as Sibbey's imitation of a court lady and as harmless as the
episodes of a silent comedy. Although the actions of the McCaslins and the
Beauchamps in this story are based on slavery, an inhuman system that will
become a foundation of injustice, the individual characters are not guilty.
Although their conventions are shown to be ridiculous, they are also shown
to result in a humane if comic gracefulness and an idyllic equilibrium.

The story is a burlesque of the Garden of Eden, yet it is also true to the
biblical form and meaning: guilt inevitably follows innocence; cruelty and
destruction are inextricably bound with freedom and love. As one reads

further in *Go Down, Moses*, one can reflect that the true focus of the opening story is not Buck, Buddy, Turl, Tennie, Sibbey, or Hubert, but Ike McCaslin. It is Ike's voice that tells the tale, although it is in his cousin Cass's idiom. Ike, past seventy, tells the story but cannot understand it; therefore, he can only repeat verbatim the words of the boy who accompanied Buck and Buddy. Perhaps this was Cass's initiation into adulthood. Ike's initiation comes later, during a bear hunt; but rather than open his eyes to the adult world with all its complexities, it seals them with blinders of fanaticism. Ike never grows beyond the self-conscious dedication of his adolescence. He can never understand the story of his older cousin because he never develops a sense of humor. While a comic view could lead to the acceptance of absurdity for fact, Ike's heroic posture can lead only to outrage and impotence—and finally to the inhumanity of what Hawthorne called the "unpardonable sin."

The next two stories universalize the situation of "Was." "The Fire and the Hearth" establishes the anguish and heroism as well as the pathos and comic dignity of Lucas Beauchamp, the son of Turl and Tennie. "Pantaloon in Black," the most tenuously connected of the stories, establishes the present condition of injustice. A powerful young black is driven mad by his wife's death, kills the white man who has been exploiting the black workers for years in a crooked dice game, and is finally lynched; ironically, the story is told by the sheriff, who misunderstands the young man's motives, to his wife, who is annoyed at being kept from her picture show. "The Old People" brings readers back to the main story line, describing Ike's ritual killing of his first deer, under the tutelage of Sam Fathers. "The Bear" deals with Ike's full initiation into manhood.

"The Bear" is confusing and incomprehensible out of context, for the story is told from Ike's point of view, and readers tend to identify with the idealistic boy. It is only gradually that one comes to see how Ike misinterprets his experience. Ike sees Sam Fathers, the bear, and the dog who is destined to catch it, as taintless and incorruptible, and he sees the woods as ideal. Sam Fathers, the illegitimate son of the Indian chief who sold the land to Carothers McCaslin, now old and the last of his line, teaches Ike humility, patience, self-reliance, and a love for the wilderness. He fails to teach Ike, even though he baptizes the boy in the blood of his first deer, that destruction is a part of life, and that to retreat from this reality is not only suicide but also an impetus to the destructive force. Ike never sees that his taintless and incorruptible bear kills farm animals and cuts a destructive path through the wilderness just like the locomotive; he never admits to himself that the hunters whom he idealizes for the remainder of his life are in fact killers. He is blind to the reality of destruction even as Sam trains the dun-colored dog that will track Old Ben.

Ike can see only the wilderness of James Fenimore Cooper; he is blind to the "heart of darkness" that is all the while before him. Part 4 of "The Bear" is well-known for the tortured, involuted style that represents Ike's mind seeking to grasp and explain an unbelievably complex, absurd, and suppressed heritage. Ike has read through the ledgers of his father and uncle, Buck and Buddy, which burlesque the chronicles of the Old Testament and portray the South in a comic microcosm. He also has discovered that his grandfather, old Carothers McCaslin, not only violated a slave but also later ordered the daughter brought to the house and had another child by her—that Tomey's Turl was a product not only of exploitation and miscegenation but of incest. Ike has come of age, and after arguing with his older cousin, Cass, he decides to repudiate a heritage founded on injustice and rapacity. Believing that Sam Fathers has set him free, he gives the land to Cass and, in imitation of Christ, becomes a carpenter.

Cass tries to explain to Ike the meaning of his responsibility. He knows that Ike is relinquishing the land for the same reason that he refused to shoot Old Ben when he had a perfect chance. The explanation is in Keat's "Ode on a Grecian Urn": Ike would forever hold the moment of his fulfillment. Cass understands that the love on the Grecian Urn had turned "Cold Pastoral," and he will accept compromise. Ike, by his attitude, not only shows a possessiveness as fierce as that of the slave owner and the capitalist but also denies life, which is complex and inevitably fluid.

In "Delta Autumn," Ike, weak and nostalgic and almost eighty years of age, goes into the woods with the grandsons of the hunters who trained him. He is left in the camp while the others go off hunting, and Roth Edmonds, grandson of Cass, asks him to deliver a packet of money. A girl carrying a small child arrives in the camp while Ike is lying in bed without his glasses or trousers. Now his blindness and impotence are brought to full realization. He learns that the girl is not only part black but also the grandniece of Lucas Beauchamp; the situation involves exploitation, miscegenation, and incest, Carothers' ancient sin all over again. Ike can only offer the girl money, the family hunting horn, and advice. His initiation, conversion, and renunciation have served only as an evasion of human responsibility. He has loved an abstraction of the past which blinded him to human necessity, although it did not finally relieve him of his responsibility. The girl recognizes that when Ike gave Cass the land, he contributed to the grandson's recklessness. She does not want money or even a husband; she knew a moment of love and is willing to recognize that it is past. All she wants is recognition. Roth evades the simple but difficult gesture by leaving camp. Ike evades it by offering empty forms and empty words. He himself has reenacted the original sin of Carothers McCaslin, who left his illegitimate child an inheritance, recognizing that this was cheaper than saying "Son" to a black.

The focus of the final story, entitled "Go Down, Moses," is not on Ike, but on the community, as Cleanth Brooks indicates. Lucas Beauchamp's grandson, Samuel, has killed a policeman in Chicago and has been electrocuted. Lucas' wife Mollie, senile and crazed by the outrage, wants the body brought home. The story shows how the leading members of the white community accept the responsibility of hiding the truth from Mollie and of bringing home the body. Sentimentality is balanced by the fine, comic characterization of Mollie.

The history of the past twenty years has dramatized the problem of leaving the race issue to the South, a position that Faulkner advocated explicitly to the press and implicitly in this story. Yet this is only one dimension of Faulkner's philosophy, just as it is a single facet of the story, and both are distorted in isolation. Marvin Klotz tried to establish the superiority of the original stories to their revision and collection in *Go Down, Moses*. While the early stories may have had greater control and a finer economy, the novel that they form is far more ambitious. In a structure that combines various attitudes and perspective, Faulkner gives a picture of the Southern situation and makes of his regional materials a metaphor of the human condition, which combines both love and destruction, which is complex and unbearable and at the same time capable of affirmation—but only when viewed from the humane vantage point that avoids fanaticism and accepts both comedy and tragedy.

GO TELL IT ON THE MOUNTAIN

Type of work: Novel
Author: James Baldwin (1924–   )
Type of plot: Social morality
Time of plot: March, 1935
Locale: Harlem, New York
First published: 1953

>
> *Principal characters:*
>
> JOHN GRIMES, a fourteen-year-old, illegitimate boy
> ELIZABETH GRIMES, his mother
> RICHARD, his father and Elizabeth's lover
> GABRIEL GRIMES, Elizabeth's husband, John's stepfather,
>   and the Deacon of the Temple of the Fire Baptized
> DEBORAH GRIMES, Gabriel's first wife
> ESTHER, Gabriel's mistress
> ROYAL, the son of Gabriel and Esther
> FLORENCE, Gabriel's sister
> FRANK, Florence's husband
> ROY, the son of Gabriel and Elizabeth and John's half
>   brother
> ELISHA, John's Sunday-school teacher

Go Tell It on the Mountain was James Baldwin's first book and first novel. A relatively short work, it continues to impress readers and critics by the economy of its form and the initial statement of Baldwin's vision of the brotherhood of man, represented in the deposition of the father figure and the initiation of the son into the company of the Saints, a religious equivalent of the human brotherhood.

Passages in Baldwin's later essays refer to the autobiographical materials used in this novel, chiefly those discussing his relationship with his father, a preacher in Harlem. The impression of unity in the book is achieved in three ways: by observing the classic unity of time and using only three related settings for the three parts; by structuring the book around Gabriel, the father; and by meticulously exploring and triumphantly concluding the struggle between John and Gabriel. This unity is especially apparent in the middle section. Part 1 shows the maneuvering for position between protagonist and antagonist, and part 3, the deposition of the father and the elevation of the son to equal status as a "saved" member of the congregation.

The extremely formal structure is intended to release a combination of universal meanings. In twenty-four hours, the actions of four members of the Grimes family, together with their past histories summoned up by their actions, reenact the Christ story from John the Baptist to St. John the Divine. Elizabeth was the mother of John the Baptist and his birth was announced to Zacharias by the Archangel Gabriel; further parallels could be developed in the almost consistent use of biblical names. The parallel is imaginative rather than literal and thus cannot be stressed obviously, but it is an effective means of stating the universal themes developed in the action of the novel, culminating in the message of love and release from bondage which is to be told "on the mountain."

The second part is by far the longest. Its setting is the Temple of the Fire Baptized, the church attended by the Grimes family on or near Lenox Avenue in Harlem. This is also the setting of the last portion of part 1 and of the first section of part 3, so that the action of part 2 is prepared at the conclusion of part 1 and concluded at the beginning of part 3. Parts 1 and 3 are comparatively short and serve to frame the middle section, just as the central chapter of the three in part 2 is framed by short chapters on either side. Parts 1 and 3 are chiefly concerned with the hero, John Grimes, and part 2 with Gabriel; John is supported by one of the two important female figures, his mother Elizabeth, and Gabriel is controlled by the other, his elder sister Florence. Her strong personality makes her the most overt doubter of Gabriel's self-sanctified status because she holds the key to his past in knowing the histories of his first wife, Deborah, of his mistress, Esther, and of his dead son, Royal. Royal is brought to life again in Roy, the eldest child of Gabriel and Elizabeth as an incarnation of old Adamic Gabriel before he was "saved."

The histories of Elizabeth and Florence are completed in their reveries of their dead lovers, Richard and Frank, in their chapters titled "Prayers" in part 2. Gabriel is thus related not only to the four female characters but also to all of the male characters but Elisha.

Florence meets her husband, Frank, in New York and loves him hopelessly, though he lives a sensual existence that reminds her painfully of her brother's. After he is killed in France during World War I, she is left with memories of her mother, her brother, her lover, and with a passionate interest in her step-nephew, John.

Elizabeth's "Prayer" shows a true love affair, delicately described and tragically concluded when she, too, goes North to New York with her lover; Richard, like Deborah, Royal, and Roy, falls foul of white society, is wrongfully accused of a crime, is acquitted by Elizabeth's efforts, but ends by committing suicide. Elizabeth is left with John.

The longest "Prayer" is Gabriel's. Filling more than a quarter the length of the book, it follows Florence's, encompasses the histories of all three characters, and is the center of the action and meaning. Gabriel's situation, after having been saved by the Lord's striking him on his way home from a debauch, is complicated. He has married in righteous fashion the blasted Deborah, who had once been so cruelly assaulted by white men that she is sterile. Gabriel, however, longs for a son. When his affair with a maid, Esther, produces Royal, a smaller image of himself, he is caught between the feeling of sin and the feeling of pride. He disowns Esther, who dies in childbirth. Royal is brought up in Gabriel's Southern hometown, and father and son meet only once. Then each offers the other protection after a lynching. After Royal has been killed in Chicago, Deborah taxes Gabriel with his fatherhood, but even in confessing it, Gabriel remains unrepentant: he is a preacher and the Lord will look after and understand him. Esther was a harlot, Deborah objects, and she warns Gabriel to seek true repentance before it is too late.

Gabriel's story is concluded in Elizabeth's "Prayer." At the conclusion of Florence's "Prayer" and of Gabriel's, the reader knows that Deborah has told Florence the secret of Royal. Also, Gabriel's dilemma with Elizabeth is very like that with Esther. Since Royal is dead and Deborah sterile, Roy, having cursed his father, is sulking at home; he is the son of the bondwoman, standing where the true heir ought to stand. Gabriel's Old Testament views have not given him the satisfaction he feels a prophet of the Lord is entitled to; readers are to understand in the irony with which Gabriel's conversion and course as a preacher have been described that Baldwin does not approve of, though he can sympathize with, a kind of religion that omits love because love seems to suggest sensuality.

Gabriel's simple views are seen in John's excursion on the morning of his birthday. He descends in the Hell of the motion-picture house across Sixth Avenue, the Inferno of good and ungodly living, contrasting with the piety and poverty of his home. Having sinned on Sixth Avenue, John returns to find a minor catastrophe and his father's prohibitions justified: Roy has been slashed with a razor during a gang war between white and black hoodlums, and his father is in a towering and righteous rage with everyone but Roy. Aunt Florence stands up to Gabriel, however, telling him that he was born wild and will die wild because nothing can be changed. Gabriel is unredeemed and, in his righteousness, unredeemable.

In Elizabeth's "Prayer," Gabriel is seen in New York after the death of Deborah, trying to change those around him and ready to begin founding his line again. Through Florence, he meets Elizabeth, and John as a baby attracts him enormously. He marries Elizabeth to forgive her her sin—Gabriel is always righteous—and they beget Roy, then Sally, with another baby coming; Gabriel is also highly sensual. The old Adam in him cannot be done away with, as Florence has warned, but his fury is not allowed to wreck the lives of others. For the Lord himself intervenes in two ways that Gabriel hardly expected: John is saved by the Lord, and Gabriel is damned in learning that Florence has Deborah's letter about Esther and Royal, and that she will surely pass it on to Elizabeth and John, if and when the need arises. Gabriel is thus defeated by his own nature, by his past, and by his stepson.

Against this towering male figure, John pits his strength during the twenty-four hours of the novel. John's battle is to reach salvation or God without acknowledging Gabriel as his father; he must reconcile flesh and spirit so as to deny Gabriel's combination of gross sensuality and righteousness, or he will simply turn into another Gabriel, a "black" angel.

John triumphs and is triumphed over in part 3, "The Threshing-Floor," which carries straight on from the dramatic conclusion to part 2 when he is suddenly stricken by the power of the Lord and finds himself thrown down upon the "threshing-floor" in the center of the Saints. The songs of the Saints return to the theme: "To walk in Jerusalem just like John." This night decides the issue whether John can walk there by somehow getting directly to the Lord and not through his stepfather. In an apocalyptic vision, he fights his last battle with the forces of darkness, represented by his father, and thus fights free of his shameful past and regains his real father's independent spirit. Richard is reborn in John as John is reborn and baptized that Sunday morning, as Elizabeth, Florence, and Gabriel realize when they all leave the Temple and walk down Lenox Avenue to meet the new day.

The completely black cast, settings, and speech are highly relevant to the themes of John's initiation and rebirth into a world of love as against sensual enjoyment, a particularly fine but necessary discrimination for a boy of fourteen in Harlem; further, the movement of the novel from the harshly realistic light of Saturday in Harlem through the darkness of the Tarrying Service on Saturday night to the clean Sunday dawn gains figurative value from the blackness of Gabriel and others. This is, then, a black novel in the truest sense: human problems achieve a special and unique coloring without ever becoming strictly racial social problems.

THE GOLD BUG

Type of work: Short story
Author: Edgar Allan Poe (1809–1849)
Type of plot: Mystery romance
Time of plot: Early nineteenth century
Locale: South Carolina
First published: 1843

> Principal characters:
> THE NARRATOR
> WILLIAM LEGRAND, the man who found the gold bug
> JUPITER, his black servant

The Story:

William Legrand has been reduced to poverty by a series of misfortunes. In order to avoid the embarrassment of meeting friends of his more prosperous days, he left New Orleans and went to live on Sullivan's Island, near Charleston, South Carolina. It was a small island, usually uninhabited except for Legrand and his black servant, Jupiter. Jupiter would not leave his master, even though he was a free man and could have found work to support himself in comfort.

Winters on the island were mild and fires were usually unnecessary, but on a night in October when a friend from Charleston visited Legrand, he found Legrand and Jupiter away from the house and a fire blazing in the fireplace. The two soon returned from a quest for entomological specimens. Legrand was in rare good humor. He had stumbled upon an entirely new specimen, a bug of gold. On his way home, he met Lieutenant G——, who took the bug to examine it. Because the friend could not examine it before morning, Legrand took an old piece of parchment from his pocket and drew a picture of the specimen.

As the friend took the drawing, Legrand's dog entered, jumped upon the guest, and licked his face in joy. When the friend finally looked at the paper, he found that the drawing resembled a human skull. Legrand, somewhat disgruntled at this slur on his drawing, took the paper back and prepared to throw it into the fire. After one last glance, however, he paled visibly, rose and seated himself at the table. Then he carefully placed the paper in his wallet. As Legrand appeared distracted and a little sulky, the friend canceled his plans for spending the night and returned to Charleston.

About a month later, the friend received a visit from old Jupiter. The servant reported that his master was not well. Going around as if in a daze, Legrand worked constantly at a cipher. Once he had eluded Jupiter and stayed away the whole day. Jupiter knew that the gold bug was to blame, for it had bitten Legrand on the day he captured it. Jupiter knew that the bug was the reason for Legrand's talk about gold in his sleep. He produced a letter from his master begging the friend to return to the island with Jupiter.

At the island, the friend found Legrand in a state of great excitement. Filled with plans for an expedition to the mainland, he asked the friend to accompany him. After getting Legrand's promise that he would consult a doctor before long, for the man was obviously deranged, the friend joined Legrand and Jupiter in their adventure. Taking the dog with them, they left that evening. Jupiter carried picks and shovels for the three. Legrand took with him the gold bug, attached to a long cord.

After traveling about two hours, they stopped at the foot of a huge tulip tree situated near an almost inaccessible hill. There Legrand commanded Jupiter to take the bug and climb the tree to the seventh limb. Jupiter obeyed, climbing out to the very tip of the limb. On the outer edge, he found a human skull, nailed to the wood. Then Legrand told him to drop the bug through the left eye of the skull. After this strange act, Jupiter climbed down. Legrand, working in feverish anxiety, then began a series of measurements. By the light of lanterns, the men, following Legrand's lead, dug out a hole four feet wide and seven feet deep. When they failed to unearth the treasure Legrand obviously thought he would find, he questioned Jupiter again about the eye through which he had dropped the gold bug. The old man, they learned, had mistakenly dropped the bug through the right eye. Again, Legrand measured and drew circles. By that time the friend shared Legrand's excitement. Again they dug, and at last they came upon an old chest, too heavy to move. Prying open the lid, their eyes fell upon gold and jewels of unbelievable value. They later computed that the total worth was over a million and a half dollars. Leaving Jupiter and the dog to guard what they could not carry, Legrand and his friend took one load home. Then they returned and, with Jupiter's help, carried the rest of the treasure back to the island.

Legrand told his friend in detail how he had solved the riddle of the treasure. The piece of parchment upon which he had drawn the picture of the gold bug had been found near the bug, on the beach. Although the paper had been blank on both sides when he drew the picture, the friend had seen the shape of a skull. He remembered then that the dog had leaped on the friend, causing the paper to come near the fire. Heat from the fire had brought out the outline of a skull. Legrand, seeing the skull when he took the parchment, had begun a feverish attempt to solve its meaning. By dipping the paper in warm water, he had found a numerical code. Deciphering had long been a hobby of his, and thus after a month, he had found the secret of the parchment. It was his belief that the treasure was a fabulous one believed to have been buried by Captain Kidd. Even after he had deciphered the numbering, transposing the figures into words, he had had trouble finding the location of the landmarks revealed in the writing. On the day he had slipped away from Jupiter, however, he had discovered the hill and the tree. On the day of their search, Jupiter's mistake about the left eye had caused an error, but the rectifying of that error had brought the treasure to light. The deciphered code had instructed that a bullet was to be dropped through the left eye of the death's head. Legrand, using the gold bug, wished only to punish his friend for suspecting his sanity.

Critical Evaluation:

"The Gold Bug," Edgar Allan Poe's most famous story, belongs to the small group which he called "tales of ratiocination," that is, tales in which logical reasoning is employed to solve a puzzle. Other Poe stories of this type are *The Murders in the Rue Morgue*, *The Mystery of Marie Roget*, and *The Purloined Letter*—a series of three in which the protagonist is Monsieur C. Auguste Dupin, an amateur detective, whose unnamed friend tells the stories. Arthur Conan Doyle's Sherlock Holmes stories were admittedly inspired by the Dupin tales, and Poe has often been called the father of the modern detective story.

Poe's ratiocinative tales differ from his others in several ways. The vocabulary of several of his tales of terror not only reveals a nervous or fearful state of mind of the narrator, but it is also intended to arouse an emotional response in the reader. The vocabulary of the ratiocinative tales, however, is consciously unemotional to stress the analytical nature of the tales. The structure of these tales also differs from that in the tales of terror. A representative terror tale builds up to a climax of action, often violent, as in *The Fall of the House of Usher* or *The Pit and the Pendulum*. The limited action of a ratiocinative tale occurs mainly in the first half of the story; most of the latter half is devoted to the explication of the mystery or puzzle given earlier. In "The Gold Bug," the action centers upon locating, digging up, and transporting the treasure, and this action is completed almost exactly halfway through the story. Nearly all of the remaining half is made up of the narrator's questions and Legrand's detailed answers or explanations concerning the parchment map and the translation of the cryptic message contained in the numbers and other characters or symbols on it.

In "The Gold Bug," then, Poe has combined the romance of finding buried treasure with the mental excitement of unraveling a mystery. Critics have pointed out inaccuracies in geography and topography, defects in character portrayal, and weak attempts at humor in Jupiter's speech; but the reader forgets or ignores these as Poe carries him along in the search first for immense wealth and then for a meaning in an enigma.

THE GOLDEN APPLES

Type of work: Interconnected short stories
Author: Eudora Welty (1909–   )
Type of plots: Regional realism
Time of plots: 1900–1940
Locale: "Morgana," Mississippi
First published: 1949

>   *Principal characters:*
>   KING MacLAIN, the wandering patriarch of the town
>   MRS. SNOWDIE HUDSON MacLAIN, his wife and an albino
>   RANDALL MacLAIN and
>   EUGENE MacLAIN, the twin sons of King and Snowdie
>   MRS. FATE RAINEY, the town gossip
>   VIRGIE RAINEY, her daughter and the protégée of Miss
>   Eckhart
>   MISS ECKHART, a half-crazed music teacher
>   LOCH MORRISON, a boy who saves a drowning girl and
>   sees things wrong and yet peculiarly right
>   CASSIE MORRISON, his sister who sees things correctly but
>   lacks depth
>   EASTER, a girl saved from drowning by Loch

The Golden Apples, first published in 1949, is a group of seven short stories, interrelated and held together by their characters; their common setting, Morgana, Mississippi; and their common theme, the wanderer's search for happiness. The stories were all published separately, but taken together they cover some forty years in the lives of the inhabitants of Morgana and form a complete drama in which they are engaged. The list of a *dramatis personae* on the first page of the book indicates that readers are to consider the work as a unified whole. The related stories are in some ways Eudora Welty's attempt to create a regional world like Faulkner's, in this case MacLain County, not Yoknapatawpha, but her focus is neither upon the Sartorises nor upon the Snopeses but on the comfortable upper-middle class and their everyday activities such as piano recitals, camping trips for the young girls, gossip between neighbors, and funerals. This world is examined from all sides, extending even to the structural device of point of view. Thus the first story, "Shower of Gold," is narrated by the gossipy Mrs. Rainey, whose matter-of-factness contrasts with the mystery of what she reveals about King MacLain and his influence upon the community. "June Recital" is revealed through the eyes of two witnesses: Loch Morrison, the young boy who sees everything wrong yet peculiarly right, and older Cassie, his sister, who sees correctly but does not share the insights or life force of her brother. "The Whole World

Knows" is revealed through the eyes of Randall MacLain, a somewhat blurred vision that discovers a certain truth as it reenacts what it observed. Whatever the point of view, Welty is able to get beneath the veneer of middle-class comfort and scratch the surface of "place" to get at the hidden lives and hidden mysteries of her characters.

The common setting is not the only unifying factor for the stories. They are held together by Yeats's poem, "The Song of the Wandering Aengus" from which the title of the collection is taken. This poem breaks into Cassie's mind as she tells her narrative, and in a very real way, it is the symbolic key to the meaning of the work as a whole. The poem itself is about a quest, a search for golden apples, representing beauty, poetry, ultimate meaning, a search that is marked by the pursuit of a vision, a mystery where a silver trout becomes a "glimmering girl" before the eyes of Aengus. The people of Morgana are also wanderers, in search of the meaning that will transform the commonness of their lives and make the name of the town as magical as it sounds in its resemblance to the name Morgan le Fay. This search reveals the mysterious beauty that lies beneath the surfaces of their lives, and is brought out by Welty in an attempt to transform them. This movement and interest is typical of most of Welty's work.

The tone of the stories is rather unlike Welty's earlier fiction, for there is not so much variety of mood here as in her early work but rather a pervasive feeling of solemnity and sadness, even in such works as "Moon Lake," in which a "silver trout," this time a girl named Easter, is presumably drowned and brought back to shore but is resurrected by Loch Morrison, a Boy Scout. Here the trout does not become a "glimmering girl" but remains a choking twelve-year-old with mud and blood coming from her mouth. The mystery of life is here, but the beauty is somewhat harder to perceive. There has been an acceptance of the symbols of Yeats, but an unwillingness to accept the direction in which the symbols lead. The search is there, but there is the sadness of the knowledge that there will be no glimmering girl.

Yet despite the solemnity and sadness, there is the affirmation of human life and its values. In *The Golden Apples*, the journey through innocence to experience and meaning is painful, and often the wanderers' knowledge is only of their predicament, not of its solution; but it is knowledge and knowledge won from experience. This affirmation is tied to the region, but the universal is symbolized in the regional, as is so often the case with Southern writers. Welty's manner of achieving this universality of the human predicament is unique. She evokes the universal by invoking the mythic and the magical. She takes a real world, Mississippi, and makes it legendary, Morgana.

The title of the book is the first hint of the pervasive use of myth and symbol. The poem from which the title is taken sets the mythical mood and the character and events are consonant with it. There is the figure of King MacLain, who seems to grow out of the character of Don McInnis in Welty's early story "Asphodel," a story that also makes use of myth for its mood of gentle fantasy. King first appears in "Shower of Gold" and reappears throughout most of the other stories, flitting in and out of the action like a golden butterfly. Morgana is in MacLain County, in fact, and thus even geographically the King's presence is to be felt. King finally comes to rest in the last story, "The Wanderers," but even there his vitality at the funeral of Mrs. Rainey is a source of amazement and admiration for Virgie Rainey. MacLain is not only king but also Zeus. There are many conscious allusions to him in this role. As a sort of wandering pagan god, he lies in wait for unsuspecting girls in the woods and populates the town with his progeny. "Sir Rabbit" is a story of such a seduction. There is something beautiful as well as slyly humorous in his comings and goings, as can be seen in all the children who have inherited their golden hair from his golden touch upon their mothers. Mrs. Rainey states in "Shower of Gold" that King has run away to the gold fields. Whenever he returns, he brings some of it with him.

There are many people in the town who are related to him. Randall and Eugene MacLain are not his only children. There are broad hints that Loch Morrison might be his child, and also Easter, the resurrected orphan girl in "Moon Lake." They both share his preoccupation with the vital forces of life and are wanderers like himself. Every one of the seven stories has a character related to him. Thus, he is intimately connected with the golden apples as a unifying symbol; indeed, he is more symbol than human and connected with the wandering search that the quest for the golden apples entails. All of his fellow seekers and roamers are brought together in the final story, "The Wanderers," and each of these wanderers, like Aengus in Yeats's poem, has his own "song."

Perhaps the most attractive and memorable of these is Virgie Rainey, whose name connects her with King in his "Shower of Gold." Her father's name is Fate, and she is the best musician in Morgana. Virgie is the protégée of Miss Eckhart, the outsider who is the music teacher for all Morgana and who remains one of the most pathetic characters in the book. Miss Eckhart belongs to the large group of Welty grotesques, lonely and isolated characters who have been warped by their lack of love. In "June Recital," Miss Eckhart escapes from a mental institution to try to burn down the house in which she had taught her many lessons, giving the town music and getting nothing in return.

Virgie is Miss Eckhart's pupil but not her disciple. Music has set her free, and she moves toward freedom by leaving Miss Eckhart to become the pianist at the silent movies and from there to various strangers passing through, to the final escape after her mother's death in "The Wanderers." She is joined as a wanderer with Randall MacLain, inheritor of his father's domain, for he is mayor of Morgana; in "The Whole World Knows," he creates tragedy by involving another in his quest. Maideen Sumrall commits suicide because Ran does not seem to be able to see beyond his own problems and thus realize that others are seekers also. Eugene MacLain discovers what it means to be a wanderer on a beach in California, where he has gone in company with a Spanish musician he met by chance. Loch Morrison is the blower of the golden horn, the Boy Scout in charge of reveille at Moon Lake. Easter is the orphan who wants to be a singer. All the wanderers have their song.

The one constant feature in all of these songs is that they are sung in silence, by solitary singers. Virgie accepts the gift of Beethoven from Miss Eckhart, but the gift does not bind her to the giver. That is the tragic and perhaps ennobling aspect of the wanderers. They give the gift of love, but love truly given separates and does not create a recognizable union. Those who truly know the value of the golden apples realize that the search is never over. What union there is remains a union in search of the unattainable. This is the community that is felt by some of the wanderers, notably Virgie. They are all victims of the search, and that is the reason for the pervasive sadness. Yet in their common circumstance as victims, they are also all heroes. Welty expressed this idea well and characteristically at the end of "The Wanderers" by referring to the myth of Medusa and Perseus. To cut off the Medusa's head was heroic, but it revealed a horror about life that is life's separateness. Life is a condition in which both the Medusa and Perseus are ever-present. The glory is in the struggle; the tragedy in the lack of completion of that struggle. The golden apples are more beautiful because they will always be on the tree.

THE GOLDEN BOWL

Type of work: Novel
Author: Henry James (1843–1916)
Type of plot: Psychological realism
Time of plot: c. 1900
Locale: England and the Continent
First published: 1904

> *Principal characters:*
> MR. VERVER, a wealthy American living in England
> MAGGIE VERVER, his daughter
> PRINCE AMERIGO, an Italian nobleman married to Maggie
> Verver
> CHARLOTTE STANT, a school friend of Maggie Verver
> MRS. ASSINGHAM, a friend of the Ververs and the Prince

The Story:

Maggie Verver was the daughter of a wealthy American widower who had devoted all his life to his daughter. The Ververs lived a lazy life. Their time was spent in collecting items to decorate their own existence and to fill a museum that Mr. Verver was giving to his native city back in the United States. They had few friends, Maggie's only confidante was Mrs. Assingham, the American-born wife of a retired British Army officer.

It was Mrs. Assingham who introduced the Ververs to Prince Amerigo, a handsome, quiet young Italian nobleman who struck Maggie's fancy. When she informed her father that she would like to marry the Prince, Mr. Verver provided a handsome dowry so that the wedding might take place.

A few days before the wedding, a painful scene occurred in Mrs. Assingham's home, where the Prince and Charlotte Stant, deeply in love with each other, met to say good-bye. Each was penniless, and a marriage had been out of the question. Since both were friends of Maggie, the present situation was painful for them. As a farewell lark, they spent the last afternoon in searching for a wedding present for Charlotte to present to Maggie. In a tiny shop, they discovered a golden bowl which Charlotte wished to purchase as a remembrance for the Prince from her. He refused it because of superstitious fears that a crack in the golden bowl might bring bad luck.

After the wedding of the Prince and Maggie, the lives of the pair coincided with the life that the Ververs had been living for years. Maggie and her father spent much of their time together. The Prince, although he did not complain,

THE GOLDEN BOWL by Henry James. By permission of the agent, Paul R. Reynolds & Son, New York, and the publishers, Charles Scribner's Sons. Copyright, 1904, by Charles Scribner's Sons. Renewed, 1932, by Henry James, Executor.

was really only a convenience that they had purchased because Maggie had reached the age when she needed to have a husband.

After a year and a half, a baby was born to the Prince and Maggie, but the child made no apparent difference in the relationships between the woman and her father or the woman and her husband. Maggie decided that her father also needed a wife. She went to Mrs. Assingham and told her friend that she planned to have Charlotte Stant marry her father. Charlotte was a quiet person aware of the love between Maggie and her father, and she was the sort of person who would be thankful to marry a wealthy man that she would cause little trouble. Neither Maggie nor Mrs. Assingham put this aspect into words, but it was tacitly understood.

Mr. Verver, anxious to please his daughter in this as in everything else, married Charlotte a short time later. This second marriage created a strange situation. Maggie and her father both took houses in London where they could be together a great deal of the time. The association of father and daughter left the Prince and Charlotte together much of the time. Maggie encouraged them to go out, to represent her and her father at balls and dinners. Maggie, however, did not know that her husband and her stepmother had been intimate before her own marriage to the Prince.

Several years went by in this manner, but slowly the fact that there was something strange in the relationships dawned upon Maggie's sensitive feelings. She eventually went to Mrs. Assingham and poured out her suspicions. Mrs. Assingham, in full knowledge of the circumstances, decided to keep silent.

Maggie resolved to say nothing of her suspicions to anyone else. Yet her attitude of indifference and her insistence in throwing the Prince and Charlotte together, aroused their suspicions that she knew they had been sweethearts and that she suspected them of being lovers after marriage.

Each one of the four speculated at length as to what the other three knew or suspected. Yet their mutual confidence and love prevented each one of them from ever asking anything of the others.

One day, Maggie went shopping for some unusual art object to present to her father on his birthday. She accidentally happened into the same shop where the Prince and Charlotte had gone several years before, and she purchased the golden bowl that they had passed over because of its flaw. The following day, the shopkeeper visited her. The name and address had told him that she was the wife of the Prince who had passed up the bowl years before. He knew that the existence of the crack would quickly come to the attention of the Prince, and so he had hastened to inform Maggie of the flaw and to return part of the purchase price. He also told her of the Prince's first visit to the shop and of the young woman who had been with him. Maggie then knew that the Prince and Charlotte had known each other before her marriage and that they had spent an afternoon together the day before she was married. She was upset. Again, she confided in Mrs. Assingham.

Having learned that there was no serious relationship between the Prince and Charlotte, Mrs. Assingham informed Maggie that she was making a great ado over nothing at all. To back up her remark, she raised the bowl above her head and smashed it to the floor, where it broke into several pieces. As she did so, the Prince entered the room and saw the fragments of the bowl. After Mrs. Assingham's departure, he tried to learn how much Maggie knew. Maggie and her husband agreed to say nothing to either Maggie's father or to Charlotte.

Charlotte, too, began to sense that something had disturbed Maggie, and she shrewdly guessed what it was. Then Maggie tried to realign the relationships of the four by proposing that she and Charlotte stay together for awhile and that the Prince and her father go to the Continent to buy art objects. This proposal was gently put forward and as gently rebuffed by the other three.

Maggie and her father began to realize that their selfishness in continuing the father-daughter relationship that they had had before her marriage was wrong. Shortly after that selfishness had been brought into the open and discussed by Maggie and Mr. Verver, Charlotte told Maggie that she wished to return to America and to take her husband with her. She bluntly informed Maggie that she was afraid that if Mr. Verver continued to live so close to his daughter, he would lose interest in his wife. Mr. Verver agreed to accompany Charlotte back to the United States. It was a difficult decision for him to make. He realized that once he was away, Charlotte would never agree to his coming back to Europe to live.

On an autumn afternoon, Mr. Verver and Charlotte went to have tea with Maggie and the Prince before leaving England. It was almost heartbreaking to Maggie to see her father's carriage take him out of sight and to know that her old way of life had really ended. The only thing that kept her from breaking down completely was the look on the Prince's face as he turned her face away from the direction her father's carriage had taken. At that moment, seeing his eyes, Maggie knew she had won her husband for herself and not for her money.

Critical Evaluation:

The Golden Bowl, along with *The Ambassadors* and *The Wings of the Dove*, is one of the novels of the triad of works upon which the high reputation of Henry James's "major phase" rests. In these novels, James's already complex style reaches new levels of sophistication as, increasingly, the writing becomes more and more intricate and convoluted as it tends toward ever-increasingly subtle levels of analysis of character and event. Gradually the "center of consciousness" in the mind of a character, which had been essential to James's earlier works, gives way to an omniscient narrative point of view, and a narrative voice that is James's own. Though it hardly appears so to the eye, James's style of this period is essentially oral—he had developed the habit of dictating his material to a secretary—and reflects his characteristically ponderous manner of speech. Seeming to move endlessly to circle or enfold a subject or an idea without ever touching it directly, James's language and technique in these late novels has been admired highly by critics who place a premium on style, while frequently being disparaged by those who stress content and clarity of thought. For James himself, the art of the novel was everything in writing, and there is little doubt that in *The Golden Bowl*, his artistry reached a peak.

With this novel, James continues the subject matter of the "international theme," which had characterized his work from its beginning, by dealing with a group of Americans in Europe. Adam Verver, in particular, can be seen as an avatar of the American Adam who recurs in James's fiction, often, as here, in search of European culture, which he will take back to his culturally barren homeland. Prince Amerigo is linked by his name to the historic connection between America and Europe, and, by his marriage to Maggie, might be seen as dramatizing a new dependence of the Old World upon the New. Yet, *The Golden Bowl* ultimately is less an international novel than such works as *The American*, *Daisy Miller*, or *The Ambassadors* because its concerns are finally more with individuals than with cultures. Though the Ververs begin in America and Adam returns there at the novel's end, neither his experience nor that of Maggie or Charlotte is essentially contingent upon the sort of conflict of cultural values that is at the heart of James's international novels and stories. Rather, the problems of love and marriage at the heart of *The Golden Bowl* are truly universal; neither their nature nor their solution depend upon an American perspective.

Like many of James's works, *The Golden Bowl* began in his notebooks with the recording of an anecdote he had heard concerning a young woman and her widower father, each of whom had taken spouses, who learned their partners were engaged in an affair. From this scant beginning, James crafted his longest and most elaborate novel, not by greatly complicating the essential material of this simple plot, but by scrupulous elaboration of the conflicts and resolutions resulting from the complex relations among his four central characters. By making his characters members of the wealthy leisure class, James frees them from the mundane worries of the world so he can focus his, and their, entire attention on the one particular problem without regard to external complications. Ultimately, the novel seeks to pose moral and philosophical questions that transcend either the psychological or social levels of the work to confront the basic question of Maggie's adjustment to a less-than-perfect world.

The golden bowl is James's metaphor for the marriage between Amerigo and Maggie, and perhaps, in its larger implications, for life itself. The bowl, not really "golden" at all, but crystal gilded with gold leaf, has the superficial appearance of perfection, but is, in fact, cracked. As a symbol of Maggie's "perfect" marriage, the bowl very clearly illustrates the flaw at the heart of the relationship—a flaw that no doubt existed even before the Prince and Charlotte resume their old love affair and that represents a potential threat to the marriage. Both Maggie and her father are guilty of treating the Prince as nothing more than one of the valuable objects they have come to Europe to purchase—they have bought the perfect marriage for Maggie. Unlike art, however, human relationships are not subject to purchase, nor can they, as in the case of Adam's marriage to Charlotte, be arranged for convenience without regard to the human factors concerned. In fact, both Maggie and her father tend to live in a small, supremely selfish world. Insulated by their money from the actuality of life, they isolate themselves from the real complexities of daily existence. Their world is, in effect, itself more "art" than "life."

The resolution of the novel turns around Maggie's positive act, but in the earlier parts of the novel, she is more passive than active. The marriage itself, for example, seems more of an arrangement between the Prince and Adam Verver than a particular choice of Maggie's—Adam wants the perfect marriage for his daughter, and Prince Amerigo wants access to the Verver millions, so they come to an agreement between themselves. Maggie apparently has little to say about it, and even, judging from her relationship to the Prince throughout most of the novel, no very great interest in the marriage. Her real desire seems to be to continue life with her father as always, rather than to begin an independent life with her husband. Only when confronted with the Prince's infidelity does Maggie recognize that she must confront this reality for all their sakes. In choosing to separate from her father in order to begin making the best of her imperfect marriage, Maggie discovers a latent ability to confront the world as it really is and to rise above the romantic idealism that had characterized her life with Adam Verver.

GONE WITH THE WIND

Type of work: Novel
Author: Margaret Mitchell (1900–1949)
Type of plot: Historical romance
Time of plot: 1861–1873
Locale: Atlanta and Tara Plantation, Georgia
First published: 1936

Principal characters:

SCARLETT O'HARA, a Georgia belle
RHETT BUTLER, an unscrupulous profiteer and her third
    husband
ASHLEY WILKES, a sensitive neighbor, loved by Scarlett
MELANIE WILKES, Ashley's wife
GERALD O'HARA, the master of Tara Plantation and
    Scarlett's father
ELLEN O'HARA, Scarlett's mother
CHARLES HAMILTON, Melanie's brother and Scarlett's first
    husband
FRANK KENNEDY, Scarlett's second husband
MISS PITTYPAT, Melanie's maiden aunt
INDIA, Ashley's sister
MAMMY, Scarlett's nurse
BONNIE BLUE, the child of Scarlett and Rhett

Gone with the Wind, one of the best-selling novels of all time, is the story of the subjugation of a proud people by war and the harsh "reconstruction" that followed. Swept along with these events is the beautiful, headstrong daughter of a wealthy plantation owner who, when reduced to poverty and hardship in the wake of Sherman's cruel and vicious destruction of the countryside, used her feminine wiles to regain her lost wealth. Having at last attained this goal, she was unable to hold the one man she really loved.

A historical romance of prodigious proportions, the first novel by an unknown author went through twelve printings within two months of publication. Its 1,037 pages enthralled millions, and the sales in a single year exceeded two million copies. The novel has been translated into more than two dozen languages and even after forty years, sales continue at a pace brisk enough to please any publisher. The motion picture lived up to Hollywood's most studied superlatives, and the photoplay has had tremendous worldwide popularity.

The unprecedented success of Margaret Mitchell's only novel may be attributed to a combination of the author's style—a sustained narrative power combined with remarkable character delineation—and the universality of her subject: the struggle for survival when the accustomed security of civilized life is abruptly swept away and the human spirit suddenly stands alone. In spite of the fast-moving narrative, one is aware of this underlying thread of universality, this familiarity with human tragedy that all men can understand.

Perhaps the most lasting impression one gets from the novel, however, is the skill with which Mitchell handles her characterizations. Scarlett O'Hara is, without question, one of the most memorable characters in fiction. So lifelike did she become in the public mind that the producers of the motion picture preferred not to risk an established actress in the role and be accused of miscasting.

The story of Scarlett O'Hara alone would be reason enough for a best-seller; many books have achieved such eminence on far less. This daughter of Irish temper and French sensibilities displays stark and bold emotions that grip the reader. One follows her intense, futile love for Ashley Wilkes, her spiteful marriage to Charles Hamilton, her opportunistic stealing of her sister's fiancé, Frank Kennedy, her grasping arrangement of convenience with Rhett Butler. One is sometimes appalled at her callous use of her sex to gain her ends; one looks in vain for some sign of lofty ideals in this woman; and yet, in spite of all of this, one finds laudable her will to survive and her contempt for her conquerors.

Three other characters stand out, admirably drawn but not quite inspiring the amount of interest created by Scarlett. Rhett Butler, dissolute son of Charleston blue bloods, is a cynical, materialistic blockade runner who consorts openly with the enemy and scoffs at patriotic ideals. Forceful and masculine, he is accustomed to taking what he wants. His one unfulfilled desire is the love of Scarlett, and this frustration finally breaks his spirit. When at last, after several years of unhappy marriage, he gains her love as Ashley defaults, Rhett, now a bitter, fleshy toper, has already reached his decision to leave her.

Ashley Wilkes, the weak-willed object of Scarlett's misguided passion, depicts the impractical idealist dependent on a stronger will to solve life's problems for him. When Scarlett observes his unstable reaction to his wife's death, she is finally able to see him as he really is. Shorn of his cavalier manners and the aura of courtly romance she had bestowed upon him, he becomes an ineffectual weakling in her eyes, and the sterility of her forbidden love is at last apparent.

Melanie, in a way the winner despite her death at the end of the novel, found happiness and tranquility in her devotion to her insecure husband. Reticent, ladylike, saccharine, but intellectually attuned to Ashley, there is never any question that she, not Scarlett, should be Ashley's wife.

High-spirited Scarlett was sixteen years old when the Civil War began. She fancied herself in love with Ashley Wilkes, the sensitive, sophisticated son at a neighboring plantation, but he did not acknowledge her love. Upon the announcement of his engagement to his soft-spoken cousin Melanie Hamilton, Scarlett impetuously married Melanie's brother Charles, to that surprised young man's pride and delight. Less than a year later, Scarlett was a war widow and an unwilling mother.

Here the novel loses the tempo of leisurely plantation life and takes on the urgency of a region at war. Leaving her father's plantation, Tara, Scarlett traveled twenty-five miles to Atlanta to stay with her dead husband's relatives. Later, as Atlanta was besieged by Sherman's troops, Scarlett returned home to Tara through the battle lines at night in a wagon provided by Rhett. With her were Melanie and Ashley's day-old son whom Scarlett had delivered as guns sounded in the distance.

Approaching Tara through the battle-scarred countryside, she saw that most of the plantation mansions had been looted and burned by the enemy. Tara had been spared as a headquarters, though the outbuildings and baled cotton had been burned and the hogs, cows, and chickens killed. Scarlett's mother, too ill with fever to be moved as the soldiers approached, died with her beloved Tara filled with Yankee conquerors. Her father's mind, unable to stand these shocks, was gone. Now the sheltered Southern belle was faced with the formidable prospect of feeding, from a plantation stripped bare by the ruthless invaders, her father, her child, two sisters, Melanie, and the few servants who remained faithfully behind when the others ran off.

These are the events that helped to shape the character of Scarlett O'Hara, and they explain the hardness and avarice that prompted many of her actions. For example, she was determined to hold on to Tara, and when the carpetbaggers arbitrarily levied an extra three-hundred-dollar tax with the expectation of taking over the property for unpaid taxes, Scarlett unhesitatingly married storeowner Frank Kennedy, who was engaged to her sister Suellen, and he dutifully paid the three-hundred-dollar tax.

Mitchell's art makes such reprehensible acts seem normal under the circumstances, for the author has skillfully brought readers along the same harsh road Scarlett has traveled and, thus exposed to the same experiences, readers understand, even condone, her responses.

Once Scarlett had learned the law of the jungle, her native abilities came into their own. Borrowing money from Rhett, she bought and successfully operated a sawmill and soon was financially secure. When Frank was killed by occupation troops, she married Rhett, who had amassed half a million dollars during the war as a blockade runner. But even the birth of a child, Bonnie Blue, did not bring happiness to this union because of the love for Ashley to which Scarlett absurdly clung. Rhett, always jealous of this will-of-the-wisp emotion, was unable to cope with what he could not understand. Ironically, Rhett overcame his love for Scarlett just as she was discovering that it was he, not Ashley, whom she loved. When she tried to tell him this, Rhett announced brusquely that she was too late, that he was leaving her forever. There was no mistaking the finality of his words but, characteristically, Scarlett, the self-confident schemer, would not accept them as such.

Gone with the Wind is not a happy book. There are flicks of humor, but for the most part, a deadly seriousness pervades the novel and in the end the callous, grasping cynicism of the leading characters mocks them and, properly, only an empty loneliness remains.

A natural question concerns the position of *Gone with the Wind* and its author in world literature. On the strength of her one novel, Mitchell certainly cannot be called a great author. Whether her outstanding book will rank as a great novel will not be decided by those who consider the question at this early date. If the work eventually achieves first rank, it will be because Scarlett O'Hara continues to convey to future readers the same essence of human behavior that we ourselves see in her now.

THE GOOD EARTH

Type of work: Novel
Author: Pearl S. Buck (1892–1973)
Type of plot: Social chronicle
Time of plot: Early twentieth century
Locale: Northern China
First published: 1931

Principal characters:
WANG LUNG, a Chinese farmer
O-LAN, his wife
LOTUS BLOSSOM, his concubine
PEAR BLOSSOM, his slave
NUNG EN, Wang Lung's oldest son
NUNG WEN, Wang Lung's second son
THE FOOL, Wang Lung's first daughter

The Story:

His father had chosen a slave girl to be the bride of Wang Lung, a slave from the house of Hwang, a girl who would keep the house clean, prepare the food, and not waste her time thinking about clothes. On the morning he led her out through the gate of the big house, they stopped at a temple and burned incense. That was their marriage.

O-lan was a good wife. She thriftily gathered twigs and wood so that they would not have to buy fuel. She mended Wang Lung's and his father's winter clothes and scoured the house. She worked in the fields beside her husband, even on the day she bore their first son.

The harvest was a good one that year. Wang Lung had a handful of silver dollars from the sale of his wheat and rice. He and O-lan bought new coats for themselves and new clothes for the baby. Together they went to pay their respects, with their child, at the home in which O-lan had once been a slave. With some of the silver dollars, Wang Lung bought a small field of rich land from the Hwangs.

The second child was born a year later. It was again a year of good harvest.

Wang Lung's third baby was a girl. On the day of her birth, crows flew about the house, mocking Wang Lung with their cries. The farmer did not rejoice when his little daughter was born, for poor farmers reared their daughters only to serve the rich. The crows had been an evil omen; the child was born feebleminded.

That summer was dry, and for months no rain fell. The harvest was poor.

After the little rice and wheat had been eaten and the ox killed for food, there was nothing for the poor peasants to do but die or go south to find work and food in a province of plenty. Wang Lung sold their furniture for a few pieces of silver, and after O-lan had borne their fourth child, dead with bruises on its neck when he saw it for the first time, the family began their journey. Falling in with a crowd of refugees, they were lucky. The refugees led them to a railroad, and with the money Wang Lung had received for his furniture, they traveled on a train to their new home.

In the city, they constructed a hut of mats against a wall, and while O-lan and the two older children begged, Wang Lung pulled a ricksha. In that way, they spent the winter, each day earning enough to buy rice for the next.

One day, an exciting thing happened. There was to be a battle between soldiers in the town and an approaching enemy. When the wealthy people in the town fled, the poor who lived so miserably broke into the houses of the rich. By threatening one fat fellow who had been left behind, Wang Lung obtained enough money to take his family home.

O-lan soon repaired the damage that the weather had done to their house during their absence; then, with jewels that his wife had managed to plunder during the looting in the city, Wang Lung bought more land from the house of Hwang. He allowed O-lan to keep two small pearls that she liked. Now Wang Lung had more land than one man could handle, and he hired one of his neighbors, Ching, as overseer. Several years later, he had six men working for him. O-lan had borne him twins, a boy and a girl, after their return from the south. She no longer went out into the fields to work but kept the new house he had built. Wang Lung's two oldest sons were sent to school in the town.

When his land was flooded and work impossible until the water receded, Wang Lung began to go regularly to a tea shop in the town. There he fell in love with Lotus Blossom and brought her home to his farm to be his concubine. O-lan would have nothing to do with the girl, and Wang Lung was forced to set up a separate establishment for Lotus in order to keep the peace.

When he found that his oldest son visited Lotus often while he was away, Wang Lung arranged to have the boy marry the daughter of a grain merchant in the town. The wedding took place shortly before O-lan, still in the prime of life, died of a chronic stomach illness. To cement the bond between the farmer and the grain merchant, Wang Lung's second son was apprenticed to Liu, the merchant, and his youngest daughter was betrothed to Liu's young son. Soon after O-lan's death, Wang Lung's father followed her. They were buried near each other on a hill on his land.

When he grew wealthy, an uncle, his wife, and his shiftless son came to live with Wang Lung. One year, there was a great flood, and although his neighbors' houses were pillaged by robbers during the confusion, Wang Lung was not bothered. Then he learned that his uncle was second to the chief of the robbers. From that time on, he had to give way to his uncle's family, for they were his insurance against robbery and perhaps murder.

At last, Wang Lung coaxed his uncle and aunt to smoke opium, and they became too involved in their dreams to bother him. There was no way, however, that he could curb their son. When the boy began to annoy the wife of Wang Lung's oldest son, the farmer rented the deserted house of Hwang, and he, with his own family, moved into town. The cousin left to join the soldiers. The uncle and aunt were left in the country with their pipes to console them.

After Wang Lung's overseer died, he did no more farming himself. From that time on, he rented his land, hoping that his youngest son would work it after his death. Yet he was disappointed. When Wang Lung took a slave young enough to be his granddaughter, the boy, who was in love with her, ran away from home and became a soldier.

When he felt that his death was near, Wang Lung went back to live on his land, taking with him only his slave, young Pear Blossom, his foolish-witted first daughter, and some servants. One day, as he accompanied his sons across the fields, he overheard them planning what they would do with their inheritance, with the money they would get from selling their father's property. Wang Lung cried out, protesting that they must never sell the land because only from it could they be sure of earning a living. He did not know that they looked at each other over his head and smiled.

Critical Evaluation:

Pearl Sydenstricker Buck referred to herself as "mentally bifocal" with respect to her American and Chinese ways of looking at things. The daughter of American missionaries in China, Buck came to know that land better than any other. She spent her early formative years in China, and that time was extremely significant in developing her ideas, viewpoints, and philosophy. She attended schools both in China and the United States and made several trips back and forth, some unwillingly as when she and her parents were expelled from China during the Boxer Rebellion of 1900.

Buck began her writing as a girl in China with articles and short stories. There is no doubt that she had a gift for making the strange, unknown, and distant appear familiar. Until the time of her first published success, *East Wind, West Wind*, very little had been written about simple Chinese life although China was becoming of increasing interest to businessmen, diplomats, and missionaries. Nevertheless, the general public thought of the Chinese in rather strange terms, not as people with whom they could easily identify. Buck's feeling for the fundamental truths of life transcended any preconceived notions that the reading public may have had about China and portrayed her people as understandable human beings who struggled for happiness and success like anyone else.

The Good Earth was published in 1931 and is probably Buck's most popular and widely read novel. It depicts a simple picture, the cycle of life from early years until death. Some Americans who first read the book thought the simple detailed descriptions of everyday Chinese life were "too Chinese" and, therefore, unappealing. Then, too, some Chinese felt that the author's portrayal of their people was inaccurate and incomplete. Most Chinese intellectuals objected to her choice of the peasant farmer as a worthy subject of a novel. They preferred to have the Western world see the intellectual and philosophical Chinese, even though that group was (and is) definitely in the minority. Buck's only answer to such criticism was that she wrote about what she knew best, and these were the people whom she saw and came to know and love during her years in the interior of China.

The theme of *The Good Earth* is an uncomplicated one with universal appeal. The author tries to show how man can rise from poverty and relative insignificance to a position of importance and wealth. In some ways, the story is the proverbial Horatio Alger tale that so many Americans know and admire. The difference with this novel and the feature that makes it unique is its setting. Wang Lung, the main character around whom the action in the novel revolves, is a poor man who knows very little apart from the fact that land is valuable, solid, and worth owning. Therefore, he spends his entire life trying to acquire as much land as he can in order to insure his own security as well as that of his family and descendants for generations to come. Ironically, he becomes like the rich he at first holds in awe. He has allowed himself to follow in their path and separate himself from the land and live above toil and dirt. The earth theme appears repeatedly throughout the book. Wang Lung's greatest joy is to look out over his land, to hold it in his fingers, and to work it for his survival. Even at the end of the novel, he returns to the old quarters he occupied on his first plot of land so that he can find the peace he knows his kinship with the land can bring him.

Buck's style is that of a simple direct narrative. There are no complicated literary techniques such as foreshadowing, flashbacks, or stream of consciousness. There are also no involved subplots to detract from the main story line. Wang Lung is, as has been noted, the central character, and all the other characters and their actions relate in one way or another to him. *The Good Earth* is structured upon characterization, and it is a book of dramatic episodes that are projected through the sensitivities and experiences of those characters. It may be said that a strength of the author's characterization is her consistency, that is to say, all of her characters act and react in keeping with their personalities. None is a stereotype, as their motives are too complex. O-lan is typically good, but there are aspects of her personality that give her depth, dimension, and originality. When she does some seemingly dishonest thing such as steal the jewels she found at the home of the plundered rich, or kill the small baby girl born to her in ill health, she is consistent with her character in the context of these situations. She is realistic and sees both acts as producing more good than evil. O-lan is courageous and faithful and, throughout the novel, she maintains a beautiful dignity that gives her a special identity of her own, even if she is an unpretty common slave.

One of the most obvious and significant Chinese customs that appears repeatedly in the novel is the submission of the wife in all things to the will of the man. Girl children were born only to be reared for someone else's house as slaves, while men were born to carry on family names, traditions, and property. This situation is based on the Chinese position that women are inferior to men. The reader cannot help but be struck by this attitude as it manifests itself in the lives of the men and women in *The Good Earth*.

The novel may be criticized as having no high point or climax. True enough, there is no point of great and significant decision. There is no one who causes Wang Lung any serious struggle. His only antagonists are the adversity of the elements and the occasional arguments he has with his lazy uncle and his worthless nephew. Dramatic interest is sustained in the novel by well-placed turning points that give the story new direction. The first is Wang Lung's marriage to O-lan and their first satisfying years together. Then, in the face of poverty, destitution, and little hope of recovery, Wang Lung demands and receives the handful of gold from the rich man and is thus able to get back to his land. At this point, readers see how much Wang Lung's land means to him and what he is willing to do to have it back. In the closing pages of the novel, the quiet servitude and devotion of Pear Blossom, his slave, brings him the only peace and contentment he is to know in his late years. While there is no moralizing as such, Pear Blossom and her relationship to her master leads one to reflect on the fruits of such hard labor and sacrifice. A simple slave girl in a house full of discord—this is all Wang Lung has.

The success of *The Good Earth* is apparent. Buck won the Pulitzer Prize for it, and it has been dramatized as well as made into a motion picture. It is widely read in many languages, undoubtedly because of its universal appeal as a clear and precise portrayal of one man's struggle for survival, success, and ultimate happiness.

THE GRANDISSIMES
A Story of Creole Life

Type of work: Novel
Author: George W. Cable (1844–1925)
Type of plot: Regional romance
Time of plot: 1804
Locale: New Orleans
First published: 1880

Principal characters:

> HONORÉ GRANDISSIME, head of the Grandissimes
> THE DARKER HONORÉ GRANDISSIME, his quadroon half
>   brother
> AGRICOLA FUSILIER, Honoré's uncle
> AURORA NANCANOU, a young widow
> CLOTILDE NANCANOU, her daughter
> JOSEPH FROWENFELD, a young American
> DR. KEENE, Joseph's physician and friend
> PALMYRE, a freed slave

The Story:

Honoré Grandissime and Aurora Nancanou, both members of the Creole aristocracy, met at a masked ball and fell in love at first sight. Each was unaware of the other's identity. Honoré was a young merchant and the head of the Grandissime family. Aurora, a young widow, was the daughter of a De Grapion. Honoré's uncle, Agricola Fusilier, had killed Aurora's husband in a duel, after he had accused Agricola of cheating at cards. Agricola won the duel, cleared his honor, and collected the gambling debt, the entire estate of Aurora's husband. Aurora and her daughter Clotilde were left penniless. Agricola gave Aurora's estate to Honoré and made him a wealthy man.

Shortly afterward, Joseph Frowenfeld, a young American immigrant, arrived in New Orleans with his parents and sisters. All were stricken with fever; only Joseph survived. The lonely young man formed a friendship with his physician, Dr. Keene. Joseph and Honoré met by chance one day and found a common interest in their concern over the injustice of slavery and the caste system of New Orleans society. Honoré's life, however, depended upon these institutions. Joseph wished to have them wiped out at once.

Deciding to earn his living as a druggist, Joseph opened a small shop and soon became friendly with his aristocratic landlord. The landlord was actually Honoré's half brother, and he bore the same name, but he was not acknowledged as a member of the family because he was a quadroon. He was called the darker Honoré.

Joseph found another new friend in old Agricola. He was also struck by the charm of Aurora and Clotilde when they called to make purchases. He learned more about Aurora from Dr. Keene. The physician told him about Palmyre, a freed slave who had once been Aurora's maid. The girl hated Agricola. One night, Joseph was awakened by pistol shots nearby. A few minutes later, Dr. Keene and several others entered the shop with the wounded Agricola; he had been stabbed, and his companions had fired upon his assailant.

Several days later, Aurora called upon her landlord in order to make some arrangements about the rent she could not pay. She knew her landlord's name was Honoré Grandissime, but she did not connect this name with the man she loved. Upon learning that they were half brothers, Aurora was upset and her family pride caused her to be harsh with Honoré.

When Dr. Keene fell sick, he asked Joseph to attend to one of his patients. The patient was Palmyre, who had been wounded as she ran away after stabbing Agricola. Joseph promised Dr. Keene to keep her trouble a secret and went to dress the wound.

Joseph paid his last visit to the wounded Palmyre, now almost recovered. Palmyre begged him to help her make the white Honoré love her. Palmyre's maid, however, misunderstanding the conversation, thought that Joseph had wronged her mistress. She struck him over the head, and Joseph reeled groggily into the street. Some passing pedestrians, seeing him emerge bleeding from Palmyre's house, drew a natural inference, and soon everyone knew about Joseph's misfortune. Only Clotilde and Honoré believed him innocent.

Public feeling was running high against the Americans, and Joseph found himself despised by most of the Creoles. Both his liberal views and his trouble at Palmyre's house were against him.

Honoré's conscience bothered him. He felt that he unjustly held Aurora's property, but he also knew he could not return it to her without ruining the finances of his family—but he made his choice. He called upon Aurora and Clotilde and presented them with their property and the income from it. Now he could not declare his love for Aurora; if he did so, his family would think he had returned the property because of love instead of a sense of justice.

On his way home from Aurora's house, Honoré met the darker Honoré with Dr. Keene. The physician had risen from his sickbed because he had heard of Honoré's call at Aurora's house. Dr. Keene, also in love with Aurora, was jealous. His exertion caused a hemorrhage of the lungs, and the two Honorés carried him home and watched over him.

While they attended the sick man, the darker Honoré proposed to his brother that they go into partnership, so that the darker Honoré's money could save the family from ruin. His brother accepted the offer; but this action turned Honoré's family against him. Agricola led an unsuccessful lynching party to find the darker Honoré. Not finding him, the mob broke the windows of Joseph's shop as a gesture against liberal views in general.

Aurora set Joseph up in business again on the ground floor of her house and made Clotilde a partner in the store. Brought together in this manner, the two young people fell in love. At the same time, the darker Honoré lay wasting away for love of Palmyre, who was trying to revenge herself upon Agricola by voodoo spells. When Agricola could no longer sleep at night, his family determined to catch Palmyre in her acts of witchcraft. They caught her accomplice, but Palmyre escaped.

Meanwhile, the darker Honoré went to Joseph's store to get some medicine for himself. Meeting Agricola, who insulted him, the darker Honoré stabbed Agricola and escaped. The wounded man was carried upstairs to Aurora's house to die; there the two families were united again at his deathbed. Agricola revealed that he had once promised to Aurora's father a marriage between Aurora and Honoré.

The darker Honoré and Palmyre escaped together to France. There he committed suicide because she still would not accept his love.

Joseph finally declared his love for Clotilde, and Aurora would not accept Honoré's offer of marriage because she thought he had made it out of obligation to Agricola. Then Honoré made his offer again as a man in love. As a last gesture of family pride, Aurora refused him, but at the same time, she threw herself into her lover's arms.

Critical Evaluation:

George Washington Cable is best known as an early regionalist who evoked a picturesque society with an amusing variety of quaint dialects, but his best work was serious in its social and moral penetration. New Orleans gave him a fascinating stage for the interaction and conflict of cultures and values as well as dialects, and his approach was that of a linguist, sociologist, and moralist, rather than an entertainer. *The Grandissimes* is based on the true story of an African prince, Bras Coupé, captured by slavers and transported to Louisiana, a story Cable had been unable to publish separately because his publishers found it "unmitigatedly distressful." Cable, who felt that fiction should "teach without telling," therefore embodied his social criticism within a romantic plot and succeeded in mitigating the distress sufficiently for a wide public; at the same time, he was able to convey a detailed and sweeping picture of New Orleans society that served as an indictment of race and caste prejudice. He later noted that any parallels his readers might find between the situation in the novel, that of the new American supremacy in 1803, and the Reconstruction period of seventy-five years later, were fully intended. Indignant reaction in New Orleans testified to the accuracy of his depiction, and his message still holds truth for modern readers.

The author analyzes in *The Grandissimes* with skill and a light, although penetrating, touch a complicated, if narrow, society. Each class or caste illustrated in the novel thinks itself above the others; from the African slave prince to the Creoles and the pure whites, each refuses to bow before the others and submits only bitterly to physical, economic, or political domination. The individuals in the book also possess a witty pride combined with a shrewd sense of self-appraisal; they know their worth and do not need to pretend to be more or less than they are. They cling to a long-standing sense of pride in family and clan as tenaciously as they cling to their old superstitions, many of which were taken from the slaves.

Cable neatly weaves a sly humor into the rich texture of his narrative, a humor that is even present in the intense discussion of deliberately narrow-minded and parochial attitudes and prejudices. Cable writes with an exquisitely graceful prose style, at once poetic and witty, realistic and fanciful. The novel introduced a new realism and breadth of vision into the literature of the South, as well as a new and highly professional standard of craftsmanship. The novel is important not only for its place in American and Southern literary history, but also because it is a superbly written and deeply felt document and a work of fiction of the highest quality.

THE GRANDMOTHERS
A Family Portrait

Type of work: Novel
Author: Glenway Wescott (1901–   )
Type of plot: Regional chronicle
Time of plot: 1830–1925
Locale: Wisconsin
First published: 1927

Principal characters:

ALWYN TOWER, a young boy
HENRY TOWER, his grandfather
ROSE TOWER, his grandmother
JIM TOWER, his uncle
EVAN TOWER, another uncle
FLORA TOWER, his aunt
RALPH TOWER, his father
MARIANNE TOWER, his mother

The Story:

During his childhood, Alwyn Tower spent many hours poring over the family albums: everything his ancestors or relatives had done was interesting to the boy. He begged his Grandmother Tower to tell him stories of her childhood and stories about her children and other relatives. Often, the old lady could not remember what he wanted to know, and sometimes she seemed reluctant to talk about the past. Yet, piece by piece, from his Grandmother Tower, his parents, his aunts and uncles, and from the albums, Alwyn learned something of what he wanted to know.

Alwyn's Grandfather Tower died when the boy was twelve years old, and so his memories of that old man were rather vague. Grandfather Tower's chief interest during his old age was his garden, where he never allowed his grandchildren to go without his permission. He had failed at farming, but he was the best gardener in that part of Wisconsin.

Grandfather Tower had come to Wisconsin from New York. Like so many others, he had planned to get rich in the new West; like so many others, he had failed. He had been a young boy full of dreams when he first cleared the wilderness for his farm. He fell in love with and married Serena Cannon and, shortly afterward, went off to the Civil War. When he returned, Serena was ill with a fever and died soon after, leaving a baby boy. Grandfather Tower could never love another as he had loved Serena. Because the boy needed a mother, however, he married Rose Hamilton, who had been jilted by his brother Leander. Serena's boy died a week before Rose bore Henry's first child. After that, life seemed unimportant to Henry Tower. There were more children, some a small pleasure to him, some a disgrace; but they seemed to be Rose's children, not his. Part of Grandfather Tower had died with Serena, and although he lived to be eighty-two years old, he had never seemed to be completely alive as far as Alwyn was concerned.

Grandmother Tower, too, had come to Wisconsin when she was a child. Growing up in the wilderness, she suffered all the hardships of the pioneers— hunger and cold and fear of Indians. When she was in her early teens, she met and fell in love with Leander Tower. When the Civil War came, Leander enlisted, and the girl went to stay with Serena Tower. While Serena lay ill with fever, the young girl cared for her and the baby. Leander returned, but he had changed. Although he could not explain himself clearly, Rose knew that he no longer wanted to marry her. After Serena's husband came home and Serena had died, Leander went to California. Rose married Serena's widower and bore his children, but like him, she was only partly alive. She never ceased to love Leander, but she was faithful to Grandfather Tower, even after Leander returned to Wisconsin. To Alwyn, she was a quiet, serene woman, resigned to life, but not unhappy with her lot.

Alwyn learned about many of his more distant relatives as he studied the albums and listened to the stories of his elders. There was his Great-Aunt Nancy Tower, who had been insane for part of her life. There was his Great-Aunt Mary Harris, who had been married three times and had traveled all over the world. Grandmother Tower said that Great-Aunt Mary was a real pioneer. She had seen her first husband killed by Southerners because he sympathized with the Union. Her second husband was a drunken sot who beat her, and often she had to beg for food to stay alive. After her second husband divorced her, she married one of the Tower men, and for the first time, she knew happiness and prosperity.

Old Leander Tower seemed to be happy only when he was helping a young boy. His younger brother Hilary had disappeared in the war, and it seemed almost as if Leander were trying to find a substitute for his brother.

Alwyn knew his father's brothers and sisters quite well. His Uncle Jim was a minister who had married a rich woman, and they took Alwyn to live with them in Chicago, giving the boy his only chance for a good education. Uncle Jim's wife persuaded her husband to give up preaching. After her death, he continued to live with her mother and sisters and to humor their whims. Alwyn liked his Uncle Jim, but he could not admire him.

Uncle Evan, a deserter in the Spanish-American War, had gone west to live after taking a new name. Once or twice he came home to visit his father, but both men seemed embarrassed during those meetings. Grandfather Tower had always been ashamed of Evan, and during the last visit Evan made, the old man refused to enter the house while his son was there.

Aunt Flora was an old maid, although she still thought of herself as a young girl. She had had many chances to marry, but she was afraid of the force of love, afraid that something hidden in her would be roused and not satisfied. It was a mysterious thing she could not understand. She turned to Alwyn, giving him her love and accepting his, for she could love the young boy wholeheartedly, having nothing to fear from him. When she was twenty-nine years old, she fell ill and died. Alwyn thought she looked happy as she took her last breath.

Alwyn's father, Ralph Tower, had always wanted to be a veterinarian, for he had a way with animals. Yet Uncle Jim had been the one chosen for an education, and after Uncle Evan deserted and went west, Ralph had to take over the farm for his father. He was never bitter, merely resigned. Perhaps he would have envied Jim if it had not been for Alwyn's mother.

His parents had one of the few really happy marriages in the family Alwyn realized as he watched them together. Alwyn knew something of the girlhood of his mother. Her parents had hated each other fiercely and had taken pleasure in showing that hatred. Alwyn's mother was a lonely child until she met Ralph Tower. Sometimes it embarrassed Alwyn to see his parents together because they revealed so much of their feeling for each other.

Alwyn realized that the Towers were one of the last pioneer families in America. He knew that in his heritage there was a deep religious feeling, a willingness to accept poverty and hardship as the will of God. His heritage was a disordered one; a deserter, an insane woman, a man and a wife who hated each other, and an uncle who lived on the wealth of his wife's mother. These people were just as much a part of him as were the others. Alwyn knew that his life would be a rearrangement of the characters of the others. He knew that he could understand himself once he understood his people.

Critical Evaluation:

In *The Grandmothers*, Glenway Wescott reveals the unknown and unseen tragedies that lie behind each person, making him what he has become. With tenderness and compassion, Wescott lays bare the hidden memories that necessarily remain unspoken between these inhibited and unintrospective characters. The tough and austere people who march through the pages of this novel, as they did across the untamed land, accept their grim fates with a sense of fatalism not far removed from classical tragedy. They all began their lives with great hopes but soon learned that life plays cruel tricks, often destroying those who seem to hold the greatest promise, the most beautiful and the most clever, and letting the others live out their empty, long lives. Through all the stories, Wescott shows a gift for bringing people to life through the use of authentic and touching period details, such as Serena Tower's hair albums and hair wreaths or Grandfather Tower's flute and deafness.

In an important sense, Alwyn Tower's quest to find his past is the quest of America; in his search to learn about his antecedents, Alwyn Tower stands for the nation looking back to the vital and strenuous days of its growth. It is clear that the author feels that only by understanding its traditions and past hardships can the country comprehend its present and future and surmount any future difficulties. The novel was an ambitious one, for it was meant to represent in one family the entire pioneer history of the United States. Yet, Wescott did not sacrifice individual characterization to his ambition for scope and symbolic representation. In fact, it is because his human beings are so filled with life and human passions that they can successfully merge into a legendary historical view. The plot is subordinated to the search for a meaning in the past; the individual stories are woven and interwoven, gradually filling in the intricate and always fascinating picture of the Tower family's often tragic history and the history of the growing American nation.

THE GRAPES OF WRATH

Type of work: Novel
Author: John Steinbeck (1902–1968)
Type of plot: Social criticism
Time of plot: 1930's
Locale: Southwest United States and California
First published: 1939

Principal characters:
TOM JOAD, JR., a former convict
PA JOAD, an Okie
MA JOAD, his wife
ROSE OF SHARON (ROSASHARN), Tom's sister
JIM CASY, a labor agitator

The Story:

Tom Joad was released from the Oklahoma state penitentiary where he had served a sentence for killing a man in self-defense. He traveled homeward through a region made barren by drought and dust storms. On the way, he met Jim Casy, a former preacher; the pair went together to the home of Tom's family. They found the Joad place deserted. While Tom and Casy were wondering what had happened, Muley Graves, a die-hard tenant farmer, came by and disclosed that all the families in the neighborhood had gone to California or were going. Tom's folks, Muley said, had gone to a relative's place to prepare for going west. Muley was the only sharecropper to stay behind.

All over the southern Midwest states, farmers, no longer able to make a living because of land banks, weather, and machine farming, had sold or were forced out of the farms they had tenanted. Junk dealers and used-car salesmen profiteered on them. Thousands of families took to the roads leading to the promised land, California.

Tom and Casy found the Joads at Uncle John's place, all busy with preparations for their trip to California. Assembled for the trip were Pa and Ma Joad; Noah, their mentally backward son; Al, the adolescent younger brother of Tom and Noah; Rose of Sharon, Tom's sister, and her husband, Connie; the Joad children, Ruthie and Winfield; and Granma and Grampa Joad. Al had bought an ancient truck to take them west. The family asked Jim Casy to go with them. The night before they started, they killed the pigs they had left and salted down the meat so that they would have food on the way.

Spurred by handbills which stated that agricultural workers were badly needed in California, the Joads, along with thousands of others, made their tortuous way, in a worn-out vehicle, across the plains toward the mountains. Grampa died of a stroke during their first overnight stop. Later, there was a long delay when the truck broke down. Small business people along the way treated the migrants as enemies; and, to add to their misery, returning migrants told the Joads that there was no work to be had in California, that conditions were even worse than they were in Oklahoma. But the dream of a bountiful West Coast urged the Joads onward.

Close to the California line, where the group stopped to bathe in a river, Noah, feeling he was a hindrance to the others, wandered away. It was there that the Joads first heard themselves addressed as *Okies*, another word for tramps.

Granma died during the night trip across the desert. After burying her, the group went into a Hooverville, as the migrants' camps were called. There they learned that work was all but impossible to find. A contractor came to the camp to sign up men to pick fruit in another county. When the Okies asked to see his license, the contractor turned the leaders over to a police deputy who had accompanied him to camp. Tom was involved in the fight that followed. He escaped, and Casy gave himself up in Tom's place. Connie, husband of the pregnant Rose of Sharon, suddenly disappeared from the group. The family was breaking up in the face of its hardships. Ma Joad did everything in her power to keep the group together.

Fearing recrimination after the fight, the Joads left Hooverville and went to a government camp maintained for transient agricultural workers. The camp had sanitary facilities, a local government made up of the transients themselves, and simple organized entertainment. During the Joads' stay at the camp, the Okies successfully defeated an attempt of the local citizens to give the camp a bad name and thus to have it closed to the migrants. For the first time since they had arrived in California, the Joads found themselves treated as human beings.

Circumstances eventually forced them to leave the camp, however, for there was no work in the district. They drove to a large farm where work was being offered. There they found agitators attempting to keep the migrants from taking the work because of unfair wages offered. The Joads, however, thinking only of food, were escorted by motorcycle police in to the farm. The entire family picked peaches for five cents a box and earned in a day just enough money to buy food for one meal. Tom, remembering the pickets outside the camp, went out at night to investigate. He found Casy, who was the leader of the agitators. While Tom and Casy were talking, deputies, who had been searching for Casy, closed in on them. The pair fled but were caught. Casy was killed. Tom received a cut on his head, but not before he had felled a deputy with an ax handle. The family concealed Tom in their shack. The rate for a box of peaches dropped, meanwhile, to two-and-a-half cents. Tom's danger and the futility of picking peaches drove the Joads on their way. They hid the injured Tom under the mattresses in the back of the truck, and then they told the suspicious guard at the entrance to the farm that the extra man they had had with them when they came was a hitchhiker who had stayed behind to pick.

The family found at last a migrant crowd encamped in abandoned boxcars along a stream. They joined the camp and soon found temporary jobs picking cotton. Tom, meanwhile, hid in a culvert near the camp. Ruthie innocently disclosed Tom's presence to another little girl. Ma, realizing that Tom was no longer safe, sent him away. Tom promised to carry on Casy's work in trying to improve the lot of the downtrodden everywhere.

The autumn rains began. Soon the stream that ran beside the camp over-flowed and water entered the boxcars. Under these all but impossible con-ditions, Rose of Sharon gave birth to a dead baby. When the rising water made their position no longer bearable, the family moved from the camp on foot. The rains had made their old car useless. They came to a barn, which they shared with a boy and his starving father. Rose of Sharon, bereft of her baby, nourished the famished man with the milk from her breasts. So the poor kept each other alive in the depression years.

Critical Evaluation:

The publication of John Steinbeck's *The Grapes of Wrath* caused a nation-wide stir in 1939. This account of the predicament of migrant workers was taken more as social document than as fiction. Some saw it as an exposé of capitalist excesses; others, as a distorted call to revolution. Frequently com-pared to *Uncle Tom's Cabin*, it was awarded the Pulitzer Prize for Literature in 1940.

Recent literary critics, taking a second look at the novel, have often lumped it with a number of other dated books of the 1930's as "proletarian fiction." A careful reader, however, recognizes that beneath this outraged account of an outrageous social situation lies a dynamic, carefully structured story that applies not only to one era or society but also to the universal human predicament.

As a social document, the novel presents such a vivid picture of oppression and misery that one tends to doubt its authenticity. Steinbeck, however, had done more than academic research. He had journeyed from Oklahoma to California, lived in a migrant camp, and worked alongside the migrants. (Peter Lisca reports that after the novel appeared, the workers sent Steinbeck a patchwork dog sewn from scraps of their clothing and wearing a tag labeled "Migrant John.") Before making the motion picture, which still stands as one of the great films of the era, Darryl F. Zanuck hired private detectives to verify Steinbeck's story; they reported that conditions were even worse than those depicted in the book. The political situation was a powder keg; Freeman Champney has remarked that "it looked as if nothing could avert an all-out battle between revolution and fascism in California's great valleys."

Social injustice was depicted so sharply that Steinbeck himself was accused of being a revolutionary. Certainly, he painted the oppressive economic system in bleak colors. Warren French argues convincingly, however, that Steinbeck was basically a reformer, not a revolutionary; that he wanted to change the attitudes and behavior of people—both migrants and economic barons—not overturn the private enterprise system. Indeed, Steinbeck observes that ownership of land is morally edifying to a man.

Steinbeck once declared that the writer must "set down his time as nearly as he can understand it" and that he should "serve as the watchdog of society . . . to satirize its silliness, to attack its injustices, to stigmatize its faults." In *The Grapes of Wrath*, he does all these things, then goes further to interpret events from a distinctly American point of view. Like Whitman, he expresses love for all men and respect for manual labor. Like Jefferson, he asserts a preference for agrarian society in which men retain a close, nourishing tie to the soil: his farmers dwindle psychologically as they are separated from their land, and the California owners become oppressors as they substitute ledgers for direct contact with the soil. Like Emerson, Steinbeck demonstrates faith in the common man and in the ideal of self-reliance. He also develops the Emersonian religious concept of an oversoul. The preacher Jim Casy muses ". . . maybe that's the Holy Sperit—the human sperit—the whole shebang. Maybe all men got one big soul ever'body's a part of it." Later, Tom Joad reassures Ma that even if he isn't physically with her, "Wherever they's a fight so hungry people can eat, I'll be there. Wherever they's a cop beatin' up a guy, I'll be there. . . . I'll be in the way kids laugh when they're hungry an' they know supper's ready. . . ."

This theme, that all men essentially belong together and are a part of one another and of a greater whole that transcends momentary reality, is what removes *The Grapes of Wrath* from the genre of timely proletarian fiction and makes it an allegory for all men in all circumstances. Warren French notes that the real story of this novel is not the Joads' search for economic security but their education, which transforms them from self-concern to a recognition of their bond with the whole human race. At first, Tom Joad is intensely individualistic, interested mainly in making his own way; Pa's primary concern is keeping bread on his table; Rose of Sharon dreams only of traditional middle-class success; and Ma, an Earth-Mother with a spine of steel, concentrates fiercely upon keeping the "fambly" together. At the end, Tom follows Casy's example in fighting for human rights; Pa, in building the dike, sees the necessity for all men to work together; Rose of Sharon forgets her grief over her stillborn child and unhesitatingly lifts a starving man to her milk-filled breast; and Ma can say "Use' ta be the fambly was fust. It ain't so now. It's anybody. Worse off we get, the more we got to do." Thus the Joads have overcome that separation which Paul Tillich equates with sin, that alienation from others which Existentialists are so fond of describing as the inescapable human condition.

It is interesting to note how much *The Grapes of Wrath*, which sometimes satirizes, sometimes attacks organized Christian religion, reflects the Bible. In structure, as critics have been quick to notice, it parallels the story of the Exodus to a "promised land." Symbolically, as Peter Lisca observes, the initials of Jim Casy are those of Jesus Christ, another itinerant preacher who rebelled against traditional religion, went into the wilderness, discovered his own gospel, and eventually gave his life in service to others.

Language, too, is frequently biblical, especially in the interchapters which, like a Greek chorus, restate, reinforce, and generalize from the specific happenings of the narrative. The cadences, repetitions, and parallel lines all echo the patterns of the Psalms—Ma Joad's favorite book.

Even the title of the novel is biblical; the exact phrase is Julia Ward Howe's, but the reference is to Jeremiah and Revelation. The grapes have been a central symbol throughout the book: first of promise, representing the fertile California valleys, but finally of bitter rage as the Midwesterners realize that they have been lured West with false bait and that they will not partake of this fertility. The wrath grows, a fearsome, terrible wrath; but, as several interchapters make clear, better wrath than despair, because wrath moves to action. Steinbeck would have his people act, in concert and in concern for one another—and finally prevail over all forms of injustice.

THE GREAT GATSBY

Type of work: Novel
Author: F. Scott Fitzgerald (1896–1940)
Type of plot: Social criticism
Time of plot: 1922
Locale: New York City and Long Island
First published: 1925

Principal characters:
NICK CARRAWAY, a young bond salesman
DAISY BUCHANAN, his cousin
TOM BUCHANAN, her husband
MYRTLE WILSON, Tom's mistress
JAY GATSBY, a racketeer of the 1920's

The Story:

Young Nick Carraway decided to forsake the hardware business of his family in the Middle West in order to sell bonds in New York City. He took a small house in West Egg on Long Island and there became involved in the lives of his neighbors. At a dinner party at the home of Tom Buchanan, he renewed his acquaintance with Tom and Tom's wife, Daisy, a distant cousin, and he met an attractive young woman, Jordan Baker. Almost at once he learned that Tom and Daisy were not happily married. It appeared that Daisy knew her husband was deliberately unfaithful.

Nick soon learned to despise the drive to the city through unkempt slums; particularly, he hated the ash heaps and the huge commercial signs. He was far more interested in the activities of his wealthy neighbors. Near his house lived Jay Gatsby, a mysterious man of great wealth. Gatsby entertained lavishly, but his past was unknown to his neighbors.

One day, Tom Buchanan took Nick to call on his mistress, a dowdy, over-plump, married woman named Myrtle Wilson, whose husband, George Wilson, operated a second-rate automobile repair shop. Myrtle, Tom, and Nick went to the apartment that Tom kept, and there the three were joined by Myrtle's sister Catherine and Mr. and Mrs. McKee. The party settled down to an afternoon of drinking, Nick unsuccessfully doing his best to get away.

A few days later, Nick attended another party, one given by Gatsby for a large number of people famous in speakeasy society. Food and liquor were dispensed lavishly. Most of the guests had never seen their host before.

At the party, Nick met Gatsby for the first time. Gatsby, in his early thirties, looked like a healthy young roughneck. He was offhand, casual, and eager to entertain his guests as extravagantly as possible. Frequently he was called away by long-distance telephone calls. Some of the guests laughed and said that he was trying to impress them with his importance.

That summer, Gatsby gave many parties. Nick went to all of them, enjoying each time the society of people from all walks of life who appeared to take advantage of Gatsby's bounty. From time to time, Nick met Jordan Baker there and when he heard that she had cheated in an amateur golf match, his interest in her grew.

Gatsby took Nick to lunch one day and introduced him to a man named Wolfshiem, who seemed to be Gatsby's business partner. Wolfshiem hinted at some dubious business deals that betrayed Gatsby's racketeering activities, and Nick began to identify the sources of some of Gatsby's wealth.

Jordan Baker told Nick the strange story of Daisy's wedding. Before the bridal dinner, Daisy, who seldom drank, became wildly intoxicated and kept reading a letter that she had just received and crying that she had changed her mind. After she had become sober, however, she went through with her wedding to Tom without a murmur. Obviously, the letter was from Jay Gatsby. At the time, Gatsby was poor and unknown; Tom was rich and influential.

Gatsby was still in love with Daisy, however, and he wanted Jordan and Nick to bring Daisy and him together again. It was arranged that Nick should invite Daisy to tea the same day he invited Gatsby. Gatsby awaited the invitation nervously.

On the eventful day, it rained. Determined that Nick's house should be presentable, Gatsby sent a man to mow the wet grass; he also sent over flowers for decoration. The tea was a strained affair at first, and both Gatsby and Daisy were shy and awkward in their reunion. Afterward, they went over to Gatsby's mansion, where he showed them his furniture, clothes, swimming pool, and gardens. Daisy promised to attend his next party.

When Daisy disapproved of his guests, Gatsby stopped entertaining. The house was shut up and the bar-crowd turned away.

Gatsby informed Nick of his origin. His true name was Gatz, and he had been born in the Middle West. His parents were poor. When he was a boy, he had become the protégé of a wealthy old gold miner and had accompanied him on his travels until the old man died. He had changed his name to Gatsby and was daydreaming of acquiring wealth and position. In the war, he had distinguished himself. After the war, he had returned penniless to the States, too poor to marry Daisy, whom he had met during the war. Later, he became a partner in a drug business. He had been lucky and had accumulated money rapidly. He told Nick that he had acquired the money for his Long Island residence after three years of hard work.

The Buchanans gave a quiet party for Jordan, Gatsby, and Nick. The group drove into the city and took a room in a hotel. The day was hot and the guests uncomfortable. On the way, Tom driving Gatsby's new yellow car, stopped at Wilson's garage. Wilson complained because Tom had not helped him in a projected car deal. He said he needed money because he was selling out and taking his wife, whom he knew to be unfaithful, away from the city.

At the hotel, Tom accused Gatsby of trying to steal his wife and also of being dishonest. He seemed to regard Gatsby's low origin with more disfavor than his interest in Daisy. During the argument, Daisy sided with both men by turns.

On the ride back to the suburbs, Gatsby drove his own car, accompanied by Daisy, who temporarily would not speak to her husband.

Following them, Nick, Jordan, and Tom stopped to investigate an accident in front of Wilson's garage. They discovered an ambulance picking up the dead body of Myrtle Wilson, struck by a hit-and-run driver in a yellow car. They tried in vain to help Wilson and then went on to Tom's house, convinced that Gatsby had struck Myrtle Wilson.

Nick learned that night from Gatsby that Daisy had been driving when the woman was hit. Gatsby, however, was willing to take the blame if the death should be traced to his car. He explained that a woman had rushed out as though she wanted to speak to someone in the yellow car and Daisy, an inexpert driver, had run her down and then collapsed. Gatsby had driven on.

In the meantime, George Wilson, having traced the yellow car to Gatsby, appeared on the Gatsby estate. A few hours later, both he and Gatsby were discovered dead. He had shot Gatsby and then killed himself.

Nick tried to make Gatsby's funeral respectable, but only one among all of Gatsby's former guests attended along with Gatsby's father, who thought his son had been a great man. None of Gatsby's racketeering associates appeared.

Shortly afterward, Nick learned of Tom's part in Gatsby's death. Wilson had visited Tom and with the help of a revolver forced him to reveal the name of the owner of the hit-and-run car. Nick vowed that his friendship with Tom and Daisy was ended. He decided to return to his people in the Middle West.

Critical Evaluation:

F. Scott Fitzgerald, the prophet of the Jazz Age, was born in St. Paul, Minnesota, to the daughter of a self-made Irish immigrant millionaire. His father was a ne'er-do-well salesman who had married above his social position. From his mother, Fitzgerald inherited the dream that was America—the promise that any young man could become anything he chose through hard work. From his father, he inherited the propensity for failure. This antithesis pervaded his own life and most of his fiction. Educated in the East, Fitzgerald was overcome with the glamor of New York and Long Island. To him, it was the "stuff of old romance," "the source of infinite possibilities." His fiction focused primarily on the lives of the rich. With the family fortune depleted by his father, Fitzgerald found himself in his early twenties an army officer in love with a southern belle, Zelda Sayre, who was socially above him. She refused his first proposal of marriage because he was too poor. Fitzgerald was determined to have her. He wrote and published *This Side of Paradise* (1920), on the basis of which Zelda married him.

Their public life for the next ten years epitomized the dizzy spiral of the 1920's—wild parties, wild spending, and wild cars—and following the national pattern, they crashed just as spectacularly in the 1930's. Zelda went mad and was committed finally to a sanitarium. Fitzgerald became a functional alcoholic. From his pinnacle in the publishing field during the 1920's, when his short stories commanded as much as fifteen hundred dollars, he fell in the 1930's to writing lukewarm Hollywood scripts. He died in Hollywood in 1940, almost forgotten and with most of his work out of print. Later revived in academic circles, Fitzgerald's place in American letters has been affirmed by a single novel—*The Great Gatsby*.

Fitzgerald once said, "America's great promise is that something's going to happen, but it never does. America is the moon that never rose." This indictment of the American Dream could well serve as an epigraph for *The Great Gatsby*. Jay Gatsby pursues his dream of romantic success without ever understanding that it has escaped him. He fails to understand that he cannot recapture the past (his fresh, new love for Daisy Buchanan) no matter how much money he makes, no matter how much wealth he displays.

The character of Gatsby was never intended by Fitzgerald to be a realistic portrayal; he is a romantic hero, always somewhat unreal, bogus, and absurd. No matter the corrupt sources of his wealth such as bootlegging and gambling (and these are only hinted at), he stands for hope, for romantic belief—for innocence. He expects more from life than the other characters who are all more or less cynical. He is an eternal juvenile in a brutal and corrupt world.

To underscore the corruption of the American Dream, Fitzgerald's characters all are finally seen as liars. Buchanan's mistress lies to her husband. Jordan Baker is a pathological liar who cheats in golf tournaments. Tom Buchanan's lie to his mistress Myrtle's husband results in the murder of Gatsby. Daisy, herself, is basically insincere; she lets Gatsby take the blame for her hit-and-run accident. Gatsby's whole life is a lie: he lies about his past and his present. He lies to himself. Nick Carraway, the Midwestern narrator, tells readers that he is the only completely honest person he knows. He panders for Gatsby, however, and in the end, he turns away from Tom Buchanan, unable to force the truth into the open. He knows the truth about Gatsby but is unable to tell the police. His affirmation of Gatsby at the end is complex; he envies Gatsby's romantic selflessness and innocence at the same time that he abhors his lack of self-knowledge.

The Great Gatsby incorporates a number of themes and motifs that unify the novel and contribute to its impact. The initiation theme governs the narrator Nick Carraway, who is a young man come East to make his fortune in stocks and bonds and who returns to the Midwest sadly disillusioned. The frontier theme is also present. Gatsby believes in the "green light," the ever-accessible future in which one can achieve what one has missed in the past. The final paragraphs of the novel state this important theme as well as it has ever been stated. Class issues are very well presented. Tom and Daisy seem accessible but when their position is threatened, they close the doors, retreating into their wealth and carelessness, letting others like Gatsby pay the vicious price in hurt and suffering. The carelessness of the rich and their followers is seen in the recurring motif of the bad driver.

Automobile accidents are ubiquitous. At Gatsby's first party, there is a smashup with drunk drivers. Jordan Baker has a near accident after which Nick calls her "a rotten driver." Gatsby is stopped for speeding but is able to fix the ticket by showing the cop a card from the mayor of New York. Finally, Myrtle Wilson is killed by Daisy, driving Gatsby's car. Bad driving becomes a moral statement in the novel.

Settings in the novel are used very well by Fitzgerald, from the splendid mansions of Long Island through the wasteland of the valley of ashes presided over by the eyes of Dr. T. J. Eckleburg (where the Wilsons live) to the New York of the Plaza Hotel or Tom and Myrtle Wilson's apartment. In each case, a variety of texture and social class is presented to the reader. Most important, however, is Fitzgerald's use of Nick as a narrator. Like Conrad before him— and from whom he learned his craft—Fitzgerald had a Romantic sensibility that controlled fictional material best through the lens of a narrator. As with Marlow in Conrad's *Heart of Darkness*, Nick relates the story of an exceptional man who fails in his dream. He is both attracted and repelled by a forceful man who dares to lead a life he could not sustain. Like Marlow, he pays tribute to his hero who is also his alter ego. Gatsby's tragedy is Nick's education. His return to the Midwest is a moral return to the safer, more solid values of the heartland. Fitzgerald himself was unable to follow such a conservative path, but he clearly felt that the American Dream should be pursued with less frantic, orgiastic, prideful convulsions of energy and spirit.

THE GREAT MEADOW

Type of work: Novel
Author: Elizabeth Madox Roberts (1886–1941)
Type of plot: Historical romance
Time of plot: 1774–1781
Locale: Western Virginia and Kentucky
First published: 1930

Principal characters:
DIONY HALL JARVIS, a pioneer wife
BERK JARVIS, her husband
EVAN MUIR, Diony's second husband
THOMAS HALL, Diony's father
ELVIRA JARVIS, Berk's mother

The Story:

Thomas Hall, the well-educated son of a tidewater Virginia family, had settled in upper Albemarle County after having lost his fortune to a dishonest relative. In the upper country, he had married a young Methodist woman who had come down into Virginia from Pennsylvania. After their marriage, Mrs. Hall bore four children, two boys and two girls.

Of all the children, the oldest girl was by far her father's favorite. She had been named Dione, out of Greek mythology, but everyone called her Diony and spelled her name with a "y." Diony, with her father's help and the use of his small library, educated herself as best she could.

During the middle 1770's, visitors occasionally stopped at the Hall house, really little more than a large cabin, as they passed from the Fincastle country or perhaps from even farther away in the cane meadows of Kentucky. Word came to the Halls in that manner of Boone, Henderson, and Harrod, and of the settlements those men had begun in the Kentucky country. The accounts of the back country held smaller charms for Diony than thoughts of visiting her rich relatives on the coasts of Virginia and Maryland; as a girl, she believed a life of balls, great houses, carriages, and fancy clothes far more enticing than the rigors of the wilderness.

Among the Halls' neighbors was a family named Jarvis. Of the several boys of the Jarvis clan, there was one who was more than six feet tall, taller even than Diony's older brother. He was the first to succumb to travelers' tales of the Kentucky country. While he was gone, he sent back word by a trapper that he hoped Diony would wait for his return before she accepted a husband. She had one suitor, a man from the tidewater, but Berk Jarvis so

---

captured her imagination that she had her father send a letter ending the suit with the man of wealth and position who had been seeking her hand.

When Berk returned, Diony quickly agreed to marry him and to go with him immediately into the wilderness, to the new settlement called Harrodsburg in the Kentucky country. Cloth was woven, garments were sewed, cattle were gathered together, kitchen utensils were selected, and seeds for a garden packed away. At last, all was in readiness for the marriage and the wilderness trek to follow immediately. Thomas Hall had had the banns cried in the Angelican Church, according to the British law of the Virginia colony, but the couple and Diony's mother wanted the Methodist minister to perform the ceremony. He did, but many of the people, including Diony and Berk, had some misgivings as to the legality of the marriage, even though the argument of the newly signed Declaration of Independence was brought forth.

After the marriage Diony, Berk, his mother, and a number of other Virginians set out on the wilderness road across the Appalachian highlands to Kentucky. They followed the trail laid out by Daniel Boone. Without accident, but with great difficulty, the party reached Harrod's fort in the wilderness. Berk bought a claim on a farm at some distance from the fort. As the months passed, the lives of the newly married couple slowly took shape. Only one shadow appeared. One day, while Diony and her mother-in-law were out of the fort, they were surprised by Indians. Before Mrs. Jarvis was killed and scalped, she managed to save Diony's life. Berk swore that he would be avenged and kill the Indian who had taken his mother's scalp.

Diony recovered from injuries received when attacked by the Indians. One day, while Berk was purposely gone from the fort, she gave birth to a boy whom they named Tom. The baby was not many weeks old when Berk set out with a party of men to aid George Rogers Clark in his expeditions against the British in the Northwest Territory. Within a few weeks, one of the party came back with an injury to his hand and the report of an Indian ambush. Berk had been taken by the Indians. Capture was at that time, even though the British gave a higher bounty for prisoners than for scalps, a certain death warrant for most prisoners.

In the weeks and months that passed after her husband's capture, Diony stayed in the cabin in the settlement and provided for herself and the baby. Help was forthcoming from Evan Muir, the man who had returned with the news of Berk's capture. In return for her nursing and cooking, Evan kept Diony and the child in meat and leather during the summer, fall, and winter. The following summer, he farmed the Jarvis homestead claim on a share basis.

Gradually the people in the settlement began to feel sure that Berk was dead, and at last a report came in that he had been killed. Still Diony refused to believe that her husband would not return. Although Evan did not press his suit for marriage, the women of the village warned Diony that it was not fair for her to continue taking his labor on her behalf without giving him the rights of a husband. Diony finally yielded to their arguments and agreed to marry Evan. She soon discovered that she really loved the man and that her passion for him was greater than it had been for Berk.

Diony and Evan moved to the Jarvis claim and lived in the house Berk had built there. For two years, they lived happily and worked steadily to improve the place. In that time, Diony gave birth to a child by Evan, another boy, who was named Michael.

One night, a call came from the edge of the clearing, and Berk Jarvis walked up to the door. Neither Diony, Evan, nor Berk knew how to resolve the predicament of a wife with two legal husbands and a child by each of them. Berk and Evan began a fierce argument, but they were interrupted by visitors from the settlement. The people from the settlement said that the frontier law was that the wife had to choose which of the husbands she would keep; then the other one had to leave for good.

After the visitors left, Evan waited silently; he felt that all he had done for Diony, his labor of three years, would speak for itself. Berk, however, began a recital of his adventures among the Indians, telling how he had traveled as a prisoner-visitor as far as Sault Sainte Marie and had finally been able to escape and return. He described his tortures in the early weeks of his captivity: the floggings, the gauntlet running, and the fear of being burned at the stake.

Late in the night, Berk finished speaking. When he had, Diony said that she had made up her mind. She chose to have Berk remain, even though Evan had been a steadier husband. She told them both to leave the cabin that night, for she wanted to be alone for a time before she faced her new start on life with her first husband.

Critical Evaluation:

Though it was her fourth published novel, *The Great Meadow* had been slowly developing in Elizabeth Madox Roberts' mind for many years. She was descended from pioneers who had settled in the Kentucky wilderness, and she wished to commemorate the part such settlers had played in transforming the great meadowland beyond the mountains into homes for themselves. She carefully considered theme, characters, style, and form. The result is a novel laid in the period of the American Revolution and the settlement of land west of the southern Appalachians, with such historical personages as Daniel Boone, James Harrod, and George Rogers Clark playing subsidiary roles. The progress of the war was briefly reported from time to time as something happening far away, except for Indian raids and skirmishes between white settlers and red men urged into battle by the British.

The dominant theme of the evolution of order out of chaos is developed in two movements: Diony Hall, an introspective but physically active young girl, seeks to control the welter of emotions and thoughts within herself as she matures into a young woman, and to find and understand the part she was intended to play in life by the great Author of Nature. She becomes a part of the other movement, that of the settlers who brought order and civilization into what had been raw wilderness. Diony is the only fully developed character in the novel, the only one seen from within as well as without. The two movements are intermeshed as the author alternately reveals Diony's thoughts and feelings and then shifts to the physical action of the story that involves Diony with the many other characters.

In style, the novel blends poetry and prose. Music abounds in ballads, hymns, the sounds of Thomas Hall's anvil, bird songs, the bells on horses' necks, and fiddle music for dancing. Images of weaving suggest the making of a historical tapestry ("the words and the wool were spun together"). Archaic locutions and dialectal words ("blowth," "frighted") give an eighteenth century folk flavor.

The principal weakness of *The Great Meadow* is the use of the Enoch Arden theme at the end when Berk returns after his long absence. For most readers, however, this ending may seem acceptable, particularly since Berk saved himself from being eaten by his captors through a convincing argument that his "thinking part" gave him his strength. This is a corollary of Diony's belief in "the power of reason over the wild life of the earth."

THE GREAT VALLEY

Type of work: Novel
Author: Mary Johnston (1870–1936)
Type of plot: Historical romance
Time of plot: 1735–1760
Locale: Virginia and Ohio
First published: 1926

Principal characters:
JOHN SELKIRK, a Scottish Presbyterian minister
JEAN SELKIRK, his wife
ANDREW SELKIRK, their son
ELIZABETH,
ROBIN, and
TAM SELKIRK, their younger children
COLONEL MATTHEW BURKE, a wealthy Virginia
landowner
CONAN BURKE, his son and later Elizabeth Selkirk's
husband
NANCY MILLIKEN SELKIRK, Andrew Selkirk's wife
STEPHEN TRABUE, a driver and guide

The Story:

John Selkirk and his family, including a spinster sister of Mrs. Selkirk, were bound for Virginia with a number of other immigrants in the small ship *Prudence.* Mr. Selkirk, a Presbyterian minister somewhat too liberal for his congregation at Thistlebrae Kirk, in Scotland, had decided to establish a new kirk in the Shenando or Great Valley of Virginia. Arriving in Williamsburg, where his oldest son Andrew was already living, he was introduced to Colonel Matthew Burke, who was developing a large tract of land in the valley and seeking settlers for it. John and Andrew Selkirk together purchased four hundred acres and prepared to set out for the valley. John had asked Colonel Burke how the Indians felt about having their lands occupied by white men but had been assured that there would be no trouble, since the lands had been obtained through treaties and since many Indians had moved farther west to find better hunting grounds.

Stephen Trabue, a friendly driver and guide, was to accompany the Selkirk family on part of the journey to the valley. As they traveled, he explained to them many of the conditions and details of daily living which they might expect in their new homes. Even Nancy Milliken, who had just become Mrs. Andrew Selkirk, would find life in the valley very difficult from that in Williamsburg, her former home.

Seven years later, John Selkirk had a congregation of two hundred in his Mt. Olivet Church, and Andrew had three hundred acres, three indentured youths to help him farm them, a grist mill, and ambitious plans for increasing his holdings and obtaining more helpers, including black slaves. John did not favor slavery, but Andrew saw nothing wrong with it as long as he treated his slaves humanely.

A few of John's Calvinist church members objected to the joyousness in his sermons. Liking fire-and-brimstone threats from the pulpit, they complained that their minister did not believe in infant damnation and was even scornful of those who thought that certain evil people were capable of practicing witchcraft.

Shortly after Colonel Burke died during a visit to the home of his son Conan, who had married Elizabeth Selkirk and settled in Burke's Tract, both Conan and John Selkirk decided to move a day's journey west into Burke's Land, an undeveloped tract which the colonel had also planned to fill with new settlers. There John established Mount Promise Church, and Conan looked forward to the growth of a thriving new community in what had been the wilderness. Some excitement was caused by a visit from a young surveyor, Mr. Washington, who reported that the French were expanding their colonization along the Ohio River and were moving eastward into Virginia lands. Also, the French had stirred up the Indians, especially the Shawnees, so that they had become a menace to the English and Scots living in the western Virginia settlements.

To the grief of her family, Jean Selkirk died after a brief illness. The Selkirks were disturbed by reports of sporadic Indian massacres and revenge killings by whites. Yet when Andrew Selkirk warned Conan to move back to Burke's Tract, Conan refused, believing that if proper precautions were taken, there was no need to fear the Indians. Not long afterward, John Selkirk was tricked into following what he thought was a lost lamb into the woods where he was shot by an Indian.

The increasing frequency of Indian attacks soon caused many settlers to flee south into North Carolina, and those who remained stayed on permanent guard. No new people moved into such areas as Burke's Land, and a guerrilla war against the marauding Indians was kept up by the Virginians, many of whose Scottish and Irish forebears had fought in much the same way to protect their Old World homes from English invaders.

In a surprise attack on Conan's homestead, a small group of Shawnees triumphed, murdering men, women, and children, scalping their victims, and taking as captives Elizabeth and two of her children, Eileen and young Andrew, Old Mother Dick, who had come with the family from their former home in

Burke's Tract, and two of the Burke servants. As the Indians and their captives moved westward, one brave, annoyed by young Andrew's screaming, tore him from Elizabeth's grasp and threw him over a cliff into Last Leap River.

For some time, the five remaining captives lived with the Indians in a village near the Ohio River. Elizabeth, who had been taken as a squaw by Long Thunder, bore him a son; but she was biding the time when she might escape with Mother Dick and Eileen, who was still too young to be claimed by some other brave as his squaw. Elizabeth finally managed to slip away from camp with her daughter and the frail but undaunted old woman. Left behind was the half-Indian baby whom a young Indian woman had promised to care for if anything happened to Elizabeth. Regretfully left with the Indians were also the black slave, Ajax, and the white servant, Barb, who might someday manage to return to Virginia.

The long, painful journey and the struggle against exhaustion and starvation were too much for Mother Dick, who died on the way. Elizabeth and Eileen, continuing their journey eastward into the rugged mountains, were constantly on guard against roving Indian bands and diligently seeking food from stream or forest to allay their hunger. At last, they reached Last Leap River, into which the baby Andrew had been thrown so long ago. Elizabeth, peering through bushes toward the river, saw a canoe heading down it, going westward. It was paddled, not by Indians as she at first feared, but by her brother Robin, the guide Stephen Trabue, and her husband Conan Burke. After the joyous reunion, Conan explained that, though Elizabeth had seen him attacked by some of the raiders and apparently killed, he had actually been rescued by neighbors after having been gravely wounded. His slowly healing wounds and the continuation of the war against the Indians and the French had prevented his and Robin's pushing toward the Ohio to rescue, if possible, the Shawnees' captives. Finally peace had come— in America, though not yet in Europe between England and France —and the word had spread to all wandering bands that now it was safe to travel in Indian territory. As soon as possible, he had set out with Robin and Stephen to search for his loved ones. As the happy group sat about a fire to eat a breakfast which was like a banquet to Elizabeth and Eileen, the famished girl clung to the belief she had had a short time before, when she wakened from a deep sleep to find her mother and her father standing above her. To her, the reunion seemed miraculously wonderful.

Critical Evaluation:

Mary Johnston intended *The Great Valley* as an epic of the opening of the American frontier, and in some respects she succeeded. It is a well-crafted and enjoyable novel, if not overly profound. An optimistic book, it does not avoid describing the hardships of the settlers' lives but stresses the positive aspects of their adventure. The beauty of the virgin land comes to symbolize in the minds of John Selkirk and his family its promise for the future.

The characters are virtuous, indomitable, and almost too noble; yet the reader feels that such people must have existed to build up the country. For Johnston's idealistic novel, at least, they are artistically right. The inner lives of the characters are not dealt with at all; Johnston pays only the most superficial attention to the psychology of her people. Their lives are entirely composed of physical acts and of desires, of hopes for the future and of hard work, and, occasionally, of memories of past life in Scotland. They are not soft people; they are capable of meeting every adversity in their paths. "Crying's good too, sometimes," says Jean Selkirk. "But I don't cry much." This is the key to her character and to most of the characters in the novel.

There is no complicated plot in *The Green Valley*; the story is that of the efforts of the Selkirk clan to establish themselves in the wilds of America. Some family members die, others marry and have children, and life moves on. The spare writing avoids melodrama. Johnston respects her characters, as they respect one another. John Selkirk respects all men, black and red as well as white, as long as they deserve respect; he refuses to countenance slavery, although his son differs from him on the issue. Even here, there is no violent disagreement. The lives of the family move forward, and its members establish a base for their descendants, which was their dream when they first sailed on the *Prudence*.